DECKER'S

PATTERNS OF

EXPOSITION 13

Randall E. Decker

Robert A. Schwegler
University of Rhode Island

HarperCollins*Publishers*

Sponsoring Editor: Patricia A. Rossi
Development Editor: Marisa L. L'Heureux
Project Coordination and Cover Design: Carnes-Lachina Publication Services, Inc.
Cover Image: HOURGLASS MEDALLION—Pieced by Angelia Tobias, Oakland,
    California, 1984. Quilted by Irene Bankhead, Oakland, California, 1987. Who'd A
    Thought It: Improvisation In African-American Quiltmaking. San Francisco Craft
    & Folk Art Museum, San Francisco, California. Photograph by Geoffry Johnson.
Production Manager: Michael Weinstein
Compositor: Omegatype Typography, Inc.
Printer and Binder: Arcata Graphics/Fairfield
Cover Printer: The Lehigh Press, Inc.

Decker's Patterns of Exposition, 13th Edition

Library of Congress Cataloging-in-Publication Data

Decker's patterns of exposition 13 / [edited by] Randall E. Decker,
    Robert A. Schwegler.
        p.   cm.
    Rev. ed of: Decker's patterns of exposition 12. c1990.
    ISBN 0-673-52118-4 (student ed.)
    ISBN 0-673-49991-X (instructor ed.)
    1. College readers. 2. Exposition (Rhetoric) I. Decker, Randall
E. II. Schwegler, Robert A. III. Decker's patterns of exposition
12. IV. Title: Patterns of exposition 13.
PE1417.P386 1991
808'.0427—dc20   91-19155
                                                            CIP

91 92 93 94 9 8 7 6 5 4 3 2 1

Contents

1 Illustrating Ideas by Use of *Example* / 23

> This columnist decides that stopping for red lights is part of a contract
> Americans have with each other. And we trust each other to honor the
> contract.

> Lewis Hill tells of a time and place where people took the proverb
> "waste not, want not" literally—sometimes with humorous results.

5 Explaining Through *Process Analysis* / *187*

A seventy-fifth wedding anniversary and a hundredth birthday coming at the same time mean little to a young boy, unless, of course, they
are accompanied by a party. Yet a party like this is likely to be filled
with old people.

This poet and novelist looks at recent arguments over American
culture and discovers that it is not the single strand people often
believe, but many strands—African, Native American, and many
others, as well as European.

What is really important for this country is the serious study of
stars—the kind that appear on the covers of magazines, on television,
and on movie screens.

The Everglades used to be one of the wonders of the world, filled with
so many birds that the sky would turn black when they took to the air
in the morning. Now, the "river of grass" is dying and Florida may
become the world's newest desert.

Suppose you moved around a bit after college and didn't get home
for a few years. By the time you got around to visiting the town where
you grew up, everything had changed. What happened to your roots,
and where can you put down new ones?

11 Using Patterns for *Argument* / 427

Argument Through Example

Looking at the case of Ted Bundy and her own experiences as a newspaper reporter, this author argues that while there are good reasons to be in favor of capital punishment, there are even better reasons to oppose it.

Argument Through Cause and Effect

How does a farmer view the effects of technology on his job? He thinks that farming is in trouble and the rest of us along with it. He also has some suggestions for solving the problem.

Argument Through Cause and Effect

Why are our public schools in such trouble? People who for many years were considered the strongest supporters of education have abandoned the schools and the results are disastrous. Nocera looks closely at experiences that are probably familiar to most of us.

Argument Through Comparison and Contrast

How good are our schools compared to those of Japan? Not very good, says this writer, and he proposes ways to improve them, including solutions that may raise the hackles of some readers.

> Dirty words have a history of violent meanings. This history, not narrow-minded sexual hangups, is what makes the words harmful and offensive.

> The martyred civil rights leader explains in this now-classic letter just why he is in Birmingham, and justifies the activities that led to his jailing.

Further Readings / 493

> Stop to reflect for a few minutes on the natural events occurring right in front of you or just over in the corner, and then you will see the kind of wonders this author records in the encounter of a spider and a hornet.

> The tragedy of AIDS calls on our deepest resources as human beings in caring for each other and in understanding ourselves.

> Writing is a magical and sacrificial act, claims this author, and she takes readers on a journey through Mexican culture and a writer's mind.

> Eating is an economic and political act with some important conse-
> quences that most of us would like to ignore. Berry has some concrete
> suggestions for changing our eating habits in order to change our
> world.

Thematic Contents

Men and Women

Work

Families and Children

Society and Social Change

Culture and Customs

Politics and Leaders

Personality and Behavior

Nature and the Environment

Morals, Crime, and Punishment

Growing Up/Getting Old

Differences

Essay Pairs

Among the selections in *Patterns of Exposition* are a number of essay pairs whose similarities in topic or theme and contrasts in perspective or style offer interesting insights. These relationships show that the strategies a writer chooses can affect the way readers come to view the subject matter of an essay. The following list identifies some sets of essays that are particularly well suited for study and discussion; there are, of course, many other interesting and revealing ways of pairing the selections in the text.

A few of the pairs illustrate different ways of using the same pattern, such as example or definition. In other sets, the patterns offer contrasting strategies for expression or alternate ways of viewing a subject.

To the Instructor

Patterns of Exposition 13 retains the basic principles and the general format of previous editions. Use of the book remains high, and we continue to poll instructor-users for evaluations of the selections and about the need for basic changes in the framework. We also reviewed the responses of students who returned questionnaires like the one at the back of this book. Although obviously we are unable to comply with all requests, we have seriously considered and fully appreciated all of them, and we have incorporated many suggestions into this new edition. We have responded, as well, to requests for added essays in some of the most heavily used sections of the book.

The annotated demonstration paragraphs located at the end of introductory sections have been rewritten for this edition. They are followed by sample paragraphs drawn from a variety of publications. These paragraphs illustrate some of the structural and stylistic variations professional writers often add while employing the basic patterns. Some of these authors are well known for their work; others less so, though the sample paragraphs may call attention to the quality of their writing.

A revised "Introduction: Reading and Writing" incorporates current theory as a basis for practical advice about the process of writing and about the ways reading can lead to and support writing. The discussion also provides practical advice about reading the selections in the text for both comprehension and awareness of technique. Included in the section is Brent Staples's well-known essay "Just Walk on By," accompanied by commentary that illustrates the activities involved in comprehension and response to reading. The discussion also outlines specific reading and writing activities that instructors may wish to assign or that students may decide to employ on their own.

Because so many instructors find it useful, we continue to retain the table of contents listing pairs of essays. Each pair provides contrasts (or similarities) in theme, approach, and style that are worth study. The essay pairs can form the focus of class discussion or writing assignments.

Although the focus of the text as a whole is on exposition and the rhetorical patterns it employs, we recognize that many instructors like to include a section on argument in their courses, and that argument often uses the same rhetorical patterns as exposition. Selections from the argument section may be added to those in the expository chapters to further illustrate the usefulness of the patterns. The argument chapter is similar in arrangement and approach to the other sections of the text.

The "Further Readings" section provides four fine contemporary selections chosen to provoke discussion of ideas and strategies. The pieces have also been chosen to suggest some of the intriguing forms and goals essays can pursue in the hands of skilled and daring writers. The essays in this section can be used on their own or along with the other sections of the book. They provide stimulus for writing and discussion as well as illustrations of strategies for students to use in their own writing.

But throughout *Patterns of Exposition 13* we have tried, as always, to make possible the convenient use of all materials in whatever ways instructors think best for their own classes. With a few exceptions, only complete essays or freestanding units of larger works have been included. With their inevitable overlap of patterns, they are more complicated than excerpts illustrating single principles, but they are also more realistic examples of exposition and more useful for other classroom purposes. Versatility has been an important criterion in choosing materials.

Thirty-six of the selections best liked in previous editions have been retained. Twenty-three selections are new, and all but a few of these are anthologized for the first time.

Their arrangement is but one of many workable orders; instructors can easily develop another if they so desire. The Thematic Contents and the table of Essay Pairs also suggest a variety of arrangements.

We have tried to vary the study questions—and undoubtedly have included far more than any one teacher will want—from the purely objective to those calling for some serious self-examination by students. (The Instructor's Manual supplements these materials.)

Suggestions for writing assignments to be developed from ideas in the essays are located immediately after each selection. But for classes in which the instructor prefers writing to be done according to the expository pattern under study at the time, regardless of subject matter, topic suggestions are located at the end of each section.

"A Guide to Terms," where matters from *Abstract* to *Unity* are briefly discussed, refers whenever possible to the essays themselves for illustrations. To permit unity and easy access, it is located at the back of the book, but there are cross-references to it in the study questions.

In all respects—size, content, arrangement, format—we have tried to keep *Patterns of Exposition 13* uncluttered and easy to use.

Acknowledgments

For their help and support, the editors would like to thank the following staff of HarperCollins College Division: Patricia Rossi and Marisa L. L'Heureux.

The second editor wishes to thank Brian Schwegler for his ideas and responses; Christopher Schwegler for his smiles; and Nancy Newman Schwegler for her love, insight, and support.

The continued success of *Patterns of Exposition* is due to a great extent to the many students and instructors who respond to question-naires and offer helpful suggestions, making the job of revision easier. For their invaluable assistance with the thirteenth edition we would especially like to thank Homai Behram, Helen Beuker, Margaret Boese, Judith M. Boschult, Charles Cochran, Katherine Dickson, Steven Hind, Kathleen Hudson, Gwendolyn S. Jones, Janet Juhnke, Muriel E. J. Klafehn, Pamela T. Pittman, Marianne F. Pollack, Jon Sams, Marci Sellers, Lucy Sheehey, Peter Sherer, June Burlingame Smith, Mark E. Tappmeyer, Dean F. Walton, and John E. Winters.

Randall E. Decker
Robert A. Schwegler

Introduction: Reading and Writing

Reading can play many roles. It can entertain or persuade; it can offer encounters with new ideas and information; or it can lead to self-discovery. For writers, however, reading can play a special role. As the eighteenth-century author Richard Steele put it, "Reading is to the mind what exercise is to the body." When you read with an eye toward writing, you use many of the same skills you employ in creating sentences and paragraphs. Reading stretches your awareness of what writers and written expression can achieve. It adds to your knowledge of writing techniques, developing and strengthening your ability to employ them in your own work.

The benefits of reading are not automatic, however. You need to be aware of the links between your reading and your writing and work to strengthen these ties. Nor are all kinds of reading equally beneficial. Most important is *active reading*, which involves not only understanding an essay but also questioning it, arguing with it, and paying attention to the writer's techniques. This book is designed to help you build bridges between reading and writing in order to improve each activity. The introduction to each section and the questions following the essays call attention to varied ways writers approach subjects and the strategies they employ, especially the patterns of exposition. At the same time, the text suggests the benefit of these strategies for your own writing.

But the value of reading goes far beyond matters of technique. Deepened understanding often leads to richness and fresh insight in expression—which is, after all, one of the highest goals of any composition class. Thus besides the study of writing techniques in a college anthology, we have a right to expect real benefit from the reading itself. Reading and thinking about new ideas or experiences are excellent ways to widen horizons and broaden our interests—and this broadening is an important phase of becoming educated. In general, therefore, each set of essays in this book progresses in complexity and depth. These challenges help our understanding reach an even higher level. In stretching our ability to comprehend, we also extend our reach (and grasp) as we compose.

Writing: Aims and Patterns

The novelist trying to give life to an imagined event and the journalist trying to present only the "bare facts" tell a story in very different ways. Their aims for writing are different, as well, from those familiar to college writers: explaining ideas and information or supporting an argument. From among the many aims of writing, this book chooses to focus on two that are familiar and important parts of our lives: exposition and argument.

Exposition is one of the basic aims of communication, more important in many situations than the other aims—entertainment, persuasion, or self-expression. Sometimes we may write to entertain, as do the novelist and to a certain extent the sportswriter; or we may try to persuade in the manner of the lawyer, the salesperson, or the preacher. We may even choose to express our beliefs and feelings in personal letters and conversation. Yet much of the writing and speaking everyday activities call for is expository in purpose, requiring us to share our knowledge of a subject. People in specialized professions are also frequent users of exposition.

Exposition means explanation, simply an *exposing* of information or ideas. Its primary function is not to tell a story or create vivid pictures for the reader, although exposition often uses narration and description among many other techniques. Its primary function is not to convey an author's feelings about a subject, though this perspective may at times be a valuable element in exposition. The primary function of exposition is not to convince or persuade, though argumentative and expository writing share many techniques and may each contain elements of the other. The primary function of exposition itself is merely *to explain*.

Beyond our need for informally written and spoken explanations, we use the processes of written exposition throughout college—in reports, term papers, and essay examinations. Most of us use exposition throughout our working lives—in letters, memoranda, and business and professional reports. Hence there are practical reasons most college composition courses are devoted primarily to study and practice in exposition. For the same reasons, this book concentrates on patterns of expository writing and other techniques commonly used.

Argument is closely related to exposition, sharing with it many techniques, including the patterns of exposition. In argument, however, we take a stand by offering a judgment of value, an interpretation of events, or a proposed course of action and then providing reasons for readers to agree with it. An argumentative essay offers an opinion, but is more than *mere* opinion. Instead, it responds to an issue or controversy by offering the author's judgment along with good reasons for readers to share it—reasons and support often presented and explained by means of the patterns of exposition.

The first ten sections of *Patterns of Exposition* explore and illustrate the basic patterns of expository writing. A section on argument follows, arranged according to the expository patterns that appear frequently in argumentative writing. The last section, "Further Readings," offers an even wider variety of composition forms and subject matter. It suggests, as well, ways in which writing can go beyond explanation and argument to explore new ideas and raise intriguing questions.

There is nothing new about the ten basic patterns of exposition; we have been using most of them since we first tried to explain why birds fly south in the winter. But mature writing depends partly on an author's being able to use *deliberately* whichever techniques will do the job best, with the least chance of misunderstanding. We study these techniques to get a clearer view of their functions and possibilities, with the aim of being able to use them more effectively in our own writing.

The patterns are above all techniques, ways of explaining or arguing. They do not determine the subject or the purpose of an essay. Rather, they help writers achieve their goals in explaining or arguing, just as the section titles in this book suggest: for instance, "Illustrating Ideas by Use of *Example*," "Explaining Through *Process Analysis*," or "Using *Definition* to Help Explain." An essay may make considerable use of one pattern, yet it is also likely to employ others. Thus, though this text at times asks you to examine and practice the techniques separately, it also tries to point out that they are seldom used separately in practical writing. After all, when we observe and practice for hours a skill involved in tennis or golf, we are not assuming that an entire game will be made up of serving or putting. In writing, we know there is no reason a process analysis should not be used to assist comparison in some explanations, no reason an illustration might not be valuably aided in certain developments by narration. In good writing, if the patterns do not overlap, it is simply because one alone is sufficient for the purpose.

The best expository writing calls attention to its subject and what the writer has to say, not to the pattern being employed. For convenience we often speak of essays according to their dominant patterns, as, for example, "a comparison-contrast essay" or a "cause-effect essay." As a writer, however, you ought to remember that your purpose for writing is most important and that you are "explaining with the help of comparison and contrast" or "analyzing a subject by looking at cause-and-effect relationships."

The importance of patterns as a means rather than an end is apparent in argumentative writing as well. The editorial writer arguing against a proposed government project might compare it to projects that have been expensive failures or might analyze cause-and-effect relationships and provide a series of examples to show the project will not meet its goals. In the argument section of this book, we can see how the expository patterns work in a different kind of writing.

Reading and the Composing Process

The contributions of reading to writing can perhaps be best understood if we look carefully at some of the many things writers do when they compose an essay or other piece of writing. We do not intend the following discussion to be a step-by-step description of the composing process, which is likely to vary from writer to writer and from task to task. Instead, we offer suggestions for effective composing that highlight as well the many ways in which reading can enrich writing.

Whatever the task—creating an expository essay, preparing a business report, or composing a news release—writing activities generally fall into three categories:

Before creation of the first full draft of an essay

During the writing of a first full draft

After the initial draft

These categories are seldom completely separate, as anyone knows who has begun rewriting parts of a first draft before it is complete or who has added new ideas and information to what was supposed to be the final version of a paper.

Before Drafting. The subject matter is important in all writing, but especially so in expository writing because it aims to explore and explain a topic. Argumentative writing also depends on the subject: the issue, disagreement, controversy, or problem being addressed. Paying attention to the subject (or trying to decide on one) is therefore where most writers begin, especially with the kinds of writing illustrated in this book.

At times a writing assignment may specify the subject, or one may come to mind with little effort. Most of the time, however, it is up to you to choose a subject, envision how readers are likely to regard it, and develop your purpose for writing. Probing your memory for subjects that interest you or that might interest readers is an obvious way to begin. Nonetheless, thinking about a subject (or any other aspect of an upcoming writing project) can be difficult because it is hard to hold fleeting ideas and bits of information in mind for close inspection. One answer is to capture ideas and details by means of pen and paper (or keyboard and screen). Once your thoughts are on paper, you can explore their relationships carefully and hold them for future use. (After all, the bane of many writers is that they forget their terrific ideas as they turn their attention to another part of the writing task.)

Lists of ideas and possible subjects can be helpful; they need not be orderly to be useful. *Grouping* related ideas and information by drawing connecting lines and circles or by generating further lists of related material can alert you to possible subjects, especially those about which you already know things worth sharing. For example, in making lists of hobbies, sports, and other leisure time activities, you might note that you like to read about adventures in the wilderness, that you like to go camping, and that you like movies about people facing challenges in remote areas and harsh climates. Circling these notes and connecting them with a line will highlight their relationship. It might also suggest as a topic area the challenges and pleasures of encountering the natural world in a relatively unspoiled form. *Freewriting* can help you discover subjects that intrigue you (and perhaps others) or that reflect values and concerns. Simply write for five to ten minutes on whatever subjects come to mind; do not stop to make changes, corrections, or revisions. Talking with others is a good practice, too, especially in *brainstorming* sessions during which the participants share and list ideas, letting one person's thoughts prompt and extend another's. All these activities help not only with discovering possible subjects but also with developing perspectives to guide exposition or argument.

Reading can be a powerful aid at this stage as well. Reading an essay exploring childhood attitudes toward elderly people can prompt your memories of related experiences that may be worth explaining and exploring. Reading an essay about differing attitudes toward work or athletics may arouse your curiosity about a subject or suggest a fresh way of looking at other common activities. But these insights may be lost unless you use pen or keyboard to record them. As you read, jot down intriguing ideas, bits of information, possible topics, and purposes for writing. Record them in a notebook or computer file you keep especially for this purpose; or simply annotate the margins of your textbook. In reading the essays in this text, pay attention also to the questions on "Meanings and Values" and the "Suggestions for Writing and Discussion" following the selections. They are designed to alert you to topics and purposes for your own writing.

Before drafting an essay you also need to turn a *subject* into a *topic* by limiting it and developing your perspective and purpose. A subject is the broad area you are writing about; a topic is the specific area you wish to explain and explore. If "work" is a subject, "ways to deal with difficult bosses" is a topic. A topic is not only limited so you can discuss it with reasonable thoroughness in the space available, it also reflects your perspective on the subject and reveals something of your purpose for writing.

Activities like listing, brainstorming, and freewriting can help you develop specific topics and ways to explore them. In addition, each of the patterns of exposition suggests questions you can use to focus on a topic and perhaps even develop a perspective (or central idea) for your writing:

Example: What are some typical instances or illustrations? What generality is illustrated by these examples?

Classification: What are the different categories? Why are the differences among the categories important?

Comparison and Contrast: What are the similarities and differences? What can we learn from the similarities and differences?

Analogy: What key points do these unlike subjects have in common? How do the similarities help us to understand either one?

Process Analysis: How does it work? How can we do it? What might we gain from understanding the operations?

Cause and Effect: What are the likely causes? Effects? How can an awareness of the possible causes and effects contribute to our understanding of people and events?

Definition: How might it be defined? In what ways does a definition aid us in understanding the importance or consequences of an idea, object, person, or event?

Description: What is its appearance and what are its characteristics? In describing the subject, what can we learn about its meaning, character, or influence?

Narration: What happened? What do the events reveal about the participants or about other events we are likely to experience?

Induction and Deduction: What generalization does the evidence suggest? What further conclusions can we draw from a generalization? How do these processes of reasoning help us understand events or social phenomena?

You may also wish to pursue a topic you encounter while reading. Try using the entries you make in a reading log as starting places for your work: "Alice Walker believes that animals have complicated thoughts and feelings. What do scientists have to say about this? What about my experiences as a pet owner?" Your answers to the "Meanings and Values" questions following the selections in this book can also be turned into probes for topics. For example, following George Orwell's essay about an execution ("A Hanging") we ask, "Why was there so much talking and laughing after the hanging was finished?" If you let your mind (or your pen) explore people's reactions to other horrifying, tragic, or unfortunate incidents, you may discover a topic that intrigues you and a way of looking at it.

Does it make any sense to cry (or even laugh as some people do) in response to a serious accident, such as a fall from a ladder, an automobile crash, or even a house on fire? I suspect we react for some physical reason and can't help responding as we do.

Developing a focus or central idea around which to build your writing is not something you should leave for the actual drafting of an essay (though you may of course find your purpose and focus changing as you prepare the draft). While exploring a possible topic, try asking questions such as, "Am I mostly interested in presenting new information on this topic, or do I really want to change readers' attitudes towards it?" and "Do I want to simply explain some steps people might take, or do I want to persuade others to take action?"

You may wish to try one or more of the following strategies. Take a moment to jot down a list of possible goals for your writing in the form of *purpose statements.*

I want to interest people in the possibility that chimpanzees and other apes are intelligent and have the ability to use language.

I hope to convince my readers that some of the recent gun control proposals are not good ideas.

Or write down some *planning statements* in order to try out possible focuses and arrangements for your essay.

I plan to start with the story of my sister's gymnastic injuries and then move on to classify the different high school sports according to the level of risk for injury they pose.

Or create statements that sum up a central idea (or argumentative proposition) you wish to convey through an essay. Try crafting statements that might form a basis for *thesis statements* designed to alert readers to the main point of an essay.

Internship programs are worth serious consideration because they provide opportunities for personal growth as well as career training.

The effects of television violence on children vary widely, often depending on the extent to which parents help children understand what appears on the screen.

Your goal at this point should be to develop your ideas while remaining open to new discoveries. The essays in this collection can help you set goals for your composing by providing examples of the many ways writers construct purposes and central ideas for their writing.

Drafting. Drafting an essay means writing out a first version following a general plan for content and arrangement. Admittedly, good essays sometimes develop from open-ended, exploratory writing during which the author discovers both a specific purpose for writing and an arrangement for carrying out that purpose. But most successful expository (and argumentative) writing follows a different path: the writer decides on a tentative arrangement (or even a detailed outline) and then begins drafting the essay, keeping the plan in mind yet remaining open to fresh ideas and directions.

Deciding on a plan is generally the first step in drafting. Each of the patterns of exposition suggests possible arrangements for your own essays, such as classification, comparison-contrast, definition, and cause-effect. These patterns are not presented for slavish imitation, but to be adapted to the needs of particular topics, purposes, and audiences, just as essays in the collection illustrate. The questions on expository or argumentative strategies following the individual selections call attention to the patterns and their many uses: in organizing whole essays, parts of essays, paragraphs, and even parts of paragraphs. The questions also highlight the tendency of most writers to employ more than one pattern, combining them to meet the needs of specific topics and audiences. Observing the strategies in use should make plain that they are not abstract patterns to be imposed on a subject but instead are flexible ways to explore ideas and information.

Putting your plans on paper (or computer disk) is a good idea. You may choose to create an informal list of the ideas and details you intend to cover, along with an indication of their order and statements of purpose for each section of the essay. Or you may decide to create a more detailed and precise plan, such as a formal outline.

Whatever approach you choose, devote some time and effort to planning. A good plan will alert you to places in the essay that need further development in the form of information and details. It will free you from having to hold an outline of the whole essay in mind as you write. It will enable you to concentrate on adding detail, organizing and developing paragraphs, or creating clear and effective sentences. At the same time, a good plan will allow you to confirm at any time that a particular paragraph or section is consistent with the overall arrangement and central idea of the essay. Plans can be revised, too, even in the middle of drafting.

Even if your writing goes according to plan, there is no need to try to polish all the details in the first draft. Crossing out sentences and paragraphs and rewriting them again and again will not ensure that the first draft is good enough to be a final draft. More likely, it will simply ensure that the first draft of your paper takes an agonizingly long time to complete. Consider spending less time on the first draft and devoting your efforts instead to later stages in the process: revising, editing, and polishing.

Many of the decisions you make while drafting have to do with techniques: opening and closing strategies, the patterns of exposition, paragraph structure, use of details, sentence structure, and so on. Careful, active reading of the essays in this book (with pen in hand for notes and responses) can help you develop a wider repertoire of writing strategies. For example, you can sharpen your awareness of the kind of detail that makes for effective paragraphs in a comparison by looking at Bruce Catton's "Grant and Lee: A Study in Contrasts." You can learn how writers balance development of the various categories in a classification by looking at the work of Desmond Morris ("Territorial Behaviour") and Peter Marsh ("Tribes"). The questions on "Expository Techniques" following these and other essays direct attention to those techniques that are especially well illustrated by the selections.

The strategies you choose for an essay ought to reflect the likely needs of your readers in addition to your subject matter and purpose(s) for writing. After all, the techniques act as guides or signals for readers. In addition, both exposition and argument exist for readers—the first to explain a subject to them, the second to persuade them. Nonetheless, the role attention to audience plays in your composing is likely to change according to where you are in the process, becoming a more pressing concern as you move through drafting into revision and editing.

After Drafting. Having completed a draft, you should set it aside, if only for a brief time. Then you can return to the essay and view it from the outside, much as a reader does. From this perspective you can begin seeing the draft essay as a whole, judging its overall effectiveness and that of its parts. The three kinds of questions following the selections in this text provide a model for reading with an eye toward revising:

Attention to *meaning* (subject, purpose, central idea or thesis)

Attention to *technique* (arrangement, detail and development, sentence and paragraph strategies)

Attention to *diction and vocabulary* (choice of words and figures of speech)

In particular, the questions on "Diction and Vocabulary" are designed to alert you to the kinds of resources accomplished writers generally employ to achieve clarity, force, and vividness in expression.

Inexperienced writers sometimes think revision means paying attention only to sentence style, wording, and clarity. These are certainly important concerns. Experienced writers, however, also make revision an opportunity for changes in content and arrangement. After revision, both small- and large-scale, writers need to edit for correctness and polish both sentences and details. These last steps are quite important in preparing an essay for readers.

A Procedure for Reading

Reading is not a simple act and may have several purposes. In both these qualities it resembles the act of writing. Moreover, like composing, reading is active, not passive. Even when our sole concern is to perceive an author's message or to glean facts and ideas from a text, we are not simply recipients of information but discoverers as well. To comprehend a piece of writing, we need to pay attention to the signals it contains and to follow their directions. We need to recognize patterns and to take note of distinctions between generalizations and supporting details.

Comprehension is seldom the sole aim of reading, except, perhaps, when we are searching for specific information to complete a task—a set of figures to include in a graph, the next step in assembling a model airplane, or the ingredients for a special punch to serve at a holiday party. In casual reading we let our imaginations roam for the pleasure of the activity. In more serious reading, when a writer challenges us with fresh ideas and arguments, we speculate on the consequences or create impassioned counterarguments, some of which we may even share in writing of our own.

One sign of good writing, then, is that it invites response. It asks readers to call on their experiences in order to understand the text and the author's vision, and it encourages (or provokes) further ideas and rejoinders from the reader. To read as a writer means to be open to the imaginative responses a text provokes and to capture them in some form—marginal notes, a writer's journal—so they can be seeds for written expression.

Writers read (or reread) in practical ways as well, often with pen in hand. They admire a particular way of closing the discussion or a strategy for explaining complex causes and effects. They make note of phrases to employ as quotations or as models for their own sentences. And they remember in particular the overall patterns of development and ways a writer combines the patterns of exposition.

Any single reading of a text, whether the first or the fifth, is likely to combine several activities. An instructor, moreover, may suggest the manner of approaching a reading and the ways to study it. Instead of a system for reading, therefore, we offer students some suggestions to be employed according to the reading situation, the reader's/writer's needs and abilities, and the nature of the text being examined.

For the First Reading:

1.   As you read for the first time, relax. Read the selection casually, as you would a magazine article, for whatever enjoyment or new ideas you get without straining. Do not stop to look up new words unless the sentences in which they are used are meaningless until you do. But have a pen or pencil in hand and mark all words or passages you are doubtful about, and then go on.

Do stop to jot down spontaneous reactions to the essay: disagreements and agreements as well as experiences and speculations of your own that the reading prompts. Try not to allow yourself to be drawn too far away from the reading by these jottings, but do capture the fleeting thoughts so you can later call them back to mind.

2.   When you have finished the first reading, put the book down; for a few minutes think over what you have read. Do not worry too much at this point about figuring out exactly what the writer has to say. The memories, feelings, and opinions that come to mind at this stage are an important part of the reading process. They can be the basis for detailed comprehension or for writing of your own. If you keep a reading log (see below), this is a time for entries exploring the text and your responses to it.

3.   Then use the dictionary to help you understand the words you have marked. Do not make the mistake of finding and trying to

memorize the first or the shortest definition of a word. Instead, examine the various meanings and look for the word's uses as a noun, verb, and modifier. *Think* about them. Pronounce the word. Use it in a few sentences. Identify it with similar words you already know. Then see how the author has used it.

4. Read and think briefly about the assigned questions and remarks following the selection. (The paragraphs in each selection are numbered for easy reference.)

For the Second Reading:

5. Reread the essay, pausing at times to think and to *question*, underlining important ideas, marking sentences or phrases that seem to you especially interesting, misleading, amusing, or well expressed. Pursue your own ideas, responses, objections, and speculations in notes in the margin or in a writing log.

6. Return to the questions at the end. You will probably find you have already provided most of the answers. If not, give the questions further thought, referring again to the essay and to "A Guide to Terms" (at the end of the book) or to earlier explanations wherever necessary for thorough understanding.

7. Reread the essay in whole or part as many times as necessary to understand any passages you find especially challenging and to observe in detail any writing strategies you might wish to employ in your own essays.

After Reading:

8. *Evaluate* the selection. What was the author trying to explain? Was the author successful in explaining? Was the endeavor worthwhile? For what point of view was the author arguing? Was the argument convincing? What lessons for writers can be drawn from the selection?

Writing in Response to Reading

As we read to understand an essay, we often have a second stream of thoughts in our minds as well—one in which we carry on a dialogue with the author, commenting on or arguing with ideas, admiring passages, or raising questions about the topic. Whether this dialogue takes place in the foreground of our attention or remains a quiet rumbling in the background depends on the content and challenges posed by the essay as well as our own attitudes. An essay that presents disquieting ideas or information is likely to bring our responses, feelings, and questions into the foreground. On the other hand, an essay that poses many difficulties in understanding may lead us to keep our judgments and ideas in the background as we work on comprehension.

Capturing this fleeting dialogue gives you a rich source of ideas and purposes for your writing as well as a way to become acquainted with writing techniques you especially admire. Here are some suggestions for writing activities that can capture your responses to an essay.

Three Questions. In the margins of an essay or in a notebook you keep to record your responses to reading, jot down brief answers to these questions, identifying each kind of answer by a letter corresponding to the question type.

> **W** (= *Why Interesting*) Why do I find this topic, passage, or example interesting?
>
> **D** (= *Detail*) Do the concrete details and the detailed explanations and arguments this author provides seem especially convincing?
>
> **M** (= *More Information*) What more would I like to know about this topic? Are other readers likely to be interested in it as well?

Marginal Notes. Use the margins of the text to record disagreements and agreements with what the author has to say or to hold shorthand references to memories and ideas that might be developed in essays of your own. As we read, many ideas for our own compositions come to mind, but unless they are recorded, even in brief form, they are likely to disappear by the time we get down to writing.

Admittedly, making extensive marginal notes can sometimes interfere with the pleasure we take in reading an essay and learning about an intriguing topic. Keep your notes short and perhaps even develop a set of abbreviations to use in them. On the other hand, an essay may be so interesting that you fail to make notes and thus miss recording ideas for later use. Try to develop a habit of stopping every page or two to see if there are any notes you wish to make.

Reading Logs. Keep a notebook of ideas, feelings, and experiences that come to mind either as you read or later as you reflect on your reading.

The log you create can be a source of ideas for essays or parts of essays in the future.

Try to label the entries according to the name of the essay. If possible, label the kinds of entries as well. Use headings that will be useful to you later; for example, "Ideas," "My Opinions," or "Possible Topics."

Double-Entry Notebooks. Draw a vertical line down the middle of the pages of a notebook. On the left side of the page, make brief notes summarizing the content of what you read. On the right side, record questions that occur to you as you read. The questions can be trivial or serious. They may be about the author, about what is coming next in the selection, or about a subject related to that under discussion. The summaries aid your understanding of what the author has to say and can be a source of information for your writing. The questions tell you about your reading process, provide insight into the ideas and problems that concern you, and can be springboards for essays of your own.

Reading and Responding to an Essay: Brent Staples, "Just Walk on By"

As you read the following essay, follow the reading procedures outlined above and use one or more of the techniques for responding in writing. Then compare your observations and responses to the commentary that follows the essay. The commentary follows the pattern of the sets of questions accompanying readings in the text: Meanings and Values, Expository Techniques, Diction and Vocabulary. Note, too, that the opening biographical note and brief introductory remarks suggest some directions and emphases for your reading. The essay is an instance of the ways examples can illustrate and explore ideas (see Section 1, "Illustrating Ideas by Use of *Example*").

BRENT STAPLES

BRENT STAPLES was born in 1951 in Chester, Pennsylvania. He received his B.A. in 1973 from Widener University and his Ph.D. (in psychology) in 1982 from the University of Chicago. He is a member of the *New York Times* editorial board, writing on matters of culture and society. He was formerly a reporter for the *Chicago Sun-Times* and an editor of the *New York Times Book Review*. Staples is the author of *Parallel Time* (1991), a memoir.

Just Walk on By

The power of examples to enable a reader to see through someone else's eyes is evident in this selection. Though many of the examples in the essay draw on a reader's sympathy, their main purpose appears to be explanatory; hence, the author accompanies them with detailed discussions. The result is a piece that is both enlightening and moving.

My first victim was a woman—white, well dressed, probably in her early twenties. I came upon her late one evening on a deserted street in Hyde Park, a relatively affluent neighborhood in an otherwise mean, impoverished section of Chicago. As I swung onto the avenue behind her, there seemed to be a discreet, uninflammatory distance between us. Not so. She cast back a worried glance. To her, the youngish black man—a broad six feet two inches with a beard and billowing hair, both hands shoved into the pockets of a bulky military jacket—seemed menacingly close. After a few more quick glimpses, she picked up her pace and was soon running in earnest. Within seconds she disappeared into a cross street.

That was more than a decade ago. I was 22 years old, a graduate 2
student newly arrived at the University of Chicago. It was in the echo
of that terrified woman's footfalls that I first began to know the
unwieldy inheritance I'd come into—the ability to alter public space
in ugly ways. It was clear that she thought herself the quarry of a
mugger, a rapist, or worse. Suffering a bout of insomnia, however, I
was stalking sleep, not defenseless wayfarers. As a softy who is
scarcely able to take a knife to a raw chicken—let alone hold it to a
person's throat—I was surprised, embarrassed, and dismayed all at
once. Her flight made me feel like an accomplice in tyranny. It also
made it clear that I was indistinguishable from the muggers who
occasionally seeped into the area from the surrounding ghetto. That
first encounter, and those that followed, signified that a vast, unnerving gulf lay between nighttime pedestrians—particularly women—
and me. And I soon gathered that being perceived as dangerous is a
hazard in itself. I only needed to turn a corner into a dicey situation,
or crowd some frightened, armed person in a foyer somewhere, or
make an errant move after being pulled over by a policeman. Where
fear and weapons meet—and they often do in urban America—there
is always the possibility of death.

In that first year, my first away from my hometown, I was to 3
become thoroughly familiar with the language of fear. At dark, shad-
owy intersections in Chicago, I could cross in front of a car stopped
at a traffic light and elicit the *thunk, thunk, thunk, thunk* of the driver—
black, white, male, or female—hammering down the door locks. On
less traveled streets after dark, I grew accustomed to but never comfortable with people who crossed to the other side of the street rather
than pass me. Then there were the standard unpleasantries with
police, doormen, bouncers, cab drivers, and others whose business it
is to screen out troublesome individuals *before* there is any nastiness.

I moved to New York nearly two years ago and I have remained 4
an avid night walker. In central Manhattan, the near-constant crowd
cover minimizes tense one-on-one street encounters. Elsewhere—visiting friends in SoHo, where sidewalks are narrow and tightly spaced
buildings shut out the sky—things can get very taut indeed.

Black men have a firm place in New York mugging literature. 5
Norman Podhoretz in his famed (or infamous) 1963 essay, "My Negro
Problem—And Ours," recalls growing up in terror of black males;
they "were tougher than we were, more ruthless," he writes—and as
an adult on the Upper West Side of Manhattan, he continues, he

cannot constrain his nervousness when he meets black men on certain streets. Similarly, a decade later, the essayist and novelist Edward Hoagland extols a New York where once "Negro bitterness bore down mainly on other Negroes." Where some see mere panhandlers, Hoagland sees "a mugger who is clearly screwing up his nerve to do more than just *ask* for money." But Hoagland has "the New Yorker's quick-hunch posture for broken-field maneuvering," and the bad guy swerves away.

I often witness that "hunch posture," from women after dark on the warrenlike streets of Brooklyn where I live. They seem to set their faces on neutral and, with their purse straps strung across their chests bandolier style, they forge ahead as though bracing themselves against being tackled. I understand, of course, that the danger they perceive is not a hallucination. Women are particularly vulnerable to street violence, and young black males are drastically overrepresented among the perpetrators of that violence. Yet these truths are no solace against the kind of alienation that comes of being ever the suspect, against being set apart, a fearsome entity with whom pedestrians avoid making eye contact. 6

It is not altogether clear to me how I reached the ripe old age of 22 without being conscious of the lethality nighttime pedestrians attributed to me. Perhaps it was because in Chester, Pennsylvania, the small, angry industrial town where I came of age in the 1960s, I was scarcely noticeable against a backdrop of gang warfare, street knifings, and murders. I grew up one of the good boys, had perhaps a half-dozen fist fights. In retrospect, my shyness of combat has clear sources. 7

Many things go into the making of a young thug. One of those things is the consummation of the male romance with the power to intimidate. An infant discovers that random flailings send the baby bottle flying out of the crib and crashing to the floor. Delighted, the joyful babe repeats those motions again and again, seeking to duplicate the feat. Just so, I recall the points at which some of my boyhood friends were finally seduced by the perception of themselves as tough guys. When a mark cowered and surrendered his money without resistance, myth and reality merged—and paid off. It is, after all, only manly to embrace the power to frighten and intimidate. We, as men, are not supposed to give an inch of our lane on the highway; we are to seize the fighter's edge in work and in play and even in love; we are to be valiant in the face of hostile forces. 8

Unfortunately, poor and powerless young men seem to take all 9
this nonsense literally. As a boy, I saw countless tough guys locked
away; I have since buried several, too. They were babies, really—a
teenage cousin, a brother of 22, a childhood friend in his mid-twen-
ties—all gone down in episodes of bravado played out in the streets.
I came to doubt the virtues of intimidation early on. I chose, perhaps
even unconsciously, to remain a shadow—timid, but a survivor.

The fearsomeness mistakenly attributed to me in public places 10
often has a perilous flavor. The most frightening of these confusions
occurred in the late 1970s and early 1980s when I worked as a
journalist in Chicago. One day, rushing into the office of a magazine
I was writing for with a deadline story in hand, I was mistaken for a
burglar. The office manager called security and, with an ad hoc posse,
pursued me through the labyrinthine halls, nearly to my editor's
door. I had no way of proving who I was. I could only move briskly
toward the company of someone who knew me.

Another time I was on assignment for a local paper and killing 11
time before an interview. I entered a jewelry store on the city's affluent
Near North Side. The proprietor excused herself and returned with
an enormous red Doberman pinscher straining at the end of a leash.
She stood, the dog extended toward me, silent to my questions, her
eyes bulging nearly out of her head. I took a cursory look around,
nodded, and bade her good night. Relatively speaking, however, I
never fared as badly as another black male journalist. He went to
nearby Waukegan, Illinois, a couple of summers ago to work on a
story about a murderer who was born there. Mistaking the reporter
for the killer, police hauled him from his car at gunpoint and but for
his press credentials would probably have tried to book him. Such
episodes are not uncommon. Black men trade tales like this all the
time.

In "My Negro Problem—And Ours," Podhoretz writes that the 12
hatred he feels for blacks makes itself known to him through a variety
of avenues—one being his discomfort with that "special brand of
paranoid touchiness" to which he says blacks are prone. No doubt he
is speaking here of black men. In time, I learned to smother the rage
I felt at so often being taken for a criminal. Not to do so would surely
have led to madness—via that special "paranoid touchiness" that so
annoyed Podhoretz at the time he wrote the essay.

I began to take precautions to make myself less threatening. I 13
move about with care, particularly late in the evening. I give a wide

berth to nervous people on subway platforms during the wee hours, particularly when I have exchanged business clothes for jeans. If I happen to be entering a building behind some people who appear skittish, I may walk by, letting them clear the lobby before I return, so as not to seem to be following them. I have been calm and extremely congenial on those rare occasions when I've been pulled over by the police.

And on late-evening constitutionals along streets less traveled by, I employ what has proved to be an excellent tension-reducing measure: I whistle melodies from Beethoven and Vivaldi and the more popular classical composers. Even steely New Yorkers hunching toward nighttime destinations seem to relax, and occasionally they even join in the tune. Virtually everybody seems to sense that a mugger wouldn't be warbling bright, sunny selections from Vivaldi's *Four Seasons*. It is my equivalent of the cowbell that hikers wear when they know they are in bear country.

Commentary

Meanings and Values. The biographical information preceding the essay indicates that the author is a well-educated and successful professional. Most readers are likely to be surprised, then, when the "I" of the essay (presumably the writer) speaks in the opening lines of a "victim," implying that he is a criminal. Moreover, the opening paragraph is likely to have an unsettling effect even for readers who are not aware of the writer's background, because it touches on subjects of considerable concern (and controversy) in our society: crime, rape, and race. The tension-filled example that opens the essay thus introduces some of the key concerns of the essay while at the same time capturing the attention of most readers.

While the opening paragraph introduces the general subject area of the essay, it does not specify the particular topic or central idea. It is not until the second paragraph that Staples makes plain the topic and the central idea he wishes to explore: the way in which African-American men are burdened by "the ability to alter public space in ugly ways." Explaining and illustrating this insight becomes the central focus of the essay.

At the same time, however, Staples does not raise the issue of race (and racism) directly. Instead, he presents it through the opening narrative example. And he employs several sentences in the second paragraph to present the central idea rather than using a single thesis statement. This somewhat indirect approach is probably part of a strategy for keeping the focus of the essay on exposition rather than argument. In our society, any conclusions about race (and racism) can easily lead to argument. Staples does have a strong point of view and he acknowledges contrasting perspectives several times in the essay. Nonetheless, his opening paragraphs manage to keep the focus of the essay on explaining and understanding rather than arguing.

Each of the examples in the essay illustrates some of the ways race serves to "alter public space in ugly ways." The examples cover a variety of social situations and acknowledge alternative ways of viewing events. Nonetheless, Staples's presentation tries to make it clear that the common thread among the events and the most adequate explanation for them is the distorting force that racism exerts on our perceptions and our society.

Expository Techniques. The essay offers several different kinds of examples. Some are relatively detailed presentations of the author's experiences (for example, paragraphs 1, 10, and 11). Others are drawn from the experiences of other people (par. 11). Some paragraphs present clusters of brief examples illustrating a point (see paragraphs 3 and 9, for instance). And several paragraphs let writers with a different point of view speak for themselves in the form of quotations and paraphrases (pars. 5 and 12).

The variety of the examples adds to both the depth and the credibility of the author's explanations. The concrete detail with which the examples are presented makes them convincing while creating sympathy for the author (and, perhaps, for others who have had similar experiences). Staples adds to the credibility of the examples by recognizing that the people who react harshly to his presence may be reacting from motives that also need to be understood and respected. Yet, though he provides balance and breadth in the examples and his explanations, Staples never loses track of his main purpose: exploring and explaining the "ugly" responses.

Many readers are likely to respond to the examples and explanations sympathetically. The essay may prompt memories of similar or parallel experiences. Other readers may wish to take issue with what Staples has to say, perhaps because they draw on different experiences or perhaps because they agree with Podhoretz's conclusion about "paranoid touchiness." The carefully chosen examples are designed to forestall this reaction, however.

Diction and Vocabulary. The language (diction) in the examples is both concrete and vivid: "The proprietor excused herself and returned with an enormous red Doberman pinscher straining at the end of a leash. She stood, the dog extended toward me, silent to my questions, her eyes bulging nearly out of her head." Much of the power of the essay depends on the author's ability to use language to enable readers to share the experiences being described. In addition, Staples uses the sentences at the end of many of the paragraphs to sum up his experiences and reinforce his conclusions. Particularly effective is the comparison that closes the essay: "It is my equivalent of the cowbell that hikers wear when they know they are in bear country."

Useful as the selections in this text can be, they are not intended as models for imitation by students. Each was written, as all expository projects should be, to give a particular audience a particular explanation. (Or, in the case of argument essays, to persuade a particular audience.) The style of some selections is much too informal for most college writing. Other styles, perhaps from a slower and more sedate age than ours, would be too stately for today. Pure imitation is not the purpose of our study.

But each of the selections does demonstrate one or more of the *patterns* of exposition and argument, which are as useful now as ever. Each can provide, too, some profitable study of other sound principles of writing—principles of effective sentences and paragraphs, mature diction, forceful introductions and closings. The consideration of all these principles, instead of being handled in separate sections, is a continuing study within the basic framework of the expository patterns. The book is designed so that instructors and students can use it in several ways.

1

Illustrating Ideas by Use of *Example*

The use of examples to illustrate an idea under discussion is the most common, and frequently the most efficient, pattern of exposition. It is a method we use almost instinctively; for instance, instead of talking in generalities about the qualities of a good city manager, we cite Harry Hibbons as an example. We may go further and illustrate Harry's virtues by a specific account of his handling of a crucial situation during the last power shortage or hurricane. In this way we put our abstract ideas into concrete form—a process that is always an aid to clarity. (As a matter of fact, with the "for instance" in this very paragraph, examples are employed to illustrate even the *use* of example.)

Lack of clear illustrations may leave readers with only a hazy conception of the points the writer has tried to make. Even worse, readers may try to supply examples from their own knowledge or experience, and these might do the job poorly or even lead them to an impression different from that intended by the author. Since writers are the ones trying to communicate, clarity is primarily their responsibility.

Not only do good examples put into clear form what otherwise might remain vague and abstract, but the writing also becomes more interesting, with a better chance of holding the reader's attention. With something specific to be visualized, a statement also becomes more convincing—but convincing within certain limitations. If we use the Volvo as an example of Swedish workmanship, the reader is probably aware that this car may not be entirely typical. Although isolated examples will not hold up well in logical argument, for ordinary purposes of explanation the Volvo example could make its point convincingly enough. In supporting an argument, however, we need either to choose an example that is clearly typical or to present several examples to show we have represented the situation fairly.

As in the selection and use of all materials for composition, of course, successful writers select and use examples cautiously, always keeping in mind the nature of their reader-audience and their own specific purpose for communicating. To be effective, each example must be pertinent, respecting the chief qualities of the generality it illustrates. Its function as an example must be either instantly obvious to the readers or fully enough developed so that they learn exactly what it illustrates, and how. Sometimes, however, illustration may be provided best by something other than a real-life example—a fictional anecdote, an analogy, or perhaps a parable that demonstrates the general idea. Here even greater care is needed to be sure these examples are both precise and clear.

Illustration is sometimes used alone as the basic means of development, but it also frequently assists other basic techniques, such as comparison and contrast. In either of its functions, authors may find their purpose best served by one well-developed example, possibly with full background information and descriptive details. But sometimes citing several shorter examples is best, particularly if the authors are attempting to show a trend or a prevalence. In more difficult explanations, of course, a careful combination of the two techniques—using both one well-developed example and several shorter examples—may be worth the extra time and effort required.

Whichever method is used, the writers are following at least one sound principle of writing: they are trying to make the general more specific, the abstract more concrete.

Sample Paragraph (Annotated)

Valley City and its suburbs have become so congested that people have begun moving to small towns two or more hours' drive away from the city center. In turn, these rapidly growing towns have begun experiencing growing pains and some strange contrasts. For instance, Palmville used to be a rural town with a dozen farms inside the city limits and its own Department of

The topic sentence—what the paragraph is about. Also the *generality* in need of specific examples.

Developed example.

Agriculture. Gradually the farms were sold and turned into tracts of one-family homes, shopping malls, and movie theaters. Now the head of the Department of Agriculture is responsible for two new pools, three golf courses (one under construction), and a physical fitness and nature trail—along with the three remaining farms. The McKetchie Family still operates its fresh fruit, vegetable, and egg stand on Route 20, only now the stand has a pizza restaurant on one side and the parking lot for the Palmville Mall on the other two sides. School

Minor examples.

enrollment has quadrupled over the past five years, and the Palmville Senior High (built in 1978) has temporary classrooms in trailers on the lawn in front of the main building. An old feed store, Abando's

Some *undeveloped examples* to show prevalence.

Groceteria, and Isaakson's Pharmacy are all that remain of the old downtown except for the City Hall. The elegant

Concluding example.

Victorian City Hall now has a towering steel and glass Civic Center on one side and the sprawling new headquarters

Figurative language. The simile emphasizes the "growing pains and strange contrasts" mentioned in the topic sentence.

for the Nedco Corporation on the other side. The beautiful old building looks as out of place as a person who dressed for a formal dinner party and arrived to find a barbecue in progress around the backyard pool.

Sample Paragraph (Example)

Something strange is happening to our weather. And it didn't just begin last summer. During the past decade, the United States has seen three of the coldest winters and four of the warmest average years ever recorded, a string of weather extremes that would occur by chance less than once in 1000 years. Elsewhere, weather has also run to extremes—with the Soviet Union and India experiencing their highest temperatures. Last winter, snow fell on the gondolas of Venice, the usually sunny beaches of the French Riviera, arid South Africa and even subtropical Brazil.

Excerpted with permission from "What's Wrong With Our Weather" by Lowell Ponte, *Reader's Digest*, November 1988. Copyright © 1988 by the Reader's Digest Association, Inc.

ANDY ROONEY

ANDREW A. ROONEY was born in 1920 in Albany, New York. Drafted into the army while still a student at Colgate University, he served in the European theater of operations as a *Stars and Stripes* reporter. After the war Rooney began what has been a prolific and illustrious career as a writer-producer for various television networks—chiefly for CBS—and has won numerous awards, including the Writers Guild Award for Best Script of the Year (six times—more than any other writer in the history of the medium) and three National Academy Emmy awards. In 1965 Rooney wrote the script for the first Telstar transatlantic satellite broadcast, which was carried by all three networks and translated into eleven other languages. As well as being the author of seven books, Rooney has contributed to *Esquire, Harper's, Playboy, Saturday Review,* and several other magazines. He is probably most familiar for his regular appearances as a commentator on the television program "60 Minutes." Rooney also writes a syndicated column, which appears in more than 250 newspapers, and has lectured on documentary writing at various universities. His most recent books are *A Few Minutes with Andy Rooney* (1981), *And More by Andy Rooney* (1982), *Pieces of My Mind* (1984), *Word for Word* (1986), and *Not That You Asked* . . . (1989). He now lives in Rowayton, Connecticut.

In and of Ourselves We Trust

"In and of Ourselves We Trust" was one of Rooney's syndicated columns. Rooney's piece uses one simple example to illustrate a generality. He draws from it a far-reaching set of conclusions: that we have a "contract" with each other to stop for red lights—and further, that our whole system of trust depends on everyone doing the right thing.

Last night I was driving from Harrisburg to Lewisburg, Pa., a distance   1
of about 80 miles. It was late, I was late, and if anyone asked me how
fast I was driving, I'd have to plead the Fifth Amendment to avoid
self-incrimination.

At one point along an open highway, I came to a crossroads with   2
a traffic light. I was alone on the road by now, but as I approached the
light, it turned red, and I braked to a halt. I looked left, right, and
behind me. Nothing. Not a car, no suggestion of headlights, but there
I sat, waiting for the light to change, the only human being, for at least
a mile in any direction.

I started wondering why I refused to run the light. I was not   3
afraid of being arrested, because there was obviously no cop anywhere around and there certainly would have been no danger in
going through it.

Much later that night, after I'd met with a group in Lewisburg   4
and had climbed into bed near midnight, the question of why I'd
stopped for that light came back to me. I think I stopped because it's
part of a contract we all have with each other. It's not only the law, but
it's an agreement we have, and we trust each other to honor it: We
don't go through red lights. Like most of us, I'm more apt to be
restrained from doing something bad by the social convention that
disapproves of it than by any law against it.

It's amazing that we ever trust each other to do the right thing,   5
isn't it? And we do, too. Trust is our first inclination. We have to make
a deliberate decision to mistrust someone or to be suspicious or
skeptical.

It's a darn good thing, too, because the whole structure of our   6
society depends on mutual trust, not distrust. This whole thing we
have going for us would fall apart if we didn't trust each other most
of the time. In Italy they have an awful time getting any money for
the government because many people just plain don't pay their
income tax. Here, the Internal Revenue Service makes some gestures
toward enforcing the law, but mostly they just have to trust that we'll
pay what we owe. There has often been talk of a tax revolt in this
country, most recently among unemployed auto workers in Michigan,
and our government pretty much admits that if there were a widespread tax revolt here, they wouldn't be able to do anything about it.

We do what we say we'll do. We show up when we say we'll   7
show up.

I was so proud of myself for stopping for that red light. And
inasmuch as no one would ever have known what a good person
I was on the road from Harrisburg to Lewisburg, I had to tell
someone.

8

Meanings and Values

1a. Explain the concept of a "contract we all have with each other" (par. 4).

b. How is the "agreement" achieved (par. 4)?

2. Why do you suppose exceeding the speed limit (par. 1) would not also
be included in the "contract"? Or is there some other reason for
Rooney's apparent inconsistency?

3. Explain the significance of the title of this selection.

Expository Techniques

1a. What generality is exemplified by the solution to Rooney's red-light
enigma?

b. In this instance, what does the generality have to do with the central
theme? (See Guide to Terms: *Unity.*)

c. Is there any disadvantage in this generality's location? Explain.

d. Does the example prove anything?

e. Do you think it is a good example of what it illustrates? Is it typical?

2. What other uses of example do you find in the selection?

3. How effective do you consider Rooney's closing? Why? (Guide: *Closings.*)

4. What, if anything, do the brief examples in paragraph 6 add to this
piece? (Guide: *Evaluation.*)

Diction and Vocabulary

1. Does it seem to you that the diction and vocabulary levels of this
selection are appropriate for the purpose intended? Why, or why not?
(Guide: *Diction.*)

2. Could this be classified as a formal essay? Why, or why not? (Guide:
Essay.)

Suggestions for Writing and Discussion

Choose one of the following passages from this selection to develop
for further discussion. You may agree or disagree, or both, but organize your ideas for most effective presentation:

1.   "[Most of us are] more apt to be restrained from doing something bad
     by the social convention that disapproves of it than by any law against
     it."

2.   "Trust is our first inclination."

3.   ". . . the whole social structure of our society depends on mutual trust,
     not distrust."

(NOTE: Suggestions for topics requiring development by use of EXAMPLE are on page
61, at the end of this section.)

LEWIS HILL

LEWIS HILL spent his early years on a Vermont farm during the
Great Depression of the 1930s. In the 1940s, he decided that he
preferred plants and trees to farming and so opened his own
nursery. During this time he started writing about gardening and
about country living, beginning a long string of publications that
now includes numerous articles and nine books. His articles have
appeared in magazines such as *Country Journal, Harrowsmith, Horticulture,* and *Diversion.* Among his books are *Country Living: A
Source Book of Projects and Friendly Advice* (1987), *Successful Perennial
Gardening* (1988), and *Fetched-Up Yankee: A New England Boyhood
Remembered* (1990).

Waste Not, Want Not

When Lewis Hill was young, properly "fetched-up" children memorized proverbs at school, recited them in verse, and read them in
embroidery hung in their homes. Thus the generality this essay
from *Fetched-Up Yankee* traces through examples of life from a rural
community is one which the people made a conscious goal for their
behavior. The examples in this selection are often humorous, yet
they also reveal the author's admiration for a way of living no
longer familiar to most of us.

Waste not, want not, is a maxim I would teach,   1
Let your watchword be dispatch, and practice what you preach.
Do not let your chances, like sunbeams pass you by,
For you'll never miss the water, 'til the well runs dry.
> —popular song by Rowland Howard

Proverbs relating to thrift were nearly as popular in School District   2
No. 9 as those that had to do with hard work. Waste was considered

a cardinal sin, as bad as lust and avarice. Not a bit of paper was thrown away until it had been thoroughly covered on both sides. Paper used on only one side was put into the scratch paper drawer and used later for figuring arithmetic problems or for practicing writing. A plain, unpainted pencil with no eraser was expected to last a minimum of one month, so we tried not to break the point too often. A fat rubber eraser was supposed to last all year, and books, nearly forever.

Water was another valuable commodity, since we had to carry it 3 each day from the Tylers' farmhouse. If any remained in the cup we'd been drinking from, it was dumped into a washbasin and used later for washing our hands. One pail of water minus the amount sloshed over us enroute from the Tylers' to school was expected to last all day.

At home, as at school, water was carefully conserved, and hot 4 water was considered precious, even though it was "het" with wood. If the kettle of water on the stove was hot, an enterprising housewife would scrub a floor, a ceiling, or a child. "No need to just let it bile away."

Douglas Anderson, who lived in the village, was asked to keep 5 an eye on the parsonage one cold winter night when the Presbyterian preacher and his wife had been called out of town. While he was filling the stoves with wood, he noticed that the water tank connected to the kitchen stove was full of mighty hot water.

His Scotch blood began to thicken, so he promptly filled up the 6 bathtub and took the first tub bath of his life. After he had dressed and was leaving, he noticed that the tank was getting well heated up again. So he went home and fetched his wife, Agnes, and she had her first tub bath, too. Naturally, nobody would have known anything about the episode, except for the fact that Doug, proud of his resourcefulness, told everyone.

There was no visible class distinction between the "haves" and 7 the "have nots" in our school, because everyone was a "have not." We all dressed more or less alike. Everybody's family owned a second-hand Ford, Chevrolet, or Plymouth that probably cost between $25 and $200. No one had electricity, and for most, indoor plumbing was a luxury that had not yet arrived. Even the toilet paper at school was a novelty, since catalogues and newspapers were the rule in our privies at home.

Most houses in the back country were in great need of paint, and 8 very few barns and sheds had ever been painted. Still, ours was not a tumbledown neighborhood. Nearly everyone kept the buildings sound, the roofs patched, and fences in good repair. Hard work accomplished much of what there was no money to buy, and because we raised most of our own food, none of us starved. Still, I think my family fully expected to see the wolf on the front steps every morning when they opened the door.

Since the government didn't subsidize poverty, our town, like 9 most, had an Overseer of the Poor who helped out destitute widows, the crippled, blind, and simple-minded. Mr. Keith bought groceries and other necessities and occasionally paid Mrs. Harvey twenty-five cents to feed a tramp. All the recipients' names were published in the town report each year, with the amount they received, so no able-bodied citizen ever applied for help, except in desperate circumstances.

Most people in our neighborhood weathered the Depression 10 rather well. Survival skills passed down from pioneer grandparents and a passion for thrift gave them a great advantage over the unemployed workers in the cities.

"Waste not, want not" was not only a slogan and a song, it was 11 also our way of life. We were not to throw away clothes or any other worldly goods for which we or someone else might ever have a possible use. Homemade clothes, which almost never fit, were handed down in each family from child to child. When there were no more children in the family to wear them, any garment still remotely wearable was passed on to a neighbor or relative, with no apology on the part of the giver or receiver.

The winter I was in sixth grade I had to wear a thick pair of wool 12 pants that had probably been sewn before the Civil War, because they looked like the tight-legged style Abraham Lincoln had worn at his inauguration. Since most everyone else was wearing wide-legged pants, I was a bit ashamed of the way I looked. Still, they were better than the knickers and long stockings I had been wearing previously.

One day near the end of the winter, though, time caught up with 13 my breeches, and they disintegrated when I caught them on the chalk tray while I was doing arithmetic problems at the blackboard. Luckily, I had on long underwear, but I was very embarrassed, nevertheless, and took a lot of ribbing from my schoolmates. That night Ma, in her big box of passed-down clothing, found another pair of pants that were not quite as old and not more than a couple of sizes too big. My ripped pants were cut into long strips to be braided into rugs.

Everybody wore clothes not only long after they had faded, but 14 also after they'd been patched and repatched and sometimes dyed.

Suits were turned inside out when the outsides got too shiny. Every housewife spent her evenings and every other spare moment mending, darning socks, turning worn collars and cuffs, repairing holes in sweaters, and sewing patches on garments that were coming apart. New clothes were so uncommon that Judah MacDougal always left the big paper labels on his overalls until they were washed so that everyone would notice they were new.

Food was never wasted, either, and leftovers from the dinner at   15
noon usually constituted the main part of that evening's supper. We always had plenty of hash, soups, and puddings that my mother concocted from leftovers, and there was still plenty for Peggy, our collie dog, and our several cats. The pigs were given all our apple and potato parings, and the chickens got any moldy bread.

Most families carried their thrift to great extremes and often   16
deposited quantities of dilapidated items in their sheds and lofts, hoping that someone would find a use for them. Our shed chamber, as the attic was called, contained large boxes of completely worn-out shoes and mismatched gloves full of holes. Several barrels of dry corncobs stood in one corner to be used for smoking meat, although we might use only eight or ten cobs each year. Neatly stacked were boxes of hopelessly rusted nails, rotten leather harness straps, broken window glass, and many pieces of heavy string and rope that were too short or too far gone for any possible use.

Also in the shed chamber, hanging on a nail, was a large rag bag   17
in which were collected clothes no longer good enough for washing windows or making rugs. These were sold for five or ten cents a bag to the peddler who came by once a year, and he, in turn, sold them to salvage companies to be used for making paper. We also religiously saved stiff old paint brushes, broken bottles, rusty tin cans, broken shoelaces, and worn-out rubber boots, for what reason I never figured out, since even the ragman didn't want them. Rummaging through the attic was one of my favorite pastimes as a boy, though, and I spent many happy hours there on rainy days.

Once I visited the children of our friends the Findlays. Their   18
ancestors, who were more recently arrived from a hard life in the British Isles than mine, had found it even more impossible to discard anything. Each room in their enormous house was like an attic—filled with catalogues, magazines, and newspapers collected over many years, bundles of peacock feathers, old guns, bottles, quarantine signs, swords and medals from the Civil War, powder kegs and horns,

cowboy spurs, bear traps, an old loom, a flax wheel, candle molds, homemade tools, and much more. It was a boy's paradise.

Just as it was considered sinful to throw away anything without   19
a good reason, likewise one was not expected to buy anything new unless he could prove to himself and his neighbors that he really needed it. Froth Hudson bought his wife, Gracie, a newfangled gasoline-powered washing machine in 1932, the year I was in the fourth grade. The neighborhood was aghast. "Gol' 'ram fool oughta have a guardian," was the common description of his folly.

"Eat it up, wear it out, make it do, or go without" was the code   20
of the Hills, and also of the Cheevers, the Andersons, the Lincolns, and just about everybody else.

Time was another commodity we must not waste, and everyone   21
had great respect for it. Being on time was as important as being frugal. To be late not only brought disgrace upon yourself and your family, but it also was considered a sin comparable to being lazy or playing pool on Sunday.

A clock was often a family's most expensive possession, and it   22
governed everyone's life. In my great-grandfather's account book, one item indicates that he paid $24 for a clock in the very early 1800s. In a time when a gallon of whiskey or a pair of shoes went for 60 cents, a casket cost $2.50, and a new house complete with cellar, two chimneys, hardwood floors, windows, and plastered walls could be built for $350, $24 was a tremendous amount.

It seems odd that the people in my neighborhood, since they had   23
no trains to catch and no time clocks to worry about, should have had such an acute sense of time, but they did. Breakfast was always on my family's table at eight, after morning chores were done. Dinner was at noon, and that didn't mean five minutes before or five minutes past. It didn't mean when the vittles were done, either, or when someone got back from the store. Supper was at five, and as with all meals, unless there was a real emergency, both the meal and the folks eating it were expected to be ready.

Most people I knew didn't go anywhere often, but when they   24
did, they planned to be early. As a teenager, I was embarrassed and uncomfortable when my family showed up a half hour early for a funeral, but we usually found several other neighbors already waiting. We arrived at my sister's high school graduation before the janitor had opened the building.

"If you can't be there on time, better not bother to go at all" and   25
"Better early than late" were phrases I heard often at home and at
school. Latecomers were stared at, commented on, and would have
had to be stone deaf not to know they were being pointed out as bad
examples of humanity.

It was expected that all neighborhood bees would start on time.   26
When Snort Finney started up his wood-sawing rig at 8:30 in the
morning, he expected the neighborhood men to have done their barn
chores, have "et" their breakfast, have laced up their boots, and be
ready to saw wood.

Sometimes a little help was necessary to meet the deadlines. "I   27
came into the house a little early one day," Herman Barker told us at
school, "and my mother was setting the clock back because she didn't
have dinner quite ready. She made me promise not to tell, and my
father thought he had set his watch wrong."

Every man valued his pocket watch, and some older folks had   28
very elaborate ones. An expensive fat gold watch in the vest pocket
of one's dress-up clothes, with a gold chain stretching across the front,
was a badge of success. Many watches had fancy engraving on the
back, and some had covers that had to be flicked open before you
could see the face. Most men, and a few boys, had pocket watches that
had cost a dollar or less. If they weren't dropped on the floor, they
would keep good time for years.

Although nearly everyone was obsessed with being on time,   29
people often lost track of the days of the week. Every home had two
or three calendars in each room, but that didn't always help. Few
homes had radios until the late 1930s, and no one saw a daily paper.
If a family didn't have children in school, each day was pretty much
like the day before, so no one seemed terribly surprised when folks
showed up for some event a day or two early or late.

One winter Sunday some years before I was born, my family was   30
on the way to church in the sleigh when they overtook Duncan
MacDonald headed for town with his team of horses and a big load
of logs on a double sled. Since Duncan was a church elder and, unlike
my family, attended faithfully, they were shocked to see him working
on the Sabbath. He was equally surprised when he turned around and
noticed them. "Where are you folks going all dressed up?" he called
as he pulled over his rig. "To church," they answered.

"Church! Why, today ain't Sunday." Then he turned pale. "By   31
gravy, it is." Turning the large load of logs around in the narrow road

wasn't easy, but he managed it. "I've got to get home and stop Hanna," he yelled back. "She's just starting to make pies."

Dunc and Hanna were quite late for church that day, but they sat 32 in their usual pew, and there was no hint, either in their expressions or conversation, that anything unusual had happened along the way.

Meanings and Values

1. In paragraph 11, Hill says, " 'Waste not, want not' was not only a slogan and a song, it was also our way of life." Do all the examples in the essay illustrate and explore this central theme? Which, if any, do not? (consider especially the examples in paragraphs 21–32). (See Guide to Terms: *Unity*.)

2a. What in the essay suggests that the author approves of the values of the people who appear in the examples?

 b. At what points, if any, does the author appear to be critical of the values? What evidence suggests that the author is being critical?

3a. Choose three humorous examples from the essay and explain why you think the humor encourages readers to be either sympathetic toward or critical of the people and their values.

 b. Explain the extent to which each of the examples might be considered ironic. (Guide: *Irony*.)

Expository Techniques

1a. Where in paragraph 11 does the author provide a concise statement of the central theme? (Guide: *Unity*.)

 b. Can this statement be considered the thesis of the entire essay? Why, or why not?

 c. Explain why readers are not likely to have trouble identifying the central theme as they read the first ten paragraphs of the essay.

2. Are there too many examples in this essay? Which, if any, could be omitted without harming the effectiveness of the essay? (Guide: *Evaluation*.)

3. Explain the role of the first sentence in paragraph 21 with regard to the essay as a whole and to the paragraphs that follow it (22–32). (Guide: *Coherence, Transition*.)

4. For each of the following paragraphs, discuss the relationship between the opening sentence and the other sentences in the paragraph: 15, 16, and 19. (Guide: *Unity*.)

Diction and Vocabulary

1. In what ways do the proverbs and colloquial expressions in each of the following paragraphs add to the essay's effectiveness: 1, 4, 19, 20, 25, and 31? (Guide: *Colloquial Expressions.*)

2a. What is meant by the passage "since catalogues and newspapers were the rule in our privies at home" (par. 7)?

 b. Why would the author bother to include this detail?

3. Use the dictionary as necessary to understand the following words: maxim, dispatch (par. 1); cardinal, avarice (2); privies (7); and knickers (12).

Suggestions for Writing and Discussion

1. Discuss the role of proverbs and brief stories (anecdotes) that make a point in your family or some other community to which you belong.

2. To what extent are the values of many people today different from those described by Hill? What values, if any, are similar?

3. To what extent are the values Hill describes characteristic of a rural community as opposed to an urban one?

(NOTE: Suggestions for topics requiring development by use of EXAMPLE are on page 61, at the end of this section.)

JANE GOODALL was born in London in 1934. After working for a short time in England, she went to Africa as an assistant to Louis Leakey, head of the National Museum of Natural History in Kenya. In 1960, she founded the Gombe Stream Research Centre in Tanzania, East Africa, which focuses on studying the behavior of animals, especially chimpanzees. In 1965, she received her Ph.D from Cambridge University. She has been awarded numerous honors for her ground-breaking research on animal behavior (ethology). Among her many publications are articles in magazines such as *National Geographic* and *Nature* as well as several books, including *In the Shadow of Man* (1971), *Grub: The Bush Baby* (1972), and *Through a Window* (1990).

The Mind of the Chimpanzee

In this selection from *Through a Window,* Goodall draws on a variety of instances from her personal experiences and field observations. With their aid, she outlines a necessarily vague picture of the mind of the chimpanzee and at the same time suggests why it is important that we continue to try to understand as much as we can about these animals that are so similar to us in many ways.

Often I have gazed into a chimpanzee's eyes and wondered what was going on behind them. I used to look into Flo's, she so old, so wise. What did she remember of her young days? David Greybeard had the most beautiful eyes of them all, large and lustrous, set wide apart. They somehow expressed his whole personality, his serene self-assurance, his inherent dignity—and, from time to time, his utter determination to get his way. For a long time I never liked to look a chimpanzee straight in the eye—I assumed that, as is the case with 1 most primates, this would be interpreted as a threat or at least as a breach of good manners. Not so. As long as one looks with gentleness, without arrogance, a chimpanzee will understand, and may even return the look. And then—or such is my fantasy—it is as though the eyes are windows into the mind. Only the glass is opaque so that the mystery can never be fully revealed.

I shall never forget my meeting with Lucy, an eight-year-old home-raised chimpanzee. She came and sat beside me on the sofa and, with her face very close to mine, searched in my eyes—for what? Perhaps she was looking for signs of mistrust, dislike, or fear, since many people must have been somewhat disconcerted when, for the first time, they came face to face with a grown chimpanzee. Whatever Lucy read in my eyes clearly satisfied her for she suddenly put one arm around my neck and gave me a generous and very chimp-like kiss, her mouth wide open and laid over mine. I was accepted.

For a long time after that encounter I was profoundly disturbed. I had been at Gombe for about fifteen years then and I was quite familiar with chimpanzees in the wild. But Lucy, having grown up as a human child, was like a changeling, her essential chimpanzeeness overlaid by the various human behaviours she had acquired over the years. No longer purely chimp yet eons away from humanity, she was man-made, some other kind of being. I watched, amazed, as she opened the refrigerator and various cupboards, found bottles and a glass, then poured herself a gin and tonic. She took the drink to the TV, turned the set on, flipped from one channel to another then, as though in disgust, turned it off again. She selected a glossy magazine from the table and, still carrying her drink, settled in a comfortable chair. Occasionally, as she leafed through the magazine she identified something she saw, using the signs of ASL, the American Sign Language used by the deaf. I, of course, did not understand, but my hostess, Jane Temerlin (who was also Lucy's "mother"), translated: "That dog," Lucy commented, pausing at a photo of a small white poodle. She turned the page. "Blue," she declared, pointing then signing as she gazed at a picture of a lady advertising some kind of soap powder and wearing a brilliant blue dress. And finally, after some vague hand movements—perhaps signed mutterings—"This Lucy's, this mine," as she closed the magazine and laid it on her lap. She had just been taught, Jane told me, the use of the possessive pronouns during the thrice weekly ASL lessons she was receiving at the time.

The book written by Lucy's human "father," Maury Temerlin,   4
was entitled *Lucy, Growing Up Human.* And in fact, the chimpanzee is
more like us than is any other living creature. There is close resemblance in the physiology of our two species and genetically, in the
structure of the DNA, chimpanzees and humans differ by only just
over one percent. This is why medical research uses chimpanzees as
experimental animals when they need substitutes for humans in the
testing of some drug or vaccine. Chimpanzees can be infected with
just about all known human infectious diseases including those, such
as hepatitis B and AIDS, to which other non-human animals (except
gorillas, orangutans and gibbons) are immune. There are equally
striking similarities between humans and chimpanzees in the anatomy and wiring of the brain and nervous system, and—although
many scientists have been reluctant to admit to this—in social behaviour, intellectual ability, and the emotions. The notion of an evolutionary continuity in physical structure from pre-human ape to modern
man has long been morally acceptable to most scientists. That the
same might hold good for mind was generally considered an absurd
hypothesis—particularly by those who used, and often misused,
animals in their laboratories. It is, after all, convenient to believe that
the creature you are using, while it may react in disturbingly human-
like ways, is, in fact, merely a mindless and, above all, unfeeling,
"dumb" animal.

When I began my study at Gombe in 1960 it was not permissible   5
—at least not in ethological circles—to talk about an animal's mind.
Only humans had minds. Nor was it quite proper to talk about animal
personality. Of course everyone knew that they *did* have their own
unique characters—everyone who had ever owned a dog or other pet
was aware of that. But ethologists, striving to make theirs a 'hard"
science, shied away from the task of trying to explain such things
objectively. One respected ethologist, while acknowledging that there
was "variability between individual animals," wrote that it was best
that this fact be "swept under the carpet." At that time ethological
carpets fairly bulged with all that was hidden beneath them.

How naive I was. As I had not had an undergraduate science   6
education I didn't realize that animals were not supposed to have
personalities, or to think, or to feel emotions or pain. I had no idea
that it would have been more appropriate to assign each of the
chimpanzees a number rather than a name when I got to know him
or her. I didn't realize that it was not scientific to discuss behaviour

in terms of motivation or purpose. And no one had told me that terms such as *childhood* and *adolescence* were uniquely human phases of the life cycle, culturally determined, not to be used when referring to young chimpanzees. Not knowing, I freely made use of all those forbidden terms and concepts in my initial attempt to describe, to the best of my ability, the amazing things I had observed at Gombe.

I shall never forget the response of a group of ethologists to some   7 remarks I made at an erudite seminar. I described how Figan, as an adolescent, had learned to stay behind in camp after senior males had left, so that we could give him a few bananas for himself. On the first occasion he had, upon seeing the fruits, uttered loud, delighted food calls: whereupon a couple of the older males had charged back, chased after Figan, and taken his bananas. And then, coming to the point of the story, I explained how, on the next occasion, Figan had actually suppressed his calls. We could hear little sounds, in his throat, but so quiet that none of the others could have heard them. Other young chimps, to whom we tried to smuggle fruit without the knowledge of their elders, never learned such self-control. With shrieks of glee they would fall to, only to be robbed of their booty when the big males charged back. I had expected my audience to be as fascinated and impressed as I was. I had hoped for an exchange of views about the chimpanzee's undoubted intelligence. Instead there was a chill silence, after which the chairman hastily changed the subject. Needless to say, after being thus snubbed, I was very reluctant to contribute any comments, at any scientific gathering, for a very long time. Looking back, I suspect that everyone was interested, but it was, of course, not permissible to present a mere "anecdote" as evidence for anything.

The editorial comments on the first paper I wrote for publication   8 demanded that every *he* or *she* be replaced with *it,* and every *who* be replaced with *which.* Incensed, I, in my turn, crossed out the *its* and *whichs* and scrawled back the original pronouns. As I had no desire to carve a niche for myself in the world of science, but simply wanted to go on living among and learning about chimpanzees, the possible reaction of the editor of the learned journal did not trouble me. In fact I won that round: the paper when finally published did confer upon the chimpanzees the dignity of their appropriate genders and properly upgraded them from the status of mere "things" to essential Being-ness.

However, despite my somewhat truculent attitude, I did want to   9 learn, and I was sensible of my incredible good fortune in being admitted to Cambridge. I wanted to get my PhD, if only for the sake of Louis Leakey and the other people who had written letters in support of my admission. And how lucky I was to have, as my supervisor, Robert Hinde. Not only because I thereby benefitted from his brilliant mind and clear thinking, but also because I doubt that I could have found a teacher more suited to my particular needs and personality. Gradually he was able to cloak me with at least some of the trappings of a scientist. Thus although I continued to hold to most of my convictions—that animals had personalities; that they could feel happy or sad or fearful; that they could feel pain; that they could strive towards planned goals and achieve greater success if they were highly motivated—I soon realized that these personal convictions were, indeed, difficult to prove. It was best to be circumspect—at least until I had gained some credentials and credibility. And Robert gave me wonderful advice on how best to tie up some of my more rebellious ideas with scientific ribbon. "You can't *know* that Fifi was jealous," he admonished on one occasion. We argued a little. And then: "Why don't you just say *If Fifi were a human child we would say she was jealous.*" I did.

It is not easy to study emotions even when the subjects are   10
human. I know how I feel if I am sad or happy or angry, and if a friend tells me that he is feeling sad, happy or angry, I assume that his feelings are similar to mine. But of course I cannot know. As we try to come to grips with the emotions of beings progressively more different from ourselves the task, obviously, becomes increasingly difficult. If we ascribe human emotions to non-human animals we are accused of being anthropomorphic—a cardinal sin in ethology. But is it so terrible? If we test the effect of drugs on chimpanzees because they are biologically so similar to ourselves, if we accept that there are dramatic similarities in chimpanzee and human brain and nervous system, is it not logical to assume that there will be similarities also in at least the more basic feelings, emotions, moods of the two species?

Meanings and Values

1. According to this essay, it is appropriate to speak of a chimpanzee's "mind"? In what ways can a chimpanzee be said to have a mind?

2. Did you come to this essay believing that chimpanzees are very similar to humans? Discuss the ways in which the essay changed or confirmed your attitudes toward chimpanzees.

3. Explain why the author was willing to go along with the changes suggested by her supervisor (para. 9) but not those suggested by the editor (par. 8).

Expository Techniques

1a.   Can the last two sentences in paragraph 1 be considered a statement of the essay's central theme? Why? (See Guide to Terms: *Unity.*)

 b.   If not, where and how in the essay is the central theme stated?

 c.   Should the central theme be stated more clearly, or is it clear enough? Be ready to defend your answer. (Guide: *Evaluation.*)

2.   Discuss the role of the short sentences in these paragraphs: 2, 5, 6, and 9.

3a.   This essay has a relatively distinctive tone. Examine paragraphs 1–2, 5–6, and 10 and then describe in your own words the tone of the essay. (Guide: *Style/Tone.*)

 b.   In what ways do the sentence structures and word choice in these paragraphs contribute to the tone? (Guide: *Syntax, Diction.*)

4.   How do the rhetorical questions in paragraph 10 help bring the selection to a close? (Guide: *Rhetorical Questions, Closings.*)

Diction and Vocabulary

1a.   Discuss how Goodall uses scientific terms in paragraph 4 to add authority and believability to her conclusions.

 b.   Are most readers likely to understand or to be put off by this language? Explain.

2.   Use the dictionary as necessary to understand the meanings of the following words: lustrous, primates (par. 1); eons (3); gibbons (4); ethological (5); erudite (7); anthropomorphic (10).

Suggestions for Writing and Discussion

1.   Tell whether you think common household pets can be said to have "minds," and provide examples to explain and illustrate your point of view.

2.   To what extent are we limited in understanding other people's minds and feelings just as we are limited in understanding those of chimpanzees?

3.   If animals have minds and feelings, can medical research using animals be justified?

(NOTE: Suggestions for topics requiring development by use of EXAMPLE are on page 61, at the end of this section.)

WILLIAM F. BUCKLEY, JR.

WILLIAM F. BUCKLEY, JR., was born in 1925 in New York, where he now lives with his wife and son. He graduated from Yale University and holds honorary degrees from a number of universities, including Seton Hall, Syracuse University, Notre Dame, and Lafayette College. He was editor in chief of *National Review* from 1955 to 1990. In addition, he has been a syndicated columnist since 1962, and host of public television's "Firing Line" since 1966. Generally considered one of the most articulate conservative writers, Buckley has published in various general circulation magazines and has received numerous honors and awards. He lectures widely and is the author of many novels and nonfiction books, among them *God and Man at Yale: The Superstitions of "Academic Freedom"* (1951), *Saving the Queen* (1976), *Stained Glass* (1978), *Who's on First* (1980), *Marco Polo, If You Can* (1982), *Atlantic High* (1982), *Overdrive: A Personal Documentary* (1983), *The Story of Henri Tod* (1984), *The Tall Ships* (1986), *See You Later, Alligator* (1985), *High Jinx* (1986), *Racing Through Paradise: A Pacific Passage* (1987), *Mongoose R.I.P.* (1988), *On the Firing Line: The Public Life of Our Public Figures* (1989), and *Tucker's Last Stand* (1990).

Why Don't We Complain?

First published in *Esquire*, "Why Don't We Complain?" is a good illustration of the grace and wit that characterize most of Buckley's writing. For students of composition, it can also provide another demonstration of the use of varied examples—some well developed, others scarcely at all—to make a single generality more specific. And the generality itself, as we can see toward the end, is of considerably broader significance than it appears at first.

It was the very last coach and the only empty seat on the entire train, so there was no turning back. The problem was to breathe. Outside,

1

the temperature was below freezing. Inside the railroad car the temperature must have been about 85 degrees. I took off my overcoat, and a few minutes later my jacket, and noticed that the car was flecked with the white shirts of the passengers. I soon found my hand moving to loosen my tie. From one end of the car to the other, as we rattled through Westchester County, we sweated; but we did not moan.

I watched the train conductor appear at the head of the car. 2 "Tickets, all tickets, please!" In a more virile age, I thought, the passengers would seize the conductor and strap him down on a seat over the radiator to share the fate of his patrons. He shuffled down the aisle, picking up tickets, punching commutation cards. *No one addressed a word to him.* He approached my seat, and I drew a deep breath of resolution. "Conductor," I began with a considerable edge to my voice. . . . Instantly the doleful eyes of my seatmate turned tiredly from his newspaper to fix me with a resentful stare: what question could be so important as to justify my sibilant intrusion into his stupor? I was shaken by those eyes. I am incapable of making a discreet fuss, so I mumbled a question about what time were we due in Stamford (I didn't even ask whether it would be before or after dehydration could be expected to set in), got my reply, and went back to my newspaper and to wiping my brow.

The conductor had nonchalantly walked down the gauntlet of 3 eighty sweating American freemen, and not one of them had asked him to explain why the passengers in that car had been consigned to suffer. There is nothing to be done when the temperature *outdoors* is 85 degrees, and indoors the air conditioner has broken down; obviously when that happens there is nothing to do, except perhaps curse the day that one was born. But when the temperature outdoors is below freezing, it takes a positive act of will on somebody's part to set the temperature *indoors* at 85. Somewhere a valve was turned too far, a furnace overstocked, a thermostat maladjusted: something that could easily be remedied by turning off the heat and allowing the great outdoors to come indoors. All this is so obvious. What is not obvious is what has happened to the American people.

It isn't just the commuters, whom we have come to visualize as 4 a supine breed who have got on to the trick of suspending their sensory faculties twice a day while they submit to the creeping dissolution of the railroad industry. It isn't just they who have given

up trying to rectify irrational vexations. It is the American people
everywhere.

A few weeks ago at a large movie theater I turned to my wife and   5
said, "The picture is out of focus." "Be quiet," she answered. I obeyed.
But a few minutes later I raised the point again, with mounting
impatience. "It will be all right in a minute," she said apprehensively.
(She would rather lose her eyesight than be around when I make one
of my infrequent scenes.) I waited. It was *just* out of focus—not
glaringly out, but out. My vision is 20–20, and I assume that is the
vision, adjusted, of most people in the movie house. So, after hectoring my wife throughout the first reel, I finally prevailed upon her to
admit that it *was* off, and very annoying. We then settled down,
coming to rest on the presumption that: (a) someone connected
with the management of the theater must soon notice the blur and
make the correction; or (b) that someone seated near the rear of the
house would make the complaint in behalf of those of us up front; or
(c) that—any minute now—the entire house would explode into
catcalls and foot stamping, calling dramatic attention to the irksome
distortion.

What happened was nothing. The movie ended, as it had begun,   6
just out of focus, and as we trooped out, we stretched our faces in a
variety of contortions to accustom the eye to the shock of normal
focus.

I think it is safe to say that everybody suffered on that occasion.   7
And I think it is safe to assume that everyone was expecting someone
else to take the initiative in going back to speak to the manager. And
it is probably true even that if we had supposed the movie would run
right through the blurred image, someone surely would have sum-
moned up the purposive indignation to get up out of his seat and file
his complaint.

But notice that no one did. And the reason no one did is because   8
we are all increasingly anxious in America to be unobtrusive, we are
reluctant to make our voices heard, hesitant about claiming our rights;
we are afraid that our cause is unjust, or that if it is not unjust, that it
is ambiguous; or if not even that, that it is too trivial to justify the
horrors of a confrontation with Authority; we still sit in an oven or
endure a racking headache before undertaking a head-on, I'm-here-
to-tell-you complaint. That tendency to passive compliance, to a
heedless endurance, is something to keep one's eyes on—in sharp
focus.

I myself can occasionally summon the courage to complain, but   9
I cannot, as I have intimated, complain softly. My own instinct is so
strong to let the thing ride, to forget about it—to expect that someone
will take the matter up, when the grievance is collective, in my
behalf—that it is only when the provocation is at a very special key,
whose vibrations touch simultaneously a complexus of nerves, aller-
gies, and passions, that I catch fire and find the reserves of courage
and assertiveness to speak up. When that happens, I get quite carried
away. My blood gets hot, my brow wet, I become unbearably and
unconscionably sarcastic and bellicose; I am girded for a total show-
down.

Why should that be? Why could not I (or anyone else) on that   10
railroad coach have said simply to the conductor, "Sir"—I take that
back: that sounds sarcastic—"Conductor, would you be good enough
to turn down the heat? I am extremely hot. In fact, I tend to get hot
every time the temperature reaches 85 degr—" Strike that last sentence. Just end it with the simple statement that you are extremely hot,
and let the conductor infer the cause.

Every New Year's Eve I resolve to do something about the   11
Milquetoast in me and vow to speak up, calmly, for my rights, and for
the betterment of our society, on every appropriate occasion. Entering
last New Year's Eve, I was fortified in my resolve because that
morning at breakfast I had had to ask the waitress three times for a
glass of milk. She finally brought it—after I had finished my eggs,
which is when I don't want it any more. I did not have the manliness
to order her to take the milk back, but settled instead for a cowardly
sulk, and ostentatiously refused to drink the milk—though I later paid
for it—rather than state plainly to the hostess, as I should have, why
I had not drunk it, and would not pay for it.

So by the time the New Year ushered out the Old, riding in on my   12
morning's indignation and stimulated by the gastric juices of resolution that flow so faithfully on New Year's Eve, I rendered my vow.
Henceforward I would conquer my shyness, my despicable disposi-
tion to supineness. I would speak out like a man against the unnecessary annoyances of our time.

Forty-eight hours later, I was standing in line at the ski repair   13
store in Pico Peak, Vermont. All I needed, to get on with my skiing,
was the loan, for one minute, of a small screwdriver, to tighten a loose
binding. Behind the counter in the workshop were two men. One was
industriously engaged in servicing the complicated requirements of

a young lady at the head of the line, and obviously he would be tied up for quite a while. The other—"Jiggs," his workmate called him—was a middle-aged man, who sat in a chair puffing a pipe, exchanging small talk with his working partner. My pulse began its telltale acceleration. The minutes ticked on. I stared at the idle shopkeeper, hoping to shame him into action, but he was impervious to my telepathic reproof and continued his small talk with his friend, brazenly insensitive to the nervous demands of six good men who were raring to ski.

Suddenly my New Year's Eve resolution struck me. It was now 14 or never. I broke from my place in line and marched to the counter. I was going to control myself. I dug my nails into my palms. My effort was only partially successful:

"If you are not too busy," I said icily, "would you mind handing 15 me a screwdriver?"

Work stopped and everyone turned his eyes on me, and I expe- 16 rienced that mortification I always feel when I am the center of centripetal shafts of curiosity, resentment, perplexity.

But the worst was yet to come. "I am sorry, sir," said Jiggs 17 deferentially, moving the pipe from his mouth. "I am not supposed to move. I have just had a heart attack." That was the signal for a great whirring noise that descended from heaven. We looked, stricken, out the window, and it appeared as though a cyclone had suddenly focused on the snowy courtyard between the shop and the ski lift. Suddenly a gigantic army helicopter materialized, and hovered down to a landing. Two men jumped out of the plane carrying a stretcher, tore into the ski shop, and lifted the shopkeeper onto the stretcher. Jiggs bade his companion good-by, was whisked out the door, into the plane, up to the heavens, down—we learned—to a nearby army hospital. I looked up manfully—into a score of man-eating eyes. I put the experience down as a reversal.

As I write this, on an airplane, I have run out of paper and need 18 to reach into my briefcase under my legs for more. I cannot do this until my empty lunch tray is removed from my lap. I arrested the stewardess as she passed empty-handed down the aisle on the way to the kitchen to fetch the lunch trays for the passengers up forward who haven't been served yet. "Would you please take my tray?" "Just a *moment*, sir!" she said, and marched on sternly. Shall I tell her that since she is headed for the kitchen *anyway*, it could not delay the feeding of the other passengers by more than two seconds necessary to stash away my empty tray? Or remind her that not fifteen minutes ago she spoke unctuously into the loudspeaker the words undoubtedly devised by the airline's highly paid public relations counselor: "If there is anything I or Miss French can do for you to make your trip more enjoyable, *please* let us—" I have run out of paper.

I think the observable reluctance of the majority of Americans to   19
assert themselves in minor matters is related to our increased sense of helplessness in an age of technology and centralized political and economic power. For generations, Americans who were too hot, or too cold, got up and did something about it. Now we call the plumber, or the electrician, or the furnace man. The habit of looking after our own needs obviously had something to do with the assertiveness that characterized the American family familiar to readers of American literature. With the technification of life goes our direct responsibility for our material environment, and we are conditioned to adopt a position of helplessness not only as regards the broken air conditioner, but as regards the overheated train. It takes an expert to fix the former, but not the latter; yet these distinctions, as we withdraw into helplessness, tend to fade away.

Our notorious political apathy is a related phenomenon. Every   20
year, whether the Republican or the Democratic Party is in office, more and more power drains away from the individual to feed vast reservoirs in far-off places; and we have less and less say about the shape of events which shape our future. From this alienation of personal power comes the sense of resignation with which we accept the political dispensations of a powerful government whose hold upon us continues to increase.

An editor of a national weekly news magazine told me a few   21
years ago that as few as a dozen letters of protest against an editorial stance of his magazine was enough to convene a plenipotentiary meeting of the board of editors to review policy. "So few people complain, or make their voices heard," he explained to me, "that we assume a dozen letters represent the inarticulate views of thousands of readers." In the past ten years, he said, the volume of mail has noticeably decreased, even though the circulation of his magazine has risen.

When our voices are finally mute, when we have finally sup-   22
pressed the natural instinct to complain, whether the vexation is trivial or grave, we shall have become automatons, incapable of feeling. When Premier Khrushchev first came to this country late in

1959, he was primed, we are informed, to experience the bitter resentment of the American people against his tyranny, against his persecutions, against the movement which is responsible for the great number of American deaths in Korea, for billions in taxes every year, and for life everlasting on the brink of disaster; but Khrushchev was pleasantly surprised, and reported back to the Russian people that he had been met with overwhelming cordiality (read: apathy), except, to be sure, for "a few fascists who followed me around with their wretched posters, and should be horsewhipped."

I may be crazy, but I say there would have been lots more posters 　 23 in a society where train temperatures in the dead of winter are not allowed to climb to 85 degrees without complaint.

Meanings and Values

1. By what means, if any, does Buckley's scolding of the American people avoid being disagreeable?

2. Restate completely what you believe to be the meaning of the last sentence of paragraph 8.

3. Why do you think the author said to "strike that last sentence" of the quoted matter in paragraph 10?

4. Explain the connection between anti-Khrushchev posters and complaining about the heat in a train (par. 23).

5a. State in your own words the central theme of this selection. (See Guide to Terms: *Unity*.)

　b. Does it seem to you that this is the best way to have developed the theme? If not, what might have been a better way?

6. On a specific-to-general continuum, where would you place "Why Don't We Complain?" Why? (Guide: *Specific/General*.)

Expository Techniques

1a. Which of the standard methods of introduction does the first paragraph demonstrate? (Guide: *Introductions*.)

　b. How successful is its use?

2a. What generality do Buckley's examples illustrate? (You may use his words or your own.)

　b. In what way, if at all, does this generality differ from his central theme?

c. In this respect, how does the writing differ from most?

3. Why do you think the Khrushchev example is kept until last? (Guide: *Emphasis*.)

4. What seems to be the purpose, or purposes, of paragraphs 4 and 12?

5. Assuming that this piece is typical of Buckley's writing, what aspects of his style or tone will probably make his writing identifiable when you next encounter it? (Guide: *Style/Tone*.)

Diction and Vocabulary

1. Explain the meaning (in par. 22) of Khrushchev's being "met with overwhelming cordiality (read: apathy)."

2. Explain the allusion to Milquetoast in paragraph 11. (Guide: *Figures of Speech*.)

3a. Were you annoyed by Buckley's liberal use of "dictionary-type" words? To what extent? Why were you annoyed?

b. Cite any such words that were used without good reason.

c. To what extent is this use a matter of style?

4. Use a dictionary as needed to understand the meanings of the following words: virile, doleful, sibilant, discreet (par. 2); gauntlet, consigned (3); supine, faculties, dissolution, rectify (4); hectoring (5); purposive (7); unobtrusive, ambiguous (8); provocation, complexus, unconscionably, bellicose, girded (9); infer (10); ostentatiously (11); impervious, reproof (13); centripetal (16); deferentially (17); unctuously (18); technification (19); apathy, phenomenon, dispensations (20); stance, plenipotentiary, inarticulated (21); automatons (22).

Suggestions for Writing and Discussion

1. Discuss, if you can, the idea that readers of American literature are familiar with the "assertiveness that characterized the American family" (par. 19).

2. An apathy such as Buckley describes, if permitted to develop to its extreme, could have disastrous results. Explore what some of these might be.

3. Buckley is generally thought to be one of the most effective spokespeople for the conservative right. Explain how you could have guessed his political views by what he says in this largely nonpolitical essay. Be specific.

4.   Does the response of the American public to recent social and political issues indicate an increase or decrease in apathy? Give examples. If you are familiar with some other country, Canada or Mexico, for instance, indicate whether its citizens are as apathetic as the people Buckley describes.

(NOTE: Suggestions for topics requiring development by use of EXAMPLE are on page 61, at the end of this section.)

BARBARA EHRENREICH

BARBARA EHRENREICH received a B.A. from Reed College and a
Ph.D. from Rockefeller University in biology. She has been active
in the women's movement and other movements for social change
for a number of years and has taught women's issues at several
universities, including New York University and the State University of New York–Old Westbury. She is a Fellow of the Institute for
Policy Studies in Washington, D.C., and is active in the Democratic
Socialists of America. A prolific author, Ehrenreich is a regular
columnist for *Ms.* and *Mother Jones* and has published articles in a
wide range of magazines, among them *Esquire*, the *Atlantic*, *Vogue*,
New Republic, the *Wall Street Journal*, *TV Guide*, the *New York Times
Magazine*, *Social Policy*, and *The Nation*. Her books include *For Her
Own Good: 150 Years of the Experts' Advice to Women* (with Deirdre
English) (1978); *The Hearts of Men: American Dreams and the Flight
from Commitment* (1983); *Remaking Love: The Feminization of Sex* (with
Elizabeth Hess and Gloria Jacobs) (1986); *Fear of Falling: The Inner
Life of the Middle Class* (1989); and *The Worst Years of Our Lives:
Irreverent Notes from a Decade of Greed* (1990).

What I've Learned from Men

The theme and strategies of this essay (first published in *Ms.*) are
similar in some striking ways to those of Buckley's piece. Nonetheless, the essays' perspectives are clearly different, reflecting the
social and political outlooks of their authors. Yet Ehrenreich, like
Buckley, provides numerous illustrations of the skillful use of examples in support of a generality. In addition, she demonstrates the
role of examples in definition as she contrasts "lady" with
"woman."

For many years I believed that women had only one thing to learn 1
from men: how to get the attention of a waiter by some means short
of kicking over the table and shrieking. Never in my life have I gotten
the attention of a waiter, unless it was an off-duty waiter whose car
I'd accidentally scraped in a parking lot somewhere. Men, however,
can summon a maître d' just by thinking the word "coffee," and this
is a power women would be well advised to study. What else would
we possibly want to learn from them? How to interrupt someone in
mid-sentence as if you were performing an act of conversational
euthanasia? How to drop a pair of socks three feet from an open
hamper and keep right on walking? How to make those weird guttural gargling sounds in the bathroom?

But now, at mid-life, I am willing to admit that there are some 2
real and useful things to learn from men. Not from all men—in fact,
we may have the most to learn from some of the men we like the least.
This realization does not mean that my feminist principles have gone
soft with age: what I think women could learn from men is how to
get *tough*. After more than a decade of consciousness-raising, assertiveness training, and hand-to-hand combat in the battle of the sexes,
we're still too ladylike. Let me try that again—we're just too *damn*
ladylike.

Here is an example from my own experience, a story that I blush 3
to recount. A few years ago, at an international conference held in an
exotic and luxurious setting, a prestigious professor invited me to his
room for what he said would be an intellectual discussion on matters
of theoretical importance. So far, so good. I showed up promptly. But
only minutes into the conversation—held in all-too-adjacent chairs—
it emerged that he was interested in something more substantial than
a meeting of minds. I was disgusted, but not enough to overcome
30-odd years of programming in ladylikeness. Every time his comments took a lecherous turn, I chattered distractingly; every time his
hand found its way to my knee, I returned it as if it were something
he had misplaced. This went on for an unconscionable period (as
much as 20 minutes); then there was a minor scuffle, a dash for the
door, and I was out—with nothing violated but my self-esteem. I, a
full-grown feminist, conversant with such matters as rape crisis coun-
seling and sexual harassment at the workplace, had behaved like a
ninny—or, as I now understand it, like a lady.

The essence of ladylikeness is a persistent servility masked as 4
"niceness." For example, we (women) tend to assume that it is our

responsibility to keep everything "nice" even when the person we are with is rude, aggressive, or emotionally AWOL. (In the above example, I was so busy taking responsibility for preserving the veneer of "niceness" that I almost forgot to take responsibility for myself.) In conversations with men, we do almost all the work: sociologists have observed that in male-female social interactions it's the woman who throws out leading questions and verbal encouragements ("So how did you *feel* about that?" and so on) while the man, typically, says "Hmmmm." Wherever we go, we're perpetually smiling—the on-cue smile, like the now-outmoded curtsy, being one of our culture's little rituals of submission. We're trained to feel embarrassed if we're praised, but if we see a criticism coming at us from miles down the road, we rush to acknowledge it. And when we're feeling aggressive or angry or resentful, we just tighten up our smiles or turn them into rueful little moues. In short, we spend a great deal of time acting like wimps.

For contrast, think of the macho stars we love to watch. Think,   5
for example, of Mel Gibson facing down punk marauders in "The Road Warrior" . . . John Travolta swaggering his way through the early scenes of "Saturday Night Fever" . . . or Marlon Brando shrugging off the local law in "The Wild One." Would they simper their way through tight spots? Chatter aimlessly to keep the conversation going? Get all clutched up whenever they think they might—just might—have hurt someone's feelings? No, of course not, and therein, I think, lies their fascination for us.

The attraction of the "tough guy" is that he has—or at least seems   6
to have—what most of us lack, and that is an aura of power and control. In an article, feminist psychiatrist Jean Baker Miller writes that "a woman's using self-determined power for herself is equivalent to selfishness [and] destructiveness"—an equation that makes us want to avoid even the appearance of power. Miller cites cases of women who get depressed just when they're on the verge of success—and of women who do succeed and then bury their achievement in self-deprecation. As an example, she describes one company's periodic meetings to recognize outstanding salespeople: when a woman is asked to say a few words about her achievement, she tends to say something like, "Well, I really don't know how it happened. I guess I was just lucky this time." In contrast, the men will cheerfully own up to the hard work, intelligence, and so on, to which they owe their success. By putting herself down, a woman avoids feeling brazenly

powerful and potentially "selfish"; she also does the traditional lady's work of trying to make everyone else feel better ("She's not really so smart, after all, just lucky").

So we might as well get a little tougher. And a good place to start 7 is by cutting back on the small acts of deference that we've been programmed to perform since girlhood. Like unnecessary smiling. For many women—waitresses, flight attendants, receptionists—smiling is an occupational requirement, but there's no reason for anyone to go around grinning when she's not being paid for it. I'd suggest that we save our off-duty smiles for when we truly feel like sharing them, and if you're not sure what to do with your face in the meantime, study Clint Eastwood's expressions—both of them.

Along the same lines, I think women should stop taking respon- 8 sibility for every human interaction we engage in. In a social encounter with a woman, the average man can go 25 minutes saying nothing more than "You don't say?" "Izzat so?" and, of course, "Hmmmm." Why should we do all the work? By taking so much responsibility for making conversations go well, we act as if we had much more at stake in the encounter than the other party—and that gives him (or her) the power advantage. Every now and then, we deserve to get more out of a conversation than we put into it: I'd suggest not offering information you'd rather not share ("I'm really terrified that my sales plan won't work") and not, out of sheer politeness, soliciting information you don't really want ("Wherever did you get that lovely tie?"). There will be pauses, but they don't have to be awkward for *you*.

It is true that some, perhaps most, men will interpret any decrease 9 in female deference as a deliberate act of hostility. Omit the free smiles and perky conversation-boosters and someone is bound to ask, "Well, what's come over *you* today?" For most of us, the first impulse is to stare at our feet and make vague references to a terminally ill aunt in Atlanta, but we should have as much right to be taciturn as the average (male) taxi driver. If you're taking a vacation from smiles and small talk and some fellow is moved to inquire about what's "bothering" you, just stare back levelly and say, the international debt crisis, the arms race, or the death of God.

There are all kinds of ways to toughen up—and potentially move 10 up—at work, and I leave the details to the purveyors of assertiveness training. But Jean Baker Miller's study underscores a fundamental principle that anyone can master on her own. We can stop acting less capable than we actually are. For example, in the matter of taking credit when credit is due, there's a key difference between saying "I was just lucky" and saying "I had a plan and it worked." If you take the credit you deserve, you're letting people know that you were confident you'd succeed all along, and that you fully intend to do so again.

Finally, we may be able to learn something from men about what   11
to do with anger. As a general rule, women get irritated: men get *mad*. We make tight little smiles of ladylike exasperation; they pound on desks and roar. I wouldn't recommend emulating the full basso profundo male tantrum, but women do need ways of expressing justified anger clearly, colorfully, and, when necessary, crudely. If you're not just irritated, but *pissed off*, it might help to say so.

I, for example, have rerun the scene with the prestigious profes-   12
sor many times in my mind. And in my mind, I play it like Bogart. I start by moving my chair over to where I can look the professor full in the face. I let him do the chattering, and when it becomes evident that he has nothing serious to say, I lean back and cross my arms, just to let him know that he's wasting my time. I do not smile, neither do I nod encouragement. Nor, of course, do I respond to his blandishments with apologetic shrugs and blushes. Then, at the first flicker of lechery, I stand up and announce coolly, "All right, I've had enough of this crap." Then I walk out—slowly, deliberately, confidently. Just like a man.

Or—now that I think of it—just like a woman.   13

Meanings and Values

1. How are most women likely to respond to the opening paragraph? How are most men likely to respond? Why?

2. The author "blush[es] to recount" her encounter with the "prestigious professor" (par. 3). Why?

3a. Define the psychological and moral problem that women face in grasping and exercising power (outlined in paragraph 6).

 b. Does the explanation of the problem and its causes offered by Ehrenreich seem reasonable to you? Be ready to explain your answer and to cite examples from your experience, if possible.

4. Is the main purpose of this essay expository or argumentative? If you have read the Buckley piece earlier in this section, you may wish to compare his aim in writing with Ehrenreich's. (See Guide to Terms: *Purpose, Argument*.)

Expository Techniques

1a. Why do you think the author chose to wait until paragraph 2 to state the essay's theme? (Guide: *Unity.*)

b. What purpose is served by the brief examples in paragraph 1, including those in the form of rhetorical questions? (Guide: *Rhetorical Questions.*)

2a. In your own words, state the problem identified in paragraph 2.

b. In what way is the example in paragraph 3 related to the statement of the problem in the preceding paragraph?

c. Specify the contrasts explored in the long example in paragraph 3.

d. Tell how this example is central to the expository purposes of the essay.

3a. Besides paragraph 3, which other parts of the essay discuss the definition of "lady" and "woman"?

b. Examine the use of contrasting pairs of quotations in paragraphs 4, 8, and 10 and be ready to explain how the author uses them to make generalities more forceful or convincing.

4a. If you have read Buckley's "Why Don't We Complain?" compare the strategies Ehrenreich and Buckley use to open their essays. (Guide: *Introductions.*)

b. To conclude their essays. (Guide: *Closings.*)

Diction and Vocabulary

1a. Discuss the ways in which the diction in paragraph 3 emphasizes the contrast between the professor's reputation and intellectual achievements and his behavior. (Guide: *Diction.*)

b. Identify the contrasts in diction in paragraph 11 and indicate the ways in which parallelism adds emphasis to them. (Guide: *Parallel Structure.*)

2. List the connotations that "lady" is likely to have for most readers and compare them with the connotations the word acquires in the course of this selection. (Guide: *Connotation/Denotation.*)

3. The following words may be unfamiliar to many readers. Use your dictionary, if necessary, to discover their meanings: maître d', guttural (par. 1); adjacent, lecherous, unconscionable, conversant (3); servility, veneer (4); simper (5); self-deprecation, brazenly (6); deference (7); taciturn (9); basso profundo (11); blandishments (12).

Suggestions for Writing and Discussion

1. If you have read Buckley's essay in this section, compare the political and social values in Ehrenreich's essay with those in Buckley's.

2. To what extent are the explanations and advice in this selection applicable solely or primarily to women? To whom else might they apply?

3. How accurate are the examples Ehrenreich provides of the way men and women converse?

(NOTE: Suggestions for topics requiring development by use of EXAMPLE follow.)

Writing Suggestions for Section 1
Example

Use one of the following statements or another suggested by them as your central theme. Develop it into a unified composition, using examples from history, current events, or personal experience to illustrate your ideas. Be sure to have your reader-audience clearly in mind, as well as your specific purpose for the communication.

1. Successful businesses keep employees at their highest level of competence.

2. In an age of working mothers, fathers spend considerable time and effort helping raise the children.

3. Family life can create considerable stress.

4. Laws holding parents responsible for their children's crimes would (or would not) result in serious injustices.

5. Letting people decide for themselves which laws to obey and which to ignore would result in anarchy.

6. Many people find horror movies entertaining.

7. Service professions are often personally rewarding.

8. Religion in the United States is not dying.

9. Democracy is not always the best form of government.

10. A successful career is worth the sacrifices it requires.

11. "An ounce of prevention is worth a pound of cure."

12. The general quality of television commercials may be improving (or deteriorating).

13. An expensive car can be a poor investment.

14. "Some books are to be tasted; others swallowed; and some few to be chewed and digested." (Francis Bacon, English scientist-author, 1561–1626)

15. Most people are superstitious in one way or another.

16. Relationships within the family are much more important than relationships outside the family.

17. New government-sponsored social welfare programs are necessary in spite of their cost (or are not necessary enough to warrant the huge costs).

2

Analyzing a Subject by *Classification*

People naturally like to sort and classify things. The untidiest urchin, moving into a new dresser of his own, will put his handkerchiefs together, socks and underwear in separate stacks, and perhaps his toads and snails (temporarily) into a drawer of their own. He may classify animals as those with legs, those with wings, and those with neither. As he gets older, he finds that schoolteachers have ways of classifying *him*, not only into a reading group but, periodically, into an "A" or "F" category, or somewhere in between. On errands to the grocery store, he discovers the macaroni in the same department as the spaghetti, the pork chops somewhere near the ham. In reading the local newspaper, he observes that its staff has done some classifying for him, putting most of the comics together and seldom mixing sports stories with the news of bridal showers. Eventually he finds courses neatly classified in the college catalogue, and he knows enough not to look for biology courses under "Social Science." (Examples again—used to illustrate a "prevalence.")

Our main interest in classification here is its use as a structural pattern for explanatory writing. Many subjects about which either students or graduates may need to write will remain a hodgepodge of facts and opinions unless they can find some system of analyzing the material, dividing the subject into categories, and classifying individual elements into those categories. Here we have the distinction usually made between the rhetorical terms *division* and *classification*—for example, dividing "meat" into pork, beef, mutton, and fowl, then classifying ham and pork chops into the category of "pork." But this distinction is one we need scarcely pause for here; once the need for analysis is recognized, the dividing and classifying become inevitable companions and result in the single scheme of "classification" itself, as we have been discussing it. The original division into parts merely sets up the system that, if well chosen, best serves our purpose.

Obviously, no single system of classification is best for all purposes. Our untidy urchin may at some point classify girls according to athletic prowess, then later by size or shape or hair color. (At the same time, of course, the girls may be placing him into one or more categories.) Other people may need entirely different systems of classification: the music instructor classifies girls as sopranos, altos, contraltos; the psychologist, according to their behavior patterns; the sociologist, according to their ethnic origins.

Whatever the purpose, for the more formal uses of classification ("formal," that is, to the extent of most academic and on-the-job writing), we should be careful to use a logical system that is complete and that follows a consistent principle throughout. It would not be logical to divide Protestantism into the categories of Methodist, Baptist, and Lutheran, because the system would be incomplete and misleading. But in classifying Protestants attending some special conference—a different matter entirely—such a limited system might be both complete and logical. In any case, the writer must be careful that classes do not overlap: to classify the persons at the conference as Methodists, Baptists, Lutherans, and clergy would be illogical, because some are undoubtedly both Lutheran, for instance, and clergy.

In dividing and classifying, we are really using the basic process of outlining. Moreover, if we are dealing with classifiable *ideas,* the resulting pattern *is* our outline, which has been our aim all along—a basic organizational plan.

This process of classification frequently does, in fact, organize much less tangible things than the examples mentioned. We might wish to find some orderly basis for discussing the South's post–Civil War problems. Division might give us three primary categories of information: economic, political, and social. But for a full-scale consideration of these, the major divisions themselves may be subdivided for still more orderly explanation: the economic information may be further divided into agriculture and industry. Now it is possible to isolate and clarify such strictly industrial matters as shortage of investment capital, disrupted transportation systems, and lack of power development.

Any plan like this seems almost absurdly obvious, of course—*after* the planning is done. It appears less obvious, however, to inexperienced writers who are dealing with a jumble of information they must explain to someone else. This is when they should be aware of the patterns at their disposal, and one of the most useful of these, alone or combined with others, is classification.

Sample Paragraph (Annotated)

Background suggesting the topic of the paragraph.

Topic announcing the division into four categories.

Classification, with each category containing a presentation of characteristics.

Palmville is not a planned town that sprang full-blown from an architect's drawing board. After all, the town has been around since 1880, and for its first ninety years it grew more or less by chance. In 1970, however, M&T Realty developed a building plan that has been followed informally by most of the other major developers. As a result, the town now has four main neighborhoods, each characterized by a different kind of housing, and each using the name originally assigned by M&T's urban planner. Brooktown is a neighborhood of modest starter homes, each with three bedrooms, $1^1/_2$ baths, a small dining area, and a one-car garage. The plain occupied by the homes is bisected by Talley's Creek (now running mostly in culverts), and is the dustiest area in town, at least by general reputation. The houses in Kingston Hills are a bit more costly. Some have three bedrooms, some four, but all have dens, dining rooms, two-car garages, and yards big enough for an in-ground pool or an elaborate patio. The streets in Brooktown and Kingston Hills are straight, but those in Paddock Estates curve gracefully around the three-acre lots of custom-built homes. Buyers get to choose from eight basic plans ranging from sprawling ranches, to oversized capes, to French Colonial chateaus. Each basic plan must be modified inside and out both to suit the homeowner's taste and to make sure that each house appears different enough to justify the ad for the development: "Unique Executive Homes on three-acre lots." In contrast, Village Green, the center of the original village, offers charming restored Victorian homes and cottages mixed with modern reproductions of homes from the same period. The homes (or the styles) may be old, but the prices are contemporary, and almost as high as the luxury homes in Paddock Estates.

Sample Paragraph (Classification)

Rock and roll is old enough now to have its generations. Some of you reading this may be part of the first (those who grew up in the fifties on Elvis and Chuck Berry), or the second (fans of the British Invasion and the Motown sound), or even the third generation (kids in the seventies for whom the members of Led Zeppelin were *eminences grises* and the Beatles were Paul McCartney's *old* band). But no matter what wave you rode in on, the chances ate pretty good that your parents didn't listen to rock, that they in fact detested it and regarded everything you listened to with the utmost disdain. I can still recall my mother's reaction to the first 45 I ever bought with my own money, the Rolling Stones' "Paint It Black," with "Stupid Girl" on the flip side. Staring in outrage at the photograph that adorned the sleeve—Mick, Keith, and the boys in their foppish, Edwardian finest—she finally exclaimed, "I suppose *that's* how you want to look!"

From "Talking 'Bout Their Generation," *Parenting Magazine* (September 1988). Reprinted by permission.

JUDITH VIORST

JUDITH VIORST was born in Newark, New Jersey, and attended
Rutgers University. Formerly a contributing editor of *Redbook* magazine, for which she wrote a monthly column, she has also been a
newspaper columnist, and in 1970 she received an Emmy award
for her contributions to a CBS television special. She has written
numerous fiction and nonfiction books for children, including *Al-
exander and the Terrible, Horrible, No Good, Very Bad Day* (1982).
Among her various books of verse and prose for adults are *It's Hard
to Be Hip Over Thirty and Other Tragedies of Married Life* (1968) (a
collection of poems), *Yes, Married: A Saga of Love and Complaint*
(1972) (prose pieces), and, more recently, *If I Were in Charge of the
World and Other Worries* (1981), *Love and Guilt and the Meaning of Life*
(1984), and *Necessary Losses* (1986).

What, Me? Showing Off?

In "What, Me? Showing Off?" first published in *Redbook*, Viorst uses
classification to explore a behavior that most of us notice readily
enough in other people but may be reluctant to acknowledge in our
own actions—showing off. Though its tone is breezy and it contains
frequent touches of humor, this essay is carefully organized and
serious in purpose. Besides classification, Viorst makes good use of
examples, definition, brief narratives, and even a short dramatic
episode.

We're at the Biedermans' annual blast, and over at the far end of the   1
living room an intense young woman with blazing eyes and a throbbing voice is decrying poverty, war, injustice and human suffering.
Indeed, she expresses such anguish at the anguish of mankind that
attention quickly shifts from the moral issues she is expounding to
how very, very, very deeply she cares about them.

She's showing off. 2

Down at the other end of the room an insistently scholarly fellow 3
has just used *angst, hubris,* Kierkegaard and *epistemology* in the same
sentence. Meanwhile our resident expert in wine meditatively sips,
then pushes away, a glass of unacceptable Beaujolais.

They're showing off. 4

And then there's us, complaining about how tired we are today 5
because we went to work, rushed back to see our son's school play,
shopped at the market and hurried home in order to cook gourmet,
and then needlepointed another dining-room chair.

And what we also are doing is showing off. 6

Indeed everyone, I would like to propose, has some sort of need 7
to show off. No one's completely immune. Not you. And not I. And
although we've been taught that it's bad to boast, that it's trashy to
toot our own horn, that nice people don't strut their stuff, seek
attention or name-drop, there are times when showing off may be
forgivable and maybe even acceptable.

But first let's take a look at showing off that *is* obnoxious, that's 8
not acceptable, that's never nice. Like showoffs motivated by a fierce,
I'm-gonna-blow-you-away competitiveness. And like narcissistic
showoffs who are willing to do anything to be—and stay—the center
of attention.

Competitive showoffs want to be the best of every bunch. 9
Competitive showoffs must outshine all others. Whatever is being
discussed, they have more—expertise or money or even aggravation—and better—periodontists or children or marriages or recipes
for pesto—and deeper—love of animals or concern for human suffering or orgasms. Competitive showoffs are people who reside in a
permanent state of sibling rivalry, insisting on playing Hertz to everyone else's Avis.

(You're finishing a story, for instance, about the sweet little card 10
that your five-year-old recently made for your birthday when the
CSO interrupts to relate how her daughter not only made her a sweet
little card, but also brought her breakfast in bed and saved her
allowance for months and months in order to buy her—obviously
much more beloved—mother a beautiful scarf for her birthday. *Grrr.*)

Narcissistic showoffs, however, don't bother to compete because 11
they don't even notice there's anyone there to compete with. They talk
nonstop, they brag, they dance, they sometimes quote Homer in
Greek, and they'll even go stand on their head if attention should flag.

Narcissistic showoffs want to be the star while everyone else is the audience. And yes, they are often adorable and charming and amusing—but only until around the age of six.

(I've actually seen an NSO get up and leave the room when the   12 conversation shifted from his accomplishments. "What's the matter?" I asked when I found him standing on the terrace, brooding darkly. "Oh, I don't know," he replied, "but all of a sudden the talk started getting so superficial." *Aagh!)*

Another group of showoffs—much more sympathetic types—are   13 showoffs who are basically insecure. And while there is no easy way to distinguish the insecure from the narcissists and competitors, you may figure out which are which by whether you have the urge to reassure or to strangle them.

Insecure showoffs show off because, as one close friend ex-   14 plained, "How will they know that I'm good unless I tell them about it?" And whatever the message—I'm smart, I'm a fine human being, I'm this incredibly passionate lover—showoffs have many different techniques for telling about it.

Take smart, for example.   15

A person can show off explicitly by using flashy words, like the   16 hubris-Kierkegaard fellow I mentioned before.

Or a person can show off implicitly, by saying not a word and   17 just wearing a low-cut dress with her Phi Beta Kappa key gleaming softly in the cleavage.

A person can show off satirically, by mocking showing off: "My   18 name is Bill Sawyer," one young man announces to every new acquaintance, "and I'm bright bright bright bright bright."

Or a person can show off complainingly: "I'm sorry my daughter   19 takes after me. Men are just so frightened of smart women."

Another way showoffs show off about smart is to drop a Very   20 Smart Name—if this brain is my friend, goes the message, I must be a brain too. And indeed, a popular showing-off ploy—whether you're showing off smartness or anything else—is to name-drop a glittery name in the hope of acquiring some gilt by association.

The theory seems to be that Presidents, movie stars, Walter   21 Cronkite and Princess Di could be friends, if they chose, with anyone in the world, and that if these luminaries have selected plain old Stanley Stone to be friends with, Stanley Stone must be one hell of a guy. (Needless to say, old Stanley Stone might also be a very dreary fellow, but if Walt and Di don't mind him, why should I?)

Though no one that I know hangs out with Presidents and movie   22
stars, they do (I too!) sometimes drop famous names.

As in: "I go to John Travolta's dermatologist."   23

Or: "I own the exact same sweater that Jackie Onassis wore in a   24
newspaper photograph last week."

Or: "My uncle once repaired a roof for Sandra Day O'Connor."   25

Or: "My cousin's neighbor's sister-in-law has a child who is   26
Robert Redford's son's best friend."

We're claiming we've got gilt—though by a very indirect associ-   27
ation. And I think that when we do, we're showing off.

Sometimes showoffs ask for cheers to which they're not entitled.   28
Sometimes showoffs earn the praise they seek. And sometimes folks
achieve great things and nonetheless do not show off about it.

Now *that's* impressive.   29

Indeed, when we discover that the quiet mother of four with   30
whom we've been talking intimately all evening has recently been
elected to the state senate—*and she never even mentioned it!*—we are
filled with admiration, with astonishment, with awe.

What self-restraint!   31

For we know damn well—*I* certainly know—that if we'd been   32
that lucky lady, we'd have worked our triumph into the conversation.
As a matter of fact, I'll lay my cards right on the table and confess that
the first time some poems of mine were published, I not only worked
my triumph into every conversation for months and months, but I
also called almost every human being I'd ever known to proclaim the
glad tidings both local and long distance. Furthermore—let me really
confess—if a stranger happened to stop me on the street and all he
wanted to know was the time or directions, I tried to detain him long
enough to enlighten him with the news that the person to whom he
was speaking was a Real Live Genuine Honest-to-God Published
Poet.

Fortunately for everyone, I eventually—it took me awhile—   33
calmed down.

Now, I don't intend to defend myself—I was showing off, I was   34
bragging and I wasn't the slightest bit shy or self-restrained, but a
golden, glowing, glorious thing had happened in my life and I had
an overwhelming need to exult. Exulting, however (as I intend to
argue farther on), may be a permissible form of showing off.

Exulting is what my child does when he comes home with an *A*   35
on his history paper ("Julius Caesar was 50," it began, "and his good

looks was pretty much demolished") and wants to read me the entire masterpiece while I murmur appreciative comments at frequent intervals.

Exulting is what my husband does when he cooks me one of his   36
cheese-and-scallion omelets and practically does a tap dance as he carries it from the kitchen stove to the table, setting it before me with the purely objective assessment that this may be the greatest omelet ever created.

Exulting is what my mother did when she took her first grandson   37
to visit all her friends, and announced as she walked into the room, "Is he gorgeous? Is that a gorgeous baby? Is that the most gorgeous baby you ever saw?"

And exulting is what that mother of four would have done if   38
she'd smiled and said, "Don't call me 'Marge' any more. Call me 'Senator.' "

Exulting is shamelessly shouting our talents or triumphs to the   39
world. It's saying: I'm taking a bow and I'd like to hear clapping. And I think if we don't overdo it (stopping strangers to say you've been published is overdoing it), and I think if we know when to quit ("Enough about me. Let's talk about you. So what do you think about me?" does not count as quitting), and I think if we don't get addicted (i.e., crave a praise-fix for every poem or *A* or omelet), and I think if we're able to walk off the stage (and clap and cheer while others take their bows), then I think we're allowed, from time to time, to exult.

Though showing off can range from very gross to very subtle,   40
and though the point of showing off is sometimes nasty, sometimes needy, sometimes nice, showoffs always run the risk of being thought immodest, of being harshly viewed as . . . well . . . showoffs. And so for folks who want applause without relinquishing their sense of modesty, the trick is keeping quiet and allowing someone else to show off *for* you.

And I've seen a lot of marriages where wives show off for   41
husbands and where husbands, in return, show off for wives. Where Joan, for instance, mentions Dick's promotion and his running time in the marathon. And where Dick, for instance, mentions all the paintings Joanie sold at her last art show. And where both of them lean back with self-effacing shrugs and smiles and never once show off about themselves.

Friends also may show off for friends, and parents for their   42
children, though letting parents toot our horns is risky. Consider, for

example, this sad tale of Elliott, who was a fearless and feisty public-interest lawyer:

"My son," his proud mother explained to his friends, "has always been independent." (Her son blushed modestly.) 43

"My son," his proud mother continued, "was the kind of person who always knew his own mind." (Her son blushed modestly.) 44

" My son," his proud mother went on, "was never afraid. He never kowtowed to those in authority." (Her son blushed modestly.) 45

"My son," his proud mother concluded, "was so independent and stubborn and unafraid of authority that we couldn't get him toilet-trained—he wet his pants till he was well past four." (Her son . . .) 46

But showing off is always a risk, whether we do it ourselves or whether somebody else is doing it for us. And perhaps we ought to consider the words Lord Chesterfield wrote to his sons: "Modesty is the only sure bait when you angle for praise." 47

And yes, of course he's right, we know he's right, he must be right. But sometimes it's so hard to be restrained. For no matter what we do, we always have a lapse or two. So let's try to forgive each other for showing off. 48

Meanings and Values

1a. Name the categories into which Viorst divides showoffs. (Note: In doing this you will need to decide if Viorst views people who say nothing about their achievements as a category of showoffs.)

b. Which of the categories does Viorst divide into subcategories? What are the subcategories?

2a. Where, if anywhere, do the categories in this essay overlap? For example, can showoffs who have a real achievement to brag about be *both* competitive and exulting?

b. If the categories overlap, is the result confusing and misleading? Why? Or is some overlap inevitable in any classification that attempts to explain human behavior?

c. Are the categories identified clearly enough in the essay? If not, how might they be made more obvious?

3. According to the examples in paragraphs 36 and 37, exulting may sometimes mean exaggerating or stretching the truth. Do you agree with Viorst that exulting should be permissible even if it means inflating one's accomplishments? Be ready to defend your answer.

4a. What is meant by the passage "people who reside in a permanent state of sibling rivalry, insisting on playing Hertz to everyone else's Avis" (par. 9)?

b. What does Viorst imply about the personalities of narcissistic showoffs when she says "they are often adorable and charming and amusing— but only until around the age of six" (par. 11)?

c. What message is the woman with the Phi Beta Kappa key conveying (par. 17)?

d. Who is "the hubris-Kierkegaard fellow I mentioned before" (par. 16)?

Expository Techniques

1a. In what order are the categories arranged? Worst to best? Most forgivable to least forgivable? Some other order?

b. Where and how is this arrangement announced to the reader?

c. Is the arrangement appropriate and effective? How else might the essay be organized?

2a. The introduction to this essay is relatively long (pars. 1–8). What does Viorst do to get readers interested in the subject? (See Guide to Terms: *Introductions*.)

b. Where in the introduction does she announce the central theme? Where else in the essay does she speak directly about the central theme?

c. Where in the introduction does she indicate the plan of organization?

d. What role do the one-sentence paragraphs play in the introduction? Do they add to its effectiveness or detract from it? (Guide: *Evaluation*.)

3a. At several places in the essay Viorst comments on its organization and summarizes the categories. Identify these places.

b. Is this commentary disruptive or does it help the reader better understand the essay? Explain.

4a. Why does paragraph 10 seem to be addressed to a female reader?

b. Can the example be easily understood by male readers or might it alienate them?

c. In the rest of the essay does Viorst take care to balance examples more likely to appeal to men with those more likely to appeal to women? Be ready to support your answer.

5a. For some of the categories the discussion consists of a general definition followed by examples. Which discussions follow this arrangement?

b. Describe briefly the organization of the remaining discussions.

c. Is this variety of approaches confusing? Helpful? Interesting? Explain your answer.

6a. Identify a section of the essay where Viorst uses parallel paragraphs and discuss their effect. (Guide: *Parallel Structure.*)

b. Do the same with parallel sentences.

c. Do the same with parallel sentence parts.

7. Examine the complicated syntax of the sentence beginning, "And I think if we don't . . ." in paragraph 39. Indicate why you think this is an appropriate or inappropriate strategy for conveying the author's point. (Guide: *Syntax.*)

Diction and Vocabulary

1a. What words or kinds of words does Viorst repeat frequently in the course of the essay?

b. What purposes does the repetition serve?

2a. To what does the phrase "gilt by association" allude? (Guide: *Figures of Speech—Allusion.*)

b. Identify as many as you can of the direct references and allusions to people, ideas, or events in the following paragraphs: pars. 3, 9, 11, 21, and 23–26.

c. Discuss the purposes of these references.

3. How is irony (understatement) used in paragraph 36? (Guide: *Irony.*) How is exaggeration used in paragraph 32?

4a. Viorst uses some devices that in many essays would seem excessively informal or careless: unusual or made-up words ("*Grrr,*" par. 10; "*Aagh,*" 12); informal phrases ("strut their stuff," 7); exclamation points; and parentheses surrounding an entire paragraph, among other things. In what ways do such devices contribute to the humor of the essay? to its overall tone? (Guide: *Style/Tone.*)

b. How do these devices help make readers willing to pay attention to the serious points about human behavior the essay makes?

5. If you are unfamiliar with any of the following words, consult your dictionary as necessary: decrying, expounding (par. 1); *angst, hubris, epistemology* (3); narcissistic (8); periodontists, sibling (9); brooding (12); cleavage (17); dermatologist (23); enlighten (32); exult (34); appreciative (35); assessment (36); shamelessly, crave (39); gross, immodest, relinquishing (40); feisty (42); kowtowed (45).

Suggestions for Writing and Discussion

1. Are there times when it might be useful or appropriate to be a competitive (narcissistic, insecure) showoff? Be ready to justify your answer and to provide specific examples.

2. Prepare an essay of your own that classifies some other human behavior according to its acceptable and unacceptable forms, like losing one's temper, being afraid, or being envious.

3. At several places in the essay, the author pokes fun at her own behavior or that of members of her family. Discuss how important this strategy is to the success of the essay and to the willingness of readers to view their own behavior in the ways Viorst describes.

(NOTE: Suggestions for topics requiring development by use of CLASSIFICATION are on page 113, at the end of this section.)

RENEE E. TAJIMA is a filmmaker and writer. She produced a documentary for public television entitled "Adopted Son: The Death of Vincent Chin." Currently she is associate editor of *The Independent Film and Video Monthly* as well as a freelance writer. With Christine Choy she runs the Film News Now Foundation. Formerly editor of *Bridge: Asian American Perspectives*, Tajima has also edited *Journey Across Three Continents: Black and African Films, Asian American Film and Video*, and *Reel Change: Guide to Social Issue Media* (2d ed.).

Lotus Blossoms Don't Bleed: Images of Asian American Women

Categories are an important tool for thinking, but unless created with care, they can become unrepresentative stereotypes. Tajima's essay reminds us of the need to be aware of how the categories presented by film and television can shape our perceptions. And she demonstrates how restrictive and harmful stereotypes can be. The classification system here is somewhat complex, consisting of two different kinds of characters, "Lotus Blossoms" and "Dragon Ladies," that appear in several different types of movie roles.

In recent years the media have undergone spectacular technical innovations. But whereas form has leaped toward the year 2000, it seems that content still straddles the turn of the last century. A reigning example of the industry's stagnation is its portrayal of Asian women. And the only real signs of life are stirring far away from Hollywood in the cutting rooms owned and operated by Asian America's independent producers.

1

The commercial media are, in general, populated by stereotyped   2
characterizations that range in complexity, accuracy, and persistence
over time. There is the hooker with a heart of gold and the steely tough
yet honorable mobster. Most of these characters are white, and may
be as one-dimensional as Conan the Barbarian or as complex as R. P.
McMurphy in *One Flew Over the Cuckoo's Nest*.

Images of Asian women, however, have remained consistently   3
simplistic and inaccurate during the sixty years of largely forgettable
screen appearances. There are two basic types: the Lotus Blossom
Baby (a.k.a. China Doll, Geisha Girl, shy Polynesian beauty), and the
Dragon Lady (Fu Manchu's various female relations, prostitutes,
devious madames). There is little in between, although experts may
differ as to whether Suzie Wong belongs to the race-blind "hooker
with a heart of gold" category, or deserves one all of her own.

Asian women in American cinema are interchangeable in ap-   4
pearance and name, and are joined together by the common language
of non-language—that is, uninterpretable chattering, pidgin English,
giggling, or silence. They may be specifically identified by national-
ity—particularly in war films—but that's where screen accuracy ends.
The dozens of populations of Asian and Pacific Island groups are
lumped into one homogeneous mass of Mama-sans.

Passive Love Interests

Asian women in film are, for the most part, passive figures who exist   5
to serve men, especially as love interests for white men (Lotus Blossoms) or as partners in crime with men of their own kind (Dragon
Ladies). One of the first Dragon Lady types was played by Anna May
Wong. In the 1924 spectacular *Thief of Bagdad* she uses treachery to
help an evil Mongol prince attempt to win the Princess of Bagdad
from Douglas Fairbanks.

The Lotus Blossom Baby, a sexual-romantic object, has been the   6
prominent type throughout the years. These "Oriental flowers" are
utterly feminine, delicate, and welcome respites from their often loud,
independent American counterparts. Many of them are the spoils of
the last three wars fought in Asia. One recent television example is
Sergeant Klinger's Korean wife in the short-lived series "AfterMash."

In the real world, this view of Asian women has spawned an   7
entire marriage industry. Today the Filipino wife is particularly in

vogue for American men who order Asian brides from picture catalogues, just as you might buy an imported cheese slicer from Spiegel's.
(I moderated a community program on Asian American women
recently. A rather bewildered young saleswoman showed up with a
stack of brochures to promote the Cherry Blossom companion service,
or some such enterprise.) Behind the brisk sales of Asian mail-order
brides is a growing number of American men who are seeking old-
fashioned, compliant wives, women they feel are no longer available
in the United States.

Feudal Asian customs do not change for the made-for-movie   8
women. Picture brides, geisha girls, concubines, and hara-kari are all
mixed together and reintroduced into any number of settings. Take
for example these two versions of Asian and American cultural
exchange:

1. It's Toko Riki on Japan's Okinawa Island during the late 1940s   9
in the film *Teahouse of the August Moon*. American occupation forces
nice guy Captain Fisby (Glenn Ford) gets a visit from Japanese yenta
Sakini (Marlon Brando).

Enter Brando: "Hey Boss, I Sonoda has a present for you."   10

Enter the gift: Japanese actress Machiko Kyo as a geisha, giggling.   11

Ford: "Who's she?"   12

Brando: "Souvenir . . . introducing Lotus Blossom geisha girl   13
first class."

Ford protests the gift. Kyo giggles.   14

Brando sneaks away with a smile: "Goodnight, Boss." Kyo,   15
chattering away in Japanese, tries to pamper a bewildered Ford who
holds up an instructive finger to her and repeats slowly, "Me . . . me
. . . no." Kyo looks confused.

2. It's San Francisco, circa 1981, in the television series "The   16
Incredible Hulk." Nice guy David Banner (Bill Bixby a.k.a. The Hulk)
gets a present from Chinese yenta Hyung (Beulah Quo).

Enter Quo: "David, I have something for you."   17

Enter Irene Sun as Tam, a Chinese refugee, bowing her head   18
shyly.

Quo: "The Floating Lotus Company hopes you will be very   19
happy. This is Tam, your mail-order bride."

Bixby protests the gift. Sun, speaking only Chinese, tries to   20
pamper a bewildered Bixby who repeats slowly in an instructive tone,
"you . . . must . . . go!" Sun looks confused.

Illicit Interracial Love

On film Asian women are often assigned the role of expendability in   21
situations of illicit Asian-white love. In these cases the most expedient
way of resolving the problems of miscegenation has been to get rid of
the Asian partner. Thus, some numbers of hyphenated (made-for-tele-
vision, wartime, wives-away-from-home) Asian women have expired
for the convenience of their home-bound soldier lovers. More pro-
gressive-minded GI's of the Vietnam era have returned to Vietnam
years later to search for the offspring of these love matches.

In 1985 the General Foods Gold Showcase proudly presented a   22
post-Vietnam version of the wilting Lotus Blossom on network tele-
vision. "A forgotten passion, a child he never knew. . . . All his tomor-
rows forever changed by *The Lady from Yesterday*." He is Vietnam vet
Craig Weston (Wayne Rogers), official father of two, and husband to
Janet (Bonnie Bedelia). She is Lien Van Huyen (Tina Chen), whom
Weston hasn't seen since the fall of Saigon. She brings the child, the
unexpected consequence of that wartime love match, to the United
States. But Janet doesn't lose her husband, she gains a son. As *New
York Times* critic John J. O'Connor points out, Lien has "the good
manners to be suffering from a fatal disease that will conveniently
remove her from the scene."

The geographic parallel to the objectification of Asian women is   23
the rendering of Asia as only a big set for the white leading actors.
What would "Shogun" be without Richard Chamberlain? The most
notable exception is the 1937 movie version of Pearl Buck's novel *The
Good Earth*. The story is about Chinese in China and depicted with
some complexity and emotion. Nevertheless the lead parts played by
Louise Rainer and Paul Muni follow the pattern of choosing white
stars for Asian roles, a problem which continues to plague Asian
actors.

*   *   *

One film that stands out as an exception because it was cast with   24
Asian people for Asian characters is *Flower Drum Song* (1961), set in
San Francisco's Chinatown. Unfortunately the film did little more
than temporarily take a number of talented Asian American actresses
and actors off the unemployment lines. It also gave birth for a while
to a new generation of stereotypes—gum-chewing Little Leaguers,
enterprising businessmen, and all-American tomboys—variations on
the then new model minority myth. *Flower Drum Song* hinted that the

assimilated, hyphenated Asian American might be much more successful in American society than the Japanese of the 1940s and the Chinese and Koreans of the 1950s, granted they keep to the task of being white American first.

The women of *Flower Drum Song* maintain their earlier image   25
with few modernizations. Miyoshi Umeki is still a picture bride. And in *Suzie Wong* actress Nancy Kwan is a hipper, Americanized version of the Hong Kong bar girl without the pidgin English. But updated clothes and setting do not change the essence of these images.

In 1985 director Michael Cimino cloned Suzie Wong to TV news   26
anchor Connie Chung and created another anchor, Tracy Tzu (Ariane), in the disastrous exploitation film *Year of the Dragon*. In it Tzu is ostensibly the only positive Asian American character in a film that vilifies the people of New York's Chinatown. The Tzu character is a success in spite of her ethnicity. Just as she would rather eat Italian than Chinese, she's rather sleep with white men than Chinese men. (She is ultimately raped by three "Chinese boys.") Neither does she bat an eye at the barrage of racial slurs fired off by her lover, lead Stanley White, the Vietnam vet and New York City cop played by Mickey Rourke.

At the outset Tzu is the picture of professionalism and sophisti-   27
cation, engaged in classic screen love/hate banter with White. The turning point comes early in the picture when their flirtatious sparring in a Chinese restaurant is interrupted by a gangland slaughter. While White pursues the culprits, Tzu totters on her high heels into a phone booth where she cowers, sobbing, until White comes to the rescue.

The standard of beauty for Asian women that is set in the movies   28
deserves mention. Caucasian women are often used for Asian roles, which contributes to a case of aesthetic imperialism for Asian women. When Asian actresses are chosen they invariably have large eyes, high cheekbones, and other Caucasian-like characteristics when they appear on the silver screen. As Judy Chu of the University of California, Los Angeles, has pointed out, much of Anna May Wong's appeal was due to her Western looks. Chu unearthed this passage from the June 1924 *Photoplay* which refers to actress Wong, but sounds a lot like a description of Eurasian model/actress Ariane: "Her deep brown eyes, while the slant is not pronounced, are typically oriental. But her Manchu mother has given her a height and poise of figure that Chinese maidens seldom have."

Invisibility

There is yet another important and pervasive characteristic of   29
Asian women on the screen, invisibility. The number of roles in the
Oriental flower and Dragon Lady categories have been few, and
generally only supporting parts. But otherwise Asian women are
absent. Asian women do not appear in films as union organizers,
or divorced mothers fighting for the custody of their children, or
fading movie stars, or spunky trial lawyers, or farm women fighting bank foreclosures; Asian women are not portrayed as ordinary
people.

Then there is the kind of invisibility that occurs when individual   30
personalities and separate identities become indistinguishable from
one another. Some memorable Asian masses are the islanders fleeing
exploding volcanoes in *Krakatoa: East of Java* (1969) and the Vietnamese villagers fleeing Coppola's airborne weaponry in various scenes
from *Apocalypse Now* (1979). Asian women populate these hordes or
have groupings of their own, usually in some type of harem situation. In *Cry for Happy* (1961), Glenn Ford is cast as an American GI
who stumbles into what turns out to be the best little geisha house
in Japan.

Network television has given Asian women even more opportu-   31
nities to paper the walls, so to speak. They are background characters
in "Hawaii 5-0," "Magnum PI," and other series that transverse the
Pacific. I've seen a cheongsam-clad maid in the soap "One Life to
Live," and assorted Chinatown types surface whenever the cops and
robbers shows revive scripts about the Chinatown Tong wars.

The most stunning exceptions to television's abuse of Asian   32
images is the phenomenon of news anchors: Connie Chung (CBS) and
Sasha Foo (CNN) have national spots, and Tritia Toyota (Los Angeles),
Wendy Tokuda (San Francisco), Kaity Tong (New York), Sandra Yep
(Sacramento), and others are reporters in large cities. All of them cover
hard news, long the province of middle-aged white men with author-
itative voices. Toyota and Yep have been able to parlay their positions
so that there is more coverage of Asian American stories at their
stations. Because of their presence on screen—and ironically, perhaps
because of the celebrity status of today's newscasters—these anchors
wield much power in rectifying Asian women's intellectual integrity
in the media. (One hopes *Year of the Dragon's* Tracy Tzu hasn't canceled
their positive effect.)

Undoubtedly the influence of these visible reporters is fortified   33
by the existence of highly organized Asian American journalists. The
West Coast–based Asian American Journalists Association has lobbied for affirmative action in the print and broadcast media. In film
and video, the same types of political initiatives have spurred a new
movement of independently produced works made by and about
Asian Americans.

Small Gems from Independents

The independent film movement emerged during the 1960s as an   34
alternative to the Hollywood mill. In a broad sense it has had little
direct impact in reversing the distorted images of Asian women,
although some gems have been produced. . . . But now Asian American independents, many of whom are women, have consciously set
out to bury sixty years of Lotus Blossoms who do not bleed and
Mama-sans who do not struggle. These women filmmakers—most of
whom began their careers only since the 1970s—often draw from
deeply personal perspectives in their work: Virginia Hashii's *Jenny*
Portrays a young Japanese American girl who explores her own
Nikkei heritage for the first time; Christine Choy's *From Spikes to
Spindles* (1976) documents the lives of women in New York's Chinatown; Felicia Lowe's *China: Land of My Father* (1979) is a film diary of
the filmmaker's own first reunion with her grandmother in China;
Renee Cho's *The New Wife* (1978) dramatizes the arrival of an immigrant bride to America; and Lana Pih Jokel's *Chiang Ching: A Dance
Journey* traces the life of dancer-actress-teacher Chiang. All these films
were produced during the 1970s and together account for only a little
more than two hours of screen time. Most are first works with the
same rough-edged quality that characterized early Asian American
film efforts.

Women producers have maintained a strong presence during the   35
1980s, although their work does not always focus on women's issues.
. . . Also in this decade veteran filmmakers Emiko Omori and Christine Choy have produced their first dramatic efforts. Omori's *The
Departure* is the story of a Japanese girl who must give up her beloved
traditional dolls in pre–World War II California. . . . In *Fei Tien: Goddess
in Flight*, Choy tries to adapt a nonlinear cinematic structure to Genny
Lim's play *Pigeons*, which explores the relationship between a Chinese American yuppie and a Chinatown "bird lady."

Perhaps the strongest work made thus far has been directed by a 36
male filmmaker, Arthur Dong. *Sewing Woman* is a small, but beautifully crafted portrait of Dong's mother, Zem Ping. It chronicles her life
from war-torn China to San Francisco's garment factories. Other films
and tapes by Asian men include Michael Uno's *Emi* (1978), a portrait
of the Japanese American writer and former concentration camp
internee Emi Tonooka; the Yonemoto brothers' neonarrative *Green
Card,* a soap-style saga of a Japanese immigrant artist seeking truth,
love, and permanent residency in Southern California; and Steve
Okazaki's *Survivors,* a documentary focusing on the women survivors
of the atomic blasts over Hiroshima and Nagasaki. All these
filmmakers are American-born Japanese. *Orientations,* by Asian Canadian Richard Fung, is the first work I've seen that provides an in-depth
look at the Asian gay community, and it devotes a good amount of
time to Asian Canadian lesbians.

Our Own Image

These film and videomakers, women and men, face a challenge far 37
beyond creating entertainment and art. Several generations of Asian
women have been raised with racist and sexist celluloid images. The
models for passivity and servility in these films and television programs fit neatly into the myths imposed on us, and contrast sharply
with the more liberating ideals of independence and activism. Generations of other Americans have also grown up with these images. And
their acceptance of the dehumanization implicit in the stereotypes of
expendability and invisibility is frightening.

Old images of Asian women in the mainstream media will likely 38
remain stagnant for a while. After sixty years, there have been few
signs of progress. However, there is hope because of the growing
number of filmmakers emerging from our own communities. Wayne
Wang in 1985 completed *Dim Sum,* a beautifully crafted feature film
about the relationship between a mother and daughter in San
Francisco's Chinatown. *Dim Sum,* released through a commercial
distributor, could be the first truly sensitive film portrayal of Asian
American women to reach a substantial national audience. In quality
and numbers, Asian American filmmakers may soon constitute a
critical mass out of which we will see a body of work that gives us a
new image, our own image.

Meanings and Values

1a.   What are the two main images of Asian women in Hollywood films (par. 3)?

b.   What are the three main roles Asian women have played in Hollywood films? (Note: See paragraphs 5, 21, and 29.)

2.   How do the roles Asian women play in recent independent productions differ from those generally created for them in Hollywood productions?

3a.   How would you characterize the *overall* tone of this essay? (See Guide to Terms: *Style/Tone.*)

b.   Identify any sections of the essay where the tone varies noticeably.

4.   Point out any passages in the essay that offer clear instances of irony, especially sarcasm or understatement. (Guide: *Irony.*)

Expository Techniques

1a.   Does Tajima offer a clear definition of each category?

b.   If not, how might the categories be introduced and defined more clearly?

2a.   Are the categories in this essay distinct or is there some overlapping?

b.   If the categories overlap, does the author acknowledge this? Where?

3a.   Would this essay be more effective if it had fewer examples? A greater number? Explain. (Guide: *Evaluation.*)

b.   Evaluate the examples in the following paragraphs for clarity and effectiveness: 8–20, 22, and 26–27.

c.   Discuss whether the examples of work by independent filmmakers provide convincing evidence that these films go beyond the stereotypes.

Diction and Vocabulary

1.   The names used to identify many of the standard character types are clichés. Point out the clichés used in this way in paragraphs 2 and 3.

2.   Explain the meaning of the following terms: "cutting rooms" (par. 1); "Mama-sans" (4); "a cheongsam-clad maid" (31).

3.   If you do not know the meanings of some of the following words, look them up in a dictionary: simplistic (par. 3); homogeneous (4); Mongol

(5); compliant (7); yenta (9); objectification (23); vilifies (26); pervasive (29).

Suggestions for Writing and Discussion

1. Discuss how movies and television have stereotyped other ethnic or social groups. Are these stereotypes always negative? Are they always harmful?

2. Immigrant groups are often subjected to negative stereotyping. Draw on your own experience and knowledge for examples of this process or do research on immigrant groups that are now considered part of the mainstream but were once treated as outsiders.

(NOTE: Suggestions for topics requiring development by use of CLASSIFICATION are on page 113, at the end of this section.)

DESMOND MORRIS

DESMOND MORRIS was born in 1928 in England and educated at Birmingham University (B.S.) and Oxford (Ph.D.). He was later researcher in animal behavior at the Department of Zoology, Oxford, and for several years served as curator of mammals at the Zoological Society of London. Morris has increasingly specialized in human behavior and now holds a Research Fellowship at Oxford, where he spends much of his time writing. He is the author of some fifty scientific papers and a dozen books. In 1967 he published *The Naked Ape*, which has sold over eight million copies and been translated into twenty-three languages. Other recent books have been *The Human Zoo* (1970); *Intimate Behaviour* (1972); *Manwatching* (1977); as co-author, *Gestures: Their Origins and Distribution* (1979); *Animal Days* (1980); *The Book of Ages* (1984); *Dogwatching* (1986); and *Catwatching* (1986).

Territorial Behaviour

"Territorial Behaviour" is a chapter from *Manwatching*. The selection is straightforward in purpose and execution: Morris's divisions of territorial behavior, though simple and obvious, provide a firm and valid structure for the writing.

A territory is a defended space. In the broadest sense, there are three kinds of human territory: tribal, family and personal.

It is rare for people to be driven to physical fighting in defence of these "owned" spaces, but fight they will, if pushed to the limit. The invading army encroaching on national territory, the gang moving into a rival district, the trespasser climbing into an orchard, the burglar breaking into a house, the bully pushing to the front of a queue, the driver trying to steal a parking space, all of these intruders are liable to be met with resistance varying from the vigorous to the savagely violent. Even if the law is on the side of the intruder, the urge to protect a territory may be so strong that otherwise peaceful citizens abandon all their usual controls and inhibitions. Attempts to evict families from their homes, no matter how socially valid the reasons, can lead to siege conditions reminiscent of the defence of a medieval fortress.

The fact that these upheavals are so rare is a measure of the success of Territorial Signals as a system of dispute prevention. It is sometimes cynically stated that "all property is theft," but in reality it is the opposite. Property, as owned space which is *displayed* as owned space, is a special kind of sharing system which reduces fighting much more than it causes it. Man is a co-operative species, but he is also competitive, and his struggle for dominance has to be structured in some way if chaos is to be avoided. The establishment of territorial rights is one such structure. It limits dominance geographically. I am dominant in my territory and you are dominant in yours. In other words, dominance is shared out spatially, and we all have some. Even if I am weak and unintelligent and you can dominate me when we meet on neutral ground, I can still enjoy a thoroughly dominant role as soon as I retreat to my private base. Be it ever so humble, there is no place like a home territory.

Of course, I can still be intimidated by a particularly dominant individual who enters my home base, but his encroachment will be dangerous for him and he will think twice about it, because he will know that here my urge to resist will be dramatically magnified and my usual subservience banished. Insulted at the heart of my own territory, I may easily explode into battle—either symbolic or real—with a result that may be damaging to both of us.

In order for this to work, each territory has to be plainly advertised as such. Just as a dog cocks its leg to deposit its personal scent on the trees in its locality, so the human animal cocks its leg symbolically all over his home base. But because we are predominantly visual animals, we employ mostly visual signals, and it is worth asking how we do this at the three levels: tribal, family and personal.

First: the Tribal Territory. We evolved as tribal animals, living in comparatively small groups, probably of less than a hundred, and we existed like that for millions of years. It is our basic social unit, a group in which everyone knows everyone else. Essentially, the tribal territory consisted of a home base surrounded by extended hunting grounds. Any neighbouring tribe intruding on our social space would be repelled and driven away. As these early tribes swelled into agricultural super-tribes, and eventually into industrial nations, their territorial defence systems became increasingly elaborate. The tiny, ancient home base of the hunting tribe became the great capital city, the primitive war-paint became the flags, emblems, uniforms and regalia of the specialized military, and the war-chants became national anthems, marching songs and bugle calls. Territorial boundary-lines hardened into fixed borders, often conspicuously patrolled and punctuated with defensive structures—forts and look-out posts, checkpoints and great walls, and, today, customs barriers.

Today each nation flies its own flag, a symbolic embodiment of its territorial status. But patriotism is not enough. The ancient tribal hunter lurking inside each citizen finds himself unsatisfied by membership in such a vast conglomeration of individuals, most of whom are totally unknown to him personally. He does his best to feel that he shares a common territorial defence with them all, but the scale of the operation has become inhuman. It is hard to feel a sense of belonging with a tribe of fifty million or more. His answer is to form sub-groups, nearer to his ancient pattern, smaller and more personally known to him—the local club, the teenage gang, the union, the specialist society, the sports association, the political party, the college fraternity, the social clique, the protest group, and the rest. Rare indeed is the individual who does not belong to at least one of these splinter groups, and take from it a sense of tribal allegiance and brotherhood. Typical of all these groups is the development of Territorial Signals—badges, costumes, headquarters, banners, slogans, and all the other displays of group identity. This is where the action is, in terms of tribal territorialism, and only when a major war breaks out does the emphasis shift upwards to the higher group level of the nation.

Each of these modern pseudo-tribes sets up its own special kind of home base. In extreme cases non-members are totally excluded, in others they are allowed in as visitors with limited rights and under a control system of special rules. In many ways they are like miniature nations, with their own flags and emblems and their own border guards. The exclusive club has its own "customs barrier": the doorman who checks your "passport" (your membership card) and prevents strangers from passing in unchallenged. There is a government:

the club committee; and often special displays of the tribal elders: the photographs or portraits of previous officials on the walls. At the heart of the specialized territories there is a powerful feeling of security and importance, a sense of shared defence against the outside world. Much of the club chatter, both serious and joking, directs itself against the rottenness of everything outside the club boundaries—in that "other world" beyond the protected portals.

In social organizations which embody a strong class system, such as military units and large business concerns, there are many territorial rules, often unspoken, which interfere with the official hierarchy. High-status individuals, such as officers or managers, could in theory enter any of the regions occupied by the lower levels in the pecking order, but they limit this power in a striking way. An officer seldom enters a sergeant's mess or a barrack room unless it is for a formal inspection. He respects those regions as alien territories even though he has the power to go there by virtue of his dominant role. And in businesses, part of the appeal of unions, over and above their obvious functions, is that with their officials, headquarters and meetings they add a sense of territorial power for the staff workers. It is almost as if each military organization and business concern consists of two warring tribes: the officers versus the other ranks, and the management versus the workers. Each has its special home base within the system, and the territorial defence pattern thrusts itself into what, on the surface, is a pure social hierarchy. Negotiations between managements and unions are tribal battles fought out over the neutral ground of a boardroom table, and are as much concerned with territorial display as they are with resolving problems of wages and conditions. Indeed, if one side gives in too quickly and accepts the other's demands, the victors feel strangely cheated and deeply suspicious that it may be a trick. What they are missing is the protracted sequence of ritual and counter-ritual that keeps alive their group territorial identity.

Likewise, many of the hostile displays of sports fans and teenage gangs are primarily concerned with displaying their group image to rival fan-clubs and gangs. Except in rare cases, they do not attack one another's headquarters, drive out the occupants, and reduce them to a submissive, subordinate condition. It is enough to have scuffles on the borderlands between the two rival territories. This is particularly clear at football matches, where the fan-club headquarters becomes temporarily shifted from the club-house to a section of the stands, and where minor fighting breaks out at the unofficial boundary line between the massed groups of rival supporters. Newspaper reports play up the few accidents and injuries which do occur on such occasions, but when they are studied in relation to the total numbers of displaying fans involved, it is clear that the serious incidents represent only a tiny fraction of the overall group behaviour. For every actual punch or kick there are a thousand war-cries, war-dances, chants and gestures.

Second: the Family Territory. Essentially, the family is a breeding unit and the family territory is a breeding ground. At the centre of this space, there is the nest—the bedroom—where, tucked up in bed, we feel at our most territorially secure. In a typical house the bedroom is upstairs, where a safe nest should be. This puts it farther away from the entrance hall, the area where contact is made, intermittently, with the outside world. The less private reception rooms, where intruders are allowed access, are the next line of defence. Beyond them, outside the walls of the building, there is often a symbolic remnant of the ancient feeding grounds—a garden. Its symbolism often extends to the plants and animals it contains, which cease to be nutritional and become merely decorative—flowers and pets. But like a true territorial space it has a conspicuously displayed boundary-line, the garden fence, wall, or railings. Often no more than a token barrier, this is the outer territorial demarcation, separating the private world of the family from the public world beyond. To cross it puts any visitor or intruder at an immediate disadvantage. As he crosses the threshold, his dominance wanes, slightly but unmistakably. He is entering an area where he senses that he must ask permission to do simple things that he would consider a right elsewhere. Without lifting a finger, the territorial owners exert their dominance. This is done by all the hundreds of small ownership "markers" they have deposited on their family territory: the ornaments, the "possessed" objects positioned in the rooms and on the walls; the furnishings, the furniture, the colours, the patterns, all owner-chosen and all making this particular home base unique to them.

It is one of the tragedies of modern architecture that there has been a standardization of these vital territorial living units. One of the most important aspects of a home is that it should be similar to other homes only in a general way, and that in detail it should have many differences, making it a *particular* home. Unfortunately, it is cheaper to build a row of houses, or a block of flats, so that all the family living-units are identical, but the territorial urge rebels against this trend and house-owners struggle as best they can to make their mark on their mass-produced properties. They do this with garden-design, with front-door colours, with curtain patterns, with wallpaper and all the other decorative elements that together create a unique and different family environment. Only when they have completed this nest-building do they feel truly "at home" and secure.

When they venture forth as a family unit, they repeat the process 13 in a minor way. On a day-trip to the seaside, they load the car with personal belongings and it becomes their temporary, portable territory. Arriving at the beach, they stake out a small territorial claim, marking it with rugs, towels, baskets and other belongings to which they can return from their seaboard wanderings. Even if they all leave it at once to bathe, it retains a characteristic territorial quality and other family groups arriving will recognize this by setting up their own "home" bases at a respectful distance. Only when the whole beach has filled up with these marked spaces will newcomers start to position themselves in such a way that the inter-base distance becomes reduced. Forced to pitch between several existing beach territories, they will feel a momentary sensation of intrusion, and the established "owners" will feel a similar sensation of invasion, even though they are not being directly inconvenienced.

The same territorial scene is being played out in parks and fields 14 and on riverbanks, wherever family groups gather in their clustered units. But if rivalry for spaces creates mild feelings of hostility, it is true to say that without the territorial system of sharing and space-limited dominance, there would be chaotic disorder.

Third: the Personal Space. If a man enters a waiting-room and sits 15 at one end of a long row of empty chairs, it is possible to predict where the next man to enter will seat himself. He will not sit next to the first man, nor will he sit at the far end, right away from him. He will choose a position about halfway between these two points. The next man to enter will take the largest gap left, and sit roughly in the middle of that, and so on, until eventually the latest newcomer will be forced to select a seat that places him right next to one of the already seated men. Similar patterns can be observed in cinemas, public urinals, airplanes, trains and buses. This is a reflection of the fact that we all carry with us, everywhere we go, a portable territory called a Personal Space. If people move inside this space, we feel threatened. If they keep too far outside it, we feel rejected. The result is a subtle series of

spatial adjustments, usually operating quite unconsciously and producing ideal compromises as far as this is possible. If a situation
becomes too crowded, then we adjust our reactions accordingly and
allow our personal space to shrink. Jammed into an elevator, a rush-
hour compartment, or a packed room, we give up altogether and
allow body-to-body contact, but when we relinquish our Personal
Space in this way, we adopt certain special techniques. In essence,
what we do is to convert these other bodies into "nonpersons." We
studiously ignore them, and they us. We try not to face them if we can
possibly avoid it. We wipe all expressiveness from our faces, letting
them go blank. We may look up at the ceiling or down at the floor,
and we reduce body movements to a minimum. Packed together like
sardines in a tin, we stand dumbly still, sending out as few social
signals as possible.

Even if the crowding is less severe, we still tend to cut down our 16
social interactions in the presence of large numbers. Careful observations of children in play groups revealed that if they are high-density
groupings there is less social interaction between the individual
children, even though there is theoretically more opportunity for such
contacts. At the same time, the high-density groups show a higher
frequency of aggressive and destructive behaviour patterns in their
play. Personal Space—"elbow room"—is a vital commodity for the
human animal, and one that cannot be ignored without risking serious trouble.

Of course, we all enjoy the excitement of being in a crowd, and 17
this reaction cannot be ignored. But there are crowds and crowds. It
is pleasant enough to be in a " spectator crowd," but not also appeal-
ing to find yourself in the middle of a rush-hour crush. The difference
between the two is that the spectator crowd is all facing in the same
direction and concentrating on a distant point of interest. Attending
a theatre, there are twinges of rising hostility towards the stranger
who sits down immediately in front of you or the one who squeezes
into the seat next to you. The shared armrest can become a polite, but
distinct, territorial boundary-dispute region. However, as soon as the
show begins, these invasions of Personal Space are forgotten and the
attention is focused beyond the small space where the crowding is
taking place. Now, each member of the audience feels himself
spatially related, not to his cramped neighbours, but to the actor
on the stage, and this distance is, if anything, too great. In the
rush-hour crowd, by contrast, each member of the pushing throng

is competing with his neighbours all the time. There is no escape to a spatial relation with a distant actor, only the pushing, shoving bodies all around.

Those of us who have to spend a great deal of time in crowded conditions become gradually better able to adjust, but no one can ever become completely immune to invasions of Personal Space. This is because they remain forever associated with either powerful hostile or equally powerful loving feelings. All through our childhood we will have been held to be loved and held to be hurt, and anyone who invades our Personal Space when we are adults is, in effect, threatening to extend his behaviour into one of these two highly charged areas of human interaction. Even if his motives are clearly neither hostile nor sexual, we still find it hard to suppress our reactions to his close approach. Unfortunately, different countries have different ideas about exactly how close is close. It is easy enough to test your own "space reaction": when you are talking to someone in the street or in any open space, reach out with your arm and see where the nearest point on his body comes. If you hail from western Europe, you will find that he is at roughly fingertip distance from you. In other words, as you reach out, your fingertips will just about make contact with his shoulder. If you come from eastern Europe, you will find you are standing at "wrist distance." If you come from the Mediterranean region, you will find that you are much closer to your companion, a little more than "elbow distance."

Trouble begins when a member of one of these cultures meets and talks to one from another. Say a British diplomat meets an Italian or an Arab diplomat at an embassy function. They start talking in a friendly way, but soon the fingertips man begins to feel uneasy. Without knowing quite why, he starts to back away gently from his companion. The companion edges forward again. Each tries in his way to set up a Personal Space relationship that suits his own background. But it is impossible to do. Every time the Mediterranean diplomat advances to a distance that feels comfortable for him, the British diplomat feels threatened. Every time the Briton moves back, the other feels rejected. Attempts to adjust this situation often lead to a talking pair shifting slowly across a room, and many an embassy reception is dotted with western-European fingertip-distance men pinned against the walls by eager elbow-distance men. Until such differences are fully understood and allowances made, these minor differences in "body territories" will continue to act as an alienation factor which may interfere in a subtle way with diplomatic harmony and other forms of international transaction.

If there are distance problems when engaged in conversation, then there are clearly going to be even bigger difficulties where people must work privately in a shared space. Close proximity of others, pressing against the invisible boundaries of our personal body-territory, makes it difficult to concentrate on non-social matters. Flatmates, students sharing a study, sailors in the cramped quarters of a ship, and office staff in crowded work-places, all have to face this problem. They solve it by "cocooning." They use a variety of devices to shut themselves off from the others present. The best possible cocoon, of course, is a small private room—a den, a private office, a study or a studio—which physically obscures the presence of other nearby territory-owners. This is the ideal situation for non-social work, but the space-sharers cannot enjoy this luxury. Their cocooning must be symbolic. They may, in certain cases, be able to erect small physical barriers, such as screens and partitions, which give substance to their invisible Personal Space boundaries, but when this cannot be done, other means must be sought. One of these is the "favoured object." Each space-sharer develops a preference, repeatedly expressed until it becomes a fixed pattern, for a particular chair, or table, or alcove. Others come to respect this, and friction is reduced. This system is often formally arranged (this is my desk, that is yours), but even where it is not, favoured places soon develop. Professor Smith has a favourite chair in the library. It is not formally his, but he always uses it and others avoid it. Seats around a messroom table, or a boardroom table, become almost personal property for specific individuals. Even in the home, father has his favourite chair for reading the newspaper or watching television. Another device is the blinkers-posture. Just as a horse that over-reacts to other horses and the distractions of the noisy race-course is given a pair of blinkers to shield its eyes, so people studying privately in a public place put on pseudo-blinkers in the form of shielding hands. Resting their elbows on the table, they sit with their hands screening their eyes from the scene on either side.

A third method of reinforcing the body-territory is to use personal markers. Books, papers and other personal belongings are scattered around the favoured site to render it more privately owned in the eyes of companions. Spreading out one's belongings is a well-known trick in public-transport situations, where a traveller tries

20

21

to give the impression that seats next to him are taken. In many contexts carefully arranged personal markers can act as an effective territorial display, even in the absence of the territory owner. Experiments in a library revealed that placing a pile of magazines on the table in one seating position successfully reserved that place for an average of 77 minutes. If a sports-jacket was added, draped over the chair, then the "reservation effect" lasted for over two hours.

In these ways, we strengthen the defences of our Personal Spaces, keeping out intruders with the minimum of open hostility. As with all territorial behaviour, the object is to defend space with signals rather than with fists and at all three levels—the tribal, the family and the personal—it is a remarkably efficient system of space-sharing. It does not always seem so, because newspapers and newscasts inevitably magnify the exceptions and dwell on those cases where the signals have failed and wars have broken out, gangs have fought, neighbouring families have feuded, or colleagues have clashed, but for every territorial signal that has failed, there are millions of others that have not. They do not rate a mention in the news, but they nevertheless constitute a dominant feature of human society—the society of a remarkably territorial animal. 22

Meanings and Values

1. What are the characteristics that enable you to classify this selection as formal, informal, or familiar? (See Guide to Terms: *Essay*.)

2a. What are some of the "socially valid" reasons that justify evicting a family from its home (par. 2)?

b. If you think there are no such valid reasons, justify your stand.

3a. List other subgroups that give members a "powerful feeling of security and importance" (par. 8).

b. What are the territorial signals of each group?

4a. In one sentence, state the central theme of this selection. (Guide: *Unity*.)

b. Does the writing have unity? Why, or why not?

5a. What was the author's apparent purpose?

b. How successfully does he accomplish this purpose?

c. How worthwhile was it? Why?

Expository Techniques

1a. Is this classification system logical, complete, and consistent in all respects? Cite any exceptions and state what is wrong.

b. What other basis can you suggest for organizing the discussion of the territorial behavior of humans? Which do you prefer? Why?

2a. Into how many categories does the author divide the solutions of people sharing cramped living or working quarters?

b. Cite two of the solutions in each division.

3a. Demonstrate the value of using examples by eliminating them entirely from any one portion of this selection, leaving only the generalities.

b. What would be the effect on the reader?

4a. It is possible (but not very rewarding) to argue about whether this selection has a one-paragraph or a five-paragraph introduction. Assuming the latter to be the author's intention, which of the standard introductory techniques does he use? (Guide: *Introductions.*)

b. How successfully does he perform the four potential functions of an introduction? Be specific.

Diction and Vocabulary

1. How can you account for the unusual spelling of some of the words, such as "behaviour" (title), "defence" (par. 2), and "colours" (par. 11)?

2. Why do you think the author considered the word *"displayed"* important enough to be italicized (par. 3)?

3a. Of what might a "symbolic" exploding into battle consist (par. 4)?

b. What makes some of the barriers listed in paragraph 20 "symbolic"?

c. Explain how the uses of "symbolic" and "symbolically" in these paragraphs and in paragraphs 5, 7, and 11 are, or are not, consistent with the discussion of "symbol" in this book. (Guide: *Symbol.*)

4a. What, if anything, is noteworthy about the diction or syntax of this selection? (Guide: *Diction and Syntax.*)

b. To what extent, if at all, is Morris's writing characterized by his style? (Guide: *Style/Tone.*) You may want to compare his style, or lack of it, with that of an author previously read.

Suggestions for Writing and Discussion

1.   Select one of the subgroups listed in answering question 3 of "Meanings and Values" and discuss it more fully—explaining, perhaps, just what the members get out of belonging.

2.   The owners of a home assert their dominance through subtle and unconscious actions as well as through objects. Discuss these actions and explain why such asserted dominance is not resented by the average visitor.

3.   Most of Morris's discussion of family territory seems to refer to family-owned homes. What are the limitations on renters, especially of apartments, in displaying their territorial signals? To what extent do you suppose a desire for greater territorial display contributes to most people's dream of one day owning their own home?

(NOTE: Suggestions for topics requiring development by use of CLASSIFICATION are on page 113, at the end of this section.)

PETER MARSH

PETER MARSH has devoted his career to studying and writing about patterns of human behavior. Currently, he is senior lecturer in social psychology at Oxford Polytechnic and co-director of the Contemporary Violence Research Unit at Oxford University. Marsh has written or co-authored numerous books, including *Rules of Disorder* (1968), *Aggro: The Illusion of Violence* (1978), *Gestures: Their Origins and Distribution* (1979) (with Desmond Morris and others), *Driving Passion: The Psychology of the Car* (1986), and *Tribes* (1988).]

Tribes[1]

"Tribes," a section from Marsh's book with the same title, looks in depth at one of the categories discussed by Desmond Morris in the preceding essay. The tribes identified in this piece, however, are not formal organizations but informal (and short-lived) social groupings based on similarities in fashion and lifestyle. The economic and cultural impact of such groups is often considerable, however, and they are characteristic features of modern society. For the student of composition, this selection demonstrates the importance of specific detail in establishing and explaining categories.

Many modern societies are now fast approaching their limits in terms of size and the impersonality which that size creates. Increasingly we witness violent reactions in massive urban developments to the alienation experienced by their inhabitants. Many young people, in particular, find no source of identity or sense of belonging in a world which often disowns them, and so turn increasingly to alternative youth cultures in which they can be *somebody*. In the harshness of economic recession, this quest for identity, coupled with the anger engendered by disadvantage, is expressed in the

[1]Editors' title.

aggression of the youth gang or in declarations of solidarity which require a clearly defined enemy. Racism, anti-Semitism, and other types of victimization of "out-groups" occur when a sense of frustration is fuelled by feelings of anonymity and detachment. For some members of our 20th-century cultures, the only way of fully understanding themselves is to establish whom they are against.

While on the one hand a sense of injustice and disenchantment 2 gives rise to tribalism, sometimes with destructive consequences, the same drive for social bonding is equally evident among the more affluent and successful members of our societies—so much so that social labelling among the new professional groups has become increasingly common. The term "Yuppie" (young, upwardly mobile professional) originated in the 1980s in the United States as a description of a new breed of rising entrepreneurs. Once the term had been coined, people started to identify with this distinctive label and positively to aspire to the lifestyle it denoted. Soon the Yuppies became a tribe of people with similar jobs, style of language, interests, tastes and attitudes. The Filofax, or "personal organizer," became more than just a high-priced diary and address book: now it was a symbol of allegiance to a cultural unit.

In the wake of the Yuppies have come other middle-class tribes, 3 each with equally distinctive acronymic nicknames, and it is now fashionable to describe people in terms of their social tribe. Up-market glossy magazines regularly carry features informing their readers about the current labels and the groups to which they refer. Although such articles are usually quite trivial, they reveal the rising need for people to define themselves in terms of their lifestyles and to feel a sense of affiliation with those who share them.

In Britain, this trend towards tribal definitions and labels was 4 undoubtedly given a boost by Peter York and his reported "discovery" of the Sloane Rangers—affluent young people who lived in fashionable areas such as that around London's Sloane Square. Writing with an appropriate sense of cynicism, he described the world of this particular section of British upper-middle-class society in the way an anthropologist might talk of a distinctive African culture. Sloanes could be identified by the fact that they wore green wellington boots and waxed jackets, drove Golf GTIs and virtually lived out their lives in wine bars. A simplistic but not totally inaccurate caricature, this description soon became much more of a reality as young people in that stratum of society identified themselves with the image and adopted both the Sloane style and the attitudes that went with it.

Young Fogeys have of course always been around in the rarefied atmosphere of Oxford, Cambridge, Harvard and other "prestige" universities, but it was only in the 1980s that the name began to be applied. Their reactionary views, traditional styles of dress and feigned disinterest in the real world of work and the professions typified them, and their distinctiveness was reinforced by the emergence of brash, stylish and energetic groups of upstarts.

Yuppies were, and still are, the antithesis of the establishment order, relying on their talents and business acumen rather than on inherited wealth or the old school tie. It is through such clear contrasts that tribal unity is made concrete. While the Yuppie, the Sloane and the Young Fogey do indeed have common interests and values, this commonality is enhanced by the experience of distance from other clearly defined collectives. As one tribe emerges, others are spawned in its shadow.

Dinkies, for example, emerged as a Yuppie splinter group, embracing an especially single-minded segment of the new professional classes. "Double Income, No Kids" couples were able to carve out a particularly identifiable stylish lifestyle because their considerable disposable income was not squandered on raising offspring and sending them to smart schools. In contrast were the Drabbies, the staid but ideologically sound tribe with several children and socially useful jobs as teachers, social workers, etc. Yummies (Young Urban Mothers), Swells (Single Women Earning Lots in London) and Spoolers (Stripped Pine, Olive Oil, Laura Ashley) also became the subject of dinner-table talk.

While the terms used to describe such tribes are rather ephemeral, they reflect the ever-increasing need for people to define themselves as members of distinct subgroups of the population. The reality of such groupings is revealed not only in the plethora of labels but more directly in new trends in market-research techniques. In order to market and sell goods effectively, major companies have to identify particular segments of the population and target their advertising accordingly. There is little point, for example, in advertising expensive designer-label jewellery in mass-circulation magazines bought by people who cannot possibly afford such luxury items; by contrast, an advertisement placed in a low-circulation "quality" magazine may produce an impressive response. Increasingly, however, the marketing people are finding that the traditional demographic measures, based primarily on social class and income levels, are not sufficiently sensitive or sophisticated. The aim of the newer methods is to identify the social tribes to which people belong and the size and characteristic features of each of those tribes. Known as "values and lifestyles analysis," the approach is little interested in knowledge simply of people's income or social background: that does not permit a sufficient distinction between the various types of potential customer, and nor does it predict with any degree of accuracy which newspapers people read, what they watch on television, or the range of articles they might be interested in purchasing.

Identifying people in terms of the discrete social groupings they   9
belong to, defined in terms of aspirations, tastes, values and particular lifestyles, allows marketing departments to determine very easily the size of the market for various products and the channels through which advertising should be directed. Where there are several segments of the population to whom a particular product might appeal, the manner in which an item is advertised can be tailored to each of them so that it appeals directly to their tribal affiliations.

This commercial realization of patterns of collective bonding is,   10
perhaps, the best evidence for tribalism in modern societies. We may make jokes about the names of trendy middle-class groupings, or prefer to think of ourselves as free, independent spirits, owing allegiance to no group in particular, but most of us in actuality find it hard to escape categorization. Modern tribes consist not merely of the ostentatious youth cults, with their elaborate hairstyles and seemingly perverse tastes in clothing. Nor is it only members of esoteric institutions, secret societies, clubs and associations who strive to achieve distinctive collective unity. All of us rely on others for our sense of self and identity. Where the scale of our culture denies us a true sense of belonging, we conspire to scale things down—to create units in which we can be human. In other words, tribes.

Meanings and Values

1a.   What three main groups does Marsh discuss in this selection?

b.   In what ways are the groups similar? (In answering this question consider traits such as social class, age, and moral or social values.)

c.   What groups does Marsh mention briefly?

2. Summarize the explanation Marsh offers in paragraphs 8–10 to support his conclusion that "the best evidence for tribalism in modern societies" is the "commercial realization" of social groups (par. 10).

3. If you have read Desmond Morris's essay "Territorial Behaviour," discuss how the kinds of tribes he identifies differ from those outlined in this selection.

4. Why does the author believe that people in modern society form tribes?

Expository Techniques

1. Where in the second paragraph is the central theme of this selection stated? (See Guide to Terms: *Unity*.)

2a. Identify the specific details Marsh uses to characterize each of the following groups: Yuppies, Sloane Rangers, Drabbies, Spoolers.

b. What objects or activities are identified in paragraphs 2, 4, and 7 that might be said to symbolize particular groups? (Guide: *Symbol*.)

3. Are the categories Marsh presents distinct enough and clear enough for the purposes of this piece? Does it matter, for example, that Dinkies might be considered a kind of Yuppie and not a distinct group? (Guide: *Purpose, Evaluation*.)

4. Groupings like those described by Marsh come and go rapidly. Is the effectiveness of the writing or the central theme of the selection likely to be undermined if some or all of its categories seem dated to a reader? Why, or why not? (Guide: *Evaluation*.)

Diction and Vocabulary

1a. To what does the name "Sloane Rangers" allude? (Guide: *Figures of Speech*.)

b. What evidence is there that Marsh or the originator of the term, Peter York, intended it to be applied ironically? (Guide: *Irony*.)

2a. In what ways is the vocabulary in this selection characteristic of writing in the social sciences, such as anthropology, sociology, or psychology?

b. In paragraphs 1, 2, and 8–10 the author employs a number of relatively technical terms. How, if at all, do they add to or reinforce the meaning of the paragraphs?

c. Do technical terms detract from the meaning or clarity of any passages, at least for the average reader? If so, which sections are most likely to trouble readers? (Guide: *Diction*.)

3. If you do not know the meaning of any of the following words, look them up in a dictionary: alienation, engendered, disadvantage, solidarity (par. 1); entrepreneurs (2); acronymic (3); cynicism, simplistic, caricature (4); rarefied, reactionary, feigned, disinterest (5); antithesis, acumen (6); staid (7); ephemeral, plethora (8); ostentatious, esoteric (10).

Suggestions for Writing and Discussion

1. Identify and discuss any new social groups based on lifestyle that have arisen since this essay was published.

2. Many would argue that it is unfair to characterize people according to the kinds of groupings Marsh presents because individuals are much more complex than his categories suggest. Based on the essay, how do you think Marsh might respond to this criticism? To what extent do you agree or disagree with the criticism?

3. Prepare an essay of your own dividing artists, entertainers, politicians, physicians, or other professionals into groups based on categories appropriate to their activities. You might, for example, decide to classify physicians according to their skill in dealing with patients or politicians according to their ability to inspire people.

(NOTE: Suggestions for topics requiring development by use of CLASSIFICATION are on page 113, at the end of this section.)

BRUCE BERGER

BRUCE BERGER was born in 1938 in Evanston, Illinois. He attended
Yale University as an undergraduate and did graduate work in
English at the University of California–Berkeley. He has published
articles, poems, and essays in a variety of places, including the *New
York Times*, *The North American Review*, *Sierra*, *Rocky Mountain Magazine*, *Sonora Review*, and *Adventure Travel*. His recent collection of
essays, *The Telling Distance: Conversations with the American Desert*
(1990), earned him the Western States Book Award.

The Assault of Squaw Peak

In this essay from *The Telling Distance*, Berger classifies people who
participate in a familiar urban phenomenon. In so doing, he raises
questions about the role that nature plays in our lives and about the
need to preserve as many natural sites as we can.

Squaw Peak, on the fringes of downtown Phoenix, is the kind of slag   1
heap most mountaineers, not to mention other mountains, look down
on. Behind a tract of ranchettes off a crosstown artery, Squaw Peak
Park is the crown of the Phoenix City Park System. From a basin of
picnic ramadas, johns and trash barrels, its shaggy pyramid rises
twelve hundred feet above the valley floor, bearing a populous trail
of switchbacks, traverses and last scrambles that winds a mile from
the parking lot to the city's beloved summit. Once a mere granite
outcropping, Squaw Peak has become that contemporary urban phenomenon, an exercise mountain. It is simultaneously a social club, a
point of reference, a spiritual escape, a vertical dog walk, a unit of
measurement, a free place to lose weight, a training ground, an
addiction, and to its more passionate admirers—and I am one—the
focus of a most curious subculture.

My introduction to Squaw Peak occurred on one of those days of   2
blustery smog that passes for winter in Phoenix. On reaching the
summit I came upon six adults speaking a tongue I couldn't identify.
Teutonic gutturals, Gallic nasals, Balkan clots of consonants, it seemed
to confound all of Europe. I selected its most American-looking
practitioner and asked. "A dialect of Swiss," the lady replied, "native
to only a few cantons. I'm not very good at it myself yet. I'm from
Chicago and only recently married into it." Through that linguistic
scramble came a clear message from Squaw Peak itself: its glory was
its people.

Motives for scaling Squaw Peak are various. A few couples are   3
less interested in the ascent than in some amorphous rock to crawl
behind for a roll in the cactus. A few first-timers hope to commune
with nature. There are various one-shot groups: geology classes, Scout
troops, outing clubs, gangs, church picnics. Some are looking for a
comfortable perch where they can let Phoenix go nonverbal; others
arrive with the problems of the world transistorized in their hands.
But the regulars are there for exercise. Imagine yourself on the summit
as a woman in a pink tank shirt and tennis shorts lurches to the top
rock, flops down and looks immediately at her watch. "Damn!
Twenty minutes and seventeen seconds."

A man in a sweat suit who has watched her last pitch says, "Still   4
haven't broken the twenty-minute barrier?"

"Yeah, but I don't think I can ever do better than this. Cloudy day,   5
Reeboks. Not much better than with hiking boots in the sun. What's
your best time?"

"Twenty-two-oh-five. You beat *me*, in any case."   6

As they split seconds an enormous hulk of a regular, minus his   7
usual overweight companion, flings himself on a neighboring rock
and squints at a stopwatch. "Finally did it," he gasps. "Took me two
months, but I broke twenty-six minutes."

"Congratulations!" says the man.   8

"Great," says the woman, "but where's your friend?"   9

"We can't seem to get our schedules together anymore," he signs.   10
"Tuesdays and Thursdays I go to the Trim 'n Slim to use the pool, and
he goes bowling on Mondays, plays bingo on Wednesdays and sees
his mother on Friday. We run into each other on weekends sometimes
and he says, 'See you on Tuesday and Thursday?' and I say, 'See you
on Monday, Wednesday and Friday?' It's hopeless."

While the trio ponders life's unfairness, a late adolescent in   11
yellow shorts, sleek as a Pentecostal, bounds to the top, grunts a
general salutation and disappears back down. He makes two round
trips every afternoon, never slowing to speak, always in the same
yellow shorts as supernaturally spotless as John Wayne's hat. Does
he have more than one pair? Wash them everyday? Possess a divine
detergent? If you know every turn, your brain needs such roughage.

Squaw Peak is no less valuable to equipment testers. It is possible,   12
when school is out, to observe a group of subteens and their adult
counselor all with shiny new red and white packs from a backpack
emporium known locally as High Indenture. Affixed to each pack is
a sleeping bag projected backward to apply maximum stress to the
bearer's spine. The sleeping bag of one little boy dangles from his
frame's bottom corner so that it swings wildly, pulling him like a sad
pendulum in its wake. More sophisticated testers climb with their
packs empty, adding weights to the outside until they attain back-
country poundage. And Squaw Peak is not forgotten once its graduates hit the trail; drilled into bone memory, it becomes a unit of
measurement. The Grand Canyon is four Squaw Peaks. The Grand
Teton is five and a half. Mt. Everest is twenty-two.

There is, of course, the doggy set. As a breed fancier I enjoy the   13
variety, the counterpoint with their owners, the aromatic pitfalls that
await the sprint back down. Most heroic is a toy poodle whose
mistress marches it daily to the summit. It is a sweating dog's fate to
look happier the hotter it gets, but this creature seems truly delighted;
under all that fluff must crouch a little rat of sheer muscle. More
elegant was an afghan I once found rounding the bends alone with
melancholy determination, hair blowing in the wind. He remained
mysterious for several turns, until I came upon an emaciated young
man with an aquiline nose and streaming blond locks, who couldn't
figure what was so hilarious when he said hello.

Casual encounters can resonate with meaning. Once at the sum-   14
mit I came upon a pack of Marlboros with each cigarette angrily
broken in half and strewn about the empty pack—an oath in litter to
live more purely. I came once upon a couple bearing two children, a
two-year-old riding a seat on his back, an infant slung on her stomach
and contentedly sucking her left breast as she climbed. I have seen
kids huffing up the trail on clunker bikes, and one late teen staggering
up with a fifteen-pound rock in his arms. In the parking lot on a day

of driving rain I was asked by a heavy-set fellow in sopping track shorts, barely slowing up, whether I had seen signs of lightning on top. "I'm out to make a record," he panted. "On my eighth lap. I'll quit after ten or an even dozen. Don't know if it's the mountain's record. It's mine. The most I've gone before is 9,000 feet. At 9,700 now. That's two Grand Canyons." And one dusk I came upon three Native Americans in track suits at a leveling of the trail, jogging in a tight circle. Muscle warm-up? Mystic rite? Two birds with one stone? Squaw Peak holds its tongue . . .

Squaw Peak on weekends is a sociological dare. The slopes are 15 alive with children unleashing aggressions built up from five consecutive days of public education, and many of them are throwing rocks. You dodge your way to the summit between cousinly gangs and downhill sprinters. On the summit you try to stay out of victory photographs, then a young voice yells to another, "Don't go yet, John, I've got to get my recorder out of your pack!" You perk up, hoping someone will blow a few bars of Scarlatti, but no, a young hand brandishes a tape deck. The sign below must be incomplete: this must be Squawk Peak. There is nothing left but to sprint back down like Nureyev the Coyote, speed-reading T-shirts, dodging dog duty, slaloming through Scout troops, family picnics, beer and dope and hot dog parties, ignoring rolling rocks, amateur police whistles and the top ten, until you can unlock your car door and fasten the safety belt.

If Squaw Peak is romantic, it is only at night. In a metropolis like 16 Phoenix, bristling with arc lights, neon lights and headlights, a shimmering twilight reigns from dusk until dawn and the trail glows like a radium dial. Few brave the mountain, and fellow hikers pass like phantoms. I have risked it occasionally, most unforgettably one night before Christmas. An unfamiliar voice sounded, *Uh-ooh-ooh-ooh!* I feared at first a clever mugger, but safe passage proved it a true owl. Christmas lights on the eaves of ranchettes crawled like coral snakes through the dark. Such night ascents prolong short winter days and extend the exercise season through the hot months, but I don't attempt Squaw Peak very often after sundown. I am not afraid of the trail, but I am terrified of the parking lot.

A friend of mine who grew up at the base of Squaw Peak 17 remembers when a trip to the summit from his house was an all-day affair. That was before motorized access made it the mountain for the man on the go. Since then it has been discovered that exercise can stave off atrophy and fat attacks, and ease the pressures of junk food, blush wines and Blue Cross payments. The hordes have arrived, devout consumers, and they believe that the only route is straight up. Switchbacks are shaved, ignored, obliterated. Whole pitches become alleys, then avenues. The more adventurous find the trail demeaning and select some nearly perpendicular alternative, launching everything loose. Rockslides become gullies, gullies become gashes, the vegetation gives up and the mountain becomes a chronic landslide. The City Park System in collaboration with volunteers has valiantly outlined the trail with rocks, strewn rubble over the cut-offs, jockeyed steps, added strategic handrails and even reared retaining walls, retarding wholesale collapse. Still, parts of Squaw Peak aren't eroding so much as they are melting like ice cream.

My affection for Squaw Peak is colored by one private association: my mother married the Arizonan who owned the undeveloped valley in back of it, just under the peak, a square mile known as Section 36. Acquired in the forties, it was once a peaceful domain where a gentleman could pull up his Lincoln and let out his poodles. Trail bikes changed all that. Signs prohibiting all but foot traffic were posted, adding the lure of the forbidden to young Knievels pioneering new ruts through the arroyos, until Section 36 sang like a swarm of electronic mosquitos. Meanwhile city taxes were spiraling, revenues held their own at zero and Frank Durham was being broken by Squaw Peak. 18

Developers offered lurid sums for the privilege of turning Section 36 into fully secured townhouses with pools and golf course, but Frank held out for cactus. I played my single card by calling Nature Conservancy in Tucson, hoping they might intervene; there followed a silence in which I imagined incredulity at anything in Phoenix worth conserving, then an explanation that they had sunk all their funds into something outside Tucson called Rancho Romero. Suddenly my stepfather ran across a newspaper photo of Mayor Driggs and associates riding through Section 36 on horseback, hoping to annex it to the open space program. With his usual flair Frank called City Hall, got Mayor Driggs on his line and growled, "What do you mean by trespassing on my land?" There followed two years of negotiations in which Section 36 was sold to the city for a fraction of its market value. Frank Durham joined the Driggs for Governor Committee, and the back of Squaw Peak, refenced, was saved as an urban refuge. 19

And Squaw Peak, beckoning darkly between downtown sky-   20
scrapers, still offers the consolations of perspective. Those consolations are necessary. Sirens howl through Phoenix like wolves all night.
City cherry pickers armed with chain saws tidy the palms by day.
Mowers, hedge clippers and radios keen to each other from back
yards. Dobermans and yappers debate the alleys. Peace in the city
seems to consist in drowning out your neighbor with the havoc of
your choice, but from the summit of Squaw Peak the voices run
together in one pure stereophonic roar. Only the pitched combustion
of a plane or the sine wave of a police car can pick itself from the din,
to lapse back into chaos. It is a fugue for a million voices, and if you
lie back with your eyes closed you can almost feel all that energy, and
even dream yourself—if you dare—its final product.

You reopen your eyes to find Western civilization splintering in   21
all directions. On many days it is hard to see beyond Sun City, and
one of the ironies of Squaw Peak is that its horizons, once achingly
pure, have blurred and vanished until you wonder whether you are
building your legs only to rot your lungs. But say a clean wind has
blown in from Los Angeles. Toward the horizon in diminishing waves
of blue stretch the mountains: the Superstitions, the McDowells,
Sierra Estrella, the South Mountains, Four Peaks, the Mazatzals, more
ranges than you can name. At their feet lies the tawny lionskin of the
Sonoran Desert, whose cactus still keep their spines out and drink
alone. And like a house pet nearby lies the better-known Camelback
Mountain, also an exercise mountain but so barbed with elec-
troguarded homes that few commoners have found the trail up its
exclusive hump.

Just out of sight at the end of the McDowells, a splinter in the   22
mind's eye, stands an improbable shaft of white. Courtesy of Mc-
Culloch Properties, the folks who brought us the London Bridge, it is
the world's tallest fountain, an ejaculation of pure ground water.
Collected over the centuries in a vast aquifer that underlies this
particular waste, it attains its consummation in one clean upward
rush into the dry Sonoran air, thence to evaporate. Its mission is not
the irrigation of life but the promotion of real estate. Into this waste
an inverted Wall of China called the Central Arizona Project has been
constructed to divert, for four billion tax dollars, what's left of the
Colorado River—but if we get lost in the Arizona mind we will never
make it off this mountain.

More immediately, great quadrangles of asphalt and green are 23
still spreading their dazzling geometry in all directions, a few of them,
like the saturated McCormick Ranch, bent on outdoing Connecticut.
High rises compound the sub-centers of Tempe and Scottsdale. The
better homes cantilever their egos into the public eye on steep hillsides, spilling prize desert into simulated mine dumps. What's left of
the Salt River Valley, assisted by the Mafia, the real estate lobby and
the Congressional delegation, is swiftly being paved or bulldozed
into dervishes of liberated topsoil. *Ave atque valley.*

Yet stand on Squaw Peak, chance a deep breath, and gaze. You 24
are at the hub of a great wheel, and flashing about you are the
accelerating spokes of the New West. They may look raw. But in the
heart of the true Phoenician, the newcomer or the native of a decade's
standing, lies the faith, the fountain, the drive of Phoenix's founding
myth, that from the recurrent ashes of itself will continue to flame the
eternally new pigeon.

Meanings and Values

1a. How close does the last sentence of paragraph 2 come to summing up
the central theme of this essay? (See Guide to Terms: *Unity.*)

b. In what way would you summarize the central theme?

2. List the various categories of climbers and others who frequent Squaw
Peak.

3. Is it the purpose of this essay to provide a formal classification of the
people who come to Squaw Peak? If not, what is the purpose of the
essay? (Guide: *Purpose.*)

Expository Techniques

1a. What part of this essay is devoted primarily to classification?

b. What does the remainder of the essay do?

c. Explain why you think the different parts of the essay do or do not
form a unified whole. (Guide: *Unity.*)

2. What does the brief narrative in paragraphs 18–19 contribute to the
essay?

3. The author offers humorous portraits of many of the people he encounters on Squaw Peak. What evidence is there that the humor is designed
to be gentle, not sharply critical?

Diction and Vocabulary

1a. What does the author mean by saying that the sounds of the city become "a fugue for a million voices" (par. 20) when heard from Squaw Peak?

  b. Is there any evidence that this statement is meant to be ironic? If so, what is it? (Guide: *Irony*).

2. Identify the figures of speech in the final paragraph and discuss their use. (Guide: *Figures of Speech*.)

3. If you do not know the meaning of some of the following words, look them up in a dictionary: slag, switchbacks, traverses (par. 1); gutturals, nasals, cantons (2); amorphous (3); Pentecostal, salutation (11); afghan (13); recorder (15); aquifer (22); cantilever (23).

Suggestions for Writing and Discussion

1. Consider classifying the kinds of people who participate in some activity: tennis players, dancers, chess players, or readers, for example.

2. If you are familiar with an urban setting similar to Squaw Peak, consider making it the basis of an essay using classification or one of the other patterns of exposition.

3. Do you agree with what seems to be the author's view of urban development? With his views on nature? How do your views differ?

(NOTE: Suggestions for topics requiring development by use of CLASSIFICATION follow.)

Writing Suggestions for Section 2
Classification

Use division and classification (into at least three categories) as your basic method of analyzing one of the following subjects from one interesting point of view. (Your instructor may have good reason to place limitations on your choice of subject.) Narrow the topic as necessary to enable you to do a thorough job.

1. College students.
2. College teachers.
3. Athletes.
4. Coaches.
5. Salespeople.
6. Hunters (or fishermen).
7. Parents.
8. Drug users.
9. Police officers.
10. Summer (or part-time) jobs.
11. Sailing vessels.
12. Game show hosts.
13. Friends.
14. Careers.
15. Horses (or other animals).
16. Television programs.
17. Motivations for study.
18. Methods of studying for exams.
19. Lies.
20. Selling techniques.
21. Tastes in clothes.
22. Contemporary music.
23. Love.
24. Ways to spend money.
25. Attitudes toward life.
26. Fast foods (or junk foods).
27. Smokers.
28. Investments.
29. Actors.
30. Books or magazines.

3

Explaining by Means of *Comparison* and *Contrast*

One of the first expository methods we used as children was *comparison,* noticing similarities of objects, qualities, and actions, or *contrast,* noticing their differences. We compared the color of the new puppies with that of their mother, contrasted our father's height with our own. Then the process became more complicated. Now we employ it frequently in college essay examinations or term papers when we compare or contrast forms of government, reproductive systems of animals, or ethical philosophies of humans. Later, in the business or professional world, we may prepare important reports based on comparison and contrast—between kinds of equipment for purchase, the personnel policies of different departments, or precedents in legal matters. Nearly all people use the process, though they may not be aware of this, many times a day—in choosing a head of lettuce, in deciding what to wear to school, in selecting a house or a friend or a religion.

In the more formal scholastic and professional uses of comparison and contrast, however, an ordered plan is needed to avoid having a mere list of characteristics or a frustrating jumble of similarities and differences. If authors want to avoid communication blocks that will prevent their "getting through" to their readers, they will observe a few basic principles of selection and development. These principles apply mostly to comparisons between two subjects only; if three or more are to be considered, they should be grouped to make the discussion easy to follow.

A *logical* comparison or contrast can be made only between subjects of the same general type. (Analogy, a special form of comparison used for another purpose, is discussed in the next section.) For example, contrasting a pine and a maple could be useful or meaningful, but little would be gained, except exercise in sentence construction, by contrasting the pine and the pansy.

Of course, logical but informal comparisons that are merely incidental to the basic structure, and hence follow no special pattern, may be made in any writing. Several of the preceding selections make limited use of comparison and contrast; Viorst does some contrasting of types of showoffs, and Desmond Morris uses some comparison between tribal territorial behavior now and in prehistoric times. But once committed to a formal, full-scale analysis by comparison and contrast, the careful writer ordinarily gives the subjects similar treatment. Points used for one should also be used for the other, and usually in the same order. All pertinent points should be explored—pertinent, that is, to the purpose of the comparison.

The purpose and the complexity of materials will usually suggest their arrangement and use. Sometimes the purpose is merely to point out *what* the likenesses and differences are, sometimes it is to show the *superiority* of one thing over another—or possibly to convince the reader of the superiority, as this is also a technique of argumentation. The purpose may be to explain the *unfamiliar* (wedding customs in Ethiopia) by comparing it to the *familiar* (wedding customs in Kansas). Or it may be to explain or emphasize some other type of *central idea*, as in most of the essays in this section.

One of the two basic methods of comparison is to present all the information on the two subjects, one at a time, and to summarize by combining their most important similarities and differences. This method may be desirable if there are few points to compare, or if the individual points are less important than the overall picture they present. Therefore, this procedure might be a satisfactory means of showing the relative difficulty of two college courses or of comparing two viewpoints concerning an automobile accident. (Of course, as in all other matters of expository arrangement, the last subject discussed is in the most emphatic position.)

However, if there are several points of comparison to be considered, or if the points are of individual importance, alternation of the material would be a better arrangement. Hence, in a detailed comparison of Oak Valley and Elm Hill hospitals, we might compare their sizes, locations, surgical facilities, staffs, and so on, always in the same order. To tell all about Oak Valley and then all about Elm Hill would create a serious communication block, requiring readers constantly to call on their memory of what was cited earlier or to turn back to the first group of facts again and again in order to make the meaningful comparisons that the author should have made for them.

Often the subject matter or the purpose itself will suggest a more casual treatment, or some combination or variation of the two basic methods. We might present the complete information on the first subject, then summarize it point by point within the complete information on the second. In other circumstances it may be desirable simply to set up the thesis of likeness or difference, and then to explain a *process* that demonstrates this thesis. And although expository comparisons and contrasts are frequently handled together, it is sometimes best to present all similarities first, then all differences—or vice versa, depending on the emphasis desired. In argument, the arrangement we choose is that which best demonstrates the superiority of one thing (or plan of action) over another. This may mean a point-by-point contrast or the presentation of a weaker alternative before a stronger one.

In any basic use of comparison (conveniently, the term is most often used in a general sense to cover both comparison and contrast), the important thing is to have a plan that suits the purpose and material thoughtfully worked out in advance.

Sample Paragraph (Annotated)

Similarity announced. Though differences are not mentioned, the word "Parents" points towards "children" and suggests that the next generation may have a different perspective.

A *contrast* that serves to emphasize how similar the outlooks of the parents are.

Parents who moved from Valley City to Palmville generally have one thing in common: they agree there is little reason to make the long drive back to the metropolis, except, perhaps, to commute to work, for special shopping, or to hear a big star in concert. The talk at neighborhood gatherings, at youth baseball games, and in the aisles at Kwik Shop often revolves around how good it is to live in Palmville and how happy everyone is to have left Valley City. A few voices can even be heard claiming that the two new malls, the industries moving to Caton Industrial Park, and new groups like the Palmville Community Symphony mean "there

Contrast announced.
(Note use of transition:
"In contrast.")

just aren't good reasons to go to Valley City anymore." In contrast, most of the town's children have their eyes set on Valley City as a distant Oz with I-104 as the Yellow Brick Road. To most it means

Point-by-point presentation of similarities in outlook that also offers point-by-point differences from the parents.

entertainment in the form of mammoth rock shows; shopping at W. P. Sowerby's Department Store or the three-tier Okono Mall; and days on the beach watching glamorous people and being seen, too. To many it means opportunity in the form of large universities, jobs with major corporations, or careers in advertising and fashion. And to a few it means escape: "Anywhere but Palmville."

The kids' own slogan used as vivid example.

Final comparison (similarity).

Both parents and children share a desire to strike out on their own, the first group to get away from Valley City, the second group to return.

Sample Paragraph (Comparison/Contrast)

Large computers have some essential attributes of an intelligent brain: they have large memories, and they have gates whose connections can be modified by experience. However, the thinking of these computers tends to be narrow. The richness of human thought depends to a considerable degree on the enormous number of wires, or nerve fibers, coming into each gate in the human brain. A gate in a computer has two, or three, or at most four wires entering on one side, and one wire coming out the other side. In the brain of an animal, the gates may have thousands of wires entering one side, instead of two or three. In the human brain, a gate may have as many as 100,000 wires entering it. Each wire comes from another gate or nerve cell. This means that every gate in the human brain is connected to as many as 100,000 other gates in other parts of the brain. During the process of thinking innumerable gates open and close throughout the brain. When one of these gates "decides" to open, the decision is the result of a complicated assessment involving inputs from thousands of other gates. This circumstance explains much of the difference between human thinking and computer thinking.

MARK TWAIN

MARK TWAIN was the pen name of Samuel Clemens (1835–1910). He was born in Missouri and became the first author of importance to emerge from "beyond the Mississippi." Although best known for bringing humor, realism, and Western local color to American fiction, Mark Twain wanted to be remembered as a philosopher and social critic. Still widely read, in most languages and in all parts of the world, are his numerous short stories (his "tall tales," in particular), autobiographical accounts, and novels, especially *Adventures of Huckleberry Finn* (1884). Ernest Hemingway called the last "the best book we've had," an appraisal with which many critics agree.

Two Ways of Seeing a River

"Two Ways of Seeing a River" (editors' title) is from Mark Twain's "Old Times on the Mississippi," which was later expanded and published in book form as *Life on the Mississippi* (1883). It is autobiographical. The prose of this selection is vivid, as is all of Mark Twain's writing, but considerably more reflective in tone than most.

Now when I had mastered the language of this water and had come to know every trifling feature that bordered the great river as familiarly as I knew the letters of the alphabet, I had made a valuable acquisition. But I had lost something, too. I had lost something which could never be restored to me while I lived. All the grace, the beauty, the poetry, had gone out of the majestic river! I still kept in mind a certain wonderful sunset which I witnessed when steamboating was new to me. A broad expanse of the river was turned to blood; in the middle distance the red hue brightened into gold, through which a solitary log came floating, black and conspicuous; in one place a long, slanting mark lay sparkling upon the water; in another the surface was broken by boiling, tumbling rings that were as many-tinted as an opal; where the ruddy flush was faintest was a smooth spot that was covered with graceful circles and radiating lines, ever so delicately

1

traced; the shore on our left was densely wooded, and the somber shadow that fell from this forest was broken in one place by a long, ruffled trail that shone like silver; and high above the forest wall a clean-stemmed dead tree waved a single leafy bough that glowed like a flame in the unobstructed splendor that was flowing from the sun. There were graceful curves, reflected images, woody heights, soft distances, and over the whole scene, far and near, the dissolving lights drifted steadily, enriching it every passing moment with new marvels of coloring.

I stood like one bewitched. I drank it in, in a speechless rapture. 2 The world was new to me and I had never seen anything like this at home. But as I have said, a day came when I began to cease from noting the glories and the charms which the moon and the sun and the twilight wrought upon the river's face; another day came when I ceased altogether to note them. Then, if that sunset scene had been repeated, I should have looked upon it without rapture and should have commented upon it inwardly after this fashion: "This sun means that we are going to have wind tomorrow; that floating log means that the river is rising, small thanks to it; that slanting mark on the water refers to a bluff reef which is going to kill somebody's steamboat one of these nights, if it keeps on stretching out like that; those tumbling 'boils' show a dissolving bar and a changing channel there; the lines and circles in the slick water over yonder are a warning that that troublesome place is shoaling up dangerously; that silver streak in the shadow of the forest is the 'break' from a new snag and he has located himself in the very best place he could have found to fish for steamboats; that tall dead tree, with a single living branch, is not going to last long, and then how is a body ever going to get through this blind place at night without the friendly old landmark?"

No, the romance and beauty were all gone from the river. All the 3 value any feature of it had for me now was the amount of usefulness it could furnish toward compassing the safe piloting of a steamboat. Since those days, I have pitied doctors from my heart. What does the lovely flush in a beauty's cheek mean to a doctor but a "break" that ripples above some deadly disease? Are not all her visible charms sown thick with what are to him the signs and symbols of hidden decay? Does he ever see her beauty at all, or doesn't he simply view her professionally and comment upon her unwholesome condition all to himself? And doesn't he sometimes wonder whether he has gained most or lost most by learning his trade?

Meanings and Values

1. No selection could better illustrate the intimate relationship of several skills with which students of writing should be familiar, especially the potentials in *point of view* (and attitude), *style,* and *tone.*

   a. What is the point of view in paragraph 1? (See Guide to Terms: *Point of View.*)

   b. Where, and how, does it change in paragraph 2?

   c. Why is the shift important to the author's contrast?

   d. Show how the noticeable change of tone is related to this change in point of view. (Guide: *Style/Tone.*)

   e. Specifically, what changes in style accompany the shift in tone and attitude?

   f. How effectively do they all relate to the central theme itself? (Remember that such effects seldom just "happen"; the writer *makes* them happen.)

2a. Is the first paragraph primarily objective or subjective? (Guide: *Objective/Subjective.*)

   b. How about the latter part of paragraph 2?

   c. Are your answers to 2a and 2b related to point of view? If so, how?

3a. Does the author permit himself to engage in sentimentality? (Guide: *Sentimentality.*) If so, how could it have been avoided without damage to his theme's development?

   b. If not, what restraints does the author use?

4. Do you think the last sentence refers only to doctors? Why, or why not?

5. List other vocations in which you assume (or perhaps know) that the beauty and romance eventually give way to practical realities; state briefly, for each, why this hardening should be expected.

Expository Techniques

1a. Where do you find a second comparison or contrast? Which is it?

   b. Is the comparison/contrast made within itself, with something external, or both? Explain.

   c. Is this part of the writing closely enough related to the major contrast to justify its use? Why, or why not?

2a. In developing the numerous points of the major contrast, would an alternating, point-to-point system have been better? Why, or why not?

b. Show how the author uses organization within the groups to assist in the overall contrast.

3a. What is the most noteworthy feature of syntax in paragraphs 1 and 2? (Guide: *Syntax.*)

b. How effectively does it perform the function intended?

4. What is gained by the apparently deliberate decision to use rhetorical questions only toward the end? (Guide: *Rhetorical Questions.*)

Diction and Vocabulary

1. Why would the colloquialism in the last sentence of paragraph 2 have been inappropriate in the first paragraph? (Guide: *Colloquial Expressions.*)

2a. Compare the quality of metaphors in the quotation of paragraph 2 with the quality of those preceding it. (Guide: *Figures of Speech.*)

b. Is the difference justified? Why, or why not?

Suggestions for Writing and Discussion

1. Select for further development one of the vocations in your answer to question 5 of "Meanings and Values." How would one's attitude be apt to change from the beginning romantic appeal?

2. Show how, if at all, Mark Twain's contrast might be used to show parallels to life itself—e.g., differences in the idealism and attitudes of youth and maturity.

3. Explore the possibility, citing examples if possible, of being able to retain both the "rapture" and the "usefulness."

(NOTE: Suggestions for topics requiring development by use of COMPARISON and CONTRAST are on page 149, at the end of this section.)

BRUCE CATTON

BRUCE CATTON (1899–1978) was a Civil War specialist whose early career included reporting for various newspapers. In 1954 he received both the Pulitzer Prize for historical work and the National Book Award. He served as director of information for the United States Department of Commerce and wrote many books, including *Mr. Lincoln's Army* (1951), *Glory Road* (1952), *A Stillness at Appomattox* (1953), *The Hallowed Ground* (1956), *America Goes to War* (1958), *The Coming Fury* (1961), *Terrible Swift Sword* (1963), *Never Call Retreat* (1966), *Waiting for the Morning Train: An American Boyhood* (1972), and *Gettysburg: The Final Fury* (1974). For five years, Catton edited *American Heritage*.

Grant and Lee: A Study in Contrasts

"Grant and Lee: A Study in Contrasts" was written as a chapter of *The American Story*, a collection of essays by noted historians. In this study, as in most of his other writing, Catton does more than recount the facts of history: he shows the significance within them. It is a carefully constructed essay, using contrast and comparison as the entire framework for his explanation.

When Ulysses S. Grant and Robert E. Lee met in the parlor of a modest house at Appomattox Court House, Virginia, on April 9, 1865, to work out the terms for the surrender of Lee's Army of Northern Virginia, a great chapter in American life came to a close, and a great new chapter began.   1

These men were bringing the Civil War to its virtual finish. To be sure, other armies had yet to surrender, and for a few days the fugitive   2

Confederate government would struggle desperately and vainly, try-ing to find some way to go on living now that its chief support was gone. But in effect it was all over when Grant and Lee signed the papers. And the little room where they wrote out the terms was the scene of one of the poignant, dramatic contrasts in American history.

They were two strong men these oddly different generals, and they represented the strengths of two conflicting currents that, through them, had come into final collision.   3

Back of Robert E. Lee was the notion that the old aristocratic concept might somehow survive and be dominant in American life.   4

Lee was tidewater Virginia, and in his background were family, culture, and tradition . . . the age of chivalry transplanted to a New World which was making its own legends and its own myths. He embodied a way of life that had come down through the age of knighthood and the English country squire. America was a land that was beginning all over again, dedicated to nothing much more com-plicated than the rather hazy belief that all men had equal rights and should have an equal chance in the world. In such a land Lee stood for the feeling that it was somehow of advantage to human society to have a pronounced inequality in the social structure. There should be a leisure class, backed by ownership of land; in turn, society itself should be keyed to the land as the chief source of wealth and influ-ence. It would bring forth (according to this ideal) a class of men with a strong sense of obligation to the community; men who lived not to gain advantage for themselves, but to meet the solemn obligations which had been laid on them by the very fact that they were privi-leged. From them the country would get its leadership; to them it could look for the higher values—of thought, of conduct, or personal deportment—to give it strength and virtue.   5

Lee embodied the noblest elements of this aristocratic ideal. Through him, the landed nobility justified itself. For four years, the Southern states had fought a desperate war to uphold the ideals for which Lee stood. In the end, it almost seemed as if the Confederacy fought for Lee; as if he himself was the Confederacy . . . the best thing that the way of life for which the Confederacy stood could ever have to offer. He had passed into legend before Appomattox. Thousands of tired, underfed, poorly clothed Confederate soldiers, long since past the simple enthusiasm of the early days of the struggle, somehow considered Lee the symbol of everything for which they had been willing to die. But they could not quite put this feeling into words. If   6 the Lost Cause, sanctified by so much heroism and so many deaths, had a living justification, its justification was General Lee.

Grant, the son of a tanner on the Western frontier, was everything 7 Lee was not. He had come up the hard way and embodied nothing in particular except the eternal toughness and sinewy fiber of the men who grew up beyond the mountains. He was one of a body of men who owed reverence and obeisance to no one, who were self-reliant to a fault, who cared hardly anything for the past but who had a sharp eye for the future.

These frontier men were the precise opposites of the tidewater 8 aristocrats. Back of them, in the great surge that had taken people over the Alleghenies and into the opening Western country, there was a deep, implicit dissatisfaction with a past that had settled into grooves. They stood for democracy, not from any reasoned conclusion about the proper ordering of human society, but simply because they had grown up in the middle of democracy and knew how it worked. Their society might have privileges, but they would be privileges each man had won for himself. Forms and patterns meant nothing. No man was born to anything, except perhaps to a chance to show how far he could rise. Life was competition.

Yet along with this feeling had come a deep sense of belonging 9 to a national community. The Westerner who developed a farm, opened a shop, or set up in business as a trader could hope to prosper only as his own community prospered—and his community ran from the Atlantic to the Pacific and from Canada down to Mexico. If the land was settled, with towns and highways and accessible markets, he could better himself. He saw his fate in terms of the nation's own destiny. As its horizons expanded, so did his. He had, in other words, an acute dollars-and-cents stake in the continued growth and development of his country.

And that, perhaps, is where the contrast between Grant and 10 Lee becomes most striking. The Virginia aristocrat, inevitably, saw himself in relation to his own region. He lived in a static society which could endure almost anything except change. Instinctively, his first loyalty would go to the locality in which that society existed. He would fight to the limit of endurance to defend it, because in defending it he was defending everything that gave his own life its deepest meaning.

The Westerner, on the other hand, would fight with an equal 11 tenacity for the broader concept of society. He fought so because everything he lived by was tied to growth, expansion, and a constantly widening horizon. What he lived by would survive or fall with the nation itself. He could not possibly stand by unmoved in the face of an attempt to destroy the Union. He would combat it with everything he had, because he could only see it as an effort to cut the ground out from under his feet.

So Grant and Lee were in complete contrast, representing two diametrically opposed elements in American life. Grant was the modern man emerging; beyond him, ready to come on the stage, was the great age of steel and machinery, of crowded cities and a restless burgeoning vitality. Lee might have ridden down from the old age of chivalry, lance in hand, silken banner fluttering over his head. Each man was the perfect champion of his cause, drawing both his strengths and his weaknesses from the people he led.   12

Yet it was not all contrast, after all. Different as they were—in background, in personality, in underlying aspiration—these two great soldiers had much in common. Under everything else, they were marvelous fighters. Furthermore, their fighting qualities were really very much alike.   13

Each man had, to begin with, the great virtue of utter tenacity and fidelity. Grant fought his way down the Mississippi Valley in spite of acute personal discouragement and profound military handicaps. Lee hung on in the trenches at Petersburg after hope itself had died. In each man there was an indomitable quality . . . the born fighter's refusal to give up as long as he can still remain on his feet and lift his two fists.   14

Daring and resourcefulness they had, too: the ability to think faster and move faster than the enemy. These were the qualities which gave Lee the dazzling campaigns of Second Manassas and Chancellorsville and won Vicksburg for Grant.   15

Lastly, and perhaps greatest of all, there was the ability, at the end, to turn quickly from war to peace once the fighting was over. Out of the way these two men behaved at Appomattox came the possibility of a peace of reconciliation. It was a possibility not wholly realized, in the years to come, but which did, in the end, help the two sections to become one nation again . . . after a war whose bitterness might have seemed to make such a reunion wholly impossible. No part of either man's life became him more than the part he played in their brief meeting in the McLean house at Appomattox. Their behavior there put all succeeding generations of Americans in their debt. Two   16 great Americans, Grant and Lee—very different, yet under everything very much alike. Their encounter at Appomattox was one of the great moments of American history.

Meanings and Values

1a. Clarify the assertions that through Lee "the landed nobility justified itself" and that "if the Lost Cause . . . had a living justification," it was General Lee (par. 6).

b. Why are these assertions pertinent to the central theme?

2a. Does it seem reasonable that "thousands of tired, underfed, poorly clothed Confederate soldiers" (par. 6) had been willing to fight for the aristocratic system in which they would never have had even a chance to be aristocrats? Why, or why not?

b. Can you think of more likely reasons why they were willing to fight?

3. Under any circumstances today might such a social structure as the South's be best for a country? Explain.

4a. What countries of the world have recently been so torn by internal war and bitterness that reunion has seemed, or still seems, impossible?

b. Do you see any basic differences between the trouble in those countries and that in America at the time of the Civil War?

5a. The author calls Lee a symbol (par. 6). Was Grant also a symbol? If so, of what? (See Guide to Terms: *Symbol*.)

b. How would you classify this kind of symbolism?

Expository Techniques

1. Make an informal list of paragraph numbers from 3 to 16, and note by each number whether the paragraph is devoted primarily to Lee, to Grant, or to direct comparison or contrast of the two. This chart will show you Catton's basic pattern of development. (Notice, for instance, how the broad information of paragraphs 4–6 and 7–9 seems almost to "funnel" down through the narrower summaries in paragraphs 10 and 11 and into paragraph 12, where the converging elements meet and the contrast is made specific.)

2. What new technique of development is started in paragraph 13?

3a. What is gained, or lost, by using one sentence for paragraph 3?

b. For paragraph 4?

4a. How many paragraphs does the introduction comprise?

b. How successfully does it fulfill the three basic requirements of a good introduction? (Guide: *Introductions.*)

5. Show how Catton has constructed the beginning of each paragraph so that there is a smooth transition from the one preceding it. (Guide: *Transition.*)

6. The author's conclusion is really only the explanation of one of his integral points—and this method, if not carefully planned, runs the risk of ending too abruptly and leaving the reader unsatisfied. How has Catton avoided this hazard? (Guide: *Closings.*)

7a. What seems to be the author's attitude toward Grant and Lee?

b. Show how his tone reflects this attitude. (Guide: *Style/Tone.*)

Diction and Vocabulary

1. Why would a use of colloquialisms have been inconsistent with the tone of this writing?

2a. List or mark all metaphors in paragraphs 1, 3, 5, 7–11, 16. (Guide: *Figures of Speech.*)

b. Comment on their general effectiveness.

3. If you are not already familiar with the following words, study their meanings as given in the dictionary and as used in this essay: virtual, poignant (par. 2); concept (4); sinewy, obeisance (7); implicit (8); tenacity (11); diametrically, burgeoning (12); aspiration (13); fidelity, profound, indomitable (14); succeeding (16).

4. Explain how the word "poignant" aptly describes this contrast of two men (par. 2).

Suggestions for Writing and Discussion

1. Find, by minor research, an incident in the life of Grant or Lee that will, in suitable essay form, illustrate one of Catton's points.

2. Select some other dramatic moment in history and show its long-range significance.

3. Select some important moment in your life and show its long-range significance.

4. Explain how someone you know symbolizes a philosophy or way of life.

(NOTE: Suggestions for topics requiring development by use of COMPARISON and CONTRAST are on page 149, at the end of this section.)

FRANK S. CROCE

FRANK S. CROCE is a practicing attorney in New Jersey. He was born in Camden, New Jersey, in 1949. Following his graduation from St. Joseph's University in 1971 he taught high school English and attended law school in the evenings at Rutgers University–Camden. Croce has published mystery stories in a variety of magazines, including *Woman's World*.

Scrambled Eggs and Cross-Purposes

Comparison and contrast is an appropriate strategy for exploring disagreements over values, particularly when no easy resolution seems possible. In this essay, taken from the *New York Times Magazine*, Frank Croce uses careful exposition both to explain a conflict and to point the way toward reconciliation. Students of writing may be especially interested in the way he gives each side a full hearing without favoring either one.

Ten years ago my mother and father split up. In the uneasy truce that 1
has followed, my father's Sunday morning visits have become a ritual. I scramble some eggs. The kids play in their pajamas. My wife dresses for Mass.

Retired now, he is youthful-appearing since he gave up the 2
chemotherapy. But he walks and speaks with a look only those who have had the cancer cut out of them can possess. The surgeon said there was a 75 percent chance the cancer would return in the next five years. If my father gets by that, he's cured. He's into his fourth year, but being a fatalist by nature, he talks loosely of when he will "check out." We don't dwell on the possibility, but maybe it accounts for the edgy overtones that accompany our conversations.

My father is still a strong union man. For nearly 43 years he cut   3
meat for a large supermarket chain. I have a clear memory of his
leaving the house one night back in those black-and-white late 1950s,
grim, pale-faced, baseball bat in hand, to protect the picket line, his
job, me. Inevitably, our talk turns to unions and politics and sports.

Family talk is taboo. And just as inevitably, we end up on oppo-   4
site sides—as we did 20 years ago when my hair was long. Experience
versus formal education; a Depression-haunted childhood versus an
adolescence in relative affluence. The debate is as predictable as a bad
sit-com. We can't agree. Only the issues have changed.

He has remained a die-hard Democrat—the party of the little   5
man. He has nothing but scorn for those who cry that unions have
ruined our industry. My feeble explanation for why corporations seek
cheaper labor in Taiwan and Korea only infuriates him further. He
defends free agency and the players' outrageous salaries as if defending John L. Lewis' struggling coal miners. I point out the contradictions in the players' stance; what kind of union allows men with the
same time on the job to make such grossly different salaries for the
same job? They are only masquerading as laborers, I say. He refuses
to budge. Our voices rise. He examines me—his son, the college
graduate, the schoolteacher, the newly admitted attorney—and sums
up his feelings in one killing phrase: "You're for the bosses."

I struggle to defend myself. A silent alarm sounds, and he pushes   6
away the coffee cup, searching for the grandchildren who will demand only that he perform his disappearing penny trick. We retreat
to the living room and the Sunday papers scattered on the floor.

I sit and contemplate. I tell myself his feelings are understand-   7
able. After 30 years, his union surrendered to the supermarket's
tactical bankruptcy—$4 chopped off the hourly rate, vacation time
reduced to two weeks and the demise of a union man's greatest
accomplishment and weapon, seniority. Then the cancer. My positions are correct. I am not wrong. He simply does not understand the
complexity of it all.

He looks up from the grandchildren swamping his chair and   8
talks wistfully about his father, the shoemaker, who always whittled.
I recall the winter visits to the county hospital, my grandfather's home
for five years after the Christmas Eve stroke left him paralyzed and
nearly speechless. "My father was a good shoemaker," he says, "but
no businessman." He says a few words in Italian I don't understand.
I offer him another cup of coffee but he shakes it off.

A look of tired puzzlement crosses his face. He kisses the children, 9
tells my wife she is looking beautiful and we walk to what he calls his
last car, a youthful, silver Camaro.

"Look," he says, pointing with his car key toward the front door. 10
"Just worry about those kids and your wife, you hear? Don't worry
about me, your mother, or nobody."

I nod and ask him if he needs anything, the password for money. 11
He lies and says his pension check will come on Wednesday. He tells
me for the hundredth time that the payments on the Camaro are
insured so that when he "croaks," I'll get the car. I laugh and tell him
he's going to live another 20 years.

It is only after closing the front door behind me that I feel the 12
hollowness of my debating victory in the kitchen. The use of verbal
acrobatics learned in law school makes me feel like a petty thief. I was
arguing issues; he was talking beliefs. The anecdotes of those beliefs
haunt me—his indignance at the Philadelphia supervisors who fired
a man for stealing a steak while corporate bigshots drained the
company dry; the childhood acquaintances who moved to suburbia
and forgot "when we all ate salami sandwiches"; his admiration for
Humphrey Bogart, who said he only wanted money so he could tell
the bigshots to go to hell.

And the most bitter, most sustaining lesson in the life of a man 13
whose marriage has failed and who has little money in the bank—it
is one he is forever telling me—the power of money to hide a multitude of sins, how it soothes and excuses and defends callous manners,
cheap tactics and even crime. It is the lesson of America, his voice
seems to chant. He has learned it well.

The kids are chaotic. I bark an order, half-obeyed. The tuition is 14
due. We need to move. There is the law school loan to pay. My wife
needs cash for the collection basket. I am almost 40. I have a
mortgage.

At 19, my father manned a PT boat in the Pacific, fighting the 15
Japanese Empire. At the same age, I sat in a college dining hall
drinking bad coffee from a Styrofoam cup, debating the issues raised
by another Asian war about as familiar to me as a television program.
I once believed that the contrast in our experiences symbolized a true
gap. No more. Book learning has fooled me. Daily the boundaries of
the gap draw closer, merging into a single line—an arc—traveling as
it must, backward to its beginnings and its end.

Meanings and Values

1a. About what issues do the author and his father disagree?

b. On what other matters do they have different perspectives?

2. What is the tone of this essay, and what does it reveal about the author's attitude toward the conflicts over values he has with his father? (See Guide to Terms: *Tone*.)

3. To what extent do the values and emotions expressed in paragraphs 13–15 at the end of the essay differ from those conveyed earlier in the selection?

4. Is the main purpose of this essay to explore and explain the difference between parent and child? To identify grounds for resolving the differences? To help readers see in the author's experience an image of relationships with their own parents? Explain.

Expository Techniques

1a. Why should paragraphs 1 and 2 be regarded as introductory? What kinds of information do they provide? (Guide: *Introductions*.)

b. Should paragraph 3 be regarded as part of the introduction? Why, or why not?

2. Which sections of the essay focus primarily on contrasts? Which look also at similarities and agreements?

3. Are there any indications in paragraph 12 that readers should consider it a turning point in the development of the essay? If so, what are they?

4. Discuss the use Croce makes of parallel examples, sentences, and phrases in paragraphs 4, 5, and 15 to emphasize contrasts. (Guide: *Emphasis, Parallel Structure*.)

Diction and Vocabulary

1. What evidence is there in the diction of paragraph 4 of the author's profession as a lawyer? (Guide: *Diction*.)

2. Choose a section of the essay in which the author reports his and his father's words indirectly and compare it to a section in which direct quotation is used. Are different purposes served by these strategies? What are they? Is one technique more effective than the other? Why? (Guide: *Purpose, Evaluation*.)

3. Identify the figures of speech in the following passages and discuss their purposes and effects (Guide: *Figures of Speech*):

a. "The debate is as predictable as a bad sit-com." (par. 4)

b. ". . . as if defending John L. Lewis' struggling coal miners." (par. 5)

c. ". . . another Asian war about as familiar to me as a television program." (par. 15)

4. What use does the father make of slang and colloquial expressions in his speech? How does this contrast with the language his son employs in writing the essay? (Guide: *Slang, Colloquial Expressions*.)

Suggestions for Writing and Discussion

1. Do conflicts between people born in the 1970s and their parents revolve around different matters from those discussed in this essay? Or is there less conflict than characterizes the relationships of the baby boom generation to which Croce belongs?

2. Can some contemporary social or political issues be viewed as the result of differences in age, experience, or social class? Consider exploring an issue and its causes in a paper of your own.

(NOTE: Suggestions for topics requiring development by COMPARISON and CONTRAST are on page 149, at the end of this section.)

DEBORAH TANNEN

DEBORAH TANNEN received her Ph.D. in linguistics from the University of California–Berkeley and now teaches at Georgetown University. As a scholar, she has explored conversational styles and differences between writing and speaking in journal articles and in several books, including *Conversational Style: Analyzing Talk Among Friends* (1984); *Talking Voices: Repetition, Dialogue, and Imagery in Conversational Discourse* (1989); and, as editor, *Spoken and Written Language: Exploring Orality and Literacy* (1982). She has shared her research with a broader audience through television shows, articles in the *New York Times Magazine*, *New York*, and the *Washington Post*, and in two books: *That's Not What I Meant! How Conversational Style Makes or Breaks Your Relations with Others* (1986) and *You Just Don't Understand: Women and Men in Conversation* (1990).

It Begins at the Beginning

In this section from her book *You Just Don't Understand*, Tannen explores some of the differences (that is, contrasts) between the ways men and women talk. As the title suggests, she begins at the beginning by looking at the different ways girls and boys use language. Tannen's overall goal, however, is not to emphasize the differences but to help build bridges of understanding.

Even if they grow up in the same neighborhood, on the same block, 1
or in the same house, girls and boys grow up in different worlds of
words. Others talk to them differently and expect and accept different
ways of talking from them. Most important, children learn how to
talk, how to have conversations, not only from their parents but from
their peers. After all, if their parents have a foreign or regional accent,
children do not emulate it: they learn to speak with the pronunciation
of the region where they grow up. Anthropologists Daniel Maltz and

Ruth Borker summarize research showing that boys and girls have very different ways of talking to their friends. Although they often play together, boys and girls spend most of their time playing in same-sex groups. And, although some of the activities they play at are similar, their favorite games are different, and their ways of using language in their games are separated by a world of difference.

Boys tend to play outside, in large groups that are hierarchically   2
structured. Their groups have a leader who tells others what to do and how to do it, and resists doing what other boys propose. It is by giving orders and making them stick that high status is negotiated. Another way boys achieve status is to take center stage by telling stories and jokes, and by sidetracking or challenging the stories and jokes of others. Boys' games have winners and losers and elaborate systems of rules that are frequently the subjects of arguments. Finally, boys are frequently heard to boast of their skill and argue about who is best at what.

Girls, on the other had, play in small groups or in pairs; the center   3
of a girl's social life is a best friend. Within the group, intimacy is key: Differentiation is measured by relative closeness. In their most frequent games, such as jump rope and hopscotch, everyone gets a turn. Many of their activities (such as playing house) do not have winners or losers. Though some girls are certainly more skilled than others, girls are expected not to boast about it, or show that they think they are better than the others. Girls don't give orders; they express their preferences as suggestions, and suggestions are likely to be accepted. Whereas boys say, "Gimme that!" and "Get outta here!" girls say, "Let's do this," and "How about doing that?" Anything else is put down as "bossy." They don't grab center stage—they don't want it—so they don't challenge each other directly. And much of the time, they simply sit together and talk. Girls are not accustomed to jockeying for status in an obvious way; they are more concerned that they be liked.

Gender differences in ways of talking have been described by   4
researchers observing children as young as three. Amy Sheldon videotaped three- to four-year-old boys and girls playing in threesomes at a day-care center. She compared two groups of three—one of boys, one of girls—that got into fights about the same play item: a plastic pickle. Though both groups fought over the same thing, the dynamics by which they negotiated their conflicts were different. In addition to illustrating some of the patterns I have just described, Sheldon's study also demonstrates the complexity of these dynamics.

While playing in the kitchen area of the day-care center, a little 5
girl named Sue wanted the pickle that Mary had, so she argued that
Mary should give it up because Lisa, the third girl, wanted it. This led
to a conflict about how to satisfy Lisa's (invented) need. Mary proposed a compromise, but Sue protested:

MARY: I cut it in half. One for Lisa, one for me, one for me.
SUE: But, Lisa wants a *whole* pickle!

Mary comes up with another creative compromise, which Sue also
rejects:

MARY: Well, it's a whole *half* pickle.
SUE: No, it isn't.
MARY: Yes, it is, a whole *half* pickle.
SUE: *I'll* give her a whole half. I'll give her a *whole whole*. I gave
her a whole one.

At this point, Lisa withdraws from the alliance with Sue, who satisfies
herself by saying, "I'm pretending I gave you one."

On another occasion, Sheldon videotaped three boys playing in 6
the same kitchen play area, and they too got into a fight about the
plastic pickle. When Nick saw that Kevin had the pickle, he demanded it for himself:

NICK: [Screams] Kevin, but the, oh, I *have* to cut! I want to cut it!
It's mine!

Like Sue, Nick involved the third child in his effort to get the pickle:

NICK: [Whining to Joe] Kevin is not letting me cut the pickle.
JOE: Oh, I know! I can pull it away from him and give it back to
you. That's an idea!

The boys' conflict, which lasted two and a half times longer than the
girls', then proceeded as a struggle between Nick and Joe on the one
hand and Kevin on the other.

In comparing the boys' and girls' pickle fights, Sheldon points 7
out that, for the most part, the girls mitigated the conflict and preserved harmony by compromise and evasion. Conflict was more
prolonged among the boys, who used more insistence, appeals to
rules, and threats of physical violence. However, to say that these little
girls and boys used *more* of one strategy or another is not to say that
they didn't use the other strategies at all. For example, the boys did

attempt compromise, and the girls did attempt physical force. The girls, like the boys, were struggling for control of their play. When Sue says by mistake, "*I'll* give her a whole half," then quickly corrects herself to say, "I'll give her a *whole whole*," she reveals that it is not really the size of the portion that is important to her, but who gets to serve it.

While reading Sheldon's study, I noticed that whereas both Nick 8 and Sue tried to get what they wanted by involving a third child, the alignments they created with the third child, and the dynamics they set in motion, were fundamentally different. Sue appealed to Mary to fulfill someone else's desire; rather than saying that *she* wanted the pickle, she claimed that Lisa wanted it. Nick asserted his own desire for the pickle, and when he couldn't get it on his own, he appealed to Joe to get it for him. Joe then tried to get the pickle by force. In both these scenarios, the children were enacting complex lines of affiliation.

Joe's strong-arm tactics were undertaken not on his own behalf 9 but, chivalrously, on behalf of Nick. By making an appeal in a whining voice, Nick positioned himself as one-down in a hierarchical structure, framing himself as someone in need of protection. When Sue appealed to Mary to relinquish her pickle, she wanted to take the one-up position of serving food. She was fighting not for the right to *have* the pickle, but for the right to *serve* it. (This reminded me of the women who said they'd become professors in order to teach.) But to accomplish her goal, Sue was depending on Mary's desire to fulfill others' needs.

This study suggests that boys and girls both want to get their way, 10 but they tend to do so differently. Though social norms encourage boys to be openly competitive and girls to be openly cooperative, different situations and activities can result in different ways of behaving. Marjorie Harness Goodwin compared boys and girls engaged in two task-oriented activities: The boys were making slingshots in preparation for a fight, and the girls were making rings. She found that the boys' group was hierarchical: The leader told the others what to do and how to do it. The girls' group was egalitarian: Everyone made suggestions and tended to accept the suggestions of others. But observing the girls in a different activity—playing house—Goodwin found that they too adopted hierarchical structures: The girls who played mothers issued orders to the girls playing children, who in turn sought permission from their play-mothers. Moreover, a girl who was a play-mother was also a kind of manager of the game. This study shows that girls know how to issue orders and operate in a hierarchical structure, but they don't find that mode of behavior appropriate when they engage in task activities with their peers. They do find it appropriate in parent-child relationships, which they enjoy practicing in the form of play.

These worlds of play shed light on the world views of women   11
and men in relationships. The boys' play illuminates why men would be on the lookout for signs they are being put down or told what to do. The chief commodity that is bartered in the boys' hierarchical world is status, and the way to achieve and maintain status is to give orders and get others to follow them. A boy in a low-status position finds himself being pushed around. So boys monitor their relations for subtle shifts in status by keeping track of who's giving orders and who's taking them.

These dynamics are not the ones that drive girls' play. The chief   12
commodity that is bartered in the girls' community is intimacy. Girls monitor their friendships for subtle shifts in alliance, and they seek to be friends with popular girls. Popularity is a kind of status, but it is founded on connection. It also places popular girls in a bind. By doing field work in a junior high school, Donna Eder found that popular girls were paradoxically—and inevitably—disliked. Many girls want to befriend popular girls, but girls' friendships must necessarily be limited, since they entail intimacy rather than large group activities. So a popular girl must reject the overtures of most of the girls who seek her out—with the result that she is branded "stuck up."

The Key Is Understanding

If adults learn their ways of speaking as children growing up in   13
separate social worlds of peers, then conversation between women and men is cross-cultural communication. Although each style is valid on its own terms, misunderstandings arise because the styles are different. Taking a cross-cultural approach to male-female conversations makes it possible to explain why dissatisfactions are justified without accusing anyone of being wrong or crazy.

Learning about style differences won't make them go away, but   14
it can banish mutual mystification and blame. Being able to understand why our partners, friends, and even strangers behave the way they do is a comfort, even if we still don't see things the same way. It

makes the world into more familiar territory. And having others understand why we talk and act as we do protects us from the pain of their puzzlement and criticism.

In discussing her novel *The Temple of My Familiar*, Alice Walker   15
explained that a woman in the novel falls in love with a man because she sees in him "a giant ear." Walker went on to remark that although people may think they are falling in love because of sexual attraction or some other force, "really what we're looking for is someone to be able to hear us."

We all want, above all, to be heard—but not merely to be heard.   16
We want to be understood—heard for what we think we are saying, for what we know we meant. With increased understanding of the ways women and men use language should come a decrease in frequency of the complaint "You just don't understand."

Meanings and Values

1. In your own words, summarize what paragraph 1 has to say about the reason girls and boys converse in different ways.

2. Create two lists, one covering the key features of boys' conversational style, one covering girls' conversational style. Keep the entries short, using single words if possible. What do these lists reveal to you about the differences Tannen is exploring?

3a. Explain how the last section of the essay (paragraphs 13–16) is related to the overall purpose of the essay and to its central theme. (See Guide to Terms: *Purpose, Unity.*)

 b. How would you describe the tone of this section? (Guide: *Style/Tone.*)

 c. How does the tone differ, if at all, from that of the rest of the selection?

Expository Techniques

1a. Discuss the use of topic sentences in paragraphs 2, 3, 11, and 12. (Guide: *Unity.*)

 b. What use does the author make of various transitional devices in these paragraphs? (Guide: *Transition.*)

 c. Discuss the ways in which the topic sentences and transitional devices support the comparison-contrast pattern employed in the essay.

2. Explain why you think the extended examples in paragraphs 4–6 are either (1) simple illustrations of the generalities offered in paragraphs

2 and 3, or (2) a way of presenting new ideas for readers to consider. Be ready to support your answer with concrete evidence from the paragraphs in question and from the rest of the essay.

3a. Does paragraph 10 present similarities, differences, or both?

b. Analyze the sentences in paragraph 10 to identify parallel structures used to emphasize the expository pattern employed in the paragraph. (Guide: *Parallel Structure.*)

4a. Where in the essay does Tannen discuss the work of other scholars?

b. What do these discussions add to the essay? How does Tannen ensure that they contribute to the unity of the selection? (Guide: *Unity.*)

Diction and Vocabulary

1a. In what ways does the inclusion of the actual language used by the children add to the effectiveness of the selection? (Guide: *Diction, Evaluation.*)

b. How would the essay be weakened if the author decided to summarize the conversations instead?

2. Discuss the use of diction in paragraphs 13–16 to emphasize the need for understanding. Pay attention as well to other strategies for achieving emphasis. (Guide: *Emphasis.*)

3. Where would you locate the style of this piece on a continuum of informal to formal? Pay particular attention to any terms you believe most readers will consider unfamiliar or technical.

4. Use the dictionary as necessary to understand the meanings of the following words: emulate (par. 1); hierarchically (2); differentiation (3); dynamics (4); mitigated, evasion (7); scenarios (8); egalitarian (10).

Suggestions for Writing and Discussion

1. Think of your experiences as a child and jot down some that either confirm or contradict what Tannen has to say about the conversational styles of children. Come to class ready to evaluate and discuss her conclusions in light of your own and your classmates' experiences.

2. Consider writing an essay using Tannen's general approach to discuss other male-female contrasts.

3. Identify and discuss reasons other than gender for differences in conversational style.

(NOTE: Suggestions for topics requiring development by use of COMPARISON and CONTRAST are on page 149, at the end of this section.)

ALICE WALKER

ALICE WALKER was born in Georgia in 1944, the youngest in a family of eight. Her parents were sharecroppers, and she attended rural schools as a child, going on eventually to attend Spelman College and Sarah Lawrence College, from which she graduated. She worked as an editor of *Ms.* magazine and taught at several colleges. At present she teaches at the University of California–Berkeley and lives in northern California. Her work as a poet, novelist, and essayist has been highly acclaimed, and one of her novels, *The Color Purple* (1982), received both a Pulitzer Prize and the American Book Award for fiction. Some of her other works are *Revolutionary Petunias and Other Poems* (1973); *In Love and Trouble* (1973), short stories; *Meridian* (1976) and *The Temple of My Familiar* (1989), novels; and *In Search of Our Mothers' Gardens* (1983) and *Living by the Word* (1988), essays.

Am I Blue?

Humans and horses might seem at first so different that any comparison would have to take the form of an analogy—a pairing of essentially unlike subjects whose limited similarities can be used for explanatory purposes (see Section 4). Walker's strategy in this essay from *Living by the Word* is just the opposite, however. She explains that despite their obvious differences, humans and animals are essentially alike, at least in important matters such as the capacity to love and to communicate.

> *"Ain't these tears in these* 1
> *eyes tellin' you?"*

For about three years my companion and I rented a small house in the 2
country that stood on the edge of a large meadow that appeared to
run from the end of our deck straight into the mountains. The mountains, however, were quite far away, and between us and them there

was, in fact, a town. It was one of the many pleasant aspects of the house that you never really were aware of this.

It was a house of many windows, low, wide, nearly floor to ceiling in the living room, which faced the meadow, and it was from one of these that I first saw our closest neighbor, a large white horse, cropping grass, flipping its mane, and ambling about—not over the entire meadow, which stretched well out of sight of the house, but over the five or so fenced-in acres that were next to the twenty-odd that we had rented. I soon learned that the horse, whose name was Blue, belonged to a man who lived in another town, but was boarded by our neighbors next door. Occasionally, one of the children, usually a stocky teen-ager, but sometimes a much younger girl or boy, could be seen riding Blue. They would appear in the meadow, climb up on his back, ride furiously for ten or fifteen minutes, then get off, slap Blue on the flanks, and not be seen again for a month or more. **3**

There were many apple trees in our yard, and one by the fence that Blue could almost reach. We were soon in the habit of feeding him apples, which he relished, especially because by the middle of summer the meadow grasses—so green and succulent since January—had dried out from lack of rain, and Blue stumbled about munching the dried stalks half-heartedly. Sometimes he would stand very still just by the apple tree, and when one of us came out he would whinny, snort loudly, or stamp the ground. This meant, of course: I want an apple. **4**

It was quite wonderful to pick a few apples, or collect those that had fallen to the ground overnight, and patiently hold them, one by one, up to his large, toothy mouth. I remained as thrilled as a child by his flexible dark lips, huge, cubelike teeth that crunched the apples, core and all, with such finality, and his high, broad-breasted *enormity;* beside which, I felt small indeed. When I was a child, I used to ride horses, and was especially friendly with one named Nan until the day I was riding and my brother deliberately spooked her and I was thrown, head first, against the trunk of a tree. When I came to, I was in bed and my mother was bending worriedly over me; we silently agreed that perhaps horseback riding was not the safest sport for me. Since then I have walked, and prefer walking to horseback riding—but I had forgotten the depth of feeling one could see in horses' eyes. **5**

I was therefore unprepared for the expression in Blue's. Blue was lonely. Blue was horribly lonely and bored. I was not shocked that this **6** should be the case; five acres to tramp by yourself, endlessly, even in the most beautiful of meadows—and his was—cannot provide many interesting events, and once rainy season turned to dry that was about it. No, I was shocked that I had forgotten that human animals and nonhuman animals can communicate quite well; if we are brought up around animals as children we take this for granted. By the time we are adults we no longer remember. However, the animals have not changed. They are in fact *completed* creations (at least they seem to be, so much more than we) who are not likely *to* change; it is their nature to express themselves. What else are they going to express? And they do. And, generally speaking, they are ignored.

After giving Blue the apples, I would wander back to the house, 7 aware that he was observing me. Were more apples not forthcoming then? Was that to be his sole entertainment for the day? My partner's small son had decided he wanted to learn how to piece a quilt; we worked in silence on our respective squares as I thought . . .

Well, about slavery: about white children, who were raised by 8 black people, who knew their first all-accepting love from black women, and then, when they were twelve or so, were told they must "forget" the deep levels of communication between themselves and "mammy" that they knew. Later they would be able to relate quite calmly, "My old mammy was sold to another good family." "My old mammy was ——— ———." Fill in the blank. Many more years later a white woman would say: "I can't understand these Negroes, these blacks. What do they want? They're so different from us."

And about the Indians, considered to be "like animals" by the 9 "settlers" (a very benign euphemism for what they actually were), who did not understand their description as a compliment.

And about the thousands of American men who marry Japanese, 10 Korean, Filipina, and other non-English-speaking women and of how happy they report they are, "*blissfully*," until their brides learn to speak English, at which point the marriages tend to fall apart. What then did the men see, when they looked into the eyes of the women they married, before they could speak English? Apparently only their own reflections.

I thought of society's impatience with the young. "Why are they 11 playing the music so loud?" Perhaps the children have listened to much of the music of oppressed people their parents danced to before they were born, with its passionate but soft cries for acceptance and love, and they have wondered why their parents failed to hear.

I do not know how long Blue had inhabited his five beautiful,   12
boring acres before we moved into our house; a year after we had
arrived—and had also traveled to other valleys, other cities, other
worlds—he was still there.

But then, in our second year at the house, something happened   13
in Blue's life. One morning, looking out the window at the fog that
lay like a ribbon over the meadow, I saw another horse, a brown one,
at the other end of Blue's field. Blue appeared to be afraid of it, and
for several days made no attempt to go near. We went away for a
week. When we returned, Blue had decided to make friends and the
two horses ambled or galloped along together, and Blue did not come
nearly as often to the fence underneath the apple tree.

When he did, bringing his new friend with him, there was a   14
different look in his eyes. A look of independence, of self-possession,
of inalienable *horse*ness. His friend eventually became pregnant. For
months and months there was, it seemed to me, a mutual feeling
between me and the horses of justice, of peace. I fed apples to them
both. The look in Blue's eyes was one of unabashed "this is *it*ness."

It did not, however, last forever. One day, after a visit to the city,   15
I went out to give Blue some apples. He stood waiting, or so I thought,
though not beneath the tree. When I shook the tree and jumped back
from the shower of apples, he made no move. I carried some over to
him. He managed to half-crunch one. The rest he let fall to the ground.
I dreaded looking into his eyes—because I had of course noticed that
Brown, his partner, had gone—but I did look. If I had been born into
slavery, and my partner had been sold or killed, my eyes would have
looked like that. The children next door explained that Blue's partner
had been "put with him" (the same expression that old people used,
I had noticed, when speaking of an ancestor during slavery who had
been impregnated by her owner) so that they could mate and she
conceive. Since that was accomplished, she had been taken back by
her owner, who lived somewhere else.

Will she be back? I asked.   16
They didn't know.   17
Blue was like a crazed person. Blue *was*, to me, a crazed person.   18
He galloped furiously, as if he were being ridden, around and around
his five beautiful acres. He whinnied until he couldn't. He tore at the
ground with his hooves. He butted himself against his single shade
tree. He looked always and always toward the road down which his
partner had gone. And then, occasionally, when he came up for

apples, or I took apples to him, he looked at me. It was a look so piercing, so full of grief, a look so *human*, I almost laughed (I felt too sad to cry) to think there are people who do not know that animals suffer. People like me who have forgotten, and daily forget, all that animals try to tell us. "Everything you do to us will happen to you; we are your teachers, as you are ours. We are one lesson" is essentially it, I think. There are those who never once have even considered animals' rights: those who have been taught that animals actually want to be used and abused by us, as small children "love" to be frightened, or women "love" to be mutilated and raped. . . . They are the great-grandchildren of those who honestly thought, because someone taught them this: "Women can't think," And "niggers can't faint." But most disturbing of all, in Blue's large brown eyes was a new look, more painful than the look of despair: the look of disgust with human beings, with life; the look of hatred. And it was odd what the look of hatred did. It gave him, for the first time, the look of a beast. And what that meant was that he had put up a barrier within to protect himself from further violence; all the apples in the world wouldn't change that fact.

And so Blue remained, a beautiful part of our landscape, very   19
peaceful to look at from the window, white against the grass. Once a friend came to visit and said, looking out on the soothing view: "And it *would* have to be a white horse; the very image of freedom." And I thought, yes, the animals are forced to become for us merely "images" of what they once so beautifully expressed. And we are used to drinking milk from containers showing "contented" cows, whose real lives we want to hear nothing about, eating eggs and drumsticks from "happy" hens, and munching hamburgers advertised by bulls of integrity who seem to command their fate.

As we talked of freedom and justice one day for all, we sat down   20
to steaks. I am eating misery, I thought, as I took the first bite. And spit it out.

Meanings and Values

1a. In which paragraphs does Walker describe what she believes to be Blue's thoughts and feelings?

  b. According to Walker, in what ways is Blue similar to a human? In what ways is he different?

2. What thematic purposes are served by the following phrases:

a. "human animals and nonhuman animals" (par. 6)

b. "who did not understand their description as a compliment" (par. 9)

c. "Am I Blue?" (title)

d. "If I had been born into slavery, and my partner had been sold or killed, my eyes would have looked like that." (par. 15)

e. "It gave him, for the first time, the look of a beast." (par. 18)

3. To what other groups does the author compare Blue and his relationships with humans in paragraphs 8–11?

Expository Techniques

1a. Why do you think Walker chose to wait until near the end of the essay (paragraph 18) for a detailed discussion of its theme? (Guide to Terms: *Unity*.)

b. To what extent does the placement of this discussion give the essay an expository rather than an argumentative purpose? (Guide: *Argument*.)

2. Discuss how the " 'images' " presented in paragraph 19 can be regarded as ironic symbols. (Guide: *Symbol, Irony*.)

3a. Describe the way Walker alters the tempo of the sentences and builds to a climax in the concluding paragraph of the essay. (Guide: *Closings*.)

b. Some readers might consider the ending effective. Others might consider it overly dramatic or distasteful. Explain which reaction you consider most appropriate. (Guide: *Evaluation*.)

Diction and Vocabulary

1. Describe the ways in which Walker uses syntax and figurative language (simile) for thematic purposes in this passage: "Blue was like a crazed person. Blue *was*, to me, a crazed person" (par. 18). (Guide: *Syntax, Figures of Speech*.)

2. In speaking of the " 'settlers,' " Walker says that this term is "a very benign euphemism for what they actually were" (par. 9). What does she mean by this comment? What other terms might be applied to them (from Walker's point of view)? Why might she have chosen not to use such terms?

3a. The title of this essay is taken from a song of the same name. In terms of the content of the essay, to what ideas or themes does it refer? Can it be considered a paradox? (Guide: *Paradox*.)

b. The quotation from the song that opens the essay points to some of the ideas discussed in the essay. What are they?

Suggestions for Writing and Discussion

1. Prepare a paper of your own explaining the regulations that safeguard the rights of animals used in experiments or outlining some common abuses in animal experimentation.

2. Walker links racism and disregard for the rights of animals. Is she correct in doing this, or is the connection farfetched?

3. Should people adopt vegetarianism for moral as well as health reasons?

4. Many people claim that in attributing human personalities to animals, we are simply fooling ourselves or being egocentric in assuming that the real meaning of events can be understood in human terms. What do you think?

(NOTE: Suggestions for topics requiring development by COMPARISON and CONTRAST follow.)

Writing Suggestions for Section 3
Comparison and *Contrast*

Base your central theme on one of the following, and develop your composition primarily by use of comparison and/or contrast. Use examples liberally for clarity and concreteness, chosen always with your purpose and reader-audience in mind.

1. Two kinds of home life.
2. The sea at two different times.
3. The innate qualities needed for success in two different careers.
4. The natural temperaments of two acquaintances.
5. Two musicians.
6. The teaching techniques of two instructors or former teachers.
7. Two methods of parental handling of teenage problems.
8. Two family attitudes toward the practice of religion.
9. Two "moods" of the same town at different times.
10. The personalities (or atmospheres) of two cities or towns of similar size.
11. Two politicians with different leadership styles.
12. Two people who approach problems in different ways.
13. Two different attitudes toward the same thing or activity: one "practical," the other romantic or aesthetic.
14. The beliefs and practices of two religions or denominations concerning one aspect of religion.
15. Two courses on the same subject: one in high school and one in college.
16. The differing styles of two players of some sport or game.
17. The hazards of frontier life and those of life today.
18. Two companies with very different styles or business philosophies.
19. Two recent movies or rock videos.
20. Two magazines focusing on similar subjects but directed at different audiences.
21. The "rewards" of two different kinds of jobs.
22. Two views of patriotism.

4

Using *Analogy* as an
Expository Device

Analogy is a special form of comparison that is used for a specific purpose: to explain something abstract or difficult to understand by showing its similarity to something concrete or easy to understand. A much less commonly used technique than logical comparison (and contrast), analogy is, nonetheless, a highly efficient means of explaining some difficult concepts or of giving added force to the explanations.

Logical comparison is made between two members of the same general class, usually assuming the same kind of interest in the subject matter of both. But in analogy we are really concerned only with the subject matter of one, using a second just to help explain the first. The two subjects, quite incomparable in most respects, are never of the same general class; if they are, we then have logical comparison, not analogy.

If the analogy is to be effective, the writer should be able to assume that the reader is familiar enough with the easier subject, or can quickly be made so, that it really helps explain the more difficult one. A common example is the explanation of the human circulatory system, which we may have trouble comprehending, by comparing the heart and arteries with a pump forcing water through the pipes of a plumbing system. This analogy has been carried further to liken the effect of cholesterol deposits on the inner walls of the arteries to that of mineral deposits that accumulate inside water pipes and eventually close them entirely. Although there is little logical similarity between a steel pipe and a human artery, the *analogical* similarity would be apparent to most readers—but the analogy might cause even greater confusion for anyone who did not know about pumps.

Distinguishing between analogy and metaphor is sometimes difficult. The difference is basically in their purpose: the function of a metaphor is merely to *describe*, to create a brief, vivid image for the reader; the function of analogy is primarily one of exposition, *to explain*, rather than to describe. In this sense, however, the function of a metaphor is actually *to suggest* an analogy: instead of showing the similarities of the heart and the pump, a metaphor might simply refer to "that faithful pump inside my chest," implying enough of a comparison to serve its purpose as description. (We can see here why some people refer to analogy as "extended" metaphor.) The analogist, when trying to explain the wide selection of college subjects and the need for balance in a course of study, could use the easily understood principle of a cafeteria, which serves Jell-O and lemon meringue pie as well as meat and potatoes. If his purpose had been only to create an image, to describe, he might have referred simply to the bewildering variety in "the cafeteria of college courses"—and that would have been a metaphor. (For still another example of the more conventional type of analogy, see the explanation of *Unity*, in the Guide to Terms.)

But as useful as analogy can be in exposition, it is a difficult technique to use in logical argument. The two subjects of an analogy, although similar in one or more ways useful for illustration, may be basically too different for any reliable conclusions to be drawn from their similarity.

Sample Paragraph (Annotated)

Introduces the *analogy*.

Uses the analogy to explain events and relationships.

Residents of Palmville have a saying: "Living here is like living in a fishbowl." It certainly does seem like everybody's business (personal or not) is open to view from all sides. When the result is gossip about people's personal lives, this characteristic of Palmville life is not very pleasant. But it does have good sides. When Jake Mollicone grew depressed because of business problems and tried to commit suicide, "nosey" neighbors were right there to save his life and help him recover, physically and mentally. When the Statler twins tried to make extra money by delivering less heating fuel than the bill showed, the rumor mill put the police on the case right away. In addition, a recent editorial in the *Palmville Gazette* suggested that extending the familiar "fishbowl" analogy might be a good idea for Palmville. The editorial pointed out that most fish tanks can be homes to a wide variety of colorful species and that the recent growth of Palmville has likewise brought together people of different backgrounds and qualities in an interesting and healthy mix. The editorial also reminded readers that when a fish tank becomes too crowded, it turns into a dirty, unhealthy environment—and the inhabitants often try to eat each other. "The lesson is clear," the paper concluded, "that while some growth is enriching and beneficial, too much expansion would be the wrong thing for life in our 'fishbowl.' "

Editorial extends the analogy. More a speculation or warning than an argument.

Sample Paragraph (Analogy)

If distant galaxies are really receding from the earth, and if more distant galaxies are receding faster than nearby ones, a remarkable picture of the universe emerges. Imagine that the galaxies were raisins scattered through a rising lump of bread dough. As the dough expanded, the raisins would be carried farther and farther apart from each other. If you were standing on one of the raisins, how would things look? You wouldn't feel any motion yourself, of course, just as you don't feel the effects of the earth's motion around the sun, but you would notice that your nearest neighbor was moving away from you. This motion would be due to the fact that the dough between you and your nearest neighbor would be expanding, pushing the two of you apart.

LOREN C. EISELEY

LOREN C. EISELEY (1907–1977) was professor of anthropology and the history of science at the University of Pennsylvania, where he also served as provost from 1959 to 1961. He was a Guggenheim Foundation Fellow and was in charge of anthropological expeditions for various universities and for the Smithsonian Institution. Eiseley, a respected naturalist and conservationist, also served on many public service boards and commissions and was awarded many honorary degrees and medals. Widely published in both scholarly and popular magazines, Eiseley also wrote several books, including *The Immense Journey* (1957), *Darwin's Century* (1959), *The Firmament of Time* (1960), *The Unexpected Universe* (1969), and *The Night Country* (1971).

The Brown Wasps

"The Brown Wasps" was selected from Eiseley's book *The Night Country*. It is an essay with a simple theme, developed through a rather intricate web of simple analogies. In reading this selection, you will see why Eiseley was—and is—widely admired for his lucid, almost poetic style, as well as for his sensitive philosophical approach to all living things.

There is a corner in the waiting room of one of the great Eastern   1
stations where women never sit. It is always in the shadow and overhung by rows of lockers. It is, however, always frequented—not so much by genuine travelers as by the dying. It is here that a certain element of the abandoned poor seeks a refuge out of the weather, clinging for a few hours longer to the city that has fathered them. In a precisely similar manner I have seen, on a sunny day in midwinter, a few old brown wasps creep slowly over an abandoned wasp nest in

a thicket. Numbed and forgetful and frost-blackened, the hum of the spring hive still resounded faintly in their sodden tissues. Then the temperature would fall and they would drop away into the white oblivion of the snow. Here in the station it is in no way different save the city is busy in its snows. But the old ones cling to their seats as though these were symbolic and could not be given up. Now and then they sleep, their gray old heads resting with painful awkwardness on the backs of the benches.

Also they are not at rest. For an hour they may sleep in the gasping exhaustion of the ill-nourished and aged who have to walk in the night. Then a policeman comes by on his round and nudges them upright.

"You can't sleep here," he growls.

A strange ritual then begins. An old man is difficult to waken. After a muttered conversation the policeman presses a coin into his hand and passes fiercely along the benches prodding and gesturing toward the door. In his wake, like birds rising and settling behind the passage of a farmer through a cornfield, the men totter up, move a few paces and subside once more upon the benches.

One man, after a slight, apologetic lurch, does not move at all. Tubercularly thin, he sleeps on steadily. The policeman does not look back. To him, too, this has become a ritual. He will not have to notice it again officially for another hour.

Once in a while one of the sleepers will not awaken. Like the brown wasps, he will have had his wish to die in the great droning center of the hive rather than in some lonely room. It is not so bad here with the shuffle of footsteps and the knowledge that there are others who share the bad luck of the world. There are also the whistles and the sounds of everyone, everyone in the world, starting on journeys. Amidst so many journeys somebody is bound to come out all right. Somebody.

Maybe it was on a like thought that the brown wasps fell away from the old paper nest in the thicket. You hold till the last, even if it is only to a public seat in a railroad station. You want your place in the hive more than you want a room or a place where the aged can be eased gently out of the way. It is the place that matters, the place at the heart of things. It is life that you want, that bruises your gray old head with the hard chairs; a man has a right to his place.

But sometimes the place is lost in the years behind us. Or sometimes it is a thing of air, a kind of vaporous distortion above a heap of rubble. We cling to a time and place because without them man is lost, not only man but life. This is why the voices, real or unreal, which speak from the floating trumpets at spiritualist seances are so unnerving. They are voices out of nowhere whose only reality lies in their ability to stir the memory of a living person with some fragment of the past. Before the medium's cabinet both the dead and the living revolve endlessly about an episode, a place, an event that has already been engulfed by time.

This feeling runs deep in life; it brings stray cats running over endless miles, and birds homing from the ends of the earth. It is as though all living creatures, and particularly the more intelligent, can survive only by fixing or transforming a bit of time into space or by securing a bit of space with its objects immortalized and made permanent in time. For example, I once saw, on a flower pot in my own living room, the efforts of a field mouse to build a remembered field. I have lived to see this episode repeated in a thousand guises, and since I have spent a large portion of my life in the shade of a nonexistent tree, I think I am entitled to speak for the field mouse. 9

One day as I cut across the field, which at that time extended on one side of our suburban shopping center, I found a giant slug feeding from a runnel of pink ice cream in an abandoned Dixie cup. I could see his eyes telescope and protrude in a kind of dim, uncertain ecstasy as his dark body bunched and elongated in the curve of the cup. Then, as I stood there at the edge of the concrete, contemplating the slug, I began to realize it was like standing on a shore where a different type of life creeps up and fumbles tentatively among the rocks and sea wrack. It knows its place and will only creep so far until something changes. Little by little as I stood there, I began to see more of this shore that surrounds the place of man. I looked with sudden care and attention at things I had been running over thoughtlessly for years. I even waded out a short way into the grass and the wild-rose thickets to see more. A huge black-belted bee went droning by and there were some indistinct scurryings in the underbrush. 10

Then I came to a sign which informed me that this field was to be the site of a new Wanamaker suburban store. Thousands of obscure lives were about to perish, the spores of puffballs would go smoking off to new fields, and the bodies of little white-footed mice would be crunched under the inexorable wheels of the bulldozers. Life disappears or modifies its appearances so fast that everything takes on an 11 aspect of illusion—a momentary fizzing and boiling with smoke rings, like pouring dissident chemicals into a retort. Here man was advancing, but in a few years his plaster and bricks would be disappearing once more into the insatiable maw of the clover. Being of an archaeological cast of mind, I thought of this fact with an obscure sense of satisfaction and waded back through the rose thickets to the concrete parking lot. As I did so, a mouse scurried ahead of me, frightened of my steps if not of that ominous Wanamaker sign. I saw him vanish in the general direction of my apartment house, his little body quivering with fear in the great open sun on the blazing concrete. Blinded and confused, he was running straight away from his field. In another week scores would follow him.

I forgot the episode then and went home to the quiet of my living room. It was not until a week later, letting myself into the apartment, that I realized I had a visitor. I am fond of plants and had several ferns standing on the floor in pots to avoid the noon glare by the south window.   12

As I snapped on the light and glanced carelessly around the room, I saw a little heap of earth on the carpet and a scrabble of pebbles that had been kicked merrily over the edge of one of the flower pots. To my astonishment I discovered a full-fledged burrow delving downward among the fern roots. I waited silently. The creature who had made the burrow did not appear. I remembered the wild field then, and the flight of the mice. No house mouse, no *Mus domesticus*, had kicked up this little heap of earth or sought refuge under a fern root in a flower pot. I thought of the desperate little creature I had seen fleeing from the wild-rose thicket. Through intricacies of pipes and attics, he, or one of his fellows, had climbed to this high green solitary room. I could visualize what had occurred. He had an image in his head, a world of seed pods and quiet, of green sheltering leaves in the dim light among the weed stems. It was the only world he knew and it was gone.   13

Somehow in his flight he had found his way to this room with drawn shades where no one would come till nightfall. And here he had smelled green leaves and run quickly up the flower pot to dabble his paws in common earth. He had even struggled half the afternoon to carry his burrow deeper and had failed. I examined the hole, but no whiskered twitching face appeared. He was gone. I gathered up the earth and refilled the burrow. I did not expect to find traces of him again.   14

Yet for three nights thereafter I came home to the darkened room   15
and my ferns to find the dirt kicked gaily about the rug and the
burrow reopened, though I was never able to catch the field mouse
within it. I dropped a little food about the mouth of the burrow, but
it was never touched. I looked under beds or sat reading with one ear
cocked for rustlings in the ferns. It was all in vain; I never saw him.
Probably he ended in a trap in some other tenant's room.

But before he disappeared, I had come to look hopefully for his   16
evening burrow. About my ferns there had begun to linger the insubstantial vapor of an autumn field, the distilled essence, as it were, of
a mouse brain in exile from its home. It was a small dream, like our
dreams, carried a long and weary journey along pipes and through
spider webs, past holes over which loomed the shadows of waiting
cats, and finally, desperately, into this room where he had played in
the shuttered daylight for an hour among the green ferns on the floor.
Every day these invisible dreams pass us on the street, or rise from
beneath our feet, or look out upon us from beneath a bush.

Some years ago the old elevated railway in Philadelphia was torn   17
down and replaced by a subway system. This ancient El with its
barnlike stations containing nut-vending machines and scattered
food scraps had, for generations, been the favorite feeding ground of
flocks of pigeons, generally one flock to a station along the route of
the El. Hundreds of pigeons were dependent upon the system. They
flapped in and out of its stanchions and steel work or gathered in
watchful little audiences about the feet of anyone who rattled the
peanut-vending machines. They even watched people who jingled
change in their hands, and prospected for food under the feet of the
crowds who gathered between trains. Probably very few among the
waiting people who tossed a crumb to an eager pigeon realized that
this El was like a food-bearing river, and that the life which haunted
its banks was dependent upon the running of the trains with their
human freight.

I saw the river stop.   18

The time came when the underground tubes were ready; the   19
traffic was transferred to a realm unreachable by pigeons. It was like
a great river subsiding suddenly into desert sands. For a day, for two
days, pigeons continued to circle over the El or stand close to the red
vending machines. They were patient birds, and surely this great river
which had flowed through the lives of unnumbered generations was
merely suffering from some momentary drought.

They listened for the familiar vibrations that had always her- 20
alded an approaching train; they flapped hopefully about the head of
an occasional workman walking along the steel runways. They
passed from one empty station to another, all the while growing
hungrier. Finally, they flew away.

I thought I had seen the last of them about the El, but there was 21
a revival and it provided a curious instance of the memory of living
things for a way of life or a locality that has long been cherished. Some
weeks after the El was abandoned, workmen began to tear it down. I
went to work every morning by one particular station, and the time
came when the demolition crews reached this spot. Acetylene torches
showered passers-by with sparks, pneumatic drills hammered at the
base of the structure, and a blind man who, like the pigeons, had clung
with his cup to a stairway leading to the change booth, was forced to
give up his place.

It was then, strangely, momentarily, one morning that I witnessed 22
the return of a little band of the familiar pigeons. I even recognized
one or two members of the flock that had lived around this particular
station before they were dispersed into the streets. They flew bravely
in and out among the sparks and the hammers and the shouting
workmen. They had returned—and they had returned because the
hubbub of the wreckers had convinced them that the river was about
to flow once more. For several hours they flapped in and out through
the empty windows, nodding their heads and watching the fall of
girders with attentive little eyes. By the following morning the station
was reduced to some burned-off stanchions in the street. My bird
friends had gone. It was plain, however, that they retained a memory
for an insubstantial structure now compounded of air and time. Even
the blind man clung to it. Someone had provided him with a chair,
and he sat at the same corner staring sightlessly at an invisible
stairway where, so far as he was concerned, the crowds were still
ascending to the trains.

I have said my life has been passed in the shade of a nonexistent 23
tree, so that such sights do not offend me. Prematurely I am one of the
brown wasps and I often sit with them in the great droning hive of
the station, dreaming sometimes of a certain tree. It was planted sixty
years ago by a boy with a bucket and a toy spade in a little Nebraska
town. That boy was myself. It was a cottonwood sapling and the boy
remembered it because of some words spoken by his father and
because everyone died or moved away who was supposed to wait

and grow old under its shade. The boy was passed from hand to hand, but the tree for some intangible reason had taken root in his mind. It was under its branches that he sheltered; it was from this tree that his memories, which are my memories, led away into the world.

After sixty years the mood of the brown wasps grows heavier   24
upon one. During a long inward struggle I thought it would do me good to go and look upon that actual tree. I found a rational excuse in which to clothe this madness. I purchased a ticket and at the end of two thousand miles I walked another mile to an address that was still the same. The house had not been altered.

I came close to the white picket fence and reluctantly, with great   25
effort, looked down the long vista of the yard. There was nothing there to see. For sixty years that cottonwood had been growing in my mind. Season by season its seeds had been floating farther on the hot prairie winds. We had planted it lovingly there, my father and I, because he had a great hunger for soil and live things growing, and because none of these things had long been ours to protect. We had planted the little sapling and watered it faithfully, and I remembered that I had run out with my small bucket to drench its roots the day we moved away. And all the years since, it had been growing in my mind, a huge tree that somehow stood for my father and the love I bore him. I took a grasp on the picket fence and forced myself to look again.

A boy with the hard bird eye of youth pedaled a tricycle slowly   26
up beside me.

"What'cha lookin' at?" he asked curiously.   27

"A tree," I said.   28

"What for?" he said.   29

"It isn't there," I said, to myself mostly, and began to walk away   30
at a pace just slow enough not to seem to be running.

"What isn't there?" the boy asked. I didn't answer. It was obvious   31
I was attached by a thread to a thing that had never been there, or certainly not for long. Something that had to be held in the air, or sustained in the mind, because it was part of my orientation in the universe and I could not survive without it. There was more than an animal's attachment to a place. There was something else, the attachment of the spirit to a grouping of events in time; it was part of our morality.

So I had come home at last, driven by a memory in the brain as   32
surely as the field mouse who had delved long ago into my flower pot or the pigeons flying forever amidst the rattle of nut-vending

machines. These, the burrow under the greenery in my living room and the red-bellied bowls of peanuts now hovering in midair in the minds of pigeons, were all part of an elusive world that existed nowhere and yet everywhere. I looked once at the real world about me while the persistent boy pedaled at my heels.

It was without meaning, though my feet took a remembered   33
path. In sixty years the house and street had rotted out of my mind. But the tree, the tree that no longer was, that had perished in its first season, bloomed on in my individual mind, unblemished as my father's words. "We'll plant a tree here, son, and we're not going to move any more. And when you're an old, old man you can sit under it and think how we planted it here, you and me, together."

I began to outpace the boy on the tricycle.   34

"Do you live here, Mister?" he shouted after me suspiciously. I 35
took a firm grasp on airy nothing—to be precise, on the bole of a great tree. "I do," I said. I spoke for myself, one field mouse, and several pigeons. We were all out of touch but somehow permanent. It was the world that had changed.

Meanings and Values

1a. How would you describe the tone of this selection? (See Guide to Terms: *Style/Tone*.)

 b. Are the tone and the pace suitable to the subject matter? Why, or why not?

 c. Is Eiseley's style compatible with the tone?

2a. What was Eiseley's apparent purpose in writing this essay? (Guide: *Evaluation*.) ("Purpose" is the key question in this evaluation: it is significant that the essay was written for inclusion in a book.)

 b. How well did he achieve his purpose?

 c. Was it worthwhile?

3. Explain how the seats were "symbolic" to the old men (par. 1). (Guide: *Symbol*.)

4. Paragraphs 2–5 give us a small but well-rounded picture of the policeman. Use your own words to describe him as fully as possible.

5a. Clarify the meaning, or meanings, of paragraph 8.

 b. How does spending much of his life "in the shade of a nonexistent tree" entitle Eiseley to speak for the field mouse (par. 9)?

c. What was it, precisely, that caused Eiseley's "obscure sense of satisfaction" (par. 11)? Why?

6a. Where would you place this essay on an objective-to-subjective continuum? Why? (Guide: *Objective/Subjective.*)

b. Could you classify it as formal? Why, or why not? (Guide: *Essay.*)

7. Select at least one passage that would be, in the hands of many writers, particularly subject to sentimentalism. (Guide: *Sentimentalism.*) Explain why you consider it overly sentimental, or how Eiseley was able to avoid that fault.

Expository Techniques

1a. What are the three major analogies that are linked in this essay?

b. Do they all have the same analogical purpose? If not, what is their relationship?

c. With what particular act does Eiseley analogically equate his own return to Nebraska, or is it an outgrowth of the whole theme to that point?

d. How effectively does each analogy achieve its purpose?

2a. The transition between paragraphs 7 and 8 is especially important. Why? (Guide: *Transitions.*)

b. By what means does Eiseley assure a smooth connection?

3. Is unity damaged by the introduction of the boy toward the end? (Guide: *Unity.*) Show how it is damaged, or explain what you think was Eiseley's purpose in using him. (The fact that the child happened along in "real life" would not have justified including him here; the author *selects* his own details.)

4a. Study the second sentence of paragraph 23 and the first sentence of paragraph 24. What, exactly, do they have in common?

b. What, if anything, is gained by this change?

5a. Did you find it difficult to get at the essence of Eiseley's meanings—in other words, did you find the essay hard to read? If so, try to determine just what caused your difficulties.

b. Could these difficulties have been readily avoided by the author without sacrificing anything of quality or message?

c. Do you think a more experienced reader than you would have had any difficulty at all?

Diction and Vocabulary

1a.   How would you describe the diction of this writing? (Guide: *Diction.*)

b.   How would you describe the syntax? (Guide: *Syntax.*)

c.   Explain why the diction and syntax, and the pace of the writing, would, or would not, be appropriate for most college papers. For most newspaper writing.

2.   Why does the author refer to the old "paper" nest in the thicket (par. 7)?

3a.   Demonstrate the meaning of the term *metaphor* by use of one or more examples from this selection. (Guide: *Figures of Speech.*)

b.   The meaning of *simile.*

c.   The meaning of *personification.*

4.   If you are not familiar with the meaning of any of the following words, consult your dictionary: sodden (par. 1); subside (4); vaporous (8); guises (9); runnel, wrack (10); inexorable, dissident, retort, insatiable, maw (11); dispersed (22).

Suggestions for Writing and Discussion

Plan and discuss, in oral or written form, one of the following passages, clarifying its meanings and implications.

1.   "We cling to a time and place because without them man is lost, not only man but life."

2.   "Life disappears or modifies its appearances so fast that everything takes on an aspect of illusion. . . ."

3.   "Every day these invisible dreams pass us on the street, or rise from beneath our feet, or look out upon us from beneath a bush."

4.   ". . . the attachment of the spirit to a grouping of events in time; it was part of our morality."

(NOTE: Suggestions for topics requiring development by use of ANALOGY are on pages 184–185, at the end of this section.)

THOMAS RAWLS

THOMAS H. RAWLS is the editor of *Harrowsmith Country Life* magazine. His column "Small Places" appeared regularly in the magazine for several years. In 1990, Rawls published a book entitled
Small Places: In Search of a Vanishing America. In it, he recorded his
visits to sixteen small towns throughout the United States as well
as his impressions of life in these communities. Among the towns
he visited were Grinnell, Iowa; Mount Hope, Ohio; International
Falls, Minnesota; Point Reyes Station, California; and Stillwater
Township, New Jersey. Rawls currently lives in Vermont.

Weeds

In this essay from *Small Places*, Rawls uses analogy primarily to give
added force to a comparison. Along the way, however, the analogy
also helps add to our understanding of the subject. In reading this
selection, pay attention to the extent to which your view of the
subject is shaped by the terms used to set up the analogy.

WEEDS—Everywhere the weeds are spreading, displacing native   1
plants. Weeds aren't necessarily just unwanted and ugly plants like
crabgrass in the flower garden, diminishing the beauty of a horticul-
tural design; nor are they merely intruders like lamb's-quarter or
tumbleweed competing with food crops on our agricultural land,
diminishing the economic value of a planting. By weeds, I mean
outsiders—plants from somewhere else, be it Europe or Asia or
wherever. They are opportunistic, rogues like burdock and thistle that
move in where man has disturbed the land. They are without natural
controls, and like loosestrife, which is invading the eastern and midwestern marshes, they may be lovely. Weeds, even ordinary ones like

plantain, are exotics, and they have remade the landscape. The result is that many areas are now dominated by fewer, similar plants that have outcompeted the distinctive, native species that once occupied special niches.

And what is true in the natural world is true in the human world. Just as the short-grass prairie was made up of particular plants suited to specific conditions, small communities near nowhere in particular were made up of people who stuck close to their hometowns, adapting to the microclimate of their locale. They came to speak with decided accents; their economies traditionally were built around the local resources—the forests for wood and for game, the hillsides for grazing, the flats for crops, the rocks underground for fuel or currency. In many cases they were Third World economies, where raw material was shipped out and manufactured goods were shipped in. The land often yielded a marginal living, and the lean life gave rise to plainspoken people proud of their ability to make a go with what was at hand, which often wasn't much.

The small communities could be insular, inbred, violent; they could be equally warm and generous. Invariably, the most ambitious of residents would in their youth strike out to play in a larger arena, and these small communities were, inevitably, depleted of talent. For the most part, our society didn't pay much attention to the drab, gnarled, fibrous-rooted people who held fast in small places. But then, the weedy riot began.

Some twenty years ago—it is hard to believe it was that long ago—the big city suddenly didn't look so attractive to a lot of people. The metropolis—American society itself—was too crowded, too noisy, too hectic, too mindlessly striving, too technocratic, too dangerous. (For some, too crowded with uncommonly hued weeds, who spoke the language in alien accents.) The unhappy, the disenchanted, the searchers, weeds all, were loosed upon rural America.

In some instances, this sowing was a good thing, some new genes into the shallow pool. Along with the nodding, mumbling dropouts came doctors, teachers, lawyers; novice farmers, down on their knees cultivating, sanctifying the soil; questing, energetic souls looking for a life's work. Many came to small places hoping to find communities where the enduring values of home and craftsmanship and respect for nature remained intact. They arrived with some notion of learning a new way—the old ways—and of fitting in.

Weeds are durable—plantain, to mention but one—and they 6
have tremendous resilience: when was the last time you actually
eradicated a dandelion? They can be beautiful—like loosestrife. But
like loosestrife and dandelions, when they move in, they tend to take
over. And where the human weeds have arrived in numbers, they
have sought dominion, and the unique environment of a small place
is altered by the new vegetation.

Over time the motivations of the newcomers seemed to change. 7
Both the early transplants and their more recently arrived cousins
have become concerned with remaking country places, altering them
to be more convenient, more consistent with the neighborhoods of
their upbringing. The intention today appears to be to improve small
places rather than adapt to them. Increasingly, economic considera-
tions have become more important than spiritual ones. A way of life
gives way to making a good living. Perhaps growing up was ever
thus, but I feel a terrible sadness about what is happening.

I am a weed, born and raised in Philadelphia, where as a youth 8
I found my pleasure in the upper deck behind first base at Connie
Mack Stadium. Now I am, by choice, a resident of a small place in
Vermont, a state where there isn't even a minor league baseball team.
I arrived here by way of Missouri, Washington, New Jersey, and
Wyoming, with other brief stops along the way, another seed carried
on the wind. I can take root only where conditions are favorable, but
being man, I can change conditions to make them favorable. That is
what my kind has done. Blending in a bit, but altering more, sometimes by our mere presence and alien background.

Before this transformation, each individual rural community 9
might have been limited, but in total, these small places offered a rich
diversity. With the spread of us weed people, homogeneity between
towns is becoming the rule. The sounds of the voices in any one place
and even the landscape itself begin to resemble those found in other
places.

Viewed another way, it seems that in every small place, one of 10
two things is happening: it is dying or it is being killed. The ones that
are dying are the out-of-the-way places that don't offer work—the
ground is too infertile even for weeds. And the young men and
women flee. A small-town sheriff said it directly: "When you lose your
youth, you lose your town."

Many are heartland towns, places out in the middle of the coun-   11
try deeply afflicted by the economic problems that plagued farmers
for a decade. Many are places populated in significant measure with
older folks, those returning to their childhood homes or retirees
simply looking to let their clocks wind down in the sort of quiet town
they've always dreamed of. The pace is right—as are the prices.
During the earning years, it is no easy matter to scratch up the income
needed to survive in one of these unpopular places, but they prove a
relatively light touch on the bank account when a fixed income is
paying the bills.

The places that are being killed are an entirely different matter—   12
popular beyond reasonable measure, growing, bursting, destroying
themselves—overrun by weeds. Many are resort towns, places
blessed by a striking natural beauty. These towns in the mountains
and on the coasts are metastasizing, the cancer of success spreading,
for example, down off the ski slopes into the once-remote villages
below. Other doomed towns are those that once were beyond the
urban fringe but soon will be no longer.

They are all seeing multitudes of new residents move in. The   13
newcomers have money, and are using it to transform the rural town
into a neo-suburb—better schools, paved roads, rising real estate
values and property taxes to match. The next generation of natives
can't afford to live in their hometowns. Their parents are selling out
(resentful but glad for the check) or making good money as a backhoe
operator or carpenter (resentful but glad for the check) or ending up
in the servant class, mowing lawns, say, or serving meals (resentful,
diminished, and unimpressed with the check).

I like the poor places. They have a down-at-the-heels look, the   14
architecture is commonplace, the food in the local eateries is greasy,
but the people are friendly and pretense is dealt with firmly. Such
communities remain most distinctive, most genuine; they successfully hold on, perhaps paradoxically because of their failure to attract
attention, to the things that made them what they always were.

In the prospering places insidious forces are at work, and that   15
saddens me. You can see that these communities were once everything a body ever could have wanted in a hometown, with dramatic
natural surroundings and often with handsome buildings as well. But
they have been caught in the pernicious grip of fashion—which is to
say, they are blind to pretense—and they are becoming parodies of
the things that originally made them so special.

TOM WOLFE

Tom Wolfe was born in 1931 and grew up in Richmond, Virginia, was graduated from Washington and Lee University, and took his doctorate at Yale. After working for several years as a reporter for the *Washington Post*, he joined the staff of the *New York Herald Tribune* in 1962. He has won two Washington Newspaper Guild Awards, one for humor and the other for foreign news. Wolfe has been a regular contributor to *New York*, *Esquire*, and other magazines. His books include *The Kandy-Kolored Tangerine-Flake Streamline Baby* (1965), *The Electric Kool-Aid Acid Test* (1968), *The Pump House Gang* (1968), *Radical Chic and Mau-Mauing the Flak Catchers* (1970), *The New Journalism* (1973), *The Painted Word* (1975), *The Right Stuff* (1977), *In Our Time* (1980), *Underneath the I-Beams: Inside the Compound* (1981), *From Bauhaus to Our House* (1981), *The Purple Decades: A Reader* (1984), and *The Bonfire of the Vanities* (1986).

O Rotten Gotham—Sliding Down into the Behavioral Sink

"O Rotten Gotham—Sliding Down into the Behavioral Sink," as used here, is excerpted from a longer selection by that title in Wolfe's book *The Pump House Gang* (1968). Here, as he frequently does, the author investigates an important aspect of modern life—seriously, but in his characteristic and seemingly freewheeling style. It is a style that is sometimes ridiculed by scholars but is far more often admired. (Wolfe, as the serious student will discover, is always in complete control of his materials and methods, using them to create certain effects, to reinforce his ideas.) In this piece his analogy is particularly noteworthy for the extensive usage he is able to get from it.

I just spent two days with Edward T. Hall, an anthropologist, watching ing thousands of my fellow New Yorkers short-circuiting themselves

1

into hot little twitching death balls with jolts of their own adrenalin. Dr. Hall says it is overcrowding that does it. Overcrowding gets the adrenalin going, and the adrenalin gets them queer, autistic, sadistic, barren, batty, sloppy, hot-in-the-pants, chancred-on-the-flankers, leering, puling, numb—the usual in New York, in other words, and God knows what else. Dr. Hall has the theory that overcrowding has already thrown New York into a state of behavioral sink. Behavioral sink is a term from ethology, which is the study of how animals relate to their environment. Among animals, the sink winds up with a "population collapse" or "massive die-off." O rotten Gotham.

It got to be easy to look at New Yorkers as animals, especially   2
looking down from some place like a balcony at Grand Central at the rush hour Friday afternoon. The floor was filled with the poor white humans, running around, dodging, blinking their eyes, making a sound like a pen full of starlings or rats or something.

"Listen to them skid," says Dr. Hall.   3

He was right. The poor old etiolate animals were out there   4
skidding on their rubber soles. You could hear it once he pointed it out. They stop short to keep from hitting somebody or because they are disoriented and they suddenly stop and look around, and they skid on their rubber-soled shoes, and a screech goes up. They pour out onto the floor down the escalators from the Pan-Am Building, from 42nd Street, from Lexington Avenue, up out of subways, down into subways, railroad trains, up into helicopters—

"You can also hear the helicopters all the way down here," says   5
Dr. Hall. The sound of the helicopters using the roof of the Pan-Am Building nearly fifty stories up beats right through. "If it weren't for this ceiling"—he is referring to the very high ceiling in Grand Central—"this place would be unbearable with this kind of crowding. And yet they'll probably never 'waste' space like this again."

They screech! And the adrenal glands in all those poor white   6
animals enlarge, micrometer by micrometer, to the size of cantaloupes. Dr. Hall pulls a Minox camera out of a holster he has on his belt and starts shooting away at the human scurry. The Sink!

Dr. Hall has the Minox up to his eye—he is a slender man, calm,   7
52 years old, young-looking, an anthropologist who has worked with Navajos, Hopis, Spanish-Americans, Negroes, Trukese. He was the most important anthropologist in the government during the crucial years of the foreign aid program, the 1950s. He directed both the Point Four training program and the Human Relations Area Files.

He wrote *The Silent Language* and *The Hidden Dimension*, two books that are picking up the kind of "underground" following his friend Marshall McLuhan started picking up about five years ago. He teaches at the Illinois Institute of Technology, lives with his wife, Mildred, in a high-ceilinged town house on one of the last great residential streets in downtown Chicago, Astor Street; he has a grown son and daughter, loves good food, good wine, the relaxed, civilized life—but comes to New York with a Minox at his eye to record!—perfect—The Sink.

We really got down in there by walking down into the Lexington   8
Avenue line subway stop under Grand Central. We inhaled those nice big fluffy fumes of human sweat, urine, effluvia, and sebaceous secretions. One old female human was already stroked out on the upper level, on a stretcher, with two policemen standing by. The other humans barely looked at her. They rushed into line. They bellied each other, haunch to paunch, down the stairs. Human heads shone through the gratings. The species North European tried to create bubbles of space around themselves, about a foot and a half in diameter—

"See, he's reacting against the line," says Dr. Hall.   9

—but the species Mediterranean presses on in. The hell with   10
bubbles of space. The species North European resents that, this male human behind him presses forward toward the booth . . . *breathing* on him, he's disgusted, he pulls out of the line entirely, the species Mediterranean resents him for resenting it, and neither of them realizes what the hell they are getting irritable about exactly. And in all of them the old adrenals grow another micrometer.

Dr. Hall whips out the Minox. Too perfect! The bottom of The Sink.   11

It is the sheer overcrowding, such as occurs in the business   12
sections of Manhattan five days a week and in Harlem, Bedford-Stuyvesant, southeast Bronx every day—sheer overcrowding is converting New Yorkers into animals in a sink pen. Dr. Hall's argument runs as follows: all animals, including birds, seem to have a built-in inherited requirement to have a certain amount of territory, space, to lead their lives in. Even if they have all the food they need, and there are no predatory animals threatening them, they cannot tolerate crowding beyond a certain point. No more than two hundred wild Norway rats can survive on a quarter acre of ground, for example, even when they are given all the food they can eat. They just die off.

But why? To find out, ethologists have run experiments on all   13
sorts of animals, from stickleback crabs to Sika deer. In one major

experiment, an ethologist named John Calhoun put some domesticated white Norway rats in a pen with four sections to it, connected by ramps. Calhoun knew from previous experiments that
the rats tend to split up into groups of ten to twelve and that the
pen, therefore, would hold forty to forty-eight rats comfortably,
assuming they formed four equal groups. He allowed them to
reproduce until there were eighty rats, balanced between male and
female, but did not let it get any more crowded. He kept them
supplied with plenty of food, water, and nesting materials. In other
words, all their more obvious needs were taken care of. A less
obvious need—space—was not. To the human eye, the pen did not
even look especially crowded. But to the rats, it was crowded
beyond endurance.

The entire colony was soon plunged into a profound behavioral   14
sink. "The sink," said Calhoun, "is the outcome of any behavioral
process that collects animals together in unusually great numbers.
The unhealthy connotations of the term are not accidental: a behavioral sink does act to aggravate all forms of pathology that can be
found within a group."

For a start, long before the rat population reached eighty, a status   15
hierarchy had developed in the pen. Two dominant male rats took
over the two end sections, acquired harems of eight to ten females
each, and forced the rest of the rats into the two middle pens. All the
overcrowding took place in the middle pens. That was where the
"sink" hit. The aristocrat rats at the end grew bigger, sleeker, healthier,
and more secure the whole time.

In The Sink, meanwhile, nest building, courting, sex behavior,   16
reproduction, social organization, health—all of it went to pieces.
Normally, Norway rats have a mating ritual in which the male chases
the female, the female ducks down into a burrow and sticks her head
up to watch the male. He performs a little dance outside the burrow,
then she comes out, and he mounts her, usually for a few seconds.
When The Sink set in, however, no more than three males—the
dominant males in the middle sections—kept up the old customs. The
rest tried everything from satyrism to homosexuality or else gave up
on sex altogether. Some of the subordinate males spent all their time
chasing females. Three or four might chase one female at the same
time, and instead of stopping at the burrow entrance for the ritual,
they would charge right in. Once mounted, they would hold on for
minutes instead of the usual seconds.

Homosexuality rose sharply. So did bisexuality. Some males   17
would mount anything—males, females, babies, senescent rats, anything. Still other males dropped sexual activity altogether, wouldn't
fight and, in fact, would hardly move except when the other rats slept.
Occasionally, a female from the aristocrat rats' harems would come
over the ramps and into the middle sections to sample life in The Sink.
When she had had enough, she would run back up the ramp. Sink
males would give chase up to the top of the ramp, which is to say, to
the very edge of the aristocratic preserve. But one glance from one of
the king rats would stop them cold and they would return to The Sink.

The slumming females from the harems had their adventures   18
and then returned to a placid, healthy life. Females in The Sink,
however, were ravaged, physically and psychologically. Pregnant rats
had trouble continuing pregnancy. The rate of miscarriages increased
significantly, and females started dying from tumors and other disor-
ders of the mammary glands, sex organs, uterus, ovaries, and Fallo-
pian tubes. Typically, their kidneys, livers, and adrenals were also
enlarged or diseased or showed other signs associated with stress.

Child-rearing became totally disorganized. The females lost the   19
interest or the stamina to build nests and did not keep them up if they
did build them. In the general filth and confusion, they would not put
themselves out to save offspring they were momentarily separated
from. Frantic, even sadistic competition among the males was going
on all around them and rendering their lives chaotic. The males began
unprovoked and senseless assaults upon one another, often in the
form of tail-biting. Ordinarily, rats will suppress this kind of behavior
when it crops up. In The Sink, male rats gave up all policing and just
looked out for themselves. The "pecking order" among males in The
Sink was never stable. Normally, male rats set up a three-class structure. Under the pressure of overcrowding, however, they broke up
into all sorts of unstable subclasses, cliques, packs—and constantly
pushed, probed, explored, tested one another's power. Anyone was
fair game, except for the aristocrats in the end pens.

Calhoun kept the population down to eighty, so that the next   20
stage, "population collapse" or "massive die-off," did not occur. But
the autopsies showed that the pattern—as in the diseases among the
female rats—was already there.

The classic study of die-off was John J. Christian's study of Sika   21
deer on James Island in the Chesapeake Bay, west of Cambridge,
Maryland. Four or five of the deer had been released on the island,

which was 280 acres and uninhabited, in 1916. By 1955 they had bred freely into a herd of 280 to 300. The population density was only about one deer per acre at this point, but Christian knew that this was already too high for the Sikas' inborn space requirements, and something would give before long. For two years the number of deer remained 280 to 300. But suddenly, in 1958, over half the deer died; 161 carcasses were recovered. In 1959 more deer died and the population steadied at about 80.

In two years, two-thirds of the herd had died. Why? It was not starvation. In fact, all the deer collected were in excellent condition, with well-developed muscles, shining coats, and fat deposits between the muscles. In practically all the deer, however, the adrenal glands had enlarged by 50 percent. Christian concluded that the die-off was due to "shock following severe metabolic disturbance, probably as a result of prolonged adrenocortical hyperactivity.... There was no evidence of infection, starvation, or other obvious cause to explain the mass mortality." In other words, the constant stress of overpopulation, plus the normal stress of the cold of the winter, had kept the adrenalin flowing so constantly in the deer that their systems were depleted of blood sugar and they died of shock.   22

Well, the white humans are still skidding and darting across the floor of Grand Central. Dr. Hall listens a moment longer to the skidding and the darting noises, and then says, "You know, I've been on commuter trains here after everyone has been through one of these rushes, and I'll tell you, there is enough acid flowing in the stomachs in every car to dissolve the rails underneath."   23

Just a little invisible acid bath for the linings to round off the day. The ulcers the acids cause, of course, are the one disease people have already been taught to associate with the stress of city life. But overcrowding, as Dr. Hall sees it, raises a lot more hell with the body than just ulcers. In everyday life in New York—just the usual, getting to work, working in massively congested areas like 42nd Street between Fifth Avenue and Lexington, especially now that the Pam-Am Building is set in there, working in cubicles such as those in the editorial offices at Time-Life, Inc., which Dr. Hall cites as typical of New York's poor handling of space, working in cubicles with low ceilings and, often, no access to a window, while construction crews all over Manhattan drive everybody up the Masonite wall with air-pressure generators with noises up to the boil-a-brain decibel level, then rushing to get home, piling into subways and trains, fighting for time and   24 for space, the usual day in New York—the whole now-normal thing keeps shooting jolts of adrenalin into the body, breaking down the body's defenses and winding up with the work-a-daddy human animal stroked out at the breakfast table with his head apoplexed like a cauliflower out of his $6.95 semi-spread Pima-cotton shirt, and nosed over into a plate of No-Kloresto egg substitute, signing off with the black thrombosis, cancer, kidney, liver, or stomach failure, and the adrenals ooze to a halt, the size of eggplants in July.

One of the people whose work Dr. Hall is interested in on this 25 score is Rene Dubos at the Rockefeller Institute. Dubos's work indicates that specific organisms, such as the tuberculosis bacillus or a pneumonia virus, can seldom be considered "the cause" of a disease. The germ or virus, apparently, has to work in combination with other things that have already broken the body down in some way—such as the old adrenal hyperactivity. Dr. Hall would like to see some autopsy studies made to record the size of adrenal glands in New York, especially of people crowded into slums and people who go through the full rush-hour-work-rush-hour cycle every day. He is afraid that until there is some clinical, statistical data on how overcrowding actually ravages the human body, no one will be willing to do anything about it. Even in so obvious a thing as air pollution, the pattern is familiar. Until people can actually see the smoke or smell the sulphur or feel the sting in their eyes, politicians will not get excited about it, even though it is well known that many of the lethal substances polluting the air are invisible and odorless. For one thing, most politicians are like the aristocrat rats. They are insulated from The Sink by practically sultanic buffers—limousines, chauffeurs, secretaries, aides-de-camp, doormen, shuttered houses, high-floor apartments. They almost never ride subways, fight rush hours, much less live in the slums or work in the Pam-Am Building.

Meanings and Values

1a.   Who are members of the "species Mediterranean"?

b.   Who belong to the "species North European"?

c.   What could account for their difference in space requirements (pars. 8–10)?

2.   Is this writing primarily objective or subjective? (See Guide to Terms: *Objective/Subjective*.) Why?

3a. Do you get the impression that the author is being unkind, "making fun" of the harried New Yorkers?

b. How, if at all, does he prevent such an impression?

4a. Compare Wolfe's style, tone, and point of view with those of Catton (Section 3). (Guide: *Style/Tone* and *Point of View*.)

b. Do these features necessarily make one author less effective than another in achieving his purposes? Explain.

Expository Techniques

1a. Using whatever criteria we have available for judging the success of analogy, appraise the effectiveness of this one.

b. Does the author work it *too* hard? Be prepared to defend your answer.

2. What are the benefits of the frequent return to what Dr. Hall is doing or saying (e.g., in pars. 3, 5, 7, 9, 11, 23)?

3. Paragraph 12 has a useful function beyond the simple information it imparts—a sort of organic relation to the coming development. Explain how this is accomplished.

4. How is the switch to Sika deer (par. 21) prepared for, and a bumpy transition avoided?

5. The preceding three questions are related in some manner to the problems of transition. How, if at all, are such problems also matters of coherence? (Guide: *Coherence*.)

6. Wolfe is adept at creating just the effect he wants, and the careful student of writing can detect a subtle change of style and pace with each change of subpurpose. (Guide: *Style/Tone*.)

a. Analyze stylistic differences, with resulting effects, between the description of chaos at Grand Central and the information about Dr. Hall in paragraph 7.

b. Analyze such differences between the Grand Central scene and the account of the laboratory experiment with rats.

c. Analyze the differences between the Grand Central scene and the final paragraph.

7. Explain how the style of the more descriptive portions is also a matter of emphasis. (Guide: *Emphasis*.)

8a. Illustrate as many as possible of the elements of effective syntax (itself a matter of style) by examples from this selection. (Guide: *Syntax*.)

b. What is gained or lost by the unusual length and design of the last sentence of paragraph 24? (We can be sure that it did not "just happen" to Wolfe—and equally sure that one of such length would be disastrous in most writing.)

Diction and Vocabulary

1.   What is the significance of the word "Gotham"?

2a. Why do you think the author refers (deliberately, no doubt) to "my fellow New Yorkers" in the first sentence?

 b. What soon could have been the effect if he had not taken such a step?

3.   Why does he consistently, after paragraph 2, refer to the people as "poor white humans," "poor human animals," etc.?

4.   In paragraph 14 he refers to the connotations of the word "sink." What are its possible connotations? (Guide: *Connotation/Denotation.*)

5.   Cite examples of verbal irony to be found in paragraphs 5, 8, 24. (Guide: *Irony.*)

6.   Which of the elements of style mentioned in your answer to question 4a of "Meanings and Values" are also matters of diction?

7.   Consult your dictionary as needed for full understanding of the following words: autistic, puling (par. 1); etiolate (4); effluvia, sebaceous (8); pathology (14); satyrism (16); senescent (17); decibel, thrombosis (24); lethal (25).

Suggestions for Writing and Discussion

1.   Carrying Wolfe's analogy still further, trace the steps by which a rise in serious crime must result from the overcrowding of "poor human animals."

2.   If you are familiar with another city, particularly during rush hours, which appears to you much like New York in this respect, describe it.

3.   If you are familiar with some area of high-density population that has solved its problem of overcrowding, explain the solution.

4.   What practical steps can the *individual* take, if forced to live and/or work in overcrowded conditions, to avoid becoming the victim of his or her own adrenals?

(NOTE: Suggestions for topics requiring development by use of ANALOGY are on pages 184–185, at the end of this section.)

JOHN HAINES

JOHN HAINES was born in Norfolk, Virginia, in 1924. He served in the United States Navy and then attended National Art School and American University. Haines was trained as a sculptor, yet has worked mostly as a poet. He has been a poet-in-residence or teacher at the Universities of Alaska, Washington, Montana, Michigan, and Idaho State as well as Oberlin College. Since the mid-1950s, Haines has lived and worked in Alaska and currently resides in Anchorage. His poetry reflects his involvement in the natural world and the culture of the Alaskan frontier. Among his publications are *Winter News* (1966), *Cicada* (1977), and *In A Dusty Light* (1977), poems; *News from the Glacier: Selected Poems 1960–1980;* and *Living Off the Country: Essays on Poetry and Place* (1981).

Snow

In this sketch, Haines takes a relatively simple analogy and uses it to explore patterns in life that we may sometimes fail to see. Haines looks to the natural world and to the lives of animals. As you read, however, you might consider the extent to which his observations apply to human lives and human society.

To one who lives in the snow and watches it day by day, it is a book 1 to be read. The pages turn as the wind blows; the characters shift and the images formed by their combinations change in meaning, but the language remains the same. It is a shadow language, spoken by things that have gone by and will come again. The same text has been written there for thousands of years, though I was not here, and will not be here in winters to come, to read it. These seemingly random ways, these paths, these beds, these footprints, these hard, round pellets in the snow: they all have meaning. Dark things may be written there, news of others lives, their sorties and excursions, their terrors and deaths. The tiny feet of a shrew or a vole make a brief, erratic pattern across the snow, and here is a hole down which the animal goes. And now the track of an ermine comes this way, swift and searching, and he too goes down that white shadow of a hole.

A wolverine, and the loping, toed-in track I followed uphill for two miles one spring morning, until it finally dropped away into another watershed and I gave up following it. I wanted to see where he would go and what he would do. But he just went on, certain of where he was going, and nothing came of it for me to see but that sure and steady track in the snowcrust, and the sunlight strong in my eyes.

Snows blows across the highway before me as I walk—little, wavering trails of it swept along like a people dispersed. The snow people—where are they going? Some great danger must pursue them. They hurry and fall; the wind gives them a push, they get up and go on again.

I was walking home from Redmond Creek one morning late in January. On a divide between two watersheds I came upon the scene of a battle between a moose and three wolves. The story was written plainly in the snow at my feet. The wolves had come in from the west, following an old trail from the Salcha River, and found the moose feeding in an open stretch of the overgrown road I was walking.

The sign was fresh, it must have happened the night before. The snow was torn up, with chunks of frozen moss and broken sticks scattered about; here and there, swatches of moose hair. A confusion of tracks in the trampled snow—the splayed, stabbing feet of the moose, the big, furred pads and spread toenails of the wolves.

I walked on, watching the snow. The moose was large and alone, almost certainly a bull. In one place he backed himself into a low, brush-hung bank to protect his rear. The wolves moved away from him—those moose feet are dangerous. The moose turned, ran on for fifty yards, and the fight began again. It became a running, broken fight that went on for nearly half a mile in the changing, rutted terrain, the red morning light coming across the hills from the sun low in the south. A pattern shifting and uncertain; the wolves relenting, running out into the brush in a wide circle, and closing again; another patch of moose hair in the trodden snow.

I felt that I knew those wolves. I had seen their tracks several times before during that winter, and once they had taken a marten from one of my traps. I believed them to be a female and two nearly grown pups. If I was right, she may have been teaching them how to hunt, and all that turmoil in the snow may have been the serious play of things that must kill to live. But I saw no blood sign that morning, and the moose seemed to have gotten the better of the fight. At the end of it he plunged away into thick alder brush. I saw his tracks, moving more slowly now, as he climbed through a low saddle, going north in the shallow, unbroken snow. The three wolves trotted east toward Banner Creek.

What might have been silence, an unwritten page, an absence, spoke   8
to me as clearly as if I had been there to see it. I have imagined a man who might live as the coldest scholar on earth, who followed each clue in the snow, writing a book as he went. It would be the history of snow, the book of winter. A thousand-year text to be read by a people hunting these hills in a distant time. Who was here, and who was gone? What were their names? What did they kill and eat? Whom did they leave behind?

Meanings and Values

1.   In your own words, state the analogy around which this essay is built.

2a.   What are the "dark things" referred to in paragraph 1?

b.   Should the situation described in the narrative in paragraphs 4–7 be considered one of the "dark things"?

3.   What important truths about nature (and perhaps human life) does the author "read" in the snow?

Expository Techniques

1a.   Does the analogy employed in this essay run throughout the entire essay or only part of it?

b.   If the analogy governs only part of the essay, where does it begin and end?

2a.   This essay has three sections: pars. 1–3, 4–7, and 8. How do they differ in strategy or purpose? (See Guide to Terms: *Purpose*.)

b.   Discuss any differences in style or tone among the three purposes of the sections. (Guide: *Style/Tone*.)

3. The themes Haines tackles in this piece might be called "philosophical" or "weighty." Does he manage to keep the essay from being difficult to understand, and if so how does he accomplish the task?

4. What expository patterns other than analogy does the author employ in this essay and where do they appear?

Diction and Vocabulary

1. Is the language in this essay more specific in some sections than in others? Which sections are the most specific and which are the most general? (Guide: *Specific/General*.)

2a. Identify the concrete language and details in paragraphs 5–7. (Guide: *Concrete/Abstract*.)

 b. Tell how the sentence structure in these paragraphs adds emphasis to the concrete details. (Guide: *Emphasis*.)

3. If you do not know the meaning of the following words, look them up in a dictionary: sorties, vole (par. 1); splayed (5); marten (7).

Suggestions for Writing and Discussion

1. Make a list of natural phenomena other than snow that can be "read" in the way Haines interprets the snow. Which of the entries on your list could be developed into an essay?

2. Are events like those Haines describes an inevitable part of the natural world? Are they an inevitable part of human society? Do you think Haines sees in the story of the wolves and the moose a pattern similar to that of human life? Do you?

(NOTE: Suggestions for topics requiring development by use of ANALOGY follow.)

Writing Suggestions for Section 4
Analogy

In any normal situation, the analogy is chosen to help explain a theme-idea that already exists—such as those in the first group below. But for classroom training, which even at best is bound to be somewhat artificial, it is sometimes permissible to work from the other direction, to develop a theme that fits some preselected analogy-symbol. Your instructor will indicate which of the groups to use.

1. State a central theme about one of the following general topics or a suitable one of your own, and develop it into a composition by use of an analogy of your own choosing.

   a. A well-organized school system.

   b. Starting a new business or other enterprise.

   c. The long-range value of programs for underprivileged children.

   d. Learning a new skill.

   e. The need for cooperation between management and labor.

   f. Today's intense competition for success.

   g. Dealing with stress.

   h. The results of ignorance.

2. Select an analogy-symbol from the following list and fashion a worthwhile theme that it can illustrate. Develop your composition as instructed.

   a. A freeway at commuting time.

   b. Building a road through a wilderness.

   c. Building a bridge across a river.

   d. A merry-go-round.

   e. A wedding.

   f. A car wash.

   g. Flood destruction of a levee.

   h. The tending of a young orchard.

   i. An animal predator stalking prey.

5

Explaining Through
Process Analysis

Process analysis explains how the steps of an operation lead to its completion. Although in one narrow sense it may be considered a kind of narration, process analysis has an important difference in purpose, and hence in approach. Other narration is mostly concerned with the story itself, or with a general concept illustrated by it, but process tells of methods that end in specified results. We might narrate a story about a rifle—its purchase, its role in colorful episodes, perhaps its eventual retirement from active service. (We could, for other purposes, *define* "rifle," or *classify* the types of rifles, and no doubt *compare* and *contrast* these types and *illustrate* by examples.) But showing how a rifle works, or how it is manufactured, or how it should be cared for—this is process, and it sometimes becomes the basic pattern of an exposition.

Most writers are especially concerned with two kinds of process, both of them apparent in the preceding example of rifles: the directional, which explains how to *do* something (how to shoot a gun or how to clean it); and the informational, which explains how something is or was *done* (how guns are manufactured). The directional process can range from the instructions on a shampoo bottle to a detailed plan showing how to make the United Nations more effective, and will often contain detailed justification for individual steps or for the process itself. The informational process, on the other hand, might explain the steps of a wide variety of operations or actions, of mental or evolutionary processes, with no how-to-do-it purpose at all—how someone went about choosing a college or how the planet Earth was formed. Informational process analysis has been seen in earlier selections: Staples explained how he keeps from frightening other people when he takes his evening walks, and Wolfe explained how the experiment with Norway rats was conducted.

Most process analyses are organized into simple, chronological steps. Indeed, the exact order is sometimes of greatest importance, as in a recipe. But occasionally there are problems in organization. The step-by-step format may need to be interrupted for descriptions, definitions, and other explanatory asides. If the process is a proposed solution, part of a problem-solution argument, then it may be necessary to justify each of the steps in turn and dismiss alternatives. And, still more of a problem, some processes defy a strict chronological treatment, because several things occur simultaneously. To explain the operating process of a gasoline engine, for example, the writer would be unable to convey at once everything that happens at the same time. Some way must be found to present the material in *general* stages, organized as subdivisions, so that the reader can see the step-by-step process through the confusion of interacting relationships.

Another difficulty in explaining by process analysis is estimating what knowledge the reader may already have. Presuming too little background may quickly lead to boredom or even irritation, with a resulting communication block; presuming too much will almost certainly leave the reader bewildered. Like a chain dependent on its weakest link for its strength, the entire process analysis can fail because of one unclear point that makes the rest incomprehensible.

Sample Paragraph (Annotated)

Process to be analyzed.

> Palmville has an unusual form of city government, at least compared with other cities in the state. Instead of an elected mayor, it has an appointed city manager responsible for all city operations and employees. This

Background on the process.

> arrangement is by no means unusual, yet Palmville also has no city council or board of supervisors. Instead, it has a Board of Proposers and a Town Meeting. How, then, are laws passed,

Reason for process analysis.

> budgets approved, and appointments made? Members of the Board of

Beginning of *informational* process. How the unusual procedure works. Begins chronologically then covers some of the key features of the process.

Proposers draw up proposals for new laws, regulations, hiring, and budgets, but they do not vote on the proposals. They send the proposals to the Town Meeting for a vote. Town Meetings are scheduled four times a year in the auditorium of the Civic Center. Only people who come to the meeting are eligible to vote on the proposals; they must be registered voters who live within the city limits. Upcoming Town Meetings are publicized through the local media. The system worked well when Palmville was a small town and there was little business to be done.

Problems and need for change in future.

Now the meetings last 8–10 hours; even so, important business often ends up being postponed until the next meeting. Although most Palmville residents enjoy the direct participation in government that the system allows, they have also begun to recognize the need for change.

Sample Paragraph (Process Analysis)

It's not the wind, though, that's the most dangerous part of a hurricane. It's the water, especially when something called the "storm surge" occurs. As the low-pressure eye of the hurricane sits over the ocean, the sea level literally rises into a dome of water. For every inch drop in barometric pressure, the ocean rises a foot higher. Now, out at sea, that means nothing. The rise is not even noticeable. But when that mound of water starts moving toward land, the situation becomes crucial. As the water approaches a shallow beach, the dome of water rises. It may rise ten to fifteen feet in an hour and span fifty miles. Like a marine bulldozer, the surge may rise up twenty feet high, crash onto land, and wash everything away. Then with six- to eight-foot waves riding atop this mound of water, the storm surge destroys buildings, trees, cars, and anything else in its path. It's this storm surge that accounts for 90 percent of the deaths during a hurricane.

JOE BUHLER AND RON GRAHAM

JOE BUHLER was born in 1950, in Vancouver, Washington. He currently teaches mathematics at Reed College in Portland, Oregon. In addition to numerous scholarly publications in the field of mathematics, Professor Buhler has published a number of essays for more general audiences. His popular writings include essays on science, juggling, and the oriental game Go.

RON GRAHAM was born in Taft, California, and at present is associated with AT&T Bell Labs in Murray Hill, New Jersey. He has had a distinguished career in mathematics, including membership in the National Academy of Sciences, and has published widely in the field. In addition, he is a past president of the International Jugglers' Association.

Give Juggling a Hand!

Originally published in the magazine *The Sciences*, this simple and straightforward process analysis nonetheless provides a good deal of information to would-be jugglers and admirers of the art. Student writers may wish to note the ways the authors keep their step-by-step directions simple and clear.

Nothing could be simpler than a game of catch. But just add another   1
ball or two and the game turns magical—the juggled balls take on a
life of their own. Suddenly, simple motions and common objects blur
into one stunning display after another.

In recent years, juggling has experienced a renaissance. Street   2
performers and skilled amateurs are practicing the ancient art in
parks, back yards and on campuses around the globe. Membership

in the largely amateur International Jugglers' Association (IJA) has more than doubled since 1979.

Juggling is actually 4000 years young. In Egypt, Asia and the 3 Americas, it was once associated with religious ritual. In medieval Europe, wandering minstrels often juggled; the very term derives from these *jongleurs*.

Amazing jugglers imported from the Orient—in particular the 4 "East Indian" Ramo Samee, who was said to string beads in his mouth while turning rings with his fingers and toes, and the Japanese artist Takashima, who manipulated a cotton ball with a stick held in his teeth—convinced 19th-century Europeans that juggling could be extraordinary show business.

Perhaps the greatest juggler of all time was variety-show virtuoso 5 Enrico Rastelli. By his death in 1931, he had taught himself to juggle eight clubs, eight plates or ten balls; he could even bounce three balls continuously on his head.

Most people assume that a skilled juggler can manage up to 20 6 objects. In fact, even five-ball juggling is very difficult and requires about a year to master. Only a few jugglers worldwide have perfected seven-ball routines. At the 1986 IJA competition, one entrant separately juggled nine rings, eight balls and seven clubs.

Jugglers use a bewildering variety of objects, including bowling 7 balls, whips, plastic swimming pools, cube puzzles, fruit, flaming torches, and playing cards. Performers trying for the largest number of objects usually choose rings, which allow a tighter traffic pattern and are stable when thrown to great heights. Several jugglers can manage ten or 11 rings, and some are trying for 12 or 13.

Clubs are the most visually pleasing objects to juggle. They're 8 especially suited for passing back and forth between performers. Because they take up a lot of space when they rotate and must be caught at one end, juggling even five is tricky. Almost nobody can manage seven, even for a few seconds.

Throughout history, all jugglers—from South Sea Islanders to 9 Aztec Indians—have used the same fundamental patterns:

The Cascade. Here, each ball travels from one hand to the other 10 and back again, following a looping path that looks like a figure eight lying on its side. The juggler starts with two balls in his right hand, using a scooping motion and releasing a ball when his throwing hand is level with his navel. As the first ball reaches its highest point, the other hand scoops and releases a second ball, and as that one reaches *its* apogee, he throws the third. Skilled jugglers can keep three, five, or even seven balls going in a cascade, but never four or six. With an even number, balls collide at the intersection of the figure eight.

The Shower. In this more difficult pattern, the balls follow a circular path as they are thrown upward by the right hand, caught by the left and quickly passed back to the right. Since the right does all the long-distance throwing, the shower is inherently asymmetrical and, therefore, inefficient; it is difficult with more than three objects. 11

The Fountain. This figure allows for a large number of balls. In a four-ball fountain, each hand juggles two balls independently in a circular motion. For symmetry, the number of balls is usually even. If the hands throw alternately and the two patterns interlock, it is surprisingly hard to discern that the fountain is made of two separate components and not one. 12

Because gravity causes objects to accelerate as they fall, a juggler has only a short time to catch and throw one ball before another drops into his hand—even if he throws high. A juggler who throws a ball eight feet in the air, for example, must catch it 1.4 seconds later, but throwing it four times that high only doubles the flight time. 13

The best way to understand juggling is to learn to do it yourself. Some people get the hang of the three-ball cascade in minutes, although most need at least a few days. Limit your sessions to ten minutes rather than frustrate yourself with a two-hour binge. 14

Step 1: One Ball. Practice throwing a ball from your right hand to your left and back, letting the ball rise to just above your head. Make the ball follow the path of a figure eight lying on its side, by "scooping" the ball and releasing it near the navel. Catch the ball at the side of your body, then repeat the sequence. 15

Step 2: Two Balls. Put one in each hand. Throw the ball in the left hand as in Step 1, and then, just as the ball passes its high point, throw the right-hand ball. Avoid releasing the second throw too early or tossing the balls to unequal heights. 16

At first it may be difficult to catch the balls. Don't worry. Focus instead on the accuracy and height of the throws. Catching will come naturally as soon as the throws are on target. If things seem hectic, try higher throws. 17

Step 3: Two Balls Reversed. Reverse the order of throws so that the sequence is right, then left. 18

Step 4: Three Balls. Now put two balls in your right hand and one   19
in your left. Try to complete Step 2 while simply holding the extra ball.
Pause, then do Step 3.

The third ball can make it difficult to catch the second throw. To   20
solve this, throw the third ball just after the second reaches its high
point. The sequence is thus right, left, right. At first it may be tough
to persuade your right hand to make its second throw. Remember:
catches are irrelevant in the beginning. Throw high, accurately and
slowly. Don't rush the tempo, and don't forget the figure-eight pattern.

Once you've mastered the three-ball cascade you'll want to try   21
other patterns. A juggler is never finished: there is always one more
ball.

Meanings and Values

1a.   If you find this essay interesting, try to explain what it is that you like
      about the piece. The topic? The authors' approach? Make your answers
      as specific as you can. (See Guide to Terms: *Evaluation*.)

 b.   If you do not find the selection interesting, try to explain the reasons
      for your response as specifically as you can and suggest some ways in
      which the essay might be improved.

2.   Explain the pun (play on words) in the title.

3a.   Tell how you think most readers are likely to view juggling before
      reading this essay.

 b.   After reading it.

Expository Techniques

1.   Should the discussion in paragraphs 10–13 be considered a directional
      process, an informational process, or both? Be ready to explain your
      answer using evidence from the text.

2a.   What strategies do the authors use to highlight the steps in the process
      described in paragraphs 14–20?

 b.   To highlight the different processes analyzed in paragraphs 9–13?

3.   Discuss the use of transitions and parallel structures in paragraphs
      15–17 to help create orderly and clear explanation. (Guide: *Transition,
      Parallel Structure*.)

4a. The opening of this essay presents considerable historical information on juggling, at least given the length of the essay. Why do you think the authors chose to begin the piece in this manner? (Guide: *Introductions.*)

b. Does this material harm the unity of the essay in any way? Why, or why not? (Guide: *Unity.*)

Diction and Vocabulary

1a. Analyze the diction in paragraph 10 and explain how it contributes to the clarity of the writing. (Guide: *Diction.*)

b. Are most readers likely to understand the term "apogee" in paragraph 10? Does its presence make the explanation confusing?

2. How do the objects listed in the first sentence of paragraph 7 and the order in which they are presented emphasize the drama and excitement that jugglers are capable of creating? (Guide: *Emphasis.*)

3. In explaining how to accomplish a three-ball cascade (pars. 14–20), the authors try to make the process seem reasonably simple and easy. How do their vocabulary choices (especially verbs) help accomplish this? (Guide: *Diction.*)

Suggestions for Writing and Discussion

1. Prepare a set of directions for some other entertaining and relaxing activity you know about. Games or exercise routines might be good subjects.

2. Are there any parts of this essay that make the process seem too simple? How might it be improved or expanded to help readers who want to give juggling a try?

3. Are many readers likely to take up juggling as a result of this essay—or at least to try it once? What elements in the essay might encourage (or discourage) such a reaction?

(NOTE: Suggestions for topics requiring development by PROCESS ANALYSIS are on pages 227–228, at the end of this section.)

DONALD M. MURRAY

DONALD M. MURRAY, born in 1924 in Boston, until recently taught
writing at the University of New Hampshire. He has served as an
editor of *Time* and, in 1954, was awarded the Pulitzer Prize for
editorials written for the Boston *Herald*. Among his published
works are novels, books of nonfiction, stories, poetry, and both
textbooks and articles on the teaching of writing.

The Maker's Eye:
Revising Your Own Manuscripts

"The Maker's Eye: Revising Your Own Manuscripts," first published in slightly different form in *The Writer*, provides an example
of directional process. The author presents his information in
chronological steps, most of them supported by direct quotations
from professional writers. Much of the advice is applicable to
student writing as well as to professional work.

When students complete a first draft, they consider the job of writing   1
done—and their teachers too often agree. When professional writers
complete a first draft, they usually feel that they are at the start of the
writing process. When a draft is completed, the job of writing can
begin.

    That difference in attitude is the difference between amateur and   2
professional, inexperience and experience, journeyman and craftsman. Peter F. Drucker, the prolific business writer, calls his first draft
"the zero draft"—after that he can start counting. Most writers share
the feeling that the first draft, and all of those which follow, are
opportunities to discover what they have to say and how best they
can say it.

To produce a progression of drafts, each of which says more and 3
says it more clearly, the writer has to develop a special kind of reading
skill. In school we are taught to decode what appears on the page as
finished writing. Writers, however, face a different category of possibility and responsibility when they read their own drafts. To them the
words on the page are never finished. Each can be changed and
rearranged, can set off a chain reaction of confusion or clarified
meaning. This is a different kind of reading, which is possibly more
difficult and certainly more exciting.

Writers must learn to be their own best enemy. They must accept 4
the criticism of others and be suspicious of it; they must accept the
praise of others and be even more suspicious of it. Writers cannot
depend on others. They must detach themselves from their own pages so
that they can apply both their caring and their craft to their own work.

Such detachment is not easy. Science fiction writer Ray Bradbury 5
supposedly puts each manuscript away for a year to the day and then
rereads it as a stranger. Not many writers have the discipline or the
time to do this. We must read when our judgment may be at its worst,
when we are close to the euphoric moment of creation.

Then the writer, counsels novelist Nancy Hale, "should be critical 6
of everything that seems to him most delightful in his style. He should
excise what he most admires, because he wouldn't thus admire it if
he weren't . . . in a sense protecting it from criticism." John Ciardi, the
poet, adds, "The last act of the writing must be to become one's own
reader. It is, I suppose, a schizophrenic process, to begin passionately
and to end critically, to begin hot and to end cold; and, more important, to be passion-hot and critic-cold at the same time."

Most people think that the principal problem is that writers are 7
too proud of what they have written. Actually, a greater problem for
most professional writers is one shared by the majority of students.
They are overly critical, think everything is dreadful, tear up page
after page, never complete a draft, see the task as hopeless.

The writer must learn to read critically but constructively, to cut 8
what is bad, to reveal what is good. Eleanor Estes, the children's book
author, explains: "The writer must survey his work critically, coolly,
as though he were a stranger to it. He must be willing to prune,
expertly and hard-heartedly. At the end of each revision, a manuscript
may look . . . worked over, torn apart, pinned together, added to,
deleted from, words changed and words changed back. Yet the book
must maintain its original freshness and spontaneity."

Most readers underestimate the amount of rewriting it usually   9
takes to produce spontaneous reading. This is a great disadvantage to
the student writer, who sees only a finished product and never
watches the craftsman who takes the necessary step back, studies the
work carefully, returns to the task, steps back, returns, steps back,
again and again. Anthony Burgess, one of the most prolific writers in
the English-speaking world, admits, "I might revise a page twenty
times." Roald Dahl, the popular children's writer, states, "By the time
I'm nearing the end of a story, the first part will have been reread and
altered and corrected at least 150 times. . . . Good writing is essentially
rewriting. I am positive of this."

Rewriting isn't virtuous. It isn't something that ought to be done.   10
It is simply something that most writers find they have to do to
discover what they have to say and how to say it. It is a condition of
the writer's life.

There are, however, a few writers who do little formal rewriting,   11
primarily because they have the capacity and experience to create and
review a large number of invisible drafts in their minds before they
approach the page. And some writers slowly produce finished pages,
performing all the tasks of revision simultaneously, page by page, rather
than draft by draft. But it is still possible to see the sequence followed
by most writers most of the time in rereading their own work.

Most writers scan their drafts first, reading as quickly as possible   12
to catch the larger problems of subject and form, then move in closer
and closer as they read and write, reread and rewrite.

The first thing writers look for in their drafts is *information*. They   13
know that a good piece of writing is built from specific, accurate, and
interesting information. The writer must have an abundance of information from which to construct a readable piece of writing.

Next writers look for *meaning* in the information. The specifics   14
must build to a pattern of significance. Each piece of specific information must carry the reader toward meaning.

Writers reading their own drafts are aware of *audience*. They put   15
themselves in the reader's situation and make sure that they deliver
information which a reader wants to know or needs to know in a
manner which is easily digested. Writers try to be sure that they
anticipate and answer the questions a critical reader will ask when
reading the piece of writing.

Writers make sure that the *form* is appropriate to the subject and   16
the audience. Form, or genre, is the vehicle which carries meaning to

the reader, but form cannot be selected until the writer has adequate information to discover its significance and an audience which needs or wants that meaning.

Once writers are sure the form is appropriate, they must then look at the *structure*, the order of what they have written. Good writing is built on a solid framework of logic, argument, narrative, or motivation which runs through the entire piece of writing and holds it together. This is the time when many writers find it most effective to outline as a way of visualizing the hidden spine by which the piece of writing is supported. [17]

The element on which writers may spend a majority of their time is *development*. Each section of a piece of writing must be adequately developed. It must give readers enough information so that they are satisfied. How much information is enough? That's as difficult as asking how much garlic belongs in a salad. It must be done to taste, but most beginning writers underdevelop, underestimating the reader's hunger for information. [18]

As writers solve development problems, they often have to consider questions of *dimension*. There must be a pleasing and effective proportion among all the parts of the piece of writing. There is a continual process of subtracting and adding to keep the piece of writing in balance. [19]

Finally, writers have to listen to their own voices. *Voice* is the force which drives a piece of writing forward. It is an expression of the writer's authority and concern. It is what is between the words on the page, what glues the piece of writing together. A good piece of writing is always marked by a consistent, individual voice. [20]

As writers read and reread, write and rewrite, they move closer and closer to the page until they are doing line-by-line editing. Writers read their own pages with infinite care. Each sentence, each line, each clause, each phrase, each word, each mark of punctuation, each section of white space between the type has to contribute to the clarification of meaning. [21]

Slowly the writer moves from word to word, looking through language to see the subject. As a word is changed, cut, or added, as a construction is rearranged, all the words used before that moment and all those that follow that moment must be considered and reconsidered. [22]

Writers often read aloud at this stage of the editing process, muttering or whispering to themselves, calling on the ear's experi- [23]

ence with language. Does this sound right—or that? Writers edit, shifting back and forth from eye to page to ear to page. I find I must do this careful editing in short runs, no more than fifteen or twenty minutes at a stretch, or I become too kind with myself. I begin to see what I hope is on the page, not what actually is on the page.

This sounds tedious if you haven't done it, but actually it is fun. Making something right is immensely satisfying, for writers begin to learn what they are writing about by writing. Language leads them to meaning, and there is the joy of discovery, of understanding, of making meaning clear as the writer employs the technical skills of language. 24

Words have double meanings, even triple or quadruple meanings. Each word has its own potential for connotation and denotation. And when writers rub one word against the other, they are often rewarded with a sudden insight, an unexpected clarification. 25

The maker's eye moves back and forth from word to phrase to sentence to paragraph to sentence to phrase to word. The maker's eye sees the need for variety and balance, for a firmer structure, for a more appropriate form. It peers into the interior of the paragraph, looking for coherence, unity, and emphasis, which make meaning clear. 26

I learned something about this process when my first bifocals were prescribed. I had ordered a larger section of the reading portion of the glass because of my work, but even so, I could not contain my eyes within this new limit of vision. And I still find myself taking off my glasses and bending my nose towards the page, for my eyes unconsciously flick back and forth across the page, back to another page, forward to still another, as I try to see each evolving line in relation to every other line. 27

When does this process end? Most writers agree with the great Russian writer Tolstoy, who said, "I scarcely ever reread my published writings, if by chance I come across a page, it always strikes me: all this must be rewritten; this is how I should have written it." 28

The maker's eye is never satisfied, for each word has the potential to ignite new meaning. This article has been twice written all the way through the writing process, and it was published four years ago. Now it is to be republished in a book. The editors make a few small suggestions, and then I read it with my maker's eye. Now it has been re-edited, re-revised, re-read, re-re-edited, for each piece of writing to the writer is full of potential and alternatives. 29

A piece of writing is never finished. It is delivered to a deadline, torn out of the typewriter on demand, sent off with a sense of accomplishment and shame and pride and frustration. If only there were a couple more days, time for just another run at it, perhaps then. . . .

Meanings and Values

1a. What is the author's point of view in this selection? (See Guide to Terms: *Point of View*.)

b. What is the relationship between his tone and the point of view? (Guide: *Style/Tone*.)

2a. What, if anything, prevents this selection from being as fascinating to read as some of the other pieces already studied?

b. Could (or should) Murray have done anything else to enliven his process analysis? If so, what might it be?

3a. What was the author's purpose in writing this selection? (Guide: *Evaluation*.)

b. How well did he succeed?

c. Was it worth doing?

Expository Techniques

1a. What standard techniques of introduction does this author use in his opening paragraph? (Guide: *Introductions*.)

b. How well does this paragraph meet the requirements of a good introduction?

2. Into which of the two basic types of process analysis can this selection be classed? Why?

3. What, if anything, is gained by the frequent use of quotations from professional writers?

4a. Are the distinctions among his eight steps of rewriting (pars. 13–20) made clear enough? Be specific.

b. Does anything about the order of these eight steps seem peculiar to you? If so, explain.

5a. Cite examples of parallel structure from paragraphs 21 and 26. (Guide: *Parallel Structure*.)

b. What is gained by such usage?

Diction and Vocabulary

1a. Cite several uses of figurative language and state what kind they are. (Guide: *Figures of Speech*.)

b. What is the main advantage in their use?

2a. What, if anything, do you find unusual about saying "a majority of their time" (par. 18)?

b. What other way, if any, do you prefer?

3. Is it clear to you how "each word has its own potential for connotation and denotation" (par. 25)? (Guide: *Connotation/Denotation*.) If it is, explain the assertion.

4. Use the dictionary as necessary to understand the meanings of the following words: prolific (par. 2); euphoric (5); excise, schizophrenic (6); spontaneity (8); genre (16); potential (29).

Suggestions for Writing and Discussion

1a. Who was the reader-audience the author apparently had in mind in writing this process analysis?

b. Explain fully why it would, or would not, be worth all the suggested time and trouble just to produce papers for your college courses.

2. Discuss the assertion that "writers begin to learn what they are writing about by writing" (par. 24). If it seems more logical (for you) to learn what you are writing about some other way, what is it?

(NOTE: Suggestions for topics requiring development by PROCESS ANALYSIS are on pages 227–228, at the end of this section.)

ANN FARADAY

ANN FARADAY studied at University College in London, where she received her Ph.D. in psychology. After additional research and training in the analysis of dreams, she developed her own method of interpretation. Much of her time is now spent lecturing on this approach to understanding dreams and on conducting research. She is the author of two books on analyzing and understanding dreams: *Dream Power* (1972) and *The Dream Game* (1974).

Unmasking Your Dream Images

Finding the right or best way to interpret dreams has been a concern of psychologists and other people for many years. In this selection from *The Dream Game*, Faraday uses process analysis along with examples to explain her approach.

There would not *be* a dream from the unconscious except as the person is confronting some issue in his conscious life—some conflict, anxiety, bafflement, fork in the road, puzzle or situation of compelling curiosity. That is, the incentive for dreaming—what cues off my particular dream on a particular night—is my need to "make something" of the world I am living in at the moment. 1

—Rollo May

[If you wish to understand and use your dreams, you can begin by writing] down at least a few recent dreams along with notes of their *themes* (falling, being chased, meeting famous people, or whatever). . . . If you are able to relate your dreams to the events or thoughts of the day—without which any dream interpretation is incomplete— then several of your dreams should be clear to you. The majority of dreams, however, depict strange and even weird images and charac- 2 ters and usually do require further work before their meanings emerge. To tie the events and thoughts of the day to these dreams is particularly important because there are always several possible interpretations of each dream symbol, and only you can find the "correct" interpretation by relating it to something that was on your mind or in your heart as you fell asleep.

In deciding whether a dream image should be understood liter- 3 ally or symbolically, the rules are:

1. If the dream character—human, animal, vegetable, or min- 4 eral—is a *real* person or thing in your life or on your mind at the time of the dream, then it should be considered literally in the first instance and taken symbolically when and only when a literal interpretation makes no sense. (Even Jung, the archexponent of elaborate dream symbolism, was insistent that dreams of a husband, wife, child, neighbor, colleague, the dog, and anyone with whom we are in intimate contact at the time of the dream almost always refer to the individuals themselves rather than to anything more subtle.) I know from my own experience that it is a mistake to interpret a dream of your car failing as a symbol of failing *drive* in yourself until you have checked the car, since the dream may well be throwing up subliminal perceptions of something wrong with the engine which you have been too busy to notice during the course of the day.

2. If a dream character or image cannot be taken literally as a real 5 person or thing in your life, then it symbolizes either someone or something in your external life, or a part of your own personality which your heart is bringing to your attention. (Jung referred to the former as an *objective* interpretation, and to the latter as a *subjective* interpretation.)

In looking for the meaning of any symbolic dream image, always 6 check first to discover whether or not it symbolizes someone or something external to yourself at the time of the dream, for we dream about the world outside us just as much as we dream of our private inner world. For example, if you dream of Vincent Price, and the real Vincent Price does not figure personally in your life at the moment, then look around to see if anyone else would fit the name. Is there perhaps a Mr. or Mrs. Price or a Vincent in your present life to whom the dream could refer? If not, then you must ask yourself what Vincent Price means to you. It could be something like costliness (a pun on his name) or showmanship (an association based on his qualities), or whatever else he may mean to you personally. Is there someone in your present life—husband, wife, colleague, neighbor, and so on—who has behaved in an extravagant (or showy or entertaining) way during the previous day or two? If there is, then your dream is probably expressing concern about your relationship with this particular person.

If you can think of no such person, then you have to consider the possibility that Vincent Price might be a part of yourself—which is nice if you admire him, and not so good if you dislike him! Have you behaved extravagantly or shown off during the past day or two? Always remember that the dream exaggerates in order to bring its point home to you; if you dream of a fascist and it turns out to represent part of your own personality, don't get too upset, for the dream is merely saying that you *feel* you behaved a bit like a fascist in the recent past, which may mean no more than some unpleasant thought about your Jewish neighbor or a dictatorial attitude toward your teenage son. If you continually dream of fascists and there are none in your life, either literally or figuratively, then it is probably fair to say that you have an inner conflict about this subject—but once again, you must remember that the dream merely reflects *your feeling* about yourself and your behavior, and your friends may not see you in this light at all. As Erich Fromm writes in his book *The Forgotten Language,* "Dreams are like a microscope through which we look at the hidden occurrences in our soul." 7

. . . I shall take several dreams from my collection to demonstrate in a practical way the various techniques you can use to discover the identities of your dream characters and images. I have chosen these few examples from thousands of dreams in order to stress what I consider the most important points in dream interpretation, but they cannot be more than guidelines at this point in the dream game. . . . I cannot interpret your dreams: you must do it for yourself; my aim is to help you make a start. Even after applying all the rules and suggestions given in this [essay], you will almost certainly find that some dreams still elude you. Don't worry about this too much; it happens to all of us. But do continue to write down your dreams, together with the events and thoughts of the day, for many of them may become clearer to you as you get to know the meanings of certain recurring symbols over a series of dreams. Very often you will find that a certain elusive symbol in one dream reveals its meaning quite openly in another dream. When this starts happening, you are ready to complete your dream glossary. . . . 8

The other principles to be borne in mind at this stage in the dream   9
game are [as follows]:

3. Even though dreams may take us back to childhood or concern   10
themselves with future possibilities, they are always triggered by
something on our minds or in our hearts at the time of the dream.
People or things that were once very intimate parts of our lives—parents, siblings, childhood home, or friends—cannot be taken literally
in our dreams if we are no longer directly involved with them. A
dream does not indulge in reminiscence for its own sake. Such characters and images appear in our dreams either because they represent
the voices of the past which still live on in us and influence our present
behavior, or to tell us that something in our present situation reminds
us of a similar situation in the past.

4. The feeling tone of a dream is always important and sometimes   11
gives the clue to the meaning of a dream symbol. For example, if I
dream of a dog passing me in the street wagging its tail and feel very
dejected in the dream because it does not respond to my friendly call,
the clue to the dream's meaning may come in remembering how upset
I was at my husband's behavior the previous evening at a "cocktail"
party—and my dream could be reflecting my heart's thought that he
was so concerned with playing the "gay dog" that he failed to pay me
any attention.

5. If you happen to know from reading books that some particular   12
symbol occurs commonly in people's dreams and has been stated by
experts to have a universal meaning, by all means take this as a
suggestion of what the symbol *might* mean if it occurs in your own
dream, for our dreams pick up and utilize symbols from anywhere in
order to make their point. Never assume that it must have this
particular meaning, however, for there might be other more personal
associations that are more important to you which actually determine
how your dreaming mind uses this particular symbol. Since the
majority of people in the West were brought up in a house, for
example, a dream house is likely to mean "living space"—a symbol
of your personality itself—but even this symbol can have different
meanings in different circumstances. Always check what the symbol
means to you—and always check on a possible literal meaning in the
first instance.

6. If the same dream image or character recurs frequently in your   13
dreams, then it is likely to have a similar meaning throughout a series
of dreams, and for this reason it is helpful to compile a dream glossary

of your own recurring symbols. You should not be surprised to discover, however, that on occasion this particular symbol has a different meaning, and can sometimes be merely part of the background with no great significance. Any symbol is influenced to a great extent by the symbols it is grouped with in any one dream, and we should always see it in the context of the dream as a whole.

7. Dreams do not come to tell us what we already know about the people in our lives or about ourselves, so if at first sight a dream seems to be doing no more than this, look deeper. At the very least, it may be clarifying the thoughts of the heart by putting them in vivid picture language or urging us to do something about a long-standing problem—but the dream may have an altogether deeper meaning which we can discover by looking again at its symbols. 14

8. A dream symbol is correctly interpreted when and only when it makes sense to the dreamer in terms of his present life situation and moves him to change his life constructively. Someone else may see a different possible interpretation, but this is only what your dream would mean *to him had he* dreamed it. Dreams do not arise arbitrarily from some universal reservoir: they arise out of the dreamer's present life experience and are meaningful to him alone. While I cannot say that the *purpose* of dreams is to move us to change our lives, I do insist that a "correct" interpretation—which means an effective interpretation—shows the way. For this reason, I suggest that anyone working on a dream successfully should conclude by writing down *briefly* what the dream means and *what he is going to do about it.* Jung made a habit of asking his patients, after they had worked together on a dream, "Now, *in one sentence,* what is the meaning of the dream?" [My colleagues and I] follow this rule in all our dream work, though we allow two or three sentences if necessary. And we conclude by asking the dreamer what practical action the dream message could lead him to take. 15

9. A dream is incorrectly (ineffectively) interpreted if the interpretation leaves the dreamer disappointed or diminished. Many psychotherapists still insist that they know the correct interpretation of your dream and believe that the message which makes sense to you may not be the one you need to see at any given moment in time—apparently quite oblivious of the fact that their colleagues, on the basis of the same dream, may be seeing quite different things for you. You must learn to trust your *own* feelings and judgment. 16

Meanings and Values

1a. According to the quotation at the beginning of this selection, what is the purpose of dreaming?

 b. Why does Faraday think most people need to learn how to interpret their dreams?

2. In your words, explain the distinction Faraday draws in paragraph 4 between interpreting dreams literally and interpreting them symbolically. (You may wish to look up the meaning of the terms *literally* and *symbolically*.)

3a. Having read this selection, do you consider the procedure explained by the author to be useful and accurate, fanciful and unreliable, or somewhere in between?

 b. Is your evaluation based on the information presented in the essay? The way the essay is written? Your view of dreams and dream interpretation? Some combination? Explain. (See Guide to Terms: *Evaluation*.)

Expository Techniques

1a. Drawing on specific evidence from the essay for support, explain why you think this selection is a directional process, an informational process, or a mixture of the two.

 b. If you consider it a combination, identify those paragraphs that are primarily directional, primarily informational, and a mixture of the two.

2a. Do the numbers indicate steps in the process? If not, what do they identify?

 b. Are the numbers used effectively? (Guide: *Evaluation*.)

3a. Identify both the brief and extended examples in these paragraphs: 4, 6, 10, and 15.

 b. Choose two of these paragraphs and discuss whether the examples are intended as illustrations for explanatory statements or as a way of showing readers how to do something.

4a. Where in the selection does the author mention other ways of interpreting dreams than the approach she thinks is correct?

 b. For what purpose does she mention these alternative approaches?

Diction and Vocabulary

1. Choose one of the longer paragraphs in this essay and explain why you think the diction is either abstract or concrete. (Guide: *Diction, Concrete/Abstract.*)

2. Consult the dictionary as needed for a full understanding of the following words, especially as they are used in this selection: subliminal (par. 4); objective, subjective (5); fascist, figuratively (7); elusive (8); arbitrarily (15).

Suggestions for Writing and Discussion

1. Discuss what dreams mean to you and how you go about interpreting them.

2. There are many different explanations of why dreams occur and what they mean. See if you can find any explanations in recent books or magazines and report on them to your classmates or in an essay.

(NOTE: Suggestions for topics requiring development by use of PROCESS ANALYSIS are on pages 227–228, at the end of this section.)

DIANE ACKERMAN

DIANE ACKERMAN was born in Waukegan, Illinois. She attended
Pennsylvania State University, receiving a B.A. in English, and
Cornell University, where she earned an M.F.A. and a Ph.D. For her
work as a writer, Ackerman has received many awards, including
the Academy of American Poets' Peter I. B. Lavan Award, and
grants from the Rockefeller Foundation and the National Endow-
ment for the Arts. Her poetry has been published in three collections, *The Planets: A Cosmic Pastoral* (1976), *Wife of Light* (1978), and
Lady Faustus (1983). Her nonfiction writing has appeared in *Twilight
of the Tenderfoot* (1980), *On Extended Wings* (1985), and *A Natural
History of the Senses* (1990). Ackerman has taught at Washington
University, New York University, Cornell, and Columbia. At present she is a staff writer at *The New Yorker*.

The Beholder's Eye

Scientific explanations can sometimes be dull to read and often
seem unrelated to our daily lives. This essay from *A Natural History
of the Senses* avoids both problems by employing lively, vivid language, surprising examples, and an imaginative approach to process analysis.

Look in the mirror. The face that pins you with its double gaze reveals   1
a chastening secret: You are looking into a predator's eyes. Most
predators have eyes set right on the front of their heads, so they can
use binocular vision to sight and track their prey. Our eyes have
separate mechanisms that gather the light, pick out an important or
novel image, focus it precisely, pinpoint it in space, and follow it; they
work like top-flight stereoscopic binoculars. Prey, on the other hand,
have eyes at the sides of their heads, because what they really need is

peripheral vision, so they can tell when something is sneaking up behind them. Something like us. If it's "a jungle out there" in the wilds of the city, it may be partly because the streets are jammed with devout predators. Our instincts stay sharp, and, when necessary, we just decree one another prey and have done with it. Whole countries sometimes. Once we domesticated fire as if it were some beautiful temperamental animal; harnessing both its energy and its light, it became possible for us to cook food to make it easier to chew and digest, and, as we found out eventually, to kill germs. But we can eat cold food perfectly well, too, and did for thousands of years. What does it say about us that, even in refined dining rooms, our taste is for meat served at the temperature of a freshly killed antelope or warthog?

Though most of us don't hunt, our eyes are still the great monopolists of our senses. To taste or touch your enemy or your food, you have to be unnervingly close to it. To smell or hear it, you can risk being farther off. But vision can rush through the fields and up the mountains, travel across time, country, and parsecs of outer space, and collect bushel baskets of information as it goes. Animals that hear high frequencies better than we do—bats and dolphins, for instance— seem to see richly with their ears, hearing geographically, but for us the world becomes most densely informative, most luscious, when we take it in through our eyes. It may even be that abstract thinking evolved from our eyes' elaborate struggle to make sense of what they saw. Seventy percent of the body's sense receptors cluster in the eyes, and it is mainly through seeing the world that we appraise and understand it. Lovers close their eyes when they kiss because, if they didn't, there would be too many visual distractions to notice and analyze—the sudden close-up of the loved one's eyelashes and hair, the wallpaper, the clock face, the dust motes suspended in a shaft of sunlight. Lovers want to do serious touching, and not be disturbed. So they close their eyes as if asking two cherished relatives to leave the room.

Our language is steeped in visual imagery. In fact, whenever we compare one thing to another, as we constantly do (consider the country expression: "It was raining harder than a cow pissing sideways on a rock"), we are relying on our sense of vision to capture the action or the mood. Seeing is proof positive, we stubbornly insist ("I saw it with my own eyes . . ."). Of course, in these days of relativity, feats of magic, and tricks of perception, we know better than to trust everything we see (". . . a flying saucer landed on the freeway . . .").

See with our naked eyes, that is. As Dylan Thomas reminds us, there are many "fibs of vision."[1] If we extend our eyes by attaching artificial lenses and other accessories to our real ones (glasses, telescopes, cameras, binoculars, scanning electron microscopes, CAT scans, X-rays, magnetic resonance imaging, ultrasound, radioisotope tracers, lasers, DNA sequencers, and so on), we trust the result a little more. But Missouri is still called the *Show Me!* state, which, as a kind of visual pun, I guess, it displays on its license plates for motorists to see. "The writing is on the wall," a politician says sagely, forgetting temporarily that it could be a forgery nonetheless. We quickly see through people whose characters are transparent. And, heaven knows, we yearn for enlightenment. "I see where you're coming from," one woman says to another in a café, "but you'd better watch out, he's bound to see what you're up to." *See for yourself!* the impatient exclaim to disbelievers. After the Bible's first imperative—"Let there be light"—God viewed each day's toil and "saw that it was good." Presumably, He, too, had to see it to believe it. Ideas dawn on us, if we're bright enough, not dim-witted, especially if we're visionary. And, when we flirt, though the common phrase sounds quite ghoulish and extreme, we give someone the eye.

The process of seeing began very simply. In the ancient seas, 4 life-forms developed faint patches of skin that were sensitive to light. They could then tell light from dark, and also the direction of the light source, but that was all. These skills turned out to be so useful that eyes evolved that could judge motion, then form, and finally a dazzling array of details and colors. One reminder of our oceanic origins is that our eyes must be constantly bathed in salt water. Some of the oldest eyes on record are those of the trilobite, one of the great success

---

[1]Among the many fibs of vision are optical illusions. A puddle forms on the highway in front of you. But, unlike a real puddle, it keeps moving farther away as you approach it. Because it is a hot summer day, with a layer of hot air sitting below a layer of cold air, a reflection (of the sky) is cast onto the road. The word "mirage" slowly forms in your mind. Its etymology means "to wonder at." When we look at something red, the lens of our eye adjusts to the same shape it needs for seeing something green that is closer. When we look at something blue, the lens changes in the opposite direction. As a result, blue things appear to recede into the background, and red things seem to leap forward. Red things seem to be contracting, while blue ones seem to be spreading out. Blue things are thought to be "cold," while pink things are thought to be "warm." And because the eye is always trying to make sense of life, if it encounters a puzzling scene it corrects the picture to what it knows. If it finds a familiar pattern, it sticks to it, regardless of how inappropriate it might be in that landscape or against that background.

stories of the Cambrian age, which we now know only through its plentiful fossil remains. As I type this, I am wearing on a chain around my neck a small trilobite fossil, set in a silver bezel. Five hundred million years ago, it thrived in the swamps, with compound faceted eyes that could see mainly sideways but, unfortunately, not up. On the other hand, the newest eyes are those we have invented, such as the electric eye (based on what we learned about the motion-detecting design of the frog's eye), or the mirror telescope (based on the contrast-judging design of the horseshoe crab's eye), or synchronous lenses for use in microsurgery, optical scanning, and severe vision problems (based on the double lens of copilia, a myopic crustacean that lives deep in the Mediterranean). Although plants do not have eyes, Loren Eiseley argues eloquently for the eye of the fungus pilobolus, which has a light-sensitive area that controls the spore cannon it aims at the brightest spot it can find.

We think of our eyes as wise seers, but all the eye does is gather light. Let's consider the light-harvesting. As we know, the eye works a lot like a camera; or rather, we invented cameras that work like our eyes. To focus a camera, you move the lens closer to or farther away from an object. The eye's rubbery, bean-shaped crystalline lens achieves the same result by changing its shape—the lens thins to focus on a distant object, which looks small; thickens to focus on a near one, which looks large. A camera can control the amount of light it allows in. The iris of the eye, which is really a muscle, changes the size of a small hole, the pupil,[2] through which the light enters the eyeball. Because fish don't have this pupillary response, in which the iris protects against sudden surges of light, and most of them do not have eyelids (since their eyes are constantly bathed in water), they're much more susceptible to dazzlement than we are. In addition to its gate-keeping function, the iris, named after the Greek word for rainbow, is what gives our eyes their color. Caucasian eyes appear blue at birth, Negro eyes brown. After death, Caucasian eyes appear greenish-brown. Blue eyes are not inherently blue, not *stained* blue like fabric: They appear blue because they have less pigment than brown eyes. When light enters "blue" eyes, the very short blue light rays scatter as they jump off tiny, nonpigmented particles; what we see are the

5

---

[2]From the Latin *pupilla*, "a little doll." When the Romans looked into one another's eyes, they saw a doll-like reflection of themselves. The old Hebrew expression for pupil is similar: *eshon ayin*, which means "little man of the eye."

scattered rays, and the eyes appear to be blue. Dark eyes have densely packed pigment molecules and absorb the blue wavelengths, at the same time reflecting other colors whose rays are longer. They therefore appear to be brown or hazel. Though on casual inspection irises may look pretty much the same, the pattern of color, starbursts, spots, and other features is so highly individual that law-enforcement people have considered using iris patterns in addition to fingerprints.

At the back of a camera, film records the images. Lining the rear 6 wall of the eyeball is a thin sheet, the retina, which includes two sorts of photosensitive cells, rods and cones. We need two because we live in the two worlds of darkness and light. A hundred and twenty-five million thin, straight rods construe the dimness, and report in black and white. Seven million plump cones examine the bright, color-packed day. There are three kinds of cones, specializing in blue, red, and green. Mixed together, the rods and cones allow the eye to respond quickly to a changing scene. One place on the retina, where the optic nerve enters the brain, has no rods or cones at all and, as a result, does not perceive light; we refer to it as our "blind spot." But right in the middle of the retina lies a small crater, the fovea, filled with highly concentrated cones, which we use for precision focusing when we want to examine an object in bright light, to drag it into sharp view and grip it with our eyes. Because the fovea is so small, it can perform its magic only on a small area (a four-inch-square snapshot at eight feet, for example). Almost every cone in a fovea has its own direct line to higher centers in the brain; elsewhere on the retina, rods and cones may serve many cells, and vision is vaguer. The eyeball moves subtly, continuously, to keep an object in front of the fovea. In dim light, the fovea's cones are almost useless; instead we must look just "off" of an object to see it clearly with the surrounding rods, not directly at it because the fovea would fail us and the object appear invisible. Because the rods see no color, we don't perceive color at night. When the retina observes something, neurons pass the word along to the brain through a series of electrochemical handshakes. In about a tenth of a second, the message reaches the visual cortex, which begins to make sense of it.

However, seeing, as we think of it, doesn't happen in the eyes but 7 in the brain. In one way, to see flamboyantly, in detail, we don't need the eyes at all. We often remember scenes from days or even years earlier, viewing them in our mind's eye, and can even picture completely imaginary events, if we wish. We see in surprising detail when we dream. Sometimes when I'm in a visually besotting landscape, somewhere out in nature and experiencing intense rapture, I lie down at night and close my eyes, and see the landscape parading across the inside of my closed lids. The first time this happened—on a 200,000-acre working cattle ranch, surrounded by pastel mesas, in the New Mexico desert—I was a little spooked. Wrung out from the rigors of the branding corral, I needed sleep, but all the day's images, gestures, and motions still blazed in my visual memory. It was not like dreaming: it was like trying to sleep with your eyes wide open during a fiesta in full swing.

The same thing happened more recently, this time in Antarctica. 8 One sunny day, we cruised through Gerlache Strait, which narrows to 1600 feet at its southern end; ice mountains towered on either side of the ship. Black jagged mountains, covered in cascading snow and ice, looked like penguins standing in familiar postures in a wash of brilliant light. While real penguins porpoised beside the boat, huge icebergs floated by, with bases of pale blue and sides of mint green. In the ship's glassed-in observation deck, people sat in armchairs at the window, some dozing. One man held out his pinky and first finger as if giving someone the evil eye, but he was measuring an iceberg. Deception Island, though distant, looked close and clear in the sterile air. A crib of ice holding a soft blue wash in its palms drifted close to the ship. Across the strait, ice calved off a glacier with a loud explosive crumble. Pastel icebergs roamed around us, some tens of thousands of years old. Great pressure can push the air bubbles out of the ice and compact it. Free of air bubbles, it reflects light differently, as blue. The waters shivered with the gooseflesh of small ice shards. Some icebergs glowed like dull peppermint in the sun—impurities trapped in the ice (phytoplankton and algae) tinted them green. Ethereal snow petrels flew around the peaks of the icebergs, while the sun shone through their translucent wings. White, silent, the birds seemed to be pieces of ice flying with purpose and grace. As they passed in front of an ice floe, they became invisible. Glare transformed the landscape with such force that it seemed like a pure color. When we went out in the inflatable motorized rafts called Zodiacs to tour the iceberg orchards, I grabbed a piece of glacial ice and held it to my ear, listening to the bubbles cracking and popping as the air trapped inside escaped. And that night, though exhausted from the day's spectacles and doings, I lay in my narrow bunk, awake with my eyes closed, while sunstruck icebergs drifted across the insides of my lids, and the

Antarctic peninsula revealed itself slowly, mile by mile, in the small theater of my closed eyes.

Because the eye loves novelty and can get used to almost any scene, even one of horror, much of life can drift into the vague background of our attention. How easy it is to overlook the furry yellow comb inside the throat of an iris, or the tiny fangs of a staple, or the red forked tongue of a garter snake, or the way intense sorrow makes people bend their bodies as if they were blowing in a high wind. Both science and art have a habit of waking us up, turning on all the lights, grabbing us by the collar and saying *Would you please pay attention!* You wouldn't think something as complexly busy as life would be so easy to overlook. But, like supreme racehorses, full of vitality, determination, and heart, we tend to miss sights not directly in our path—the colorful crowds of people on either side, the shapes left in the thickly rutted track, and the permanent spectacle of the sky, that ever-present, ever-changing pageant overhead.

Meanings and Values

1. One purpose of this essay is to explain how our eyes work. What are its other purposes? (See Guide to Terms: *Purpose.*)

2. What does the author mean by each of the following phrases or sentences?

    a. "However, seeing, as we think of it, doesn't happen in the eyes but in the brain." (par. 7)

    b. "The face that pins you with its double gaze . . ." (par. 1)

    c. "Animals that hear high frequencies better than we do—bats and dolphins, for instance—seem to see richly with their ears, hearing geographically . . ." (par. 2)

    d. "We think of our eyes as wise seers, but all the eye does is gather light." (par. 5)

    e. "Because the eye loves novelty and can get used to almost any scene, even one of horror, much of life can drift into the vague background of our attention." (par. 9)

Expository Techniques

1. What strategies does the author use to open this essay? (Guide: *Intro-ductions.*)

2. Why does Ackerman wait until paragraph 4 to begin focusing directly on the process of seeing?

3a. Each of the first three paragraphs in the essay draws its examples (for the most part) from a different source. What are the different kinds of examples in these paragraphs?

b. What is the central theme of each of the first three paragraphs, and how are the examples in each paragraph related to its theme? (Guide: *Unity*.)

4. Discuss the author's use of analogy as a pattern of exposition in paragraphs 5–6. Tell how she combines analogy with process analysis. (See Section 4, *Analogy*).

5a. In what ways does this essay differ from a typical scientific explanation you might expect to encounter in a textbook?

b. In what ways is it similar?

Diction and Vocabulary

1. Discuss how the author uses concrete diction in paragraph 8, not to paint pretty pictures but to isolate and describe physical phenomena. (Guide: *Concrete/Abstract*.)

2. Identify the figure of speech in each of the following passages:

a. " . . . in the small theater of my closed eyes." (par. 8)

b. "Both science and art have a habit of waking us up, turning on all the lights, grabbing us by the collar and saying *Would you please pay attention!*" (par. 9)

c. "The waters shivered with the gooseflesh of small ice shards." (par. 8)

3. Study the author's use of the following words, consulting the dictionary if necessary: chastening, peripheral (par. 1); monopolists, parsecs, motes (2); imagery, relativity, sagely (3); bezel, synchronous, myopic (4); crystalline, pupillary, pigment (5); photosensitive, construe (6); besotting, rapture, mesas (7); calved, shards, translucent, floe (8).

Suggestions for Writing and Discussion

1. To what extent do our other senses reflect our role as predator rather than prey?

2. Look up information about the way our other senses work (hearing, smelling, touching, tasting). Consider sharing this information in an essay of your own.

3. Have you ever had the experience of the visions of the day replaying themselves in your mind as you try to sleep? Is Ackerman's description of the phenomenon exaggerated or accurate according to your experience?

(NOTE: Suggestions for topics requiring development by use of PROCESS ANALYSIS are on pages 227–228, at the end of this section.)

JESSICA MITFORD

JESSICA MITFORD was born in 1917, the daughter of an English peer.
Her brother was sent to Eton, but she and her six sisters were
educated at home by their mother. At the age of nineteen Mitford
left home, eventually making her way to the United States in 1939.
Since 1944 she has been an American citizen, and is now living in
San Francisco. She did not begin her writing career until she was
thirty-eight. Her books are *Lifeitselfmanship* (1956); her autobiogra-
phy, *Daughters and Rebels* (1960); the bestseller *The American Way of
Death* (1963); *The Trial of Dr. Spock* (1969); *Kind and Usual Punishment*
(1973), a devastating study of the American penal system; *A Fine
Old Conflict* (1977); and *Poison Penmanship* (1979). Mitford's articles
have appeared in the *Atlantic, Harper's,* and *McCall's.*

To Dispel Fears of Live Burial

"To Dispel Fears of Live Burial" (editors' title) is a portion of *The
American Way of Death,* a book described in the *New York Times* as a
"savagely witty and well-documented exposé." The "savagely
witty" style, evident in this selection, does not obscure the fact of
its being a tightly organized, step-by-step process analysis.

Embalming is indeed a most extraordinary procedure, and one must 1
wonder at the docility of Americans who each year pay hundreds of
millions of dollars for its perpetuation, blissfully ignorant of what it
is all about, what is done, how it is done. Not one in ten thousand has
any idea of what actually takes place. Books on the subject are
extremely hard to come by. They are not to be found in most libraries
or bookshops.

In an era when huge television audiences watch surgical opera- 2
tions in the comfort of their living rooms, when, thanks to the animated cartoon, the geography of the digestive system has become

familiar territory even to the nursery school set, in a land where the satisfaction of curiosity about almost all matters is a national pastime, the secrecy surrounding embalming can, surely, hardly be attributed to the inherent gruesomeness of the subject. Custom in this regard has within this century suffered a complete reversal. In the early days of American embalming, when it was performed in the home of the deceased, it was almost mandatory for some relative to stay by the embalmer's side and witness the procedure. Today, family members who might wish to be in attendance would certainly be dissuaded by the funeral director. All others, except apprentices, are excluded by law from the preparation room.

A close look at what does actually take place may explain in large   3
measure the undertaker's intractable reticence concerning a procedure that has become his major *raison d'être*. Is it possible he fears that public information about embalming might lead patrons to wonder if they really want this service? If the funeral men are loath to discuss the subject outside the trade, the reader may, understandably, be equally loath to go on reading at this point. For those who have the stomach for it, let us part the formaldehyde curtain. . . .

The body is first laid out in the undertaker's morgue—or rather,   4
Mr. Jones is reposing in the preparation room—to be readied to bid the world farewell.

The preparation room in any of the better funeral establishments   5
has the tiled and sterile look of a surgery, and indeed the embalmer-restorative artist who does his chores there is beginning to adopt the term "dermasurgeon" (appropriately corrupted by some mortician-writers as "demisurgeon") to describe his calling. His equipment, consisting of scalpels, scissors, augers, forceps, clamps, needles, pumps, tubes, bowls and basins, is crudely imitative of the surgeon's as is his technique, acquired in a nine- or twelve-month post-high-school course in an embalming school. He is supplied by an advanced chemical industry with a bewildering array of fluids, sprays, pastes, oils, powders, creams, to fix or soften tissue, shrink or distend it as needed, dry it here, restore the moisture there. There are cosmetics, waxes and paints to fill and cover features, even plaster of Paris to replace entire limbs. There are ingenious aids to prop and stabilize the cadaver: A Vari-Pose Head Rest, the Edwards Arm and Hand Positioner, the Repose Block (to support the shoulders during the embalming), and the Throop Foot Positioner, which resembles an old-fashioned stocks.

Mr. John H. Eckels, president of the Eckels College of Mortuary   6
Science, thus describes the first part of the embalming procedure: "In
the hands of a skilled practitioner, this work may be done in a
comparatively short time and without mutilating the body other than
by slight incision—so slight that it scarcely would cause serious
inconvenience if made upon a living person. It is necessary to remove
the blood, and doing this not only helps in the disinfecting, but
removes the principal cause of disfigurements due to discoloration."

Another textbook discusses the all-important time element: "The   7
earlier this is done, the better, for every hour that elapses between
death and embalming will add to the problems and complications
encountered. . . ." Just how soon should one get going on the embalming? The author tells us, "On the basis of such scanty information
made available to this profession through its rudimentary and haphazard system of technical research, we must conclude that the best
results are to be obtained if the subject is embalmed before life is
completely extinct—that is, before cellular death has occurred. In the
average case, this would mean within an hour after somatic death."
For those who feel that there is something a little rudimentary, not to
say haphazard, about this advice, a comforting thought is offered by
another writer. Speaking of fears entertained in early days of premature burial, he points out, "One of the effects of embalming by
chemical injection, however, has been to dispel fears of live burial."
How true; once the blood is removed, chances of live burial are indeed
remote.

To return to Mr. Jones, the blood is drained out through the veins   8
and replaced by embalming fluid pumped in through the arteries. As
noted in *The Principles and Practices of Embalming*, "Every operator has
a favorite injection and drainage point—a fact which becomes a
handicap only if he fails or refuses to forsake his favorites when
conditions demand it." Typical favorites are the carotid artery, femo-
ral artery, jugular vein, subclavian vein. There are various choices of
embalming fluid. If Flextone is used, it will produce a "mild, flexible
rigidity. The skin retains a velvety softness, the tissues are rubbery
and pliable. Ideal for women and children." It may be blended with
B. and G. Products Company's Lyf-Lyk tint, which is guaranteed to
reproduce "nature's own skin texture . . . the velvety appearance of
living tissue." Suntone comes in three separate tints: Suntan; Special
Cosmetic Tint, a pink shade "especially indicated for young female
subjects"; and Regular Cosmetic Tint, moderately pink.

About three to six gallons of dyed and perfumed solution of   9
formaldehyde, glycerin, borax, phenol, alcohol and water are soon
circulating through Mr. Jones, whose mouth has been sewn together
with a "needle directed upward between the upper lip and gum and
brought out through the left nostril," with the corners raised slightly
"for a more pleasant expression." If he should be bucktoothed, his
teeth are cleaned with Bon Ami and coated with colorless nail polish.
His eyes, meanwhile, are closed with flesh-tinted eye caps and eye
cement.

The next step is to have at Mr. Jones with a thing called a trocar.   10
This is a long, hollow needle attached to a tube. It is jabbed into the
abdomen, poked around the entrails and chest cavity, the contents of
which are pumped out and replaced with "cavity fluid." This done,
and the hole in the abdomen sewn up, Mr. Jones's face is heavily
creamed (to protect the skin from burns which may be caused by
leakage of the chemicals), and he is covered with a sheet and left
unmolested for a while. But not for long—there is more, much more,
in store for him. He has been embalmed, but not yet restored, and the
best time to start the restorative work is eight to ten hours after
embalming, when the tissues have become firm and dry.

The object of all this attention to the corpse, it must be remem-   11
bered, is to make it presentable for viewing in an attitude of healthy
repose. "Our customs require the presentation of our dead in the
semblance of normality . . . unmarred by the ravages of illness, disease or mutilation," says Mr. J. Sheridan Mayer in his *Restorative Art*.
This is rather a large order since few people die in the full bloom of
health, unravaged by illness and unmarked by some disfigurement.
The funeral industry is equal to the challenge: "In some cases the
gruesome appearance of a mutilated or disease-ridden subject may
be quite discouraging. The task of restoration may seem impossible
and shake the confidence of the embalmer. This is the time for intestinal fortitude and determination. Once the formative work is begun
and affected tissues are cleaned or removed, all doubts of success
vanish. It is surprising and gratifying to discover the results which
may be obtained."

The embalmer, having allowed an appropriate interval to elapse,   12
returns to the attack, but now he brings into play the skill and
equipment of sculptor and cosmetician. Is a hand missing? Casting
one in plaster of Paris is a simple matter. "For replacement purposes,
only a cast of the back of the hand is necessary; this is within the ability

of the average operator and is quite adequate." If a lip or two, a nose or an ear should be missing, the embalmer has at hand a variety of restorative waxes with which to model replacements. Pores and skin texture are simulated by stippling with a little brush, and over this cosmetics are laid on. Head off? Decapitation cases are rather routinely handled. Ragged edges are trimmed, and head joined to torso with a series of splints, wires and sutures. It is a good idea to have a little something at the neck—a scarf or high collar—when time for viewing comes. Swollen mouth? Cut out tissue as needed from inside the lips. If too much is removed, the surface contour can easily be restored by padding with cotton. Swollen necks and cheeks are reduced by removing tissue through vertical incisions made down each side of the neck. "When the deceased is casketed, the pillow will hide the suture incisions . . . as an extra precaution against leakage, the suture may be painted with liquid sealer."

The opposite condition is more likely to present itself—that of emaciation. His hypodermic syringe now loaded with massage cream, the embalmer seeks out and fills the hollowed and sunken areas by injection. In this procedure the backs of the hands and fingers and the under-chin area should not be neglected.   13

Positioning the lips is a problem that recurrently challenges the ingenuity of the embalmer. Closed too tightly, they tend to give a stern, even disapproving expression. Ideally, embalmers feel, the lips should give the impression of being ever so slightly parted, the upper lip protruding slightly for a more youthful appearance. This takes some engineering, however, as the lips tend to drift apart. Lip drift can sometimes be remedied by pushing one or two straight pins through the inner margin of the lower lip and then inserting them between the two front upper teeth. If Mr. Jones happens to have no teeth, the pins can just as easily be anchored in his Armstrong Face Former and Denture Replacer. Another method to maintain lip closure is to dislocate the lower jaw, which is then held in its new position by a wire run through holes which have been drilled through the upper and lower jaws at the midline. As the French are fond of saying, *il faut souffrir pour être belle.*[1]   14

If Mr. Jones has died of jaundice, the embalming fluid will very likely turn him green. Does this deter the embalmer? Not if he has   15

---

[1]You have to suffer if you want to be beautiful (Editors' note).

intestinal fortitude. Masking pastes and cosmetics are heavily laid on, burial garments and casket interiors are color-correlated with particular care, and Jones is displayed beneath rose-colored lights. Friends will say, "How *well* he looks." Death by carbon monoxide, on the other hand, can be rather a good thing from the embalmer's viewpoint: "One advantage is the fact that this type of discoloration is an exaggerated form of a natural pink coloration." This is nice because the healthy glow is already present and needs but little attention.

The patching and filling completed, Mr. Jones is now shaved,   16
washed and dressed. Cream-based cosmetic, available in pink, flesh, suntan, brunette and blond, is applied to his hands and face, his hair is shampooed and combed (and, in the case of Mrs. Jones, set), his hands manicured. For the horny-handed son of toil special care must be taken; cream should be applied to remove ingrained grime, and the nails cleaned. "If he were not in the habit of having them manicured in life, trimming and shaping is advised for better appearance—never questioned by kin."

Jones is now ready for casketing (this is the present participle of   17
the verb "to casket"). In this operation, his right shoulder should be depressed slightly "to turn the body a bit to the right and soften the appearance of lying flat on the back." Positioning the hands is a matter of importance, and special rubber positioning blocks may be used. The hands should be cupped slightly for a more lifelike, relaxed appearance. Proper placement of the body requires a delicate sense of balance. It should lie as high as possible in the casket, yet not so high that the lid, when lowered, will hit the nose. On the other hand, we are cautioned, placing the body too low "creates the impression that the body is in a box."

Jones is next wheeled into the appointed slumber room where a   18
few last touches may be added—his favorite pipe placed in his hand or, if he was a great reader, a book propped into position. (In the case of little Master Jones a Teddy bear may be clutched.) Here he will hold open house for a few days, visiting hours 10 A.M. to 9 P.M.

Meanings and Values

1a.   What is the author's tone? (See Guide to Terms: *Style/Tone.*)

  b.   Try to analyze the effect this tone had, at first reading, on your impressions of the subject matter itself.

c. Form a specific comparison between this effect of tone and the effect of "tone of voice" in spoken language.

2. Why was it formerly "almost mandatory" for some relative to witness the embalming procedure (par. 2)?

3a. Do you believe that public information about this procedure would cost mortuaries much embalming business (par. 3)? Why, or why not?

b. Why *do* people subject their dead to such a process?

4. Use the three-part system of evaluation to judge the success of this process analysis. (Guide: *Evaluation.*)

Expository Techniques

1a. What is the central theme? (Guide: *Unity.*)

b. Which parts of the writing, if any, do not contribute to the theme, thus damaging unity?

c. What other elements of the writing contribute to, or damage, unity?

2a. Beginning with paragraph 4, list or mark the transitional devices that help to bridge paragraphs. (Guide: *Transition.*)

b. Briefly explain how coherence is aided by such interparagraph transitions.

3. In this selection, far more than in most, emphasis can best be studied in connection with style. In fact, the two are almost indistinguishable here, and few, if any, of the other methods of achieving emphasis are used at all. (Guide: *Emphasis* and *Style/Tone.*) Consider each of the following stylistic qualities (some may overlap; others are included in diction) and illustrate, by examples, how each creates emphasis.

a. Number and selection of details—e.g., the equipment and "aids" (par. 5).

b. Understatement—e.g., the "chances of live burial" (par. 7).

c. Special use of quotations—e.g., "that the body is in a box" (par. 17).

d. Sarcasm and/or other forms of irony—e.g., "How *well* he looks" (par. 15). (Guide: *Irony.*)

Diction and Vocabulary

1. Much of the essay's unique style (with resulting emphasis) comes from qualities of diction. Use examples to illustrate the following. (Some may be identical to those of the preceding answer, but they need not be.)

a.   Choice of common, low-key words to achieve sarcasm through under-
     statement—e.g., "This is nice . . ." (par. 15).

b.   Terms of violence—e.g., "returns to the attack" (par. 12).

c.   Terms of the living—e.g., "will hold open house" (par. 18).

d.   The continuing use of "Mr. Jones."

2a. Illustrate the meaning of "connotation" with examples of quotations
     from morticians. (Guide: *Connotation/Denotation.*)

b.   Are these also examples of "euphemism"?

c.   Show how the author uses these facts to her own advantage—i.e.,
     again, to achieve emphasis.

3a. Comment briefly on the quality and appropriateness of the metaphor
     that ends the introduction. (Guide: *Figures of Speech.*)

b.   Is this, in any sense, also an allusion? Why, or why not?

4.   Use the dictionary as needed to understand the meanings of the
     following words: docility, perpetuation (par. 1); inherent, mandatory
     (2); intractable, reticence, *raison d'être* (3); ingenious (5); rudimentary,
     cellular, somatic (7); carotid artery, femoral artery, subclavian vein (8);
     semblance (11); simulated, stippling, sutures (12); emaciation (13);
     dispel (7, title).

Suggestions for Writing and Discussion

1.   What evidence can you find that "the satisfaction of curiosity about
     almost all matters is a national pastime" (par. 2)? Is this a good thing
     or not? Why?

2.   Burial customs differ widely from country to country, sometimes from
     area to area in this country. If you can, describe one of the more
     distinctive customs and, if possible, show its sources—e.g., the climate,
     "old country" tradition.

3.   What do you foresee as near- and far-future trends or radical changes
     in American burial practices? Why?

4.   You may wish to develop further your answers to question 3 of
     "Meanings and Values"—the rationale of a large majority of people
     who do use this mortuary "service" for their departed relatives.

5.   If you like, explain your personal preferences and the reasons for them.

(NOTE: Suggestions for topics requiring development by PROCESS ANALYSIS follow.)

Writing Suggestions for Section 5
Process Analysis

1. From one of the following topics develop a central theme into an *informational* process analysis, showing:

a. How you selected a college.

b. How you selected your future career or major field of study.

c. How your family selected a home.

d. How an unusual sport is played.

e. How religious faith is achieved.

f. How gasoline is made.

g. How the air (or water) in _____ becomes polluted.

h. How lightning kills.

i. How foreign policy is made.

j. How political campaigns are financed.

k. How _____ Church was rebuilt.

l. How fruit blossoms are pollinated.

m. How a computer chip is designed or made.

2. Select a specific reader-audience and write a *directional* process analysis on one of the following topics, showing:

a. How to *do* any of the processes suggested by topics 1a–e. (This treatment will require a different viewpoint, completely objective, and may require a different organization.)

b. How to overcome shyness.

c. How to overcome stage fright.

d. How to make the best use of study time.

e. How to write a college composition.

f. How to sell an ugly house.

g. How to prepare livestock or any other entry for a fair.

h. How to start a club (or some other kind of recurring activity).

i.   How to reduce the number of highway accidents in an area.

j.   How to survive a tornado (or other natural disaster).

k.   How to select a car.

l.   How to sail a boat.

m.   How to set up a fish tank and keep the fish alive and healthy.

n.   How to collect baseball cards.

6

Analyzing *Cause and Effect* Relationships

Unlike process analysis, which merely tells *how,* causal analysis seeks to explain *why.* The two may be combined, but they need not be—many people have driven a car successfully after being told how to do it, never knowing or caring why the thing moved when they turned a key and worked a pedal or two.

Some causes and effects are not very complicated; at least their explanation requires only a simple statement. A car may sit in the garage for a while because its owner has no money for a license tag, and sometimes this is explanation enough. But frequently a much more thorough analysis is required, and this may even become the basic pattern of an exposition.

To explain fully the causes of a war or a depression or election results, the writer must seek not only *immediate* causes (the ones encountered first) but also *ultimate* causes (the basic, underlying factors that help to explain the more apparent ones). Business or professional people, as well as students, often have a pressing need for this type of analysis. How else could they fully understand or report on a failing sales campaign, diminishing church membership, a local increase in traffic accidents, or teenage use of drugs? The immediate cause of a disastrous warehouse fire could be faulty electrical wiring, but this might be attributed in turn to the company's unwise economy measures, which might be traced even further to undue pressures on the management to show large profits. The written analysis might logically stop at any point, of course, depending entirely on its purpose and the reader-audience for which it is intended.

Similarly, both the immediate and ultimate *effects* of an action or situation may, or may not, need to be fully explored. If a five percent pay raise is granted, what will be the immediate effect on the cost of production, leading to what ultimate effects on prices and, in some cases, on the economy of a business, a town, or perhaps the entire nation?

In earlier sections of this book we have seen several examples of causal analysis. In Section 1, for instance, Buckley gives some attention to both immediate and ultimate causes of American apathy, and in Section 4, Wolfe is concerned with both immediate and ultimate effects of overcrowding.

Causal analysis is one of the chief techniques of reasoning; and if the method is used at all, the reader must always have confidence in its thoroughness and logic. Here are some ways to avoid the most common faults in causal reasoning:

1. Never mistake the fact that something happens with or after another occurrence as evidence of a causal relationship—for example, that a black cat crossing the road caused the flat tire a few minutes later, or that a course in English composition caused a student's nervous breakdown that same semester.

2. Consider all possibly relevant factors before attributing causes. Perhaps studying English did result in a nervous breakdown, but the cause may also have been ill health, trouble at home, the stress of working while attending college, or the anguish of a love affair. (The composition course, by providing an "emotional" outlet, may even have helped postpone the breakdown!)

3. Support the analysis by more than mere assertions: offer evidence. It would not often be enough to *tell* why Shakespeare's wise Othello believed the villainous Iago—the dramatist's lines should be used as evidence, possibly supported by the opinions of at least one literary scholar. If you are explaining that capital punishment deters crime, do not expect the reader to take your word for it—give before-and-after statistics or the testimony of reliable authorities.

4. Be careful not to omit any links in the chain of causes or effects unless you are certain that the readers for whom the writing is intended will automatically make the right connections themselves—and this is frequently a dangerous assumption. To unwisely omit one or more of the links might leave the reader with only a vague, or even erroneous, impression of the causal connection, possibly invalidating all that follows and thus making the entire writing ineffective.

5. Be honest and objective. Writers (or thinkers) who bring their old prejudices to the task of causal analysis, or who fail to see the probability of *multiple* causes or effects, are almost certain to distort their analyses or to make them so superficial, so thin, as to be almost worthless.

Ordinarily the method of causal analysis is either to work logically from the immediate cause (or effect) down toward the most basic, or to start with the basic and work up toward the immediate. But after at least analyzing the subject and deciding what the purpose requires in the paragraph or entire composition, the writer will usually find that a satisfactory pattern suggests itself.

Sample Paragraph (Annotated)

A question introduces the phenomenon to be explained.

An *ultimate cause,* though a negative one.

The ultimate cause does not provide a satisfactory explanation for the choice of Palmville.

Immediate causes.

Use of the survey adds authority to the explanation.

Why has Palmville grown so rapidly over the past decade? In response to a survey conducted last year by the Chamber of Commerce, most new residents said the reason they moved to Palmville was to escape from the living conditions in Valley City and its nearest suburbs, especially congestion, air pollution, and high housing costs. Other towns nearby have not grown as rapidly as Palmville, however. On the survey, people also indicated why they chose to move here rather than to other towns in Nocatowie County, such as Lopestown, El Caton, or Fillmore Glen. People say they came to Palmville because of the location. Interstate 104 runs through the town on its way to Valley City, making commuting possible, though taxing. They came because M&T Realty spent a good deal on ads in the *Valley City Times* telling about affordable three-bedroom homes in the town. They came for the good

Taken together, the immediate causes provide a satisfactory explanation for the choice of Palmville.

schools and the nearby lakes and parks. Finally, almost all those surveyed said that they came in part because they were already familiar with the name of the town from the region's most famous agricultural product: The Palmville Onion.

Sample Paragraph (Cause/Effect)

Rap [music] started in discos, not the midtown glitter palaces like Studio 54 or New York, New York, but at Mel Quinn's on 42nd Street and Club 371 in the Bronx, where a young Harlemite who called himself D. J. Hollywood spun on the weekends. It wasn't unusual for black club jocks to talk to their audiences in the jive style of the old personality deejays. Two of the top black club spinners of the day, Pete (D. J.) Jones and Maboya, did so. Hollywood, just an adolescent when he started, created a more complicated, faster style, with more rhymes than his older mentors and call-and-response passages to encourage reaction from the dancers. At local bars, discos, and many illegal after-hours spots frequented by street people, Hollywood developed a huge word-of-mouth reputation. Tapes of his parties began appearing around the city on the then new and incredibly loud Japanese portable cassette players flooding into America. In Harlem, Kurtis Blow, Eddie Cheeba, and D. J. Lovebug Star-ski; in the Bronx, Junebug Star-ski, Grandmaster Flash, and Melle

Mel; in Brooklyn, three kids from the projects called Whodini; and in Queens, Russell and Joey, the two youngest sons from the middle-class Simmons household—all shared a fascination with Hollywood's use of the rhythmic breaks in his club mixes and his verbal dexterity. These kids would all grow up to play a role in the local clubs and, later, a few would appear on the national scene to spread Hollywood's style. Back in the 1970s, while disco reigned in the media, the Black Main Streets of New York were listening to D. J. Hollywood, and learning.

Nelson George, *The Death of Rhythm and Blues.*

BOB GREENE, born in 1947, in Columbus, Ohio, is a columnist for the *Chicago Tribune* and writes regularly for *Esquire* magazine. His daily reports and commentary are syndicated to more than 120 other newspapers in the United States. His articles have appeared in *Newsweek, Harper's, Rolling Stone, New Times,* the *New York Times,* and other publications, and his commentary has been featured on the CBS television and radio networks. Greene has written numerous books, including *We Didn't Have None of Them Fat Funky Angels on the Wall of Heartbreak Hotel* (1971), *Billion Dollar Baby* (1974), *Johnny Deadline, Reporter* (1976), *Good Morning, Merry Sunshine* (1984), *Cheeseburgers* (1985), *Be True to Your School: A Diary of 1964* (1986), and *Homecoming: When the Soldiers Returned from Vietnam* (1989).

Thirty Seconds

Much has been written about the broad influence of television on our lives and culture. In this essay, however, Bob Greene looks at some of the specific consequences a television commercial had for a man who participated in it. In doing so, he also attests to the remarkable power of the medium. "Thirty Seconds" first appeared in Greene's "American Beat" column in *Esquire.*

It's funny how a man can live his whole life—a life filled with heroism   1
and downfalls, fatherhood and courage and pain and introspection—
and no one notices. No one outside the man's family and his small
group of friends.

It's funny what television can do. Take the same man. Film a TV   2
commercial that is brilliantly conceived and executed, and the man
becomes known and revered in every corner of the nation. He is the

same person; nothing at all about him has changed. Nothing except the most important thing of all: he has been televised.

Novelists can write one hundred thousand words, two hundred 3 thousand words, and not cause a ripple. For Bill Demby, it took only fifty-seven words, written by someone else and spoken by an announcer during a thirty-second television commercial, to totally revise his life.

Here are the words: "When Bill Demby was in Vietnam, he 4 dreamed of coming home and playing a little basketball. A dream that all but died when he lost both legs to a Vietcong rocket. But then researchers discovered that a Du Pont plastic could make truly lifelike artificial limbs. Now Bill's back, and some say he hasn't lost a step."

There was a tag line promoting Du Pont. The fifty-seven words 5 about Bill Demby and the Du Pont tag line weren't what was so significant, of course. What was significant was the film footage of Demby—his artificial legs visible to the camera—competing in a game of playground basketball with able-bodied men. It began airing in the fall of 1987, and it became one of those commercials that people think about and talk to their friends about. It won a Clio award from the advertising industry; Demby was featured on the ABC program *20/20*. He went from being completely anonymous to truly famous in a matter of weeks.

When I caught up with him he was heading for a small college 6 in the Midwest to make an address to the students. The basketball arena had been reserved for the event because an overflow crowd was expected.

"I walked into a McDonald's the other day to get something to 7 eat," Bill Demby said. "This guy said hello to me and I said hi back. I thought he was just a friendly guy. But then he said, 'I liked the commercial.' "

Demby, now thirty-eight, was driving a truck on a road outside 8 Quang Tri, Vietnam, on March 26, 1971, when a Vietcong rocket hit the vehicle. A twenty-year-old Army private at the time, he lost both legs below the knee. He spent the next year in Walter Reed hospital in Washington, and then tried to put his life back together.

Nothing very spectacular happened. He had problems with 9 alcohol and drugs. A promising athlete before going to Vietnam, Demby—with the help of artificial legs—began trying to play sports again. He was in Nashville in 1987 at a basketball tournament spon-

sored by the U.S. Amputee Athletic Association when he was invited
to audition for a Du Pont commercial. Du Pont had manufactured
some of the materials used in certain prostheses, and had sent representatives of its advertising agency to the amputee tournament.

"I was very wary about doing it," Demby said. "I knew that on   10
television, they can go into the cutting room and put things together
any way they want. As far as the world was concerned at that point,
Bill Demby didn't exist. As an amputee, usually I kept to myself."

Demby and four other disabled men wearing prostheses played   11
basketball with personnel from the BBD&O ad agency looking on,
and all five men submitted to informal interviews. Before long,
Demby was told that he had been selected from the five to be the star
of the Du Pont spot.

He was far from thrilled. "Actually, I called them up and said I   12
was not interested in doing the commercial," Demby said.

I asked him why that was. For the first time in our conversation,   13
he seemed to hesitate, as if a little embarrassed. Finally he said:

" I don't like to take my pants off in front of people." Meaning he 14
doesn't like people to look at his artificial legs. Any people, much less
millions upon millions of television viewers.

But in the end he decided to say yes. The commercial was shot   15
on a basketball court in New York City, on Columbus Avenue between
Seventy-sixth and Seventy-seventh streets, in late August 1987. "They
told us that we were just supposed to play basketball, and that they'd
film it," Demby said. "The other guys weren't actors—they were just
players from the neighborhood. Players without physical disabilities.

"We played basketball from 7:00 in the morning until 6:30 at   16
night. I got very tired. They had rented a room for me at the Warwick
Hotel, and when the filming was over I just went to my room, took a
shower, and fell asleep with the television set on. When I woke up the
next morning the TV was still going. I didn't think much about what
had happened. I just thought I had played some pickup basketball
and they had filmed it, and now I would go back to my regular life. I
went home that day. I felt that nothing had changed."

The advertising agency put the commercial together quickly.   17
Demby and his family, who live near Washington, D.C., received a
telephone call advising them to watch the CBS *Sunday Morning* broadcast on September 13, 1987. That was the day the commercial first
aired.

"My wife and daughter and I sat in front of the TV set," Demby   18
said. "The commercial came on. The wonderful feeling . . . there are
no words to describe it."

The first time Demby realized that something unusual was up   19
came within a few weeks. "I was walking down the street in Washington, and this real huge guy started staring right into my eyes. I was
kind of scared. He said, 'It's you. It's you.' I didn't know what he was
talking about. I thought that maybe he was going to rob me or
something. I said, 'No, no.' And then the guy said, 'You're the one in
the commercial. It's the best one I've ever seen.' "

Since that moment, Demby has become used to the public recog-   20
nition. Sometimes he doesn't much like it. "On occasion it still sur-
prises me when people look at me," he said. "It shouldn't, but it does.
Once in a while when someone will ask me about the commercial I'll
find myself saying, 'No, that was my twin brother.' "

There are other times, though . . .   21

"A man came up to me—a man who had been having a lot of   22
troubles. He explained the details of his troubles. He told me he had
given up on everything. He said that seeing me in the commercial had
turned him around. He thanked me for changing his life. Me.

"I walked away so that he wouldn't see me cry."   23

Soon everything was happening for Demby. He went to a New   24
York Knicks basketball game—he had never even been inside Madi-
son Square Garden before—and the crowd gave him a long standing
ovation. Moses Malone and Patrick Ewing shook his hand.

He began to be invited to speak before large groups, such as the   25
college audience he was on his way to address when I joined him. The
20/20 segment was filmed. The irony, of course, was that he was the
same man he had been for the almost twenty years after he had
returned from Vietnam. But because of those thirty seconds on the Du
Pont commercial (a sixty-second version also ran), for the first time in
his life people were treating him as if he were special.

"It was very hard to get used to," Demby said. He was inter-   26
viewed by newspapers and magazines; suddenly people saw him as
a symbol of bravery and hope. He knew that if the commercial had
not been broadcast, the same people would stare right through him
as though he were invisible. Now they adored him.

Not everything made him feel great. "For a long time, I had been   27
hesitant to tell people that I had lost my legs in Vietnam," he said. "I'd
always wear long pants, even when I was playing sports. But now
everyone knows what my legs look like.

"And my past problem with alcohol and PCP . . . that was my   28
private problem, and now it's out. My daughter was eight years old,
and she didn't know about it. She probably never would have, if the
commercial hadn't been filmed and people hadn't started talking
about me. She was very hurt by it. I tried to explain. I told her, 'It was
just a bad part in Daddy's life. He was weak.' "

There is one aspect of the commercial that Demby virtually never   29
volunteers to talk about. The standard line is that the film crew just
shot the pickup basketball game and edited the footage down. The
most emotional moment in the commercial comes when Demby is
knocked to the ground, hard, by an opposing player. On his back, he
stares up. Then he gets to his feet. It is one of those magical television
instants—a second or two of film that gives the audience goose bumps
and stays with them for a long time.

"That didn't happen during the game," Demby said. "We had   30
been playing all day, and finally the director, Rick Levine, called me
aside. He said he needed something else. He asked me if I would mind
if he had one of the players knock me down."

It must have been quite a question. Imagine saying to a man with   31
artificial legs: "Listen, we know you've been playing basketball for
hours, but would it be okay if we had you jump in the air and then
we pushed you to the concrete so that you land on your back? We'll
only need to do it a few times."

Demby thought about it and said yes. He figured that Levine   32
must know what he was doing. It paid off; without that sequence—
especially the expression in Demby's eyes after he hits the ground—
the commercial would lose its strongest surge of visceral humanity
and power. Still, though: imagine asking the question.

Now, with all that has happened to Demby, you have to remind   33
yourself that there were four other finalists for the starring role in the
commercial, and that if BBD&O had selected any one of those four,
today no one would know who Bill Demby is. Demby said that he has
not heard from or seen the other four since auditioning. He got the
thirty seconds; they didn't.

He does his best to keep it in perspective. There are days now 34 when he feels it would be impossible to be any more famous and respected. "But I know that just as fast as this has come, it can leave. It could turn out to be a very temporary thing.

"I have a tendency to think we're all sort of crazy. The idea that 35 thirty seconds could completely change a man's life." He tries not to lose sight of the fact that with or without the commercial, he would still be Bill Demby.

He is finally accepting the idea that strangers will approach him 36 and tell him how much they admire him. "That's just society, though," he said. "That's just people reacting to what they've seen on their television screen.

"I keep having this thought. One of these days the commercial is 37 going to stop running. They all do.

"And not long after that, someone is going to say to someone else, 38 'Hey, do you remember that guy—the amputee who played basketball in that commercial?'

"And the other guy will hesitate for a second and then say, 'Yeah, 39 I think so. What was his name?' "

Meanings and Values

1a.   List the positive effects of the commercial.

 b.   The negative effects.

 c.   Explain why you think the author wants us to consider the commercial on the whole as either harmful or beneficial.

2a.   Is the primary focus of this essay on what happened to Bill Demby as a result of the commercial? Or is it on the power of television to affect our lives and attitudes? Be ready to support your answer with evidence from the essay.

 b.   How would you describe the main purpose or purposes of the essay? (See Guide to Terms: *Purpose*.)

 c.   If you believe the essay has more than one important purpose, explain why it should (or should not) be considered unified. (Guide: *Unity*.)

3.   The subject of this essay is one that many writers might be tempted to handle in a sentimental manner. To what extent does Greene's treatment avoid sentimentality, if at all? (Guide: *Sentimentality*.)

4.   Do you remember seeing this commercial on television? Does your memory of the commercial and its effectiveness agree with Greene's account?

Expository Techniques

1a. In which parts of the essay does Greene discuss causes?

  b. Effects?

2. Should paragraphs 1–3 or 1–6 be considered the introduction to this essay? Why?

3a. Identify the uses of parallelism in the first two paragraphs of the essay. (Guide: *Parallel Structure.*)

  b. How does the author use parallel structures to emphasize the central theme of the essay? (Guide: *Emphasis.*)

4. At several places in the essay, Greene talks about the men who were considered for the commercial but not chosen. To what extent do these discussions detract from the essay's unity or contribute to its central theme? (Guide: *Unity.*)

5. In what ways does Greene's frequent use of quotations from Bill Demby add to the effectiveness of the essay? (Guide: *Evaluation.*)

Diction and Vocabulary

1. Discuss how Greene uses diction and sentence structure to create drama and tension in paragraphs 29, 31, and 32. (Guide: *Diction, Syntax.*)

2. If you do not know the meaning of any of the following words, look them up in the dictionary: introspection (par. 1); prostheses (9); visceral (32).

Suggestions for Writing and Discussion

1. The commercial described in this essay may represent a growing interest in the effects of the Vietnam war on both those who fought in it and those who did not. What other evidence of this growing interest can you identify?

2. Is Demby's prediction about his anonymity after the commercial stops running likely to come true (pars. 37–39)? Why, or why not?

3. If you believe television is as powerful as Greene suggests, can you cite some other examples of its effects?

(NOTE: Suggestions for topics requiring development by analysis of CAUSE AND EFFECT are on pages 265–266, at the end of this section.)

NANCY MAIRS

NANCY MAIRS was born in Long Beach, California, in 1943. She graduated from Wheaton College in 1964 and worked from 1966 to 1972 as a technical editor at the Smithsonian Astrophysical Observatory, the MIT Press, and Harvard Law School. She has lived in Tucson, Arizona, since 1972. Mairs has been a teacher of composition in both high school and college and has received an M.F.A. in creative writing and a Ph.D. in English literature. A volume of her poems, *In All the Rooms of the Yellow House* (1984), was given first prize for poetry in the Western States Book Awards. A volume of her essays entitled *Plaintext: Deciphering a Woman's Life* appeared in 1986 and another, *Carnal Acts,* was published in 1990. She has also written a memoir, *Remembering the Bone House* (1989).

On Being a Scientific Booby

In this essay from *Plaintext*, Nancy Mairs looks back at her freshman college course in biology and forward toward her daughter's college career. Mairs's discussion of her difficult experiences in biology class should be easy to understand for any student who has struggled with a particular teacher or course. In addition to cause and effect, the essay makes use of comparison and examples.

My daughter is dissecting a chicken. Her first. Her father, whose job   1
this usually is, has been derelict in his duties, and my hands are now too weak to dissect much more than a zucchini. If she wants dinner (and she does), she will make this pale, flabby carcass into eight pieces I can fit into the skillet. I act as coach. To encourage her, I tell her that her great-great-grandfather was a butcher. This is true, not something I have made up to con her into doing a nasty job.

Now that she's gotten going, she is having a wonderful time. She   2
has made the chicken crow and flap and dance all over the cutting
board, and now it lies quiet under her short, strong fingers as she slices
the length of its breastbone. She pries back the ribs and peers into the
cavity. "Oh, look at its mesenteries!" she cries. I tell her I thought
mesentery was something you got from drinking the water in Mexico.
She pokes at some filmy white webs. Mesenteries, she informs me, are
the membranes that hold the chicken's organs in place. My organs too.
She flips the chicken over and begins to cut along its spine. As her
fingers search out joints and the knife severs wing from breast, leg
from thigh, she gives me a lesson in the comparative anatomy of this
chicken and the frog she and her friend Emily have recently dissected
at school.

I am charmed by her enthusiasm and self-assurance. Since she   3
was quite small, she has talked of becoming a veterinarian, and now
that she is approaching adulthood, her purpose is growing firmer.
During this, her junior year in a special high school, she is taking a
college-level introductory course in biology. I took much the same
course when I was a freshman in college. But if I entered that course
with Anne's self-confidence, and I may very well have done so, I
certainly had none of it by the time I wrote the last word of my final
examination in my blue book and turned it in the following spring.
As the result of Miss White and the quadrat report, I am daunted to
the point of dysfunction by the notion of thinking or writing "scien-
tifically."

That woman—damn that woman!—turned me into a scientific   4
cripple, and did so in the name of science at a prestigious women's
college that promised to school me in the liberal arts that I might "have
life and have it abundantly." And really, I have had it abundantly, so
I suppose I oughtn't to complain if it's been a little short in *Paramecia*
and *Amanita phalloides* and *Drosophila melanogaster,* whose eyes I have
never seen.

Still. Miss White should not have been allowed to teach freshman   5
biology because she had a fatal idiosyncrasy (fatal, that is, to the
courage of students, not to herself, though I believe she is dead now
of some unrelated cause): She could not bear a well-written report.
One could be either a writer or a scientist but not both, she told me
one November afternoon, the grey light from a tall window sinking
into the grain of the dark woodwork in her cramped office in the old
Science Building, her fingers flicking the sheets of my latest lab

write-up. She was washing her hands of me, I could tell by the weariness of her tone. She didn't even try to make me a scientist. For that matter, she didn't even point to a spot where I'd gone wrong and show me what she wanted instead. She simply wrinkled her nose at the odor of my writing, handed me the sheets, and sent me away. We never had another conference. At the end of the semester, I wrote my quadrat report, and Miss White failed it. She allowed me to rewrite it. I wrote it again, and she failed it again. Neither of us went for a third try.

All the same, I liked my quadrat, which was a twenty-by-twenty   6
plot in the College Woods behind the Library. Mine was drab compared to some others: Pam Weprin's, I remember, had a brook running through it, in which she discovered goldfish. It turned out that her magical discovery had a drab explanation: In a heavy rain the water from Peacock Pond backed up and spilled its resident carp into the brook. Even so, her quadrat briefly held an excitement mine never did. Mine was, in fact, as familiar as a living room, since i had spent large portions of my youth tramping another such woods sixty miles north. The lichen grew on the north side of the trees. In the rain the humus turned black and rank. Afterwards, a fallen log across one corner would sprout ears of tough, pale fungus.

Each freshman biology student received a quadrat. There were   7
enough of us that we had to double up, but I never met my quadrat-mate or even knew her name. It occurs to me now that I ought to have found out, ought to have asked her what she got on her quadrat report, but I was new to failure and knew no ways to profit from it. I simply did as I was told—visited my quadrat to observe its progress through the seasons and wrote up my observations—and then discovered that I had somehow seen and spoken wrong. I wish now that I had kept the report. I wonder exactly what I said in it. Probably something about ears of fungus, Good God.

With a D+ for the first semester I continued, perversely, to like   8
biology, but I also feared it more and more. Not the discipline itself. I pinned and opened a long earthworm, marveling at the delicately tinted organs. I dissected a beef heart, carefully, so as not to spoil it for stuffing and roasting at the biology department's annual beef-heart feast. For weeks I explored the interior of my rat, which I had opened neatly, like the shutters over a window. He was a homely thing, stiff, his fur yellow and matted from formaldehyde, and because he was male, not very interesting. Several students got pregnant females, and

I envied them the intricate organs, the chains of bluish-pink fetuses. At the end of each lab, I would reluctantly close the shutters, swaddle my rat in his plastic bag, and slip him back into the crock.

No, biology itself held more fascination and delight than fear. But with each report I grew more terrified of my own insidious poetic nature, which Miss White sniffed out in the simplest statement about planaria or left ventricles. Years later, when I became a technical editor and made my living translating the garbled outbursts of scientists, I learned that I had done nothing much wrong. My understanding was limited, to be sure, but Miss White would have forgiven me ignorance, even stupidity I think, if I had sufficiently muddled the language. As it was, I finished biology with a C–, and lucky I was to get it, since the next year the college raised the passing grade from C– to C. I have always thought, indeed, that the biology department awarded me a passing grade simply so that they wouldn't have to deal with me another year. 9

And they didn't. Nor did anyone else. I never took another science course, although I surprised myself long afterward by becoming, perforce and precipitously, a competent amateur herpetologist. My husband arrived home one afternoon with a shoebox containing a young bull snake, or gopher snake as this desert variety is called, which he had bought for a quarter from some of his students at a school for emotionally disturbed boys so that they wouldn't try to find out how long a snake keeps wriggling without its head. This was Ferdinand, who was followed by two more bull snakes, Squeeze and Beowulf, and by a checkered garter snake named Winslow J. Tweed, a black racer named Jesse Owens, a Yuma king snake named Hrothgar, and numerous nameless and short-lived blind snakes, tiny and translucent, brought to us by our cats Freya, Burton Rustle, and Vanessa Bell. I grew so knowledgeable that when my baby boa constrictor, Crictor, contracted a respiratory ailment, I found that I was more capable of caring for him than were any of the veterinarians in the city. In fact, I learned, veterinarians do not do snakes; I could find only one to give Crictor the shot of a broad-spectrum antibiotic he needed. 10

So I do do snakes. I have read scientific treatises on them. I know that the Latin name for the timber rattlesnake is *Crotalus horridus horridus*. I know that Australia has more varieties of venomous snakes than any other continent, among them the lethal sea snakes and the willfully aggressive tiger snake. I know how long one is likely to live 11 after being bitten by a mamba (not long). I read the treatises; but I don't, of course, write them. Although as a technical editor I grew proficient at unraveling snarls in the writing of scientists, I have never, since Miss White, attempted scientific experimentation or utterance.

Aside from my venture into herpetology, I remain a scientific booby. I mind my stupidity. I feel diminished by it. And I know now that it is unnecessary, the consequence of whatever quirk of fate brought me into Miss White's laboratory instead of Miss Chidsey's or Dr. McCoy's. Miss White, who once represented the whole of scientific endeavor to me, was merely a woman with a hobbyhorse. I see through her. Twenty years later, I am now cynical enough to write a quadrat report badly enough to pass her scrutiny, whereas when I had just turned seventeen I didn't even know that cynicism was an option—knowledge that comes, I suppose, from having life abundantly. I've learned, too, that Miss White's bias, though unusually strong, was not peculiar to herself but arose from a cultural rift between the humanities and the sciences resulting in the assumption that scientists will naturally write badly, that they are, in fact, rhetorical boobies. Today I teach technical writing. My students come to me terrified of the word-world from which they feel debarred, and I teach them to breach the boundaries in a few places, to step with bravado at least a little way inside. Linguistic courage is the gift I can give them.

In return, they give me gifts that I delight in—explanations of vortex centrifuges, evaluations of copper-smelting processes, plans for extracting gums from paloverde beans. These help me compensate for my deficiencies, as do the works of the popularizers of science. Carl Sagan, Loren Eiseley, Lewis Thomas and his reverential reflections subtitled *Notes of a Biology Watcher*, Stephen Jay Gould, James Burke and Jacob Bronowski, Pierre Teilhard de Chardin, John McPhee, who has made me love rocks, Isaac Asimov, Elaine Morgan. I watch television too. *Nova*, *Odyssey*, *The Undersea World of Jacques Cousteau*, *The Body in Question*. But always I am aware that I am having translated for me the concepts of worlds I will never now explore for myself. I stand with my toes on the boundaries, peering, listening.

Anne has done a valiant job with the chicken. She's had a little trouble keeping its pajamas on, and one of the thighs has a peculiar trapezoidal shape, but she's reduced it to a workable condition. I brown it in butter and olive oil. I press in several cloves of garlic and then splash in some white wine. As I work, I think of the worlds Anne is going to explore. Some of them are listed in the college catalogues

12

13

14

she's begun to collect: "Genetics, Energetics, and Evolution"; "Histology of Animals"; "Vertebrate Endocrinology"; "Electron Microscopy"; "Organic Synthesis"; "Animal Morphogenesis."

Anne can write. No one has yet told her that she can be a scientist   15
or a writer but not both, and I trust that no one ever will. The complicated world can ill afford such lies to its children. As she plunges from my view into the thickets of calculus, embryology, and chemical thermodynamics, I will wait here for her to send me back messages. I love messages.

Meanings and Values

1a.   Summarize Miss White's view of the relationship between scientists and writers, that is, between science and good writing.

 b.   Summarize the author's view of the relationship.

2a.   Identify the causes that led to the author's becoming "a scientific cripple."

 b.   Point out evidence in the story that indicates that the author is not quite the "scientific booby" she claims to be.

3.   What is the "cultural rift" that Mairs discusses in paragraph 12? To what extent do your experiences confirm or fail to confirm the existence of such a split?

4.   Are many readers likely to recognize the authors and television programs mentioned in paragraph 13? What effect are these references likely to have on readers who recognize most or all of them? On readers who recognize few or none of them?

Expository Techniques

1a.   What incident does Mairs use to open the essay?

 b.   How is it related to the subject and theme of the essay? (See Guide to Terms: *Unity*.)

2.   In what ways are the opening and closing of the essay related? (Guide: *Introductions, Closings*.)

3.   Discuss how the essay makes use of the following patterns:

 a.   narrative

 b.   comparison

 c.   example

4.   Despite the presence of these other patterns, why should this piece be classified as a cause-effect essay?

Diction and Vocabulary

1a.   The names of some of the snakes and cats in paragraph 10 are allusions. Identify as many of the allusions as you can. (Guide: *Figures of Speech*.)

 b.   What do these allusions suggest about the author's attitude toward both language and science?

2a.   Identify the metaphor in the closing paragraph. (Guide: *Figures of Speech*.)

 b.   Why is it appropriate for this essay?

3a.   In what ways is the diction in paragraphs 6 and 8 characteristic of a writer (and poet) rather than a scientist? (Guide: *Diction*.)

 b.   How might the diction be altered to turn the passages into good scientific writing?

4a.   Is an understanding of the scientific terms the author uses necessary to grasp the meaning of the essay?

 b.   If not, what roles do they play?

5.   If you do not understand the following phrases, consult a dictionary: "daunted to the point of dysfunction" (par. 3); "perforce and precipitously" (10); "a scientific booby" (12, title); "a woman with a hobbyhorse" (12).

Suggestions for Writing and Discussion

1.   In what ways do your experiences in science classes resemble or differ from the author's?

2.   Why are science magazines and television shows so popular?

3.   Prepare an essay of your own telling how a particular class or teacher made you love (or hate) an area of study.

(NOTE: Suggestions for topics requiring development by analysis of CAUSE AND EFFECT are on pages 265–266, at the end of this section.)

SUSAN PERRY AND JIM DAWSON

SUSAN PERRY is a former staff writer for Time-Life, Inc., and now works full-time as a freelance writer specializing in health, business, and women's issues. Her articles have appeared in such publications as *Ms.,* the *Washington Post,* and the *Minneapolis Star.*

JAMES DAWSON is a science reporter who writes regularly for the *Minneapolis Star-Tribune.* Recently Perry and Dawson co-authored *The Secrets Our Body Clocks Reveal* (1988).

What's Your Best Time of Day?

This essay, published as a magazine article, is drawn from *The Secrets Our Body Clocks Reveal.* The piece opens with examples of some puzzling behaviors, looks at their causes in the rhythms of our bodies, then examines some further effects of these rhythms. Along the way it provides some practical advice for taking the best advantage of the biological patterns that help govern our lives. As might be expected, the authors draw on a variety of patterns to accomplish these tasks, including classification, process, and the use of examples.

Every fall, Jane, a young mother and part-time librarian, begins to eat   1
more and often feels sleepy. Her mood is also darker, especially when
she awakens in the morning; it takes all her energy just to drag herself
out of bed. These symptoms persist until April, when warmer weather
and longer days seem to lighten her mood and alleviate her cravings
for food and sleep.

Joseph, a 48-year-old engineer for a Midwestern computer com-   2
pany, feels cranky early in the morning. But as the day progresses, he
becomes friendlier and more accommodating.

248

All living organisms, from mollusks to men and women, exhibit 3 biological rhythms. Some are short and can be measured in minutes or hours. Others last days or months. The peaking of body temperature, which occurs in most people every evening, is a daily rhythm. The menstrual cycle is a monthly rhythm. The increase in sexual drive in the autumn—not in the spring, as poets would have us believe—is a seasonal, or yearly, rhythm.

The idea that our bodies are in constant flux is fairly new—and 4 goes against traditional medical training. In the past, many doctors were taught to believe the body has a relatively stable, or homeostatic, internal environment. Any fluctuations were considered random and not meaningful enough to be studied.

As early as the 1940s, however, some scientists questioned the 5 homeostatic view of the body. Franz Halberg, a young European scientist working in the United States, noticed that the number of white blood cells in laboratory mice was dramatically higher and lower at different times of day. Gradually, such research spread to the study of other rhythms in other life forms, and the findings were sometimes startling. For example, the time of day when a person receives X-ray or drug treatment for cancer can affect treatment benefits and ultimately mean the difference between life and death.

This new science is called chronobiology, and the evidence sup- 6 porting it has become increasingly persuasive. Along the way, the scientific and medical communities are beginning to rethink their ideas about how the human body works, and gradually what had been considered a minor science just a few years ago is being studied in major universities and medical centers around the world. There are even chronobiologists working for the National Aeronautics and Space Administration, as well as for the National Institutes of Health and other government laboratories.

With their new findings, they are teaching us things that can 7 literally change our lives—by helping us organize ourselves so we can work *with* our natural rhythms rather than against them. This can enhance our outlook on life as well as our performance at work and play.

Because they are easy to detect and measure, more is known of 8 daily—or circadian (Latin for "about a day")—rhythms than other types. The most obvious daily rhythm is the sleep/wake cycle. But there are other daily cycles as well: temperature, blood pressure, hormone levels. Amid these and the body's other changing rhythms, you are simply a different person at 9 A.M. than you are at 3 P.M. How you feel, how well you work, your level of alertness, your sensitivity to taste and smell, the degree with which you enjoy food or take pleasure in music—all are changing throughout the day.

Most of us seem to reach our peak of alertness around noon. Soon   9
after that, alertness declines, and sleepiness may set in by midafternoon.

Your short-term memory is best during the morning—in fact,   10
about 15 percent more efficient than at any other time of day. So, students, take heed: when faced with a morning exam, it really does pay to review your notes right before the test is given.

Long-term memory is different. Afternoon is the best time for   11
learning material that you want to recall days, weeks or months later. Politicians, business executives or others who must learn speeches would be smart to do their memorizing during that time of day. If you are a student, you would be wise to schedule your more difficult classes in the afternoon, rather than in the morning. You should also try to do most of your studying in the afternoon, rather than late at night. Many students believe they memorize better while burning the midnight oil because their short-term recall is better during the wee hours of the morning than in the afternoon. But short-term memory won't help them much several days later, when they face the exam.

By contrast, we tend to do best on cognitive tasks—things that   12
require the juggling of words and figures in one's head—during the morning hours. This might be a good time, say, to balance a checkbook.

Your manual dexterity—the speed and coordination with which   13
you perform complicated tasks with your hands—peaks during the afternoon hours. Such work as carpentry, typing or sewing will be a little easier at this time of day.

What about sports? During afternoon and early evening, your   14
coordination is at its peak, and you're able to react the quickest to an outside stimulus—like a baseball speeding toward you at home plate. Studies have also shown that late in the day, when your body temperature is peaking, you will *perceive* a physical workout to be easier and less fatiguing—whether it actually is or not. That means you are more likely to work harder during a late-afternoon or early-evening workout, and therefore benefit more from it. Studies involving swimmers, runners, shot-putters and rowing crews have shown consistently that performance is better in the evening than in the morning.

In fact, all of your senses—taste, sight, hearing, touch and smell— may be at their keenest during late afternoon and early evening. That could be why dinner usually tastes better to us than breakfast and why bright lights irritate us at night. 15

Even our perception of time changes from hour to hour. Not only does time seem to fly when you're having fun, but it also seems to fly even faster if you are having that fun in the late afternoon or early evening, when your body temperature is also peaking. 16

While all of us follow the same general pattern of ups and downs, the exact timing varies from person to person. It all depends on how your "biological" day is structured—how much of a morning or night person you are. The earlier your biological day gets going, the earlier you are likely to enter—and exit—the peak times for performing various tasks. An extreme morning person and an extreme night person may have circadian cycles that are a few hours apart. 17

Each of us can increase our knowledge about our individual rhythms. Learn how to listen to the inner beats of your body; let them set the pace of your day. You will live a healthier—and happier—life. As no less an authority than the Bible tells us, "To every thing there is a season, and a time to every purpose under heaven." 18

Meanings and Values

1. In what ways are the patterns illustrated or discussed in the first three paragraphs similar to each other?

2. According to the explanations in this essay, what are the best times to undertake the following activities, and why:

   a. play a sport

   b. balance a checkbook

   c. learn a speech

   d. prepare for an exam

Expository Techniques

1. What functions do the examples that open the essay perform for readers? (Guide: *Introductions.*)

2a. Where in the essay do the authors use classification and for what purposes is it employed?

b. Where and for what purposes do the authors use process analysis?

3. Would this essay be more effective if discussions of the causes and the effects were more clearly separated? Why, or why not? (Guide: *Evaluation*.)

4. Discuss the arrangement of paragraphs 9–12, paying special attention to parallel structures and transitions within and between paragraphs. (Guide: *Unity, Parallel Structure*.)

Diction and Vocabulary

1. In what ways does the diction in paragraphs 1 and 2 emphasize the contrasts being illustrated? (Guide: *Diction*.)

2. Discuss how the authors provide explanations of the following scientific or otherwise unfamiliar terms in the text so that readers will not have to pause to look them up: homeostatic (par. 4); circadian (8); cognitive tasks (12); manual dexterity (13).

3. Does the allusion that concludes the essay seem appropriate? Why, or why not? Try looking up the passage in the Bible (Ecclesiastes 3:1) to see if its original meaning is similar to the one it has in the context of this essay.

Suggestions for Writing and Discussion

1. Do your experiences confirm what the authors say about the cycles that guide our behavior? Provide examples that either support or contradict the essay's conclusions.

2. How might typical academic or work schedules be altered to take into account the patterns described in this selection? What common practices seem particularly in need of change given the information provided here?

(NOTE: Suggestions for topics requiring development by analysis of CAUSE AND EFFECT are on pages 265–266, at the end of this section.)

ELLEN GOODMAN

ELLEN GOODMAN was born in 1941 in Boston, where she now lives. She was graduated cum laude from Radcliffe College and then spent a year at Harvard on a Nieman Fellowship. Goodman has been with the *Boston Globe* as a reporter since 1967 and, since 1974, has been a full-time columnist. Her "At Large" columns are now published in over two hundred newspapers across the country, and her commentaries have been broadcast on both television and radio. Goodman's work has also appeared in *McCall's,* the *Village Voice, Family Circle, Harper's Bazaar,* and many other publications, and she has been the recipient of various journalistic honors and awards, including the 1980 Pulitzer Prize for distinguished commentary. Her columns have been collected in *Close to Home* (1979), *Turning Points* (1979), *At Large* (1981), *Keeping in Touch* (1986), and *Making Sense* (1990).

Children Lost and Found

Expository writing often focuses on a surprising phenomenon or problem then looks at its causes (and sometimes effects). This is the general approach taken by Goodman in her concise and effective essay, originally a newspaper column. As you read, pay attention also to her ability to provide brief yet compelling examples.

In a supermarket in Maine there is a poster of a girl. It says that she is missing. There are other such faces: boys and girls, three years old, eleven years old, eight years old, hanging like "the most wanted" in public places. Some are on the highway toll gates, others on the Chicago subways, or on milk cartons, or on gas bills. All of them are missing.

In New Jersey last winter, they began fingerprinting 44,000 school children. In North Carolina, they put microdots into the molars of some children. At Tufts University, they developed a technique for toothprints. These are in case, just in case, children are ever missing.

Over the past year or more, the alarm about the abduction of children has been raised everywhere. A television special or two, a talk show or a hundred. A hot line: Dial 800-THE-LOST. Congress declared a National Missing Children's Day. The media rounded up the usual statistics: 1.5 million children missing, 50,000 a year abducted. 3

It has taken all this time for the facts to catch up with our bleakest fears. 4

Now, just now, we hear that there are not 50,000 children a year abducted by strangers. Child Find in New York has altered their estimate to 600 such kidnappings, and the FBI says 67 were reported in 1984. Nor are there 1.5 million missing children in this country. The FBI estimates, rather, 32,000. 5

Among the missing, the overwhelming majority—two thirds, three quarters, 90 percent (there are different figures from different people)—are runaways and, as they say now, throwaways. Of the rest, perhaps as many as 90 percent have been taken by one parent from another in a disintegrating family. 6

Are those children all at risk? Absolutely, but this is not the fear that grips most parents who let a child walk to school for the first time, who leave the children alone in the house, who lose a preschooler in the shopping center, who wait for a child to come home from school, and wait and wait. It is the strangers that we fear. 7

It is impossible to exaggerate the pain of those parents who have lost a child. It is incalculable, inconsolable. But it is easy to exaggerate the risk, and in these months, the fear has been fanned out of all proportion to the reality. 8

I think it's worth asking why. Why, now, is there such a receptive audience for this primal anxiety? It isn't just the misused statistics that causes an epidemic of concern. There must be some particular vulnerability in parents today. 9

The terror of losing a child is a staple of mythology as well as nightmares. Village folklore was full of stories about strangers who stole children. Gypsies were the vagrants and suspects. In those days, communities were tight enough that the only strangers were rootless outsiders. 10

Today, more and more of us are outsiders, strangers on our own streets. The cities are bigger, neighborhoods less stable. The ratio of 11 strangers to friends, strangers to families, has changed dramatically. This is, I think, at the root of our insecurity.

In this same world, we routinely place our children in the hands 12 of people we hardly know. The doctor at the clinic, the teacher at school, the swimming counselor, the bus driver. It is not a coincidence that the fear of child abduction is heightened at a time when more of us leave small children in day care outside their home and family than ever before.

When we tell our children—as we must—to beware of strangers, 13 the number of people wearing that label is much larger than it once was. The more time they spend away from us, the more unknown their world, the more easily our anxiety can be tapped.

The victims of abduction deserve their priority, deserve all the 14 sophisticated methods of discovery in our arsenal. But the victims of hysteria should wonder about the strangeness of our lives. Fear grows irrationally in a world without communities where we know the names of children only when they appear on a milk carton, on a tollbooth or on a poster in a supermarket.

Meanings and Values

1a. State in your own words the phenomenon or problem whose causes Goodman investigates.

 b. What evidence does she offer to show that the problem is significant and that its causes are worth investigating?

2. List the causes Goodman identifies, labeling them as immediate and ultimate.

3. Is her explanation of the causes convincing? Why, or why not? (See Guide to Terms: *Evaluation.*)

Expository Techniques

1a. What strategy does Goodman use to begin the essay? (Guide: *Introductions.*)

 b. To conclude it. (Guide: *Conclusions.*)

2. What is the role of the rhetorical question in paragraph 9? (Guide: *Rhetorical Questions.*)

3a. As is often the case in newspaper columns, the paragraphs in this essay are relatively short. What is their average length?

b. Which ones, if any, might be combined?

c. Which might be expanded, and what could be added to them?

Diction and Vocabulary

1a. What is the effect of the repetition of the words "missing" and "abducted" in paragraphs 1–5?

b. The repetition of the word "strangers" and similar words in paragraphs 10–14?

2. How do the transitional devices in paragraphs 4–8 announce and emphasize the contrast the author is making? (Guide: *Transition.*)

Suggestions for Writing and Discussion

1. Discuss a common fear or problem you feel is exaggerated, and try to identify the reasons (causes) people are so concerned about it.

2. If you have read William Severini Kowinski's "Kids in the Mall: Growing Up Controlled" (pp. 257–262), compare his view of the way children are raised and educated in our society with Goodman's.

3. What other explanations might there be for the widespread fear of kidnapping?

(NOTE: Suggestions for topics requiring development by analysis of CAUSE AND EFFECT are on pages 265–266, at the end of this section.)

WILLIAM SEVERINI KOWINSKI

WILLIAM SEVERINI KOWINSKI grew up in Greensburg, Pennsylvania. In 1964, the year before the first mall was built in Greensburg, he left to attend Knox College in Illinois. While attending Knox he spent a semester studying in the fiction and poetry workshops at the University of Iowa. Kowinski was a writer and editor for the Boston *Phoenix* and the Washington *Newsworks* and has written articles for a number of national newspapers and magazines including *Esquire, New Times,* and the *New York Times Magazine.* His book *The Malling of America: An Inside Look at the Great Consumer Paradise* (1985) is based on his travels to malls throughout the United States and Canada.

Kids in the Mall: Growing Up Controlled

Over the past twenty years, the number, size, and variety of suburban shopping malls have grown at astonishing rates, replacing, in many cases, both plazas and urban shopping districts. They are now important economic and cultural forces in American and Canadian society. In this chapter from *The Malling of America,* Kowinski looks at some of the ways malls have affected the teenagers who spend much of their time shopping, working, or just hanging around at the mall.

Butch heaved himself up and loomed over the group. "Like it was   1
different for me," he piped. "My folks used to drop me off at the shopping mall every morning and leave me all day. It was like a big free baby-sitter, you know? One night they never came back for me.

"Kids in the Mall: Growing Up Controlled" (pp. 349–) from *The Malling of America* by William Severini Kowinski. Copyright © 1985 by William Severini Kowinski. By permission of William Morrow and Company.

Maybe they moved away. Maybe there's some kind of a Bureau of Missing Parents I could check with."

—Richard Peck
Secrets of the Shopping Mall, a
novel for teenagers

From his sister at Swarthmore, I'd heard about a kid in Florida whose   2
mother picked him up after school every day, drove him straight to the mall, and left him there until it closed—all at his insistence. I'd heard about a boy in Washington who, when his family moved from one suburb to another, pedaled his bicycle five miles every day to get back to his old mall, where he once belonged.

These stories aren't unusual. The mall is a common experience   3
for the majority of American youth; they have probably been going there all their lives. Some ran within their first large open space, saw their first fountain, bought their first toy, and read their first book in a mall. They may have smoked their first cigarette or first joint or turned them down, had their first kiss or lost their virginity in the mall parking lot. Teenagers in America now spend more time in the mall than anywhere else but home and school. Mostly it is their choice, but some of that mall time is put in as the result of two-paycheck and single-parent households, and the lack of other viable alternatives. But are these kids being harmed by the mall?

I wondered first of all what difference it makes for adolescents to   4
experience so many important moments in the mall. They are, after all, at play in the fields of its little world and they learn its ways; they adapt to it and make it adapt to them. It's here that these kids get their street sense, only it's mall sense. They are learning the ways of a large-scale artificial environment: its subtleties and flexibilities, its particular pleasures and resonances, and the attitudes it fosters.

The presence of so many teenagers for so much time was not   5
something mall developers planned on. In fact, it came as a big surprise. But kids became a fact of mall life very early, and the International Council of Shopping Centers found it necessary to commission a study, which they published along with a guide to mall managers on how to handle the teenage incursion.

The study found that "teenagers in suburban centers are bored   6
and come to the shopping centers mainly as a place to go. Teenagers in suburban centers spent more time fighting, drinking, littering and walking than did their urban counterparts, but presented fewer over-

all problems." The report observed that "adolescents congregated in groups of two to four and predominantly at locations selected by them rather than management." This probably had something to do with the decision to install game arcades, which allow management to channel these restless adolescents into naturally contained areas away from major traffic points of adult shoppers.

The guide concluded that mall management should tolerate and 7 even encourage the teenage presence because, in the words of the report, "The vast majority support the same set of values as does shopping center management." *The same set of values* means simply that mall kids are already preprogrammed to be consumers and that the mall can put the finishing touches to them as hard-core, lifelong shoppers just like everybody else. That, after all, is what the mall is about. So it shouldn't be surprising that in spending a lot of time there, adolescents find little that challenges the assumption that the goal of life is to make money and buy products, or that just about everything else in life is to be used to serve those ends.

Growing up in a high-consumption society already adds inesti- 8 mable pressure to kids' lives. Clothes consciousness has invaded the grade schools, and popularity is linked with having the best, newest clothes in the currently acceptable styles. Even what they read has been affected. "Miss [Nancy] Drew wasn't obsessed with her wardrobe," noted *The Wall Street Journal*. "But today the mystery in teen fiction for girls is what outfit the heroine will wear next." Shopping has become a survival skill and there is certainly no better place to learn it than the mall, where its importance is powerfully reinforced and certainly never questioned.

The mall as a university of suburban materialism, where Valley 9 Girls and Boys from coast to coast are educated in consumption, has its other lessons in this era of change in family life and sexual mores and their economic and social ramifications. The plethora of products in the mall, plus the pressure on teens to buy them, may contribute to the phenomenon that psychologist David Elkind calls "the hurried child": kids who are exposed to too much of the adult world too quickly, and must respond with a sophistication that belies their still-tender emotional development. Certainly the adult products marketed for children—form-fitting designer jeans, sexy tops for preteen girls—add to the social pressure to look like an adult, along with the home-grown need to understand adult finances (why mothers must work) and adult emotions (when parents divorce).

Kids spend so much time at the mall partly because their parents   10
allow it and even encourage it. The mall is safe, it doesn't seem to
harbor any unsavory activities, and there is adult supervision; it is,
after all, a controlled environment. So the temptation, especially for
working parents, is to let the mall be their babysitter. At least the kids
aren't watching TV. But the mall's role as a surrogate mother may be
more extensive and more profound.

Karen Lansky, a writer living in Los Angeles, has looked into the   11
subject and she told me some of her conclusions about the effects on
its teenaged denizens of the mall's controlled and controlling environment. "Structure is the dominant idea, since true 'mall rats' lack
just that in their home lives," she said, "and adolescents about to make
the big leap into growing up crave more structure than our modern
society cares to acknowledge." Karen pointed out some of the elements malls supply that kids used to get from their families, like
warmth (Strawberry Shortcake dolls and similar cute and cuddly
merchandise), old-fashioned mothering ("We do it all for you," the
fast-food slogan), and even home cooking (the "homemade" treats at
the food court).

The problem in all this, as Karen Lansky sees it, is that while   12
families nurture children by encouraging growth through the assumption of responsibility and then by letting them rest in the bosom
of the family from the rigors of growing up, the mall as a structural
mother encourages passivity and consumption, as long as the kid
doesn't make trouble. Therefore all they learn about becoming adults
is how to act and how to consume.

Kids are in the mall not only in the passive role of shoppers—they   13
also work there, especially as fast-food outlets infiltrate the mall's
enclosure. There they learn how to hold a job and take responsibility,
but still within the same value context. When *CBS Reports* went to Oak
Park Mall in suburban Kansas City, Kansas, to tape part of their
hour-long consideration of malls, "After the Dream Comes True,"
they interviewed a teenaged girl who worked in a fast-food outlet
there. In a sequence that didn't make the final program, she described
the major goal of her present life, which was to perfect the curl on top
of the ice-cream cones that were her store's specialty. If she could do
that, she would be moved from the lowly soft-drink dispenser to the
more prestigious ice-cream division, the curl on top of the status
ladder at her restaurant. These are the achievements that are important at the mall.

Other benefits of such jobs may also be overrated, according to   14
Laurence D. Steinberg of the University of California at Irvine's social
ecology department, who did a study on teenage employment. Their
jobs, he found, are generally simple, mindlessly repetitive and boring.
They don't really learn anything, and the jobs don't lead anywhere.
Teenagers also work primarily with other teenagers; even their supervisors are often just a little older than they are. "Kids need to spend
time with adults," Steinberg told me. "Although they get benefits
from peer relationships, without parents and other adults it's one-
sided socialization. They hang out with each other, have age-segre-
gated jobs, and watch TV."

Perhaps much of this is not so terrible or even so terribly different.   15
Now that they have so much more to contend with in their lives,
adolescents probably need more time to spend with other adolescents
without adult impositions, just to sort things out. Though it is more
concentrated in the mall (and therefore perhaps a clearer target), the
value system there is really the dominant one of the whole society.
Attitudes about curiosity, initiative, self-expression, empathy, and
disinterested learning aren't necessarily made in the mall; they are
mirrored there, perhaps a bit more intensely—as through a glass
brightly.

Besides, the mall is not without its educational opportunities.   16
There are bookstores, where there is at least a short shelf of classics at
great prices, and other books from which it is possible to learn more
than how to do sit-ups. There are tools, from hammers to VCRs, and
products, from clothes to records, that can help the young find and
express themselves. There are older people with stories, and places to
be alone or to talk one-on-one with a kindred spirit. And there is
always the passing show.

The mall itself may very well be an education about the future. I   17
was struck with the realization, as early as my first forays into
Greengate,[1] that the mall is only one of a number of enclosed and
controlled environments that are part of the lives of today's young.
The mall is just an extension, say, of those large suburban schools—
only there's Karmelkorn instead of chem lab, the ice rink instead of
the gym: It's high school without the impertinence of classes.

---

[1]Greengate Mall in Greensburg, Pennsylvania, where Kowinski began his research
on malls (Editors' note).

Growing up, moving from home to school to the mall—from 18
enclosure to enclosure, transported in cars—is a curiously continuous
process, without much in the way of contrast or contact with unen-
closed reality. Places must tend to blur into one another. But whatever
differences and dangers there are in this, the skills these adolescents
are learning may turn out to be useful in their later lives. For we seem
to be moving inexorably into an age of pre-planned and regulated
environments, and this is the world they will inherit.

Still, it might be better if they had more of a choice. One teenaged 19
girl confessed to *CBS Reports* that she sometimes felt she was missing
something by hanging out at the mall so much. "But I'm here," she
said, "and this is what I have."

Meanings and Values

1. Why do malls have a marked effect on children and teenagers?

2a. Do teenagers who spend their time in malls display any obviously
unusual behavior? If so, in what ways do they behave?

b. If not, how might one describe their behavior?

3a. What question does this essay attempt to answer? Where in the essay
is the question asked?

b. Other than providing an answer to the question, what purpose or
purposes does this selection have? (See Guide to Terms: *Purpose*.)

4a. What does Kowinski see as the major effects of malls on teenagers?

b. What other, less important effects (if any) does he identify?

c. Discuss whether or not the author presents enough evidence to convince most readers that he has correctly identified the effects.

5a. Where in the essay does Kowinski consider causes other than the mall
environment for the attitudes and behaviors of teenagers?

b. Explain how the alternative explanation either undermines or adds to
his view of the malls.

Expository Techniques

1. What strategies does the author employ in the introduction (pars. 1–3)
to help convince readers of the importance of reading and thinking

about what happens to teenagers as a result of the time they spend at malls? (Guide: *Introductions*.)

2. Discuss how the author uses examples, quotations from authorities, and various strategies of emphasis in paragraphs 8, 9, 11, 13, and 14 to indicate whether or not the effects of malls can be considered harmful. (Guide: *Emphasis*.)

3a. Which sections of the essay are devoted *primarily* to exploring the effects of the mall environment?

b. Which are devoted *primarily* to discussing whether or not the effects are harmful?

c. What use does the author make of qualification in presenting his conclusions in paragraphs 15 and 17–19? (Guide: *Qualification*.)

d. Explain why this strategy adds to or weakens your confidence in his conclusions.

4. Explain how parallelism in paragraphs 17 and 18 helps emphasize similarities in the environments. (Guide: *Parallel Structure*.)

Diction and Vocabulary

1a. Who is the Nancy Drew alluded to in paragraph 8? (Guide: *Allusion*.)

b. What is the purpose of this allusion?

2a. What transitional devices are used to tie together paragraphs 7–9? (Guide: *Transition*.)

b. Which are used to link paragraphs 10–13?

3. If you do not know the meaning of some of the following words, look them up in the dictionary: loomed, piped (par. 1); viable (3); resonances, fosters (4); incursion (5); inestimable (8); mores, ramifications, plethora (9); surrogate (10); denizens (11); nurture (12); socialization (14); impositions, empathy, disinterested (15); kindred (16); forays, impertinence (17); inexorably (18).

Suggestions for Writing and Discussion

1. Were malls as important to you as they were to some of the people Kowinski describes in his essay? Based on your experience and observations, does Kowinski appear to be overstating the effects of malls on teenagers?

2.   Prepare an essay exploring the roles malls have played in your social life. If you grew up in a town without a mall, write about some other place in which you and people your age gathered.

3.   If you have read Marie Winn's essay "Television Addiction" in Section 7, apply her definition of *addiction* in an essay of your own on malls ("Mall Addiction," perhaps) or on some other influential force in contemporary life like cars or rock music.

(NOTE: Suggestions for topics requiring development by analysis of CAUSE AND EFFECT follow.)

Writing Suggestions for Section 6
Cause and Effect

Analyze the immediate and ultimate causes and/or effects of one of the following subjects, or another suggested by them. (Be careful that your analysis does not develop into a mere listing of superficial "reasons.")

1. The ethnic makeup of a neighborhood.

2. Some *minor* discovery or invention.

3. The popularity of some modern singer or other celebrity.

4. The popularity of some fad of clothing or hair style.

5. The widespread fascination for antique cars (or guns, furniture, dishes, etc.).

6. The widespread enjoyment of fishing or hunting.

7. Student cheating.

8. Too much pressure (on you or an acquaintance) for good school grades.

9. Your being a member of some minority ethnic or religious group.

10. Your association, as an outsider, with members of such a group.

11. The decision of some close acquaintance to enter the religious life.

12. Some unreasonable fear or anxiety that afflicts you or someone you know well.

13. The reluctance of many women today to enter what used to be primarily women's professions such as nursing.

14. Your tendency toward individualism.

15. The popularity of computer games.

16. The mainstreaming of handicapped children.

17. The appeal of careers that promise considerable financial rewards.

18. The appeal of a recent movie or current television series.

19. The willingness of some people to sacrifice personal relationships for professional success.

20. The disintegration of a marriage or family.

21. A family's move (or reluctance to move) to a new home.

22. A candidate's success in a local or national election.

23. A recent war or international conflict.

24. A trend in the national economy.

7

Using *Definition* to Help Explain

Few writing faults can cause a more serious communication block between writer and reader than using key terms that can have various meanings or shades of meaning. To be useful rather than detrimental, such terms must be adequately defined.

Of the two basic types of definition, only one is our special concern as a pattern of exposition. But the other, the simpler form, is often useful to clarify meanings of concrete or noncontroversial terms. This simple process is similar to that used most in dictionaries: either providing a synonym (for example, cinema: a motion picture), or placing the word in a class and then showing how it differs from others of the same class (for example, metheglin: an alcoholic liquor made of fermented honey—here the general class is "liquor," and the differences between metheglin and other liquors are that it is "alcoholic" and "made of fermented honey").

With many such abstract, unusual, or coined terms, typical readers are too limited by their own experiences and opinions (and no two sets are identical) for writers to expect understanding of the exact sense in which the terms are used. They have a right, of course, to use such abstract words any way they choose—as long as their readers know what that way is. The importance of making this meaning clear becomes crucial when the term is used as a key element of the overall explanation. And sometimes the term being defined is even more than a key element: it may be the subject itself, for purposes of either explanation or argument.

Extended definition, unlike the simple, dictionary type, follows no set and formal pattern. Often readers are not even aware of the process. Because it is an integral part of the overall subject, extended definition is written in the same tone as the rest of the exposition (or argument), usually with an attempt to interest the readers, as well as to inform or persuade them.

There are some expository techniques peculiar to definition alone. The purpose may be served by giving the background of the term. Or the definition may be clarified by negation, sometimes called "exclusion" or "differentiation," by showing what is *not* meant by the term. Still another way is to enumerate the characteristics of what is defined, sometimes isolating an essential one for special treatment.

To demonstrate the possibilities in these patterns, we can use the term *juvenile delinquency*, which might need defining in some contexts since it certainly means different things to different people. (Where do we draw the line, for instance, between "childish pranks" and antisocial behavior, or between delinquent and non-delinquent experimentation with sex or marijuana?) We might show how attitudes toward juvenile crime have changed: "youthful high spirits" was the label for some of our grandfathers' activities that would be called "delinquency" today. Or we could use negation, eliminating any classes of juvenile wrongdoing not considered delinquency in the current discussion. Or we could simply list characteristics of the juvenile delinquent or isolate one of these—disrespect for authority or lack of consideration for other people—as a universal.

But perhaps the most dependable techniques for defining are the basic expository patterns already studied. Writers could illustrate their meaning of *juvenile delinquency* by giving *examples* from their own experience, from newspaper accounts, or from other sources. (Every one of the introductions to the eleven sections of this book, each a definition, relies greatly on illustration by example.) They could analyze the subject by *classification* of types or degrees of delinquency. They could use the process of *comparison* and *contrast*, perhaps between delinquent and nondelinquent youth. Showing the *causes* and *effects* of juvenile crime could help explain their attitudes toward it, and hence its meaning for them. They might choose to use *analogy*, perhaps comparing the child to a young tree growing grotesque because of poor care and attention. Or a step-by-step analysis of the *process* by which a child becomes delinquent might, in some cases, help explain the intended meaning.

Few extended definitions would use all these methods, but the extent of their use must always depend on three factors: (1) the term itself, since some are more elusive and subject to misunderstanding than others; (2) the function the term is to serve in the writing, since it would be foolish to devote several pages to defining a term that serves only a casual or unimportant purpose; and (3) the prospective reader-audience, since writers want to avoid insulting the intelligence or background of their readers, yet want to go far enough to be sure of their understanding.

But this, of course, is a basic challenge in any good writing—analyzing the prospective readers and writing for the best effect on *them*.

Sample Paragraph (Annotated)

The subject to be defined is clearly announced. After all, few readers are likely to know what *Buhna* means, let alone *Buhna Bash*.

Some of the *characteristics*.

Background of the term.

Negation or *exclusion* to indicate what the term does not mean.

Analogy with a brief example.

Every year on August 17, Palmville celebrates Buhna Bash, also known as Buhna Days or the Buhna Festival. Most of the day revolves around picnics, sports (including baseball, volleyball, and tennis tournaments), and the Palmville Onion Parade. The latter is presided over by the Onion of Ceremonies (winner of a costume contest). Where did the name Buhna come from? In part from Karl Buhler, the town's first settler, who helped incorporate the city in 1880. And in part from Salvador Nana, who was the first farmer in the region to cultivate the now-famous large, sweet onion called the Palmville Onion. The day may be a Bash, but it is a bash without alcohol and with plenty of laughter and exercise. For Palmville residents, Buhna Bash is like New Year's because it is a time of high spirits and hope for the coming year—often accompanied by optimistic resolutions.

Sample Paragraph (Definition)

This is *orienteering*, a mixture of marathon, hike, and scavenger hunt, a cross-country race in which participants must locate a series of markers set in unfamiliar terrain by means of map and compass. The course, which may range from an acre of city park to twenty square miles of wilderness, is dotted with anywhere from four to fifteen "controls," red-and-white flags whose general locations are marked on the map by small circles. At each control there is a paper punch that produces a distinctive pattern on a card the racer carries. In most events the order in which the card must be punched is fixed; the route taken to reach each control, however, is up to the participant.

Excerpt from "Marathoning with Maps" by Linton Robinson from *Science*, published by The American Association for the Advancement of Science. Reprinted by permission.

MARIE WINN

MARIE WINN was born in Czechoslovakia, and emigrated with her family to the United States, where she attended the New York City schools. She graduated from Radcliffe College and also attended Columbia University. Winn has written eleven books, all of them about children, and has been a frequent contributor to the *New York Times* and various other newspapers and periodicals. Her most recent books are *Children Without Childhood* (1983) and *Unplugging the Plug-In Drug* (1987).

Television Addiction

"Television Addiction" is the title of a chapter in Marie Winn's highly regarded book *The Plug-In Drug* (1977), and our selection is an excerpt from that chapter. It will be seen that a careful definition of the term *addiction*, and a careful application of it to TV viewing, particularly by the young, is of utmost importance to the author's main point, as indicated by the book's title. The selection is a fairly typical use of extended definition.

The word "addiction" is often used loosely and wryly in conversa- 1
tion. People will refer to themselves as "mystery book addicts" or "cookie addicts." E. B. White writes of his annual surge of interest in gardening: "We are hooked and are making an attempt to kick the habit." Yet nobody really believes that reading mysteries or ordering seeds by catalogue is serious enough to be compared with addictions to heroin or alcohol. The word "addiction" is here used jokingly to denote a tendency to overindulge in some pleasurable activity.

People often refer to being "hooked on TV." Does this, too, fall 2
into the lighthearted category of cookie eating and other pleasures

that people pursue with unusual intensity, or is there a kind of television viewing that falls into the more serious category of destructive addiction?

When we think about addiction to drugs or alcohol, we frequently focus on negative aspects, ignoring the pleasures that accompany drinking or drug-taking. And yet the essence of any serious addiction is a pursuit of pleasure, a search for a "high" that normal life does not supply. It is only the inability to function without the addictive substance that is dismaying, the dependence of the organism upon a certain experience and an increasing inability to function normally without it. Thus a person will take two or three drinks at the end of the day not merely for the pleasure drinking provides, but also because he "doesn't feel normal" without them.

An addict does not merely pursue a pleasurable experience and need to experience it in order to function normally. He needs to *repeat* it again and again. Something about that particular experience makes life without it less than complete. Other potentially pleasurable experiences are no longer possible, for under the spell of the addictive experience, his life is peculiarly distorted. The addict craves an experience and yet he is never really satisfied. The organism may be temporarily sated, but soon it begins to crave again.

Finally a serious addiction is distinguished from a harmless pursuit of pleasure by its distinctly destructive elements. A heroin addict, for instance, leads a damaged life: his increasing need for heroin in increasing doses prevents him from working, from maintaining relationships, from developing in human ways. Similarly an alcoholic's life is narrowed and dehumanized by his dependence on alcohol.

Let us consider television viewing in the light of the conditions that define serious addictions.

Not unlike drugs or alcohol, the television experience allows the participant to blot out the real world and enter into a pleasurable and passive mental state. The worries and anxieties of reality are as effectively deferred by becoming absorbed in a television program as by going on a "trip" induced by drugs or alcohol. And just as alcoholics are only inchoately aware of their addiction, feeling that they control their drinking more than they really do ("I can cut it out any time I want—I just like to have three or four drinks before dinner"), people similarly overestimate their control over television watching. Even as they put off other activities to spend hour after hour watching television, they feel they could easily resume living in a different, less passive style. But somehow or other while the television set is present in their homes, the click doesn't sound. With television pleasures available, those other experiences seem less attractive, more difficult somehow.

A heavy viewer (a college English instructor) observes: 8

"I find television almost irresistible. When the set is on, I cannot 9 ignore it. I can't turn it off. I feel sapped, will-less, enervated. As I reach out to turn off the set, the strength goes out of my arms. So I sit there for hours and hours."

The self-confessed television addict often feels he "ought" to 10 do other things—but the fact that he doesn't read and doesn't plant his garden or sew or crochet or play games or have conversations means that those activities are no longer as desirable as television viewing. In a way a heavy viewer's life is as imbalanced by his television "habit" as a drug addict's or an alcoholic's. He is living in a holding pattern, as it were, passing up the activities that lead to growth or development or a sense of accomplishment. This is one reason people talk about their television viewing so ruefully, so apologetically. They are aware that it is an unproductive experience, that almost any other endeavor is more worthwhile by any human measure.

Finally it is the adverse effect of television viewing on the lives 11 of so many people that defines it as a serious addiction. The television habit distorts the sense of time. It renders other experiences vague and curiously unreal while taking on a greater reality for itself. It weakens relationships by reducing and sometimes eliminating normal opportunities for talking, for communicating.

And yet television does not satisfy, else why would the viewer 12 continue to watch hour after hour, day after day? "The measure of health," writes Lawrence Kubie, "is flexibility . . . and especially the freedom to cease when sated."[1] But the television viewer can never be sated with his television experiences—they do not provide the true nourishment that satiation requires—and thus he finds that he cannot stop watching.

[1]Lawrence Kubie, *Neurotic Distortion and the Creative Process* (Lawrence: University of Kansas Press, 1958).

Meanings and Values

1. Would you classify this as formal or informal writing? Why? (See Guide to Terms: *Essay.*)

2. Is it primarily objective or subjective? Why? (Guide: *Objective/Subjective.*)

3. Using our three-question method, evaluate this selection, giving particular attention to the third question. (Guide: *Evaluation.*)

4a. What do you think would be Winn's reply to the assertion that television is such an important element in contemporary culture that time spent watching it is seldom wasted?

b. Do you think you would agree with her answer? Explain.

Expository Techniques

1a. What is the first technique of definition used in this selection? Where is it used?

b. Why is it important to get this aspect of the subject over first?

2a. Which paragraphs are devoted to an enumeration of the characteristics of addiction?

b. What are the characteristics of addiction, according to the author?

3a. What major pattern of exposition does the latter half of the selection utilize?

b. How important is definition of the term prior to this development? Why?

c. Would it have been better if the author had presented a more orderly, point-by-point discussion of this latter material? Why, or why not?

Diction and Vocabulary

1a. Is there anything distinctive about Winn's diction, as demonstrated in this piece? (Guide: *Diction.*) (You may wish to compare it with that of Wolfe in Section 4.)

b. Does your answer to question 1a indicate that Winn's style is inferior in some way? Explain.

2. Use the dictionary as necessary to understand the meanings of the following words: wryly (par. 1); organism (3); sated (4); inchoately (7); enervated (9).

Suggestions for Writing and Discussion

1. Even assuming that a person has a terrible TV habit, what does it really matter (to the person or to others) whether the habit qualifies as an addiction?

2. What other pastimes can you think of that fit, or nearly fit, Winn's criteria for addiction? Do they have any redeeming qualities that TV viewing does not offer?

3. Why do people often worry about the amount of time spent watching TV but seldom about the amount of time spent reading books or magazines? Explain.

(NOTE: Suggestions for topics requiring development by use of DEFINITION are on page 309, at the end of this section.)

PERRI KLASS

PERRI KLASS is both a physician and a writer. She is the author of numerous articles and stories in such publications as the *New York Times, Self, Esquire, Vogue, Mademoiselle, Christopher Street*, and the *Boston Globe Magazine*. In addition, she has been a writer for *Discover* magazine, contributing a regular column, "Vital Signs." Her books include *Recombinations* (1985), *I Am Having an Adventure* (1986), *A Not Entirely Benign Procedure: Four Years as a Medical Student* (1987), and *Other Women's Children* (1990).

Anatomy and Destiny

Feminism is a term that continues to have "various meanings or shades of meaning" for both women and men. In this essay, first published in *Ms.*, Perri Klass considers some of its meanings—historical, practical, and idealistic—in settings that were once the almost exclusive preserves of men: medical school and the practice of medicine.

When I was a medical student, writing about being a medical student, I had two different editors ask me whether professors had taught anatomy with *Playboy* pinups instead of diagrams, or lecturers had made offensive jokes about women. There seemed to be a sort of common knowledge about the medical school experience that my articles didn't incorporate. In fact, I went through medical school without encountering that sort of nonsense, and if a lecturer did occasionally try a would-be witty, would-be provocative remark about women, he got roundly hissed for his trouble—it's very satisfying to hiss a lecturer, and few of them keep their composure well during the process.

There were, however, other, more subtle, ways in which medical 2
school made me aware that I and my kind were newcomers. There
was, above all, the unending parade of male lecturers. There was the
pervasive (and almost unconscious) practice of using the generic *he*
for the doctor in any clinical anecdote, and the generic *she* for the
patient (provided it wasn't prostate trouble, of course). I can still
remember a day when one of our rare female lecturers said to us
something on the order of, "So one day someone will come in with
these symptoms, and you'll get an orthopedist to look at the patient
with you, and she'll tell you such and such," and the women in the
audience burst into applause.

So we hissed sexist jokes and we applauded the use of the female 3
pronoun. Did that mean that the women with whom I went to medical
school considered themselves feminists? I can't say, but I do know
this: many of us felt poised, as women entering a traditionally (and
sometimes militantly) male profession, between gratitude to the
women who had fought their way through before us on the one hand,
and a desire to identify with our new brotherhood on the other.

Most people who go to medical school want very badly to be 4
doctors. It takes a great deal of effort to get to medical school, let alone
to get through. Wanting to be a doctor means identifying with the
people up ahead of you, the group you are trying to join, and up until
very recently, that group has been a brotherhood, in every sense of the
word. For some women, the word *feminist* may have been unwel-
come, a reminder that they might never be fully accepted into that
brotherhood, an awkward and public attempt to make an ideology
out of a fact of life. And yet, I think my class was still close enough to
the pioneers who had gone before for us to understand that we owed
our opportunity, our comparatively easy path, entirely to those reso-
lute embattled pioneers. The graffiti in the women's bathroom in the
dormitory at my medical school read, "Every time you sit down here,
thank the women who have come before you."

I have taken for granted that I was a feminist ever since I was in 5
junior high school, but I have never seen myself as a banner-carrier.
Certainly in college and in graduate school there were women who
would have considered me a fellow traveler at best: because I did not
live a truly politically correct life, because I was not more active in
women's causes. I never minded this and it never kept me from
considering myself a feminist; others could carry the banners but I

would march; I would acknowledge the debt I owed to other women and to the Women's Movement. I was a feminist, but I was not The Feminist.

When I got to medical school, I discovered that I was a radical 6 feminist. By medical school standards I was in fact The Feminist, or one of them. It didn't take much; there was almost no one person, and certainly no group, to carry the banner or smile patronizingly at my lack of seriousness. I found myself running the medical school women's association, along with a friend. Our activities were far short of revolutionary; we used to invite speakers to come and talk once a week. We covered topics of obvious relevance to women—battered women, midwifery—and also medical topics that we thought might be relevant—alcoholism, child abuse—and we also invited a number of women physicians to come talk about their training and their lives. The talks were generally very well attended, by both female and male students, and they were fun, but not particularly radical. Still, one day when I and a couple of other women from our class were talking to the women who had directed the organization before us about possible speakers and other activities (develop a women's medical directory of the area? get involved with a study that was being done of the medical school's failure to give tenure to women?), one of my classmates said abruptly that she didn't want to help run the organization since it was clear that the group was going to be headed by some radical people. It wasn't that I minded the label. I was vaguely thrilled to find myself finally something other than a weak-minded fellow traveler. But it was disconcerting not to know when I was doing something "extreme."

I was once called to the office of the director of medical school 7 admissions along with the heads of some other student groups to discuss his concern because the women's organization was writing to female applicants, offering encouragement and information, even offering to put them up when they came for interviews. He pointed out that the Hispanic and black student groups were making similar offers to their constituents, and he wanted to put a stop to all these separate letters. Among other things, he said, it just wasn't fair—no one was writing to the white men. There was a pause, and then I said, in unison with one of the other students present, "And yet, somehow they keep coming!" The lesson, in the end, was that medicine is fundamentally a conservative world, that medical students as a group are a far more conservative context for any kind of political thinking than college students or graduate students.

Most female medical students, as I remember, were highly aware of the sex ratios on the hospital teams on which they worked. And I remember a sense of betrayal when a female resident or attending physician proved ineffective, unpleasant, uninspiring. I also remember how different it felt the first time I was ever in an operating room with an all-female group: the orthopedic resident, the surgical intern, the medical student (me), the scrub nurse, *and* the patient. And in fact it was nothing like the usual operating room drama; there was less yelling, more courtesy, more collegiality and less strict hierarchy. That distinction has held up in a fair number of operating rooms since then. 8

You can't help feeling these differences, whatever the association you choose to claim with feminism. However wary you may be of the word, medical school is an educational experience, and one of the courses everyone gets, like it or not, is an introduction to sexual politics. Many of the men, of course, don't quite realize it's going on. 9

Now I am doing a residency in pediatrics, a field that has traditionally had a relatively high percentage of women. In my own program there are many female residents. When the list of interns came out for next year, several of us reviewed with fascination the list of the people who would take over our position at the very bottom of the totem pole. Only later did we realize that none of us had thought to count how many of the new interns were male and how many female—the most striking evidence, we all agreed, that we are in a situation where that really isn't an issue. When half or more of the residents are female, a female resident doesn't feel she is by definition on probation. Polarizations of male and female doctor styles are acknowledged; residents are regularly twitted for being macho. 10

Many of the young female doctors I work with today would call themselves feminists. Their feminism involves a sense of entitlement, and that is also valuable. In a way the victory is the sense of entitlement, the feeling that you belong. You need both—you need a balance of a rock-hard confidence that you belong in medicine, and also an awareness that you only got there because the women ahead of you battered down the doors. With that confidence and that awareness, the hope is you can enjoy your position, preserve it for those who will come next, and also preserve the challenge to the traditional style that is one of the greatest contributions women bring to medicine. 11

Meanings and Values

1.   Why might some women in medical school prefer not to be called "feminists"?

2.   How does the "all-female" operating room the author describes in paragraph 8 differ from other operating rooms according to her?

3.   What kind of feminist does the author define herself as in paragraph 5?

4a.   According to whose standards was Klass "a radical feminist" (par. 6)?

 b.   In your opinion, do the activities she describes in paragraphs 6 and 7 justify the label? Be ready to defend your answer.

5.   If the purpose of this essay is not to define "feminist" in a general sense, what is its purpose (or purposes)? (See Guide to Terms: *Purpose.*)

Expository Techniques

1.   Where in this selection does Klass make clear her intention to consider the meanings of feminism in a particular professional context?

2a.   What examples does Klass offer of her feminist activities in medical school?

 b.   In what ways does she qualify her presentation to indicate that she does not consider her activities to have been especially radical? (Guide: *Qualification.*)

3a.   Having explained the need for feminism in medical school and given examples of the changes that come with the presence of women, why would Klass spend the last three paragraphs describing some of the successful effects of the feminist movement on the profession?

 b.   Do these paragraphs threaten the unity of the essay in any way? (Guide: *Unity.*)

 c.   How, if at all, do they extend the definition of *feminism* Klass develops in the course of the piece?

 d.   In what way do they constitute an effective conclusion? (Guide: *Closings.*)

4.   What use does the author make of definition by negation and by enumeration of characteristics in paragraphs 5–8?

Diction and Vocabulary

1a.   Discuss the use of diction in paragraph 1 to convey the writer's view of a lecturer who makes sexist remarks. (Guide: *Diction.*)

b. How does the author use irony in paragraph 7 to answer the director's concern about the lack of fairness to white males? (Guide: *Irony.*)

2a. Contrast the positive denotations and connotations of the diction in paragraph 11 with the uncertain or negative meanings conveyed by the diction in paragraph 4. (Guide: *Connotation and Denotation.*)

b. What thematic concerns do the differences in diction highlight?

3. If you do not know the meaning of any of the following words, look them up in the dictionary: pervasive, generic, prostate, orthopedist (par. 2); militantly (3); ideology, embattled (4); patronizingly, mid-wifery (6); collegiality (8); entitlement (11).

Suggestions for Writing and Discussion

1. Look over the articles in a recent edition of the magazine *Ms.* Would Klass's essay be considered radical or moderate if it appeared in the context of the articles you examined? If it appeared in a recent edition of *Glamour? National Review?*

2. How, if at all, does your understanding of feminism differ from Klass's?

3. To what extent has our society gone beyond a need for feminism? Or was there ever a need for the feminist movement?

(NOTE: Suggestions for topics requiring development by use of DEFINITION are on page 309, at the end of this section.)

ROGER WELSCH

ROGER WELSCH was a professor of English and anthropology at the University of Nebraska–Lincoln when he decided to move to a small tree farm in the central Plains. Since then he has made a living as a writer and television and radio columnist and has begun his "rural education." His essays on rural life have been collected in *It's Not the End of the Earth but You Can See It from Here: Tales of the Great Plains* (1990). His other books include *Treasury of Nebraska Pioneer Folklore* (1966); *Shingling the Fog and Other Plains Lies* (1980); *Mister, You Got Yourself a Horse: Tales of Old-Time Horse Trading* (1981); *Omaha Tribal Myths and Trickster Tales* (1981); and *Cather's Kitchens: Foodways in Literature and Life* (1987) and *Catfish at the Pump: Humor and the Frontier* (1987) (both with Linda K. Welsch).

Gypsies

As the title suggests, this essay offers a definition of a group of people rather than a term or concept. In addition, one of Welsch's tasks is to redefine a group whose reputation over the centuries has often been less than positive.

I was once talking with a Lakota wise man, Richard Fool Bull, wondering at his ability to sense what seemed to me to be mystic occurrences. Magic things seemed to happen to him fairly regularly. A hundred years ago they would have been called "visions" by the Indians. A thousand years ago they would have been called "miracles" even in our culture, but Mr. Fool Bull accepted them as a normal part of life.

"They *are* a normal part of life," he laughed when I expressed my amazement. "They happen all the time."

"To you maybe, Mr. Fool Bull, but not to me." 3

"Oh yes, to you too," he said, nodding seriously. "That is the sad 4
thing about white culture. You see, Roger, it is not a matter of me being
trained to see such things; *you* have been trained not to see them."

That's not a new idea. In anthropology classes it is a common 5
teaching trick, for example, to tell students that there are still peoples
of this world who do not know the connection between sexual intercourse and pregnancy. That usually excites astonishment in the
class—how can anyone not understand a cause-and-effect that obvious?

The professor lets the students throw around their obvious cul- 6
tural superiority for a few minutes and then asks, "What is the result
of eating asparagus?" It is rare that anyone responds with a serious
response. "Your urine smells to high heaven for a couple of hours,
that's what. Now, why is it you think these people are so stupid
because they have not realized an association that spans nine months
while you have never figured out a very obvious cause-and-effect
relationship that takes place over only a few minutes?" The fact of the
matter is, very obvious things, most not at all mystical, happen
around us all the time and we manage to remain totally oblivious to
them.

I enjoy the regular—every few months or so—articles that appear 7
in the Omaha or Rising City newspapers that run pretty much along
these lines:

The Bleaker County Savings and Loan lost an estimated $900 in an unusual
fraud perpetrated against teller Judy Hockworthy last Thursday. According
to Ms. Hockworthy six or seven swarthy people—probably Indians or Iranians—came in to the office at 48th and Caldwell Streets looking for change
for the parking meter and a fifty-dollar bill with an L in the serial number.
Ms. Hockworthy reported that the men spoke broken English and the
women were dressed in loose, colorful clothing. The men had seventeen
one-hundred-dollar bills for which they wanted the change for the parking
meter and the fifty-dollar bills.
After several changes of the bills, the alleged defrauders left the office and
drove away in late-model pickup trucks, all with campers on the beds and all
with Illinois license plates.
The police have no suspects.

I love those stories. For one thing, I think it's wonderful that these 8
skilled con men get away with what they do in large part because they
have plenty of money in their hands when they enter the bank. The

thesis in our society, evidently, is, "Anyone who has lots of money is obviously to be trusted" when every indication should tell us exactly the opposite.

But there is a deeper, philosophical reason for my affection for   9
these enduring, widespread petty bilkers. You see, I like coyotes. I don't care if coyotes take 15 percent of the lambs and calves on western ranges. To me coyotes represent something very important— that creatures under the pressure of full warfare can survive. Out here coyotes are hunted with high-power rifles, traps, exploding baits, poison, airplanes, calls, chumming, and mobs. And yet survive. They *prosper!* That prospect gives coyotes like me a lot of hope, you see.

Well, newspaper stories like that are about human coyotes, I   10
guess. Gypsies. That's who those "Indians or Iranians" are, Gypsies. Through a thousand years of resistance, through wars and contempt and murder and expulsion, the Gypsies survive. Before Hitler murdered the Jews, he murdered the Gypsies.

And yet here they are, still with us, and so skillfully concealed   11
that most Americans haven't the foggiest notion they are still here.

Before I forget, let me tell you what happened in Germany. The   12
Gypsies were almost totally eradicated in Germany, and do you know what happened after the Second World War? The Gypsies *swarmed* into Germany. Where would they be safer than where they had only a few years before been pariahs? They could still be hated in England or Sweden, but not in Germany. Gypsy caravans parked illegally under Autobahn overpasses and in department-store parking lots because the gypsies knew that here, where they had been most abused, now they would be most tolerated.

I admired especially the ones camped illegally under the over-   13
passes. Can you imagine a better place to set up camp? Families sat at picnic tables and enjoyed supper even when it was raining like crazy or when the sun was blazing, peacefully watching the traffic whiz by. Overpass railings were festooned with wet laundry, a kind of Gypsy flag of resistance.

Gypsies are still visible throughout Europe, where their distinc-   14
tive clothing and wagons and a long tradition make them easily recognized by the citizens of the countries they travel. In America Gypsies are almost invisible. Americans see them not as "Gypsies" but "slightly peculiar, dark people—maybe Iranians or Indians." The average American perceives their pickup trucks with inevitable

camper toppers and "For Sale" signs as something strange—but almost never as "Gypsies"!

What I love about American Gypsies is that they are seen only rarely, and then briefly, like comets. I, for one, feel graced when I have the chance to see them, even if only in passing on the highway. 15

Fremont, Nebraska, used to be a popular place for Gypsies to stop and for all I know may still be. It is on Highway 30, the Lincoln Highway, and that was the main artery for cross-country travel for many years. For the still nomadic Gypsies, the long, open stretches of the Lincoln Highway must have been like a hometown. And Fremont is about halfway across America, so it was a logical meeting and resting place for the eternal travelers. 16

As a boy I once read a newspaper report of a time when two rival Gypsy bands wound up at a Gypsy cemetery in Fremont at the same time—both paying respect, as I recall, to the hallowed memory of the same patriarch of the tribe. The result was memorable. My recollection is that something like four hundred shots were fired, and when the police finally sorted things out after the pitched battle, they amassed a huge pile of knives, clubs, guns, brass knuckles, and other weapons of choice. 17

Now, I am not a violent guy and you probably wonder what possible saving grace I could deduce from a violent encounter like that. Well, what I found *glorious* about it was that not a single person was hurt. It was all posturing, maneuvering, threatening, and bluster. Coyotes at play. 18

I've spoken with quite a few people in Fremont about the Gypsies in the old days, and there are a lot of stories. The Gypsies often asked to camp at farms and farmers would usually give them permission in order to avoid later retribution, but they made sure the chickens and children were put to bed early and the mother and father stayed up late to keep an eye on things. 19

Older farm women who remember when Gypsies would camp near their farmsteads tell me that the Gypsy women and children would often come to the house asking for eggs or milk and they were usually given those simple things. Later inspection revealed that the next day tools, cooking utensils, dogs, and even horses or cows showed up missing—or perhaps I should say didn't show up missing. 20

Today, savvy merchants close up the store the minute they hear that the Gypsies are in town. For those too slow or inexperienced to 21 close up shop, the experience is usually that ten or twelve women with voluminous clothing sweep into the store and scatter throughout the aisles. Merchandise disappears within the ample folds of the clothing. The ensuing shouting, arguing, and linguistic confusion makes it impossible for the merchant, security, or even the police to sort out one woman from another, let alone retrieve pilfered goods, and the inventory is shot to hell for the rest of the year.

All except the new car and truck dealers. They love to see the   22 Gypsies come to town. The Gypsies frequently buy new vehicles in Fremont, and their mode of operation is always the same. They come onto the lot, point to the vehicle they want, ask how much it is, and without any haggling whatsoever pay the price in cash.

Now, I know what's going to happen when folks read this.   23 Latter-day Gypsies are going to say that I have slandered their people, that Gypsies never steal, that all the stories are fictions, that Gypsies actually travel around the world doing good deeds wherever they can. Well, anyone who tries to sell that sort of nonsense does the Gypsies a gross disservice. By lying about their people, they deny their heritage. I have no sympathy for people like that. Just as surely as Gypsies have leavened the cultural loaf of western civilization with their music, art, and food, they have enriched us all with their irrepressible resistance to change, their thousands of years of resistance to authority and order not their own.

There will be non-Gypsies who say I am a real jerk for suggesting   24 that common thievery is anything but common thievery and the Gypsies should learn to behave like Americans if they intend to live in this glorious land of the free, home of the brave. They should learn that nothing is more rewarding than money earned by the sweat of your brow—sort of like Ivan Boesky or Donald Trump or Don King, I guess. No, the Gypsies offer another alternative—survival by wit.

I don't condone cheating and thievery normally, but in the case   25 of the Gypsies it is a cultural inheritance and its cleverness makes me glad to be a member of the same species as the Gypsies.

I used to think that one of the things I wanted to do in my life   26 was to spend an afternoon or evening in a Gypsy camp. My fantasy was that I would spot a bunch of Gypsy pickup trucks in a small park some day, somewhere on the Plains—I know what to look for, after all. I imagined that what I would do on that occasion is walk into the camp with a couple of chickens and maybe a battered banjo I wouldn't mind losing over my shoulder. That way I could trade the chickens for something to eat—something *Gypsy*—and play my banjo in exchange for some of their legendary music.

Unfortunately, the closest I have come to realizing that fantasy is one time when some friends and I stopped for a picnic lunch in a public parking place at a large park in South Dakota. We were eating and I was eyeing ten or twelve pickup campers on the other side of the parking lot. I suspected they might be Gypsies. 27

As we were eating, two five- or six-year-old children approached us from the direction of the trucks. They were beautiful children—dark-skinned with enormous, black eyes. Obviously they were Gypsies. "Would you like a cookie?" I asked them. 28

They nodded yes. 29

I held out the sack, but to my surprise they backed away a couple steps. No, they explained, they would not take the cookies as a gift. They would accept them only if they could buy them from me. 30

Hummm. Maybe these weren't Gypsies. Gypsies steal, I thought. They don't *buy*. I was put mentally off balance. 31

"How much you want for the cookies, Mister?" one of the children asked. 32

These were great big chocolate chip cookies, and I had a big bag of about sixty or seventy of them; they had cost me maybe eight dollars early that morning at the grocery store. "Tell you what, young man," I said. "How about a penny. Will you pay a penny for a cookie this big?" 33

He smiled and nodded yes, and I felt like a real prince for being such a nice guy with these kids. And I felt like a real dope for all the things I had said in the past about Gypsies being—how shall I say it?—shrewd operators. 34

The little boy handed me a penny, and I gave him a cookie. His little friend handed me a penny, and I gave him a cookie too. Gosh, what a pleasant little vignette, I thought. 35

Then suddenly, out of nowhere, I was surrounded by eighty little children, all with pennies, all wanting cookies. So we wound up selling our entire supper, all of it—cookies, sandwiches, candy bars, chips, everything, for something like eighty-five cents! 36

These folks were Gypsies, all right—kids and all. I had been had, but good. I had fallen for exactly the routine I had watched other people fall for for decades—my junior deceivers had confused me with their impressive wealth, they had let me believe that I was being the clever party to the exchange, they had come at me from a direction 37

I would have never thought of looking into, and when it was all over, I still wasn't sure what had happened to me, how much I had lost, how it had ever developed, why I had been such a dope.

And I loved it. Every minute of it. I have savored the moment 38 over and over for these twenty years now. Outwitted by the Gypsies, I was, and not just by Gypsies but by two five-year-old Gypsies.

I still keep an old banjo around the house, and a few chickens, 39 just in case.

Meanings and Values

1. In your own words, summarize Welsch's attitudes towards Gypsies.

2. How would you characterize the tone of this essay? (See Guide to Terms: *Style/Tone.*)

3. How would you characterize the purpose of this essay? (Guide: *Purpose.*)

4. Estimate the importance of tone in helping the essay achieve its purpose.

Expository Techniques

1. Tell where the essay makes use of each of the following definition techniques:

   a. background

   b. negation

   c. enumeration

   d. analogy

2. Welsch mentions other definitions of Gypsies as part of his attempt to redefine the group and change readers' attitudes. Where does he mention these other definitions and what are they?

3a. At first, paragraphs 1–7 may appear to be only loosely related to the rest of the essay. Discuss whether they contribute to or undermine the unity of the selection. (Guide: *Unity.*)

   b. How, if at all, can these paragraphs be considered part of an effective introduction?

4. What is the central theme of this essay, and in what ways is it communicated to readers?

5. Which examples in the body of the essay are most successful in creating admiration (or at least respect) for Gypsies? Which are least successful? Why? (Guide: *Evaluation.*)

Diction and Vocabulary

1. Study the word choice in paragraphs 10 and 13 and explain how Welsch uses it to invite sympathy and admiration for his subjects. Pay special attention to repetition and to the connotation of words. (Guide: *Connotation/Denotation.*)

2a. What are the synonyms Welsch offers in paragraphs 1–6 for the phenomenon he refers to first as "mystic occurrences"?

 b. Offer a definition of the phenomenon yourself using any of the definition strategies discussed in the introduction to Section 7.

3. If you do not know the meaning of any of the following words, look them up in a dictionary: bilkers (par. 9); festooned (13); patriarch, amassed (17); posturing (18); retribution (19); vignette (35).

Suggestions for Writing and Discussion

1. Try to think of any other group (or practices) that might be defended in a manner similar to the way Welsch defends Gypsies. List the kinds of things you might cover in an essay on the topic.

2. At several places in the essay, Welsch defends his outlook against possible criticisms (see paragraphs 23–25). What other criticisms might there be of his outlook in the essay?

(NOTE: Suggestions for topics requiring development by use of DEFINITION are on page 309, at the end of this section.)

KESAYA NODA

KESAYA E. NODA was born in California and raised in rural New Hampshire. She did not learn Japanese until she graduated from high school, but then spent two years living and studying in Japan. After college, she wrote *The Yamato Colony*, based on her research into the history of the California community to which her grandparents came as immigrants and in which her parents were raised. Following this, she worked and traveled in Japan for another year. Noda earned a master's degree from the Harvard Divinity School. She now teaches at Lesley College in Cambridge, Massachusetts.

Growing Up Asian in America

The act of definition in this essay is one of self-definition, both of an individual and, by implication, of a cultural group. This complex task is accomplished in an especially clear manner. In reading, pay attention to the different kinds of expository patterns Noda employs, including comparison and narration. Note, too, how clearly she makes the different pieces of the essay fit together.

Sometimes when I was growing up, my identity seemed to hurtle toward me and paste itself right to my face. I felt that way, encountering the stereotypes of my race perpetuated by non-Japanese people (primarily white) who may or may not have had contact with other Japanese in America. "You don't like cheese, do you?" someone would ask. "I know your people don't like cheese." Sometimes questions came making allusions to history. That was another aspect of the identity. Events that had happened quite apart from the me who stood silent in that moment connected my face with an incomprehensible past. "Your parents were in California? Were they in those camps during the war?" And sometimes there were phrases or nicknames: "Lotus Blossom." I was sometimes addressed or referred to as racially Japanese, sometimes as Japanese American, and sometimes as an Asian woman. Confusions and distortions abounded.

How is one to know and define oneself? From the inside—within a context that is self defined, from a grounding in community and a connection with culture and history that are comfortably accepted? Or from the outside—in terms of messages received from the media and people who are often ignorant? Even as an adult I can still see two sides of my face and past. I can see from the inside out, in freedom. And I can see from the outside in, driven by the old voices of childhood and lost in anger and fear.

I Am Racially Japanese

A voice from my childhood says: "You are other. You are less than. You are unalterably alien." This voice has its own history. We have indeed been seen as other and alien since the early years of our arrival in the United States. The very first immigrants were welcomed and sought as laborers to replace the dwindling numbers of Chinese, whose influx had been cut off by the Chinese Exclusion Act of 1882. The Japanese fell natural heir to the same anti-Asian prejudice that had arisen against the Chinese. As soon as they began striking for better wages, they were no longer welcomed.

I can see myself today as a person historically defined by law and custom as being forever alien. Being neither "free white," nor "African," our people in California were deemed "aliens, ineligible for citizenship," no matter how long they intended to stay here. Aliens ineligible for citizenship were prohibited from owning, buying, or leasing land. They did not and could not belong here. The voice in me remembers that I am always a *Japanese* American in the eyes of many. A third-generation German American is an American. A third-generation Japanese American is a Japanese American. Being Japanese means being a danger to the country during the war and knowing how to use chopsticks. I wear this history on my face.

I move to the other side. I see a different light and claim a different context. My race is a line that stretches across ocean and time to link me to the shrine where my grandmother was raised. Two high, white banners lift in the wind at the top of the stone steps leading to the shrine. It is time for the summer festival. Black characters are written against the sky as boldly as the clouds, as lightly as kites, as sharply as the big black crows I used to see above the fields in New Hampshire. At festival time there is liquor and food, ritual, discipline, and abandonment. There is music and drunkenness and invocation. There is hope. Another season has come. Another season has gone.

I am racially Japanese. I have a certain claim to this crazy place   6
where the prayers intoned by a neighboring Shinto priest (standing in for my grandmother's nephew who is sick) are drowned out by the rehearsals for the pop singing contest in which most of the villagers will compete later that night. The village elders, the priest, and I stand respectfully upon the immaculate, shining wooden floor of the outer shrine, bowing our heads before the hidden powers. During the patchy intervals when I can hear him, I notice the priest has a stutter. His voice flutters up to my ears only occasionally because two men and a woman are singing gustily into a microphone in the compound, testing the sound system. A prerecorded tape of guitars, samisens, and drums accompanies them. Rock music and Shinto prayers. That night, to loud applause and cheers, a young man is given the award for the most *netsuretsu*—passionate, burning—rendition of a song. We roar our approval of the reward. Never mind that his voice had wandered and slid, now slightly above, now slightly below the given line of the melody. Netsuretsu. Netsuretsu.

In the morning, my grandmother's sister kneels at the foot of the   7
stone stairs to offer her morning prayers. She is too crippled to climb the stairs, so each morning she kneels here upon the path. She shuts her eyes for a few seconds, her motions as matter of fact as when she washes rice. I linger longer than she does, so reluctant to leave, savoring the connection I feel with my grandmother in America, the past, and the power that lives and shines in the morning sun.

Our family has served this shrine for generations. The family's   8
need to protect this claim to identity and place outweighs any individual claim to any individual hope. I am Japanese.

I Am a Japanese American

"Weak." I hear the voice from my childhood years. "Passive," I hear.   9
Our parents and grandparents were the ones who were put into those camps. They went without resistance; they offered cooperation as proof of loyalty to America. "Victim," I hear. And, "Silent."

Our parents are painted as hard workers who were socially 10
uncomfortable and had difficulty expressing even the smallest opinion. Clean, quiet, motivated, and determined to match the American
way; that is us, and that is the story of our time here.

"Why did you go into those camps," I raged at my parents, 11
frightened by my own inner silence and timidity. "Why didn't you do
anything to resist? Why didn't you name it the injustice it was?"
Couldn't our parents even think? Couldn't they? Why were we so
passive?

I shift my vision and my stance. I am in California. My uncle is 12
in the midst of the sweet potato harvest. He is pressed, trying to get
the harvesting crews onto the field as quickly as possible, worried
about the flow of equipment and people. His big pickup is pulled off
to the side, motor running, door ajar. I see two tractors in the yard in
front of an old shed; the flat bed harvesting platform on which the
workers will stand has already been brought over from the other field.
It's early morning. The workers stand loosely grouped and at ease,
but my uncle looks as harried and tense as a police officer trying to
unsnarl a New York City traffic jam. Driving toward the shed, I pull
my car off the road to make way for an approaching tractor. The front
wheels of the car sink luxuriously into the soft, white sand by the
roadside and the car slides to a dreamy halt, tail still on the road. I try
to move forward. I try to move back. The front bites contentedly into
the sand, the back lifts itself at a jaunty angle. My uncle sees me and
storms down the road, running. He is shouting before he is even near me.

"What's the matter with you," he screams. "What the hell are you 13
doing?" In his frenzy, he grabs his hat off his head and slashes it
through the air across his knee. He is beside himself. "Don't you know
how to drive in sand? What's the matter with you? You've blocked
the whole roadway. How am I supposed to get my tractors out of
here? Can't you use your head? You've cut off the whole roadway,
and we've got to get out of here."

I stand on the road before him helplessly thinking, "No, I don't 14
know how to drive in sand. I've never driven in sand."

"I'm sorry, uncle," I say, burying a smile beneath a look of sincere 15
apology. I notice my deep amusement and my affection for him with
great curiosity. I am usually devastated by anger. Not this time.

During the several years that follow I learn about the people and 16
the place, and much more about what has happened in this California
village where my parents grew up. The issei, our grandparents, made

this settlement in the desert. Their first crops were eaten by rabbits and ravaged by insects. The land was so barren that men walking from house to house sometimes got lost. Women came here too. They bore children in 114 degree heat, then carried the babies with them into the fields to nurse when they reached the end of each row of grapes or other truck farm crops.

I had had no idea what it meant to buy this kind of land and make 17 it grow green. Or how, when the war came, there was no space at all for the subtlety of being who we were—Japanese Americans. Either/or was the way. I hadn't understood that people were literally afraid for their lives then, that their money had been frozen in banks; that there was a five-mile travel limit; that when the early evening curfew came and they were inside their houses, some of them watched helplessly as people they knew went into their barns to steal their belongings. The police were patrolling the road, interested only in violators of curfew. There was no help for them in the face of thievery. I had not been able to imagine before what it must have felt like to be an American—to know absolutely that one is an American— and yet to have almost everyone else deny it. Not only deny it, but challenge that identity with machine guns and troops of white American soldiers. In those circumstances it was difficult to say, "I'm a Japanese American." "American" had to do.

But now I can say that I am a Japanese American. It means I have 18 a place here in this country, too. I have a place here on the East Coast, where our neighbor is so much a part of our family that my mother never passes her house at night without glancing at the lights to see if she is home and safe; where my parents have hauled hundreds of pounds of rocks from fields and arduously planted Christmas trees and blueberries, lilacs, asparagus, and crab apples; where my father still dreams of angling a stream to a new bed so that he can dig a pond in the field and fill it with water and fish. "The neighbors already came for their Christmas tree?" he asks in December. "Did they like it? Did they like it?"

I have a place on the West Coast where my relatives still farm, 19 where I heard the stories of feuds and backbiting, and where I saw that people survived and flourished because fundamentally they trusted and relied upon one another. A death in the family is not just a death in a family; it is a death in the community. I saw people help each other with money, materials, labor, attention, and time. I saw men gather once a year, without fail, to clean the grounds of a ninety-year-old woman who had helped the community before, during, and after the war. I saw her remembering them with birthday cards sent to each of their children.

I come from a people with a long memory and a distinctive grace. 20
We live our thanks. And we are Americans. Japanese Americans.

I Am a Japanese American Woman

Woman. The last piece of my identity. It has been easier by far for me 21
to know myself in Japan and to see my place in America than it has
been to accept my line of connection with my own mother. She was
my dark self, a figure in whom I thought I saw all that I feared most
in myself. Growing into womanhood and looking for some model of
strength, I turned away from her. Of course, I could not find what I
sought. I was looking for a black feminist or a white feminist. My
mother is neither white nor black.

My mother is a woman who speaks with her life as much as 22
with her tongue. I think of her with her own mother. Grandmother
had Parkinson's disease and it had frozen her gait and set her
fingers, tongue, and feet jerking and trembling in a terrible dance.
My aunts and uncles wanted her to be able to live in her own home.
They fed her, bathed her, dressed her, awoke at midnight to take
her for one last trip to the bathroom. My aunts (her daughters-in-
law) did most of the care, but my mother went from New Hampshire to California each summer to spend a month living with
grandmother, because she wanted to and because she wanted to
give my aunts at least a small rest. During those hot summer days,
mother lay on the couch watching the television or reading, cooking foods that grandmother liked, and speaking little. Grandmother thrived under her care.

The time finally came when it was too dangerous for grand- 23
mother to live alone. My relatives kept finding her on the floor beside
her bed when they went to wake her in the mornings. My mother flew
to California to help clean the house and make arrangements for
grandmother to enter a local nursing home. On her last day at home,
while grandmother was sitting in her big, overstuffed armchair, hair
combed and wearing a green summer dress, my mother went to her
and knelt at her feet. "Here, Mamma," she said. "I've polished your
shoes." She lifted grandmother's legs and helped her into the shiny
black shoes. My grandmother looked down and smiled slightly. She

left her house walking, supported by her children, carrying her pocket book, and wearing her polished black shoes. "Look, Mamma," my mom had said, kneeling. "I've polished your shoes."

Just the other day, my mother came to Boston to visit. She had recently lost a lot of weight and was pleased with her new shape and her feeling of good health. "Look at me, Kes," she exclaimed, turning toward me, front and back, as naked as the day she was born. I saw her small breasts and the wide, brown scar, belly button to pubic hair, that marked her because my brother and I were both born by Caesarean section. Her hips were small. I was not a large baby, but there was so little room for me in her that when she was carrying me she could not even begin to bend over toward the floor. She hated it, she said.

"Don't I look good? Don't you think I look good?"

I looked at my mother, smiling and as happy as she, thinking of all the times I have seen her naked. I have seen both my parents naked throughout my life, as they have seen me. From childhood through adulthood we've had our naked moments, sharing baths, idle conversations picked up as we moved between showers and closets, hurried moments at the beginning of days, quiet moments at the end of days.

I know this to be Japanese, this ease with the physical, and it makes me think of an old, Japanese folk song. A young nursemaid, a fifteen-year-old girl, is singing a lullaby to a baby who is strapped to her back. The nursemaid has been sent as a servant to a place far from her own home. "We're the beggars," she says, "and they are the nice people. Nice people wear fine sashes. Nice clothes."

> If I should drop dead,
> bury me by the roadside!
> I'll give a flower
> to everyone who passes.
>
> What kind of flower?
> The cam-cam-camellia {tsun-tsun-tsubaki}
> watered by Heaven:
> alms water.[1]

The nursemaid is the intersection of heaven and earth, the intersection of the human, the natural world, the body, and the soul. In this

[1]Patia R. Isaku, *Mountain Storm, Pine Breeze: Folk Song in Japan* (Tucson: University of Arizona Press, 1981), 41.

song, with clear eyes, she looks steadily at life, which is sometimes so very terrible and sad. I think of her while looking at my mother, who is standing on the red and purple carpet before me, laughing, without any clothes.

I am my mother's daughter. And I am myself.   29

I am a Japanese American woman.   30

Epilogue

I recently heard a man from West Africa share some memories of his   31
childhood. He was raised Muslim, but when he was a young man, he found himself deeply drawn to Christianity. He struggled against this inner impulse for years, trying to avoid the church yet feeling pushed to return to it again and again. "I would have done *anything* to avoid the change," he said. At last, he became Christian. Afterwards he was afraid to go home, fearing that he would not be accepted. The fear was groundless, he discovered, when at last he returned—he had separated himself, but his family and friends (all Muslim) had not separated themselves from him.

The man, who is now a professor of religion, said that in the   32
Africa he knew as a child and a young man, pluralism was embraced rather than feared. There was "a kind of tolerance that did not deny your particularity," he said. He alluded to zestful, spontaneous debates that would sometimes loudly erupt between Muslims and Christians in the village's public spaces. His memories of an atheist who harangued the villagers when he came to visit them once a week moved me deeply. Perhaps the man was an agricultural advisor or inspector. He harassed the women. He would say:

"Don't go to the fields! Don't even bother to go to the fields. Let God take care of you. He'll send you the food. If you believe in God, why do you need to work? You don't need to work! Let God put the seeds in the ground. Stay home."

The professor said, "The women laughed, you know? They just   33
laughed. Their attitude was, 'Here is a child of God. When will he come home?' "

The storyteller, the professor of religion, smiled the most fantas-   34
tic, tender smile as he told this story. "In my country, there is a deep affirmation of the oneness of God," he said. "The atheist and the women were having quite different experiences in their encounter,

though the atheist did not know this. He saw himself as quite separate from the women. But the women did not see themselves as being separate from him. 'Here is a child of God,' they said. 'When will he come home?' "

Meanings and Values

1.   Define in your own words each of the identities Noda outlines for herself.

2.   How can the last section of the essay, "Epilogue" (pars. 31–34), be said to harmonize these identities or at least to suggest a way of building bridges among them?

3.   Discuss how the opening section of this essay (pars. 1–2) explains the author's need to define herself and suggests indirectly that each of us needs to go through a similar process.

Expository Techniques

1a.   Apart from definition, what expository technique does Noda use to organize this essay as a whole?

 b.   What expository pattern does she employ in paragraphs 3–8?

 c.   What pattern does she use in paragraphs 9–20?

 d.   What pattern or patterns organize paragraphs 21–28?

 e.   What pattern helps conclude the essay in paragraphs 31–34?

2.   This essay makes use of a variety of expository patterns. Explain why it is accurate (or inaccurate) to refer to the overall pattern as one of definition. Be ready to defend your answer with evidence from the text.

3a.   Tell how paragraph 2 helps predict and justify the organization of the essay.

 b.   Why is this kind of paragraph a useful part of the essay?

 c.   For what kinds of essays might a paragraph like this be neither useful nor necessary?

4.   Discuss the use of subtitles in organizing the essay. In what ways are they linked to the overall definition pattern? (See Guide to Terms: *Unity*.)

Diction and Vocabulary

1. Each of the major sections in the body of the essay uses a different cluster of terms to explore and define a particular part of the author's identity. Tell what the clusters of terms are in each section.

2. Tell how the diction in paragraphs 22–28 contributes to their effectiveness. (Consider also the contribution made by the choice of details.) (Guide: *Diction*.)

3. If you do not know the meanings of some of the following terms, look them up in a dictionary: context (par. 2); influx (3); invocation (5); Shinto, samisens (6); issei (16); arduously (18); pluralism, spontaneous, harangued (32).

Suggestions for Writing and Discussion

1. If you believe that all people have multiple identities, try defining yours in an essay. If you can, try harmonizing them as well or at least discuss the relationships among them.

2. At the end of the essay, Noda endorses a kind of "pluralism." To what extent is our society already guided by such an attitude? Do we often look at people and events with an opposite attitude? Give some examples. What might be some of the practical consequences (good and bad) of a thoroughgoing pluralism in our society? Is such an attitude really possible for a large society to adopt?

(NOTE: Suggestions for topics requiring development by use of DEFINITION are on page 309, at the end of this section.)

MARGARET ATWOOD

MARGARET ATWOOD was born in Ottawa, Ontario, in 1939. After attending college in Canada, she went to graduate school at Harvard University. She has had a distinguished career as a novelist, poet, and essayist, and is generally considered to be one of the central figures in contemporary Canadian literature and culture. Atwood's international reputation as a writer rests on her novels, including *The Edible Woman* (1960), *Surfacing* (1972), *Life Before Man* (1979), *Bodily Harm* (1982), *The Handmaid's Tale* (1986), and *Cat's Eye* (1989); and her short stories, including *Bluebeard's Egg and Other Stories* (1986), though she has written poetry, television plays, and children's books as well. Her essays were collected in the volume *Second Words* (1982) and have continued to appear in magazines such as *Ms., Harper's, The Humanist, The New Republic,* and *Architectural Digest.* As an essayist, Atwood frequently writes about issues in contemporary culture and society, including the nature of Canadian culture and relationships between Canada and the United States.

Pornography

In the following essay, Atwood addresses the question of pornography with a directness and originality that are characteristic of her work. This essay originally appeared in *Chatelaine Magazine,* a mass-circulation women's magazine. As you read the selection, consider how well it addresses both the concerns of its original audience and the concerns about pornography a somewhat wider audience might have.

When I was in Finland a few years ago for an international writers' conference, I had occasion to say a few paragraphs in public on the subject of pornography. The context was a discussion of political repression, and I was suggesting the possibility of a link between the two. The immediate result was that a male journalist took several large bites out of me. Prudery and pornography are two halves of the same coin, said he, and I was clearly a prude. What could you expect from an Anglo-Canadian? Afterward, a couple of pleasant Scandinavian men asked me what I had been so worked up about. All "pornography" means, they said, is graphic depictions of whores, and what was the harm in that?

Not until then did it strike me that the male journalist and I had two entirely different things in mind. By "pornography," he meant naked bodies and sex. I, on the other hand, had recently been doing the research for my novel *Bodily Harm*, and was still in a state of shock from some of the material I had seen, including the Ontario Board of Film Censors' "outtakes." By "pornography," I meant women getting their nipples snipped off with garden shears, having meat hooks stuck into their vaginas, being disemboweled; little girls being raped; men (yes, there are some men) being smashed to a pulp and forcibly sodomized. The cutting edge of pornography, as far as I could see, was no longer simple old copulation, hanging from the chandelier or otherwise: it was death, messy, explicit and highly sadistic. I explained this to the nice Scandinavian men. "Oh, but that's just the United States," they said. "Everyone knows they're sick." In their country, they said, violent "pornography" of that kind was not permitted on television or in movies; indeed, excessive violence of any kind was not permitted. They had drawn a clear line between erotica, which earlier studies had shown did not incite men to more aggressive and brutal behavior toward women, and violence, which later studies indicated did.

Some time after that I was in Saskatchewan, where, because of the scenes in *Bodily Harm*, I found myself on an open-line radio show answering questions about "pornography." Almost no one who phoned in was in favor of it, but again they weren't talking about the same stuff I was, because they hadn't seen it. Some of them were all set to stamp out bathing suits and negligees, and, if possible, any depictions of the female body whatsoever. God, it was implied, did not approve of female bodies, and sex of any kind, including that practised by bumblebees, should be shoved back into the dark, where it belonged. I had more than a suspicion that *Lady Chatterley's Lover*, Margaret Laurence's *The Diviners*, and indeed most books by most serious modern authors would have ended up as confetti if left in the hands of these callers.

For me, these two experiences illustrate the two poles of the 4 emotionally heated debate that is now thundering around this issue. They also underline the desirability and even the necessity of defining the terms. "Pornography" is now one of those catchalls, like "Marxism" and "feminism," that have become so broad they can mean almost anything, ranging from certain verses in the Bible, ads for skin lotion and sex tests for children to the contents of Penthouse, Naughty '90s postcards and films with titles containing the word *Nazi* that show vicious scenes of torture and killing. It's easy to say that sensible people can tell the difference. Unfortunately, opinions on what constitutes a sensible person vary.

But even sensible people tend to lose their cool when they start 5 talking about this subject. They soon stop talking and start yelling, and the name-calling begins. Those in favor of censorship (which may include groups not noticeably in agreement on other issues, such as some feminists and religious fundamentalists) accuse the others of exploiting women through the use of degrading images, contributing to the corruption of children, and adding to the general climate of violence and threat in which both women and children live in this society; or, though they may not give much of a hoot about actual women and children, they invoke moral standards and God's supposed aversion to "filth," "smut" and deviated *preversion*, which may mean ankles.

The camp in favor of total "freedom of expression" often comes 6 out howling as loud as the Romans would have if told they could no longer have innocent fun watching the lions eat up Christians. It too may include segments of the population who are not natural bedfellows: those who proclaim their God-given right to freedom, including the freedom to tote guns, drive when drunk, drool over chicken porn and get off on videotapes of women being raped and beaten, may be waving the same anticensorship banner as responsible liberals who fear the return of Mrs. Grundy, or gay groups for whom sexual emancipation involves the concept of "sexual theatre." *Whatever turns you on* is a handy motto, as is *A man's home is his castle* (and if it includes a dungeon with beautiful maidens strung up in chains and bleeding from every pore, that's his business).

Meanwhile, theoreticians theorize and speculators speculate. Is 7 today's pornography yet another indication of the hatred of the body, the deep mind-body split, which is supposed to pervade Western Christian society? Is it a backlash against the women's movement by men who are threatened by uppity female behavior in real life, so like to fantasize about women done up like outsize parcels, being turned into hamburger, kneeling at their feet in slavelike adoration or sucking off guns? Is it a sign of collective impotence, of a generation of men who can't relate to real women at all but have to make do with bits of celluloid and paper? Is the current flood just a result of smart marketing and aggressive promotion by the money men in what has now become a multibillion-dollar industry? If they were selling movies about men getting their testicles stuck full of knitting needles by women with swastikas on their sleeves, would they do as well, or is this penchant somehow peculiarly male? If so, why? Is pornography a power trip rather than a sex one? Some say that those ropes, chains, muzzles and other restraining devices are an argument for the immense power female sexuality still wields in the male imagination: you don't put these things on dogs unless you're afraid of them. Others, more literary, wonder about the shift from the 19th-century Magic Woman or Femme Fatale image to the lollipop-licker, airhead or turkey-carcass treatment of women in porn today. The proporners don't care much about theory; they merely demand product. The antiporners don't care about it in the final analysis either; there's dirt on the street, and they want it cleaned up, now.

It seems to me that this conversation, with its *You're-a-prude/You're-a-pervert* dialectic, will never get anywhere as long as we continue to think of this material as just "entertainment." Possibly we're deluded by the packaging, the format: magazine, book, movie, theatrical presentation. We're used to thinking of these things as part of the "entertainment industry," and we're used to thinking of ourselves as free adult people who ought to be able to see any kind of "entertainment" we want to. That was what the First Choice pay-TV debate was all about. After all, it's only entertainment, right? Entertainment means fun, and only a killjoy would be antifun. What's the harm? 8

This is obviously the central question: *What's the harm?* If there isn't any real harm to any real people, then the antiporners can tsk-tsk and/or throw up as much as they like, but they can't rightfully expect more legal controls or sanctions. However, the no-harm position is far from being proven. 9

(For instance, there's a clear-cut case for banning—as the federal government has proposed—movies, photos and videos that depict 10 children engaging in sex with adults: real children are used to make the movies, and hardly anybody thinks this is ethical. The possibilities for coercion are too great.)

To shift the viewpoint, I'd like to suggest three other models for 11
looking at "pornography"—and here I mean the violent kind.

Those who find the idea of regulating pornographic materials 12
repugnant because they think it's Fascist or Communist or otherwise not in accordance with the principles of an open democratic society should consider that Canada has made it illegal to disseminate material that may lead to hatred toward any group because of race or religion. I suggest that if pornography of the violent kind depicted these acts being done predominantly to Chinese, to blacks, to Catholics, it would be off the market immediately, under the present laws. Why is hate literature illegal? Because whoever made the law thought that such material might incite real people to do real awful things to other real people. The human brain is to a certain extent a computer: garbage in, garbage out. We only hear about the extreme cases (like that of American multimurderer Ted Bundy) in which pornography has contributed to the death and/or mutilation of women and/or men. Although pornography is not the only factor involved in the creation of such deviance, it certainly has upped the ante by suggesting both a variety of techniques and the social acceptability of such actions. Nobody knows yet what effect this stuff is having on the less psychotic.

Studies have shown that a large part of the market for all kinds 13
of porn, soft and hard, is drawn from the 16-to-21-year-old population of young men. Boys used to learn about sex on the street, or (in Italy, according to Fellini movies) from friendly whores, or, in more genteel surroundings, from girls, their parents, or, once upon a time, in school, more or less. Now porn has been added, and sex education in the schools is rapidly being phased out. The buck has been passed, and boys are being taught that all women secretly like to be raped and that real men get high on scooping out women's digestive tracts.

Boys learn their concept of masculinity from other men: is this 14
what most men want them to be learning? If word gets around that rapists are "normal" and even admirable men, will boys feel that in order to be normal, admirable and masculine they will have to be rapists? Human beings are enormously flexible, and how they turn out depends a lot on how they're educated, by the society in which they're immersed as well as by their teachers. In a society that adver-

tises and glorifies rape or even implicitly condones it, more women get raped. It becomes socially acceptable. And at a time when men and the traditional male role have taken a lot of flak and men are confused and casting around for an acceptable way of being male (and, in some cases, not getting much comfort from women on that score), this must be at times a pleasing thought.

It would be naïve to think of violent pornography as just harmless entertainment. It's also an educational tool and a powerful propaganda device. What happens when boy educated on porn meets girl brought up on Harlequin romances? The clash of expectations can be heard around the block. She wants him to get down on his knees with a ring, he wants her to get down on all fours with a ring in her nose. Can this marriage be saved? 15

Pornography has certain things in common with such addictive substances as alcohol and drugs: for some, though by no means for all, it induces chemical changes in the body, which the user finds exciting and pleasurable. It also appears to attract a "hard core" of habitual users and a penumbra of those who use it occasionally but aren't dependent on it in any way. There are also significant numbers of men who aren't much interested in it, not because they're undersexed but because real life is satisfying their needs, which may not require as many appliances as those of users. 16

For the "hard core," pornography may function as alcohol does for the alcoholic: tolerance develops, and a little is no longer enough. This may account for the short viewing time and fast turnover in porn theatres. Mary Brown, chairwoman of the Ontario Board of Film Censors, estimates that for every one mainstream movie requesting entrance to Ontario, there is one porno flick. Not only the quantity consumed but the quality of explicitness must escalate, which may account for the growing violence: once the big deal was breasts, then it was genitals, then copulation, then that was no longer enough and the hard users had to have more. The ultimate kick is death, and after that, as the Marquis de Sade so boringly demonstrated, multiple death. 17

The existence of alcoholism has not led us to ban social drinking. On the other hand, we do have laws about drinking and driving, excessive drunkenness and other abuses of alcohol that may result in injury or death to others. 18

This leads us back to the key question: what's the harm? Nobody knows, but this society should find out fast, before the saturation 19 point is reached. The Scandinavian studies that showed a connection between depictions of sexual violence and increased impulse toward it on the part of male viewers would be a starting point, but many more questions remain to be raised as well as answered. What, for instance, is the crucial difference between men who are users and men who are not? Does using affect a man's relationship with actual women, and, if so, adversely? Is there a clear line between erotica and violent pornography, or are they on an escalating continuum? Is this a "men versus women" issue, with all men secretly siding with the proporners and all women secretly siding against? (I think not; there *are* lots of men who don't think that running their true love through the Cuisinart is the best way they can think of to spend a Saturday night, and they're just as nauseated by films of someone else doing it as women are.) Is pornography merely an expression of the sexual confusion of this age or an active contributor to it?

Nobody wants to go back to the age of official repression, when   20 even piano legs were referred to as "limbs" and had to wear pantaloons to be decent. Neither do we want to end up in George Orwell's *1984*, in which pornography is turned out by the State to keep the proles in a state of torpor, sex itself is considered dirty and the approved practise it only for reproduction. But Rome under the emperors isn't such a good model either.

If all men and women respected each other, if sex were consid-   21 ered joyful and life-enhancing instead of a wallow in germ-filled glop, if everyone were in love all the time, if, in other words, many people's lives were more satisfactory for them than they appear to be now, pornography might just go away on its own. But since this is obviously not happening, we as a society are going to have to make some informed and responsible decisions about how to deal with it.

Meanings and Values

1.   Why does Atwood believe it is important now to define the term "pornography"?

2.   Why does the author consider the debates she summarizes in paragraphs 5–7 to be unproductive and perhaps even irritating?

3.   Atwood talks about "three other models for looking at 'pornography' " (par. 11). What are they?

4. In paragraph 19, the author speaks of "erotica" and "violent pornography." Does she offer a concise definition for either term in the course of the essay? If not, construct your own definitions.

Expository Techniques

1a. What is to be gained by opening an essay with extreme examples such as those in paragraph 2? (See Guide to Terms: *Introductions*.)

  b. What might be lost?

  c. Is the strategy effective in this case? (Guide: *Evaluation*.)

2a. What use does Atwood make of comparison in this essay?

  b. How does she use classification?

3. Which of the standard techniques of definition does she employ? (See the introduction to Section 7.)

4a. Characterize Atwood's tone in this essay. Consider especially her attitude toward the various participants in the debate she summarizes in paragraphs 5–8. (Guide: *Style/Tone*.)

  b. Does the tone vary throughout the essay? If so, in what ways does it vary?

  c. Explain how tone might be considered one strategy for offering the author's own definition and encouraging others to agree with it.

Diction and Vocabulary

1. One characteristic of this essay is the way the author compresses evocative words and details into dense but interesting paragraphs. Choose one such paragraph (6, 7, 12, or 13, for example) and discuss how the denotations, connotations, and sensory images conveyed by the words contribute to the overall effect of the paragraph. (Guide: *Connotation/Denotation*.)

2a. For what purposes does Atwood employ so many rhetorical questions in paragraph 7? (Guide: *Rhetorical Questions*.)

  b. How does the diction in the paragraph also contribute to these purposes? (Guide: *Diction*.)

3. If you do not know the meaning of any of the following words, look them up in the dictionary: graphic (par. 1); erotica (2); constitutes (4); impotence (7); dialectic (8); coercion (10); repugnant (12); condones (14); penumbra (16); copulation (17); continuum (19); pantaloon, torpor (20).

Suggestions for Writing and Discussion

1. Develop your own essay defining pornography, or consider other topics that have accumulated similar multiple meanings and generated controversy: abuse (various kinds), violence (on TV and elsewhere), or censorship.

2. Does Atwood represent fairly the various points of view on pornography? What objections might be raised to her portraits? To her conclusions in this essay?

(NOTE: Suggestions for topics requiring development by use of DEFINITION follow.)

Writing Suggestions for Section 7
Definition

Develop a composition for a specified purpose and audience, using whatever methods and expository patterns will help convey a clear understanding of your meaning of one of the following terms:

1. Country music.
2. Conscience.
3. Religion.
4. Bigotry.
5. Success.
6. Empathy.
7. Family.
8. Hypocrisy.
9. Humor.
10. Sophistication.
11. Naiveté.
12. Cowardice.
13. Wisdom.
14. Integrity.
15. Morality.
16. Greed.
17. Social poise.
18. Intellectual (the person).
19. Pornography (if your opinions differ appreciably from Margaret Atwood's).
20. Courage.
21. Patriotism.
22. Equality (or equal opportunity).
23. Loyalty.
24. Stylishness (in clothing or behavior).
25. Fame.

8

Explaining with the Help of *Description*

Exposition, as well as argument, can be made more vivid, and hence more understandable, with the support of description. Most exposition does contain some elements of description, and at times description carries almost the entire burden of the explanation, becoming a basic pattern for the expository purpose.

Description is most useful in painting a word-picture of something concrete, such as a scene or a person. Its use is not restricted, however, to what we can perceive with our senses; we can also describe (or attempt to describe) an abstract concept, such as an emotion or a quality or a mood. But most attempts to describe fear, for instance, still resort to the physical—a "coldness around the heart," perhaps—and in such concrete ways communicate the abstract to the reader.

In its extreme forms, description is either *objective* or *impressionistic* (subjective), but most of its uses are somewhere between these extremes. Objective description is purely factual, uncolored by any feelings of the author; it is the type used for scientific papers and most business reports. But impressionistic description, as the term implies, at least tinges the purely factual with the author's personal impressions; instead of describing how something *is*, objectively, the author describes how it *seems*, subjectively. Such a description might refer to the "blazing heat" of an August day. Somewhat less impressionistic would be "extreme heat." But the scientist would describe it precisely as "115 degrees Fahrenheit," and this would be purely objective reporting, unaffected by the impressions of the author. (No examples of the latter are included in this section, but many textbooks for other courses utilize the technique of pure objective description, as do encyclopedias. The Ackerman essay in Section 5 provides some good examples of objective description, although not entirely unmixed with colorful impressionistic details.)

The first and most important job in any descriptive endeavor is to select the details to be included. There are usually many from which to choose, and writers must constantly keep in mind the kind of picture they want to paint with words—for *their* purpose and *their* audience. Such a word-picture need not be entirely visual; in this respect writers have more freedom than artists, for writers can use strokes that will add the dimensions of sound, smell, and even touch. Such strokes, if made to seem natural enough, can help create a vivid and effective image in the reader's mind.

Most successful impressionistic description focuses on a single *dominant impression*. Of the many descriptive details ordinarily available for use, the author selects those that will help create a mood or atmosphere or emphasize a feature or quality. But more than the materials themselves are involved, for even diction can often assist in creating the desired dominant impression. Sometimes syntax is also an important factor, as in the use of short, hurried sentences to help convey a sense of urgency or excitement.

Actual structuring of passages is perhaps less troublesome in description than in most of the other patterns. But some kind of orderliness is needed for the sake of both readability and a realistic effect. (Neither objective nor impressionistic description can afford not to be realistic, in one manner or another.) In visual description, orderliness is usually achieved by presenting details as the eye would find them—that is, as arranged in space. We could describe a person from head to toe, or vice versa, or begin with the most noticeable feature and work from there. A scenic description might move from near to far or from far to near, from left to right or from right to left. It might also start with a broad, overall view, gradually narrowing to a focal point, probably the most significant feature of the scene. These are fairly standard kinds of description; but as the types and occasions for using description vary widely, so do the possibilities for interesting treatment. In many cases, writers are limited only by their own ingenuity.

But ingenuity should not be allowed to produce *excessive* description, an amazingly certain path to reader boredom. A few well-chosen details are better than profusion. Economy of words is desirable in any writing, and description is no exception. Appropriate use of figurative language and careful choice of strong nouns and verbs will help prevent the need for strings of modifiers, which are wasteful and can seem amateurish.

Even for the experienced writer, however, achieving good description remains a constant challenge; the beginner should not expect to attain this goal without working at it.

Sample Paragraph (Description)

Background.

Interpretation of the photograph.

Generally objective description of the photograph, though "almost smell" is certainly impressionistic.

The details of the photograph are presented objectively, but the description is filled with impressionistic observations about the dancer's moods and the emotional "temperature" of the scene.

The theme of this year's Amateur Photography Contest sponsored by the Palmville *Gazette* was "Snapshots of Palmville." There were two "Top Shot" award winners. Emily Grezibel looked to the past with a black-and-white photograph of Ericson's Feed Store. The peeling white paint on the front of the old clapboard building gleams in the hot midday sun and little puffs of dust follow the footsteps of the elderly farmer in dark bib overalls as he passes in front of the Blue Seal Feeds sign. One can almost smell the dust and the scents of feed, fertilizer, and oil hanging in the air. The title sums up the photograph's theme: "Fading." Brian Alonzo's color photograph "Saturday Night" is the other winner. Taken in the parking lot of the Palmville Mall, it shows a group of teenagers dancing to the music of a boom box sitting on the hood of a shiny, cherry-red convertible. Several of the couples dancing in the foreground appear to be singing along with the music and the dancers are frozen in the middle of joyous, athletic dance steps. Other teenagers sit on hoods of bright blue, turquoise, and yellow cars in a semicircle behind the dancers, clapping and smiling. The silent yet exciting sounds of the music seem to radiate

314

The central theme of the paragraph is the contrast between the generations and their outlooks.

from the entire picture. The whole scene is illuminated by the arc lights of the parking lot, making the picture seem a festival celebrating the energy and hopefulness of the next generation of Palmville citizens.

Sample Paragraph (Description)

It's no winter without an ice storm. When Robert Frost gazed at bowed-over birch trees and tried to think that boys had bent them playing, he knew better: "Ice-storms do that." They do that and a lot more, trimming disease and weakness out of the tree—the old tree's friend, as pneumonia used to be the old man's. Some of us provide life-support systems for our precious shrubs, boarding them over against the ice, for the ice storm takes the young or unlucky branch or birch as well as the rotten or feeble. One February morning we look out our windows over yards and fields littered with kindling, small twigs and great branches. We look out at a world turned into one diamond, ten thousand carats in the line of sight, twice as many facets. What a dazzle of spinning refracted light, spider webs of cold brilliance attacking our eyeballs! All winter we wear sunglasses to drive, more than we do in summer, and never so much as after an ice storm, with its painful glaze reflecting from maple and birch, granite boulder and stone wall, turning electric wires into bright silver filaments. The

snow itself takes on a crust of ice, like
the finish of a clay pot, that carries our
weight and sends us swooping and
sliding. It's worth your life to go for the
mail. Until sand and salt redeem the
highway, Route 4 is quiet. We cancel the
appointment with the dentist, stay
home, and marvel at the altered
universe, knowing that midday sun will
strip ice from tree and roof and restore
our ordinary white winter world.

SHARON CURTIN

SHARON CURTIN, a native of Douglas, Wyoming, was raised in a family of ranchers and craftspeople. Curtin, a feminist and political leftist, has worked as a nurse in New York and California but now devotes most of her time to writing and to operating a small farm in Virginia.

Aging in the Land of the Young

"Aging in the Land of the Young" is the first part of Curtin's article by that title, as it appeared in the *Atlantic* in July 1972. It is largely a carefully restructured composite of portions of her book *Nobody Ever Died of Old Age*, also published in 1972. It illustrates the subjective form of description, generally known as impressionistic description.

Old men, old women, almost 20 million of them. They constitute 10 1
percent of the total population, and the percentage is steadily growing. Some of them, like conspirators, walk all bent over, as if hiding
some precious secret, filled with self-protection. The body seems to
gather itself around those vital parts, folding shoulders, arms, pelvis
like a fading rose. Watch and you see how fragile old people come to
think they are.

Aging paints every action gray, lies heavy on every movement, 2
imprisons every thought. It governs each decision with a ruthless and
single-minded perversity. To age is to learn the feeling of no longer
growing, of struggling to do old tasks, to remember familiar actions.
The cells of the brain are destroyed with thousands of unfelt tiny
strokes, little pockets of clotted blood wiping out memories and

abilities without warning. The body seems slowly to give up, randomly stopping, sometimes starting again as if to torture and tease with the memory of lost strength. Hands become clumsy, frail transparencies, held together with knotted blue veins.

Sometimes it seems as if the distance between your feet and the floor were constantly changing, as if you were walking on shifting and not quite solid ground. One foot down, slowly, carefully force the other foot forward. Sometimes you are a shuffler, not daring to lift your feet from the uncertain earth but forced to slide hesitantly forward in little whispering movements. Sometimes you are able to "step out," but this effort—in fact the pure exhilaration of easy movement—soon exhausts you. ³

The world becomes narrower as friends and family die or move away. To climb stairs, to ride in a car, to walk to the corner, to talk on the telephone; each action seems to take away from the energy needed to stay alive. Everything is limited by the strength you hoard greedily. Your needs decrease, you require less food, less sleep, and finally less human contact; yet this little bit becomes more and more difficult. You fear that one day you will be reduced to the simple acts of breathing and taking nourishment. This is the ultimate stage you dread, the period of helplessness and hopelessness, when independence will be over. ⁴

There is nothing to prepare you for the experience of growing old. Living is a process, an irreversible progression toward old age and eventual death. You see men of eighty still vital and straight as oaks; you see men of fifty reduced to gray shadows in the human landscape. The cellular clock differs for each one of us, and is profoundly affected by our own life experiences, our heredity, and perhaps most important, by the concepts of aging encountered in society and in oneself. ⁵

The aged live with enforced leisure, on fixed incomes, subject to many chronic illnesses, and most of their money goes to keep a roof over their heads. They also live in a culture that worships youth. ⁶

A kind of cultural attitude makes me bigoted against old people; it makes me think young is best; it makes me treat old people like outcasts. ⁷

Hate that gray? Wash it away! ⁸
Wrinkle cream. ⁹
Monkey glands. ¹⁰

Face-lifting.   11
Look like a bride again.   12
Don't trust anyone over thirty.   13
I fear growing old.   14
Feel Young Again!   15

I am afraid to grow old—we're all afraid. In fact, the fear of   16
growing old is so great that every aged person is an insult and a threat
to the society. They remind us of our own death, that our body won't
always remain smooth and responsive, but will someday betray us
by aging, wrinkling, faltering, failing. The ideal way to age would be
to grow slowly invisible, gradually disappearing, without causing
worry or discomfort to the young. In some ways that does happen.
Sitting in a small park across from a nursing home one day, I noticed
that the young mothers and their children gathered on one side, and
the old people from the home on the other. Whenever a youngster
would run over to the "wrong" side, chasing a ball or just trying to
cover all the available space, the old people would lean forward and
smile. But before any communication could be established, the
mother would come over, murmuring embarrassed apologies, and
take her child back to the "young" side.

Now, it seemed to me that the children didn't feel any particular   17
fear and the old people didn't seem to be threatened by the children.
The division of space was drawn by the mothers. And the mothers
never looked at the old people who lined the other side of the park
like so many pigeons perched on the benches. These well-dressed
young matrons had a way of sliding their eyes over, around, through
the old people; they never looked at them directly. The old people may
as well have been invisible; they had no reality for the youngsters,
who were not permitted to speak to them, and they offended the
aesthetic eye of the mothers.

My early experiences were somewhat different; since I grew up   18
in a small town, my childhood had more of a nineteenth-century
flavor. I knew a lot of old people, and considered some of them
friends. There was no culturally defined way for me to "relate" to old
people, except the rules of courtesy which applied to all adults. My
grandparents were an integral and important part of the family and
of the community. I sometimes have a dreadful fear that mine will be
the last generation to know old people as friends, to have a sense of

what growing old means, to respect and understand man's mortality and his courage in the face of death. Mine may be the last generation to have a sense of living history, of stories passed from generation to generation, of identity established by family history.

Meanings and Values

1. What is the general tone of this writing? (See Guide to Terms: *Style/Tone*.)

2. If you find it depressing to read about aging, try to analyze why (especially in view of the fact that you are very likely many years from the stage of "a fading rose").

3. Why do you suppose it is more likely to be the mothers than the children who shun old people (pars. 16–17)?

4a. Has this author avoided the excesses of sentimentality? (Guide: *Sentimentality*.) If not, where does she fail?

 b. If she does avoid sentimentality, try to discover how.

Expository Techniques

1a. Why should this writing be classed as primarily impressionistic, rather than objective?

 b. What is the dominant impression?

2a. Analyze the role that selection of details plays in creating the dominant impression.

 b. Provide examples of the type of details that could have been included but were not.

 c. Are such omissions justifiable?

3a. Paragraph 5 ends the almost pure description to begin another phase of the writing. What is it?

 b. How has the author provided for a smooth transition between the two? (Guide: *Transition*.)

4a. What particular method of gaining emphasis has been used effectively in one portion of the selection? (Guide: *Emphasis*.)

 b. How might the material have been presented if emphasis were not desired?

5. Which previously studied patterns of exposition are also used in this writing? Cite paragraphs where each may be found.

Diction and Vocabulary

1a.   The author sometimes changes person—e.g., "they" to "you" after paragraph 2. Analyze where the changes occur.

b.   What justification, if any, can you find for each change?

2a.   Which two kinds of figures of speech do you find used liberally to achieve this description? (Guide: *Figures of Speech.*)

. b.   Cite three or more examples of each.

c.   As nearly as you can tell, are any of them clichés? (Guide: *Clichés.*)

Suggestions for Writing and Discussion

1.   If Curtin is correct in her fears expressed in the last two sentences, what could be the consequences for society in general?

2.   Discuss the pros and cons of placing old people in rest homes, rather than letting them live alone or taking them to live with the family. What other alternatives, if any, does the family have?

3.   If you know some very old person who (apparently) is not as affected by aging as the ones the author describes, what seems to account for this difference?

4.   If many people at age sixty-five to seventy-five are still efficient at their jobs, as is often argued, what practical reasons are there for forcing retirement at that age?

(NOTE: Suggestions for topics requiring development by use of DESCRIPTION are on pages 351–352, at the end of this section.)

JOYCE MAYNARD was born in 1953 and spent her childhood in Durham, New Hampshire, where her father taught at the nearby University of New Hampshire. At 19, while she was still a sophomore at Yale University, her first book appeared: *Looking Backward: A Chronicle of Growing Up Old in the Sixties* (1973). Maynard was a reporter for the *New York Times* and currently writes a syndicated newspaper column. She also writes monthly for *Mademoiselle* and *Harrowsmith* magazines and has published a novel, *Baby Love* (1981). Many of her columns were reprinted in the collection *Domestic Affairs* (1988).

The Yellow Door House

Permanence, continuity, and change are some of the ideas explored through description in this essay, originally published as one of the author's columns. Comparison plays an important part in the exposition as well, particularly in juxtaposing Maynard's memories of the house with its present reality.

I've known only two homes in my life: the one I live in now, with my husband and children, and another one, just sixty miles from here, where I grew up. My father's dead now, and even before that, my parents were divorced and my mother moved away from our old house. But though she rents the house out nine months of the year and hasn't spent a winter there for thirteen years, she hasn't sold our old house yet. It's still filled with our old belongings from our old life. And though my mother has another house now, and a good life, with another man, in a new place, she still comes back to the old house for a couple of months every summer. Every year I ask her, "Have you considered putting the house on the market?" And every summer the answer is "not yet." 1

My children call the place where I grew up the yellow door house. 2
They love the place, with its big, overgrown yard, the old goldfish
pond, the brick walkway, the white picket fence. On the front door
there's a heavy brass knocker my sons like to bang on to announce
their arrival for visits with their grandmother, and French windows
on either side that I was always cautioned against breaking as a child.
(As now I caution my children.) There's a brass mail slot I used to pass
messages through to a friend waiting on the other side. Now my
daughter Audrey does the same.

It's a big house, a hip-roofed colonial, with ceilings higher than 3
anybody needs, and a sweeping staircase rising up from the front hall,
with a banister that children more adventurous than my sister and I
(mine, for instance) are always tempted to slide on. There are plants
everywhere, paintings my father made, Mexican pottery, and a band
of tin Mexican soldiers—one on horseback, one playing the flute, one
the tuba. We bought those soldiers on the first trip I ever made to New
York City. They cost way too much, but my mother said we could get
them if we took the bus home instead of flying. So we did.

One room of the yellow door house is wood paneled and lined 4
with books. There used to be a big overstuffed armchair in it that I'd
settle into with my cookies and milk, when I came home from school,
to do my homework or watch "Leave It to Beaver." (That chair is in
my house now.) There's a porch with a swing out back, and a sunny
corner in the kitchen where I always ate my toast—grilled in the oven,
sometimes with cinnamon sugar and sometimes jam, but always the
way my mother made it, buttered on both sides. My mother is a
wonderful, natural cook, who would announce, on a typical night,
three different dessert possibilities, all homemade. Now I wouldn't
think of eating a third piece of blueberry pie. But the old habits return
when I walk into my mother's kitchen. The first thing I do is go see
what's in the refrigerator.

It's been fourteen years since I lived in the yellow door house, 5
but I could still make my way around it blindfolded. There are places
where the house could use some work now, and my mother never was
the best housekeeper. I open a drawer in the big Welsh dresser in the
dining room, looking for a safety pin, and so much spills out (though
not safety pins) that I can't close it again. A person can choose from
five different kinds of cookies in this house. There's a whole closetful
of fabric scraps and antique lace. Eight teapots. But no yardstick, no
light bulbs, no scissors.

My children's favorite place in the house is the attic. The front 6
half used to be the studio where my father painted, at night, when
he came home from his job as an English teacher. The paintings and
paints are long gone now; but my father was a lover of art supplies
and hopelessly extravagant when it came to acquiring them, so
every once in a while, even now, thirteen years since he's been here,
I'll come upon a box of unopened pastels, or watercolor pencils, or
the kind of art gum eraser he always used. I'll pick up a stub of an
oil pastel and hold it up to my nose, and a wave of feeling will wash
over me that almost makes my knees weak. Cadmium yellow light.
Cerulean blue. Suddenly I'm ten years old again, sitting on the
grass in a field a couple of miles down the road from here, with a
sketch pad on my lap and my father beside me, drawing a picture
of Ski Jump Hill.

Beyond the room that was my father's studio is the part of our 7
attic where my mother—a hoarder, like me—has stored away just
about every toy we ever owned, and most of our old dresses. A ripped
Chinese umbrella, a broken wicker rocker, a hooked rug she started
and never finished, an exercise roller, purchased around 1947, meant
to undo the damage of all those blueberry pies. Songs I wrote when I
was nine. My sister's poems. My mother's notes from college English
class. My father's powerfully moving proclamations of love to her,
written when she was eighteen and he was thirty-eight, when she was
telling him she couldn't marry him and he was telling her she must.

Every time we come to the yellow door house to visit, Audrey 8
and Charlie head for the attic—and though we have mostly cleaned
out my old Barbies now (and a Midge doll, whose turned-up nose had
been partly nibbled off by mice), we never seem to reach the end of
the treasures: My homemade dollhouse furniture (I packed it away,
room by room, with notes enclosed, to the daughter I knew I would
someday have, describing how I'd laid out the rooms.) An old
wooden recorder. A brass doll bed. Wonderfully detailed doll clothes
my mother made for us every Christmas (at the time, I longed for
store-bought). One year she knit a sweater, for a two-inch-tall bear,
using toothpicks for knitting needles. Another year she sewed us
matching skirts from an old patchwork quilt.

The little town where I grew up (and where I used to know just 9
about everyone) has been growing so fast that my mother hardly
knows anyone on our street anymore. A house like hers has become
so desirable that within days of her arrival this summer, my mother

got a call from a realtor asking if she'd be interested in selling. He named as a likely asking price a figure neither one of us could believe. My parents bought the house, thirty years ago, for a fifth of that amount, and still, they sometimes had to take out loans to meet the mortgage payments.

For years now, I have been telling my mother that it makes little   10
sense to hold on to the yellow door house (and to worry about tenants, make repairs, put away the Mexican tin soldiers every Labor Day and take them out again every Fourth of July). But I suddenly realized, hearing about this realtor's call, that when the day comes that my mother sells the house, I will be deeply shaken. I doubt if I will even want to drive down our old street after that, or even come back to the town, where I scarcely know anybody anymore. I don't much want to see some other family inventing new games, new rituals, in our house. Don't want to know where they put their Christmas tree, or what sort of paintings they hang on their walls. It would be crazy—impossible—to pack up and haul away all those dress-up clothes and bits of costume jewelry and boxes of old book reports and crumbs of pastels. But neither do I relish the thought of someday having to throw them out.

My mother's yellow door house is a perfect place to play hide-   11
and-seek, and last weekend, when I was there visiting with my three children, that's what my two sons and I did. I found a hiding place in the wood-paneled room, behind the couch. I scrunched myself up so small that several minutes passed without my sons' finding me, even though they passed through the room more than once.

Many families have rented the house since my mother ceased to   12
make it her full-time home, but the smell—I realized—hasn't changed. Listening to my children's voices calling out to me through the rooms, I studied a particular knothole in the paneling, and it came back to me that this knothole had always reminded me of an owl. I ran my finger over the wood floors and the upholstery on the side of the couch, and noted the dust my mother has always tended to leave in corners. I heard the sewing machine whirring upstairs: my mother, sewing doll clothes with Audrey. I smelled my mother's soup on the stove. And for a moment, I wanted time to freeze.

But then I let myself make a small noise. "We found you, we   13
found you," my boys sang out, falling into my arms. And then we all had lunch, with my mother's chocolate chip cookies for dessert—and headed back to the house I live in now. Whose door is green.

Meanings and Values

1.   Where in the opening paragraph does Maynard introduce the themes of change and continuity?

2.   List the kinds of memories the objects in the attic call up in the author's mind (pars. 6–8).

3.   What does the author believe will be lost if her mother sells the house?

4a.   What is meant by the phrase "I wanted time to freeze" in paragraph 12?

b.   What actions does the author take in the next paragraph that undermine this wish and the values implied by it?

Expository Techniques

1a.   Identify the subjects Maynard describes in each of the paragraphs following the opening.

b.   Do these paragraphs generally focus on a single scene (or subject) or on several? Be ready to support your answer with examples from the text.

c.   Can the descriptions in paragraphs 4 and 10 be considered unified? Why, or why not? (See Guide to Terms: *Unity*.)

2.   What use does Maynard make of comparison in paragraphs 2, 12, and 13 to convey themes of continuity, permanence, and change?

Diction and Vocabulary

1a.   Identify the concrete diction in paragraph 6 and discuss how it contributes to the effectiveness of the passage. (Guide: *Evaluation*.)

b.   What are the technical terms used in the passage, and how do they contribute to its effect? (Guide: *Diction*.)

2a.   Why does the author mention the television program "Leave It to Beaver" (par. 4)?

b.   In what ways has her life been similar to the life of the family depicted in the series?

c.   In what ways has it differed?

Suggestions for Writing and Discussion

1.   Do many people today have a chance to return to the homes and apartments in which they grew up? Is it likely that many spent their

entire childhoods living in a single house or apartment? How are the childhood memories of people whose families moved often likely to differ from those of Maynard? Are their values likely to differ also?

2. Prepare an essay describing one or more places where you lived as a child. In the course of the description deal with questions of change, loss, growth, continuity, and related matters.

(NOTE: Suggestions for topics requiring development by use of DESCRIPTION are on pages 351–352, at the end of this section.)

GEORGE SIMPSON

GEORGE SIMPSON, born in Virginia in 1950, received his B.A. in
journalism from the University of North Carolina. He went to work
for *Newsweek* in 1972 and in 1978 became public affairs director for
that magazine. Before joining *Newsweek*, Simpson worked for two
years as a writer and editor for the *Carolina Financial Times* in Chapel
Hill, North Carolina, and as a reporter for the *News-Gazette* in
Lexington, Virginia. He received the Best Feature Writing award
from Sigma Delta Chi in 1972 for a five-part investigative series on
the University of North Carolina football program. He has written
stories for the *New York Times, Sport, Glamour*, the *Winston-Salem
Journal*, and *New York*.

The War Room at Bellevue

"The War Room at Bellevue" was first published in *New York*
magazine. The author chose, for good reason, to stay strictly within
a time sequence as he described the emergency ward. This essay is
also noteworthy for the cumulative descriptive effect, which was
accomplished almost entirely with objective details.

Bellevue. The name conjures up images of an indoor war zone: the   1
wounded and bleeding lining the halls, screaming for help while
harried doctors in blood-stained smocks rush from stretcher to
stretcher, fighting a losing battle against exhaustion and the crushing
number of injured. "What's worse," says a longtime Bellevue nurse,
"is that we have this image of being a hospital only for . . ." She
pauses, then lowers her voice; "for crazy people."

Though neither battlefield nor Bedlam is a valid image, there is   2
something extraordinary about the monstrous complex that spreads
for five blocks along First Avenue in Manhattan. It is said best by the

head nurse in Adult Emergency Service: "If you have any chance for survival, you have it here." Survival—that is why they come. Why do injured cops drive by a half-dozen other hospitals to be treated at Bellevue? They've seen the Bellevue emergency team in action.

9:00 P.M. It is a Friday night in the Bellevue emergency room. The after-work crush is over (those who've suffered through the day, only to come for help after the five-o'clock whistle has blown) and it is nearly silent except for the mutter of voices at the admitting desk, where administrative personnel discuss who will go for coffee. Across the spotless white-walled lobby, ten people sit quietly, passively, in pastel plastic chairs, waiting for word of relatives or to see doctors. In the past 24 hours, 300 people have come to the Bellevue Adult Emergency Service. Fewer than 10 percent were true emergencies. One man sleeps fitfully in the emergency ward while his heartbeat, respiration, and blood pressure are monitored by control consoles mounted over his bed. Each heartbeat trips a tiny bleep in the monitor, which attending nurses can hear across the ward. A half hour ago, doctors in the trauma room withdrew a six-inch stiletto blade from his back. When he is stabilized, the patient will be moved upstairs to the twelve-bed Surgical Intensive Care Unit.

9:05 P.M. An ambulance backs into the receiving bay, its red and yellow lights flashing in and out of the lobby. A split second later, the glass doors burst open as a nurse and an attendant roll a mobile stretcher into the lobby. When the nurse screams, "Emergency!" the lobby explodes with activity as the way is cleared to the trauma room. Doctors appear from nowhere and transfer the bloodied body of a black man to the treatment table. Within seconds his clothes are stripped away, revealing a tiny stab wound in his left side. Three doctors and three nurses rush around the victim, each performing a task necessary to begin treatment. Intravenous needles are inserted into his arms and groin. A doctor draws blood for the lab, in case surgery is necessary. A nurse begins inserting a catheter into the victim's penis and continues to feed in tubing until the catheter reaches the bladder. Urine flows through the tube into a plastic bag. Doctors are glad not to see blood in the urine. Another nurse records pulse and blood pressure.

The victim is in good shape. He shivers slightly, although the trauma room is exceedingly warm. His face is bloodied, but shows no major lacerations. A third nurse, her elbow propped on the treatment table, asks the man a series of questions, trying to quickly outline his

3

4

5

medical history. He answers abruptly. He is drunk. His left side is swabbed with yellow disinfectant and a doctor injects a local anesthetic. After a few seconds another doctor inserts his finger into the wound. It sinks in all the way to the knuckle. He begins to rotate his finger like a child trying to get a marble out of a milk bottle. The patient screams bloody murder and tries to struggle free.

Meanwhile in the lobby, a security guard is ejecting a derelict who   6
has begun to drink from a bottle hidden in his coat pocket. "He's a regular, was in here just two days ago," says a nurse. "We checked him pretty good then, so he's probably okay now. Can you believe those were clean clothes we gave him?" The old man, blackened by filth, leaves quietly.

9:15 P.M. A young Hispanic man interrupts, saying his pregnant   7
girl friend, sitting outside in his car, is bleeding heavily from her vagina. She is rushed into an examination room, treated behind closed doors, and rolled into the observation ward, where, much later in the night, a gynecologist will treat her in a special room—the same one used to examine rape victims. Nearby, behind curtains, the neurologist examines an old white woman to determine if her headaches are due to head injury. They are not.

9:45 P.M. The trauma room has been cleared and cleaned merci-   8
lessly. The examination rooms are three-quarters full—another overdose, two asthmatics, a young woman with abdominal pains. In the hallway, a derelict who has been sleeping it off urinates all over the stretcher. He sleeps on while attendants change his clothes. An ambulance—one of four that patrol Manhattan for Bellevue from 42nd Street to Houston, river to river—delivers a middle-aged white woman and two cops, the three of them soaking wet. The woman has escaped from the psychiatric floor of a nearby hospital and tried to drown herself in the East River. The cops fished her out. She lies on a stretcher shivering beneath white blankets. Her eyes stare at the ceiling. She speaks clearly when an administrative worker begins routine questioning. The cops are given hospital gowns and wait to receive tetanus shots and gamma globulin—a hedge against infection from the befouled river water. They will hang around the E.R. for another two hours, telling their story to as many as six other policemen who show up to hear it. The woman is rolled into an examination room, where a male nurse speaks gently: "They tell me you fell into the river." "No," says the woman, "I jumped. I have to commit suicide." "Why?" asks the nurse. "Because I'm insane and I can't help

[it]. I have to die." The nurse gradually discovers the woman has a history of psychological problems. She is given dry bedclothes and placed under guard in the hallway. She lies on her side, staring at the wall.

The pace continues to increase. Several more overdose victims   9
arrive by ambulance. One, a young black woman, had done a strip-tease on the street just before passing out. A second black woman is semiconscious and spends the better part of her time at Bellevue alternately cursing at and pleading with the doctors. Attendants find a plastic bottle coated with methadone in the pocket of a Hispanic O.D. The treatment is routinely the same, and sooner or later involves vomiting. Just after doctors begin to treat the O.D., he vomits great quantities of wine and methadone in all directions. "Lovely business, huh?" laments one of the doctors. A young nurse confides that if there were other true emergencies, the overdose victims would be given lower priority. "You can't help thinking they did it to themselves," she says, "while the others are accident victims."

10:30 P.M. A policeman who twisted his knee struggling with an   10
"alleged perpetrator" is examined and released. By 10:30, the lobby is jammed with friends and relatives of patients in various stages of treatment and recovery. The attendant who also functions as a trans-lator for Hispanic patients adds chairs to accommodate the overflow. The medical walk-in rate stays steady—between eight and ten pa-tients waiting. A pair of derelicts, each with battered eyes, appear at the admitting desk. One has a dramatically swollen face laced with black stitches.

11:00 P.M. The husband of the attempted suicide arrives. He thanks   11
the police for saving his wife's life, then talks at length with doctors about her condition. She continues to stare into the void and does not react when her husband approaches her stretcher.

Meanwhile, patients arrive in the lobby at a steady pace. A young   12
G.I. on leave has lower-back pains; a Hispanic man complains of pains in his side; occasionally parents hurry through the adult E.R. carrying children to the pediatric E.R. A white woman of about 50 marches into the lobby from the walk-in entrance. Dried blood covers her right eyebrow and upper lip. She begins to perform. "I was assaulted on 28th and Lexington, I was," she says grandly, "and I don't have to take it *anymore*. I was a bride 21 years ago and, God, I was beautiful then." She has captured the attention of all present. "I was there when the

boys came home—on Memorial Day—and I don't have to take this kind of treatment."

As midnight approaches, the nurses prepare for the shift change. 13 They must brief the incoming staff and make sure all reports are up-to-date. One young brunet says, "Christ, I'm gonna go home and take a shower—I smell like vomit."

11:50 P.M. The triage nurse is questioning an old black man about 14 chest pains, and a Hispanic woman is having an asthma attack, when an ambulance, its sirens screaming full tilt, roars into the receiving bay. There is a split-second pause as everyone drops what he or she is doing and looks up. Then all hell breaks loose. Doctors and nurses are suddenly sprinting full-out toward the trauma room. The glass doors burst open and the occupied stretcher is literally run past me. Cops follow. It is as if a comet has whooshed by. In the trauma room it all becomes clear. A half-dozen doctors and nurses surround the lifeless form of a Hispanic man with a shotgun hole in his neck the size of your fist. Blood pours from a second gaping wound in his chest. A respirator is slammed over his face, making his chest rise and fall as if he were breathing. "No pulse," reports one doctor. A nurse jumps on a stool and, leaning over the man, begins to pump his chest with her palms. "No blood pressure," screams another nurse. The ambulance driver appears shaken, "I never thought I'd get here in time," he stutters. More doctors from the trauma team upstairs arrive. Wrappings from syringes and gauze pads fly through the air. The victim's eyes are open yet devoid of life. His body takes on a yellow tinge. A male nurse winces at the gunshot wound. "This guy really pissed off somebody," he says. This is no ordinary shooting. It is an execution. IV's are jammed into the body in the groin and arms. One doctor has been plugging in an electrocardiograph and asks everyone to stop for a second so he can get a reading. "Forget it," shouts the doctor in charge. "No time." "Take it easy, Jimmy," someone yells at the head physician. It is apparent by now that the man is dead, but the doctors keep trying injections and finally they slit open the chest and reach inside almost up to their elbows. They feel the extent of the damage and suddenly it is all over. "I told 'em he was dead," says one nurse, withdrawing. "They didn't listen." The room is very still. The doctors are momentarily disgusted, then go on about their business. The room clears quickly. Finally there is only a male nurse and the still-warm body, now waxy-yellow, with huge ribs exposed on both sides of the chest and giant holes in both sides of the neck. The nurse speculates that this is yet another murder in a Hispanic political struggle that has brought many such victims to Bellevue. He marvels at the extent of the wounds and repeats, "This guy was really blown away."

Midnight. A hysterical woman is hustled through the lobby   15
into an examination room. It is the dead man's wife, and she is nearly delirious. "I know he's dead, I know he's dead," she screams over and over. Within moments the lobby is filled with anxious relatives of the victim, waiting for word on his condition. The police are everywhere asking questions, but most people say they saw nothing. One young woman says she heard six shots, two louder than the other four. At some point, word is passed that the man is, in fact, dead. Another woman breaks down in hysterics; everywhere young Hispanics are crying and comforting each other. Plainclothes detectives make a quick examination of the body, check on the time of pronouncement of death, and begin to ask questions, but the bereaved are too stunned to talk. The rest of the uninvolved people in the lobby stare dumbly, their injuries suddenly paling in light of a death.

12:30 A.M. A black man appears at the admissions desk and says   16
he drank poison by mistake. He is told to have a seat. The ambulance brings in a young white woman, her head wrapped in white gauze. She is wailing terribly. A girl friend stands over her, crying, and a boyfriend clutches the injured woman's hands, saying, "I'm here, don't worry, I'm here." The victim has fallen downstairs at a friend's house. Attendants park her stretcher against the wall to wait for an examination room to clear. There are eight examination rooms and only three doctors. Unless you are truly an emergency, you will wait. One doctor is stitching up the eyebrow of a drunk who's been punched out. The friends of the woman who fell down the stairs glance up at the doctors anxiously, wondering why their friend isn't being treated faster.

1:10 A.M. A car pulls into the bay and a young Hispanic asks if a   17
shooting victim has been brought here. The security guard blurts out, "He's dead." The young man is stunned. He peels his tires leaving the bay.

1:20 A.M. The young woman of the stairs is getting stitches in a   18
small gash over her left eye when the same ambulance driver who

brought in the gunshot victim delivers a man who has been stabbed in the back on East 3rd Street. Once again the trauma room goes from 0 to 60 in five seconds. The patient is drunk, which helps him endure the pain of having the catheter inserted through his penis into his bladder. Still he yells, "That hurts like a bastard," then adds sheepishly, "Excuse me, ladies." But he is not prepared for what comes next. An X-ray reveals a collapsed right lung. After just a shot of local anesthetic, the doctor slices open his side and inserts a long plastic tube. Internal bleeding had kept the lung pressed down and prevented it from reinflating. The tube releases the pressure. The ambulance driver says the cops grabbed the guy who ran the eight-inch blade into the victim's back. "That's not the one," says the man. "They got the wrong guy." A nurse reports that there is not much of the victim's type blood available at the hospital. One of the doctors says that's okay, he won't need surgery. Meanwhile blood pours from the man's knife wound and the tube in his side. As the nurses work, they chat about personal matters, yet they respond immediately to orders from either doctor. "How ya doin'?" the doctor asks the patient. "Okay," he says. His blood spatters on the floor.

So it goes into the morning hours. A Valium overdose, a woman who fainted, a man who went through the windshield of his car. More overdoses. More drunks with split eyebrows and chins. The doctors and nurses work without complaint. "This is nothing, about normal, I'd say," concludes the head nurse. "No big deal." 19

Meanings and Values

1a. What is the author's point of view? (See Guide to Terms: *Point of View*.)

 b. How is this reflected by the tone? (Guide: *Style/Tone*.)

2a. Does Simpson ever slip into sentimentality—a common failing when describing the scenes of death and tragedy? (Guide: *Sentimentality*.) If so, where?

 b. If not, how does he avoid it?

3a. Cite at least six facts learned from reading this piece that are told, not in general terms, but by specific, concrete details—e.g., that a high degree of cleanliness is maintained at Bellevue, illustrated by "the spotless white-walled lobby" (par. 3) and "the trauma room has been cleared and cleaned mercilessly" (par. 8).

 b. What are the advantages of having facts presented in this way?

Expository Techniques

1.   How do you think the author went about selecting details, from among the thousands that must have been available to him?

2a. Do you consider the writing to be primarily objective or impressionistic?

 b. Clarify any apparent contradictions.

 c. What is the dominant impression, if any?

3.   What is the value of using a timed sequence in such a description?

4.   Does it seem to you that any of this description is excessive—i.e., unnecessary to the task at hand?

5a. List, in skeletal form, the facts learned about the subject from reading the two-paragraph introduction.

 b. How well does it perform the three basic purposes of an introduction? (Guide: *Introductions.*)

6a. What is the significance of the rhetorical question in paragraph 2? (Guide: *Rhetorical Questions.*)

 b. Why is it rhetorical?

7.   Is the short closing effective? (Guide: *Closings.*) Why, or why not?

Diction and Vocabulary

1a. Cite the clichés in paragraphs 4, 5, 8, and 14. (Guide: *Clichés.*)

 b. What justification, if any, can you offer for their use?

2.   Cite the allusion in paragraph 2, and explain its meaning and source. (Guide: *Figures of Speech.*)

3a. Simpson uses some slang and other colloquialisms. Cite as many of these as you can. (Guide: *Colloquial Expressions.*)

 b. Is their use justified? Why, or why not?

4.   Why is "alleged perpetrator" placed in quotation marks (par. 10)?

Suggestions for Writing and Discussion

1.   Explain why "neither battlefield nor Bedlam is a valid image" of the emergency room at Bellevue (pars. 1, 2).

2.   Do you think it is right and/or understandable that O.D.'s should be given lower priorities than "true emergencies" (par. 9)? Defend your views.

3.   If you have had a job that to the outsider might seem hectic or hazardous, or both, were the personnel also able to "chat about personal matters" while the work was in progress? What were the circumstances?

(NOTE: Suggestions for topics requiring development by use of DESCRIPTION are on pages 351–352, at the end of this section.)

MARGARET BOURKE-WHITE

MARGARET BOURKE-WHITE (1904–1971) was born in New York City. She studied at Columbia University, the University of Michigan, and Cornell University, from which she received her B.A. in 1927. Her work as a photographer for *Fortune* and *Life* magazines made her famous. Her photographs are now part of the permanent collections of many major art museums throughout the world. Among her numerous books are *Eyes on Russia* (1931), *They Called It Purple Heart Valley* (1944), and *Portrait of Myself* (1963).

Dust Changes America

In her report on the devastating drought and dust storms of the mid-1930s, Bourke-White chose to provide a panorama of scenes rather than one or two detailed portraits. The individual snapshots add up to a convincing, moving examination of the personal and economic devastation caused by the drought. By relying heavily on description (along with comparison and examples), Bourke-White is able to give readers an understanding of events probably unlike anything they have ever experienced.

Vitamin K they call it—the dust which sifts under the door sills, and stings in the eyes, and seasons every spoonful of food. The dust storms have distinct personalities, rising in formation like rolling clouds, creeping up silently like formless fog, approaching violently like a tornado. Where has it come from? It provides topics of endless speculation. Red, it is the topsoil from Oklahoma; brown, it is the fertile earth of western Kansas; the good grazing land of Texas and New Mexico sweeps by as a murky yellow haze. Or, tracing it locally, "My uncle will be along pretty soon," they say; "I just saw his farm go by."

The town dwellers stack their linen in trunks, stuff wet cloths 2
along the window sills, estimate the tons of sand in the darkened air
above them, paste cloth masks on their faces with adhesive tape, and
try to joke about Vitamin K. But on the farms and ranches there is an
attitude of despair.

By coincidence I was in the same parts of the country where last 3
year I photographed the drought. As short a time as eight months ago
there was an attitude of false optimism. "Things will get better," the
farmers would say. "We're not as hard hit as other states. The government will help out. This can't go on." But this year there is an
atmosphere of utter hopelessness. Nothing to do. No use digging out
your chicken coops and pigpens after the last "duster" because the
next one will be coming along soon. No use trying to keep the house
clean. No use fighting off that foreclosure any longer. No use even
hoping to give your cattle anything to chew on when their food crops
have literally blown out of the ground.

It was my job to avoid dust storms, since I was commissioned by 4
an airplane company to take photographs of its course from the air,
but frequently the dust storms caught up with us, and as we were
grounded anyway, I started to photograph them. Thus I saw five
dust-storm states from the air and from the ground.

In the last several years there have been droughts and sand 5
storms and dusters, but they have been localized, and always one
state could borrow from another. But this year the scourge assumes
tremendous proportions. Dust storms are bringing distress and death
to 300,000 square miles; they are blowing over all of Kansas, all of
Nebraska and Wyoming, strips of the Dakotas, about half of Colorado, sections of Iowa and Missouri, the greater part of Oklahoma,
and the northern panhandle of Texas, extending into the eastern parts
of New Mexico.

Last year I saw farmers harvesting the Russian thistle. Never 6
before had they thought of feeding thistles to cattle. But this prickly
fodder became precious for food. This year even the Russian thistles
are dying out and the still humbler soap weed becomes as vital to the
farmer as the fields of golden grain he tended in the past. Last year's
thistle-fed cattle dwindled to skin and bone. This year's herds on their
diet of soap weed develop roughened hides, ugly growths around the
mouth, and lusterless eyes.

Years of the farmers' and ranchers' lives have gone into the 7
building up of their herds. Their herds were like their families to them.

When AAA officials spotted cows and steers for shooting during the cattle-killing days of last summer, the farmers felt as though their own children were facing the bullets. Kansas, a Republican state, has no love for the AAA. This year winds whistled over land made barren by the drought and the crop-conservation program. When Wallace removed the ban on the planting of spring wheat he was greeted by cheers. But the wheat has been blown completely out of the ground. Nothing is left but soap weed, or the expensive cotton-seed cake, and after that—bankruptcy.

The storm comes in a terrifying way. Yellow clouds roll. The wind 8 blows such a gale that it is all my helper can do to hold my camera to the ground. The sand whips into my lens. I repeatedly wipe it away trying to snatch an exposure before it becomes completely coated again. The light becomes yellower, the wind colder. Soon there is no photographic light, and we hurry for shelter to the nearest farmhouse.

Three men and a woman are seated around a dust-caked lamp, 9 on their faces grotesque masks of wet cloth. The children have been put to bed with towels tucked over their heads. My host greets us: "It takes grit to live in this country." They are telling stories: A bachelor harnessed the sandblast which ripped through the keyhole by holding his pots and pans in it until they were spick and span. A pilot flying over Amarillo got caught in a sand storm. His motor clogged; he took to his parachute. It took him six hours to shovel his way back to earth. And when a man from the next county was struck by a drop of water, he fainted, and it took two buckets of sand to revive him.

The migrations of the farmer have begun. In many of the worst- 10 hit counties 80 per cent of the families are on relief. In the open farm country one crop failure follows another. After perhaps three successive crop failures the farmer can't stand it any longer. He moves in with relatives and hopes for a job in Arizona or Illinois or some neighboring state where he knows he is not needed. Perhaps he gets a job as a cotton picker, and off he goes with his family, to be turned adrift again after a brief working period.

We passed them on the road, all their household goods piled on 11 wagons, one lucky family on a truck. Lucky, because they had been able to keep their truck when the mortgage was foreclosed. All they owned in the world was packed on it; the children sat on a pile of bureaus topped with mattresses, and the sides of the truck were strapped up with bed springs. The entire family looked like a Ku Klux

Klan meeting, their faces done up in masks to protect them from the whirling sand.

Near Hays, Kansas, a little boy started home from school and never arrived there. The neighbors looked for him till ten at night, and all next day a band of two hundred people searched. At twilight they found him, only a quarter of a mile from home, his body nearly covered with silt. He had strangled to death. The man who got lost in his own ten-acre truck garden and wandered around choking and stifling for eight hours before he found his house considered himself lucky to escape with his life. The police and sheriffs are kept constantly busy with calls from anxious parents whose children are lost, and the toll is mounting of people who become marooned and die in the storms. 12

But the real tragedy is the plight of the cattle. In a rising sand storm cattle quickly become blinded. They run around in circles until they fall and breathe so much dust that they die. Autopsies show their lungs caked with dust and mud. Farmers dread the birth of calves during a storm. The newborn animals will die within twenty-four hours. 13

And this same dust that coats the lungs and threatens death to cattle and men alike, that ruins the stock of the storekeeper lying unsold on his shelves, that creeps into the gear shifts of automobiles, that sifts through the refrigerator into the butter, that makes housekeeping, and gradually life itself, unbearable, this swirling drifting dust is changing the agricultural map of the United States. It piles ever higher on the floors and beds of a steadily increasing number of deserted farmhouses. A half-buried plowshare, a wheat binder ruffled over with sand, the skeleton of a horse near a dirt-filled water hole are stark evidence of the meager life, the wasted savings, the years of toil that the farmer is leaving behind him. 14

Meanings and Values

1a. Identify those places in the essay where Bourke-White gives evidence of the farmers' optimism in the face of disaster.

b. Does the report, on the whole, offer grounds for hope or optimism? Be ready to support your answer with specific references to the text.

2. Is it necessary to know what AAA was or who Wallace was to understand the meaning of paragraph 7?

3.   Where does the essay fall on a subjective-objective continuum? Why? (See Guide to Terms: *Objective/Subjective.*)

Expository Techniques

1.   Discuss how Bourke-White uses concrete details in paragraphs 3 and 11–12 to indicate the economic and personal costs of the drought.

2a.   For what purpose does the author include the example of the Russian thistle (par. 6)? (Guide: *Purpose.*)

 b.   Why is its placement within the essay significant?

3.   Are the various scenes and examples in this essay arranged in any particular order? Do they, for example, move from relatively general to more specific or more emotionally moving?

4a.   Discuss the role of humor in paragraphs 1–2 and 9.

 b.   Does the humor in these paragraphs undermine the unity of the essay?

 c.   If not, tell how it contributes to the central theme.

Diction and Vocabulary

1a.   Tell how the author uses diction and sentence structure in the last paragraph of the essay to create a series of "snapshots." (Guide: *Diction, Syntax.*)

 b.   Why is this such an effective way to conclude the essay? (Guide: *Closings, Evaluation.*)

2.   The examples in paragraphs 11–12 have considerable emotional impact. To what extent does *understatement* contribute to this effect? (Guide: *Irony.*)

3.   How does the verb tense in paragraphs 8–9 contribute to the vividness of the scene?

Suggestions for Writing and Discussion

1.   Talk with family members or friends about their memories of the Depression or drought of the 1930s. Report their memories to the class.

2.   Discuss how more recent disasters or human tragedies could be made the subject of essays.

(NOTE: Suggestions for topics requiring development by use of DESCRIPTION are on pages 351–352, at the end of this section.)

E. B. WHITE

E. B. WHITE, distinguished essayist, was born in Mount Vernon, New York, in 1899 and died in 1985 in North Brooklin, Maine. A graduate of Cornell University, White worked as a reporter and advertising copywriter, and in 1926 he joined the staff of the *New Yorker* magazine. After 1937 he did most of his writing at his farm in Maine, for many years contributing a regular column, "One Man's Meat," to *Harper's* magazine and freelance editorials for the "Notes and Comments" column of the *New Yorker*. White also wrote children's books, two volumes of verse, and, with James Thurber, *Is Sex Necessary?* (1929). With his wife, Katherine White, he compiled *A Subtreasury of American Humor* (1941). Collections of his own essays include *One Man's Meat* (1942), *The Second Tree from the Corner* (1953), *The Points of My Compass* (1962), and *Essays of E. B. White* (1977). In 1959 he revised and enlarged William Strunk's *The Elements of Style*, a textbook still widely used in college classrooms. White received many honors and writing awards for his crisp, highly individual style and his sturdy independence of thought.

Once More to the Lake

In this essay White relies primarily on description to convey his sense of the passage of time and the power of memory. The vivid scenes and the clear yet expressive prose in this essay are characteristic of his writing.

August 1941

One summer, along about 1904, my father rented a camp on a lake in   1
Maine and took us all there for the month of August. We all got
ringworm from some kittens and had to rub Pond's Extract on our
arms and legs night and morning, and my father rolled over in a canoe

with all his clothes on; but outside of that the vacation was a success and from then on none of us ever thought there was any place in the world like that lake in Maine. We returned summer after summer—always on August 1 for one month. I have since become a salt-water man, but sometimes in summer there are days when the restlessness of the tides and the fearful cold of the sea water and the incessant wind that blows across the afternoon and into the evening make me wish for the placidity of a lake in the woods. A few weeks ago this feeling got so strong I bought myself a couple of bass hooks and a spinner and returned to the lake where we used to go, for a week's fishing and to revisit old haunts.

I took along my son, who had never had any fresh water up his   2
nose and who had seen lily pads only from train windows. On the journey over to the lake I began to wonder what it would be like. I wondered how time would have marred this unique, this holy spot—the coves and streams, the hills that the sun set behind, the camps and the paths behind the camps. I was sure that the tarred road would have found it out, and I wondered in what other ways it would be desolated. It is strange how much you can remember about places like that once you allow your mind to return into the grooves that lead back. You remember one thing, and that suddenly reminds you of another thing. I guess I remembered clearest of all the early mornings, when the lake was cool and motionless, remembered how the bedroom smelled of the lumber it was made of and of the wet woods whose scent entered through the screen. The partitions in the camp were thin and did not extend clear to the top of the rooms, and as I was always the first up I would dress softly so as not to wake the others, and sneak out into the sweet outdoors and start out in the canoe, keeping close along the shore in the long shadows of the pines. I remembered being very careful never to rub my paddle against the gunwale for fear of disturbing the stillness of the cathedral.

The lake had never been what you would call a wild lake. There   3
were cottages sprinkled around the shores, and it was in farming country although the shores of the lake were quite heavily wooded. Some of the cottages were owned by nearby farmers, and you would live at the shore and eat your meals at the farmhouse. That's what our family did. But although it wasn't wild, it was a fairly large and undisturbed lake and there were places in it that, to a child at least, seemed infinitely remote and primeval.

I was right about the tar: it led to within half a mile of the shore. 4
But when I got back there, with my boy, and we settled into a camp near a farmhouse and into the kind of summertime I had known, I could tell that it was going to be pretty much the same as it had been before—I knew it, lying in bed the first morning, smelling the bedroom and hearing the boy sneak quietly out and go off along the shore in a boat. I began to sustain the illusion that he was I, and therefore, by simple transposition, that I was my father. This sensation persisted, kept cropping up all the time we were there. It was not an entirely new feeling, but in this setting it grew much stronger. I seemed to be living a dual existence. I would be in the middle of some simple act, I would be picking up a bait box or laying down a table fork, or I would be saying something, and suddenly it would be not I but my father who was saying the words or making the gesture. It gave me a creepy sensation.

We went fishing the first morning. I felt the same damp moss 5
covering the worms in the bait can, and saw the dragonfly alight on the tip of my rod as it hovered a few inches from the surface of the water. It was the arrival of this fly that convinced me beyond any doubt that everything was as it always had been, that the years were a mirage and that there had been no years. The small waves were the same, chucking the rowboat under the chin as we fished at anchor, and the boat was the same boat, the same color green and the ribs broken in the same places, and under the floorboards the same fresh-water leavings and débris—the dead helgramite, the wisps of moss, the rusty discarded fishhook, the dried blood from yesterday's catch. We stared silently at the tips of our rods, at the dragonflies that came and went. I lowered the tip of mine into the water, tentatively, pensively dislodging the fly, which darted two feet away, poised, darted two feet back, and came to rest again a little farther up the rod. There had been no years between the ducking of this dragonfly and the other one—the one that was part of memory. I looked at the boy, who was silently watching his fly, and it was my hands that held his rod, my eyes watching. I felt dizzy and didn't know which rod I was at the end of.

We caught two bass, hauling them in briskly as though they were 6
mackerel, pulling them over the side of the boat in a businesslike manner without any landing net, and stunning them with a blow on the back of the head. When we got back for a swim before lunch, the

lake was exactly where we had left it, the same number of inches from the dock, and there was only the merest suggestion of a breeze. This seemed an utterly enchanted sea, this lake you could leave to its own devices for a few hours and come back to, and find that it had not stirred, this constant and trustworthy body of water. In the shallows, the dark, water-soaked sticks and twigs, smooth and old, were undulating in clusters on the bottom against the clean ribbed sand, and the track of the mussel was plain. A school of minnows swam by, each minnow with its small individual shadow, doubling the attendance, so clear and sharp in the sunlight. Some of the other campers were in swimming, along the shore, one of them with a cake of soap, and the water felt thin and clear and unsubstantial. Over the years there had been this person with the cake of soap, this cultist, and here he was. There had been no years.

Up to the farmhouse to dinner through the teeming, dusty field,   7
the road under our sneakers was only a two-track road. The middle track was missing, the one with the marks of the hooves and the splotches of dried, flaky manure. There had always been three tracks to choose from in choosing which track to walk in; now the choice was narrowed down to two. For a moment I missed terribly the middle alternative. But the way led past the tennis court, and something about the way it lay there in the sun reassured me; the tape had loosened along the backline, the alleys were green with plantains and other weeds, and the net (installed in June and removed in September) sagged in the dry noon, and the whole place steamed with midday heat and hunger and emptiness. There was a choice of pie for dessert, and one was blueberry and one was apple, and the waitresses were the same country girls, there having been no passage of time, only the illusion of it as in a dropped curtain—the waitresses were still fifteen; their hair had been washed, that was the only difference—they had been to the movies and seen the pretty girls with the clean hair.

Summertime, oh, summertime, pattern of life indelible, the fade-   8
proof lake, the woods unshatterable, the pasture with the sweetfern and the juniper forever and ever, summer without end; this was the background, and the life along the shore was the design, their tiny docks with the flagpole and the American flag floating against the white clouds in the blue sky, the little paths over the roots of the trees leading from camp to camp and the paths leading back to the out-houses and the can of lime for sprinkling, and at the souvenir counters at the store the miniature birch-bark canoes and the postcards that

showed things looking a little better than they looked. This was the American family at play, escaping the city heat, wondering whether the newcomers in the camp at the head of the cove were "common" or "nice," wondering whether it was true that the people who drove up for Sunday dinner at the farmhouse were turned away because there wasn't enough chicken.

It seemed to me, as I kept remembering all this, that those times and those summers had been infinitely precious and worth saving. There had been jollity and peace and goodness. The arriving (at the beginning of August) had been so big a business in itself, at the railway station the farm wagon drawn up, the first smell of the pine-laden air, the first glimpse of the smiling farmer, and the great importance of the trunks and your father's enormous authority in such matters, and the feel of the wagon under you for the long ten-mile haul, and at the top of the last long hill catching the first view of the lake after eleven months of not seeing this cherished body of water. The shouts and cries of the other campers when they saw you, and the trunks to be unpacked, to give up their rich burden. (Arriving was less exciting nowadays, when you sneaked up in your car and parked it under a tree near the camp and took out the bags and in five minutes it was all over, no fuss, no loud wonderful fuss about trunks.)

9

Peace and goodness and jollity. The only thing that was wrong now, really, was the sound of the place, an unfamiliar nervous sound of the outboard motors. This was the note that jarred, the one thing that would sometimes break the illusion and set the years moving. In those other summertimes all motors were inboard; and when they were at a little distance, the noise they made was a sedative, an ingredient of summer sleep. They were one-cylinder and two-cylinder engines, and some were make-and-break and some were jump-spark, but they all made a sleepy sound across the lake. The one-lungers throbbed and fluttered, and the twin-cylinder ones purred and purred, and that was a quiet sound, too. But now the campers all had outboards. In the daytime, in the hot mornings, these motors made a petulant, irritable sound; at night, in the still evening when the afterglow lit the water, they whined about one's ears like mosquitoes. My boy loved our rented outboard, and his great desire was to achieve single-handed mastery over it, and authority, and he soon learned the trick of choking it a little (but not too much), and the adjustment of the needle valve. Watching him I would remember the things you could do with the old one-cylinder engine with the heavy

10

flywheel, how you could have it eating out of your hand if you got really close to it spiritually. Motorboats in those days didn't have clutches, and you would make a landing by shutting off the motor at the proper time and coasting in with a dead rudder. But there was a way of reversing them, if you learned the trick, by cutting the switch and putting it on again exactly on the final dying revolution of the flywheel, so that it would kick back against compression and begin reversing. Approaching a dock in a strong following breeze, it was difficult to slow up sufficiently by the ordinary coasting method, and if a boy felt he had complete mastery over his motor, he was tempted to keep it running beyond its time and then reverse it a few feet from the dock. It took a cool nerve, because if you threw the switch a twentieth of a second too soon you would catch the flywheel when it still had speed enough to go up past center, and the boat would leap ahead, charging bull-fashion at the dock.

We had a good week at the camp. The bass were biting well and 11 the sun shone endlessly, day after day. We would be tired at night and lie down in the accumulated heat of the little bedrooms after the long hot day and the breeze would stir almost imperceptibly outside and the smell of the swamp drift in through the rusty screens. Sleep would come easily and in the morning the red squirrel would be on the roof, tapping out his gay routine. I kept remembering everything, lying in bed in the mornings—the small steamboat that had a long rounded stern like the lip of a Ubangi, and how quietly she ran on the moon-light sails, when the older boys played their mandolins and the girls sang and we ate doughnuts dipped in sugar, and how sweet the music was on the water in the shining night, and what it had felt like to think about girls then. After breakfast we would go up to the store and the things were in the same place—the minnows in a bottle, the plugs and spinners disarranged and pawed over by the youngsters from the boys' camp, the Fig Newtons and the Beeman's gum. Outside, the road was tarred and cars stood in front of the store. Inside, all was just as it had always been, except there was more Coca-Cola and not so much Moxie and root beer and birch beer and sarsaparilla. We would walk out with the bottle of pop apiece and sometimes the pop would backfire up our noses and hurt. We explored the streams, quietly, where the turtles slid off the sunny logs and dug their way into the soft bottom; and we lay on the town wharf and fed worms to the tame bass. Everywhere we went I had trouble making out which was I, the one walking at my side, the one walking in my pants.

One afternoon while we were there at that lake a thunderstorm 12
came up. It was like the revival of an old melodrama that I had seen
long ago with childish awe. The second-act climax of the drama of the
electrical disturbance over a lake in America had not changed in any
important respect. This was the big scene, still the big scene. The
whole thing was so familiar, the first feeling of oppression and heat
and a general air around camp of not wanting to go very far away. In
mid-afternoon (it was all the same) a curious darkening of the sky,
and a lull in everything that had made life tick; and then the way the
boats suddenly swung the other way at their moorings with the
coming of a breeze out of the new quarter, and the premonitory
rumble. Then the kettle drum, then the snare, then the bass drum
and cymbals, then crackling light against the dark, and the gods
grinning and licking their chops in the hills. Afterward the calm,
the rain steadily rustling in the calm lake, the return of light and
hope and spirits, and the campers running out in joy and relief to
go swimming in the rain, their bright cries perpetuating the death-
less joke about how they were getting simply drenched, and the
children screaming with delight at the new sensation of bathing in
the rain, and the joke about getting drenched linking the generations in a strong indestructible chain. And the comedian who
waded in carrying an umbrella.

When the others went swimming, my son said he was going in, 13
too. He pulled his dripping trunks from the line where they had hung
all through the shower and wrung them out. Languidly, and with no
thought of going in, I watched him, his hard little body, skinny and
bare, saw him wince slightly as he pulled up around his vitals the
small, soggy, icy garment. As he buckled the swollen belt, suddenly
my groin felt the chill of death.

Meanings and Values

1a. Why does White decide to return to the lake?

   b. Can the lake be considered a personal symbol for White? (See Guide
   to Terms: *Symbol*.)

   c. If so, what does it symbolize?

2a. In what ways have the lake and its surroundings remained the same
   since White's boyhood? Be specific.

   b. In what ways have they changed?

3a.   At one point in the essay White says, "I seemed to be living a dual existence" (par. 4). What is the meaning of this statement?

b.   How does this "dual existence" affect his point of view in the essay? (Guide: *Point of View.*)

c.   Is the "dual existence" emphasized more in the first half of the essay or the second half? Why?

4a.   Where would you place this essay on an objective-to-subjective continuum? (Guide: *Objective/Subjective.*)

b.   Is this a formal or an informal essay? Explain. (Guide: *Essay.*)

5a.   After spending a day on the lake, White remarks, "There had been no years" (par. 6). What other direct or indirect comments does he make about time and change? Be specific.

b.   How are these comments related to the central theme of the essay? (Guide: *Unity.*)

6a.   What is the tone of the essay? (Guide: *Style/Tone.*)

b.   Does the tone change or remain the same throughout the essay?

7a.   What is meant by the closing phrase of the essay, "suddenly my groin felt the chill of death" (par. 13)?

b.   Is this an appropriate way to end the essay? Why, or why not?

Expository Techniques

1a.   If you agree that the lake is a personal symbol for White, explain how he enables readers to understand its significance. (Guide: *Symbol.*)

b.   Is he successful in doing this? (Guide: *Evaluation.*)

2a.   In the first part of the essay White focuses on the unchanged aspects of the lake; in the second part he begins acknowledging the passage of time. Where does this shift in attitude take place?

b.   What strategies, including transitional devices, does White use to signal to the reader the shift in attitude? Be specific.

3.   How does White use the discussion of outboard motors and inboard motors (par. 10) to summarize the differences between life at the lake in his youth and at the time of his return with his son? Explain.

4.   Many of the descriptive passages in this essay convey a dominant impression, usually an emotion or mood. Choose a paragraph from the essay and discuss how the author's choice of details, variety of syntax, and diction help create a dominant impression. Be specific. (Guide: *Syntax and Diction.*)

5a. In many places the author combines description and comparison. Select a passage from the essay and discuss in detail how he combines the patterns.

b. In what ways is the combination of description and comparison appropriate to the theme and the point of view of the essay?

6. White has often been praised for the clarity and variety of his prose style. To what extent are these qualities the result of syntax and of the variety of strategies he uses to achieve emphasis? (Choose a sample paragraph, such as 6, 9, or 12, to illustrate your answer.) (Guide: *Emphasis and Syntax.*)

Diction and Vocabulary

1. To what extent are the qualities of White's style mentioned in your answer to question 6 of "Expository Techniques" matters of diction? (Guide: *Diction.*)

2a. How much do the connotations of the words used in paragraph 8 contribute to the dominant impression the author is trying to create? (Guide: *Connotation/Denotation.*)

b. In paragraph 10?

3a. Why would the author refer to the person with the cake of soap as "this cultist" (par. 6)?

b. In what sense can a tennis court steam "with midday heat and hunger and emptiness" (par. 7)?

4. What kind of paradox is presented in this passage: ". . . the waitresses were the same country girls, there having been no passage of time, only the illusion of it as in a dropped curtain—the waitresses were still fifteen; their hair had been washed, that was the only difference—they had been to the movies and seen the pretty girls with the clean hair" (par. 7)? (Guide: *Paradox.*)

5a. Is the diction in this passage sentimental: "Summertime, oh, summertime, pattern of life indelible, the fade-proof lake, the woods unshatterable, the pasture with the sweetfern and the juniper forever and ever, summer without end . . ." (par. 8)? (Guide: *Sentimentality.*)

b. If so, why would the author choose to use this style in the passage?

c. Does the passage contain an allusion? If so, what is alluded to and why? (Guide: *Figures of Speech.*)

6. Study the author's uses of the following words, consulting the dictionary as needed: incessant, placidity (par. 1); gunwale (2); primeval (3); transposition (4); helgramite, pensively (5); petulant (10); premonitory (12); languidly (13).

Suggestions for Writing and Discussion

1. Choose some place you remember from your childhood and have seen recently, and write a description of it comparing its present appearance with your memories of it.

2. Prepare a description of some object or place that symbolizes the passage of time and try to control the tone of your description so it reflects your attitudes toward time and change.

3. Discuss your relationship with your parents (or your children) insofar as that relationship includes experiences similar to the ones White describes in "Once More to the Lake."

4. If you have taken a summer vacation like the one recorded by White, compare your experiences and the setting to those in the essay. How much has our civilization—and our vacations—changed since the time of the events in the essay?

(NOTE: Suggestions for topics requiring development by use of DESCRIPTION follow.)

Writing Suggestions for Section 8
Description

1. Primarily by way of impressionistic description that focuses on a single dominant impression, show and explain the mood, or atmosphere, of one of the following:

   a. A country fair.

   b. A ball game.

   c. A rodeo.

   d. A wedding.

   e. A funeral.

   f. A busy store.

   g. A ghost town.

   h. A cave.

   i. A beach in summer (or winter).

   j. An antique shop.

   k. A party.

   l. A family dinner.

   m. A traffic jam.

   n. Reveille.

   o. An airport (or a bus depot).

   p. An automobile race (or a horse race).

   q. A home during one of its rush hours.

   r. The last night of Christmas shopping.

   s. A natural scene at a certain time of day.

   t. The campus at examination time.

   u. A certain person at a time of great emotion—e.g., joy, anger, grief.

2. Using objective description as your basic pattern, explain the functional qualities or the significance of one of the following:

   a. A house for sale.

   b. A public building.

   c. A dairy barn.

d. An ideal workshop (or hobby room).

e. An ideal garage.

f. A fast-food restaurant.

g. The layout of a town (or airport).

h. The layout of a farm.

i. A certain type of boat.

9

Using *Narration* as an Expository Technique

Attempts to classify the functions of narration seem certain to develop difficulties and end in arbitrary and sometimes fuzzy distinctions. These need not distress us, however, if we remember that narration remains narration—a factual or fictional report of a sequence of events—and that our only reason for trying to divide it into categories is to find some means of studying its uses.

In a sense, as we have already seen in Section 5, exposition by process analysis makes one important, if rather narrow, use of narration, since it explains in sequence how specific steps lead to completion of some process. At the other extreme is narration that has very little to do with exposition: the story itself is the important thing, and instead of a series of steps leading obviously to a completed act, events *develop* out of each other and build suspense, however mild, through some kind of conflict. This use of narration includes the novel and the short story, as well as some news and sports reporting. Because we are studying exposition, however, we must avoid getting too involved with these uses of narration; they require special techniques, the study of which would require a whole course or, in fact, several courses.

Between the extremes of a very usable analysis of process and very intriguing narration for the story's sake—and often seeming to blur into one or the other—is narration for *explanation*'s sake, to explain a concept that is more than process and that might have been explained by one of the other patterns of exposition. Here only the form is narrative; the function is expository.

Fortunately, the average student seldom needs to use narration for major explanatory purposes, as it has been used in each of the following selections. But to learn the handling of even minor or localized narration, the best procedure (short of taking several college courses, or at least one that concentrates on the narrative form) is simply to observe how successful writers use it to perform various functions. Localized narration can sometimes be helpful in developing any of the other major patterns of exposition—e.g., as in the Buckley essay (Section 1) or in Catton's (Section 3).

The most common problems can be summarized as follows:

1. *Selection of details.* As in writing description, the user of narration always has far more details available than can or should be used. Good unity demands the selection of only those details that are most relevant to the purpose and the desired effect.

2. *Time order.* The writer can use straight chronology, relating events as they happen (the usual method in minor uses of narration), or the flashback method, leaving the sequence temporarily in order to go back and relate some now-significant happening of a time prior to the main action. If flashback is used, it should be deliberate and for a valid reason—not merely because the episode was neglected at the beginning.

3. *Transitions.* The lazy writer of narration is apt to resort to the transitional style of a three-year-old: ". . . and then we . . . and then she . . . and then we. . . ." Avoiding this style may tax the ingenuity, but invariably the result is worth the extra investment of time and thought.

4. *Point of view.* This is a large and complex subject if dealt with fully, as a course in narration would do. Briefly, however, the writer should decide at the beginning whether the reader is to experience the action through a character's eyes (and ears and brain) or from an overall, objective view. This decision makes a difference in how much can be told, whose thoughts or secret actions can be included. The writer must be consistent throughout the narrative and include only information that could logically be known through the adopted point of view.

5. *Dialogue.* Presumably the writer already knows the mechanics of using quotations. Beyond these, the problems are to make conversation as natural-sounding as possible and yet to keep it from rambling through many useless details—to keep the narrative moving forward by *means* of dialogue.

As in most patterns of writing, the use of expository narration is most likely to be successful if the writer constantly keeps the purpose and audience in mind, remembering that the only reason for using the method in the first place—for doing *any* writing—is to communicate ideas. Soundness, clarity, and interest are the best means of attaining this goal.

Sample Paragraph (Annotated)

Central theme announced (reason for the narrative).

The story of Palmville's oil well is often told to newcomers in order to reveal the character of the town and, incidentally, to explain why city government policy is set by a Town Meeting rather than by a city council. In 1953, several successful oil wells were drilled in neighboring Yutawpa County, setting off an "Oil Rush" in this part of the state. The mayor at the time, Norbert Flax, was gripped by "Oil Fever" and devised a plan for city-funded drilling in what is now Anna May Wong Park. A citizen's group led by Herbert and Ellie Gomez opposed the plan, arguing that it would simply waste taxpayers' money. Recognizing that the mayor had the City Council on his side, Ellie and Herbert organized a campaign against the proposal, built around the theme of greater citizen participation in government and complete with marches, placards, and chants of "Par-Ti-Ci-Pa-Tion!" The wells were dry, the city had to triple the tax rate to pay off the debt, and growth in population and jobs was stunted for two decades. Since the debacle, citizen participation has been a key element in Palmville's government, the town has a city manager rather than a mayor, and all major policy decisions are made by the Town Meeting.

Narrative in generally chronological order.

Told from an "objective" point of view, not through the eyes of participants.

Sample Paragraph (Narration)

For anyone who has looked up from the sullen South Georgia shore [island near Antarctica] towards the soaring, razor-edged peaks and the terrible chaos of glaciers topped by swirling clouds and scoured by mighty winds, the knowledge of the crossing made by these three men adds a wider dimension to an already awe-inspiring sight. How they did it, God only knows, but they crossed the island in thirty-six hours. They were fortunate that the weather held, although many times great banks of fog rolled in from the open sea, creeping towards them over the snow and threatening to obscure their way. Confronted by precipices of ice and walls of rock they had often to retrace their steps adding many miles to the journey. They walked almost without rest. At one point they sat down in an icy gully, the wind blowing the drift around them, and so tired were they that Worsely and Crean fell asleep immediately. Shackleton, barely able to keep himself awake, realized that to fall asleep under such conditions would prove fatal. After five minutes he woke the other two, saying that they had slept for half an hour.

Edwin Mickleburgh, *Beyond the Frozen Sea: Visions of Antarctica*. New York: St. Martin's Press, 1987.

MARTIN GANSBERG

MARTIN GANSBERG, born in Brooklyn, New York, in 1920, received a Bachelor of Social Sciences degree from St. John's University. He has been an editor and reporter for the *New York Times* since 1942, including a three-year period as editor of its international edition in Paris. He also served on the faculty of Fairleigh Dickinson University. Gansberg has written for many magazines, including *Diplomat, Catholic Digest, Facts,* and *U.S. Lady.*

38 Who Saw Murder Didn't Call the Police

"38 Who Saw Murder ..." was written for the *New York Times* in 1964, and for obvious reasons it has been anthologized frequently since then. Cast in a deceptively simple news style, it still provides material for serious thought, as well as a means of studying the use and technique of narration.

For more than half an hour 38 respectable, law-abiding citizens in Queens watched a killer stalk and stab a woman in three separate attacks in Kew Gardens. 1

Twice their chatter and the sudden glow of their bedroom lights interrupted him and frightened him off. Each time he returned, sought her out, and stabbed her again. Not one person telephoned the police during the assault; one witness called after the woman was dead. 2

That was two weeks ago today. 3

Still shocked is Assistant Chief Inspector Frederick M. Lussen, in charge of the borough's detectives and a veteran of 25 years of homicide investigations. He can give a matter-of-fact recitation on many murders. But the Kew Gardens slaying baffles him—not be- 4 cause it is a murder, but because the "good people" failed to call the police.

"As we have reconstructed the crime," he said, "the assailant had 5
three chances to kill this woman during a 35-minute period. He returned twice to complete the job. If we had been called when he first attacked, the woman might not be dead now."

This is what the police say happened beginning at 3:20 A.M. in the 6
staid, middle-class, tree-lined Austin Street area:

Twenty-eight-year-old Catherine Genovese, who was called 7
Kitty by almost everyone in the neighborhood, was returning home from her job as manager of a bar in Hollis. She parked her red Fiat in a lot adjacent to the Kew Gardens Long Island Rail Road Station, facing Mowbray Place. Like many residents of the neighborhood, she had parked there day after day since her arrival from Connecticut a year ago, although the railroad frowns on the practice.

She turned off the lights of her car, locked the door, and started 8
to walk the 100 feet to the entrance of her apartment at 82–70 Austin Street, which is in a Tudor building, with stores in the first floor and apartments on the second.

The entrance to the apartment is in the rear of the building 9
because the front is rented to retail stores. At night the quiet neighborhood is shrouded in the slumbering darkness that marks most residential areas.

Miss Genovese noticed a man at the far end of the lot, near a 10
seven-story apartment house at 82–40 Austin Street. She halted. Then, nervously, she headed up Austin Street toward Lefferts Boulevard, where there is a call box to the 102nd Police Precinct in nearby Richmond Hill.

She got as far as a street light in front of a bookstore before the 11
man grabbed her. She screamed. Lights went on in the 10-story apartment house at 82–67 Austin Street, which faces the bookstore. Windows slid open and voices punctuated the early-morning stillness.

Miss Genovese screamed: "Oh, my God, he stabbed me! Please 12
help me! Please help me!"

From one of the upper windows in the apartment house, a man 13
called down: "Let that girl alone!"

The assailant looked up at him, shrugged and walked down 14
Austin Street toward a white sedan parked a short distance away. Miss Genovese struggled to her feet.

Lights went out. The killer returned to Miss Genovese, now 15
trying to make her way around the side of the building by the parking
lot to get to her apartment. The assailant stabbed her again.

"I'm dying!" she shrieked. "I'm dying!" 16

Windows were opened again, and lights went on in many apart- 17
ments. The assailant got into his car and drove away. Miss Genovese
staggered to her feet. A city bus, Q-10, the Lefferts Boulevard line to
Kennedy International Airport, passed. It was 3:35 A.M.

The assailant returned. By then, Miss Genovese had crawled to 18
the back of the building, where the freshly painted brown doors to
the apartment house held out hope for safety. The killer tried the first
door; she wasn't there. At the second door, 82–62 Austin Street, he saw
her slumped on the floor at the foot of the stairs. He stabbed her a
third time—fatally.

It was 3:50 by the time the police received their first call, from a 19
man who was a neighbor of Miss Genovese. In two minutes they were
at the scene. The neighbor, a 70-year-old woman, and another woman
were the only persons on the street. Nobody else came forward.

The man explained that he had called the police after much 20
deliberation. He had phoned a friend in Nassau County for advice
and then he had crossed the roof of the building to the apartment of
the elderly woman to get her to make the call.

"I didn't want to get involved," he sheepishly told the police. 21

Six days later, the police arrested Winston Moseley, a 29-year-old 22
business-machine operator, and charged him with homicide. Moseley
had no previous record. He is married, has two children and owns a
home at 133–19 Sutter Avenue, South Ozone Park, Queens. On
Wednesday, a court committed him to Kings County Hospital for
psychiatric observation.

When questioned by the police, Moseley also said that he had 23
slain Mrs. Annie May Johnson, 24, of 146–12 133rd Avenue, Jamaica,
on Feb. 29 and Barbara Kralik, 15, of 174–17 140th Avenue, Springfield
Gardens, last July. In the Kralik case, the police are holding Alvin L.
Mitchell, who is said to have confessed to that slaying.

The police stressed how simple it would have been to have gotten 24
in touch with them. "A phone call," said one of the detectives, "would
have done it." The police may be reached by dialing "O" for operator
or SPring 7–3100.

Today witnesses from the neighborhood, which is made up of 25
one-family homes in the $35,000 to $60,000 range with the exception

of the two apartment houses near the railroad station, find it difficult
to explain why they didn't call the police.

A housewife, knowingly if quite casually, said, "We thought it   26
was a lover's quarrel." A husband and wife both said, "Frankly, we
were afraid." They seemed aware of the fact that events might have
been different. A distraught woman, wiping her hands on her apron,
said, "I didn't want my husband to get involved."

One couple, now willing to talk about that night, said they heard   27
the first screams. The husband looked thoughtfully at the bookstore
where the killer first grabbed Miss Genovese.

"We went to the window to see what was happening," he said,   28
"but the light from our bedroom made it difficult to see the street."
The wife, still apprehensive, added: "I put out the light and we were
able to see better."

Asked why they hadn't called the police, she shrugged and   29
replied: "I don't know."

A man peeked out from the slight opening in the doorway to his   30
apartment and rattled off an account of the killer's second attack. Why
hadn't he called the police at the time? "I was tired," he said without
emotion. "I went back to bed."

It was 4:25 A.M. when the ambulance arrived to take the body of   31
Miss Genovese. It drove off. "Then," a solemn police detective said,
"the people came out."

Meanings and Values

1a. What is Gansberg's central (expository) theme?

 b. How might he have developed this theme without using narration at
     all? Specify what patterns of exposition he could have used instead.

 c. Would any of them have been as effective as narration *for the purpose*?
     Why, or why not?

2.   Show how this selection could be used as an illustration in an explan-
     atory discussion of abstract and concrete writing. (See Guide to Terms:
     Concrete/Abstract.)

3a. Why has this narrative account of old news (the murder made its only
     headlines in 1964) retained its significance to this day?

 b. Are you able to see in this event a paradigm of any larger condition or
     situation? If so, explain, using examples as needed to illustrate your
     ideas.

4.   If you have read Wolfe's essay (Section 4), do you think Dr. Hall would have been surprised at this New York case of noninvolvement? Why, or why not?

Expository Techniques

1a.   What standard introductory technique is exemplified in the first paragraph? (Guide: *Introductions.*)

b.   How effective do you consider it?

c.   If you see anything ironic in the fact stated there, explain the irony. (Guide: *Irony.*)

2a.   Where does the main narration begin?

b.   What, then, is the function of the preceding paragraphs?

3a.   Study several of the paragraph transitions within the narration itself to determine Gansberg's method of advancing the time sequence (to avoid overuse of "and then"). What is the technique?

b.   Is another needed? Why, or why not?

4a.   What possible reasons do you see for the predominant use of short paragraphs in this piece?

b.   Does this selection lose any effectiveness because of the short paragraphs?

5.   Undoubtedly, the author selected with care the few quotations from witnesses that he uses. What principle or principles do you think applied to his selection?

6.   Explain why you think the quotation from the "solemn police detective" was, or was not, deliberately and carefully chosen to conclude the piece. (Guide: *Closings.*)

7a.   Briefly identify the point of view of the writing. (Guide: *Point of View.*)

b.   Is it consistent throughout?

c.   Show the relation, as you see it, between this point of view and the author's apparent attitude toward his subject matter.

8a.   Does he permit himself any sentimentality? If so, where? (Guide: *Sentimentality.*)

b.   If not, specifically what might he have included that would have slipped into melodrama or sentimentality?

Diction and Vocabulary

1a.   Why do you think the author used no difficult words in this narration?

b.   Do you find the writing at all belittling to college people because of this fact? Why, or why not?

Suggestions for Writing and Discussion

1.   Use both developed and undeveloped examples to show the prevalence, among individuals, of an anti-involvement attitude today. Or, if you prefer, show that this accusation is unjustified.

2.   If this narration can be regarded as a paradigm (see question 3b of "Meanings and Values"), select one example from the larger subject and develop it on whatever theme you choose. Your example could be from international affairs, if you like (and if you don't mind becoming the center of a controversy)—e.g., the recent cries of "Murder!" from numerous small countries. If you prefer, go into more distant (and therefore less controversial) history for your example.

3.   If such a crime as the Genovese murder were happening in an area or a situation where police were not so instantly available, what do you think an observer should do about it? What would *you* do? Justify your stand fully.

(NOTE: Suggestions for topics requiring development by NARRATION are on page 388, at the end of this section.)

ANNIE DILLARD

ANNIE DILLARD was born in 1945 in Pittsburgh, Pennsylvania. She received a B.A. and an M.A. from Hollins College. Formerly a professor of English at Western Washington State College, she now teaches at Wesleyan University. Her book *Pilgrim at Tinker Creek* (1974), based on her experiences living in the Roanoke Valley of Virginia, was awarded the Pulitzer Prize for general nonfiction. She has also published a book of poems, *Tickets for a Prayer Wheel* (1974); two volumes of literary criticism, *Living by Fiction* (1982) and *Conversations with Chinese Writers* (1984); and two collections of brief narratives and meditations on nature and experience, *Holy the Firm* (1978) and *Teaching a Stone to Talk* (1982). Her most recent books are *An American Childhood* (1987) and *The Writing Life* (1984).

Prologue

In this essay, a chapter from the opening section of *An American Childhood*, Dillard uses parallel narratives to show how she and her father awoke to consciousness of themselves and their values. Such awakenings are often turning points, but as this essay shows through comparison, their meaning often differs from person to person.

In 1955, when I was ten, my father's reading went to his head. 1

My father's reading during that time, and for many years before 2 and after, consisted for the most part of *Life on the Mississippi*. He was a young executive in the old family firm, American Standard; sometimes he traveled alone on business. Traveling, he checked into a hotel, found a bookstore, and chose for the night's reading, after what I fancy to have been long deliberation, yet another copy of *Life on the Mississippi*. He brought all these books home. There were dozens of copies of *Life on the Mississippi* on the living-room shelves. From time to time, I read one.

Down the Mississippi hazarded the cub riverboat pilot, down the   3
Mississippi from St. Louis to New Orleans. His chief, the pilot Mr.
Bixby, taught him how to lay the boat in her marks and dart between
points; he learned to pick a way fastidiously inside a certain snag and
outside a shifting shoal in the black dark; he learned to clamber down
a memorized channel in his head. On tricky crossings the leadsmen
sang out the soundings, so familiar I seemed to have heard them the
length of my life: "Mark four! . . . Quarter-less-four! . . . Half three! . . .
Mark three! . . . Quarter-less . . ." It was an old story.

When all this reading went to my father's head, he took action.   4
From Pittsburgh he went down the river. Although no one else that
our family knew kept a boat on the Allegheny River, our father did,
and now he was going all the way with it. He quit the firm his
great-grandfather had founded a hundred years earlier down the
river at his family's seat in Louisville, Kentucky; he sold his own
holdings in the firm. he was taking off for New Orleans.

New Orleans was the source of the music he loved: Dixieland   5
jazz, O Dixieland. In New Orleans men would blow it in the air and
beat it underfoot, the music that hustled and snapped, the music
whose zip matched his when he was a man-about-town at home in
Pittsburgh, working for the family firm; the music he tapped his foot
to when he was a man-about-town in New York for a few years after
college working for the family firm by day and by night hanging out
at Jimmy Ryan's on Fifty-second Street with Zutty Singleton, the black
drummer who befriended him, and the rest of the house band. A
certain kind of Dixieland suited him best. They played it at Jimmy
Ryan's, and Pee Wee Russell and Eddie Condon played it too—New
Orleans Dixieland chilled a bit by its journey up the river, and
smoothed by its sojourns in Chicago and New York.

Back in New Orleans where he was headed they would play the   6
old stuff, the hot, rough stuff—bastardized for tourists maybe, but still
the big and muddy source of it all. Back in New Orleans where he was
headed the music would smell like the river itself, maybe, like a
thicker, older version of the Allegheny River at Pittsburgh, where he
heard the music beat in the roar of his boat's inboard motor; like a
thicker, older version of the wide Ohio River at Louisville, Kentucky,
where at his family's summer house he'd spent his boyhood summers
mucking about in boats.

Getting ready for the trip one Saturday, he roamed around our   7
big brick house snapping his fingers. He had put a record on: Sharkey
Bonano, "Li'l Liza Jane." I was reading Robert Louis Stevenson on the
sunporch: *Kidnapped.* I looked up from my book and saw him outside;
he had wandered out to the lawn and was standing in the wind
between the buckeye trees and looking up at what must have been a
small patch of wild sky. Old Low-Pockets. He was six feet four, all
lanky and leggy; he had thick brown hair and shaggy brows, and a
mild and dreamy expression in his blue eyes.

When our mother met Frank Doak, he was twenty-seven: witty,   8
boyish, bookish, unsnobbish, a good dancer. He had grown up an
only child in Pittsburgh, attended Shady Side Academy, and Washington and Jefferson College in Pennsylvania, where he studied history. He was a lapsed Presbyterian and a believing Republican.
"Books make the man," read the blue bookplate in all his books.
"Frank Doak." The bookplate's woodcut showed a square-rigged
ship under way in a steep following sea. Father had hung around jazz
in New York, and halfheartedly played the drums; he had smoked
marijuana, written poems, begun a novel, painted in oils, imagined a
career as a riverboat pilot, and acted for more than ten seasons in
amateur and small-time professional theater. At American Standard,
Amstan Division, he was the personnel manager.

But not for long, and never again; Mother told us he was quitting   9
to go down the river. I was sorry he'd be leaving the Manufacturers'
Building downtown. From his office on the fourteenth floor, he often
saw suicides, which he reported at dinner. The suicides grieved him,
but they thrilled us kids. My sister Amy was seven.

People jumped from the Sixth Street bridge into the Allegheny   10
River. Because the bridge was low, they shinnied all the way up the
steel suspension cables to the bridge towers before they jumped.
Father saw them from his desk in silhouette, far away. A man vigor-
ously climbed a slanting cable. He slowed near the top, where the
cables hung almost vertically; he paused on the stone tower, seeming
to sway against the sky, high over the bridge and the river below.
Priests, firemen, and others—presumably family members or pass-
ersby—gathered on the bridge. In about half the cases, Father said,
these people talked the suicide down. The ones who jumped kicked
off from the tower so they'd miss the bridge, and fell tumbling a long
way down.

Pittsburgh was a cheerful town, and had far fewer suicides than   11
most other cities its size. Yet people jumped so often that Father and
his colleagues on the fourteenth floor had a betting pool going. They
guessed the date and time of day the next jumper would appear. If a
man got talked down before he jumped, he still counted for the betting
pool, thank God; no manager of American Standard ever wanted to
hope, even in the smallest part of himself, that the fellow would go
ahead and jump. Father said he and the other men used to gather at
the biggest window and holler, "No! Don't do it, buddy, don't!" Now
he was leaving American Standard to go down the river, and he was
a couple of bucks in the hole.

While I was reading *Kidnapped* on this Saturday morning, I heard   12
him come inside and roam from the kitchen to the pantry to the bar,
to the dining room, the living room, and the sunporch, snapping his
fingers. He was snapping the fingers of both hands, and shaking his
head, to the record—"Li'l Liza Jane"—the sound that was beating, big
and jivey, all over the house. He walked lightly, long-legged, like a
soft-shoe hoofer barely in touch with the floor. When he played the
drums, he played lightly, coming down soft with the steel brushes that
sounded like a Slinky falling, not making the beat but just sizzling
along with it. He wandered into the sunporch, unseeing; he was
snapping his fingers lightly, too, as if he were feeling between them a
fine layer of Mississippi silt. The big buckeyes outside the glass
sunporch walls were waving.

A week later, he bade a cheerful farewell to us—to Mother, who   13
had encouraged him, to us oblivious daughters, ten and seven, and
to the new baby girl, six months old. He loaded his twenty-four-foot
cabin cruiser with canned food, pushed off from the dock of the
wretched boat club that Mother hated, and pointed his bow down-
stream, down the Allegheny River. From there it was only a few miles
to the Ohio River at Pittsburgh's point, where the Monongahela came
in. He wore on westward down the Ohio; he watched West Virginia
float past his port bow and Ohio past his starboard. It was 138 river
miles to New Martinsville, West Virginia, where he lingered for some
races. Back on the move, he tied up nights at club docks he'd seen on
the charts; he poured himself water for drinks from dockside hoses.
By day he rode through locks, twenty of them in all. He conversed
with the lockmasters, those lone men who paced silhouetted in overalls on the concrete lock-chamber walls and threw the big switches

that flooded or drained the locks: "Hello, up there!" "So long, down there!"

He continued down the river along the Kentucky border with Ohio, bumping down the locks. He passed through Cincinnati. He moved along down the Kentucky border with Indiana. After 640 miles of river travel, he reached Louisville, Kentucky. There he visited relatives at their summer house on the river. 14

It was a long way to New Orleans, at this rate another couple of months. He was finding the river lonesome. It got dark too early. It was September; people had abandoned their pleasure boats for the season; their children were back in school. There were no old salts on the docks talking river talk. People weren't so friendly as they were in Pittsburgh. There was no music except the dreary yacht-club jukeboxes playing "How Much Is That Doggie in the Window?" Jazz had come up the river once and for all; it wasn't still coming, he couldn't hear it across the water at night rambling and blowing and banging along high and tuneful, sneaking upstream to Chicago to get educated. He wasn't free so much as loose. He was living alone on beans in a boat and having witless conversations with lockmasters. He mailed out sad postcards. 15

From phone booths all down the Ohio River he talked to Mother. She told him that she was lonesome, too, and that three children—maid and nanny or no—were a handful. She said, further, that people were starting to talk. She knew Father couldn't bear people's talking. For all his dreaminess, he prized respectability above all; it was our young mother, whose circumstances bespoke such dignity, who loved to shock the world. After only six weeks, then—on the Ohio River at Louisville—he sold the boat and flew home. 16

I was just waking up then, just barely. Other things were changing. The highly entertaining new baby, Molly, had taken up residence in a former guest room. The great outer world hove into view and began to fill with things that had apparently been there all along: mineralogy, detective work, lepidopterology, ponds and streams, flying, society. My younger sister Amy and I were to start at private school that year: the Ellis School, on Fifth Avenue. I would start dancing school. 17

Children ten years old wake up and find themselves here, discover themselves to have been here all along; is this sad? They wake 18 like sleepwalkers, in full stride; they wake like people brought back from cardiac arrest or from drowning: *in medias res*, surrounded by familiar people and objects, equipped with a hundred skills. They know the neighborhood, they can read and write English, they are old hands at the commonplace mysteries, and yet they feel themselves to have just stepped off the boat, just converged with their bodies, just flown down from a trance, to lodge in an eerily familiar life already well under way.

I woke in bits, like all children, piecemeal over the years. I   19
discovered myself and the world, and forgot them, and discovered them again. I woke at intervals until, by that September when Father went down the river, the intervals of waking tipped the scales, and I was more often awake than not. I noticed this process of waking, and predicted with terrifying logic that one of these years not far away I would be awake continuously and never slip back, and never be free of myself again.

Consciousness converges with the child as a landing tern touches   20
the outspread feet of its shadow on the sand: precisely, toe hits toe. The tern folds its wings to sit; its shadow dips and spreads over the sand to meet and cup its breast.

Like any child, I slid into myself perfectly fitted, as a diver meets   21
her reflection in a pool. Her fingertips enter the fingertips on the water, her wrists slide up her arms. The diver wraps herself in her reflection wholly, sealing it at the toes, and wears it as she climbs rising from the pool, and ever after.

I never woke, at first, without recalling, chilled, all those other   22
waking times, those similar stark views from similarly lighted preci-pices: dizzying precipices from which the distant, glittering world revealed itself as a brooding and separated scene—and so let slip a queer implication, that I myself was both observer and observable, and so a possible object of my own humming awareness. Whenever I stepped into the porcelain bathtub, the bath's hot water sent a shock traveling up my bones. The skin on my arms pricked up, and the hair rose on the back of my skull. I saw my own firm foot press the tub, and the pale shadows waver over it, as if I were looking down from the sky and remembering this scene forever. The skin on my face tightened, as it had always done whenever I stepped into the tub, and remembering it all drew a swinging line, loops connecting the dots, all the way back. You again.

Meanings and Values

1. How do the father's reading activities (pars. 2 and 3) contrast with his life as a businessman?

2. In the context of the essay, what does this phrase mean: "my father's reading went to his head" (par. 1)?

3. Tell how each of the following reacted (or would be likely to react) to the actions of the father in leaving his young family for a trip on the river:

   a. His wife.

   b. The author as a child.

   c. Neighbors and friends (i.e., "people" [par. 16]).

   d. Most readers of the essay.

   e. The author as an adult.

4. In what ways is the story of the "jumpers" (pars. 9–11) parallel to and different from the narrative of the father?

5. In your own words, summarize what you believe the author wants us to think her father learned about himself and his values from the trip on the river.

Expository Techniques

1a. Which part of this essay is devoted primarily to the narrative of the father?

   b. To the narrative of the author as a child?

2a. From what narrative are the events presented in paragraph 3 taken?

   b. Which paragraphs other than paragraph 3 provide background information for the father's story (including events prior to the main narrative)?

3. Which paragraphs in the story of the author as a child are devoted mainly to presenting events and which to generalizing about them? Which mix telling and generalizing?

4. Discuss how the author manages in paragraph 16 to explain her father's reasons for returning home and to suggest what he had learned about himself—without generalizing directly about either.

5. From what point of view or points of view is this essay narrated? Be ready to provide examples to support your answer. (See Guide to Terms: *Point of View* and the introduction to Section 9, p. 354.)

Diction and Vocabulary

1a.   Compare the diction in paragraphs 15 and 19. In which is the diction more concrete and specific? More abstract and general? Identify words and phrases that support your conclusion. (Guide: *Concrete/Abstract, Specific/General.*)

b.   Paragraph 15 is part of the narrative of the author's father and paragraph 19 is from the narrative of the author as a child. What differences in the purposes of these two segments of the essay are reflected in their diction? (Guide: *Purpose.*)

2.   Identify the similes in paragraphs 20 and 21 and discuss the ways in which the author's use of these figures of speech is appropriate or inappropriate to her purpose in these sections of the essay. (Guide: *Purpose.*)

3.   Do some of the details in the conclusion (par. 22) call up memories of your own experiences, either as a child or as an adult? Describe your memories briefly and identify the details that prompt them.

4a.   What does the term *in medias res* (par. 18) mean? Does its use here add to or detract from the effectiveness of the writing?

b.   If you do not know the meaning of any of the following terms, look them up in the dictionary: hazarded, marks, shoal, soundings (par. 3); bastardized (6); hoofer (12); salts (15); hove, lepidopterology (17); tern (20).

Suggestions for Writing and Discussion

1.   Our earliest childhood memories are often of events that involve a growing awareness of ourselves and others. Such events and what they reveal about the way humans develop can make good subjects for expository essays.

2.   How are readers who grew up in relatively affluent surroundings likely to respond to this essay? How are readers who grew up in families with modest means (or less) likely to respond? Does the author take into account the social class of her family in recreating or commenting on the events in the narrative?

3.   What common activities do men undertake to escape from responsibilities or act out in middle age the dreams of their youth? What common activities do women undertake?

(NOTE: Suggestions for topics requiring development by NARRATION are on page 388, at the end of this section.)

GEORGE ORWELL

GEORGE ORWELL (1903–1950), whose real name was Eric Blair, was a British novelist and essayist, well known for his satire. He was born in India and educated at Eton in England; he was wounded while fighting in the Spanish Civil War. Later he wrote the books *Animal Farm* (1945), a satire on Soviet history, and *1984* (1949), a vivid picture of life in a projected totalitarian society. He was, however, also sharply aware of injustices in democratic societies and was consistently socialistic in his views. Many of Orwell's essays are collected in *Critical Essays* (1946), *Shooting an Elephant and Other Essays* (1950), and *Such, Such Were the Joys* (1953).

A Hanging

"A Hanging" is typical of Orwell's essays in its setting— Burma— and in its subtle but biting commentary on colonialism, on capital punishment, even on one aspect of human nature itself. Although he is ostensibly giving a straightforward account of an execution, the author masterfully uses descriptive details and dialogue to create atmosphere and sharply drawn characterizations. The essay gives concrete form to a social message that is often delivered much less effectively in abstract generalities.

It was in Burma, a sodden morning of the rains. A sickly light, like 1 yellow tinfoil, was slanting over the high walls into the jail yard. We were waiting outside the condemned cells, a row of sheds fronted with double bars, like small animal cages. Each cell measured about ten feet by ten and was quite bare within except for a plank bed and a pot for drinking water. In some of them brown, silent men were squatting at the inner bars, with their blankets draped round them.

These were the condemned men, due to be hanged within the next week or two.

One prisoner had been brought out of his cell. He was a Hindu, a puny wisp of a man, with a shaven head and vague liquid eyes. He had a thick, sprouting mustache, absurdly too big for his body, rather like the mustache of a comic man on the films. Six tall Indian warders were guarding him and getting him ready for the gallows. Two of them stood by with rifles and fixed bayonets, while the others handcuffed him, passed a chain through his handcuffs and fixed it to their belts, and lashed his arms tight to his sides. They crowded very close about him, with their hands always on him in a careful, caressing grip, as though all the while feeling him to make sure he was there. It was like men handling a fish which is still alive and may jump back into the water. But he stood quite unresisting, yielding his arms limply to the ropes, as though he hardly noticed what was happening.

Eight o'clock struck and a bugle call, desolately thin in the wet air, floated from the distant barracks. The superintendent of the jail, who was standing apart from the rest of us, moodily prodding the gravel with his stick, raised his head at the sound. He was an army doctor, with a grey toothbrush mustache and a gruff voice. "For God's sake, hurry up, Francis," he said irritably. "The man ought to have been dead by this time. Aren't you ready yet?"

Francis, the head jailer, a fat Dravidian in a white drill suit and gold spectacles, waved his black hand. "Yes sir, yes sir," he bubbled. "All iss satisfactorily prepared. The hangman iss waiting. We shall proceed."

"Well, quick march, then. The prisoners can't get their breakfast till this job's over."

We set out for the gallows. Two warders marched on either side of the prisoner, with their rifles at the slope; two others marched close against him, gripping him by arm and shoulder, as though at once pushing and supporting him. The rest of us, magistrates and the like, followed behind. Suddenly, when we had gone ten yards, the procession stopped short without any order or warning. A dreadful thing had happened—a dog, come goodness knows whence, had appeared in the yard. It came bounding among us with a loud volley of barks and leapt round us wagging its whole body, wild with glee at finding so many human beings together. It was a large woolly dog, half Airedale, half pariah. For a moment it pranced around us, and then, before anyone could stop it, it had made a dash for the prisoner, and jumping up tried to lick his face. Everybody stood aghast, too taken aback even to grab the dog.

"Who let that bloody brute in here?" said the superintendent 7 angrily. "Catch it, someone!"

A warder detached from the escort, charged clumsily after the 8 dog, but it danced and gambolled just out of his reach, taking everything as part of the game. A young Eurasian jailer picked up a handful of gravel and tried to stone the dog away, but it dodged the stones and came after us again. Its yaps echoed from the jail walls. The prisoner, in the grasp of the two warders, looked on incuriously, as though this was another formality of the hanging. It was several minutes before someone managed to catch the dog. Then we put my handkerchief through its collar and moved off once more, with the dog still straining and whimpering.

It was about forty yards to the gallows. I watched the bare brown 9 back of the prisoner marching in front of me. He walked clumsily with his bound arms, but quite steadily, with that bobbing gait of the Indian who never straightens his knees. At each step his muscles slid neatly into place, the lock of hair on his scalp danced up and down, his feet printed themselves on the wet gravel. And once, in spite of the men who gripped him by each shoulder, he stepped lightly aside to avoid a puddle on the path.

It is curious; but till that moment I had never realized what it 10 means to destroy a healthy, conscious man. When I saw the prisoner step aside to avoid the puddle, I saw the mystery, the unspeakable wrongness, of cutting a life short when it is in full tide. This man was not dying, he was alive just as we are alive. All the organs of his body were working—bowels digesting food, skin renewing itself, nails growing, tissues forming—all toiling away in solemn foolery. His nails would still be growing when he stood on the drop, when he was failing through the air with a tenth-of-a-second to live. His eyes saw the yellow gravel and the grey walls, and his brain still remembered, foresaw, reasoned—even about puddles. He and we were a party of men walking together, seeing, hearing, feeling, understanding the same world; and in two minutes, with a sudden snap, one of us would be gone—one mind less, one world less.

The gallows stood in a small yard, separate from the main 11 grounds of the prison, and overgrown with tall prickly weeds. It was a brick erection like three sides of a shed, with planking on top, and above that two beams and a crossbar with the rope dangling. The hangman, a greyhaired convict in the white uniform of the prison, was waiting beside his machine. He greeted us with a servile crouch as we entered. At a word from Francis the two warders, gripping the prisoner more closely than ever, half led, half pushed him to the gallows and helped him clumsily up the ladder. Then the hangman climbed up and fixed the rope round the prisoner's neck.

We stood waiting, five yards away. The warders had formed in a   12
rough circle round the gallows. And then, when the noose was fixed, the prisoner began crying out to his god. It was a high, reiterated cry of "Ram! Ram! Ram! Ram!" not urgent and fearful like a prayer or cry for help, but steady, rhythmical, almost like the tolling of a bell. The dog answered the sound with a whine. The hangman, still standing on the gallows, produced a small cotton bag like a flour bag and drew it down over the prisoner's face. But the sound, muffled by the cloth, still persisted, over and over again: "Ram! Ram! Ram! Ram! Ram!"

The hangman climbed down and stood ready, holding the lever.   13
Minutes seemed to pass. The steady, muffled crying from the prisoner went on and on, "Ram! Ram! Ram!" never faltering for an instant. The superintendent, his head on his chest, was slowly poking the ground with his stick; perhaps he was counting the cries, allowing the prisoner a fixed number—fifty, perhaps, or a hundred. Everyone had changed colour. The Indians had gone grey like bad coffee, and one or two of the bayonets were wavering. We looked at the lashed, hooded man on the drop, and listened to his cries—each cry another second of life; the same thought was in all our minds; oh, kill him quickly, get it over, stop that abominable noise!

Suddenly the superintendent made up his mind. Throwing up   14
his head he made a swift motion with his stick. " Chalo! " he shouted almost fiercely.

There was a clanking noise, and then dead silence. The prisoner   15
had vanished, and the rope was twisting on itself. I let go of the dog, and it galloped immediately to the back of the gallows; but when it got there it stopped short, barked, and then retreated into a corner of the yard, where it stood among the weeds, looking timorously out at us. We went round the gallows to inspect the prisoner's body. He was dangling with his toes pointed straight downwards, very slowly revolving, as dead as a stone.

The superintendent reached out with his stick and poked the bare   16
brown body; it oscillated slightly. "*He's* all right," said the superintendent. He backed out from under the gallows, and blew out a deep

breath. The moody look had gone out of his face quite suddenly. He glanced at his wrist-watch. "Eight minutes past eight. Well, that's all for this morning, thank God."

The warders unfixed bayonets and marched away. The dog, sobered and conscious of having misbehaved itself, slipped after them. We walked out of the gallows yard, past the condemned cells with their waiting prisoners, into the big central yard of the prison. The convicts, under the command of warders armed with lathis, were already receiving their breakfast. They squatted in long rows, each man holding a tin pannikin, while two warders with buckets marched around ladling out rice; it seemed quite a homely, jolly scene, after the hanging. An enormous relief had come upon us now that the job was done. One felt an impulse to sing, to break into a run, to snigger. All at once everyone began chattering gaily.

The Eurasian boy walking beside me nodded towards the way we had come, with a knowing smile: "Do you know, sir, our friend (he meant the dead man) when he heard his appeal had been dismissed, he pissed on the floor of his cell. From fright. Kindly take one of my cigarettes, sir. Do you not admire my new silver case, sir? From the boxwallah, two rupees eight annas. Classy European style."

Several people laughed—at what, nobody seemed certain.

Francis was walking by the superintendent, talking garrulously: "Well, sir, all has passed off with the utmost satisfactoriness. It was all finished—flick! Like that. It iss not always so—oah, no! I have known cases where the doctor was obliged to go beneath the gallows and pull the prissoner's legs to ensure decease. Most disagreeable!"

"Wriggling about, eh? That's bad," said the superintendent.

"Ach, sir, it iss worse when they become refractory! One man, I recall, clung to the bars of hiss cage when we went to take him out. You will scarcely credit, sir, that it took six warders to dislodge him, three pulling at each leg. We reasoned with him, 'My dear fellow,' we said, 'think of all the pain and trouble you are causing to us!' But no, he would not listen! Ach, he wass very troublesome!"

I found that I was laughing quite loudly. Everyone was laughing. Even the superintendent grinned in a tolerant way. "You'd better all come out and have a drink," he said quite genially. "I've got a bottle of whisky in the car. We could do with it."

We went through the big double gates of the prison into the road. "Pulling at his legs!" exclaimed a Burmese magistrate suddenly, and burst into a loud chuckling. We all began laughing again. At that moment Francis' anecdote seemed extraordinarily funny. We all had a drink together, native and European alike, quite amicably. The dead man was a hundred yards away.

Meanings and Values

1. What was the real reason for the superintendent's impatience?

2. On first impression it may have seemed that the author gave undue attention to the dog's role in this narrative.

    a. Why was the episode such a "dreadful thing" (par. 6)?

    b. Why did the author think it worth noting that the dog was excited at "finding so many human beings together"?

    c. Of what significance was the dog's trying to lick the prisoner's face?

3. Explain how the prisoner's stepping around a puddle could have given the author a new insight into what was about to happen (par. 10).

4. Why was there so much talking and laughing after the hanging was finished?

5. What is the broadest meaning of Orwell's last sentence?

Expository Techniques

1. Cite examples of both objective and impressionistic description in the first paragraph.

2a. What is the primary time order used in this narrative?

 b. If there are any exceptions, state where.

3. Considering the relatively few words devoted to them, several of the characterizations in this essay are remarkably vivid—a result, obviously, of highly discriminating selection of details from the multitude of those that must have been available to the author. For each of the following people, list the character traits that we can observe, and state whether these impressions come to us through details of description, action, and/or dialogue.

    a. The prisoner.

    b. The superintendent.

    c. Francis.

    d. The Eurasian boy.

4a. Why do you think the author included so many details of the preparation of the prisoner (par. 2)?

b. Why did he include so many details about the dog and his actions?

c. What is gained by the assortment of details in paragraph 10?

5. The tone of writing such as this can easily slip into sentimentality or even melodrama without the author's realizing what is happening. (See Guide to Terms: *Sentimentality*.) Select three places in this narrative where a less-skilled writer might have had such trouble, and note by what restraints Orwell avoided sentimentality.

Diction and Vocabulary

1. A noteworthy element of Orwell's style is his occasional use of figurative language. Cite six metaphors and similes, and comment on their choice and effectiveness.

2. Orwell was always concerned with the precise effects that words could give to meaning and style.

a. Cite at least six nonfigurative words that seem to you particularly well chosen for their purpose.

b. Show what their careful selection contributes to the description of atmosphere or to the subtle meanings of the author.

c. How is this attention to diction a matter of style? (Guide: *Style/Tone*.)

Suggestions for Writing and Discussion

1. Select *one* of the points of controversy over capital punishment and present both sides with equal objectivity.

2. Consider the dilemma of a person whose "duty" seems to require one course of action and whose "conscience" just the opposite course. Use concrete illustrations to show how serious such dilemmas can be.

3. Examine the moral right, or lack of it, of the people of one country to impose their laws on the people of another country.

4. Discuss one benefit of colonialism to the people colonized. Use specific illustrations.

5. Explain how, in your own experience, a seemingly minor incident led to much deeper insight into a matter not fully understood before.

(NOTE: Suggestions for topics requiring development by NARRATION are on page 388, at the end of this section.)

GARY SOTO

A poet, short story writer, and essayist, GARY SOTO also teaches English and Chicano Studies at the University of California–Berkeley. He has published six volumes of poetry, a short story collection, and four collections of essays. His most recent volume of essays, *A Summer Life*, appeared in 1990. An earlier collection, *Living Up the Street* (1985), received a Before Columbus Foundation American Book Award. Soto has also been honored by the Fresno Area Council of English Teachers for the inspiration his writings have provided to young people from the San Joaquin Valley.

The Locket

Combining narration with comparison, this essay from *A Summer Life* uses toys to highlight stages in an "awakening." The events in the essay should be similar enough to incidents and patterns in most readers' lives so that the selection offers us ways of understanding our own adolescence.

I never liked jewelry. My sister Debra did. Twenty Bazooka comic   1
strips and a dollar—after a three-week binge of reading teenage romances while waiting for the mailman—brought her a gold-plated locket, studded with plastic pearls and a fake diamond. I wanted her to choose the miniature binoculars because I helped her chew at least seven pieces of pink bubble gum and gave her a clean dime in exchange for our once-a-week pudding dessert. We were always selling desserts to each other. We were always short a dime or a quarter, and our only bargaining chip was dessert, especially the pudding mother served in gold-rimmed goblets, the kind kings and queens used in Robin Hood movies.

I wanted Debra to choose the binoculars. My head was large, but   2
my eyes were small as a cat's, maybe even smaller. I could look
through both lenses with one eye, and what I wanted was a better
look at our neighbor, a junior college student who swam in an
aluminum-sided doughboy pool. She used a ladder to get in, and
often just stood on the ladder fiddling with her top and snapping her
bikini bottom back into place. I could spy on her from behind our
fence, the binoculars to my right eye because that one seemed to work
better.

But Debra chose the locket. When it arrived in a business-sized   3
envelope, I waved it at her and said, "It's here." Angrily, she snatched
it from me and took it to her room. I ate an afternoon bowl of Cocoa
Puffs and watched a movie about giant ants no flame thrower could
stop. I looked at her bedroom door now and then, wondering what
was going on. Later, just before the ants got fried with a laser, she came
out stinking of perfume, the locket around her brown neck. She didn't
look at me as she went out the front door and crossed the street to see
her friend, Jill.

My sister was eleven. She still clacked the plastic faces of Barbie   4
and Ken together, made them hug, made them cry and run back to
each other, stiff arms extended, faces wet with pretend tears from the
bathroom sink. But she and Jill played with them less and less. Now
they were going for the real thing: boys with washed faces.

In spite of the plastic pearls and the chip of glass centered in the   5
middle, the locket made her look grown-up. I didn't tease her, and
she didn't tease me about wearing rummage-sale baseball cleats.

All summer Debra wore the locket, and Jill wore one, too, an   6
expensive one her mother had bought at Penney's. But Debra didn't
care. She loved the locket whose metal chain left her neck green.
Mother admired the locket, said it made her look elegant. That summer, Debra began to complain less and less about doing the dishes.

When a pearl fell out, she glued it back in. Another lost its grip   7
and rolled into the floor furnace. She vacuumed the furnace of its
ghostly lint, and shook out the bag and ran her fingers through the
stinking hair, lint, broken potato chips, Cocoa Puffs, Cheerios, staples,
bits of Kleenex, dead ants, and blue, flowery marble. She searched
through the debris until, miraculously, she found the tiny pearl. She
glued it back into place and gave her locket a rest.

One day, while Debra was at the playground swimming, I snuck   8
into her bedroom to peek in the locket because I knew she kept

something in the frame. She was always snapping it open and closed, always feeling pretty happy when she looked down at her breasts, twin mounds that had begun to cast small shadows. When I opened it, slowly because the clasp looked fragile, I saw a face that was mostly an eyeball looking at me. I stared back at the eyeball, and after a moment realized that it was Paul of the Beatles. It was Paul's eyeball, a bit droopy, a bit sad like his songs. Paul was favored by the girls who rode their bikes up and down the block singing "Michelle, ma belle."

A few days later I checked the locket again. Paul's eyeball was gone, and now I was staring at a smiling Herman and the Hermits. Herman looked happy. His hair was long and soft, and his teeth were large and charmingly crooked. I smiled wide and thought for a moment that I looked like Herman. A few days later it was back to Paul in a new picture that she had cut out of a magazine. I thumbed through the magazine, emptied of all the famous pop stars, and looked around the room. Almost everything was pink. The furry rug, the canopy bed, the bottles of perfume and nail polish, the much-hugged pillow, everything except the chest of drawers which she intended to paint by fall. I left in a hurry when I heard Debra's bike skid to a halt in the driveway.

All summer it was Paul's eyeball, Herman's teeth, and one time Paul Revere with his colonial hat. Debra began to polish her nails and walk more slowly, erect as a ladder. By fall, the chest of drawers was pink and Mother was no longer worried about the green around her neck where the chain rested—an allergic reaction to cheap metal. Debra no longer wore the locket. She was saving Bazooka comics for a camera that came with a free roll of film. She had her first boyfriend and wanted to take his picture on the sly, wanted more than a droopy eyeball or toothy smile. She wanted the entire face, and some of the neck.

Meanings and Values

1a. In what ways can Debra be said to treat the locket as a symbol? What does it symbolize to her? (See Guide to Terms: *Symbol*.)

 b. How does the speaker's attitude toward the locket differ from his sister's?

 c. What does Debra's abandonment of interest in the locket indicate?

2. Summarize what this essay has to say about differences (and similarities) between girls' and boys' attitudes toward the opposite sex and sexuality.

Expository Techniques

1. Instead of speaking directly about the feelings and attitudes of his sister and himself as adolescents, Soto focuses on the way they interact with a variety of toys. Identify the various toys Soto uses in this way, and tell what they reveal about him and his sister at various stages of development.

2. What use does the writer make of comparison to highlight and explore major themes in the essay?

3. Discuss the author's use of concrete detail in the following paragraphs: 7, 9, and 10. (Guide: *Concrete/Abstract*.)

4. What strategy does he employ to conclude the essay? (Guide: *Closings*.)

Diction and Vocabulary

1. Why does Soto mention the color scheme in his sister's room (pars. 9–10)?

2. Discuss the diction that the author uses to describe the locket and reactions to it, focusing especially on paragraphs 4–6. In what ways does the choice of language comment on the changes in his sister's outlook and other people's attitudes toward her? (Guide: *Diction*.)

Suggestions for Writing and Discussion

1. Consider writing an essay that draws on your experiences with a sibling or a friend and that highlights patterns of psychological and social development.

2. Does awakening sexuality still involve behaviors similar to the ones Soto describes? What differences are there now, if any?

3. Consider how an essay like this might differ if it were written from the perspective of a sister.

(NOTE: Suggestions for topics requiring development by NARRATION are on page 388, at the end of this section.)

DONALD HALL

DONALD HALL, poet, essayist, biographer, literary critic, and text-book writer, was born in Connecticut in 1928. In 1975, he left his teaching position at the University of Michigan to move to a farm in New Hampshire and devote his time to writing. Among his more than forty books of poetry, prose, and anthologies are *Kicking the Leaves* (1978) and *The Happy Man* (1986), poems; *String Too Short to Be Saved* (1961), *Seasons at Eagle Pond* (1987), and *Here at Eagle Pond* (1990), prose; *The Oxford Book of Children's Verse in America* (1985), anthology; and *Writing Well* (7th edition, 1991, with Sven Birkerts) and *A Writer's Reader* (6th edition, 1991, with Donald Emblen), textbooks.

The Embrace of Old Age

The title of this essay from *Here at Eagle Pond* takes on several different meanings for readers by the end of the selection. Likewise, the insights into youth and aging that Hall offers become richer and more complex as the essay progresses and even more apparent on rereading. Most interesting, perhaps, is the distance between what Hall saw as a youth and what he knows now.

When I spent my summers here [Wilmot, New Hampshire] as a boy, 1 my grandparents took me everywhere they went. We had no car. We didn't hitch up the horse to go to a drive-in movie, but we rode behind Riley to church on Sunday morning, and on Sunday night returned in the buggy for Christian Endeavor. We attended annual social events, in July the Church Fair and in August Old Home Day. Although my grandparents lived without anything that passes for entertainment in the 1990s—no car, no television, no VCR, no restaurants, no cocktail parties—they were remarkably cheerful. My grandfather especially had a fortunate temperament. He liked his work, and a little amusement went a long way. Occasionally we hitched up Riley for a special occasion: a family reunion, an auction, an eightieth birthday party, a funeral, a long-delayed visit to a dying cousin. When I was fourteen years old we went to Willard and Alice Buzzle's diamond wedding anniversary.

In preparation, my grandmother made three blueberry pies and   2
a bagful of ginger snaps; my grandfather dusted the horse carriage, wiped off the harness, and curried Riley. Because the buggy's iron rims rattled on its wooden wheels—a dry August—we drove it across the railroad tracks to Eagle Pond and urged Riley against his better judgment to wade, pulling the carriage into shallow water. We sat there for a few minutes as I delighted in the strangeness, sitting still in the buggy in the pond's shallows while the wood swelled tight inside the rims. Then we drove back to the farm to dress and set out.

Willard and Alice were older than my grandparents, who were   3
in their sixties. I remembered the Buzzles from Old Home Day: They were *old*. Alice had been seventeen when she was married, which made her ninety-two on her seventy-fifth wedding anniversary. Willard was exactly one hundred, married the day he turned twenty-five, which of course made today's celebration double. Diamond wedding anniversaries were rare enough; today we added a simultaneous one hundredth birthday party. Three weekly newspapers sent photographer-reporters to the Danbury Grange.

Horses and buggies were uncommon on the roads, though horse   4
farmers were not unknown in 1943. The war kept traffic down, but a few dark square cars passed us on Route 4. My grandfather kept the buggy's right wheels on the shoulder, and I watched sand spin off the wheels like Fourth of July nightworks fountains. When we arrived at the Grange Hall, it was decorated red, white, and blue. As we alighted my grandfather spoke in Riley's ear and tied him loosely to a young maple, so that he could bend his neck to eat grass. Inside, the Grange walls were covered with photographs of past Grange presidents, and there was an American flag beside the stage in the front, the drawn curtain showing a view of Mount Kearsage painted by a local artist in 1906. We were early, of course, and so was everyone else. My grandmother cut her pies and set the pieces out on a long table covered with pies and cookies. Willard and Alice's sons Clarence and Frank scurried about, old men who moved with the sprightly energy

of children anxious to please. Then a shout from the door told us that the bridal couple had arrived. I looked out to see Willard's Model A parked at the front door, driven by their surviving daughter Ada. Bride and bridegroom tottered up the steps, walking with canes held in outside hands so that they could join inside arms. They gripped each other fiercely, as if each were convinced that the other needed help. Willard looked the frailer as he climbed the Grange steps on his hundredth birthday and his seventy-fifth wedding anniversary, wavering over the worn wood stairs.

At the opened double doors Clarence and Frank took charge, each grasping one parent, and led them into the hall, where my grandmother at the organ belted out the Wedding March. Now the ancient small parents, on the arms of ancient small sons, with ancient daughter in the rear, walked slowly the length of the hall between the folding chairs set up for the ceremony, waving and acknowledging our waves like conquerors returned from the war that was not over. When Alice and Willard reached the end of the hall, my grandmother's fingers switched to "Happy Birthday." Everyone sang while a huge cake, big enough for everyone present, was wheeled into the crowd, topped with a hundred candles and the figurines of a bride and groom. Willard and Alice conspired with Ada, Clarence, and Frank to blow out the candles, taking many breaths, after a pause for a wish.

And I thought, What could they wish for? Not for a long life! Maybe for an easy winter? I studied Willard's infirmity. The skin of his hands was brown with liver spots, flesh hung like turkey wattles from his neck, and everything about him shook: his arms, his head on its frail stem, and his bony knees visibly trembling against his trouser legs. I felt horror—as if it were indecent to be alive with no future, each day merely a task for accomplishment. My vision of old age shook me as Willard shook.

Our minister, Kate's brother my uncle Luther, was host and master of ceremonies for half an hour of reminiscences and songs: "The Old Oaken Bucket," "When You and I Were Young, Maggie," "Down by the Old Mill Stream." Luther read two telegrams, one for the wedding and one for the birthday, from President Franklin Delano Roosevelt. When we broke to eat I heaped my paper plate with hermits and brownies and cherry pie, not forgetting a piece of wedding cake. Returning for seconds, I gathered the last piece of my grandmother's blueberry.

Then I was bored. I was rarely bored in my grandparents' company but today they paid me no mind. They had done introducing me and I had done with comments on how tall I was. Now they stood with other old people recollecting together. And I felt separate, separated especially because I understood that I was the *only one* in this crowd able to see clearly the futility and ugliness of old age. 8

So I prowled around the building, exploring the stage behind the painted curtain, finding a closet full of ancient costumes, trying on a top hat and derby. Then I opened a door I had not entered before, a green room to the side of the stage, and walked into the dimness without sensing the presence of others. In low light from a shaded window I saw two bodies embracing as they leaned against a wardrobe. I was embarrassed, I suppose because notions of embracing had begun to occupy me day and night. I started to back out, then saw that it was Willard and Alice who clung to each other, having crept from their thronged relatives and neighbors to this privacy. Their twin canes leaned on a box while their arms engaged each other. For a quick moment it was as if I saw, beyond the ancients in the green room, a young couple, seventy-five years back, who found a secret place to kiss and hug in. 9

Then I heard what she said: "Alice, Alice, Alice." She spoke urgently, "Alice, Alice," as if she were warning herself of something. At that moment I felt my grandfather's hand on my shoulder—it was time to go home; he had sought me out—and when I looked up I saw that he had heard. It was not until we were driving home that he mentioned it. I listened as he spoke—his voice controlled, as if he made a neutral observation, about the weather perhaps, that although the day was bright he wouldn't be surprised if it rained—saying, "Kate, Willard didn't know who Alice was." 10

Meanings and Values

1a. How would you describe the tone of the essay as it is established by the title and the opening paragraph? (See Guide to Terms: *Style/Tone*.)

b. How does the tone shift in the last paragraph?

2a. In your own words, state the central theme of the selection. (Guide: *Unity*.)

b. Identify those places where the writer seems to state the central theme either directly or ironically. (Guide: *Irony*.)

c.   Would the selection be more or less effective if the writer had chosen
     to state the central theme more clearly near the beginning of the essay?
     Why, or why not? (Guide: *Evaluation*.)

Expository Techniques

1a.   Many of the details and observations in paragraphs 2, 3, and 8 are
      typical of a fourteen-year-old boy. Which are they? (Guide: *Persona*.)

b.   What evidence is there that the narrative is presented to a considerable
      extent from the perspective of a fourteen-year-old? (Guide: *Point of
      View*.)

c.   To what extent does the point of view shape the presentation of events
      in paragraph 9? How does the writer signal to us that a youthful
      perspective is at work?

d.   In what ways are the power and the surprise of the concluding para-
      graph the result of the use of this point of view?

2a.   Reread the essay to identify any clues it contains that foreshadow the
      eventual revelation about Willard.

b.   Explain why most readers are not likely to notice these clues during
      the first encounter with the essay.

c.   Why might the selection have been less effective in conveying its theme
      if the author had provided more obvious foreshadowing?

Diction and Vocabulary

1.   Discuss how the diction and the choice of details in paragraphs 2–5
      and 6 create a sense of an old-fashioned festival. (Guide: *Diction*.)

2.   Examine and discuss Hall's use of the following in paragraph 6:

a.   Rhetorical questions. (Guide: *Rhetorical Questions*.)

b.   Diction.

c.   Varied sentence structure and length.

d.   Simile. (Guide: *Figures of Speech*.)

3.   Identify the figure of speech in the following sentence and discuss its
      relationship to the essay's central theme: "Now the ancient small
      parents, on the arms of ancient small sons, with ancient daughter in
      the rear, walked slowly the length of the hall between the folding chairs
      set up for the ceremony, waving and acknowledging our waves like
      conquerors returned from the war that was not over" (par. 5).

Suggestions for Writing and Discussion

1. If you have read Sharon Curtin's "Aging in the Land of the Young" (pp. 316–319), compare its treatment of old age and attitudes toward the elderly with the treatment provided in this essay.

2. In class, discuss how present-day relationships between children (or teenagers) and the elderly compare to the close relationship Hall had with his grandparents.

(NOTE: Suggestions for topics requiring development by NARRATION follow.)

Writing Suggestions for Section 9
Narration

Use narration as at least a partial pattern (e.g., in developed examples or in comparison) for one of the following expository themes or another suggested by them. Avoid the isolated personal account that has little broader significance. Remember, too, that development of the essay should itself make your point, without excessive moralizing.

1. People can still succeed without a college education.

2. The frontiers are not all gone.

3. When people succeed in communicating, they can learn to get along with each other.

4. Even with "careful" use of capital punishment, innocent people can be executed.

5. Sports don't always build character.

6. Physical danger can make us more aware of ourselves and our values.

7. Conditioning to the realities of the job is as important to the police officer as professional training.

8. It is possible for employees themselves to determine when they have reached their highest level of competence.

9. Wartime massacres are not a new development.

10. "Date rape" and sexual harassment on the job are devastating and generally unexpected.

11. Both heredity and environment shape personality.

12. Physical and mental handicaps can be overcome in some ways, but they are still a burden.

13. Toxic wastes pose a problem for many communities.

14. Hunting is a worthwhile and challenging sport.

15. Lack of money places considerable stress on a family or a marriage.

16. Exercise can become an obsession.

17. People who grow up in affluent surroundings don't understand what it is like to worry about money, to be hungry, or to live in a dangerous neighborhood.

18. Some jobs are simply degrading, either because of the work or because of the fellow workers.

10

Reasoning by Use of *Induction* and *Deduction*

Induction and deduction, important as they are in argumentation, may also be useful methods of exposition. They are often used simply to explain a stand or conclusion, without any effort or need to win converts.

Induction is the process by which we accumulate evidence until, at some point, we can make the "inductive leap" and thus reach a useful *generalization.* The science laboratory employs this technique; hundreds of tests and experiments and analyses may be required before the scientist will generalize, for instance, that a disease is caused by a certain virus. It is also the primary technique of the prosecuting attorney who presents pieces of inductive evidence, asking the jury to make the inductive leap and conclude that the accused did indeed kill the victim.

Even the commonplace "process of elimination" also may be considered a form of induction. If it can be shown, for instance, that "A" does not have the strength to swing the murder weapon, that "B" was in a drunken sleep at the time of the crime, and that "C" had recently become blind and could not have found her way to the boathouse, then we may be ready for the inductive leap—that the foul deed must have been committed by "X," the only other person on the island. (The use of this kind of induction implies an added obligation, of course, to make certain that all the possibilities but *one* have been eliminated: if we fail to note that "Y," a visitor on a neighboring island, and his boat were unaccounted for that evening, then our conclusion is invalid.)

On a more personal level, of course, we all learned to use induction at a very early age. We may have disliked the taste of orange juice, winter squash, and carrots, and we were not too young to make a generalization: orange-colored food tastes bad.

Whereas induction is the method of reaching a potentially useful generalization (for example, Professor Melville always gives an "F" to students who cut his class three times), *deduction* is the method of *using* such a generality, now accepted as a fact (for example, if we cut this class again today, we will get an "F"). Working from a generalization already formulated—by ourselves, by someone else, or by tradition—we may deduce that a specific thing or circumstance that fits into the generality will act the same. Hence, if convinced that orange-colored food tastes bad, we will be reluctant to try pumpkin pie.

A personnel manager may have discovered over the years that electronics majors from Central College are invariably well trained in their field. His induction may have been based on the evidence of observations, records, and the opinions of fellow Rotary members; and, perhaps without realizing it, he has made the usable generalization about the training of Central College electronics majors. Later, when he has an application from Nancy Ortega, a graduate of Central College, his *de*ductive process will probably work as follows: Central College turns out well-trained electronics majors; Ortega was trained at Central; therefore, Ortega must be well trained. Here he has used a generalization to apply to a specific case.

Put in this simplified form (which, in writing, it seldom is),[1] the deductive process is also called a "syllogism"—with the beginning generality known as the "major premise" and the specific that fits into the generality known as the "minor premise." For example:

Major premise—Orange-colored food is not fit to eat.
Minor premise—Pumpkin pie is orange-colored.
Conclusion—Pumpkin pie is not fit to eat.

Frequently, however, the validity of one or both of the premises may be questionable, and here is one of the functions of *in*duction: to give needed support—with evidence such as opinions of experts,

---

[1]Neither induction nor deduction is confined to a particular order of presentation. If we use specific evidence to *reach* a generalization, it is induction regardless of which part is stated first in a written or spoken account. (Very likely, both a prosecutor's opening remarks and a medical researcher's written reports first present their generalizations and then the inductive evidence by which they have been reached.) But if we use a generality in which to *place* a specific, it is still deduction, however stated. (Hence the reasoning of the personnel manager might be: "Ortega must be well trained because she was educated at C.C., and there's where they really know how to do it.")

statistics, and results of experiments or surveys—to the *de*ductive syllogism, whether stated or implied. Deductive reasoning, in whatever form presented, is only as sound as both its premises. The child's conviction that orange-colored food is not fit to eat was not necessarily true; therefore, the conclusion about pumpkin pie is not very trustworthy. The other conclusions, that we will automatically get an "F" by cutting Melville's class and that Ortega is well trained in electronics, can be only as reliable as the original generalizations that were used as deductive premises. If the generalizations themselves were based on flimsy or insufficient evidence, any future deduction using them is likely to be erroneous.

These two faults are common in induction: (1) the use of *flimsy* evidence—mere opinion, hearsay, or analogy, none of which can support a valid generalization—instead of verified facts or opinions of reliable authorities; and (2) the use of *too little* evidence, leading to a premature inductive leap.

The amount of evidence needed in any situation depends, of course, on purpose and audience. The success of two Central College graduates might be enough to convince some careless personnel director that all Central electronics graduates would be good employees, but two laboratory tests would not convince medical researchers that they had learned anything worthwhile about a disease-causing virus. The authors of the Declaration of Independence, in justifying their argument for rebellion to a wide variety of readers and listeners, explained why they considered the king tyrannical, by listing twenty-eight despotic acts of his government, each of which was a verifiable fact, a matter of public record.

Induction and deduction are highly logical processes, and any trace of weakness can seriously undermine an exposition that depends on their reasonableness. (Such weakness can, of course, be even more disastrous in argument.) Although no induction or deduction ever reaches absolute, 100 percent certainty, we should try to get from these methods as high a degree of *probability* as possible. (We can never positively prove, for instance, that the sun will rise in the east tomorrow, but thousands of years of inductive observation and theorizing make the fact extremely probable—and certainly sound enough for any working generalization.)

Students using induction and deduction in compositions, essay examinations, or term papers—showing that Stephen Crane was a naturalistic writer, or that our national policies are unfair to revolutionary movements—should always assume that they will have a skeptical audience that wants to know the logical basis for *all* generalizations and conclusions.

Sample Paragraph (Annotated)

The report to the committee follows an *inductive* pattern.

The evidence presented in the body of the paragraph becomes the basis for an *inductive generalization*.

Two *inductive generalizations*.

The generalizations become the basis for an informal *deductive* syllogism pointing toward an action that probably needs to be taken.

Having built four new elementary schools in the last five years, members of the Palmville School Board were convinced they had solved the problem with overcrowding that had plagued the public schools ever since the mid-1970s. As a result, they were disappointed when School Superintendent Marisa LaRoux made her mid-July Projected Enrollment Report. She pointed out that the town's population has expanded by several hundred more families than were projected because the good weather this year spurred home building and the low mortgage rates encouraged buyers. In addition, more families are deciding to have two or more children, bringing the average number of children per family to 1.9, much higher than the figure of 1.65 used in the past to calculate demands for school services. The superintendent also admitted that the decades-old policy of calculating a family of two as a family without children has proven to be a serious mistake because it ignored the many children growing up in single-parent families. Based on this information, the superintendent concluded that the overcrowding problem would continue this year and probably for many years in the future. Chairperson Clifton Washington summed up the school board's response this way: "The schools are overcrowded now, and if more students are going to be coming to us asking for instruction, then we'd better get back into the school-building business."

Sample Paragraph (Induction)

Roaming the site, I can't help noticing that when men start cooking, the hardware gets complicated. Custom-built cookers—massive contraptions of cast iron and stainless steel—may cost $15,000 or more; they incorporate the team's barbecue philosophy. "We burn straight hickory under a baffle," Jim Garts, coleader of the Hogaholics, points out as he gingerly opens a scorching firebox that vents smoke across a water tray beneath a 4-by-8-foot grill. It's built on a trailer the size of a mobile home. Other cookers have been fashioned from a marine diesel engine; from a '76 Datsun, with grilling racks instead of front seats, a chimney above the dash, and coals under the hood; and as a 15-foot version of Elvis Presley's guitar (by the Graceland Love Me Tenderloins). It's awesome ironmongery.

Daniel Cohen, "Cooking-off for Fame and Fortune," *Smithsonian,* September 1988, p. 132.

Sample Paragraph (Deduction)

It is an everyday fact of life that competitors producing similar products assert that their own goods or services are better than those of their rivals. Every product advertised—from pain relievers to fried chicken—is claimed to be better than its competitors. If all these companies sued for libel, the courts would be so overloaded with cases that they would grind to a halt. For years courts dismissed criticisms of businesses, products, and performances as expressions of opinion. When a restaurant owner sued a guidebook to New York restaurants for giving his establishment a bad review, he won a $20,000 verdict in compensatory damages and $5 in punitive damages. But this was overturned by the court of appeals. The court held that, with the exception of one item, the allegedly libelous statements were expressions of opinion, not fact. Among these statements were that the "dumplings, on our visit, resembled bad ravioli . . . chicken with chili was rubbery and the rice . . . totally insipid. . . ." Obviously, it would be impossible to prove the nature of the food served at that particular meal. What is tender to one palate may be rubbery to another. The one misstatement of fact, that the Peking duck was served in one dish instead of three, was in my opinion, a minor and insignificant part of the entire review. Had the review of the restaurant been considered as a whole . . . , this small misstatement of fact would have been treated as *de minimis*. That is a well-established doctrine requiring that minor matters not be considered by the courts. In this case, the court held that the restaurant was a public figure and had failed to prove actual malice.

ISHMAEL REED

Born in Buffalo in 1938, ISHMAEL REED attended public schools in the city and the University of Buffalo. At present, he lives in Oakland, California. Reed is a prolific writer whose works include novels, plays, essays, and songs. In addition, he works as a television producer, magazine editor, and publisher. He has also taught at Harvard, Yale, and Dartmouth and is currently a lecturer at the University of California–Berkeley. Two of Reed's books have been nominated for National Book Awards, and in 1978 the Studio Museum in Harlem awarded him the Lewis H. Michaux Literary Prize. Among his publications are *The Free Lance Pall Bearers* (1967), *Mumbo Jumbo* (1978), and *Reckless Eyeballing* (1986) (novels); *Conjure* (1972) and *Catechism of D Neoamerican Hoodoo Church* (1970) (poems); and *Shrovetide in New Orleans* (1979) and *Writin' Is Fightin'* (1988) (essays).

America: The Multinational Society

"America: The Multinational Society" is an ambitious but nonetheless clearly structured and easily followed essay. The selection opens with a line of inductive reasoning ending in a generalization. Then it employs a mirror image of the process, an inductive "process of elimination" of sorts, designed to disprove competing generalizations. Following this, the essay undertakes a third line of inductive reasoning ending in a generalization that becomes the basis for an informal syllogism. Despite this, most readers should have little trouble understanding Reed's reasoning, though they may reject his conclusions. His energetic, imaginative style may likewise please some readers and irritate others.

At the annual Lower East Side Jewish Festival yesterday, a Chinese   1
woman ate a pizza slice in front of Ty Thuan Duc's Vietnamese

grocery store. Beside her a Spanish-speaking family patronized a cart with two signs: "Italian Ices" and "Kosher by Rabbi Alper." And after the pastrami ran out, everybody ate knishes.

(*New York Times*, 23 June 1983)

On the day before Memorial Day, 1983, a poet called me to 2 describe a city he had just visited. He said that one section included mosques, built by the Islamic people who dwelled there. Attending his reading, he said, were large numbers of Hispanic people, forty thousand of whom lived in the same city. He was not talking about a fabled city located in some mysterious region of the world. The city he'd visited was Detroit.

A few months before, as I was leaving Houston, Texas, I heard it 3 announced on the radio that Texas's largest minority was Mexican American, and though a foundation recently issued a report critical of bilingual education, the taped voice used to guide the passengers on the air trams connecting terminals in Dallas Airport is in both Spanish and English. If the trend continues, a day will come when it will be difficult to travel through some sections of the country without hearing commands in both English and Spanish; after all, for some western states, Spanish was the first written language and the Spanish style lives on in the western way of life.

Shortly after my Texas trip, I sat in an auditorium located on the 4 campus of the University of Wisconsin at Milwaukee as a Yale professor—whose original work on the influence of African cultures upon those of the Americas has led to his ostracism from some monocultural intellectual circles—walked up and down the aisle, like an old-time southern evangelist, dancing and drumming the top of the lectern, illustrating his points before some serious Afro-American intellectuals and artists who cheered and applauded his performance and his mastery of information. The professor was "white." After his lecture, he joined a group of Milwaukeeans in a conversation. All of the participants spoke Yoruban, though only the professor had ever traveled to Africa.

One of the artists told me that his paintings, which included 5 African and Afro-American mythological symbols and imagery, were hanging in the local McDonald's restaurant. The next day I went to McDonald's and snapped pictures of smiling youngsters eating hamburgers below paintings that could grace the walls of any of the country's leading museums. The manager of the local

McDonald's said, "I don't know what you boys are doing, but I like it," as he commissioned the local painters to exhibit in his restaurant.

Such blurring of cultural styles occurs in everyday life in the United States to a greater extent than anyone can imagine and is probably more prevalent than the sensational conflict between people of different backgrounds that is played up and often encouraged by the media. The result is what the Yale professor, Robert Thompson, referred to as a cultural bouillabaisse, yet members of the nation's present educational and cultural Elect still cling to the notion that the United States belongs to some vaguely defined entity they refer to as "Western civilization," by which they mean, presumably, a civilization created by the people of Europe, as if Europe can be viewed in monolithic terms. Is Beethoven's Ninth Symphony, which includes Turkish marches, a part of Western civilization, or the late nineteenth- and twentieth-century French paintings, whose creators were influenced by Japanese art? And what of the cubists, through whom the influence of African art changed modern painting, or the surrealists, who were so impressed with the art of the Pacific Northwest Indians that, in their map of North America, Alaska dwarfs the lower forty-eight in size?

Are the Russians, who are often criticized for their adoption of "Western" ways by Tsarist dissidents in exile, members of Western civilization? And what of the millions of Europeans who have black African and Asian ancestry, black Africans having occupied several countries for hundreds of years? Are these "Europeans" members of Western civilization, or the Hungarians, who originated across the Urals in a place called Greater Hungary, or the Irish, who came from the Iberian Peninsula?

Even the notion that North America is part of Western civilization because our "system of government" is derived from Europe is being challenged by Native American historians who say that the founding fathers, Benjamin Franklin especially, were actually influenced by the system of government that had been adopted by the Iroquois hundreds of years prior to the arrival of large numbers of Europeans.

Western civilization, then, becomes another confusing category like Third World, or Judeo-Christian culture, as man attempts to impose his small-screen view of political and cultural reality upon a complex world. Our most publicized novelist recently said that Western civilization was the greatest achievement of mankind, an attitude that flourishes on the street level as scribbles in public restrooms: "White Power," "Niggers and Spics Suck," or "Hitler was a prophet," the latter being the most telling, for wasn't Adolph Hitler the archetypal monoculturalist who, in his pig-headed arrogance, believed that one way and one blood was so pure that it had to be protected from alien strains at all costs? Where did such an attitude, which has caused so much misery and depression in our national life, which has tainted even our noblest achievements, begin? An attitude that caused the incarceration of Japanese-American citizens during World War II, the persecution of Chicanos and Chinese Americans, the near-extermination of the Indians, and the murder and lynchings of thousands of Afro-Americans.

Virtuous, hardworking, pious, even though they occasionally   10 would wander off after some fancy clothes, or rendezvous in the woods with the town prostitute, the Puritans are idealized in our schoolbooks as "a hardy band" of no-nonsense patriarchs whose discipline razed the forest and brought order to the New World (a term that annoys Native American historians). Industrious, responsible, it was their "Yankee ingenuity" and practicality that created the work ethic. They were simple folk who produced a number of good poets, and they set the tone for the American writing style, of lean and spare lines, long before Hemingway. They worshiped in churches whose colors blended in with the New England snow, churches with simple structures and ornate lecterns.

The Puritans were a daring lot, but they had a mean streak. They   11 hated the theater and banned Christmas. They punished people in a cruel and inhuman manner. They killed children who disobeyed their parents. When they came in contact with those whom they considered heathens or aliens, they behaved in such a bizarre and irrational manner that this chapter in the American history comes down to us as a late-movie horror film. They exterminated the Indians, who taught them how to survive in a world unknown to them, and their encounter with the calypso culture of Barbados resulted in what the tourist guide in Salem's Witches' House refers to as the Witchcraft Hysteria.

The Puritan legacy of hard work and meticulous accounting led   12 to the establishment of a great industrial society; it is no wonder that the American industrial revolution began in Lowell, Massachusetts, but there was the other side, the strange and paranoid attitudes toward those different from the Elect.

The cultural attitudes of that early Elect continue to be voiced in 13
everyday life in the United States: the president of a distinguished
university, writing a letter to the *Times,* belittling the study of African
civilizations; the television network that promoted its show on the
Vatican art with the boast that this art represented "the finest achievements of the human spirit." A modern up-tempo state of complex
rhythms that depends upon contacts with an international community can no longer behave as if it dwelled in a "Zion Wilderness"
surrounded by beasts and pagans.

When I heard a schoolteacher warn the other night about the 14
invasion of the American educational system by foreign curriculums,
I wanted to yell at the television set, "Lady, they're already here." It
has already begun because the world is here. The world has been
arriving at these shores for at least ten thousand years from Europe,
Africa, and Asia. In the late nineteenth and early twentieth centuries,
large numbers of Europeans arrived, adding their cultures to those of
the European, African, and Asian settlers who were already here, and
recently millions have been entering the country from South America
and the Caribbean, making Yale Professor Bob Thompson's bouillabaisse richer and thicker.

One of our most visionary politicians said that he envisioned a 15
time when the United States could become the brain of the world, by
which he meant the repository of all of the latest advanced information systems. I thought of that remark when an enterprising poet
friend of mine called to say that he had just sold a poem to a computer
magazine and that the editors were delighted to get it because they
didn't carry fiction or poetry. Is that the kind of world we desire? A
humdrum homogenous world of all brains but no heart, no fiction,
no poetry; a world of robots with human attendants bereft of imagination, of culture? Or does North America deserve a more exciting
destiny? To become a place where the cultures of the world crisscross.
This is possible because the United States is unique in the world: The
world is here.

Meanings and Values

1a. What inductive generalization based on the opening paragraphs of the
essay does Reed offer in paragraph 6?

b. What generalization representing the views of the "present educational and cultural Elect" does he offer in the same paragraph?

c.   Summarize in your own words the inductive generalization presented in paragraph 12.

2.   In several places in the essay, especially in paragraph 9, Reed directs some harsh comments at those who reach conclusions about American culture that differ from his. Are these comments likely to alienate a majority of his readers? If not, what in the tone and content of his remarks keeps them from seeming unacceptable? (See Guide to Terms: *Tone*.)

3a.   Some elements of this selection are characteristic of a formal essay and others of an informal essay. Identify elements belonging to each category. (Guide: *Essay*.)

b.   In what ways does this mixing of qualities add to or detract from the effectiveness of the selection? (Guide: *Evaluation*.)

Expository Techniques

1a.   Evaluate the quality of the inductive evidence that Reed presents in paragraphs 1–5. Is it believable or flimsy? Is there enough evidence to justify the leap to a generalization? (See the introduction to Section 10.)

b.   Evaluate the quality of the evidence presented in paragraphs 6–8 that the author uses to undermine the conclusion that there is a " 'Western civilization' . . . created by the people of Europe" (par. 6).

2.   Identify the generalization in paragraph 9 that the author calls into question.

3.   Should the quotation that begins the essay be considered part of the pattern of reasoning or simply a device to get the reader's attention? Explain.

4.   What role do the rhetorical questions in paragraph 6 play? (Guide: *Rhetorical Questions*.)

Diction and Vocabulary

1.   Locate the paragraphs in which the word "Elect" appears and discuss the ways in which Reed uses it to link the outlook of the Puritans to that of people who believe that American culture is (or ought to be) homogeneous and "Western."

2.   Discuss the use Reed makes of diction in establishing both the positive and the negative qualities of the Puritans. (Guide: *Diction*.)

3.   In discussing the contributions of various cultures to American society and elsewhere in the essay, Reed uses a number of terms that readers may find unfamiliar. If you do not know what some of these words

mean, look them up in the dictionary: knishes (par. 1); Yoruban (4); bouillabaisse, monolithic (6); Urals (7); archetypal, incarceration (9); patriarchs (10); Zion (13); bereft (15).

Suggestions for Writing and Discussion

1. If you have taken or are taking a course in Western civilization or Western literature, explain why you think Reed's criticisms do or do not apply to the content and perspective of the course.

2. What ethnic groups or cultures (including those discussed by Reed) do you believe are excluded from mainstream American culture? Are some of the cultures that Reed discusses actually a part of what most of us consider American culture?

3. Should high school and college curriculums pay more attention to African and Asian cultures?

4. If you belong to an ethnic group or culture that you believe is excluded from mainstream American society, prepare a paper explaining the special and different features of the culture.

(NOTE: Suggestions for topics requiring development by INDUCTION and DEDUCTION are on page 425, at the end of this section.)

BARBARA EHRENREICH received a B.A. from Reed College and a
Ph.D. from Rockefeller University in biology. She has been active
in the women's movement and other movements for social change
for a number of years and has taught women's issues at several
universities, including New York University and the State University of New York–Old Westbury. She is a Fellow of the Institute for
Policy Studies in Washington, D.C., and is active in the Democratic
Socialists of America. A prolific author, Ehrenreich is a regular
columnist for *Ms.* and *Mother Jones* and has published articles in a
wide range of magazines, among them *Esquire,* the *Atlantic, Vogue,
New Republic,* the *Wall Street Journal, TV Guide,* the *New York Times
Magazine, Social Policy,* and *The Nation.* Her books include *For Her
Own Good: 150 Years of the Experts' Advice to Women* (with Deirdre
English) (1978); *The Hearts of Men: American Dreams and the Flight
from Commitment* (1983); *Remaking Love: The Feminization of Sex* (with
Elizabeth Hess and Gloria Jacobs) (1986); *Fear of Falling: The Inner
Life of the Middle Class* (1989); and *The Worst Years of Our Lives:
Irreverent Notes from a Decade of Greed* (1990).

Star Dreck

Ehrenreich's humorous example of inductive and deductive reasoning offers some pointed criticisms of our values. It also points
out the ease with which logic can be twisted and misdirected. Thus
the essay serves as a caution for both writers and readers.

When I was a kid, we knew very little about the stars, and much of   1
what we did know was imprecise and speculative in nature. But such
is the beauty of the human mind—forever reaching, forever grasping—that we now know far more than we can possibly absorb or

usefully apply, and certainly far more than I ever expected to know in my own lifetime: not only what they eat for breakfast and what their favorite colors are, but their secret self-doubts and worries, their hair-management problems, and the names and locations of their unclaimed progeny.

As in all expanding fields, we are faced with what the scholars call an "information explosion," which is already taxing the resources of the available media. In the old days, there were only a few specialized journals, with titles like *Silver Screen* and *Swooning Starlets*. But today there are dozens of publications, such as *People* and *Us*, which make fast-breaking discoveries accessible even to the person of limited educational attainment. For the intellectual elite, we have such challenging sources as *Vanity Fair* and *Interview*, which provide the depth of analysis that is sadly lacking on *Entertainment Tonight*.

Of course there are still a few throwbacks who have failed to appreciate our expanding knowledge of the stars. They point out that most Americans are profoundly ignorant—prone to believe that Botswana is in Florida or that the *Yellow Pages* is a "great book." But retro-pedants like Allan Bloom never bother to quiz us on Burt and Loni's baby problem, or the tribulations of Cher's unfortunately monikered "Bagel Boy." They forget that, as far as the majority of the world's population is concerned, star trivia *is* Western civilization.

I don't want to boast, but I do try to keep abreast. Once, for example, I had the opportunity to shake the bejeweled hand of a very major star. But I didn't—not because I was shy; but because *I knew too much about her*: her former husband's megavitamin problem, her hairdresser's recent breakdown, her ill-concealed rivalry with Joan Collins. There was simply nothing left to say.

Theory, as usual, lags behind the frenetic accumulation of new data, but already a few broad paradigmatic principles are beginning to emerge. There are three of them, just as there are three fundamental forces (not counting the fourth), three Stooges, and three Rambos. The first one is: all stars are related to each other.

It didn't used to be this way in the old days, when the average star was the abused daughter of an alcoholic Mississippian. But in the last two decades, the stars have undergone a sudden and astonishing genetic convergence: there's Jamie Lee Curtis (daughter of Janet Leigh and Tony), Carrie Fisher (daughter of Debbie Reynolds and Eddie), Michael Douglas (son of Kirk), Jeff Bridges (son of Lloyd), Charlie Sheen (son of Martin), Emilio Estevez (brother of Charlie), and so on.

Frankly, no one knows what this means, although the search is on for the "star gene," which could then be transferred, by familiar bioengineering techniques, to piglets, mice, and intestinal bacteria.

The second principle, which is again the result of very recent 7 research, is that *all stars work out*. Whether this is a response to the inevitable muscular weakening caused by inbreeding, or merely an attempt to fill in the empty hours between interviews for *Premiere*, no one knows, but it all began with Jane (daughter of Henry, sister of Peter).

The third and final principle, which we owe in part to the 8 dedicated researchers at *Star* and similar journals, is that all stars—and especially those who do not work out—have had near-fatal encounters with cocaine (Richard Dreyfuss), alcohol (Don Johnson), food (Elizabeth Taylor), or the lack of it (Dolly Parton). Here again, inbreeding may be at work, but the net result is the unique life cycle of the star, which is not dissimilar to the classic saga of the hero as charted by Joseph Campbell: birth, abuse, the struggle against substances at Betty Ford—followed by redemption and inspiring appearances in "Just Say No" ads.

But as our knowledge increases, so does our frustration. Ameri- 9 cans, after all, do not like knowing things (such as the location of Botswana) that they cannot do anything about. So, I say, give us some way of applying our ever-growing knowledge: let us *vote* on the lives of the stars!

After all, we're better informed about the lives of the stars than 10 we are about such dreary matters as deficit management and the balance of trade. In fact, we are probably in a better position to make star decisions than the stars themselves. Consider that tragic misstep: Bruce's marriage to Julianne—which led to the dullest album of his career and the temporary removal of his earring. One hundred million American women were prepared to say, "No, don't do it. Wait for a Jersey Girl. Or, better yet, wait for me to move to Jersey and become one!" But we couldn't do a thing.

Imagine if we could have a referendum on Barbra and Don (hold 11 out, Barb, he's just a bimbo!). Or a plebiscite on Michael Jackson's pigmentation (he'd be able to wear one of those "Black by Popular Demand" T-shirts!). Imagine the debates, the mass rallies and marches, the furious exchanges in the op-ed pages!

But of course the stars wouldn't accept that. They might rebel. 12 They'd go underground—get fat, go back to the substances of their youth, and hide out in unmarked mobile homes in Culver City. I guess there are some things that humankind just wasn't meant to tinker with—some things that will always fill our souls with helpless awe, and show us how insignificant and meaningless our own lives are in the grand scheme of things. And no matter how much we may learn about them, that is the function of the stars.

Meanings and Values

1. What two meanings does the word "stars" have in the opening paragraph?

2. What process of reasoning is illustrated (in fragmented form) in paragraph 9?

3. Try to identify as many targets of the author's ironic criticism as you can in paragraphs 9–12. (Hint: The most important targets are our own habits and values.)

4a. Is it possible to identify a central theme for this essay? If so, what is it?

 b. If not, can the essay still be considered unified? (Guide: *Unity*.) What are some of its important themes?

Expository Techniques

1. In which paragraph does the author introduce the first of her generalizations, derived, she suggests, from a process of induction?

2. In which paragraphs does she announce and illustrate the rest of the deductive generalizations?

3a. From what kinds of sources are most of the examples in the essay probably drawn? Be specific.

 b. Do you consider it likely that Ehrenreich means to poke fun at these sources? Why?

4a. What reasons do we have for suspecting that the speaker in this essay is not the author?

 b. Describe the character and attitudes of the persona created for this essay. (Guide: *Persona*.)

Diction and Vocabulary

1. How does the pun in the opening paragraph (a play on the word "stars") serve to surprise readers and undermine their sense of what the essay is about?

2a. In several passages in the essay, Ehrenreich uses scholarly and scientific language to discuss topics often found in gossip columns or popular magazines. Locate several examples of this use of language.

b. For what purpose or purposes does the author employ this contrast between content and style? (Guide: *Style*.)

3a. There are numerous allusions in paragraphs 5, 7, and 8. Identify their sources. (Note: Some of the allusions refer to scholars and scientific theories.)

b. What general purpose do these allusions serve?

4. If you do not know the meaning of some of the following words, look them up in the dictionary: progeny (par. 1); pedants, tribulations (3); frenetic, paradigmatic (5); plebiscite (11).

Suggestions for Writing and Discussion

1. Do you object to Ehrenreich's poking fun at magazines like *People*? What can be said in favor of them?

2. What does this essay have to say about the things people in our country value most? Do you think this view of our values is an accurate one?

3. If this essay can use reasoning to reach absurd conclusions, shouldn't we consider reasoning an unreliable method for making decisions?

(NOTE: Suggestions for topics requiring development by INDUCTION and DEDUCTION are on page 425, at the end of this section.)

PETE HAMILL

PETE HAMILL was born in 1935 in Brooklyn, New York. He attended Pratt Institute and the University of the Americas. After spending time as a sheet metal worker and an advertising designer, he began working as a reporter. During his career he has written for the *Saturday Evening Post, Newsday,* the *New York Post,* and the *New York Daily News.* He is now a columnist for the *Village Voice.* Hamill has published novels and screenplays and written numerous articles for magazines such as *Cosmopolitan,* the *New York Times Magazine, Playboy,* and the *Reader's Digest.*

The Neverglades

This essay (from *Esquire* magazine) offers several inductive gener-alizations and a syllogism with an imaginative twist: Its conclusion is not (yet) clear. Along with the clear pattern of reasoning, the author offers vivid, carefully chosen language and details.

I first saw the Everglades in the spring of 1954. I was a kid then, poorly   1
disguised as a sailor of the United States Navy, and my guide was the craziest woman I've ever known. She had a bottle-green 1940 Ford, and one morning in Pensacola she told me to take a week's leave. She was going to show me Key West. I did what I was told and off we went. She drove, barrel-assing south along the coast from Pensacola, swearing at truck drivers and tourists, drinking Jax beer all the way. We slept on a deserted beach, with palm fronds rattling above us in the breeze. We danced to Hank Williams and Webb Pierce in a shit-kicker bar in citrus country and had to fight our way out. We had coconut juice for breakfast. We looked at garish sunsets in the gigantic

Gulf evenings. Since there was no radio, she talked all the way. I never
laughed as much again.

Then, before dawn, at Naples, she turned onto the Tamiami Trail.   2
And stopped talking.

In memory, a lavender wash covered the world. We parked and   3
stepped out of the car. I looked out at a flat, empty prairie, its
monotony relieved by the occasional silhouettes of nameless trees
against the blank early-morning sky.

"What is this?" I asked. "Where are we?"   4

"Listen," she whispered.   5

And I heard them, far off, almost imperceptible at first: thin, high,   6
and then like the sound of a million whips cutting the air. They came
over the edge of the horizon and then the sky was black with them.
Birds. Thousands of them. Tens of thousands. Maybe a million. I
shivered in fear and awe. The woman held my city-boy's hand. And
then the vast dense flock was gone. The great molten ball of the sun
oozed over the horizon.

"We're in The Everglades," she said.   7

I don't know what happened to that wild and lovely woman. I'm   8
certain that old '40 Ford was long ago hammered into scrap. But that
moment in The Everglades has stayed with me across all the decades.
It was as if someone had torn a hole in time that morning, and for one
scary moment I stepped into the beginnings of the earth, before man,
before cement and gasoline, before history. The Everglades are like
that: so primeval that they can make you feel as if you are the first
human ever to see them. Eventually, we made it to U.S. 1 and hurtled
down the old two-lane highway, over the sea and into the luminous
terrain of the Keys.

But I couldn't get The Everglades out of my head. Back in   9
Pensacola, I found and read a copy of Marjory Stoneman Douglas's
lyrical 1947 book, *The Everglades: River of Grass*. I saw Budd Schulberg's
wonderful movie, *Wind Across The Everglades*. In the years that followed, I drove across them again, took small boats down into Florida
Bay, where the waters of the Glades empty, traveled with a tour guide
into the eerie stands of mangrove at the edge of the land. Then,
somehow, life became too busy for wandering through wild places.
Twenty years went by. When I saw the Glades again, it was from
twenty-thousand feet, on my way somewhere else.

Still, they were always *there*, part of America, part of my youth,   10
a wet, uncharted vastness in my imagination. Occasionally, I would

read stories about the problems of the Glades and how they were drying up. Once in a while, there would be a piece on television, showing thousands of acres on fire. More and more frequently, there were predictions that the whole system might be dying. I decided I'd better go back before The Everglades joined all the other marvels that have been beaten out of the world I knew while I was young.

The first stop was Miami, which, like every other city in southern Florida, lives off this ecosystem. "If The Everglades die, Miami dies, too," said Joe Podgor, of Friends of The Everglades. "It's as simple as that." 11

I moved around the next few days, and it was clear even to a man with urban astigmatism that Podgor and the others were right: The Glades are in trouble. 12

The facts are easy enough to find. Over many thousands of years, nature created a splendid system here. Fresh water from summer rains gathered in small lakes in central Florida (near Orlando). This water drained into the Kissimmee River, which in turn fed Lake Okeechobee, a shallow body of fresh water that covers 730 square miles. The overflow spilled over the southern lip of the lake and formed a fifty-mile-wide river that moved slowly and subtly south, 150 miles across southern Florida to the sea above the Keys. This was a slow process; the river moved down a gradual slope of one and a half inches to the mile before reaching Florida Bay. Clouds sucked moisture from these rich wetlands, blew north, and rained upon the lakes and rivers in a perpetual natural cycle. The great insight of Marjory Stoneman Douglas was to recognize The Everglades as a wide, shallow, sheetlike river, not a swamp. 13

Water is at the heart of the system. It feeds the Biscayne Aquifer, the gigantic underground cavern that supplies fresh water to Miami and other thirsty coastal towns. And it has given life to a magnificent array of creatures. When the first Spaniards arrived in 1513, an estimated five million alligators lived in the Glades, along with un-counted crocodiles; this lush habitat is one of the few on earth where these cousins exist together. The sloughs (freshwater rivers running through the saw-grass prairies) were thick with largemouth bass and bluegills. There were herds of deer, thousands of raccoons, opossums, otter, mink, and black bear and fox, along with the beautiful Florida panther. There were twenty-six kinds of snakes. In the bays and rivers you could see the manatee, huge and homely and shy. In Florida Bay, there were stone crabs, dolphins, sharks, and barracuda. And always, there were the birds. 14

I wasn't the first human to see the sky blacken with birds; I only   15
felt that way. Once they came in the millions: dozens of species,
including flamingos, great white herons, ibis, snowy egrets, pelicans,
roseate spoonbills, and bald eagles with seven-foot wingspans, living
in nests that were nine feet deep. When John James Audubon passed
through in 1832, he was astonished. A century later, a drive along the
eighty-five miles of the Tamiami Trail from Miami to Naples left cars
encrusted with *guano.*

Most of those birds are gone now—in the past fifty years, about   16
90 percent have vanished—along with many of the other living
creatures. Only 10 percent of the ibis are left; the wood stork could be
completely gone by the year 2000. There are only thirty known Florida
panthers left alive; many fell to disease caused by the destruction of
the ecosystem; many to speeding automobiles. Fisherman can no
longer eat catfish or largemouth bass; they are loaded with mercury.
The manatee has been smashed and shredded in the hundreds by
powerboats. Ninety percent of the alligators are gone; in the 1880s
alone, two and a half million were slaughtered for their hides. It is
more and more difficult to see crocodiles, too; it's believed that only
six hundred remain.

The problem, of course, was—and is—man.   17

Man came to The Everglades. Man stripped away the wild or-   18
chids. Man hunted down the egrets for their plumes to satisfy the
fashions of the turn of the last century. Man walked into the forests
with saws and axes in the Forties and Fifties and destroyed the stands
of knot-free cypress trees (cousins of the redwood). Man carted away
the corpses of mahogany trees and live oak and gumbo-limbo, which
had stood on hammocks above the saw-grass, providing shelter for
raccoons and otter and deer. Man saw The Everglades as a mere
swamp to be drained, planted, lived upon, tamed. He attacked and
attacked and attacked.

A small band—Ernest Coe, Marjory Douglas, Art Marshall—saw   19
early that disaster was imminent. Beginning in the 1930s, they lobbied
politicians. In 1947, President Truman finally set aside 1.4 million
acres for The Everglades National Park. This was only a fraction of
the original four thousand square miles that made up the natural
Everglades, but it at least offered sanctuary to the creatures who had
been so ferociously mauled by the bloody hand of man.

Now even this vast, silent preserve is threatened. "Some people   20
think it's already too late to save The Everglades," Joe Podgor said

one night at dinner. "I hope they're wrong. But if they're right, then all of southern Florida is doomed."

The fatal wounds would be self-inflicted. In the Fifties, when I first passed through the region, about a million people depended upon water generated by The Everglades. Today the population is 4.5 million, with another 600 arriving every day. "Florida is adding one Tampa to its population every year," Podgor explained, "and they all use water." If the consequences are alarming, the images are banal: millions of people bathing, flushing, filling swimming pools, washing dogs. Few of them believe they could be transforming this great green place into a desert. But they are. According to the South Florida Water Management Corporation, per capita water use in the area is two hundred gallons of fresh water a *day*. That water is sucked up from the Biscayne Aquifer. It travels south from Okeechobee through canals. It is drained from The Everglades. It is manufactured in desalinization plants. And still, there is not enough. 21

To supply that water, man tampered with nature. First, an immense dike was constructed around Lake Okeechobee, back in the 1920s; the purpose of this earthen manacle was to prevent flooding and to reclaim part of The Everglades for agriculture. In some ways, it worked. More than two million acres were drained and planted and developed for human itinerants lusting for the sun. Everybody cheered, particularly the real estate racketeers. The Tamiami Trail was constructed in the 1920s, effectively placing another dike across the Glades, and a second highway, Alligator Alley, was erected across the great slow river in the Sixties. Canals and dikes were sliced south into the saw grass. Then, in the early '60s, after Castro took Cuba, the sugar barons came upon the land. Eventually, more than 430,000 acres of sugarcane were planted in the drained Everglades south of Okeechobee, their existence subsidized by huge government handouts (and free water, paid for by the city dwellers), their overflow of phosphorus and nitrogen pumped back into the lake. The spirit of this was essentially: *Up yours Fidel, we'll grow our own sugar!* 22

North of the lake, a vast dairy industry began to thrive; it, too, dumped its waste into the waters. After Disney World arrived, in 1971, even more millions of water-sucking bipeds were drawn to the region, with the real estate developers and civic boosters prancing in orgasmic frenzies of welcome. Worst of all, the loopy geniuses of the U.S. Army Corps of Engineers decided to straighten out the lazy curves of the Kissimmee River, gouging a new course through the 23 savanna and palmetto trees, transforming it by 1971 into a fifty-two-mile concrete ditch that was romantically named C-38.

The result of all this: disaster. Vast algae blooms soon appeared   24
in the lake. Hundreds of thousands of fish died. Even the developers
could see that Okeechobee was being choked by chemicals and cow
shit. Some citizens rose in anger; there were articles, studies, meetings,
protests.

In 1983, under Governor Bob Graham, the state decided to take   25
action. For the first time in the nation's history, a major water project
was put in reverse. The Kissimmee was partially restored to its old
course, complete with marshes to filter the nutrients (the total cost
will be $275 million); the sugar barons were told to stop pumping swill
into the lake. It was a good beginning; it wasn't enough.

For everybody involved knew that there was one certain way to   26
save The Everglades, and nobody would dare try it. They needed only
to force the principles of capitalism on the sugar barons. That is, cut
the $3-billion-a-year federal subsidy in the world marketplace. Out in
the world, sugar sells for thirteen to fourteen cents a pound; our
domestic sugar barons are getting twenty-four cents a pound. This is
all done under the familiar theory of socialism for the owners, capitalism for the workers. And in Florida, those workers are underpaid
migrants from the Caribbean. The Florida sugar growers were allowed to pump their discharges into a part of the Glades reserved for
wildlife; the theory was that these marshes would act as a sieve.

But that didn't happen. Phosphorus and other nutrients began   27
creating cattails, which are foreign to the area, and are now growing
at the rate of four acres a day; saw grass and other native plants are
being choked to death by these intruders, and the entire food chain
has been disrupted. Worse, the slow, steady flow of water down-
stream is being stopped, starving the lower Glades. All of this has been
compounded by a long drought, which some feel was caused by the
disruption of the ecosystem. No wading birds have nested in the
Loxahatchee National Wildlife Refuge for two years; a few years ago
there were thirty thousand. In addition, the once-rich Everglades
muck, upon which the farms and sugar plantations were built, is
drying up and blowing away; of the original fifteen, only five feet of
this primeval soil remains, and by the end of the century, the rest of it
could be gone. That would leave a rocky limestone desert, no longer
suitable for agriculture, but almost certain to be transformed into

another plastic extension of Condoland. By the time that happens, The Everglades could be dead.

Walking along the Anhinga Trail in the park not long ago, I saw a lone alligator dozing on the banks of a canal. In the Taylor Slough, there were pond lilies and spears of green pickerelweed and dense coverings of water lettuce, which in the natural order of things, would die, decay, and become part of the muck and the peat below. In the distance, a dozen unseen birds chattered in their different idioms, while insects droned and chirped. I touched a blade of saw grass, its fine toothy edges raw against my fingers. This was no longer the great wild place I first glimpsed as a boy. But it was enough, one small fragment left to us that told the awesome tale of the beginning of the world. If we let this die, it would be an obscenity. 28

Meanings and Values

1. This essay offers an inductive generalization at the end of paragraphs 11–12. What is it?

2a. How does the evidence in the preceding paragraphs contribute to the generalization?

  b. What role is played by the evidence in paragraphs 1–10?

3. Can paragraph 17 be considered an inductive generalization? If so, where does the author present the evidence on which it is based?

4a. State in your own words the syllogism underlying paragraph 20.

  b. Does the author believe the conclusion is inevitable?

  c. If not, what does he think can be done?

Expository Techniques

1. What strategy does Hamill use in paragraphs 1–7 to open the essay? (See Guide to Terms: *Introductions*.)

2. What pattern of exposition is employed in paragraphs 13–14?

3. What expository pattern shapes the relationship of paragraphs 15–16?

4. Paragraph 15 echoes an earlier section of the essay. What is the purpose of this strategy?

5. Discuss the special roles played by paragraphs, 2, 4, 5, and 17. What contributes to their effectiveness?

6.   What use does Hamill make of cause-effect analysis in the latter part of the essay?

Diction and Vocabulary

1a.   Discuss how the author uses diction to emphasize the contrasts between paragraphs 1 and 3. (Guide: *Diction.*)

 b.   How does the sentence structure contribute to this effect? (Guide: *Syntax.*)

2.   Examine the following paragraphs to see how Hamill uses concrete details and word choice to create scenes that are like paintings: 3, 6, and 28. (Guide: *Concrete/Abstract.*)

3.   Examine the strategy Hamill uses to introduce the sentences in paragraph 18. What emphasis does it provide? (Guide: *Emphasis.*)

4.   If you do not know the meaning of some of the following words, look them up in a dictionary: wash (par. 3); primeval, luminous (8); ecosystem (11); astigmatism (12); aquifer (14); banal (21); bipeds, orgasmic (23); sieve (26).

Suggestions for Writing and Discussion

1.   Do some research into the current state of the Everglades to determine how well efforts to preserve it are succeeding.

2.   Examine and report on the effects of development and/or preservation on an area familiar to you.

3.   Is it important to preserve historical sites as well as natural sites? Can some of the arguments in favor of one effort be used to support the other?

(NOTE: Suggestions for topics requiring development by INDUCTION and DEDUCTION are on page 425, at the end of this section.)

BRAD EDMONDSON

Brad Edmondson was born in Nokomis, Florida, in 1959. He
attended Deep Springs College and Cornell University and received his B.A. in history from Cornell in 1981. As a freelance writer,
he has had articles published in the *Utne Reader*, the *Washington
Post*, and the *Atlantic*. He is currently editor in chief of *American
Demographics* magazine.

Making Yourself at Home

As a process of reasoning, induction can help us arrive at answers
to important questions. As a pattern for exposition, it can enable
readers to participate in the process along with the author. That is
the strategy Edmondson employs in this essay, inviting readers to
search for answers along with him.

I was riding a bicycle along a country road near my home in upstate   1
New York a few years ago. It was a beautiful Saturday afternoon in
early summer, the creeks flowing fresh, the air warm but not too
humid, and the last trilliums of the season dotting the woods with
white and pink blossoms. Legs pumping away at the pedals, I sped
past startled woodchucks and the fat buds of tiger lilies about to burst
in the roadside ditches.

This ride, one of my favorites, went past four old cemeteries,   2
three Iroquois settlement sites, two active Quaker meetinghouses,
and one ancient (but still working) Coke machine. Many of the names
on the mailboxes along the route were the same as the names on the
gravestones. I liked the idea of a long chain of farm families stretching
endlessly into the past and future with my family in the middle, and
everyone united by their common knowledge of this land. Never

mind the fact that I seldom talked to my neighbors and that I had lived in my rented farmhouse for only a few months. The idea was none-theless attractive as I rode along in solitude.

Then things got even better—I came upon a garage sale. It's   3
always entertaining to poke through someone else's possessions and try to get a sense of how they live. For a nickel, I rode off with a three-inch orange plaster alligator. It was a souvenir of Florida, the place where I had grown up. It was an impulse purchase. I didn't understand the impulse until years later.

The alligator ended up on my desk at an alternative weekly   4
newspaper in Ithaca, New York. Ithaca is a classic example of a college town, and I am a classic example of someone who came to such a town as a student, fell in love with it, and refused to leave. My desk, the editor's desk, was one of the focal points of the community. I knew about the local politicians, the local artists, and all the local pancake breakfasts. I loved the 60-hour work weeks devoted to the endless process of gathering and disseminating news in the community. The orange gator held down the pages of my appointment book and entertained me while I talked on the phone. Then one day a colleague brought me another alligator, a plastic one on a keychain. Add it to your collection, she said.

I don't collect these, I said, and how do you know I'm from   5
Florida?

You talk about it all the time, she said. You miss Florida.   6

Now I had two alligators. And as the months went by, people   7
gave me alligator wind-up toys, drinking glasses, postcards, and even a hideous stuffed baby cayman. My work area became a small natural history museum. I found myself immersed in the life of one home-town while surrounded by reminders of another. I began daydream-ing about Florida even as I worked hard at promoting community life in Ithaca. I began wondering where I really belonged. Where were my roots?

Today this question is becoming acute for me and for many of the   8
people I know. As I muddle away from youth into middle age, the realization is dawning that this is not merely a rehearsal. This is the one life I have on Earth, and anything lacking in it now may soon become a permanent regret. So I wonder: Where is the best place to spend the time I have? Where is my true home?

The question of roots is a highly personal matter that increasingly   9
seems to bother many Americans, particularly people in their mid-20s

to early 40s (read: baby boomers). This is especially true of a certain group that Barbara Ehrenreich describes in her book *Fear of Falling* (1989, Pantheon): "people whose economic and social status is based on education, rather than the ownership of capital or property." People in this "professional middle class" (or PMC) tend to stick to themselves, according to Ehrenreich. Most spend their young adult years in college, where they typically acquire mates, best friends, and a shared code of values. Once they grow up, PMC members seek to establish their status and distinguish themselves from the working class or the less educated element of the middle class—the backgrounds from which many of them originally came. This is done partly through their consumer choices. They are especially fond of things that are "natural," "authentic," or "the best," like cashmere sweaters or single-malt Scotch.

This bunch sounds a lot like my circle of friends. Most of us   10
arrived in Ithaca from some other place, and decided to stay. We are all reasonably comfortable in our nice houses and apartments, reliable cars, and regular vacations. We are writers, planners, professors, and lawyers who spend a lot of time talking on the phone and chatting in restaurants.

The problem for this group—my group—is that our over-devel-   11
oped work ethic, our primary emphasis on ideas, and our global network of friends and colleagues make us a uniquely rootless minority. We often find ourselves like the man in David Byrne's song "Once in a Lifetime," living in one place, dreaming of another, unable to commit to either, and obsessed by the question "Well, how did I get here?"

The place I grew up in was Nokomis, Florida, a small bayside   12
town about 25 miles south of Sarasota. In my earliest memories, the road to Sarasota is a two-lane blacktop, a passenger train runs once a day, and the airport has a dirt runway. The hard, constant sun makes everyone move slowly. When it sets each evening, the local radio station signs off.

That was in 1960, when Sarasota County had a total population   13
of 77,000. Not knowing anything else, I didn't know what I had; I saw little value in small beachfront pavilions that sold alligator postcards, a mayor who wore short-sleeved shirts, or the vast silent pine forests, pastures, and swamps that stretched beyond the outskirts of town. Like many small-town children, I concentrated on my schoolwork and couldn't wait to get out of Nokomis.

Roots are so basic to us that we often don't notice them until   14
they're missing. After I left for college, the Florida that I knew as a
child was obliterated. Sarasota County's population is now about
275,000, and the pastures and forests where I once rambled have been
replaced by subdivisions and shopping centers. I still go home to see
my folks, but the Nokomis I grew up in is really just a memory. I feel
like a stranger in the Sunbelt boomtown that Sarasota County has
become.

Pining for one place while living in another is a typically Amer-   15
ican state of mind. In 1790, most Americans lived on the Atlantic
seaboard and dreamed about life back home in England. In 1890, new
settlers in the Midwest and West wrote long, melancholy letters to
their families in the East and Europe. As a nation we've always
celebrated the urge to pack up and move somewhere else in search of
greater opportunity, even if it also meant enduring a personal loss.

You can see America's uprooted nature most vividly today in the   16
Sunbelt. The shift of our population to the west and south is not new,
but it has gained momentum in the last 40 years. Three states—California, Texas, and Florida—contain one quarter of the U.S. population
and will account for half of all U.S. population growth in the next
decade. These areas will also claim much of the economic growth. But
the economic advantages of living in a high-growth area are tempered
by the fact that these places often seem completely fragmented. The
sprawling cities have no center and little sense of community or
history.

The rise of the Sunbelt in recent years has been accompanied by   17
the decline of rural America. Until 1920, a majority of Americans lived
in small towns and on farms. Today, 77 percent of Americans are
packed into metropolitan areas of more than 100,000 people. Meanwhile, many tightly knit city neighborhoods and ethnic enclaves have
disintegrated as a result of urban renewal, crime, and suburbaniza-
tion. The steady growth of new suburbs, with their malls and fast food
joints, symbolizes the rootless pattern of American life.

Yet it's interesting to note that more than three quarters of Ameri-   18
cans say they would rather not live in a metropolitan area. In 1985,
only 23 percent of Americans told the Gallup Organization that they
wanted to live in a large metropolitan area. The rest, given their
druthers, would live in a city of 10,000 to 100,000 residents (29 percent), a rural area (25 percent), or a small town (23 percent).

This is one sign that many Americans are beginning to yearn for   19
a greater sense of rootedness in their lives. Another is the strong
evidence that African-Americans are returning to their roots in the
southern states. The percentage of blacks living there rose between
1980 and 1988, after 70 straight years of decline. Also, some small cities
and rural towns are booming. These tend to be places such as culturally vibrant college towns and state capitals, scenic retirement areas,
and rural counties that are close to big cities.

On television and in the mainstream press, we are constantly told   20
that regional and national borders are becoming meaningless. The
future, it seems, will be a place where the whole world joins in one
economy, watches the same TV programs, wears the same brand of
jeans, and dances the same dances. I know people here in Ithaca who
routinely FAX documents to Amsterdam. They converse on a regular
basis with people in Tokyo and Seattle. Yet walking home, they like
to appreciate the sunset outlining the tops of trees on neighboring hills
and maybe pick up some homemade Italian sausage from a corner
grocer named Gus. The perfect evening for these folks is a dinner at
a new ethnic restaurant (perhaps Ethiopian or Indian), a concert of
"world music" like klezmer or salsa, and a mug of hometown-brewed
beer in an old-fashioned tavern. They want a secure place in both the
global economy and the local neighborhood.

Across America, things that were once taken for granted are now   21
treasured—from regional cuisine and ethnic music to clean air and
friendly neighborhoods. Almost every morning, we are jolted awake
by what the media says about rising ethnic nationalism in Eastern
Europe or the religious reawakening in the Islamic world. All over the
world, it seems, people are trying to reassert their identities and return
to their roots. Safe in our little enclaves, my friends and I sit around
and wonder where we might fit into all of this.

We are the people who are always talking about finding a place   22
we can truly call home and at the same time dreaming of visiting Tibet
or living in Paris. We're junkies for international news, yet we'll
happily spend more for something made by a local business. We're
passionate about community issues, but forever thinking about moving away to get a better job, more money, or some other abstraction.
The state of being in one place and thinking about another is our
natural habitat.

Actually, most Americans aren't that far removed from their 23 roots. About one person in six changes residences each year, according to the Census Bureau, but the average distance moved is only about six miles. Almost two thirds of the 39 million people who moved in 1983 stayed within the boundaries of one county. Fewer than 10 percent of them went to a different region.

Of course, the economic winds of change do blow away some 24 people who would prefer to stay in their hometowns. The Census Bureau reports that 13 states will actually lose population in the next decade, and all but two of them are in the Rustbelt. Buffalo, New York, is still losing about 250 people a week. But the unemployed metalworker driving south in a U-Haul truck is not your typical rootless American. People who actually cut their roots and move to another state tend to be younger, wealthier, and better-educated than those who stay put. Interstate migrants are more likely to be the people considered winners in our society.

These are the same people who have recently developed an 25 insatiable appetite for ethnic foods, regional crafts, "country" fashions, and nostalgic portrayals of small-town life. A rash of new magazines such as *Country Living, Midwest Living,* and *Wigwag* have arisen that idealize rural and small-town America for an audience of mid-scale to upscale readers. The most coveted couches, draperies, and clothing are in something called "Santa Fe Style." Any product, restaurant, or entertainment that can sell itself as an "authentic" example of some regional or folk culture is halfway to the bank. It doesn't matter if you have any direct experience with the culture or not.

America's winners are discovering that something important is 26 missing from their lives. They need to be part of a community, and they're trying to purchase the feeling. Meanwhile, the more mundane life of real communities goes on around them in bowling leagues, church groups, local committees, and pancake breakfasts. But this is a life they either can't or won't accept.

As we move into the 1990s, however, more and more people will 27 be in a position to join real communities instead of pining after imaginary ones. Thanks to some powerful socioeconomic forces, it has become much more difficult for the average American to pull up stakes and move on.

The first and most important reason for this is that the nation is 28 getting older. One third of people in their twenties move every year, according to the Census Bureau, but that share drops to one fifth for people in their early thirties and fewer than one in 10 for Americans aged 45 or older. The typical 45-year-old has lived in his or her residence for about eight years, and will move only once or twice more. Thanks to the baby boom's relentless march through life, the median age of the U.S. population will rise from 33 today to 36 in ten years.

Young people move to get better jobs, but older people tend to 29 stay put regardless of their careers. When you're raising kids or balancing your needs with those of your spouse, moving is a much more complex and painful prospect than it was when it was just you and your Volkswagen.

Another reason Americans are staying put is that moving has 30 become terribly expensive. The average cost of relocating a home-owning employee and family rose 11 percent between 1988 and 1989, to about $41,000, according to Runzheimer International. And just imagine how hard it must be to move if you don't have a company that will pay for everything.

It boils down to this: In the "global" 1990s, the vast majority of 31 Americans will be staying put. Most of us will stay in our hometowns because we want to, and a few of us will stay because we can't afford not to. But the reasons don't really matter. What matters is that we're staying. Make the best of it.

Stuck in traffic one gray February afternoon, dreaming about 32 Florida, I heard an ad on the radio. "There are only 105 days until swimsuit season begins, so buy your treadmill now and get in shape for summer," said the announcer. The special price: $799.

Later that day I read an article about a sociologist named Ray 33 Oldenburg who specializes in studying neighborhood bars. By his count, the number of taverns in the United States has shrunk from 152,000 in 1950 to fewer than 50,000 today. Similar erosion has taken place in the number of neighborhood diners, pool halls, beauty par-lors, and general stores.

I put these two things together. Why should anyone spend 34 hundreds of dollars on a treadmill when they could simply button up their coat and walk down to the local tavern or diner for a little conversation with their neighbors? Why buy a treadmill and embark on a solitary march to nowhere?

Of course people might have lots of reasons not to walk around 35 their neighborhood or hang around in bars and diners. They might get beaten up. It's cold outside. They have to watch the kids. They can't stand the cigarette smoke. A treadmill, on balance, seems like a lot less trouble. Yet these reasons all boil down to fear of the unknown and a desire for two of advertising's most effective lures: "comfort" and "convenience." By purchasing the treadmill and exercising while watching television, you can avoid the complex and unpredictable nature of human contact. You can stay instead in the comfort of your own living room, with the convenience of never leaving it. Advertising reinforces this decision, making the treadmill into something that you feel you need.

But why not put the $800 that a treadmill would cost into a   36
savings account and go for a walk each evening instead? You can say hello to strangers and find out all the neighborhood gossip. Walk regularly, and you'll discover that real community still exists, a community you've been too busy to notice. Maybe you can even promote and preserve the sense of community that is slipping away in many places across America.

Ray Oldenburg says he is concerned about "the loss of informal,   37
public gathering places where people can feel at home." He calls taverns, diners, and community centers the "third places" between work and home. These hangouts are vital for informal public discourse, grass-roots democracy, and the nurturing of friendships, he says. Oldenburg did a lot of thinking for his new book, *The Great Good Place* (Paragon House, $19.95), in a coffee shop near his home in Pensacola, Florida.

Community grows out of discovering and nurturing the things   38
you share with your neighbors. People often refer to it as the soul of a place. But it takes time to get to know your neighbors. Communities, by definition, happen in public. Their beauty and importance comes from small, seemingly insignificant things like conversations with strangers, neighborhood groups that lobby local politicians, and flower boxes hanging from windows. Their pleasure comes from things that happen slowly, over periods of months or years, to people who are involved every day. You can't merely observe a community— you have to be in it.

You can spend $20 a plate for Cajun blackened redfish at some   39
stuck-up downtown bistro, or you can go down to the local fire station for a Friday night fish fry, get a more satisfying dinner for $6.50 (plus slaw, a roll, and a beer), and meet your real-life neighbors in the process. It's your choice. You can stay inside and watch television

while walking on an electric treadmill, or you can convince your neighbors to join you in a regular evening stroll.

Of course, there is another reason why people might resist put- 40 ting down roots by participating in the life of their community. The fact is that commitment to a community is often a pain in the ass. If you don't believe me, go to the next monthly meeting of your city government. The hall will be full of bores, boors, and people who smell bad. They will come from all races and classes. They will argue passionately in the hallways, and the arguments won't always end well.

But any commitment means that you'll have to put up with some 41 discomfort. If you don't like this kind of unpleasantness, you can always stay within the deodorized confines of the PMC and spend your evenings buying things out of mail-order catalogs. You can keep the riffraff away, just as an earlier generation did, by scurrying to a new outlying housing development and mixing only with your own kind. But is this really the kind of person you want to be?

Not me. I hope to stay in Ithaca, but I want to make a commitment 42 to whatever community I live in. This means not having your fun alone. It means talking to strangers, organizing block parties and neighborhood festivals, noticing the geese flying north, visiting the same woods every year when the wildflowers are blooming, and saying yes to working on local beautification or crime watch commit- tees.

Over time, the rewards of nurturing your roots are great. For one 43 thing, you get to be a part of a lot of world-class pancake breakfasts.

Meanings and Values

1. In what way can the questions raised in paragraphs 7 and 8 be considered important parts of the process of induction?

2a. Where in the essay does the author provide generalizations to answer the questions raised in paragraph 8?

b. Why might these be considered inductive generalizations?

3a. What two lifestyles does the author contrast in the second half of the essay?

b. What does he see as the advantages and disadvantages of each?

c. What leads him to decide in favor of one?

Expository Techniques

1. Discuss the relationship between the examples in the introduction (pars. 1–6) and the questions raised in paragraphs 7 and 8.

2. Identify the expository patterns in these paragraphs and discuss their use: 9, 12–13, 20–22, 25, and 32–34.

3. Examine and evaluate the use of transitional devices in paragraphs 20 and 21 and the use of similar devices *within* sentences in paragraph 22. (See Guide to Terms: *Transition*.)

4. Some of the paragraphs in this essay are filled with specific details. Identify several such paragraphs and discuss the effectiveness of this strategy. (Guide: *Specific/General, Evaluation*.)

Diction and Vocabulary

1. In discussing contrasting lifestyles in the second half of the essay, the author chooses words carefully to make one more attractive than the other. Choose several passages and point out how the diction is used in this way. (Guide: *Diction*.)

2. If you do not know the meanings of some of the following words, look them up in a dictionary: trilliums (par. 1); enclaves (17); klezmer, salsa (20).

Suggestions for Writing and Discussion

1. Do you agree with the conclusions Edmondson reaches? What other solutions might there be to the problem of "roots"?

2. Do most people have a need to feel rooted in a community? Or is it a concern primarily for the PMC?

(NOTE: Suggestions for topics requiring development by INDUCTION and DEDUCTION follow.)

Writing Suggestions for Section 10
Induction and *Deduction*

Choose one of the following unformed topics and shape your central theme from it. This could express the view you prefer or an opposing view. Develop your composition primarily by use of induction, alone or in combination with deduction. Unless otherwise directed by your instructor, be completely objective and limit yourself to exposition, rather than engaging in argumentation.

1. Little League baseball (or the activities of 4-H clubs, Boy Scouts, Girl Scouts, etc.) as a molder of character.

2. Conformity as an expression of insecurity.

3. Pop music as a mirror of contemporary values.

4. The status symbol as a motivator to success.

5. The liberal arts curriculum and its relevance to success in a career.

6. Student opinion as the guide to better educational institutions.

7. The role of public figures (including politicians, movie stars, and business people) in shaping attitudes and fashions.

8. The values of education, beyond dollars and cents.

9. Knowledge and its relation to wisdom.

10. The right of individuals to select the laws they obey.

11. Television commercials as a molder of morals.

12. The "other" side of one ecological problem.

13. The value of complete freedom from worry.

14. The threat of nuclear war and public policy.

15. Raising mentally retarded children at home.

16. Fashionable clothing as an expression of power (or a means of attaining status).

11

Using Patterns for *Argument*

Argument and exposition have many things in common. They both use the basic patterns of exposition; they share a concern for the audience; and they often deal with similar subjects, including social trends (changing relationships between men and women, the growth of the animal rights movement), recent developments (the creation of new strains of plants through genetic manipulation, medical treatment of the terminally ill), and issues of widespread concern (the quality of education, the effects of pollution). As a result, the study of argument is a logical companion to the study of exposition. Yet the two kinds of writing have very different purposes.

Expository writing shares information and ideas; it explores issues and explains problems. In exposition we select facts and ideas to give an accurate picture of a subject and arrange them as clearly as we can, emphasizing features likely to interest readers. To explain the importance of knowing how to use computers, for instance, an essay might provide examples of the roles of computers in business, industry, education, and research; it might describe the uses of computers for personal budgeting, recordkeeping, and entertainment; and it might emphasize that more everyday tasks than we realize are already heavily dependent on computers.

Argumentative writing, however, has a different motivation. It asks readers to choose one side of an issue or take a particular action, whether it is to buy a product, vote for a candidate, or build a new highway. In argument we select facts and ideas that provide strong support for our point of view and arrange this evidence in the most logical and persuasive order, taking care to provide appropriate background information and to acknowledge and refute opposing points of view. The evidence we choose is determined to a great extent by the attitudes and needs of the people we are trying to convince. For example, suppose we want to argue successfully that a high school or college ought to give all students advanced training in computer use. Our essay would need to provide examples of benefits to students that are great enough to justify the considerable expenses for equipment and staff. (Examples of greatly increased job opportunities and improved learning skills would make good evidence; discussions of how computers can be used for personal recordkeeping and managing household finances would not be likely to persuade school officials facing tight budgets.) And an effective essay would also answer possible objections to the proposal: Will only a limited number of students really benefit from advanced computer training? Are computers developing so rapidly that only large businesses and specialized institutes can afford to provide up-to-date training?

At the heart of an argumentative essay is the opinion we want readers to share or the action we want them to take. In argument this central theme is called the *thesis* or *proposition* and is often expressed concisely in a *thesis statement* designed to alert readers to the point of the argument. Some writers like to arrive at a sharply focused thesis early in the process of composing and use it to guide the selection and arrangement of evidence. Others settle on a tentative ("working") thesis, which they revise as the essay takes shape. In either case, checking frequently to see that factual evidence and supporting ideas or arguments are clearly linked to the thesis is a good way for writers to make sure their finished essays are coherent, unified arguments.

The purpose of a simple argumentative essay often falls into one of three categories. Some essays ask readers to agree with a value judgment ("The present city government is corrupt and ineffective"). Others propose a specific action ("Money from the student activity fee at this college should be used to establish and staff a fitness program available to all students"). And still others advance an opinion quite different from that held by most people ("Contrary to what many people believe, investing in stocks and bonds is not just for the wealthy—it is for people who want to become wealthy, too"). In situations calling for more complex arguments, however, writers should feel free to combine these purposes as long as the relationship among them is made clear to the reader. In a complex argument, for instance, we might *first* show that the city government is inefficient and corrupt and *then* argue that it is better to change the city charter to eliminate the opportunities for the abuse of power than it is to try to vote a new party into office or to support a reform faction within the existing political machine.

Another distinction is normally made between *logical argument* (usually called, simply, *argument*) and *persuasive argument* (usually termed *persuasion*). Whereas logical argument appeals to reason, persuasive argument appeals to the emotions. The aim of both, however, is to convince, and they are nearly always blended into whatever mixture seems most likely to do the convincing. After all, reason and emotion are both important human elements—and we may have to persuade someone even to listen to our logic. The emphasis on one or the other, of course, should depend on the subject and the audience.

Some authorities make a slightly different distinction: they say we argue merely to get people to change their minds, and we use persuasion to get them to *do* something about it—for example, to vote a Republican ticket, not just agree with the party platform. But this view is not entirely inconsistent with the other. We can hardly expect to change a *mind* by emotional appeal, but we can hope to get someone to *act* because of it.

The choice of supporting evidence for an argument depends in part on the subject and in part on the audience and situation. There is a good deal of evidence to support the argument that industry should turn to labor-saving machines and new work arrangements to increase its competitiveness. Company executives looking for ways to increase profits are likely to find almost all of this evidence persuasive, but workers and union leaders worried about loss of jobs and cuts in wages will probably be harder to persuade. Writers addressing the second group would need to choose evidence to show that industrial robots and work rules calling for fewer people would lead to increased sales, not lower wages and fewer jobs. And if the changes might actually cause layoffs, writers would have to show that without the changes a company might be forced to shut down entirely, throwing everyone out of work.

Variety in evidence gives the writer a chance to present an argument fully and at the same time helps persuade readers. Examples, facts and figures, statements from authorities, personal experience or the experience of other people—all these can be valuable sources of support. The basic patterns of exposition, too, can be viewed as ways to support arguments. For instance, to persuade people to take sailing (hang-gliding, skin-diving) lessons, we might tell the story of the inexperienced sailor who almost drowned even though she was sailing in a "safe" boat on a small lake. Or we might combine this narrative with a discussion of how lack of knowledge causes sailing accidents, with a classification of the dangers facing beginning sailors, or with examples of things that can go wrong while sailing. Most writers choose to combine patterns on the grounds that variety helps convince readers, just as three pieces of evidence are more convincing than one—as long as all three point to the same conclusion.

All the expository patterns can also be used to arrange factual evidence and supporting ideas or arguments, though some patterns are more useful than others. Entire arguments structured as narratives are rare, except for stories designed to show what the world will be like if we do not change our present nuclear, military, or technological policies. But example, comparison and contrast, cause and effect, definition, and induction or deduction are frequently used to organize arguments. A series of *examples* can be an effective way of showing that a government social policy does not work and in fact hurts the people it is supposed to serve. *Cause and effect* can organize argument over who is to blame for a problem or over the possible consequences of a new program. *Comparison* and *contrast* can guide choices among competing products, among ways of disposing of toxic waste, or among directions for national economic policy. *Definition* is helpful when a controversy hinges on the interpretation of a key term or when the meaning of an important word is itself the subject of disagreement. *Induction* and *deduction* are useful in argument because they provide the kind of careful, logical reasoning necessary to convince many readers, especially those who may at first have little sympathy for the writer's opinion.

An argument need not be restricted to a single pattern. The choice of a pattern or a combination of patterns depends on the subject, the specific purpose, and the kinds of evidence needed to convince the audience to which the essay is directed. Some arguments about complicated, significant issues make use of so many patterns that they can be called *complex arguments.*

In addition to using the patterns of exposition, most argumentative essays also arrange evidence according to its potential impact on the audience. Three of the most common arrangements are ascending order, refutation-proof, and con-pro. In *ascending order*, the strongest, most complex, or most emotionally moving evidence comes last, where it can build on the rest of the evidence in the essay and is likely to have the greatest impact on the reader. *Refutation-proof* acknowledges opposing points of view early in the essay and then goes on to show why the author's outlook is superior. *Con-pro* presents an opposing point of view and then refutes it, continuing until all opposition has been dealt with and all positive arguments voiced; this strategy is particularly useful when there is strong opposition to the writer's thesis. The strategies can be combined, of course, as in a refutation-proof essay that builds up to its strongest evidence.

Accuracy and fairness in argument are not only morally correct, they can also be a means of persuasion. Accuracy in the use of facts, figures, quotations, and references can encourage readers to trust what an author has to say. And writers who are able to acknowledge and refute opposing arguments fairly and without hostility add strength to their own arguments and may even win the respect of those who disagree with them.

But the most important elements of effective argument are careful choice of evidence and clear, logical reasoning. It is never possible to arrive at absolute proof—argument, after all, assumes that there are at least two sides to the matter under discussion—yet a carefully constructed case will convince many readers. At the same time, a flaw in logic can undermine an otherwise reasonable argument and destroy a reader's confidence in its conclusions. The introduction to Section 10, "Reasoning by Use of *Induction* and *Deduction*," discusses some important errors to avoid in reasoning or in choosing evidence. Here are some others:

Post hoc ergo propter hoc ("After this therefore because of this")—Just because one thing happened *after* does not mean that the first event caused the second. In arguing without detailed supporting evidence that a recent drop in the crime rate is the result of a newly instituted anticrime policy, a writer might be committing this error, because there are other equally plausible explanations: a drop in the unemployment rate, for example, or a reduction in the number of people in the fifteen to twenty-five age bracket, the segment of the population that is responsible for a high proportion of all crimes.

Begging the question—A writer "begs the question" when he or she assumes the truth of something that is still to be proven. An argument that begins this way, "The recent, unjustified rise in utility rates should be reversed by the state legislature," assumes that the rise is "unjustified," though this important point needs to be proven.

Ignoring the question—A writer may "ignore the question" by shifting attention away from the issue at hand to some loosely related or even irrelevant matter: for example, "Senator Jones's plan for encouraging new industries cannot be any good because in the past he has opposed tax cuts for corporations" (this approach shifts attention away from the merits of Senator Jones's proposal). A related problem is the *ad hominem* (toward the person) argument, which substitutes a personal attack for a discussion of the issue in question.

In composing argumentative essays, therefore, writers need to pay attention not only to what is necessary to convince an audience but also to the integrity of the evidence and arguments they advance in support of a thesis.

Sample Paragraph (Annotated)

The issue is outlined briefly.

Thesis statement.

Evidence and *supporting arguments.* (These five points will themselves need much more evidence, of course, in presenting the actual argument.)

The latest state proposal to divert more water from agricultural to residential uses might be expected to gain support from rapidly urbanizing Palmville. Speaking through their Town Meeting, however, the citizens of the town argue that the state should not meddle with arrangements that have contributed so much to the economic and social health of the region. The report of the Town Meeting contained these arguments: (1) Farming in the Palmville area constitutes an important element in the state's food supply which would be expensive to replace. (2) Farms and support industries provide a large proportion of the jobs of Palmville residents. (3) The farms are an important part of the social fabric of the town and the region, providing, among other things, healthful summer employment for many of the town's youth. (4) Diverting water from the farms would cause many to be sold to real estate developers, thus increasing the population *and* the demand for water. (5) The town's zoning plan will limit growth over the next decade and should slow the increasing demand for water. Whether state officials will be persuaded by these arguments remains to be seen, but Palmville residents hope to prevent changes that might threaten the community they have built so carefully.

Sample Paragraphs (Argument)

Still, the nearly two decades since Congress created Earth Day have left no doubt that our system of environmental regulation badly needs an overhaul. Overloaded with unrealistic deadlines and sweeping legislation during the 1970s, battered by budget cuts during the '80s, the Environmental Protection Agency now needs to devise a regulatory approach that's flexible and effective, and that relies as much on market-based incentives as rigid penalties. As perverse as this may sound, the EPA needs to stop trying to ban pollution and start letting companies pay for the privilege of polluting.

The basic idea is to turn pollution into a cost that, like any other expense, the company will want to minimize. This can be done directly by imposing a fee or tax on the pollutants released into the environment. It can be done indirectly by making companies pay for pollution permits. The government could even auction off the permits (a nice "revenue enhancer"). Alternatively, companies with low pollution levels could sell pollution rights to companies with poorer controls—financially rewarding the "clean" companies and penalizing the laggards. All of these schemes would force companies to pay for their pollution, giving them an incentive to find and use the most cost-effective preventive technology.

From "Grime and Punishment," *The New Republic*, February 20, 1989. Reprinted by permission.

ANNA QUINDLEN

ANNA QUINDLEN is a reporter and writer best known for her column which appears regularly in the *New York Times* and is nationally syndicated. After graduating from Barnard College in 1974 she worked as a general assignment and city hall reporter at the *New York Times*, as writer of the "About New York" column, and finally as deputy metropolitan editor. Her novel, *Object Lessons*, was published in 1991.

Execution

Few issues have been argued as extensively in writing as the death penalty, yet this essay, originally a newspaper column, is fresh in both outlook and technique. Student writers might note that in choosing to build much of the essay around an extended example, Quindlen acknowledges the importance of specificity and concreteness in persuasive writing. Of particular interest, too, are her use of examples drawn from two sources likely to be familiar to readers: newspaper reporting and television.

Ted Bundy and I go back a long way, to a time when there was a series 1
of unsolved murders in Washington State known only as the Ted murders. Like a lot of reporters, I'm something of a crime buff. But the Washington Ted murders—and the ones that followed in Utah, Colorado, and finally in Florida, where Ted Bundy was convicted and sentenced to die—fascinated me because I could see myself as one of the victims. I looked at the studio photographs of young women with long hair, pierced ears, easy smiles, and I read the descriptions: polite, friendly, quick to help, eager to please. I thought about being ap-

proached by a handsome young man asking for help, and I knew if I had been in the wrong place at the wrong time I would have been a goner. By the time Ted finished up in Florida, law enforcement authorities suspected he had murdered dozens of young women. He and the death penalty seemed made for each other.

The death penalty and I, on the other hand, seem to have nothing 2 in common. But Ted Bundy has made me think about it all over again, now that the outlines of my sixties liberalism have been filled in with a decade as a reporter covering some of the worst back alleys in New York City and three years as a mother who, like most, would lay down her life for her kids. Simply put, I am opposed to the death penalty. I would tell that to any judge or lawyer undertaking the voir dire[1] of jury candidates in a state in which the death penalty can be imposed. That is why I would be excused from such a jury. In a rational, completely cerebral way, I think the killing of one human being as punishment for the killing of another makes no sense and is inherently immoral.

But whenever my response to an important subject is rational and 3 completely cerebral, I know there is something wrong with it—and so it is here. I have always been governed by my gut, and my gut says I am hypocritical about the death penalty. That is, I do not in theory think that Ted Bundy, or others like him, should be put to death. But if my daughter had been the one clubbed to death as she slept in a Tallahassee sorority house, and if the bite mark left in her buttocks had been one of the prime pieces of evidence against the young man charged with her murder, I would with the greatest pleasure kill him myself.

The State of Florida will not permit the parents of Bundy's victims 4 to do that, and, in a way, that is the problem with an emotional response to capital punishment. The only reason for a death penalty is to exact retribution. Is there anyone who really thinks that it is a deterrent, that there are considerable numbers of criminals out there who think twice about committing crimes because of the sentence involved? The ones I have met in my professional duties have either sneered at the justice system, where they can exchange one charge for another with more ease than they could return a shirt to a clothing store, or they have simply believed that it is the other guy who will get caught, get convicted, get the stiffest sentence. Of course, the death

---

[1]Examination of the competence of a prospective juror (Editors' note).

penalty would act as a deterrent by eliminating recidivism, but then so would life without parole, albeit at greater taxpayer expense.

I don't believe deterrence is what most proponents seek from the death penalty anyhow. Our most profound emotional response is to want criminals to suffer as their victims did. When a man is accused of throwing a child from a high-rise terrace, my emotional—some might say hysterical—response is that he should be given an opportunity to see how endless the seconds are from the thirty-first story to the ground. In a civilized society that will never happen. And so what many people want from the death penalty, they will never get.

Death is death, you may say, and you would be right. But anyone who has seen someone die suddenly of a heart attack and someone else slip slowly into the clutches of cancer knows that there are gradations of dying.

I watched a television reenactment one night of an execution by lethal injection. It was well done; it was horrible. The methodical approach, people standing around the gurney waiting, made it more awful. One moment there was a man in a prone position; the next moment that man was gone. On another night I watched a television movie about a little boy named Adam Walsh, who disappeared from a shopping center in Florida. There was a reenactment of Adam's parents coming to New York, where they appeared on morning talk shows begging for their son's return, and in their hotel room, where they received a call from the police saying that Adam had just been found: not all of Adam, actually, just his severed head, discovered in the waters of a Florida canal. There is nothing anyone could do that is bad enough for an adult who took a six-year-old boy away from his parents, perhaps tortured, then murdered him and cut off his head. Nothing at all. Lethal injection? The electric chair? Bah.

And so I come back to the position that the death penalty is wrong, not only because it consists of stooping to the level of the killers, but also because it is not what it seems. Just before one of Ted Bundy's execution dates was postponed pending further appeals, the father of his last known victim, a twelve-year-old girl, said what almost every father in his situation must feel. "I wish they'd bring him back to Lake City," said Tom Leach of the town where Kimberly Leach lived and died, "and let us all have at him." But the death penalty does not let us all have at him in the way Mr. Leach seems to mean. What he wants is for something as horrifying as what happened to his child to happen to Ted Bundy. And that is impossible.

Meanings and Values

1a. According to Quindlen, what two purposes do people believe the death penalty can serve?

b. Does she believe it can effectively serve either purpose?

2a. Tell what you think the phrase "sixties liberalism" is likely to mean to most readers. (See Guide to Terms: *Connotation/Denotation.*)

b. Does the essay provide any clear evidence that Quindlen is either liberal or conservative in her political and social outlook? If so, what is the evidence?

3. How does the author try to show that she is not unthinking and naive in her opposition to the death penalty and is, in fact, entitled to speak with authority?

4a. How does Quindlen answer one of the most common arguments made on behalf of capital punishment, that it helps deter crime?

b. Explain why you find her answer satisfactory or unsatisfactory.

Argumentative Techniques

1. Why does the author wait until the second paragraph to state the thesis of the essay?

2a. Identify the examples Quindlen presents in paragraphs 1, 3, 5, 6, and 7.

b. To what extent do the examples in paragraphs 1, 3, and 7 function as a refutation? (Guide: *Refutation.*)

c. How successful is the author in convincing readers that these examples accurately represent her view of the complexity of the issue and are more than simply strategies to refute opposing arguments? Be ready to support your evaluation with examples from the text. (Guide: *Evaluation.*)

3. Tell how the essay uses comparison in paragraphs 1–3 and 6.

Diction and Vocabulary

1a. In the fourth paragraph, Quindlen argues against using the death penalty as a deterrent. How does the wording of the second sentence exclude opposing arguments?

b. What flaw in logic, if any, does this assertion contain? (See the introduction to Section 11, pp. 431–32.)

2a. Identify several instances of colloquial expressions in this essay that keep it from being completely formal. (Guide: *Colloquial Expressions*.)

b. Does the colloquial language add to or detract from the effectiveness of the essay? How? (Guide: *Evaluation*.)

c. What effect are technical terms such as *voir dire* (par. 2) and *recidivism* (par. 4) likely to have on readers?

Suggestions for Writing and Discussion

1. Have TV specials and docudramas, such as those mentioned in the essay, become important forces shaping our moral outlooks? Discuss some programs that you or your classmates remember, identifying their moral perspectives and considering their likely effects on viewers.

2. To what extent is punishment of any sort a deterrent for crime? Are some punishments more effective than others? Besides deterrence, what ends can punishment serve?

3. Prepare an essay arguing for (or against) a mandatory life sentence without parole as an alternative for capital punishment.

(NOTE: Suggestions for topics requiring development by use of ARGUMENT are on page 491, at the end of this section.)

NOEL PERRIN

NOEL PERRIN was born in 1927 in New York. He farms and raises beef cattle in Thetford, Vermont. He also teaches American literature at Dartmouth College. Perrin writes essays for the *New Yorker* and a number of other magazines. In addition, he has published several books of essays, including *In All Weathers* (1973), *First Person Rural* (1978), *Second Person Rural* (1980), *Third Person Rural* (1983), and *A Reader's Delight* (1989).

War on the Farm

"War on the Farm" was first published in *Harrowsmith*, a magazine focusing on rural and small-town living. Few city-dwellers and suburbanites know much about farming, but all of us eat. For people living in both urban and rural areas, therefore, Perrin's look at the negative consequences of technology in farming and the possible responses to it strikes close to home.

> Even while we talk some chemist at Columbia   1
> Is stealthily contriving wool from jute
> That when let loose upon the grazing world
> Will put ten thousand farmers out of sheep.

Robert Frost wrote those lines in 1932, and it's a lot more than ten   2
thousand farmers that have been put out of sheep in the ensuing 53 years. Even those who still raise them do much better selling Easter lambs than they do selling wool. I find with my own handful of sheep that the cost of getting them sheared generally exceeds the value of the fleeces.

But things are even worse than Frost knew. Having put most 3
sheep farmers out of business, the chemists went to work on the jute
farmers, and they have got a good many of them, too. When I first
bought a hundred pounds of feed for my first cow, it came in a burlap
sack—made, of course, of jute. Nice things, burlap sacks. They had a
dozen uses around the farm, such as storing fleeces and holding
apples en route to the cider mill. They were biodegradable besides.
And the jute they were made of formed a leading cash crop in central India.

Now when I buy a hundred pounds of grain, it comes in a 4
particularly nasty kind of woven plastic sack. Nasty (you mustn't, for
example, ever put a fleece in one—it contaminates the wool) and
practically immortal. Last summer I mowed a field for a neighbor, a
field he'd let go for two years and before that had kept a couple of
cows in. At some point at least three years ago, he had left an empty
plastic grain bag lying on the ground. When I mowed over it—it was
hidden in weeds—it took me ten minutes with a pair of pliers to clear
my cutter bar.

And then what to do with the pieces? I didn't dare burn them— 5
God knows what I would have put in the atmosphere. In the end I
took them home in a paper bag to help fill up our town landfill.

Almost everything farmers do is threatened by technology. Often 6
it's direct replacement: artificial maple flavor, orlon socks instead of
cotton, synthetic "bacon bits," every kind of Lifesaver but two flavored with something made in a factory rather than grown on a farm.

Equally often, technology merely perverts true farming. People 7
still raise chickens in order to get eggs—but those people are not
exactly farmers any more. And no child would recognize the places
they operate as farms. Indeed, children are carefully kept away from
modern, 50,000-inmate chicken houses. Being young and innocent,
they might think it was cruel to treat hens that way. They might even
want to release them.

It can be argued, and often is, that all these changes represent 8
progress. Cheap food and cheap clothing are supplied by the chemists
and the agrifactories, and if that means an end to traditional farming,
well, times change.

Naturally I don't agree, and I am not alone. The tremendous rise 9
in demand for natural foods over the last ten years represents a
horrified recoil by hundreds of thousands, perhaps even millions of
consumers. They have come to distrust not only junk food but the
whole larger category of tech food. They are thinking primarily about

their own health (and their own taste buds), of course, but some of
them also like the idea of supporting farms. Some of them deliberately
seek out farmers' markets for that reason.

But what about farmers themselves? What do they do to keep the   10
grazing world alive? I see three common responses. And then there's
a fourth one I don't often see, but wish I did.

The commonest response is to try to meet the factory on its own   11
ground. Do you want to save your farm? Automate it. Reduce costs.
If you're in the sheep business, for example, you might try to develop
sheep-shearing robots so as to help keep the price of wool competitive
with the price of polyester.

This is no fantasy. Australian farmers are in the process of devel-   12
oping such robots right now, just as Florida farmers, with an assist from
the aerospace industry, are in the process of developing citrus-picking
robots. (*Big* farmers in Australia and Florida, that is.) An expensive robot
makes no sense at all if you have 30 sheep or one small grove of orange
trees—but it might if you have 6,000 sheep or a square mile of citrus.

It might. And in the long run it might not, too. If you fight   13
technology with technology, technology fights back. The result is
what used to be called a vicious circle and is now called escalation.
The nuclear arms race is a familiar example. And that, at least, has no
built-in tilt toward the U.S., the USSR, or any other nuclear power. But
when the orlon factory gets its robots, it will be able to use them more
efficiently than the sheep station, since it is dependent neither on
weather nor on the inherent one-at-a-time complexity of living creatures such as sheep. The chief result of robotizing sheep farms will be
to reduce the number of shepherds still further, just as the chief result
of Holsteinizing and milk-parlorizing dairy farms has been drastically to reduce the number of dairy farmers.

A second response is to concede defeat on the main battleground,   14
and to look for little specialty markets that technology hasn't yet
bothered with, or can't at the moment handle. Take wool. *I* don't make
any money on my fleeces, which are ordinary ones. But there are a
small number of farmers who produce special high-quality wool for
the tiny hand-spinning market, and they get quite a decent price per
pound. Maple sugar is never again going to have the role as a bulk
sweetener that it once did, and even cane sugar is losing ground fast.
Chemicals and corn syrup are what the Pepsicola Company buys. But
there remains a luxury market for maple syrup, and a health market
both for it and for brown sugar.

The third response, one possibly only for part-time farmers, is to 15 ignore or at least downplay the economic side of farming and to concentrate on its pleasures as a way of life. This way you needn't compete with high-tech at all. If you want to shear your ewes with hand clippers because it's just damn well an interesting thing to do, you are free to. Obviously you would have only a handful of ewes, or it would cease to be an interesting thing to do. And while you'd still hope to sell the wool, the fact that your return for the time you put in breeding, raising and shearing the sheep might come to 36 cents an hour simply doesn't matter. Your financial state is still better than that of the paddle tennis player, whose return is something like minus $8 per hour, or even the TV viewer at minus 18 cents an hour.

I am this third kind of farmer myself, and I certainly don't mean 16 to criticize play farms. (I hate the name, though. More accurately they should be called owner-subsidized farms. We in the third class do plenty of hard work. It just happens to differ from most late-20th-century work in being deeply satisfying.)

But what I have to note is that high-tech will eventually get most 17 of us, too. Two of my own principal crops are maple syrup and firewood. I'll be able to go on making syrup for the luxury market when reverse osmosis—which isn't economic on my small scale—has completely triumphed. I'll just make even less money per hour spent sugaring. But when whole-tree chippers complete *their* triumph, and pressed by the industry, states begin to pass laws saying the only legal stoves are those that burn chips, have fans, and theoretically pollute less, then where will the market for my cut and split logs be? Just about where the market for goosedown will be when Thinsulate® completes *its* triumph.

What we need is a fourth response: not turning the farm into a 18 sort-of factory, not settling for the economic crumbs left by technology, not pretending we're living fifty or a hundred years ago. We need to fight.

Farmers, of course, *do* fight—dumping milk, seeking quotas, 19 trying to protect price supports. But mostly they fight the wrong battles. Where we should be fighting hardest is in the courts and in the newspapers, and what we should be attacking is the reckless use of technology. We should be trying to make the reckless users pay the true costs of what they do.

To what extent are artificial cherry and tangerine flavors in 20 Lifesavers actually life-damagers? How many people have had allergic reactions? A very few suits might make it economic to use real cherry and tangerine flavors. What about all the beef the fast-food chains import from Central America? What does it contain? It is well known that when a dangerous pesticide or herbicide is banned in the United States, the companies that make it merely shift their markets overseas. DDT, for example, is freely sold in Central America, and freely used in farming. I suspect we don't need a quota on beef; we merely need to make the chemical companies liable for any damage they do to human health in particular and the health of the ecosystem in general. Organic beef might suddenly turn out to be a good buy.

What about plastic grain bags and, for that matter, polyester 21 pants? If the true costs of dealing with the wastes put out by the factories that make these things are factored in, not to mention the costs of getting rid of the sacks and the pants later, are burlap and wool really more expensive?

What about those cheap broiler chickens, raised on hormones? If 22 it's the case, as it seems to be (it's not yet proved), that they play merry hell with the hormonal balance of some of the people who eat them— if the little girls who begin to menstruate at five years old have been thus cruelly affected by eating too much biochemical chicken—then those chickens aren't really cheap at all. The health costs have just deftly been passed on to the public. If the producers had to assume them, then a decently raised farm chicken might turn out to be less per pound. These are some of the battles I'd like to see fought.

There is one caution I need instantly to add. It is easy to get 23 paranoid on a subject like this, and it is easy (for me, anyway) to forget the many good things technology has done for farming and for human life in general. So let me grant that sometimes the new synthetic really is better in every way than the old natural product. Let me further grant that the producers are not villains out to destroy rural life but just businessmen out to make money. And in the case of the scientists who make the actual discoveries, the motive isn't money (usually), but pure disinterested irresponsible curiosity. As Frost says of scientific ingenuity in the same poem I began with, it is something

> Which for no sordid self-aggrandizement,
> For nothing but its own blind satisfaction
> (In this it is as much like hate as love)
> Works in the dark as much against us as for us.

It does work for us. It also works against us. All I'm saying is that in the latter case we'd better resist. Otherwise we may find ourselves with no farms, and eventually the human race may find itself with no habitable world.

Meanings and Values

1a. What does Perrin see as the problem or challenge facing farmers (and, perhaps, the rest of us)?

b. What does he see as its negative effects?

2a. What general action does the author propose as a response to the problem?

b. What examples of specific responses does he offer?

3. Explain what Perrin means by saying "technology merely perverts true farming" (par. 7).

Argumentative Techniques

1. What strategy does Perrin use to begin the essay? (See Guide to Terms: *Introductions*.)

2. Does the author manage to convince readers other than farmers of the importance of his topic? If so, how does he accomplish this task?

3a. What are "three common responses" (par. 10) of farmers to technology and where in the essay does Perrin explain them?

b. What strategies (including expository patterns) does he employ to argue against them?

4a. Where in the essay does Perrin acknowledge opposing points of view other than the "three common responses"? (Guide: *Refutation*.)

b. What strategies does he employ to refute them?

c. Could the refutations be made more effective? If so, how might they be changed?

5. Discuss the use Perrin makes of rhetorical questions in the following paragraphs: 5, 10, 11, 19–21. (Guide: *Rhetorical Questions*.)

Diction and Vocabulary

1a. Discuss how Perrin uses diction, especially the connotations of words, to sway his readers' opinions in the following paragraphs: 3–4, 7, 12, and 21. (Guide: *Diction, Connotation/Denotation*.)

b. Does he rely on language alone for persuasion? If not, what other means does he employ in these paragraphs? Be specific in your answers.

2. If you do not know the meaning of some of the following words, look them up in a dictionary: jute (par. 1); inherent (13); ewes (15); subsidized (16); osmosis (17); pesticide, herbicide (20).

Suggestions for Writing and Discussion

1. Many people believe technology aids rather than threatens farming. If you know something about this topic, consider writing an essay that takes a position different from Perrin's. Or consider doing some research into the pros and cons of technology in farming.

2. Most environmental issues have two (or more) sides. Take a topic (such as the Greenhouse effect or water pollution), read about it in some general interest magazines, identify an issue, and prepare a paper either outlining the pros and cons or taking a stand.

(NOTE: Suggestions for topics requiring development by use of ARGUMENT are on page 491, at the end of this section.)

JOSEPH NOCERA

JOSEPH NOCERA was born in Providence, Rhode Island. He received his B.S. in journalism from Boston University in 1974. His articles have appeared in a wide variety of newspapers and magazines including the *Wall Street Journal,* the *New York Times Book Review, Texas Monthly, New Republic,* and *Esquire.* In addition, he was on the staff of the *New England Monthly* and is currently a columnist for *GQ.* At present, he is working on a book on the history of personal finance. He lives in Northampton, Massachusetts.

How the Middle Class Has Helped Ruin the Public Schools

The common wisdom is that people with middle-class incomes and middle-class jobs tend to value education highly. The title of this essay (from the *Washington Monthly*) is thus likely to surprise many readers. Nocera's arguments are likewise surprising, though the detailed evidence that he presents means that they ought to be taken seriously, though not automatically given assent. As you read, therefore, try to judge the quality of his argument by analyzing the evidence and thinking of other interpretations and possible causes than the ones the author identifies.

I moved to Northampton, Massachusetts, with my family two and a half years ago to take a job with a magazine. I've since learned a lot about the attractions of small-town life. I live in a place where I never have to lock my car, where a "traffic jam" means having to wait for   1

447

the light to change twice, where the cost of things is a good 20 percent less than it is in, say, Boston.

While I don't deny the appeal of this life, the truth is, I've always   2
thought of myself as a city boy. I still do.

So why am I here? It's not the job: I no longer do much work for   3
the magazine that brought me to Northampton, nor is my wife
employed in the local economy. And while I can toss off a half-dozen
persuasive reasons for living here—good friends I don't want to leave
behind; the low cost of housing—I know in my heart of hearts that
these are only partial explanations. There is another reason, one that
looms larger in my mind than any other, one that I always feel a bit
ashamed to admit to. I am talking about The Schools.

The public schools here are quite good—not the best in the region,   4
perhaps (that distinction belongs to nearby Amherst), but good nonetheless. One can argue forever as to why this is so; my own belief is
that places like Northampton and Amherst, little cities with populations between 30,000 and 50,000, are the perfect size for good school
systems. They are large enough to have the critical mass and money
needed for decent facilities, but small enough so that there is very little
bureaucratic (or union) rigmarole standing between teachers and
students. Also, teachers still have status and respect in a small town—
including yuppified small towns like mine—that they don't have in
larger places.

Most important, there is a large group of white middle-class   5
parents deeply involved in the public school system. One of the givens
about American public education is that parental involvement is one
of the two or three critical factors that determine whether a school
system will be good or bad. Historically, that vigilance is provided by
the educated class: predominately white, overwhelmingly middle-class
people who know how to "fight city hall" and aren't afraid to do so.

The result is that when my oldest child was ready to enter   6
kindergarten this past September, I had no qualms about sending her
to public school. I now fully expect that she'll stay in the public school
system, as will my other children as they grow older. It would be hard
to overstate my relief when I first realized that this was going to be
possible. For one thing, my wife and I were suddenly spared a
daunting financial burden. But since I was also anxious for my children to get a taste of the democratic experience that the public schools
provide, it was satisfying to know that their education would not
suffer for that experience.

That sense of relief has done something else to me, though: It's 7 planted me here as firmly as any job might have. Perhaps more firmly, since these days parents are more likely to shift jobs than shift their kids into a different, untried school system. A decent public school today is something to be treasured, and if you've found one for your kids, you don't abandon it lightly.

So over the past year or so, as I've daydreamed about moving to 8 a big city, I've gradually come to the conclusion that I just can't do it. Not anytime soon, anyway. And the reason is The Schools. The thought of what it would cost to send my children to a private elementary school is sobering enough. But then when I think about the other option—sending them to public school—I shudder. I can't imagine sending my children to a big-city public school system.

Look at them, for God's sake: Boston is a shambles, wrecked by 9 the busing tragedies of the 1970s. In Boston, 40 percent of the kids who enter ninth grade will drop out before graduation. Washington is not much better, a system clogged with bureaucrats, where union grievances generate more passion than any seventh grade history lesson. New York? You can scarcely pick up an edition of the *Times* without reading about some new outrage: teachers robbed and beaten in their classrooms; an alcoholic principal who is absent more than he is present; a district school board dealing cocaine; and on and on. The destruction of the large public school systems in America is one of the great tragedies of our time. And because schools are so important, the cities, by permitting their destruction, have effectively abandoned people like me.

Or perhaps I'm being too easy on myself. Perhaps it is more 10 accurate to say that it is people like me who have done the abandoning. Isn't it obvious today that big-city public school systems began their decline at precisely the moment when the white middle class began fleeing them? It seems awfully obvious to me. You can talk all you want about the debilitating effects of busing or ill-equipped teachers, but to my mind, the most debilitating factor by far in the disintegration of the public schools was the unwillingness of the white middle class, *as a class,* to do what they had always done: stand and fight to keep the schools good. I don't mean to sound too self-flagellatory, but I know in my soul that when I decided to stay in Northampton so that my children could go to school here, I was making the same moral choice that hundreds of thousands had made before me. I too was choosing not to stand and fight.

One of the most compelling arguments about the Vietnam War   11
is that it lasted as long as it did because of its "classist" nature. The
central thesis is that because neither the decision-makers in the government *nor anyone they knew* had children fighting and dying in
Vietnam, they had no personal incentive to bring the war to a halt.
The government's generous college-deferment system, steeped as it
was in class distinctions, allowed the white middle class to avoid the
tragic consequences of the war. And the people who did the fighting
and dying in place of the college-deferred were those whose voices
were least heard in Washington: the poor and the disenfranchised.

I bring this up because I believe that the decline of the public   12
schools is rooted in the same cause. Just as with the Vietnam War, as
soon as the white middle class no longer had a stake in the public
schools, the surest pressure on school systems to provide a decent
education instantly disappeared. Once the middle class was gone, no
mayor was going to get booted out of office because the schools were
bad. No incompetent teacher had to worry about angry parents
calling for his or her head "downtown." No third-rate educationalist
at the local teachers college had to fear having his or her methods
criticized by anyone that mattered.

The analogy to the Vietnam War can be extended even to the   13
extent of the denial. It amuses me sometimes to hear people like
myself decry the state of the public schools. We bemoan the lack of
money, the decaying facilities, the absurd credentialism, the high
foolishness of the school boards. We applaud the burgeoning reform
movement. And everything we say is deeply, undeniably true. We can
see every problem with the schools clearly except one: the fact that
our decision to abandon the schools has helped create all the other
problems. One small example: In the early 1980s, Massachusetts
passed one of those tax cap measures, called Proposition $2\frac{1}{2}$, which
has turned out to be a force for genuine evil in the public schools.
Would Proposition $2\frac{1}{2}$ have passed had the middle class still had a
stake in the schools? I wonder. I also wonder whether 20 years from
now, in the next round of breast-beating memoirs, the exodus of the
white middle class from the public schools will finally be seen for
what it was. Individually, every parent's rationale made impeccable
sense—"I can't deprive my children of a decent education"—but
collectively, it was a deeply destructive act.

The main reason the white middle class fled, of course, is race, or   14
more precisely, the complicated admixture of race and class and good

intentions gone awry. The fundamental good intention—which even today strikes one as both moral and right—was to integrate the public classroom, and in so doing, to equalize the resources available to all school children. In Boston, this was done through enforced busing. In Washington, it was done through a series of judicial edicts that attempted to spread the good teachers and resources throughout the system. In other big city districts, judges weren't involved; school committees, seeing the handwriting on the wall, tried to do it themselves.

However moral the intent, the result almost always was the 15 same. The white middle class left. The historic parental vigilance I mentioned earlier had had a lot to do with creating the two-tiered system—one in which schools attended by the kids of the white middle class had better teachers, better equipment, better everything than those attended by the kids of the poor. This did not happen because the white middle-class parents were racists, necessarily; it happened because they knew how to manipulate the system and were willing to do so on behalf of their kids. Their neighborhood schools became little havens of decent education, and they didn't much care what happened in the other public schools.

In retrospect, this behavior, though perfectly understandable, 16 was tragically short-sighted. When the judicial fiats made those safe havens untenable, the white middle class quickly discovered what the poor had always known: There weren't enough good teachers, decent equipment, and so forth to go around. For that matter, there weren't even enough good *students* to go around; along with everything else, middle-class parents had to start worrying about whether their kids were going to be mugged in school.

Faced with the grim fact that their children's education was 17 quickly deteriorating, middle-class parents essentially had two choices: They could stay and pour the energy that had once gone into improving the neighborhood school into improving the entire school system—a frightening task, to be sure. Or they could leave. Invariably, they chose the latter.

And it wasn't just the white middle class that fled. The black 18 middle class, and even the black poor who were especially ambitious for their children, were getting out as fast as they could too, though not to the suburbs. They headed mainly for the parochial schools, which subsequently became integration's great success story, even as the public schools became integration's great failure.

There is no place in America where all this played out as starkly   19
and as sadly as in Boston. I was living there during that city's terrible
busing ordeal of the mid-1970s, just finishing up college, when Judge
Arthur Garrity's busing plan took effect in 1974. I remember feeling
a sense of contempt, of real moral superiority, toward the people who
opposed busing, easy enough to do when you're young and single
and your mind is uncluttered with worries about the upbringing of
your flesh and blood. *Those people are racists,* I thought. *Their excuses
are all smokescreens.* And of course, many of the most violent opponents
of busing *were* racists, and many of their excuses *were* smokescreens.
I don't condone that racism in any way, but one of the things I
understand now that I didn't then was that the poor whites were
lashing out at least in part out of a sense of their own impotence. The
white parents whose kids were bused were those who had absolutely
no other choice. They saw their kids being treated as guinea pigs, and
they didn't like it. What parent would?

Another thing I can see now that I didn't then was how keenly   20
the opponents of busing felt the class divide. "Thousands of letters
poured into [Judge Garrity's] chambers," writes J. Anthony Lukas in
Common Ground, his great book about the Boston busing crisis. "Many
of the angriest letters and phone calls emphasized the judge's remote-
ness from Boston, his long residence in affluent Wellesley, where his
family and friends were exempt from his court order."

My own memory is that it became difficult for even the once-   21
sainted Ted Kennedy to enter Southie after the buses began rolling.
Where did Ted Kennedy's kids go to school? the anti-busing forces
used to taunt. Where did Mayor Kevin White's kids go to school? Not
to any public school in Boston, that's for sure. To believe that integration was the only moral course does not mean that Garrity's busing
orders were the only moral option. Perhaps it *was* the only way, given
the legendary intransigence of the Boston School Committee. But now
that I am a parent and view these matters through a different prism,
Garrity's orders strike me as unnecessarily cruel, as if he were pun-
ishing the school children for the actions of their elders. Besides, to
return to the Vietnam parallel, wouldn't it have made a huge difference in how integration was implemented if Judge Garrity's or Ted
Kennedy's or Kevin White's kids had been enrolled in the Boston
schools? However deeply they felt about the busing crisis, they could
never have the personal stake of someone whose child was being
bused.

Here's what happened in Boston: In 1972, there were 96,000 22
students enrolled in the public schools, of whom 60 percent were
white. Sixteen years later, only 57,000 students remain, and less than
a quarter of them are white.

Think about that for a minute. Even given that the school age 23
population declined over that period, you're still looking at a lot of
students who have left the school system, almost all of them the sons
and daughters of the white middle class. Or, to put it another way,
those students who have left represent 75,000 or so parents who in
effect have dropped out of the Boston public school system.

It takes, I believe, a strong dose of denial to believe that those 24
75,000 middle-class parents would not have made a difference. Since
the white middle class left, the system has simply fallen apart. Can
this really be sheer coincidence? I think not.

One painful result of this massive exodus of the white middle 25
class is that those few who did stay and fight wound up feeling like
suckers. In his book, Lukas tells the story of one such couple, Colin
and Joan Diver, whose son Brad was in elementary school. Colin
Diver was a lawyer who worked for Mayor White and lived in
Boston's South End. Happily for them, their son was enrolled in one
of those wonderful little havens, a good, innovative, integrated public
school, called Bancroft, whose recent transformation showed exactly
the kind of effect an involved white middle class can have.

Over time, however, the quality of the Divers' little school was 26
eroded by one after another of Garrity's decrees. Was Garrity's heart
in the right place? Of course it was. Did that do the Divers any good?
Of course not. In frustration, parents began moving their kids out of
the school. Those who remained, like the Divers, were worn down.

By 1976, two years after busing began, it had come to this: "Many 27
Bancroft students were in academic difficulties, with reading scores a
particular focus of concern. Joan and Colin were dismayed to learn
that Brad's reading scores had actually declined. For a child of Brad's
promise, that was plainly unacceptable. Joan and Colin wondered
once again whether they were sacrificing their children's future on
the altar of their social principles." Soon afterwards, the Divers decided they too had to leave.

Here is the rub, of course. Here is what makes each middle-class 28
parent's personal, wrenching decision to move so understandable
and ultimately so forgivable. *Parents aren't willing to sacrifice their*

children on the altar of their social principles. How can they? It's one thing to sacrifice yourself, but quite another to offer up your children, about whom you have overwhelming feelings of protection and in whom you invest your most deeply felt hopes and dreams.

I don't mean to suggest that it can ever be otherwise. How do you 29 counteract one of humanity's most strongly felt emotions? But that's also why the state of the big-city public school systems can seem so hopeless to me at times. Unless you have an involved middle class— unless you have that parental vigilance—it is difficult to see how things are going to change.

Where is the impetus for change to come from? Just as it is too 30 much to ask Ted Kennedy to send his kids to public school, it is also probably too much to expect the parents with kids still in public school to pick up where the middle class left off. In Boston recently, as court-ordered busing was about to end, the school committee held a series of public hearings. The *Boston Globe* ran a story on the hearings, noting that even though three-quarters of the students are now black, Hispanic, or Asian, "the typical speaker [at the sparsely attended hearings] was a white, well-educated and middle-class parent." The reporter found this fact "ironic," but she also quoted a consultant who got to the heart of the matter: "When you're talking about the underclass," he said, "these people don't see themselves as part of the mainstream. When you talk about reforms that are good, they think you're not talking about them."

No, if the public schools are ever going to get better, the forces for 31 change are going to have to come from people outside the system. In effect, we have to find a way to replace the clout exercised by vigilant parents with some other, equally powerful force. What might that be?

One possibility ought to be America's urban black leadership, 32 which has been as much at fault in the decline of the public schools as the white middle class. That is their shame. It would take only a few eloquent black voices to turn the state of the schools into the moral cause it ought to be.

Then there's the education reform movement itself, which has 33 gained considerable steam these past few years. As laudable as this is, we ought not kid ourselves about the reasons why. One, the most compelling, is that the schools have gotten so bad that radical measures now are acceptable in a way they weren't even 10 years ago. Another is that statewide reforms help the Northamptons as much as the Bostons—perhaps more so since out here in the sticks we have a better chance of making sure they are implemented. You can live in the suburbs and still have a personal stake in reform.

But the reforms have gained momentum also because they seem   34
so obviously *right*. It's criminal that the unions and the bureaucrats now regularly put their own interests ahead of their students. It's absurd for unions to automatically protect bad teachers and for schools to require master's degrees for pay raises instead of demonstrated ability. It's infuriating the way the whole system is designed to discourage better, more idealistic people from becoming teachers. No one denies any of these things any more. The system has gotten warped, and if there is one thing the white middle class can do from the outside, it is to actively back the reforms that will unwarp it.

In the meantime, the exodus continues. I was in Washington not   35
long ago looking up old friends who had lived in the city when I had—people who had loved the city the way I did. I couldn't help but notice that most of them didn't live in Washington anymore. They lived in Bethesda. They lived in Chevy Chase. They lived in Alexandria. These were generally people who had sneered at suburbia a decade ago but were now making their peace with the suburbs. "It's nice here," they told me halfheartedly, and I knew exactly what they meant. But they also admitted, invariably, that they had moved to gain access to The Schools, and as I listened to them say those words, I could hear the guilt. It is in the sound of that guilt, I think, that one can find hope.

I fervently pray the day will come when the big-city public   36
schools get decent again. If that were to happen, I would gladly move back to the city and put my children in the schools. I would become an involved middle-class parent. In the meantime, I will watch closely from the sidelines, applauding when progress is made, grimacing when there are setbacks. But I also know that until they change, I won't be back. Yes, I've done the right thing for my kids, but I'll never feel good about it. I'll always feel as if I'm an unindicted co-conspirator in the one great crime of my class.

Meanings and Values

1a.   What is the thesis of this essay and where is it stated? (See Guide to Terms: *Thesis*.)

  b.   How might paragraphs 30–35 be said to have a separate thesis from the rest of the essay?

    c.   Explain why paragraphs 30–35 ought to be considered a unified part of the whole essay.

    2.   What causes does Nocera cite to explain the middle class's abandonment of the public schools?

    3.   Why does the author believe that public schools are worth preserving and improving?

    4.   What evidence does Nocera offer to argue that the decline of public schools is not caused solely by racism?

    5a.   What does Nocera think ought to be done?

    b.   What evidence does he offer to support this conclusion?

Argumentative Techniques

    1a.   Why did Nocera choose to begin the essay by talking about his own experiences?

    b.   Is this strategy effective? (Guide: *Evaluation.*)

    c.   What other ways of introducing the essay might he have chosen? Be specific. (Guide: *Introductions.*)

    2.   How does the author introduce his discussions of each of the causes that led to the abandonment of the public schools? (Guide: *Transition.*)

    3a.   In addition to the personal examples from Northampton, this essay draws on Massachusetts for examples in several places: paragraphs 9, 13, 14, 19–27, and 30. From where are other examples drawn?

    b.   Are most readers likely to feel that these examples are representative of their own experiences and applicable to their own towns? If so, explain how Nocera tries to make clear their representative nature.

    c.   If not, which might be eliminated and replaced by examples from other cities and towns?

Diction and Vocabulary

    1a.   To what extent is the diction in the following paragraphs meant to appeal to our emotions and values: 9, 13, 19, 25, and 34?

    b.   Are these appeals adequately supported by evidence? If so, what is the evidence?

    c.   If not, argue whether the diction in these paragraphs is a legitimate tool of argument or an inappropriate attempt to sway readers' opinions. (Guide: *Evaluation.*)

2. If you do not know the meaning of some of the following terms, look them up in the dictionary: vigilance (par. 5); daunting (6); flagellatory (10); disenfranchised (11); admixture (14); fiats (16); subsequently (18); intransigence (21); laudable (33); unindicted (36).

Suggestions for Writing and Discussion

1. This essay touches on all sorts of potentially explosive topics: race, class, integration, taxation, education, and so on. If the author's views in one or more of these efforts differ sharply from yours, jot down your thoughts and then look over what you have written as a possible source for essay topics. If you agree with the author, but see ways that his ideas could be extended or modified, jot down your ideas in order to use them as a basis for an essay.

2. Is schooling the only thing about our cities and towns that is affected by the desire of parents to provide the best experiences they can for their children? What other effects on town government, town services, and town policies are traceable to parents acting on behalf of their children? Are these effects always beneficial for the society as a whole?

(NOTE: Suggestions for topics requiring development by use of ARGUMENT are on page 491, at the end of this section.)

RICHARD LYNN

RICHARD LYNN was born in London, England, in 1930. He received a B.A. from King's College, Cambridge, in 1953 and was awarded a Ph.D. in 1956. He has taught at Exeter University and the Economic and Social Research Institute, Dublin, and is currently a professor of psychology at the University of Ulster. Among his books are *Personality and National Character* (1971), *An Introduction to the Study of Personality* (1971), *The Entrepreneur* (1974), and, most recently, *Educational Achievement in Japan* (1988).

Why Johnny Can't Read, but Yoshio Can

This essay was first published in the *National Review,* a magazine noted for its advocacy of conservative social, economic, and political policies. In the selection, Lynn compares the Japanese educational system to those of the United States and England in order to argue for changes in the latter two systems. Of particular interest in this essay is the way the comparison pattern lends itself to arguments urging the adoption of policies that have worked in another setting.

There can be no doubt that American schools compare poorly with Japanese schools. In the latter, there are no serious problems with poor discipline, violence, or truancy; Japanese children take school seriously and work hard. Japanese educational standards are high, and illiteracy is virtually unknown. 1

The evidence of Japan's high educational standards began to appear as long ago as the 1960s. In 1967 there was published the first of a series of studies of educational standards in a dozen or so 2

458

economically developed nations, based on tests of carefully drawn representative samples of children. The first study was concerned with achievement in math on the part of 13- and 18-year-olds. In both age groups the Japanese children came out well ahead of their coevals in other countries. The American 13-year-olds came out second to last for their age group; the American 18-year-olds, last. In both age groups, European children scored about halfway between the Japanese and the Americans.

Since then, further studies have appeared, covering science as well as math. The pattern of results has always been the same: the Japanese have generally scored first, the Americans last or nearly last, and the Europeans have fallen somewhere in between. In early adolescence, when the first tests are taken, Japanese children are two or three years ahead of American children; by age 18, approximately 98 per cent of Japanese children surpass their American counterparts. 3

Meanwhile, under the Reagan Administration, the United States at least started to take notice of the problem. In 1983 the President's report, *A Nation at Risk*, described the state of American schools as a national disaster. A follow-up report issued by the then-secretary of education, Mr. William Bennett, earlier this year[1] claims that although some improvements have been made, these have been "disappointingly slow." 4

An examination of Japan's school system suggests that there are three factors responsible for its success, which might be emulated by other countries: a strong national curriculum, stipulated by the government; strong incentives for students; and the stimulating effects of competition between schools. 5

The national curriculum in Japan is drawn up by the Department of Education. It covers Japanese language and literature, math, science, social science, music, moral education, and physical education. From time to time, the Department of Education requests advice on the content of the curriculum from representatives of the teaching profession, industry, and the trade unions. Syllabi are then drawn up, setting out in detail the subject matter that has to be taught at each grade. These syllabi are issued to school principals, who are responsible for ensuring that the stipulated curriculum is taught in their schools. Inspectors periodically check that this is being done. 6

[1]1988, the year this essay was first published (Editors' note).

The Japanese national curriculum ensures such uniformly high 7
standards of teaching that almost all parents are happy to send their
children to the local public school. There is no flight into private
schools of the kind that has been taking place in America in recent
years. Private schools do exist in Japan, but they are attended by less
than 1 per cent of children in the age range of compulsory schooling
(six to 15 years).

This tightly stipulated national curriculum provides a striking 8
contrast with the decentralized curriculum of schools in America.
Officially, the curriculum in America is the responsibility of school
principals with guidelines from state education officials. In practice,
even school principals often have little idea of what is actually being
taught in the classroom.

America and Britain have been unusual in leaving the curriculum 9
so largely in the hands of teachers. Some form of national curriculum
is used throughout Continental Europe, although the syllabus is
typically not specified in as much detail as in Japan. And now Britain
is changing course: legislation currently going through Parliament
will introduce a national curriculum for England and Wales, with the
principal subjects being English, math, science, technology, a foreign
language, history and geography, and art, music, and design. It is
envisioned that the new curriculum will take up approximately 70 per
cent of teaching time, leaving the remainder free for optional subjects
such as a second foreign language, or extra science.

Under the terms of the new legislation, schoolchildren are going 10
to be given national tests at the ages of seven, 11, 14, and 16 to ensure
that the curriculum has been taught and that children have learned it
to a satisfactory standard. When the British national curriculum
comes into effect, America will be left as the only major economically
developed country without one.

To achieve high educational standards in schools it is necessary to 11
have motivated students as well as good teachers. A national curriculum acts as a discipline on teachers, causing them to teach efficiently,
but it does nothing to provide incentives for students, an area in which
American education is particularly weak.

One of the key factors in the Japanese education system is that 12
secondary schooling is split into two stages. At the age of 11 or 12,
Japanese children enter junior high school. After three years there,
they take competitive entrance examinations for senior high schools.

In each locality there is a hierarchy of public esteem for these senior high schools, from the two or three that are regarded as the best in the area, through those considered to be good or average, down to those that (at least by Japanese standards) are considered to be poor.

The top schools enjoy national reputations, somewhat akin to   13
the famous English schools such as Eton and Harrow. But in England the high fees exacted by these schools mean that very few parents can afford them. Consequently there are few candidates for entry, and the entrance examinations offer little incentive to work for the great mass of children. By contrast, in Japan the elite senior high schools are open to everyone. While a good number of these schools are private (approximately 30 per cent nationwide, though in some major cities the figure is as high as 50 per cent), even these schools are enabled, by government subsidies, to keep their fees within the means of a large proportion of parents. The public schools also charge fees, but these are nominal, amounting to only a few hundred dollars a year, and loans are available to cover both fees and living expenses.

Thus children have every expectation of being able to attend the   14
best school they can qualify for; and, hence, the hierarchical rankings of senior high schools act as a powerful incentive for children preparing for the entrance examinations. There is no doubt that Japanese children work hard in response to these incentives. Starting as early as age ten, approximately half of them take extra tuition on weekends, in the evenings, and in the school holidays at supplementary coaching establishments known as *juku*, and even at that early age they do far more homework than American children. At about the age of 12, Japanese children enter the period of their lives known as *examination hell*: during this time, which lasts fully two years, it is said that those who sleep more than five hours a night have no hope of success, either in school or in life. For, in addition to conferring great social and intellectual status on their students, the elite senior high schools provide a first-rate academic education, which, in turn, normally enables the students to get into one of the elite universities and, eventually, to move into a good job in industry or government.

Although Japanese children are permitted to leave school at the   15
age of 15, 94 per cent of them proceed voluntarily to the senior high schools. Thus virtually all Japanese are exposed in early adolescence to the powerful incentive for academic work represented by the senior-high-school entrance examinations. There is nothing in the

school systems of any of the Western countries resembling this powerful incentive.

The prestige of the elite senior high schools is sustained by the 16 extensive publicity they receive from the media. Each year the top hundred or so schools in Japan are ranked on the basis of the percentage of their pupils who obtain entry to the University of Tokyo, Japan's most prestigious university. These rankings are widely reported in the print media, and the positions of the top twenty schools are announced on TV news programs, rather like the scores made by leading sports teams in the United States and Europe. At a local level, more detailed media coverage is devoted to the academic achievements of all the schools in the various localities, this time analyzed in terms of their pupils' success in obtaining entry to the lesser, but still highly regarded, local universities.

Thus, once Japanese 15-year-olds have been admitted to their 17 senior high schools, they are confronted with a fresh set of incentives in the form of entrance examinations to universities and colleges, which are likewise hierarchically ordered in public esteem. After the University of Tokyo, which stands at the apex of the status hierarchy, come the University of Kyoto and ten or so other highly prestigious universities, including the former Imperial Universities in the major provincial cities and the technological university of Hitosubashi, whose standing and reputation in Japan resembles that of the Massachusetts Institute of Technology in the United States.

Below these top dozen institutions stand some forty or so less 18 prestigious but still well-regarded universities. And after these come numerous smaller universities and colleges of varying degrees of standing and reputation.

To some extent the situation in Japan has parallels in the United 19 States and Europe, but there are two factors that make the importance of securing admission to an elite university substantially greater in Japan than in the West. In the first place, the entire Japanese system is geared toward providing lifelong employment, both in the private sector and in the civil service. It is practically unheard of for executives to switch from one corporation to another, or into public service and then back into the private sector, as in the United States and Europe. Employees are recruited directly out of college, and, needless to say, the major corporations and the civil service recruit virtually entirely from the top dozen universities. The smaller Japanese corporations operate along the same lines, although they widen their recruitment net to cover the next forty or so universities in the prestige hierarchy. Thus, obtaining entry to a prestigious university is a far more vital step for a successful career in Japan than it is in the United States or Europe.

Secondly, like the elite senior high schools, the elite universities are meritocratic. The great majority of universities are public institutions, receiving substantial government subsidies. Again, as with the senior high schools, fees are quite low, and loans are available to defray expenses. In principle and to a considerable extent in practice, any young Japanese can get into the University of Tokyo, or one of the other elite universities, provided only that he or she is talented enough and is prepared to do the work necessary to pass the entrance examinations. Knowing this, the public believes that *all* the most talented young Japanese go to one of these universities—and, conversely, that anyone who fails to get into one of these schools is necessarily less bright. Avoiding this stigma is, of course, a further incentive for the student to work hard to get in.

The third significant factor responsible for the high educational standards in Japan is competition among schools. This operates principally among the senior high schools, and what they are competing for is academic reputation. The most prestigious senior high school in Japan is Kansei in Tokyo, and being a teacher at Kansei is something like being a professor at Harvard. The teachers' self-esteem is bound up with the academic reputation of their schools—a powerful motivator for teachers to teach well.

In addition to this important factor of self-esteem, there is practical necessity. Since students are free to attend any school they can get into, if a school failed to provide good-quality teaching, it would no longer attract students. In business terms, its customers would fade away, and it would be forced to close. Thus the essential feature of the competition among the Japanese senior high schools is that it exposes the teachers to the discipline of the free-enterprise system. In the case of the public senior high schools, the system can be regarded as a form of market socialism in which the competing institutions are state-owned but nevertheless compete against each other for their customers. Here the Japanese have been successfully operating the kind of system that Mikhail Gorbachev may be feeling his way toward introducing in the Soviet Union. The Japanese private senior high schools add a further capitalist element to the system insofar as they offer their educational services more or less like firms operating in a conventional market.

The problem of how market disciplines can be brought to bear   23
on schools has been widely discussed in America and also in Britain ever since Milton Friedman raised it a quarter of a century or so ago, but solutions such as Friedman's voucher proposal seem as distant today as they did then. Although the proposal has been looked at sympathetically by Republicans in the United States and by Conservatives in Britain, politicians in both countries have fought shy of introducing it. Probably they have concluded that the problems of getting vouchers into the hands of all parents, and dealing with losses, fraud, counterfeits, and so forth, are likely to be too great for the scheme to be feasible.

The Japanese have evolved a different method of exposing   24
schools to market forces. Subsidies are paid directly to the schools on a per-capita basis in accordance with the number of students they have. If a school's rolls decline, so do its incomes, both from subsidies and from fees. This applies to both the public and private senior high schools, although the public schools obviously receive a much greater proportion of their income as subsidies and a smaller proportion from fees.

A similar scheme is being introduced in Britain. The Thatcher   25
government is currently bringing in legislation that will permit public schools to opt out of local-authority control. Those that opt out will receive subsidies from the central government on the basis of the number of students they have. They will then be on their own, to sink or swim.

There is little doubt that this is the route that should be followed   26
in America. The exposure of American schools to the invigorating stimulus of competition, combined with the introduction of a national curriculum and the provision of stronger incentives for students, would work wonders. Rather than complaining about Japanese aggressiveness and instituting counterproductive protectionist measures, Americans ought to be looking to the source of Japan's power.

Meanings and Values

1. What is the issue or problem Lynn identifies in paragraphs 1–4?
2. Summarize briefly the main reasons Lynn offers for the success of the Japanese school system.

3a. How does the curriculum in Japanese schools contrast with those in American and British schools?

b. How does the Japanese system motivate students to excel, in contrast to the American and British systems?

4a. One possible weakness in this argument is that the author pays little attention to opposing points of view. Think of some reasonable objections a North American reader might have to the Japanese educational system. Try to identify some practical difficulties that stand in the way of the reforms the author proposes based on the Japanese model.

b. Explain how you think the author might respond to these objections and possible problems.

Argumentative Techniques

1. What kinds of evidence does the author offer to demonstrate the seriousness of the problem he describes in the opening of the essay? (See Guide to Terms: *Argument*.)

2. Why might the author have chosen to summarize his main supporting arguments in paragraph 5, early in the essay?

3a. Discuss the strategies Lynn employs in paragraphs 11 and 21, which act as transitions between major segments of the essay. (Guide: *Transition*.)

b. Tell how these two paragraphs, along with paragraphs 5 and 6, contribute to the overall coherence of the essay. (Guide: *Coherence*.)

4. How would you describe the tone of the essay? In what ways does it add to the persuasiveness of the argument? (Guide: *Tone*.)

Diction and Vocabulary

1a. Examine the diction in paragraphs 7, 14, and 22 to decide whether it is designed to appeal primarily to readers' emotions, reason, or both. (See the introduction to Section 11, p. 427, and Guide: *Diction*.)

b. On the whole, would you characterize the writing in this selection as objective or subjective? Why? (Guide: *Objective/Subjective*.)

2. Identify the uses Lynn makes of parallel structures and contrasts in diction to emphasize the seriousness of the problem described in paragraphs 2 and 3. (Guide: *Parallel Structure*.)

3. Point out the transitional devices used in paragraphs to emphasize contrasts between the Japanese educational system and those of Britain and America. (Guide: *Transition*.)

Suggestions for Writing and Discussion

1. In what other ways do you think North Americans can learn from the economic or social systems of other countries? In discussing this issue, pay particular attention to countries such as Japan that have been especially successful in the last decade.

2. Prepare an essay in which you take issue with the recommendations in this essay and propose some educational reforms of your own that you believe would be just as effective—or even more so.

3. Using comparison as a strategy, argue for some solutions to a local problem such as disposal of solid waste, improvement of the transportation system, better administration of school athletics, or control of drug and alcohol abuse.

(NOTE: Suggestions for topics requiring development by use of ARGUMENT are on page 491, at the end of this section.)

BARBARA LAWRENCE

BARBARA LAWRENCE was born in Hanover, New Hampshire. After
receiving a B.A. in French literature from Connecticut College, she
worked as an editor on *McCall's, Redbook, Harper's Bazaar,* and the
New Yorker. During this period she also took an M.A. in philosophy
from New York University. Currently a professor of humanities at
the State University of New York's College at Old Westbury, Lawrence has published criticism, poetry, and fiction in *Choice, Common-
weal, Columbia Poetry,* the *New York Times,* and the *New Yorker.*

Four-Letter Words Can Hurt You

"Four-Letter Words Can Hurt You" first appeared in the *New York
Times* and was later published in *Redbook.* In arguing against the
"earthy, gut-honest" language often preferred by her students,
Lawrence also provides a thoughtful, even scholarly, extended
definition of *obscenity* itself. To accomplish her purpose, the author
makes use of several other patterns as well.

Why should any words be called obscene? Don't they all describe   1
natural human functions? Am I trying to tell them, my students
demand, that the "strong, earthy, gut-honest"—or, if they are fans of
Norman Mailer, the "rich, liberating, existential"—language they use
to describe sexual activity isn't preferable to "phony-sounding, middle-class words like 'intercourse' and 'copulate'?" "Cop You Late!"
they say with fancy inflections and gagging grimaces. "Now, what is
that supposed to mean?"

Well, what is it supposed to mean? And why indeed should one   2
group of words describing human functions and human organs be

acceptable in ordinary conversation and another, describing presumably the same organs and functions, be tabooed—so much so, in fact, that some of these words still cannot appear in print in many parts of the English-speaking world?

The argument that these taboos exist only because of "sexual 3 hangups" (middle-class, middle-age, feminist), or even that they are a result of class oppression (the contempt of the Norman conquerors for the language of their Anglo-Saxon serfs), ignores a much more likely explanation, it seems to me, and that is the sources and functions of the words themselves.

The best known of the tabooed sexual words, for example, comes 4 from the German *ficken,* meaning "to strike"; combined according to Partridge's etymological dictionary *Origins,* with the Latin sexual verb *futuere:* associated in turn with the Latin *fustis,* "a staff or cudgel"; the Celtic *buc,* "a point, hence to pierce"; the Irish *bot,* "the male member"; the Latin *battuere,* "to beat"; the Gaelic *batair,* "a cudgeller"; the Early Irish *bualaim,* "I strike"; and so forth. It is one of what etymologists sometimes called "the sadistic group of words for the man's part in copulation."

The brutality of this word, then, and its equivalents ("screw," 5 "bang," etc.) is not an illusion of the middle class or a crotchet of Women's Liberation. In their origins and imagery these words carry undeniably painful, if not sadistic, implications, the object of which is almost always female. Consider, for example, what a " screw" actually does to the wood it penetrates; what a painful, even mutilating, activity this kind of analogy suggests. "Screw" is particularly interesting in this context, since the noun, according to Partridge, comes from words meaning "groove," "nut," "ditch," "breeding sow," "scrofula" and "swelling," while the verb, besides its explicit imagery, has antecedent associations to "write on," "scratch," "scarify," and so forth—a revealing fusion of a mechanical or painful action with an obviously denigrated object.

Not all obscene words, of course, are as implicitly sadistic or 6 denigrating to women as these, but all that I know seem to serve a similar purpose: to reduce the human organism (especially the female organism) and human functions (especially sexual and procreative) to their least organic, most mechanical dimension; to substitute a trivializing or deforming resemblance for the complex human reality of what is being described.

Tabooed male descriptives, when they are not openly denigrat- 7
ing to women, often serve to divorce a male organ or function from
any significant interaction with the female. Take the word "testes,"
for example, suggesting "witnesses" (from the Latin *testis*) to the
sexual and procreative strengths of the male organ; and the obscene
counterpart of this word, which suggests little more than a mechanical shape. Or compare almost any of the "rich," "liberating" sexual
verbs, so fashionable today among male writers, with that much-de-
rived Latin word "copulate" ("to bind or join together") or even that
Anglo-Saxon phrase (which seems to have had no trouble surviving
the Norman Conquest) "make love."

How arrogantly self-involved the tabooed words seem in com- 8
parison to either of the other terms, and how contemptuous of the
female partner. Understandably so, of course, if she is only a "skirt,"
a "broad," a "chick," a "pussycat" or a "piece." If she is, in other
words no more than her skirt, or what her skirt conceals; no more than
a breeder, or the broadest part of her; no more than a piece of a human
being or a "piece of tail."

The most severely tabooed of all the female descriptives, inciden- 9
tally, are those like a "piece of tail," which suggests (either explicitly
or through antecedents) that there is no significant difference between
the female channel through which we are all conceived and born and
the anal outlet common to both sexes—a distinction that pornogra-
phers have always enjoyed obscuring.

This effort to deny women their biological identity, their individ- 10
uality, their humanness, is such an important aspect of obscene language that one can only marvel at how seldom, in an era preoccupied
with definitions of obscenity, this fact is brought to our attention. One
problem, of course, is that many of the people in the best position to
do this (critics, teachers, writers) are so reluctant today to admit that
they are angered or shocked by obscenity. Bored, maybe, unimpressed, aesthetically displeased, but—no matter how brutal or denigrating the material—never angered, never shocked.

And yet how eloquently angered, how piously shocked many of 11
these same people become if denigrating language is used about any
minority group other than women; if the obscenities are racial or
ethnic, that is, rather than sexual. Words like "coon," "kike," "spic,"
"wop," after all, deform identity, deny individuality and humanness in
almost exactly the same way that sexual vulgarisms and obscenities do.

No one that I know, least of all my students, would fail to question   12
the values of a society whose literature and entertainment rested
heavily on racial or ethnic pejoratives. Are the values of a society
whose literature and entertainment rest as heavily as ours on sexual
pejoratives any less questionable?

Meanings and Values

1a.   Explain the meaning of *irony* by use of at least one illustration from the
      latter part of this essay. (See Guide to Terms: *Irony.*)

 b.   What kind of irony is it?

2a.   Inasmuch as the selection itself includes many of the so-called "strong,
      earthy, gut-honest" words, could anyone logically call it obscene? Why,
      or why not?

 b.   To what extent, if at all, does the author's point of view help determine
      your answer to question 2a? (Guide: *Point of View.*)

3a.   Compose, in your own words, a compact statement of Lawrence's
      thesis. (Guide: *Thesis.*)

 b.   Are all parts of the essay completely relevant to this thesis? Justify your
      answer.

 c.   Does the writing have unity?

4.   Evaluate this composition by use of our three-question system. (Guide:
      Evaluation.)

Argumentative Techniques

1.   What is the purpose of this essay? (Guide: *Purpose.*)

2a.   What objection to her opinion does the author refute in paragraph 3,
      and how does she refute it? (Guide: *Refutation.*)

 b.   Where else in the essay does she refute opposing arguments?

3a.   Are the evidence and supporting arguments in this essay arranged in
      a refutation-proof pattern?

 b.   If not, describe the arrangement of the essay.

4a.   Which of the methods "peculiar to definition alone" (see the introduc-
      tion to Section 7) does the author employ in developing this essay?

 b.   Which of the regular patterns of exposition does she also use?

 c.   Explain your reasons and cite examples to justify your answers to 4a
      and 4b.

5a. Which of the standard techniques of introduction are used? (Guide: *Introductions*.)

b. Which methods are used to close the essay? (Guide: *Closing*.)

Diction and Vocabulary

1a. How, if at all, is this discussion of words related to *connotation*? (Guide: *Connotation/Denotation*.)

b. To what extent would connotations in this matter depend on the setting and circumstances in which the words are used? Cite illustrations to clarify your answer.

2. In view of the fact that the author uses frankly many of the "gut-honest" words, why do you suppose she plainly avoids others, such as in paragraphs 4 and 7?

3. The author says that a "kind of analogy" is suggested by some of the words discussed (par. 5). If you have studied Section 4 of this book, does her use of the term *analogy* seem in conflict with what you believed it to mean? Explain.

4. Study the author's uses of the following words, consulting the dictionary as needed: existential, grimaces (par. 1); etymological, cudgel (4); sadistic (4–6); crotchet, scrofula, explicit, antecedent, scarify (5); denigrated (5–7, 10–11); aesthetically (10); pejoratives (12).

Suggestions for Writing and Discussion

1. Why is it the so-called middle class that is so often accused of having sexual hangups—and hence all sorts of sex-related taboos?

2. Probably most people using obscene language (obscene, at least, by Lawrence's definition) are not aware of the etymology of the words. Can they, therefore, be accused of denigrating women—or is ignorance a suitable defense, as it is not in legal matters?

3. Does the author make a justifiable comparison between obscene words and ethnic pejoratives? Using illustrations for specificity, carry the comparison further to show why it is sound, or explain why you consider it a weak comparison.

(NOTE: Suggestions for topics requiring development by use of ARGUMENT are on page 491, at the end of this section.)

MARTIN LUTHER KING, JR.

MARTIN LUTHER KING, JR. (1929–1968), was a Baptist minister, the president of the Southern Christian Leadership Conference, and a respected leader in the nationwide movement for equal rights for blacks. He was born in Atlanta, Georgia, and earned degrees from Morehouse College (A.B., 1948), Crozer Theological Seminary (B.D., 1951), Boston University (Ph.D., 1955), and Chicago Theological Seminary (D.D., 1957). He held honorary degrees from numerous other colleges and universities and was awarded the Nobel Peace Prize in 1964. Some of his books are *Stride Toward Freedom* (1958), *Strength to Love* (1963), and *Why We Can't Wait* (1964). King was assassinated April 4, 1968, in Memphis, Tennessee.

Letter from Birmingham Jail[1]

This letter, written to King's colleagues in the ministry, is a reasoned explanation for his actions during the civil rights protests in Birmingham. It is a good example of both persuasion and logical argument. Here the two are completely compatible, balancing each other in rather intricate but convincing and effective patterns.

[1] This response to a published statement by eight fellow clergymen from Alabama (Bishop C. C. J. Carpenter, Bishop Joseph A. Durick, Rabbi Hilton L. Grafman, Bishop Paul Hardin, Bishop Holan B. Harmon, the Reverend George M. Murray, the Reverend Edward V. Ramage, and the Reverend Earl Stallings) was composed under somewhat constricting circumstances. Begun on the margins of the newspaper in which the statement appeared while I was in jail, the letter was continued on scraps of writing paper supplied by a friendly Negro trusty, and concluded on a pad my attorneys were eventually permitted to leave me. Although the text remains in substance unaltered, I have indulged in the author's prerogative of polishing it for publication.—King's note.

MY DEAR FELLOW CLERGYMEN:

While confined here in the Birmingham city jail, I came across your recent statement calling my present activities "unwise and untimely." Seldom do I pause to answer criticism of my work and ideas. If I sought to answer all the criticisms that cross my desk, my secretaries would have little time for anything other than such correspondence in the course of the day, and I would have no time for constructive work. But since I feel that you are men of genuine good will and that your criticisms are sincerely set forth, I want to try to answer your statement in what I hope will be patient and reasonable terms.

I think I should indicate why I am here in Birmingham, since you have been influenced by the view which argues against "outsiders coming in." I have the honor of serving as president of the Southern Christian Leadership Conference, an organization operating in every southern state, with headquarters in Atlanta, Georgia. We have some eighty-five affiliated organizations across the South, and one of them is the Alabama Christian Movement for Human Rights. Frequently we share staff, educational, and financial resources with our affiliates. Several months ago the affiliate here in Birmingham asked us to be on call to engage in a nonviolent direct-action program if such were deemed necessary. We readily consented, and when the hour came, we lived up to our promise. So I, along with several members of my staff, am here because I was invited here. I am here because I have organizational ties here.

But more basically, I am in Birmingham because injustice is here. Just as the prophets of the eighth century B.C. left their villages and carried their "thus saith the Lord" far beyond the boundaries of their home towns, and just as the Apostle Paul left his village of Tarsus and carried the gospel of Jesus Christ to the far corners of the Greco-Roman world, so am I compelled to carry the gospel of freedom beyond my own home town. Like Paul, I must constantly respond to the Macedonian call for aid.

Moreover, I am cognizant of the interrelatedness of all communities and states. I cannot sit idly by in Atlanta and not be concerned about what happens in Birmingham. Injustice anywhere is a threat to justice everywhere. We are caught in an inescapable network of mutuality, tied in a single garment of destiny. Whatever affects one directly, affects all indirectly. Never again can we afford to live with the narrow, provincial "outside agitator" idea. Anyone who lives inside the United States can never be considered an outsider within its bounds.

You deplore the demonstrations taking place in Birmingham. But your statement, I am sorry to say, fails to express a similar concern for the conditions that brought about the demonstrations. I am sure that none of you would want to rest content with the superficial kind of social analysis that deals merely with effects and does not grapple with underlying causes. It is unfortunate that demonstrations are taking place in Birmingham, but it is even more unfortunate that the city's white power structure left the Negro community with no alternative.

In any nonviolent campaign there are four basic steps: collection of the facts to determine whether injustices exist; negotiation; self-purification; and direct action. We have gone through all these steps in Birmingham. There can be no gainsaying the fact that racial injustice engulfs this community. Birmingham is probably the most thoroughly segregated city in the United States. Its ugly record of brutality is widely known. Negroes have experienced grossly unjust treatment in the courts. There have been more unsolved bombings of Negro homes and churches in Birmingham than in any other city in the nation. These are the hard, brutal facts of the case. On the basis of these conditions, Negro leaders sought to negotiate with the city fathers. But the latter consistently refused to engage in good-faith negotiation.

Then, last September, came the opportunity to talk with leaders of Birmingham's economic community. In the course of the negotiations, certain promises were made by the merchants—for example, to remove the stores' humiliating racial signs. On the basis of these promises, the Reverend Fred Shuttlesworth and the leaders of the Alabama Christian Movement for Human Rights agreed to a moratorium on all demonstrations. As the weeks and months went by, we realized that we were the victims of a broken promise. A few signs, briefly removed, returned; the others remained.

As in so many past experiences, our hopes had been blasted, and the shadow of deep disappointment settled upon us. We had no alternative except to prepare for direct action, whereby we would present our very bodies as a means of laying our case before the conscience of the local and the national community. Mindful of the difficulties involved, we decided to undertake a process of self-purification. We began a series of workshops on nonviolence, and we repeatedly asked ourselves: "Are you able to accept blows without retaliating?" "Are you able to endure the ordeal of jail?" We decided to schedule our direct-action program for the Easter season, realizing that except for Christmas, this is the main shopping period of the year. Knowing that a strong economic-withdrawal program would be the by-product of direct action, we felt that this would be the best time to bring pressure to bear on the merchants for the needed change.

9   Then it occurred to us that Birmingham's mayoral election was coming up in March, and we speedily decided to postpone action until after election day. When we discovered that the Commissioner of Public Safety, Eugene "Bull" Connor, had piled up enough votes to be in the run-off, we decided again to postpone action until the day after the run-off so that the demonstrations could not be used to cloud the issues. Like many others, we waited to see Mr. Connor defeated, and to this end we endured postponement after postponement. Having aided in this community need, we felt that our direct-action program could be delayed no longer.

10   You may well ask, "Why direct action? Why sit-ins, marches, and so forth? Isn't negotiation a better path?" You are quite right in calling for negotiation. Indeed, this is the very purpose of direct action. Nonviolent direct action seeks to create such a crisis and foster such a tension that a community which has constantly refused to negotiate is forced to confront the issue. It seeks so to dramatize the issue that it can no longer be ignored. My citing the creation of tension as part of the work of the nonviolent-resister may sound rather shocking. But I must confess that I am not afraid of the word "tension." I have earnestly opposed violent tension, but there is a type of constructive, nonviolent tension which is necessary for growth. Just as Socrates felt that it was necessary to create a tension in the mind so that individuals could rise from the bondage of myths and half-truths to the unfettered realm of creative analysis and objective appraisal, so must we see the need for nonviolent gadflies to create the kind of tension in society that will help men rise from the dark depths of prejudice and racism to the majestic heights of understanding and brotherhood.

11   The purpose of our direct-action program is to create a situation so crisis-packed that it will inevitably open the door to negotiation. I therefore concur with you in your call for negotiation. Too long has our beloved Southland been bogged down in a tragic effort to live in monologue rather than dialogue.

12   One of the basic points in your statement is that the action that I and my associates have taken in Birmingham is untimely. Some have

asked: "Why didn't you give the new city administration time to act?"
The only answer that I can give to this query is that the new Birmingham administration must be prodded about as much as the outgoing one, before it will act. We are sadly mistaken if we feel that the election of Albert Boutwell as mayor will bring the millennium to Birmingham. While Mr. Boutwell is a much more gentle person than Mr. Connor, they are both segregationists, dedicated to maintenance of the status quo. I have hoped that Mr. Boutwell will be reasonable enough to see the futility of massive resistance to desegregation. But he will not see this without pressure from devotees of civil rights. My friends, I must say to you that we have not made a single gain in civil rights without determined legal and nonviolent pressure. Lamentably, it is an historical fact that privileged groups seldom give up their privileges voluntarily. Individuals may see the moral light and voluntarily give up their unjust posture; but, as Reinhold Niebuhr has reminded us, groups tend to be more immoral than individuals.

We know through painful experience that freedom is never vol-   13
untarily given by the oppressor; it must be demanded by the oppressed. Frankly, I have yet to engage in a direct-action campaign that was "well timed" in the view of those who have not suffered unduly from the disease of segregation. For years now I have heard the word "Wait!" It rings in the ear of every Negro with piercing familiarity. This "Wait" has almost always meant "Never." We must come to see, with one of our distinguished jurists, that "justice too long delayed is justice denied."

We have waited for more than 340 years for our constitutional   14
and God-given rights. The nations of Asia and Africa are moving with jetlike speed toward gaining political independence, but we still creep at horse-and-buggy pace toward gaining a cup of coffee at a lunch counter. Perhaps it is easy for those who have never felt the stinging darts of segregation to say, "Wait." But when you have seen vicious mobs lynch your mothers and fathers at will and drown your sisters and brothers at whim; when you have seen hate-filled policemen curse, kick, and even kill your black brothers and sisters; when you see the vast majority of your twenty million Negro brothers smothering in an airtight cage of poverty in the midst of an affluent society; when you suddenly find your tongue twisted and your speech stammering as you seek to explain to your six-year-old daughter why she can't go to the public amusement park that has just been advertised on television, and see tears welling up in her eyes when she is told

that Funtown is closed to colored children, and see ominous clouds of inferiority beginning to form in her little mental sky, and see her beginning to distort her personality by developing an unconscious bitterness toward white people; when you have to concoct an answer for a five-year-old son who is asking, "Daddy, why do white people treat colored people so mean?"; when you take a cross-country drive and find it necessary to sleep night after night in the uncomfortable corners of your automobile because no motel will accept you; when you are humiliated day in and day out by nagging signs reading "white" and "colored"; when your first name becomes "nigger," your middle name becomes "boy" (however old you are) and your last name becomes "John," and your wife and mother are never given the respected title "Mrs."; when you are harried by day and haunted by night by the fact that you are a Negro, living constantly at tiptoe stance, never quite knowing what to expect next, and are plagued with inner fears and outer resentments; when you are forever fighting a degenerating sense of "nobodiness"—then you will understand why we find it difficult to wait. There comes a time when the cup of endurance runs over, and men are no longer willing to be plunged into the abyss of despair. I hope, sirs, you can understand our legitimate and unavoidable impatience.

You express a great deal of anxiety over our willingness to break laws. This is certainly a legitimate concern. Since we so diligently urge people to obey the Supreme Court's decision of 1954 outlawing segregation in the public schools, at first glance it may seem rather paradoxical for us consciously to break laws. One may well ask: "How can you advocate breaking some laws and obeying others?" The answer lies in the fact that there are two types of laws: just and unjust. I would be the first to advocate obeying just laws. One has not only a legal but a moral responsibility to obey just laws. Conversely, one has a moral responsibility to disobey unjust laws. I would agree with St. Augustine that "an unjust law is no law at all." 15

Now, what is the difference between the two? How does one determine whether a law is just or unjust? A just law is a man-made code that squares with the moral law or the law of God. An unjust law is a code that is out of harmony with the moral law. To put it in the terms of St. Thomas Aquinas: An unjust law is a human law that is not rooted in eternal law and natural law. Any law that uplifts human personality is just. Any law that degrades human personality is unjust. All segregation statutes are unjust because segregation 16 distorts the soul and damages the personality. It gives the segregator a false sense of superiority and the segregated a false sense of inferiority. Segregation, to use the terminology of the Jewish philosopher Martin Buber, substitutes an "I-it" relationship for an "I-thou" relationship and ends up relegating persons to the status of things. Hence segregation is not only politically, economically, and sociologically unsound, it is morally wrong and sinful. Paul Tillich has said that sin is separation. Is not segregation an existential expression of man's tragic separation, his awful estrangement, his terrible sinfulness? Thus it is that I can urge men to obey the 1954 decision of the Supreme Court, for it is morally right; and I can urge them to disobey segregation ordinances, for they are morally wrong.

Let us consider a more concrete example of just and unjust laws.   17
An unjust law is a code that a numerical or power majority group compels a minority group to obey but does not make binding on itself. This is *difference* made legal. By the same token, a just law is a code that a majority compels a minority to follow and that it is willing to follow itself. This is *sameness* made legal.

Let me give another explanation. A law is unjust if it is inflicted   18
on a minority that, as a result of being denied the right to vote, had no part in enacting or devising the law. Who can say that the legislature of Alabama which set up that state's segregation laws was democratically elected? Throughout Alabama all sorts of devious methods are used to prevent Negroes from becoming registered voters, and there are some counties in which, even though Negroes constitute a majority of the population, not a single Negro is registered. Can any law enacted under such circumstances be considered democratically structured?

Sometimes a law is just on its face and unjust in its application.   19
For instance, I have been arrested on a charge of parading without a permit. Now, there is nothing wrong in having an ordinance which requires a permit for a parade. But such an ordinance becomes unjust when it is used to maintain segregation and to deny citizens the First Amendment privilege of peaceful assembly and protest.

I hope you are able to see the distinction I am trying to point out.   20
In no sense do I advocate evading or defying the law, as would the rabid segregationist. That would lead to anarchy. One who breaks an unjust law must do so openly, lovingly, and with a willingness to accept the penalty. I submit that an individual who breaks a law that conscience tells him is unjust, and who willingly accepts the penalty

of imprisonment in order to arouse the conscience of the community over its injustice, is in reality expressing the highest respect for the law.

Of course, there is nothing new about this kind of civil disobedi- 21
ence. It was evidenced sublimely in the refusal of Shadrach, Meshach, and Abednego to obey the laws of Nebuchadnezzar, on the ground that a higher moral law was at stake. It was practiced superbly by the early Christians, who were willing to face hungry lions and the excruciating pain of chopping blocks rather than submit to certain unjust laws of the Roman Empire. To a degree, academic freedom is a reality today because Socrates practiced civil disobedience. In our own nation, the Boston Tea Party represented a massive act of civil disobedience.

We should never forget that everything Adolf Hitler did in 22
Germany was "legal" and everything the Hungarian freedom fighters did in Hungary was "illegal." It was "illegal" to aid and comfort a Jew in Hitler's Germany. Even so, I am sure that, had I lived in Germany at the time, I would have aided and comforted my Jewish brothers. If today I lived in a Communist country where certain principles dear to the Christian faith are suppressed, I would openly advocate disobeying that country's anti-religious laws.

I must make two honest confessions to you, my Christian and 23
Jewish brothers. First, I must confess that over the past few years I have been gravely disappointed with the white moderate. I have almost reached the regrettable conclusion that the Negro's great stumbling block in his stride toward freedom is not the White Citizen's Counciler or the Ku Klux Klanner, but the white moderate, who is more devoted to "order" than to justice; who prefers a negative peace which is the absence of tension to a positive peace which is the presence of justice; who constantly says, "I agree with you in the goal you seek, but I cannot agree with your methods of direct action"; who paternalistically believes he can set the timetable for another man's freedom; who lives by a mythical concept of time and who constantly advises the Negro to wait for a "more convenient season." Shallow understanding from people of good will is more frustrating than absolute misunderstanding from people of ill will. Lukewarm acceptance is much more bewildering than outright rejection.

I had hoped that the white moderate would understand that law 24
and order exist for the purpose of establishing justice and that when they fail in this purpose they become the dangerously structured

dams that block the flow of social progress. I had hoped that the white moderate would understand that the present tension in the South is a necessary phase of the transition from an obnoxious negative peace, in which the Negro passively accepted his unjust plight, to a substantive and positive peace, in which all men will respect the dignity and worth of human personality. Actually, we who engage in nonviolent direct action are not the creators of tension. We merely bring to the surface the hidden tension that is already alive. We bring it out in the open, where it can be seen and dealt with. Like a boil that can never be cured so long as it is covered up but must be opened with all its ugliness to the natural medicines of air and light, injustice must be exposed, with all the tension its exposure creates, to the light of human conscience and the air of national opinion, before it can be cured.

In your statement you assert that our actions, even though peace- 25
ful, must be condemned because they precipitate violence. But is this a logical assertion? Isn't this like condemning a robbed man because his possession of money precipitated the evil act of robbery? Isn't this like condemning Socrates because his unswerving commitment to truth and his philosophical inquiries precipitated the act by the misguided populace in which they made him drink hemlock? Isn't this like condemning Jesus because his unique God-consciousness and never-ceasing devotion to God's will precipitated the evil act of crucifixion? We must come to see that, as the federal courts have consistently affirmed, it is wrong to urge an individual to cease his efforts to gain his basic constitutional rights because the quest may precipitate violence. Society must protect the robbed and punish the robber.

I had also hoped that the white moderate would reject the myth 26
concerning time in relation to the struggle for freedom. I have just received a letter from a white brother in Texas. He writes: "All Christians know that the colored people will receive equal rights eventually, but it is possible that you are in too great a religious hurry. It has taken Christianity almost two thousand years to accomplish what it has. The teachings of Christ take time to come to earth." Such an attitude stems from a tragic misconception of time, from the strangely irrational notion that there is something in the very flow of time that will inevitably cure all ills. Actually, time itself is neutral; it can be used either destructively or constructively. More and more I feel that the people of ill will have used time much more effectively than have the people of good will. We will have to repent in this

generation not merely for the hateful words and actions of the bad people, but for the appalling silence of the good people. Human progress never rolls in on wheels of inevitability; it comes through the tireless efforts of men willing to be co-workers with God, and without this hard work, time itself becomes an ally of the forces of social stagnation. We must use time creatively, in the knowledge that the time is always ripe to do right. Now is the time to make real the promise of democracy and transform our pending national elegy into a creative psalm of brotherhood. Now is the time to lift our national policy from the quicksand of racial injustice to the solid rock of human dignity.

You speak of our activity in Birmingham as extreme. At first I was rather disappointed that fellow clergymen would see my nonviolent efforts as those of an extremist. I began thinking about the fact that I stand in the middle of two opposing forces in the Negro community. One is a force of complacency, made up in part of Negroes who, as a result of long years of oppression, are so drained of self-respect and a sense of "somebodiness" that they have adjusted to segregation; and in part of a few middle-class Negroes who, because of a degree of academic and economic security and because in some ways they profit by segregation, have become insensitive to the problems of the masses. The other force is one of bitterness and hatred, and it comes perilously close to advocating violence. It is expressed in the various black nationalist groups that are springing up across the nation, the largest and best-known being Elijah Muhammad's Muslim movement. Nourished by the Negro's frustration over the continued existence of racial discrimination, this movement is made up of people who have lost faith in America, who have absolutely repudiated Christianity, and who have concluded that the white man is an incorrigible "devil." 27

I have tried to stand between these two forces, saying that we need emulate neither the "do-nothingism" of the complacent nor the hatred and despair of the black nationalist. For there is the more excellent way of love and nonviolent protest. I am grateful to God that, through the influence of the Negro church, the way of nonviolence became an integral part of our struggle. 28

If this philosophy had not emerged, by now many streets of the South would, I am convinced, be flowing with blood. And I am further convinced that if our white brothers dismiss as "rabble-rousers" and "outside agitators" those of us who employ nonviolent 29 direct action, and if they refuse to support our nonviolent efforts, millions of Negroes will, out of frustration and despair, seek solace and security in black-nationalist ideologies—a development that would inevitably lead to a frightening racial nightmare.

Oppressed people cannot remain oppressed forever. The yearn-   30
ing for freedom eventually manifests itself, and that is what has happened to the American Negro. Something within has reminded him of his birthright of freedom, and something without has re-minded him that it can be gained. Consciously or unconsciously, he has been caught up by the *Zeitgeist,* and with his black brothers of Africa and his brown and yellow brothers of Asia, South America, and the Caribbean, the United States Negro is moving with a sense of great urgency toward the promised land of racial justice. If one recognizes this vital urge that has engulfed the Negro community, one should readily understand why public demonstrations are taking place. The Negro has many pent-up resentments and latent frustrations, and he must release them. So let him march; let him make prayer pilgrimages to the city hall; let him go on freedom rides—and try to understand why he must do so. If his repressed emotions are not released in nonviolent ways, they will seek expression through violence; this is not a threat but a fact of history. So I have not said to my people, "Get rid of your discontent." Rather, I have tried to say that this normal and healthy discontent can be channeled into the creative outlet of nonviolent direct action. And now this approach is being termed extremist.

But though I was initially disappointed at being categorized as   31
an extremist, as I continued to think about the matter I gradually gained a measure of satisfaction from the label. Was not Jesus an extremist for love: "Love your enemies, bless them that curse you, do good to them that hate you, and pray for them which despitefully use you, and persecute you." Was not Amos an extremist for justice: "Let justice roll down like waters and righteousness like an everflowing stream." Was not Paul an extremist for the Christian gospel: "I bear in my body the marks of the Lord Jesus." Was not Martin Luther an extremist: "Here I stand; I cannot do otherwise, so help me God." And John Bunyan: "I will stay in jail to the end of my days before I make a butchery of my conscience." And Abraham Lincoln: "This nation can-not survive half slave and half free." And Thomas Jefferson: "We hold these truths to be self-evident, that all men are created equal . . ." So the question is not whether we will be extremists, but what kind of

extremists we will be. Will we be extremists for hate or for love? Will we be extremists for the preservation of injustice or for the extension of justice? In that dramatic scene on Calvary's hill three men were crucified. We must never forget that all three were crucified for the same crime—the crime of extremism. Two were extremists for immorality, and thus fell below their environment. The other, Jesus Christ, was an extremist for love, truth, and goodness, and thereby rose above his environment. Perhaps the South, the nation, and the world are in dire need of creative extremists.

I had hoped that the white moderate would see this need. 32 Perhaps I was too optimistic; perhaps I expected too much. I suppose I should have realized that few members of the oppressor race can understand the deep groans and passionate yearnings of the oppressed race, and still fewer have the vision to see that injustice must be rooted out by strong, persistent, and determined action. I am thankful, however, that some of our white brothers in the South have grasped the meaning of this social revolution and committed themselves to it. They are still all too few in quantity, but they are big in quality. Some—such as Ralph McGill, Lillian Smith, Harry Golden, James McBride Dabbs, Anne Braden, and Sarah Patton Boyle—have written about our struggle in eloquent and prophetic terms. Others have marched with us down nameless streets of the South. They have languished in filthy, roach-infested jails, suffering the abuse and brutality of policemen who view them as "dirty nigger-lovers." Unlike so many of their moderate brothers and sisters, they have recognized the urgency of the moment and sensed the need for powerful "action" antidotes to combat the disease of segregation.

Let me take note of my other major disappointment. I have been 33 so greatly disappointed with the white church and its leadership. Of course, there are some notable exceptions. I am not unmindful of the fact that each of you has taken some significant stands on this issue. I commend you, Reverend Stallings, for your Christian stand on this past Sunday, in welcoming Negroes to your worship service on a nonsegregated basis. I commend the Catholic leaders of this state for integrating Spring Hill College several years ago.

But despite these notable exceptions, I must honestly reiterate 34 that I have been disappointed with the church. I do not say this as one of those negative critics who can always find something wrong with the church. I say this as a minister of the gospel, who loves the church;

who was nurtured in its bosom; who has been sustained by its spiritual blessings and who will remain true to it as long as the cord of life shall lengthen.

When I was suddenly catapulted into the leadership of the bus   35
protest in Montgomery, Alabama, a few years ago, I felt we would be supported by the white church. I felt that the white ministers, priests, and rabbis of the South would be among our strongest allies. Instead, some have been outright opponents, refusing to understand the freedom movement and misrepresenting its leaders; all too many others have been more cautious than courageous and have remained silent behind the anesthetizing security of stained glass windows.

In spite of my shattered dreams, I came to Birmingham with the   36
hope that the white religious leadership of this community would see the justice of our cause and, with deep moral concern, would serve as the channel through which our just grievances could reach the power structure. I had hoped that each of you would understand. But again I have been disappointed.

I have heard numerous southern religious leaders admonish   37
their worshipers to comply with a desegregation decision because it is the law, but I have longed to hear white ministers declare: "Follow this decree because integration is morally right and because the Negro is your brother." In the midst of blatant injustices inflicted upon the Negro, I have watched white churchmen stand on the sideline and mouth pious irrelevancies and sanctimonious trivialities. In the midst of a mighty struggle to rid our nation of racial and economic injustice I have heard many ministers say: "Those are social issues, with which the gospel has no real concern." And I have watched many churches commit themselves to a completely otherworldly religion which makes a strange, un-Biblical distinction between body and soul, between the sacred and the secular.

I have traveled the length and breadth of Alabama, Mississippi,   38
and all the other southern states. On sweltering summer days and crisp autumn mornings I have looked at the South's beautiful churches with their lofty spires pointing heavenward. I have beheld the impressive outlines of her massive religious-education buildings. Over and over I have found myself asking: "What kind of people worship here? Who is their God? Where were their voices when the lips of Governor Barnett dripped with words of interposition and nullification? Where were they when Governor Wallace gave a clarion call for defiance and hatred? Where were their voices of support when

bruised and weary Negro men and women decided to rise from the dark dungeons of complacency to the bright hills of creative protest?"

Yes, these questions are still in my mind. In deep disappointment I have wept over the laxity of the church. But be assured that my tears have been tears of love. There can be no deep disappointment where there is not deep love. Yes, I love the church. How could I do otherwise? I am in the rather unique position of being the son, the grandson, and the great-grandson of preachers. Yes, I see the church as the body of Christ. But, oh! How we have blemished and scarred that body through social neglect and through fear of being nonconformists. [39]

There was a time when the church was very powerful—in the time when the early Christians rejoiced at being deemed worthy to suffer for what they believed. In those days the church was not merely a thermometer that recorded the ideas and principles of popular opinion; it was a thermostat that transformed the mores of society. Whenever the early Christians entered a town, the people in power became disturbed and immediately sought to convict the Christians for being "disturbers of the peace" and "outside agitators." But the Christians pressed on, in the conviction that they were "a colony of heaven," called to obey God rather than man. Small in number, they were big in commitment. They were too God-intoxicated to be "astronomically intimidated." By their effort and example they brought an end to such ancient evils as infanticide and gladiatorial contests. [40]

Things are different now. So often the contemporary church is a weak, ineffectual voice with an uncertain sound. So often it is an archdefender of the status quo. Far from being disturbed by the presence of the church, the power structure of the average community is consoled by the church's silent—and often even vocal—sanction of things as they are. [41]

But the judgment of God is upon the church as never before. If today's church does not recapture the sacrificial spirit of the early church, it will lose its authenticity, forfeit the loyalty of millions, and be dismissed as an irrelevant social club with no meaning for the twentieth century. Every day I meet young people whose disappointment with the church has turned into outright disgust. [42]

Perhaps I have once again been too optimistic. Is organized religion too inextricably bound to the status quo to save our nation and the world? Perhaps I must turn my faith to the inner spiritual [43] church, the church within the church, as the true *ekklesia*[2] and the hope of the world. But again I am thankful to God that some noble souls from the ranks of organized religion have broken loose from the paralyzing chains of conformity and joined us as active partners in the struggle for freedom. They have left their secure congregations and walked the streets of Albany, Georgia, with us. They have gone down the highways of the South on tortuous rides for freedom. Yes, they have gone to jail with us. Some have been dismissed from their churches, have lost the support of their bishops and fellow ministers. But they have acted in the faith that right defeated is stronger than evil triumphant. Their witness has been the spiritual salt that has preserved the true meaning of the gospel in these troubled times. They have carved a tunnel of hope through the dark mountain of disappointment.

I hope the church as a whole will meet the challenge of this   44
decisive hour. But even if the church does not come to the aid of justice, I have no despair about the future. I have no fear about the outcome of our struggle in Birmingham, even if our motives are at present misunderstood. We will reach the goal of freedom in Birmingham and all over the nation, because the goal of America is freedom. Abused and scorned though we may be, our destiny is tied up with America's destiny. Before the pilgrims landed at Plymouth, we were here. Before the pen of Jefferson etched the majestic words of the Declaration of Independence across the pages of history, we were here. For more than two centuries, our forebears labored in this country without wages; they made cotton king; they built the homes of their masters while suffering gross injustice and shameful humiliation—and yet out of a bottomless vitality they continued to thrive and develop. If the inexpressible cruelties of slavery could not stop us, the opposition we now face will surely fail. We will win our freedom because the sacred heritage of our nation and the eternal will of God are embodied in our echoing demands.

Before closing I feel impelled to mention one other point in your   45
statement that has troubled me profoundly. You warmly commended the Birmingham police force for keeping "order" and "preventing violence." I doubt that you would have so warmly commended the police force if you had seen its dogs sinking their teeth into unarmed, nonviolent Negroes. I doubt that you would so quickly commend the

---

[2]The Greek New Testament word for the early Christian church (Editors' note).

policemen if you were to observe their ugly and inhumane treatment of Negroes here in the city jail; if you were to watch them push and curse old Negro women and young Negro girls; if you were to see them slap and kick old Negro men and young boys; if you were to observe them, as they did on two occasions, refuse to give us food because we wanted to sing our grace together. I cannot join you in your praise of the Birmingham police department.

It is true that the police have exercised a degree of discipline in handling the demonstrators. In this sense they have conducted themselves rather "nonviolently" in public. But for what purpose? To preserve the evil system of segregation. Over the past few years I have consistently preached that nonviolence demands that the means we use must be as pure as the ends we seek. I have tried to make clear that it is wrong to use immoral means to attain moral ends. But now I must affirm that it is just as wrong, or perhaps even more so, to use moral means to preserve immoral ends. Perhaps Mr. Connor and his policemen have been rather nonviolent in public, as was Chief Pritchett in Albany, Georgia, but they have used the moral means of nonviolence to maintain the immoral end of racial injustice. As T. S. Eliot has said, "The last temptation is the greatest treason: To do the right deed for the wrong reason." 46

I wish you had commended the Negro sit-inners and demonstrators of Birmingham for their sublime courage, their willingness to suffer, and their amazing discipline in the midst of great provocation. One day the South will recognize its real heroes. They will be the James Merediths, with the noble sense of purpose that enables them to face jeering and hostile mobs, and with the agonizing loneliness that characterizes the life of the pioneer. They will be old, oppressed, battered Negro women, symbolized in a seventy-two-year-old woman in Montgomery, Alabama, who rose up with a sense of dignity and with her people decided not to ride segregated buses, and who responded with ungrammatical profundity to one who inquired about her weariness: "My feets is tired, but my soul is at rest." They will be the young high school and college students, the young ministers of the gospel and a host of their elders, courageously and nonviolently sitting in at lunch counters and willingly going to jail for conscience' sake. One day the South will know that when these disinherited children of God sat down at lunch counters, they were in reality standing up for what is best in the American dream and for the most sacred values in our Judaeo-Christian heritage, thereby 47 bringing our nation back to those great wells of democracy which were dug deep by the founding fathers in their formulation of the Constitution and the Declaration of Independence.

Never before have I written so long a letter. I'm afraid it is much   48
too long to take your precious time. I can assure you that it would have been much shorter if I had been writing from a comfortable desk, but what else can one do when he is alone in a narrow jail cell, other than write long letters, think long thoughts, and pray long prayers?

If I have said anything in this letter that overstates the truth and   49
indicates an unreasonable impatience, I beg you to forgive me. If I have said anything that understates the truth and indicates my having a patience that allows me to settle for anything less than brotherhood, I beg God to forgive me.

I hope this letter finds you strong in the faith. I also hope that   50
circumstances will soon make it possible for me to meet each of you, not as an integrationist or a civil-rights leader but as a fellow clergyman and a Christian brother. Let us all hope that the dark clouds of racial prejudice will soon pass away and the deep fog of misunderstanding will be lifted from our fear-drenched communities, and in some not too distant tomorrow the radiant stars of love and brotherhood will shine over our great nation with all their scintillating beauty.

Yours for the cause of Peace and Brotherhood,
MARTIN LUTHER KING, JR.

Meanings and Values

1a. Does King's purpose in this essay go beyond responding to the criticism of the white clergymen?

  b. If so, what is his broader purpose?

2. Reconstruct as many of the arguments in the clergymen's letter as you can by studying King's refutation of their accusations.

3. What arguments are used in the essay to justify the demonstrations?

4. Summarize the distinction King makes between just and unjust laws.

5a. What kind of behavior did King expect from the white moderates?

  b. Why was he disappointed?

6. How does King defend himself and his followers against the accusation that their actions lead to violence?

7. What is the thesis of this essay?

8.   Like many other argumentative essays, this was written in response to a specific situation; yet it is widely regarded as a classic essay. What qualities give the essay its broad and lasting appeal?

Argumentative Techniques

1.   How does King establish his reasonableness and fairness so that his audience will take the arguments in the essay seriously even if they are inclined at the start to reject his point of view?

2.   Identify as many of the expository patterns as you can in this essay and explain what each contributes to the argument. (Guide: *Unity*.)

3a.   What standard techniques of refutation are used in this essay to deal with the accusations made by the clergymen? (Guide: *Refutation*.)

  b.   Are any other strategies of refutation used in the essay?

4a.   State the argument in paragraph 6 as a syllogism. (See the introduction to Section 10, "Reasoning by Use of *Induction* and *Deduction*.")

  b.   Do the same with the argument in paragraphs 15–22.

5.   Identify several examples of inductive argument in this essay.

6.   At what points in the argument does King use several examples, where one would do, in order to strengthen the argument through variety in evidence?

Diction and Vocabulary

1.   Locate an example of each of the following figures of speech in the essay and explain what it contributes to the argument. (Guide: *Figures of Speech*.)

  a.   Metaphor.

  b.   Allusion.

  c.   Simile.

  d.   Paradox.

2a.   Discuss what resources of syntax King uses to construct a 28-line sentence in paragraph 14—without confusing the reader. (Guide: *Syntax*.)

  b.   Choose a paragraph that displays considerable variety in sentence length and structure and show how King uses variety in sentence style to convey his point. (Guide: *Style/Tone*.)

3.   Choose two paragraphs, each with a different tone, and discuss how the diction of the passages differs and how the diction in each case contributes to the tone. (Guide: *Diction*.)

4. In many passages King uses the resources of diction and syntax to add emotional impact to logical argument. Choose such a passage and discuss how it mingles logic and emotion.

Suggestions for Writing and Discussion

1. Use some of King's arguments to construct a defense of a more recent act of protest or to encourage people to protest a policy you consider unjust. Or, if you wish, draw on his arguments to attack a recent protest on the grounds that it does not meet the high standards he sets.

2. Discuss the practical consequences of King's distinction between just and unjust laws.

3. To what extent does the racism against which King was protesting still exist in our society? Has it been replaced by other forms of discrimination?

(NOTE: Suggestions for topics requiring development by use of ARGUMENT follow.)

Writing Suggestions for Section 11
Argument

Choose one of the following topic areas, identify an issue (a conflict or problem) within it, and prepare an essay that tries to convince readers to share your opinion about the issue and to take any appropriate action. Use a variety of evidence in your essay, and choose any pattern of development you consider proper for the topic, for your thesis, and for the intended audience.

1. Gun control.
2. The quality of education in American elementary and secondary schools.
3. Treatment of critically ill newborn babies.
4. Hunting.
5. Euthanasia.
6. Censorship in public schools and libraries.
7. College athletics.
8. The problem of toxic waste or a similar environmental problem.
9. Careers versus family responsibilities.
10. The separation of church and state.
11. Law on the drinking age or on drunk driving.
12. Evolution versus creationism.
13. Arms control.
14. Government spending on social programs.
15. The quality of television programming.
16. The impact of divorce.
17. The effects of television viewing on children.
18. Professional sports.
19. Violence in service of an ideal or belief.
20. Scholarship and student loan policies.
21. Low pay for public service and the "helping" professions.
22. Cheating in college courses.
23. Drug and alcohol abuse.
24. Product safety and reliability.
25. Government economic or social policy.

FURTHER READINGS

ROBERT FINCH

ROBERT FINCH was born in 1943. He lives on Cape Cod, Massachu-
setts, and spends much of his time thinking and writing about it.
His many articles have appeared in magazines such as Blair and
Ketchum's *Country Journal, Orion, Nature Quarterly, Sanctuary,* and
Diversion. His essays have been published in two volumes: *Common
Ground: A Naturalist's Guide to Cape Cod* (1981) and *Outlands* (1986).
This essay has a relatively narrow focus. In it, Finch records "a
remarkable encounter between a spider and a yellow hornet," an
intense drama which he manages to convey vividly. As is the case
with the best writing about nature, this essay also becomes a
meditation on human behavior and allows us to see ourselves
reflected in and against the natural world and its complex inhabitants.

Death of a Hornet

For the past half hour I have been watching a remarkable encounter   1
between a spider and a yellow hornet, in which I was an unwitting
catalyst. I have found several of these hornets in my study recently,
buzzing and beating themselves against the glass doors and windows, having crawled out, I presume, from the cracks between the
still-unplastered sheets of rock lath on the ceiling. Usually I have
managed to coax them out the door with a piece of paper or a book,
but this morning my mind was abstracted with innumerable small
tasks, so when another one of these large insects appeared, buzzing
violently like a yellow and black column of electricity slowly sizzling
up the window pane above my desk, I rather absentmindedly
whacked it with a rolled-up bus schedule until it fell, maimed but still
alive, onto the window sill.

My sill is cluttered with natural objects and apparatus used for   2
studying and keeping insects and other forms of local wildlife—various small jars, a microscope box, a dissecting kit, an ancient phoebe's

---

nest that was once built on our front-door light, an aquarium pump, pieces of coral and seaweed, etc.—none of which has been used for several months. They now serve largely as an eclectic substrate for several large, messy spider webs.

In one corner is a rather large, irregular, three-dimensional web occupying a good quarter-cubic-foot of space. It was into this web that the stricken hornet fell, catching about halfway down into the loose mesh and drawing out from her reclusiveness in the corner a nondescript brownish house spider with a body about three-eighths of an inch long. The hornet hung, tail down, twirling tenuously from a single web-thread, while its barred yellow abdomen throbbed and jabbed repeatedly in instinctive attack. The motion could not really be called defensive, as the hornet was surely too far gone to recover, but it was as if it was determined to inflict whatever injury it could on whatever might approach it in its dying. Defense, in insects as in us, it seems, is not founded on the ability to survive but on the resolution to keep from forgiving as long as possible. 3

The spider rushed out along her strands to investigate the commotion and stopped about an inch short of this enormous creature, three or four times her own size, with what seemed a kind of "Oh, Lord, why me?" attitude, the stance of a fisherman who suddenly realizes he has hooked a wounded shark on his flounder line. 4

Whether or not her momentary hesitation reflected any such human emotion, the spider immediately set out to secure her oversized prey. After making a few tentative feints toward the hornet and apparently seeing that it could do no more than ineffectually thrust its stinger back and forth, she approached more deliberately, made a complete circuit around the hanging beast, and suddenly latched onto it at its "neck." 5

At this point I went and got a magnifying glass and stationed myself to observe more closely. The spider did indeed seem to be fastening repeatedly onto the thin connection between the hornet's head and thorax—a spot, I theorized, that might be more easily injected with the spider's paralyzing venom. 6

While she remained attached, all motion in the spider's legs and body ceased, adding to the impression that some intense, concealed activity was taking place at the juncture. If so, it proved effective, for within a very few minutes almost all throbbing in the hornet's abdomen had stopped, and only the flickering of its rear legs indicated that any life remained. 7

During this process, the spider's movements were still very   8
cautious, but also somehow gentle, never violent or awkward as my
whacking had been, but almost as solicitous, as if ministering to the
stricken hornet, as carefully and as gently as possible ending its
struggles and its agony. Her graceful arched legs looked, through the
glass, like miniature, transparent, bent soda straws, with dark spots
of pigment at the joints.

At this point the spider seemed to have made the hornet *hers*—   9
her object, her possession—and her movements became more confident, proprietary, almost perfunctory in contrast. She no longer
seemed aware of the hornet as something apart from her, foreign to
the web, but rather as a part of it now, ready to be assimilated. She
now appeared to begin dancing around the paralyzed insect, her rear
legs moving rapidly and rhythmically in a throwing motion towards
the object in the center. I did not see any silk coming out of her
abdomen, and her legs did not actually appear to touch the spinnerets
there, but gradually a light film of webbing, like a thin, foggy sheen,
became visible around the hornet's mid-section.

She would spin for several seconds, then climb an inch or two   10
and attach a strand to a piece of webbing overhead. I thought at first
that she was merely securing the hornet from its rather unstable
attachment, but after she had done this a few times, I saw that, with
each climb upward, the hornet itself also moved a small fraction of an
inch up and to the side.

It was soon clear that the spider was maneuvering this enormous   11
insect in a very definite and deliberate manner, using her spun cables
like a system of block and tackle, hoisting and moving her prey
through the seemingly random network of spun silk.

In between these bouts of spinning and hoisting, the spider   12
occasionally stopped and again approached the hornet, now totally
motionless and with one of its darkly veined wings bound to its
barred side. She would place herself head down (the usual position
for a spider in a web when not spinning) just above the hornet's head
and, again becoming totally motionless, as if in some paralysis of
ecstasy, seemed to attach her mouth parts to those of her prey's, as
though engaged in some long, drawn-out death kiss. The two insects
would remain attached so for ten to fifteen seconds at a time, after
which the spider would again resume her hoisting and fastening. Was
this some further injection of venom taking place, or was she beginning to suck the juices from the wasp's still-living body even as she

was moving it somewhere? I was struck, mesmerized, by this alternation of intimate, motionless contact of prey and predator, and the businesslike, bustling manipulation of an inert object by its possessor.

All in all, the spider has moved the hornet about two inches to the side and one inch upward from the point where it landed, out of the center portion of the web and nearer the window frame, where now she crouches motionless behind it, perhaps using it to conceal herself while waiting for another prey. I pulled myself away from the corner and put down the magnifying glass, feeling strangely drained from having been drawn in so strongly to watch such concentrated activity and dispassionate energy. There is something about spiders that no insect possesses, that makes it seem right that they are not true insects but belong to a more ancient order of being. I like them in my home, but they will not bear too close watching.   13

I look back at the window corner and see that the characters of the drama are still there, once more in miniature tableau. All is quiet again; the spider remains crouched behind its mummified prey, in that waiting game that spiders have perfected, where memory and hope play no part. There is only the stillness of an eternal present and the silent architecture of perfectly strung possibilities.   14

ANDREW HOLLERAN

ANDREW HOLLERAN is a novelist and essay writer. His articles have appeared in *New York* magazine, *Christopher Street*, and other publications. He has published two novels: *Dancer from the Dance* (1978) and *Nights in Aruba* (1983). A collection of his essays, *Ground Zero*, was published in 1988. "Bedside Manners" is taken from it. The essay begins with personal events, but quickly moves to consider the relationships between sickness and health and between living and dying that set boundaries on all human lives. Its movement thus resembles the ripples from a stone thrown in the water. In the end, Holleran asks readers to consider not simply the narrower meanings of "the plague" but also the larger challenges it poses.

Bedside Manners

"There is no difference between men so profound," wrote Scott Fitz- 1
gerald, "as that between the sick and the well."

There are many thoughts that fill someone's head as he walks 2
across town on a warm July afternoon to visit a friend confined to a
hospital room—and that is one of them. Another occurs to you as you
wait for the light to change and watch the handsome young basketball
players playing on the public court behind a chicken wire fence:
Health is everywhere. The world has a surreal quality to it when you
are on your way to the hospital to visit someone you care for who is
seriously ill: Everyone in it, walking down the sidewalk, driving by
in cars, rushing about on a basketball court with sweat-stained chests,
exhausted faces, and wide eyes, seems to you extremely peculiar.
They are peculiar because they are free: walking under their own
power, nicely dressed, sometimes beautiful. Beauty does not lose its
allure under the spell of grief. The hospital visitor still notices the
smooth chests of the athletes in their cotton shorts as they leap to
recover the basketball after it bounces off the rim. But everything

seems strangely quiet—speechless—as if you were watching a movie on television with the sound turned off, as if everyone else in the world but you is totally unaware of something: that the act of walking across York Avenue under one's own power is essentially miraculous.

Every time he enters a hospital, the visitor enters with two 3 simultaneous thoughts: He hates hospitals, and only people working in them lead serious lives. Everything else is selfish. Entering a hospital he always thinks, *I should work for a year as a nurse, an aide, a volunteer helping people, coming to terms with disease and death.* This feeling will pass the moment he leaves the hospital. In reality the visitor hopes his fear and depression are not evident on his face as he walks down the gleaming, silent hall from the elevator to his friend's room. He is trying hard to stay calm.

The door of the room the receptionist downstairs has told the 4 visitor his friend is in is closed—and on it are taped four signs that are not on any of the other doors and are headlined, WARNING. The visitor stops as much to read them as to allow his heartbeat to subside before going in. He knows—from the accounts of friends who have already visited—he must don a robe, gloves, mask, and even a plastic cap. He is not sure if the door is closed because his friend is asleep inside or because the door to this room is always kept closed. So he pushes it open a crack and peers in. His friend is turned on his side, a white mound of bed linen, apparently sleeping.

The visitor is immensely relieved. He goes down the hall and asks 5 a nurse if he may leave the *Life* magazine he brought for his friend and writes a note to him saying he was here. Then he leaves the hospital and walks west through the summer twilight as if swimming through an enchanted lagoon. The next day—once more crossing town—he is in that surreal mood, under a blue sky decorated with a few photogenic, puffy white clouds, certain that no one else knows . . . knows he or she is absurdly, preposterously, incalculably fortunate to be walking on the street. He feels once again that either the sound has been turned off or some other element (his ego, perhaps with all its anger, ambition, jealousy) has been removed from the world. The basketball players are different youths today but just as much worth pausing to look at. He enters the hospital one block east more calmly this time and requests to see his friend—who is allowed only two visitors at a time, and visits lasting no more than ten minutes. He goes upstairs, peeks around the door, and sees his friend utterly awake. The visitor's heart races as he steps back and puts on the gloves, mask, cap, and robe he has been told his friends all look so comical in. He smiles because he hopes the photograph that made him bring the copy of *Life* to the hospital—Russian women leaning against a wall in Leningrad in bikinis and winter coats, taking the sun on a February day—has amused his friend as much as it tickled him.

"Richard?" the visitor says as he opens the door and peeks in. His friend blinks at him. Two plastic tubes are fixed in his nostrils bringing him oxygen. His face is emaciated and gaunt, his hair longer, softer in appearance, wisps rising above his head. But the one feature the visitor cannot get over are his friend's eyes. His eyes are black, huge, and furious. Perhaps because his face is gaunt or perhaps because they really are larger than usual, they seem the only thing alive in his face; as if his whole being were distilled and concentrated, poured, drained, into his eyes. They are shining, alarmed, and—there is no other word—furious. He looks altogether like an angry baby—or an angry old man—or an angry bald eagle. 6

And just as the hospital visitor is absorbing the shock of these livid eyes, the sick man says in a furious whisper, "Why did you bring me that dreadful magazine? I hate *Life* magazine! With that stupid picture! I wasn't amused! I wasn't amused at all! You should never have brought that dreck into this room!" 7

The visitor is momentarily speechless: It is the first time in their friendship of ten years that anything abusive or insulting has ever been said; it is as astonishing as the gaunt face in which two huge black eyes burn and shine. But he sits down and recovers his breath and apologizes. The visitor thinks, *He's angry because I haven't visited him till now. He's angry that he's here at all, that he's sick.* And they begin to talk. They talk of the hospital food (which he hates too), of the impending visit of his mother (whose arrival he dreads), of the drug he is taking (which is experimental), and of the other visitors he has had. The patient asks the visitor to pick up a towel at the base of the bed and give it to him. The visitor complies. The patient places it across his forehead—and the visitor, who, like most people, is unsure what to say in this situation, stifles the question he wants to ask, *Why do you have a towel on your forehead?* The patient finally says, "Don't you think I look like Mother Teresa?" And the visitor realizes his friend has made a joke—as he did years ago in their house on Fire Island: doing drag with bedspreads, pillow cases, towels, whatever was at hand. The visitor does not smile—he is so unprepared for a joke in these circumstances—but he realizes, with relief, he is forgiven. 8

He realizes what people who visit the sick often learn: It is the patient who puts the visitor at ease. In a few moments his ten minutes are up. He rises and says, "I don't want to tire you." He goes to the door and once beyond it he turns and looks back. His friend says to him, "I'm proud of you for coming."

"Oh—!" the visitor says and shakes his head. "Proud of *me* for coming!" he tells a friend later that evening, after he has stripped off his gown and mask and gone home, through the unreal city of people in perfect health. "Proud of me! Can you imagine! To say that to me, to make *me* feel good! When he's the one in bed!" The truth is he is proud of himself the next time he visits his friend, for he is one of those people who looks away when a nurse takes a blood test and finds respirators frightening. He is like almost everyone—everyone except these extraordinary people who work in hospitals, he thinks, as he walks into the building. The second visit is easier, partly because it is the second, and partly because the patient is better—the drug has worked.

But he cannot forget the sight of those dark, angry eyes and the plastic tubes and emaciated visage—and as he goes home that evening, he knows there is a place whose existence he was not aware of before: the foyer of death. It is a place many of us will see at least once in our lives. Because modern medicine fights for patients who a century ago would have died without its intervention, it has created an odd place between life and death. One no longer steps into Charon's boat to be ferried across the River Styx—ill people are now detained, with one foot in the boat and the other still on shore. It is a place where mercy looks exactly like cruelty to the average visitor. It is a place that one leaves, if one is only a visitor, with the conviction that ordinary life is utterly miraculous, so that, going home from the hospital on the subway, one is filled with things one cannot express to the crowd that walks up out of the station or throngs the street of the block where he lives. But if the people caught in the revolving door between health and death could speak, would they not say—as Patrick Cowley reportedly did as he watched the men dancing to his music while he was fatally ill, "Look at those stupid queens. Don't they *know*?" Guard your health. It is all you have. It is the thin line that stands between you and hell. It is your miraculous possession. Do nothing to threaten it. Treat each other with kindness. Comfort your suffering friends. Help one another. Revere life. Do not throw it away for the momentous pleasures of lust, or even the obliteration of loneliness.

Many homosexuals wonder how they will die: where, with 11 whom. Auden went back to Oxford, Santayana to the Blue Nuns in Rome. We are not all so lucky. Some men afflicted with AIDS returned to die in their family's home. Others have died with friends. Some have died bitterly and repudiated the homosexual friends who came to see them; others have counted on these people. Volunteers from the Gay Men's Health Crisis have cooked, cleaned, shopped, visited, taken care of people they did not even know until they decided to help. One thing is sure—we are learning how to help one another. We are discovering the strength and goodness of people we knew only in discotheques or as faces on Fire Island. We are following a great moral precept by visiting the sick. We are once again learning the awful truth Robert Penn Warren wrote years ago: "Only through the suffering of the innocent is the brotherhood of man confirmed." The most profound difference between men may well be that between the sick and the well, but compassionate people try to reach across the chasm and bridge it. The hospital visitor who conquers his own fear of something facing us all takes the first step on a journey that others less fearful than he have already traveled much further on: They are combining eros and agape as they rally round their stricken friends. As for the courage and dignity and sense of humor of those who are sick, these are beyond praise, and one hesitates where words are so flimsy. As for a disease whose latency period is measured in years, not months, there is no telling which side of the line dividing the sick and the well each of us will be on before this affliction is conquered. We may disdain the hysteria of policemen and firemen who call for masks, and people who ask if it is safe to ride the subway, and television crews who will not interview AIDS patients. For they are not at risk—those who are, are fearlessly helping their own. This is the greatest story of the plague.

GLORIA ANZALDÚA

GLORIA ANZALDÚA is a writer who explores and celebrates her
Spanish and Indian heritage in poetry and in prose. She was a
co-editor of the collection *This Bridge Called My Back: Writing by
Radical Women of Color* (1983). In 1987, she published *Borderlands/La
Frontera: The New Mestiza*. In addition, she is a contributing editor
of the journal *Sinister Wisdom*. "Tlilli, Tlapalli" is a section of *Bor-
derlands/La Frontera*. The mixture of cultures and beliefs in this
selection may make it difficult to follow in places, but most readers
will find the journey rewarding. Along the way they will encounter
insights into the sources of Anzaldúa's writing that may suggest
ways of looking at their own writing and their own experiences.
The ways of looking at life, poetry, reality, and magic in a culture
different from mainstream American culture can shed light on the
ways most Americans view these aspects of life. At the very least,
the essay can be a source of disagreement that sharpens the readers'
own beliefs. We have chosen not to translate the passages written
in Spanish because we believe that the untranslated passages allow
students in a class to approach (and understand) the text in different
ways depending on their knowledge of Spanish (or their lack of
knowledge). These different perceptions may be in themselves
instructive and may be the source of fruitful discussions.

Tlilli, Tlapalli: The Path of the Red and Black Ink

> "Out of poverty, poetry;
> out of suffering, song."
>
> —a Mexican saying

When I was seven, eight, nine, fifteen, sixteen years old, I would read
in bed with a flashlight under the covers, hiding my self-imposed
insomnia from my mother. I preferred the world of the imagination
to the death of sleep. My sister, Hilda, who slept in the same bed with
me, would threaten to tell my mother unless I told her a story.

1

2

I was familiar with *cuentos*—my grandmother told stories like the   3
one about her getting on top of the roof while down below rabid
coyotes were ravaging the place and wanting to get at her. My father
told stories about a phantom giant dog that appeared out of nowhere
and sped along the side of the pickup no matter how fast he was
driving.

Nudge a Mexican and she or he will break out with a story. So,   4
huddling under the covers, I made up stories for my sister night after
night. After a while she wanted two stories per night. I learned to give
her installments, building up the suspense with convoluted complications until the story climaxed several nights later. It must have been
then that I decided to put stories on paper. It must have been then that
working with images and writing became connected to night.

Invoking Art

In the ethno-poetics and performance of the shaman, my people, the   5
Indians, did not split the artistic from the functional, the sacred from
the secular, art from everyday life. The religious, social, and aesthetic
purposes of art were all intertwined. Before the Conquest, poets
gathered to play music, dance, sing, and read poetry in open-air places
around the *Xochicuahuitl, el Arbol Florido,* Tree-in-Flower. (The
Coaxihuitl or morning glory is called the snake plant and its seeds,
known as *ololiuhqui,* are hallucinogenic.[1]) The ability of story (prose
and poetry) to transform the storyteller and the listener into something or someone else is shamanistic. The writer, as shape-changer, is
a *nahual,* a shaman.

In looking over the book from which this essay was taken, I see   6
a mosaic pattern (Aztec-like) emerging, a weaving pattern, thin here,
thick there. I see a preoccupation with the deep structure, the underlying structure, with the gesso underpainting that is red earth, black
earth. I can see the deep structure, the scaffolding. If I can get the bone
structure right, then putting flesh on it proceeds without too many
hitches. The problem is that the bones often do not exist prior to the
flesh, but are shaped after a vague and broad shadow of its form is
discerned or uncovered during beginning, middle, and final stages of
the writing. Numerous overlays of paint, rough surfaces, smooth

[1] R. Gordon Wasson, *The Wondrous Mushroom: Mycolatry in Mesoamerica* (New York, NY: McGraw-Hill Book Company, 1980), 59, 103.

surfaces make me realize I am preoccupied with texture as well. Too, I see the barely contained color threatening to spill over the boundaries of the object it represents and into other "objects" and over the borders of the frame. I see a hybridization of metaphor, different species of ideas popping up here, popping up there, full of variations and seeming contradictions, though I believe in an ordered, structured universe where all phenomena are interrelated and imbued with spirit. This book seems an assemblage, a montage, a beaded work with several leitmotifs and with a central core, now appearing, now disappearing in a crazy dance. The whole thing has had a mind of its own, escaping me and insisting on putting together the pieces of its own puzzle with minimal direction from my will. It is a rebellious, willful entity, a precocious girl-child forced to grow up too quickly, rough, unyielding, with pieces of feather sticking out here and there, fur, twigs, clay. My child, but not for much longer. This female being is angry, sad, joyful, is *Coatlicue*, dove, horse, serpent, cactus. Though it is a flawed thing—a clumsy, complex, groping blind thing—for me it is alive, infused with spirit. I talk to it; it talks to me.

I make my offerings of incense and cracked corn, light my candle.   7
In my head I sometimes will say a prayer—an affirmation and a voicing of intent. Then I run water, wash the dishes or my underthings, take a bath, or mop the kitchen floor. This "induction" period sometimes takes a few minutes, sometimes hours. But always I go against a resistance. Something in me does not want to do this writing. Yet once I'm immersed in it, I can go fifteen to seventeen hours in one sitting and I don't want to leave it.

My "stories" are acts encapsulated in time, "enacted" every time   8
they are spoken aloud or read silently. I like to think of them as performances and not as inert and "dead" objects (as the aesthetics of Western culture think of art works). Instead, the work has an identity; it is a "who" or a "what" and contains the presences of persons, that is, incarnations of gods or ancestors or natural and cosmic powers. The work manifests the same needs as a person, it needs to be "fed," *la tengo que bañar y vestir.*

When invoked in rite, the object/event is "present"; that is,   9
"enacted," it is both a physical thing and the power that infuses it. It is metaphysical in that it "spins its energies between gods and humans" and its task is to move the gods. This type of work dedicates itself to managing the universe and its energies. I'm not sure what it

is when it is at rest (not in performance). It may or may not be a "work" then. A mask may only have the power of presence during a ritual dance and the rest of the time it may merely be a "thing." Some works exist forever invoked, always in performance. I'm thinking of totem poles, cave paintings. Invoked art is communal and speaks of every-day life. It is dedicated to the validation of humans; that is, it makes people hopeful, happy, secure, and it can have negative effects as well, which propel one towards a search for validation.[2]

The aesthetic of virtuosity, art typical of Western European cul-   10
tures, attempts to manage the energies of its own internal system such as conflicts, harmonies, resolutions and balances. It bears the presence of qualities and internal meanings. It is dedicated to the validation of itself. Its task is to move humans by means of achieving mastery in content, technique, feeling. Western art is always whole and always "in power." It is individual (not communal). It is "psychological" in that it spins its energies between itself and its witness.[3]

Western cultures behave differently toward works of art than do   11
tribal cultures. The "sacrifices" Western cultures make are in housing their art works in the best structures designed by the best architects; and in servicing them with insurance, guards to protect them, conser-vators to maintain them, specialists to mount and display them, and the educated and upper classes to "view" them. Tribal cultures keep art works in honored and sacred places in the home and elsewhere. They attend them by making sacrifices of blood (goat or chicken), libations of wine. They bathe, feed, and clothe them. The works are treated not just as objects, but also as persons. The "witness" is a participant in the enactment of the work in a ritual, and not a member of the privileged classes.[4]

Ethnocentrism is the tyranny of Western aesthetics. An Indian   12
mask in an American museum is transported into an alien aesthetic system where what is missing is the presence of power invoked through performance ritual. It has become a conquered thing, a dead "thing" separated from nature and, therefore, its power.

Modern Western painters have "borrowed," copied, or otherwise   13
extrapolated the art of tribal cultures and called it cubism, surrealism,

---

[2]Robert Plant Armstrong, *The Powers of Presence: Consciousness, Myth, and Affecting Presence* (Philadelphia, PA: University of Pennsylvania Press, 1981), 11, 20.

[3]Armstrong, 10.

[4]Armstrong, 4.

symbolism. The music, the beat of the drum, the Blacks' jive talk. All taken over. Whites, along with a good number of our own people, have cut themselves off from their spiritual roots, and they take our spiritual art objects in an unconscious attempt to get them back. If they're going to do it, I'd like them to be aware of what they are doing and to go about doing it the right way. Let's all stop importing Greek myths and the Western Cartesian split point of view and root ourselves in the mythological soil and soul of this continent. White America has only attended to the body of the earth in order to exploit it, never to succor it or to be nurtured in it. Instead of surreptitiously ripping off the vital energy of people of color and putting it to commercial use, whites could allow themselves to share and exchange and learn from us in a respectful way. By taking up *curanderismo,* Santeria, shamanism, Taoism, Zen, and otherwise delving into the spiritual life and ceremonies of multi-colored people, Anglos would perhaps lose the white sterility they have in their kitchens, bathrooms, hospitals, mortuaries, and missile bases. Though in the conscious mind, black and dark may be associated with death, evil, and destruction, in the subconscious mind and in our dreams, white is associated with disease, death, and hopelessness. Let us hope that the left hand, that of darkness, of femaleness, of "primitiveness," can divert the indifferent, right-handed, "rational" suicidal drive that, unchecked, could blow us into acid rain in a fraction of a millisecond.

Ni cuicani: I, the Singer

For the ancient Aztecs, *tlilli, tlapalli, la tinta negra y roja de sus códices*   14 (the black and red ink painted on codices) were the colors symbolizing *escritura y sabiduría* (writing and wisdom).[5] They believed that through metaphor and symbol, by means of poetry and truth, communication with the Divine could be attained, and *topan* (that which is above—the gods and spirit world) could be bridged with *mictlán* (that which is below—the underworld and the region of the dead).

Poet: she pours water from the mouth of the pump, lowers the handle then   15 lifts it, lowers, lifts. Her hands begin to feel the pull from the entrails, the live

[5]Miguel Leon-Portilla, *Los Ansiguos Mexicanos: A traves de sus cronicas y cantares* (Mexico, D.F.: Fondo de Cultura Economica, 1961), 19, 22.

animal resisting. A sigh rises up from the depths, the handle becomes a wild thing in her hands, the cold sweet water gushes out, splashing her face, the shock of nightlight filling the bucket.

An image is a bridge between evoked emotion and conscious knowledge; words are the cables that hold up the bridge. Images are more direct, more immediate than words, and closer to the unconscious. Picture language precedes thinking in words; the metaphorical mind precedes analytical consciousness. 16

The Shamanic State

When I create stories in my head, that is, allow the voices and scenes to be projected in the inner screen of my mind, I "trance." I used to think I was going crazy or that I was having hallucinations. But now I realize it is my job, my calling, to traffic in images. Some of these film-like narratives I write down; most are lost, forgotten. When I don't write the images down for several days or weeks or months, I get physically ill. Because writing invokes images from my unconscious, and because some of the images are residues of trauma which I then have to reconstruct, I sometimes get sick when I *do* write. I can't stomach it, become nauseous, or burn with fever, worsen. But, in reconstructing the traumas behind the images, I make "sense" of them, and once they have "meaning" they are changed, transformed. It is then that writing heals me, brings me great joy. 17

To facilitate the "movies" with soundtracks, I need to be alone, or in a sensory-deprived state. I plug up my ears with wax, put on my black cloth eye-shades, lie horizontal and unmoving, in a state between sleeping and waking, mind and body locked into my fantasy. I am held prisoner by it. My body is experiencing events. In the beginning it is like being in a movie theater, as pure spectator. Gradually I become so engrossed with the activities, the conversations, that I become a participant in the drama. I have to struggle to "disengage" or escape from my "animated story," I have to get some sleep so I can write tomorrow. Yet I am gripped by a story which won't let me go. Outside the frame, I am film director, screenwriter, camera operator. Inside the frame, I am the actors—male and female—I am desert sand, mountain, I am dog, mosquito. I can sustain a four- to six-hour "movie." Once I am up, I can sustain several "shorts" of anywhere between five and thirty minutes. Usually these "narratives" are the 18

feels very much like being a Chicana, or being queer—a lot of squirming, coming up against all sorts of walls. Or its opposite: nothing defined or definite, a boundless, floating state of limbo where I kick my heels, brood, percolate, hibernate, and wait for something to happen.

Living in a state of psychic unrest, in a Borderland, is what makes poets write and artists create. It is like a cactus needle embedded in the flesh. It worries itself deeper and deeper, and I keep aggravating it by poking at it. When it begins to fester I have to do something to put an end to the aggravation and to figure out why I have it. I get deep down into the place where it's rooted in my skin and pluck away at it, playing it like a musical instrument—the fingers pressing, making the pain worse before it can get better. Then out it comes. No more discomfort, no more ambivalence. Until another needle pierces the skin. That's what writing is for me, an endless cycle of making it worse, making it better, but always making meaning out of the experience, whatever it may be.

> My flowers shall not cease to live;
> my songs shall never end:
> I, a singer, intone them;
> they become scattered, they are spread about.
>
> —*Cantares mexicanos*

To write, to be a writer, I have to trust and believe in myself as a speaker, as a voice for the images. I have to believe that I can communicate with images and words and that I can do it well. A lack of belief in my creative self is a lack of belief in my total self and vice versa—I cannot separate my writing from any part of my life. It is all one.

When I write it feels like I'm carving bone. It feels like I'm creating my own face, my own heart—a Nahuatl concept. My soul makes itself through the creative act. It is constantly remaking and giving birth to itself through my body. It is the learning to live with *la Coatlicue* that transforms living in the Borderlands from a nightmare into a numinous experience. It is always a path/state to something else.

In *Xóchitl* in *Cuícatl*[7]

---

[7]In *Xóchitl* in *Cuícatl* is Nahuatl for flower and song, *flor y canto*.

She writes while other people sleep. Something is trying to come out. She fights the words, pushes them down, down, a woman with morning sickness in the middle of the night. How much easier it would be to carry a baby for nine months and then expel it permanently. These continuous multiple pregnancies are going to kill her. She is the battlefield for the pitched fight between the inner image and the words trying to recreate it. *La musa bruja* has no manners. Doesn't she know, nights are for sleeping?

She is getting too close to the mouth of the abyss. She is teetering on the edge, trying to balance while she makes up her mind whether to jump in or find a safer way down. That's why she makes herself sick—to postpone having to jump blindfolded into the abyss of her own being and there in the depths confront her face, the face underneath the mask.

To be a mouth—the cost is too high—her whole life enslaved to that devouring mouth. *Todo pasaba por esa boca, el viento, el fuego, los mares y la Tierra.* Her body, a crossroads, a fragile bridge, cannot support the tons of cargo passing through it. She wants to install 'stop' and 'go' signal lights, instigate a curfew, police Poetry. But something wants to come out.

Blocks (*Coatlicue* states) are related to my cultural identity. The   35
painful periods of confusion that I suffer from are symptomatic of a larger creative process: cultural shifts. The stress of living with cultural ambiguity both compels me to write and blocks me. It isn't until I'm almost at the end of the blocked state that I remember and recognize it for what it is. As soon as this happens, the piercing light of awareness melts the block and I accept the deep and the darkness and I hear one of my voices saying, "I am tired of fighting. I surrender. I give up, let go, let the walls fall. On this night of the hearing of faults, *Tlazolteotl, diosa de la cara negra,* let fall the cockroaches that live in my hair, the rats that nestle in my skull. Gouge out my lame eyes, rout my demon from its nocturnal cave. Set torch to the tiger that stalks me. Loosen the dead faces gnawing at my cheekbones. I am tired of resisting. I surrender. I give up, let go, let the walls fall."

And in descending to the depths I realize that down is up, and I   36
rise up from and into the deep. And once again I recognize that the internal tension of oppositions can propel (if it doesn't tear apart) the mestiza writer out of the *metate* where she is being ground with corn and water, eject her out as *nahual,* an agent of transformation, able to modify and shape primordial energy and therefore able to change herself and others into turkey, coyote, tree, or human.

I sit here before my computer, *Amiguita,* my altar on top of the   37
monitor with the *Virgen de Coatlalopeuh* candle and copal incense burning. My companion, a wooden serpent staff with feathers, is to

my right while I ponder the ways metaphor and symbol concretize the spirit and etherealize the body. The Writing is my whole life, it is my obsession. This vampire which is my talent does not suffer other suitors.[8] Daily I court it, offer my neck to its teeth. This is the sacrifice that the act of creation requires, a blood sacrifice. For only through the body, through the pulling of flesh, can the human soul be trans- formed. And for images, words, stories to have this transformative power, they must arise from the human body—flesh and bone—and from the Earth's body—stone, sky, liquid, soil. This work, these images, piercing tongue or ear lobes with cactus needle, are my offerings, are my Aztecan blood sacrifices.

[8]Nietzsche, in *The Will to Power*, says that the artist lives under a curse of being vampirized by his talent.

WENDELL BERRY

WENDELL BERRY was born in 1934 in Henry City, Kentucky. He earned his B.A. (1956) and his M.A. from the University of Kentucky, where he has also taught in the English Department. Berry is a poet, novelist, and essayist. His works have been published in the *Nation, Prairie Schooner, Chelsea Review,* and numerous other journals and magazines. Among his many books are *The Unsettling of America* (1977) and *What Are People For?* (1990). Deeply concerned with the fate of the soil and of those farmers who work with it, Berry has written eloquently and often about both concerns. This essay, written in 1989 and published in *What Are People For?*, takes what will be for most readers an unusual (and interesting) approach. Most of us look upon eating as a necessity and, often, as a pleasure. Berry, however, asks us to view it as an economic and political act with important consequences. In addition, he proposes some steps we might take if we wish to follow his advice and "eat responsibly."

The Pleasures of Eating

Many times, after I have finished a lecture on the decline of American   1
farming and rural life, someone in the audience has asked, "What can city people do?"

"Eat responsibly," I have usually answered. Of course, I have   2
tried to explain what I meant by that, but afterwards I have invariably felt that there was more to be said than I had been able to say. Now I would like to attempt a better explanation.

I begin with the proposition that eating is an agricultural act.   3
Eating ends the annual drama of the food economy that begins with planting and birth. Most eaters, however, are no longer aware that this is true. They think of food as an agricultural product, perhaps, but they do not think of themselves as participants in agriculture. They think of themselves as "consumers." If they think beyond that, they recognize that they are passive consumers. They buy what they want—or what they have been persuaded to want—within the limits

514

of what they can get. They pay, mostly without protest, what they are charged. And they mostly ignore certain critical questions about the quality and the cost of what they are sold: How fresh is it? How pure or clean is it, how free of dangerous chemicals? How far was it transported, and what did transportation add to the cost? How much did manufacturing or packaging or advertising add to the cost? When the food product has been manufactured or "processed" or "pre-cooked," how has that affected its quality or price or nutritional value?

Most urban shoppers would tell you that food is produced on 4 farms. But most of them do not know what farms, or what kinds of farms, or where the farms are, or what knowledge or skills are involved in farming. They apparently have little doubt that farms will continue to produce, but they do not know how or over what obstacles. For them, then, food is pretty much an abstract idea—something they do not know or imagine—until it appears on the grocery shelf or on the table.

The specialization of production induces specialization of con- 5 sumption. Patrons of the entertainment industry, for example, entertain themselves less and less and have become more and more passively dependent on commercial suppliers. This is certainly true also of patrons of the food industry, who have tended more and more to be *mere* consumers—passive, uncritical, and dependent. Indeed, this sort of consumption may be said to be one of the chief goals of industrial production. The food industrialists have by now persuaded millions of consumers to prefer food that is already prepared. They will grow, deliver, and cook your food for you and (just like your mother) beg you to eat it. That they do not yet offer to insert it, prechewed, into your mouth is only because they have found no profitable way to do so. We may rest assured that they would be glad to find such a way. The ideal industrial food consumer would be strapped to a table with a tube running from the food factory directly into his or her stomach.

Perhaps I exaggerate, but not by much. The industrial eater is, in 6 fact, one who does not know that eating is an agricultural act, who no longer knows or imagines the connections between eating and the land, and who is therefore necessarily passive and uncritical—in short, a victim. When food, in the minds of eaters, is no longer associated with farming and with the land, then the eaters are suffering a kind of cultural amnesia that is misleading and dangerous. The current version of the "dream home" of the future involves "effortless" shopping from a list of available goods on a television monitor and heating precooked food by remote control. Of course, this implies and depends on a perfect ignorance of the history of the food that is consumed. It requires that the citizenry should give up their hereditary and sensible aversion to buying a pig in a poke. It wishes to make the selling of pigs in pokes an honorable and glamorous activity. The dreamer in this dream home will perforce know nothing about the kind or quality of this food, or where it came from, or how it was produced and prepared, or what ingredients, additives, and residues it contains—unless, that is, the dreamer undertakes a close and constant study of the food industry, in which case he or she might as well wake up and play an active and responsible part in the economy of food.

There is, then, a politics of food that, like any politics, involves   7
our freedom. We still (sometimes) remember that we cannot be free if our minds and voices are controlled by someone else. But we have neglected to understand that we cannot be free if our food and its sources are controlled by someone else. The condition of the passive consumer of food is not a democratic condition. One reason to eat responsibly is to live free.

But if there is a food politics, there are also a food esthetics and a   8
food ethics, neither of which is dissociated from politics. Like industrial sex, industrial eating has become a degraded, poor, and paltry thing. Our kitchens and other eating places more and more resemble filling stations, as our homes more and more resemble motels. "Life is not very interesting," we seem to have decided. "Let its satisfactions be minimal, perfunctory, and fast." We hurry through our meals to go to work and hurry through our work in order to "recreate" ourselves in the evenings and on weekends and vacations. And then we hurry, with the greatest possible speed and noise and violence, through our recreation—for what? To eat the billionth hamburger at some fast-food joint hellbent on increasing the "quality" of our life? And all this is carried out in a remarkable obliviousness to the causes and effects, the possibilities and the purposes, of the life of the body in this world.

One will find this obliviousness represented in virgin purity in   9
the advertisements of the food industry, in which food wears as much makeup as the actors. If one gained one's whole knowledge of food from these advertisements (as some presumably do), one would not

know that the various edibles were ever living creatures, or that they all come from the soil, or that they were produced by work. The passive American consumer, sitting down to a meal of pre-prepared or fast food, confronts a platter covered with inert, anonymous substances that have been processed, dyed, breaded, sauced, gravied, ground, pulped, stained, blended, prettified, and sanitized beyond resemblance to any part of any creature that ever lived. The products of nature and agriculture have been made, to all appearances, the products of industry. Both eater and eaten are thus in exile from biological reality. And the result is a kind of solitude, unprecedented in human experience, in which the eater may think of eating as, first, a purely commercial transaction between him and a supplier and then as a purely appetitive transaction between him and his food.

And this peculiar specialization of the act of eating is, again, of   10
obvious benefit to the food industry, which has good reasons to obscure the connection between food and farming. It would not do for the consumer to know that the hamburger she is eating came from a steer who spent much of his life standing deep in his own excrement in a feedlot, helping to pollute the local streams, or that the calf that yielded the veal cutlet on her plate spent its life in a box in which it did not have room to turn around. And, though her sympathy for the slaw might be less tender, she should not be encouraged to meditate on the hygienic and biological implications of mile-square fields of cabbage, for vegetables grown in huge monocultures are dependent on toxic chemicals—just as animals in close confinement are dependent on antibiotics and other drugs.

The consumer, that is to say, must be kept from discovering that,   11
in the food industry—as in any other industry—the overriding concerns are not quality and health, but volume and price. For decades now the entire industrial food economy, from the large farms and feedlots to the chains of supermarkets and fast-food restaurants, has been obsessed with volume. It has relentlessly increased scale in order to increase volume in order (presumably) to reduce costs. But as scale increases, diversity declines; as diversity declines, so does health; as health declines, the dependence on drugs and chemicals necessarily increases. As capital replaces labor, it does so by substituting machines, drugs, and chemicals for human workers and for the natural health and fertility of the soil. The food is produced by any means or any shortcut that will increase profits. And the business of the cosmeticians of advertising is to persuade the consumer that food so pro-

duced is good, tasty, healthful, and a guarantee of marital fidelity and long life.

It is possible, then, to be liberated from the husbandry and wifery 12 of the old household food economy. But one can be thus liberated only by entering a trap (unless one sees ignorance and helplessness as the signs of privilege, as many people apparently do). The trap is the ideal of industrialism: a walled city surrounded by valves that let merchandise in but no consciousness out. How does one escape this trap? Only voluntarily, the same way that one went in: by restoring one's consciousness of what is involved in eating; by reclaiming responsibility for one's own part in the food economy. One might begin with the illuminating principle of Sir Albert Howard's *The Soil and Health,* that we should understand "the whole problem of health in soil, plant, animal, and man as one great subject." Eaters, that is, must understand that eating takes place inescapably in the world, that it is inescapably an agricultural act, and that how we eat determines, to a considerable extent, how the world is used. This is a simple way of describing a relationship that is inexpressibly complex. To eat responsibly is to understand and enact, so far as one can, this complex relationship. What can one do? Here is a list, probably not definitive:

1. Participate in food production to the extent that you can. If you 13 have a yard or even just a porch box or a pot in a sunny window, grow something to eat in it. Make a little compost of your kitchen scraps and use it for fertilizer. Only by growing some food for yourself can you become acquainted with the beautiful energy cycle that revolves from soil to seed to flower to fruit to food to offal to decay, and around again. You will be fully responsible for any food that you grow for yourself, and you will know all about it. You will appreciate it fully, having known it all its life.

2. Prepare your own food. This means reviving in your own mind 14 and life the arts of kitchen and household. This should enable you to eat more cheaply, and it will give you a measure of "quality control": you will have some reliable knowledge of what has been added to the food you eat.

3. Learn the origins of the food you buy, and buy the food that is 15 produced closest to your home. The idea that every locality should be, as much as possible, the source of its own food makes several kinds of sense. The locally produced food supply is the most secure, the freshest, and the easiest for local consumers to know about and to influence.

4. Whenever possible, deal directly with a local farmer, gardener, or orchardist. All the reasons listed for the previous suggestion apply here. In addition, by such dealing you eliminate the whole pack of merchants, transporters, processors, packagers, and advertisers who thrive at the expense of both producers and consumers. 16

5. Learn, in self-defense, as much as you can of the economy and technology of industrial food production. What is added to food that is not food, and what do you pay for these additions? 17

6. Learn what is involved in the *best* farming and gardening. 18

7. Learn as much as you can, by direct observation and experience if possible, of the life histories of the food species. 19

The last suggestion seems particularly important to me. Many people are now as much estranged from the lives of domestic plants and animals (except for flowers and dogs and cats) as they are from the lives of the wild ones. This is regrettable, for these domestic creatures are in diverse ways attractive; there is much pleasure in knowing them. And farming, animal husbandry, horticulture, and gardening, at their best, are complex and comely arts; there is much pleasure in knowing them, too. 20

It follows that there is great *dis*pleasure in knowing about a food economy that degrades and abuses those arts and those plants and animals and the soil from which they come. For anyone who does know something of the modern history of food, eating away from home can be a chore. My own inclination is to eat seafood instead of red meat or poultry when I am traveling. Though I am by no means a vegetarian, I dislike the thought that some animal has been made miserable in order to feed me. If I am going to eat meat, I want it to be from an animal that has lived a pleasant, uncrowded life outdoors, on bountiful pasture, with good water nearby and trees for shade. And I am getting almost as fussy about food plants. I like to eat vegetables and fruits that I know have lived happily and healthily in good soil, not the products of the huge, bechemicaled factory-fields that I have seen, for example, in the Central Valley of California. The industrial farm is said to have been patterned on the factory production line. In practice, it looks more like a concentration camp. 21

The pleasure of eating should be an *extensive* pleasure, not that of the mere gourmet. People who know the garden in which their vegetables have grown and know that the garden is healthy will remember the beauty of the growing plants, perhaps in the dewy first light of morning when gardens are at their best. Such a memory 22 involves itself with the food and is one of the pleasures of eating. The knowledge of the good health of the garden relieves and frees and comforts the eater. The same goes for eating meat. The thought of the good pasture and of the calf contentedly grazing flavors the steak. Some, I know, will think it bloodthirsty or worse to eat a fellow creature you have known all its life. On the contrary, I think it means that you eat with understanding and with gratitude. A significant part of the pleasure of eating is in one's accurate consciousness of the lives and the world from which food comes. The pleasure of eating, then, may be the best available standard of our health. And this pleasure, I think, is pretty fully available to the urban consumer who will make the necessary effort.

I mentioned earlier the politics, esthetics, and ethics of food. But to speak of the pleasure of eating is to go beyond those categories. Eating with the fullest pleasure—pleasure, that is, that does not depend on ignorance—is perhaps the profoundest enactment of our connection with the world. In this pleasure we experience and celebrate our dependence and our gratitude, for we are living from mystery, from creatures we did not make and powers we cannot comprehend. When I think of the meaning of food, I always remember these lines by the poet William Carlos Williams, which seem to me merely honest: 23

> There is nothing to eat,
>   seek it where you will,
>   but the body of the Lord.
> The blessed plants
>   and the sea, yield it
>   to the imagination
> intact.

A Guide to Terms

Abstract (See *Concrete/Abstract*.)
Allusion (See *Figures of Speech*.)
Analogy (See Section 4.)
Argument is writing that uses factual evidence and supporting ideas to convince readers to share the author's opinion on an issue or to take some action the writer considers appropriate or necessary. Like exposition, argument conveys information; however, it does so not to explain but to induce readers to favor one side in a conflict or to choose a particular course of action.

Some arguments appeal primarily to reason, others primarily to emotion. Most, however, mix reason and emotion in whatever way is appropriate for the issue and the audience. (See Section 11.)

Support for an argument can take a number of forms:

1. *Examples*—Real-life examples, or hypothetical examples (used sparingly) can be convincing evidence if they are typical and if the author provides enough of them to illustrate all the major points in the argument or combines them with other kinds of evidence. (See Quindlen, Nocera, Perrin.) Some examples are *specific*, referring to particular people or events. (See Nocera, Quindlen.) Others are *general*, referring to kinds of events or people, usually corresponding in some way to the reader's experiences.

2. *Facts and figures*—Detailed information about a subject, particularly if presented in statistical form, can help convince readers by showing that the author's perspective on an issue is consistent with what is known about the subject. (See Nocera,

Lynn.) But facts whose accuracy is questionable or statistics that are confusing can undermine an argument.

    3. *Authority*—Supporting an argument with the ideas or the actual words of someone who is recognized as an expert can be an effective strategy as long as the author can show that the expert is a reliable witness and can combine the expert's opinion with other kinds of evidence that point in the same direction.

    4. *Personal experience*—Examples drawn from personal experience or the experience of friends can be more detailed and vivid (and hence more convincing) than other kinds of evidence, but a writer should use this kind of evidence sparingly because readers may sometimes suspect that it represents no more than one person's way of looking at events. When combined with other kinds of evidence, however, examples drawn from personal experience can be an effective technique for persuasion. (See Nocera, Perrin.)

    In addition, all the basic expository patterns can be used to support an argument. (See Section 11.)

Cause (See Section 6.)

Central Theme (See *Unity.*)

Classification (See Section 2.)

Clichés are tired expressions, perhaps once fresh and colorful, that have been overused until they have lost most of their effectiveness and become trite or hackneyed. The term is also applied, less commonly, to trite ideas or attitudes.

    We may need to use clichés in conversation, of course, where the quick and economical phrase is an important and useful tool of expression—and where no one expects us to be constantly original. We are fortunate, in a way, to have a large accumulation of clichés from which to draw. To describe someone, without straining our originality very much, we can always declare that he is *as innocent as a lamb, as thin as a rail,* or *as fat as a pig;* that he is *as dumb as an ox, as sly as a fox,* or *as wise as an owl;* that he is *financially embarrassed* or *has a fly in the ointment* or *his ship has come in;* or that, *last but not least, in this day and age,* the *Grim Reaper* has taken him to *his eternal reward.* There is indeed *a large stockpile* from which we can draw for ordinary conversation. But the trite expression, written down on paper, is a permanent reminder that the writer is either lazy or not aware of the dullness of stereotypes—or, even more damaging, it is a clue that the ideas themselves may be threadbare, and therefore can be adequately expressed in threadbare language.

Occasionally, of course, a writer can use obvious clichés deliberately (see Lawrence, par. 1; Ehrenreich, "Star"). But usually to be fully effective, writing must be fresh, and should seem to have been written specifically for the occasion. Clichés, however fresh and appropriate at one time, have lost these qualities.

Closings are almost as much of a problem as introductions, and they are equally important. The function of a closing is simply "to close," of course, but this implies somehow tying the entire writing into a neat package, giving the final sense of unity to the whole endeavor, and thus leaving the reader with a sense of satisfaction instead of an uneasy feeling that there ought to be another page. There is no standard length for closings. A short composition may be effectively completed with one sentence—or even without any real closing at all, if the last point discussed is a strong or climactic one. A longer piece of writing, however, may end more slowly, perhaps through several paragraphs.

A few types of weak endings are so common that warnings are in order here. Careful writers will avoid these faults: (1) giving the effect of suddenly tiring and quitting; (2) ending on a minor detail or an apparent afterthought; (3) bringing up a new point in the closing; (4) using any new qualifying remark in the closing (if writers want their opinions to seem less dogmatic or generalized, they should go back to do their qualifying where the damage was done); (5) ending with an apology of any kind (authors who are not interested enough to become at least minor experts in their subject should not be wasting the reader's time).

Of the several acceptable ways of giving the sense of finality to a paper, the easiest is the *summary*, but it is also the least desirable for most short papers. Readers who have read and understood something only a page or two before probably do not need to have it reviewed for them. Such a review is apt to seem merely repetitious. Longer writings, of course, such as research or term papers, may require thorough summaries.

Several other closing techniques are available to writers. The following, which do not represent all the possibilities, are useful in many situations, and they can frequently be employed in combination:

1. *Using word signals*—e.g., *finally, at last, thus, and so, in conclusion,* as well as more original devices suggested by the subject itself. (See Buhler and Graham, Simpson.)

2. *Changing the tempo*—usually a matter of sentence length or pace. This is a very subtle indication of finality, and it is difficult to achieve. (For examples of modified use, see Simpson, Walker.)

3. *Restating the central idea of the writing*—sometimes a "statement" so fully developed that it practically becomes a summary itself. (See Catton, Marsh.)

4. *Using climax*—a natural culmination of preceding points or, in some cases, the last major point itself. This is suitable, however, only if the materials have been so arranged that the last point is outstanding. (See Catton, Lawrence, Walker.)

5. *Making suggestions,* perhaps mentioning a possible solution to the problem being discussed—a useful technique for exposition as well as for argument, and a natural signal of the end. (See Berry, Perrin.)

6. *Showing the topic's significance,* its effects, or the universality of its meaning—a commonly used technique that, if carefully handled, is an excellent indication of closing. (See Buckley, Lawrence, Noda, Tannen.)

7. *Echoing the introduction*—a technique that has the virtue of improving the effect of unity by bringing the development around full circle, so to speak. The echo may be a reference to a problem posed or a significant expression, quotation, analogy, or symbol used in the introduction or elsewhere early in the composition. (See Buckley, Ehrenreich, "Men.")

8. *Using some rhetorical device*—a sort of catchall category, but a good supply source that includes several very effective techniques: pertinent quotations, anecdotes and brief dialogues, metaphors, allusions, ironic comments, and various kinds of witty or memorable remarks. All, however, run the risk of seeming forced and hence amateurish; but properly handled, they make for an effective closing. (See White, Hill, Lawrence, Simpson, King.)

Coherence is the quality of good writing that results from the presentation of all parts in logical and clear relations.

Coherence and unity are usually studied together and, indeed, are almost inseparable. But whereas unity refers to the relation of parts to the central theme (see *Unity*), coherence refers to their relations with each other. In a coherent piece of writing, each sentence, each paragraph, each major division seems to grow out of those preceding it.

Several transitional devices (see *Transition*) help to make these relations clear, but far more fundamental to coherence is the sound organization of materials. From the first moment of visualizing the subject materials in pattern, the writer's goal must be clear and logical development. If it is, coherence is almost ensured.

Colloquial Expressions are characteristic of conversation and informal writing, and they are normally perfectly appropriate in those contexts. However, most writing done for college, business, or professional purposes is considered "formal" writing; and for such usage, colloquialisms are too informal, too *folksy* (itself a word most dictionaries would label "colloq.").

Some of the expressions appropriate only for informal usage are *kid* (for child), *boss* (for employer), *flunk*, *buddy*, *snooze*, *gym*, *a lot of*, *phone*, *skin flicks*, *porn*. In addition, contractions such as *can't* and *I'd* are usually regarded as colloquialisms and are never permissible in, for instance, a research or term paper.

Slang is defined as a low level of colloquialism, but it is sometimes placed "below" colloquialism in respectability; even standard dictionaries differ as to just what the distinction is. (Some of the examples in the preceding paragraph, if included in dictionaries at all, are identified both ways.) At any rate, slang generally comprises words either coined or given novel meanings in an attempt at colorful or humorous expression. Slang soon becomes limp with overuse, however, losing whatever vigor it first had. In time, slang expressions either disappear completely or graduate to more acceptable colloquial status and thence, possibly, into standard usage. (That is one way in which our language is constantly changing.) But until their "graduations," slang and colloquialism have an appropriate place in formal writing only if used sparingly and for special effect. Because dictionaries frequently differ in matters of usage, the student should be sure to use a standard edition approved by the instructor. (For further examples, see Viorst; Wolfe; Hill; Simpson, pars. 8, 16, 17.)

Comparison (See Section 3.)
Conclusions (See *Closings*.)

Concrete and **Abstract** words are both indispensable to the language, but a good rule in most writing is to use the concrete whenever possible. This policy also applies, of course, to sentences that express only abstract ideas, which concrete examples can often make clearer and more effective. Many expository and argumentative paragraphs are constructed with an abstract topic sentence and its concrete support. (See *Unity*.)

A concrete word names something that exists as an entity in itself, something that can be perceived by the human senses. We can see, touch, hear, and smell a horse—hence *horse* is a concrete word. But a horse's *strength* is not. We have no reason to doubt that strength exists, but it does not have an independent existence: something else must *be* strong or there is no strength. Hence *strength* is an abstract word.

Purely abstract reading is difficult for average readers; with no concrete images provided, they are constantly forced to make their own. Concrete writing helps readers to visualize and is therefore easier and faster to read.

(See *Specific/General* for further discussion.)

Connotation and **Denotation** both refer to the meanings of words. Denotation is the direct, literal meaning as it would be found in a dictionary, whereas connotation refers to the response a word *really* arouses in the reader or listener. (See Wolfe, par. 14; Lawrence.)

There are two types of connotation: personal and general. Personal connotations vary widely, depending on the experiences and moods that an individual associates with the word. (This corresponds with personal symbolism; see *Symbol*.) *Waterfall* is not apt to have the same meaning for the happy young honeymooners at Yosemite as it has for the grieving mother whose child has just drowned in a waterfall. General connotations are those shared by many people. *Fireside*, far beyond its obvious dictionary definition, generally connotes warmth and security and good companionship. *Mother*, which denotatively means simply "female parent," means much more connotatively.

A word or phrase considered less distasteful or offensive than a more direct expression is called a *euphemism*, and this is also a matter of connotation. (See Mitford.) The various expressions used instead of the more direct "four-letter words" referring to daily bathroom events are examples of euphemisms. (See

Wolfe's "mounting.") *Remains* is often used instead of *corpse*, and a few newspapers still have people *passing away* and being *laid to rest*, rather than *dying* and being *buried*.

But a serious respect for the importance of connotations goes far beyond euphemistic practices. Young writers can hardly expect to know all the different meanings of words for all their potential readers, but they can at least be aware that words do *have* different meanings. Of course, this is most important in persuasive writing—in political speeches, in advertising copywriting, and in any endeavor where some sort of public image is being created. When President Franklin Roosevelt began his series of informal radio talks, he called them "fireside chats," thus putting connotation to work. An advertising copywriter trying to evoke the feeling of love and tenderness associated with motherhood is not seriously tempted to use *female parent* instead of *mother*.

In exposition, where the primary purpose is to explain, the writer ordinarily tries to avoid words that may have emotional overtones, unless these can somehow be used to increase understanding. In argument, however, a writer may on occasion wish to appeal to the emotions.

Contrast (See Section 3.)

Deduction (See Section 10.)

Denotation (See *Connotation/Denotation*.)

Description (See Section 8.)

Diction refers simply to "choice of words," but, not so simply, it involves many problems of usage, some of which are explained under several other headings in this guide, e.g., *Clichés, Colloquial Expressions, Connotation/Denotation, Concrete/Abstract*—anything, in fact, that pertains primarily to word choices. But the characteristics of good diction may be more generally classified as follows:

1. *Accuracy*—the choice of words that mean exactly what the author intends.

2. *Economy*—the choice of the simplest and fewest words that will convey the exact meaning intended.

3. *Emphasis*—the choice of fresh, strong words, avoiding clichés and unnecessarily vague or general terms.

4. *Appropriateness*—the choice of words that suit the subject matter, the prospective reader-audience, and the purpose of the writing.

(For contrasts of diction see Welsch, Walker, Eiseley, King, Soto, Anzaldúa, Quindlen.)

Division (See Section 2.)

Effect (See Section 6.)

Emphasis is almost certain to fall *somewhere*, and the author should be the one to decide where. A major point, not some minor detail, should be emphasized.

Following are the most common ways of achieving emphasis. Most of them apply to the sentence, the paragraph, or the overall writing—all of which can be seriously weakened by emphasis in the wrong places.

1. By *position*—the most emphatic position is usually at the end, the second most emphatic at the beginning. (There are a few exceptions, including news stories and certain kinds of scientific reports.) The middle, therefore, should be used for materials that do not deserve special emphasis. (See Buckley, for saving the most significant example until last; Catton, par. 16; and Hall, for the long-withheld revelation of the real central theme.)

A sentence in which the main point is held until the last is called a *periodic sentence*, e.g., "After a long night of suspense and horror, the cavalry arrived." In a *loose sentence*, the main point is disposed of earlier and followed by dependencies, e.g., "The calvary arrived after a long night of suspense and horror." (See Edmundson, par. 32, first sentence, for an effective periodic sentence that acts as a transition between sections of an essay.)

2. By *proportion*—Ordinarily, but not necessarily, important elements are given the most attention and thus automatically achieve a certain emphasis.

3. By *repetition*—Words and ideas may sometimes be given emphasis by reuse, usually in a different manner. If not cautiously handled, however, this method can seem merely repetitious, not emphatic. (See Atwood; Ehrenreich, "Star," provides an ironic example of the strategy.)

4. By *flat statement*—Although an obvious way to achieve emphasis is simply to *tell* the reader what is most important, it is often least effective, at least when used as the only method. Readers have a way of ignoring such pointers as "most important" and "especially true." (See Catton, par. 16.)

5. By *mechanical devices*—Emphasis can be achieved by using italics (underlining), capital letters, or exclamation points.

But too often these devices are used, however unintentionally, to cover deficiencies of content or style. Their employment can quickly be overdone and their impact lost. (For a limited and therefore emphatic use of italics and capitalization, see Faraday.)

6. By *distinctiveness of style*—The author can emphasize subtly with fresh and concrete words or figures of speech, crisp or unusual structures, and careful control of paragraph or sentence lengths. (These methods are used in many essays in this book: see Buckley; Twain, who changes style radically for the second half of his essay; Catton; Haines; Wolfe; Curtin, pars. 7–15.) *Verbal irony* (see *Irony*), including *sarcasm* (see Buckley, Atwood) and the rather specialized form known as *understatement*, if handled judiciously, is another valuable means of achieving distinctiveness of style and increasing emphasis. (See Wolfe, Mitford, Ehrenreich, "Star.")

Essay refers to a brief prose composition on a single topic, usually, but not always, communicating the author's personal ideas and impressions. Beyond this, because of the wide and loose application of the term, no really satisfactory definition has been universally accepted.

Classifications of essay types have also been widely varied and sometimes not very meaningful. One basic and useful distinction, however, is between *formal* and *informal* essays, although many defy classification even in such broad categories as these. It is best to regard the two types as opposite ends of a continuum, along which most essays may be placed.

The formal essay usually develops an important theme through a logical progression of ideas, with full attention to unity and coherence, and in a serious tone. Although the style is seldom completely impersonal, it is literary rather than colloquial. (For examples of essays that are somewhere near the "formal" end of the continuum, see Buckley, Lynn, Eiseley, Catton, Winn, Lawrence. Note that the Declaration of Independence, a completely formal document, is not classifiable as an "essay" at all.)

The informal, or personal, essay is less elaborately organized and more chatty in style. First-person pronouns, contractions, and other colloquial or even slang expressions are often freely used. Informal essays are less serious in apparent purpose than formal essays. Although most do contain a worthwhile message or observation of some kind, an important purpose of many is to entertain. (See Wolfe; Reed, who treats a serious subject in an informal and idiosyncratic manner.)

The more personal and intimate informal essays may be classifiable as *familiar* essays, although, again, there is no well-established boundary. Familiar essays pertain to the author's own experience, ideas, or prejudices, frequently in a light and humorous style. (See Viorst, Curtin, White, Greene, Mairs.)

Evaluation of a literary piece, as for any other creative endeavor, is meaningful only when based somehow on the answers to three questions: (1) What was the author's purpose? (2) How successfully was it fulfilled? (3) How worthwhile was it?

An architect could hardly be blamed for designing a poor gymnasium if the commission had been to design a library. Similarly, an author who is trying to explain for us why women are paid less than men cannot be faulted for failing to make the reader laugh. An author whose purpose is simply to amuse (a worthy goal) should not be condemned for teaching little about trichobothria. (Nothing prevents the author from trying to explain pornography through the use of humor, or trying to amuse by comparing two Civil War generals, but in these situations the purpose has changed—and grown almost unbearably harder to achieve.)

An architect who was commissioned to design a gymnasium, and who, in fact, designed one, however, could be justifiably criticized on whether the building is successful and attractive *as a gymnasium*. If an author is trying to show how definitions of feminism are changing (as is Klass), the reader has a right to expect sound reasoning and clear expository prose; and varied, detailed support ought to be expected in an essay that looks at the physical basis of human behavior (Perry and Dawson, Ackerman).

Many things are written and published that succeed very well in carrying out the author's intent—but simply are not worthwhile. Although this is certainly justifiable grounds for unfavorable criticism, readers should first make full allowance for their own limitations and perhaps their narrow range of interests, evaluating the work as nearly as possible from the standpoint of the average reader for whom the writing was intended.

Figures of Speech are short, vivid comparisons, either stated or implied; but they are not literal comparisons (e.g., "Your car is like my car," which is presumably a plain statement of fact). Figures of speech are more imaginative. They imply analogy but, unlike analogy, are used less to inform than to make quick and forceful impressions. All figurative language is a comparison of unlikes, but the unlikes do have some interesting point of likeness, perhaps one never noticed before.

A *metaphor* merely suggests the comparison and is worded as if the two unlikes are the same thing—e.g., "the language of the river" and "was turned to blood" (Twain, par. 1) and "a great chapter in American life" (Catton, par. 1). (For some of the many other examples in this book, see Eiseley, Hamill, King.)

A *simile* (which is sometimes classified as a special kind of metaphor) expresses a similarity directly, usually with the word *like* or *as* (Eiseley, par. 4).

A *personification*, which is actually a special type of either metaphor or simile, is usually classified as a "figure" in its own right. In personification, inanimate things are treated as if they had the qualities or powers of a person. Some people would also label as personification any characterization of inanimate objects as animals, or of animals as humans.

An *allusion* is literally any casual reference, any alluding, to something, but rhetorically it is limited to a figurative reference to a famous or literary person, event, or quotation, and it should be distinguished from the casual reference that has a literal function in the subject matter. Hence casual mention of Judas Iscariot's betrayal of Jesus is merely a reference, but calling a modern traitor a "Judas" is an allusion. A rooster might be referred to as "the Hitler of the barnyard," or a lover as a "Romeo." Many allusions refer to mythological or biblical persons or places. (See Buckley, par. 11; Wolfe, title and par. 1; and Simpson, par. 2, for a discussion of some commonly employed allusions.)

Irony and paradox (both discussed under their own headings) and analogy (see Section 4) are also frequently classed as figures of speech, and there are several other less common types that are really subclassifications of those already discussed.

General (See *Specific/General*.)
Illustration (See Section 1.)
Impressionistic Description (See Section 8.)
Induction (See Section 10.)

Introductions give readers their first impressions, which often turn out to be the lasting ones. In fact, unless an introduction succeeds in somehow attracting a reader's interest, he or she probably will read no further. The importance of the introduction is one reason that writing it is nearly always difficult.

When the writer remains at a loss to know how to begin, it may be a good idea to forget about the introduction for a while and go ahead with the main body of the writing. Later the writer may find that a suitable introduction has suggested itself or even that the way the piece begins is actually introduction enough.

Introductions may vary in length from one sentence in a short composition to several paragraphs or even several pages in longer and more complex expositions and arguments, such as research papers and reports of various kinds.

Good introductions in expository writing have at least three and sometimes four functions:

1. *To identify the subject and set its limitations,* thus building a solid foundation for unity. This function usually includes some indication of the central theme, letting the reader know what point is to be made about the subject. Unlike the other forms of prose, which can often benefit by some degree of mystery, exposition has the primary purpose of explaining, so the reader has a right to know from the beginning just *what* is being explained.

2. *To interest the readers,* and thus ensure their attention. To be sure of doing this, writers must analyze their prospective readers and the readers' interest in their subject. The account of a new X-ray technique would need an entirely different kind of introduction if written for doctors than if written for the campus newspaper.

3. *To set the tone* of the rest of the writing. (See *Style/Tone.*) Tone varies greatly in writing, just as the tone of a person's voice varies with the person's mood. One function of the introduction is to let the reader know the author's attitude since it may have a subtle but important bearing on the communication.

4. *Frequently,* but not always, *to indicate the plan of organization.* Although seldom important in short, relatively simple compositions and essay examinations, this function of introductions can be especially valuable in more complex papers.

These are the necessary functions of an introduction. For best results, keep these guidelines in mind: (1) Avoid referring to the title, or even assuming that the reader has seen it. Make the introduction do all the introducing. (2) Avoid crude and uninteresting beginnings, such as "This paper is about. . . ." (3) Avoid going too abruptly into the main body—smooth transition is at least as important here as anywhere else. (4) Avoid overdoing the introduction, either in length or in extremes of style.

Fortunately, there are many good ways to introduce expository writing (and argumentative writing), and several of the most useful are illustrated by the selections in this book. Many writings, of course, combine two or more of the following techniques for interesting introductions.

1. *Stating the central theme,* which is sometimes fully enough explained in the introduction to become almost a preview-summary of the exposition or argument to come. (See Tajima, Noda, Tannen, Viorst.)

2. *Showing the significance of the subject,* or stressing its importance. (See Catton, Wolfe, Simpson.)

3. *Giving the background of the subject,* usually in brief form, in order to bring the reader up to date as early as possible for a better understanding of the matter at hand. (See Buhler and Graham, Lynn.)

4. *"Focusing down"* to one aspect of the subject, a technique similar to that used in some movies, showing first a broad scope (of subject area, as of landscape) and then progressively narrowing views until the focus is on one specific thing (perhaps the name "O'Grady O'Connor" on a mailbox by a gate—or the silent sufferers on Buckley's train). (See also Rooney.)

5. *Using a pertinent rhetorical device* that will attract interest as it leads into the main exposition—e.g., an anecdote, analogy, allusion, quotation, or paradox. (See Welsch, Simpson.)

6. *Using a short but vivid comparison or contrast* to emphasize the central idea. (See Murray.)

7. *Posing a challenging question,* the answering of which the reader will assume to be the purpose of the writing. (See Lawrence.)

8. *Referring to the writer's experience with the subject,* perhaps even giving a detailed account of that experience. Some writings are simply continuations of experience so introduced, perhaps with the expository purpose of making the telling entirely evident only at the end or slowly unfolding it as the account progresses. (See White, Goodall.)

9. *Presenting a startling statistic or other fact* that will indicate the nature of the subject to be discussed. (See Goodman, Ackerman.)

10. *Making an unusual statement* that can intrigue as well as introduce. (See Wolfe, Gansberg, Ehrenreich, "Star.")

11. *Making a commonplace remark* that can draw interest because of its very commonness in sound or meaning.

Irony, in its verbal form sometimes classed as a figure of speech, consists of saying one thing on the surface but meaning exactly (or nearly) the opposite—e.g., "this beautiful neighborhood of ours" may mean that it is a dump. (For other illustrations, see Wolfe, Mitford, Walker.)

Verbal irony has a wide range of tones, from the gentle, gay, or affectionate to the sharpness of outright *sarcasm* (see Buckley), which is always intended to cut. It may consist of only a word or phrase, it may be a simple *understatement* (see Mitford, Ehrenreich, "Star"), or it may be sustained as one of the major components of satire.

Irony can be an effective tool of exposition if its tone is consistent with the overall tone and if the writer is sure that the audience is bright enough to recognize it. In speech, a person usually indicates by voice or eye-expression that he is not to be taken literally; in writing, the words on the page have to speak for themselves. (See Klass, par. 7.)

In addition to verbal irony, there is also an *irony of situation*, in which there is a sharp contradiction between what is logically expected to happen and what does happen—e.g., a man sets a trap for an obnoxious neighbor and then gets caught in it himself. Or the ironic situation may simply be some discrepancy that an outsider can see while those involved cannot. (See Lawrence, pars. 11–12.)

Logical Argument (See Section 11.)

Loose Sentences (See *Emphasis*.)

Metaphor (See *Figures of Speech*.)

Narration (See Section 9.)

Objective writing and **Subjective** writing are distinguishable by the extent to which they reflect the author's personal attitudes or emotions. The difference is usually one of degree, as few writing endeavors can be completely objective or subjective.

Objective writing, seldom used in its pure form except in business or scientific reports, is impersonal and concerned almost entirely with straight narration, with logical analysis, or with the description of external appearances. (For somewhat objective writing, see Simpson, Staples, par. 1.)

Subjective writing (in description called "impressionistic"—see Section 8) is more personalized, more expressive of the beliefs, ideals, or impressions of the author. Whereas in objective writing the emphasis is on the object being written about, in subjective writing the emphasis is on the way the author sees and interprets the object. (For some of the many examples in this book, see Twain, Wolfe, Mitford, Haines, Soto, Welsch, Lawrence, Staples, after par. 1, Eiseley, Ehrenreich, Klass.)

Paragraph Unity (See *Unity.*)

Parallel Structure refers in principle to the same kind of "parallelism" that is studied in grammar: the principle that coordinate elements should have coordinate presentation, as in a pair or a series of verbs, prepositional phrases, gerunds. It is often as much a matter of "balance" as it is of parallelism.

But the principle of parallel structure, far from being just a negative "don't mix" set of rules, is also a positive rhetorical device. Many writers use it as an effective means of stressing variety of profusion in a group of nouns or modifiers, or of emphasizing parallel ideas in sentence parts, in two or more sentences, or even in two or more paragraphs. At times it can also be useful stylistically, to give a subtle poetic quality to the prose.

(For illustrations of parallel parts within a sentence, see Murray, pars. 21, 26; Wolfe, pars. 1, 4; of parallel sentences themselves, see Catton, par. 14; of both parallel parts and parallel sentences, see Twain, Maynard, Viorst; of parallel paragraphs, see Tannen.)

Periodic Sentence (See *Emphasis.*)

Persona refers to a character created as the speaker in an essay or the narrator of a story. The attitudes and character of a persona often differ from those of the author, and their persona may be created as a way of submitting certain values or perspectives to examination and criticism. The speaker in Ehrenreich's "Star Dreck" is clearly a persona and advocates actions that the author would consider abhorrent if put into practice.

Personification (See *Figures of Speech.*)

Point of View in *argument* means the author's opinion on an issue or the thesis being advanced in an essay. In *exposition,* however, point of view is simply the position of the author in relation to the subject matter. Rhetorical point of view in exposition has little in common with the grammatical sort and differs somewhat from point of view in fiction.

A ranch in a mountain valley is seen differently by the ranch hand working at the corral, by the gardener deciding where to plant the petunias, by the artist or poet viewing the ranch from the mountainside, and by the geographer in a plane above, map-sketching the valley in relation to the entire range. It is the same ranch but the positions and attitudes of the viewers are different.

So it is with expository prose. The position and attitude of the author are the important lens through which the reader sees the subject. Consistency is important, because if the lens is changed without sufficient cause and explanation, the reader will become disconcerted, if not annoyed.

Obviously, since the point of view is partially a matter of attitude, the tone and often the style of writing are closely linked to it. (See *Style/Tone*.)

The expository selections in this book provide examples of numerous points of view. Dillard's and Twain's are those of authority in their own fields of experience; Mitford's is as the debunking prober; Ehrenreich's is that of the angry observer of human behavior. In each of these (and the list could be extended to include all the selections in the book), the subject would seem vastly different if seen from some other point of view.

Process Analysis (See Section 5.)

Purpose that is clearly understood by the author before beginning to write is essential to both unity and coherence. A worthwhile practice, certainly in the training stages, is to write down the controlling purpose before even beginning to outline. Some instructors require both a statement of purpose and a statement of central theme or thesis. (See *Unity*, *Thesis*.)

The most basic element of a statement of purpose is the commitment to "explain" or, in some assignments, to "convince" (argument). But the statement of purpose, whether written down or only decided upon, goes further—e.g., "to argue that 'dirty words' are logically offensive because of the sources and connotations of the words themselves" (Lawrence).

Qualification is the tempering of broad statements to make them more valid and acceptable, the authors themselves admitting the probability of exceptions. This qualifying can be done inconspicuously, to whatever degree needed, by the use of *possibly, nearly always* or *most often, usually* or *frequently, sometimes* or *occasionally.* Instead of saying, "Chemistry is the most valuable field of study," it would probably be more accurate and defensible to say that it is for *some* people, or that it *can* be the most valuable. (For examples of qualification, see Klass.)

Refutation of opposing arguments is an important element in most argumentative essays, especially where the opposition is strong enough or reasonable enough to provide a real alternative to the author's opinion. A refutation consists of a brief summary of the opposing point of view along with a discussion of its inadequacies, a discussion which often helps support the author's own thesis.

Here are three commonly used strategies for refutation:

1. *Pointing out weaknesses in evidence*—If an opposing argument is based on inaccurate, incomplete, or misleading evidence, or if the argument does not take into account some new evidence that contradicts it, then the refutation should point out these weaknesses.

2. *Pointing out errors in logic*—If an opposing argument is loosely reasoned or contains major flaws in logic, then the refutation should point these problems out to the reader.

3. *Questioning the relevance of an argument*—If an opposing argument does not directly address the issue under consideration, then the refutation should point out that even though the argument may well be correct, it is not worth considering because it is not relevant.

Refutations should always be moderate in tone and accurate in representing opposing arguments; otherwise, readers may feel that the writer has treated the opposition unfairly and as a result judge the author's own argument more harshly.

Rhetorical Questions are posed with no expectation of receiving an answer; they are merely structural devices for launching or furthering a discussion or for achieving emphasis. (See Quindlen, pars. 4, 7; Hall, par. 6; Lawrence; Ehrenreich, "Men," par. 1; Reed, pars. 6, 7.)

Sarcasm (See *Irony*.)

Satire, sometimes called "extended irony," is a literary form that brings wit and humor to the serious task of pointing out frailties or evils of human institutions. It has thrived in Western literature since the time of the ancient Greeks, and English literature of the eighteenth century was particularly noteworthy for the extent and quality of its satire. Broadly, two types are recognized: *Horatian satire*, which is gentle, smiling, and aims to correct by invoking laughter and sympathy, and *Juvenalian satire*, which is sharper and points with anger, contempt, and/or moral indignation to corruption and evil.

Sentimentality, also called *sentimentalism*, is an exaggerated show of emotion, whether intentional or caused by lack of restraint. An author can sentimentalize almost any situation, but the trap is most dangerous when writing of timeworn emotional symbols or scenes—e.g., a broken heart, mother love, a lonely death, the conversion of a sinner. However sincere the author may be, if readers are not fully oriented to the worth and uniqueness of the situation described, they may be either resentful or amused at any attempt to play on their emotions. Sentimentality is, of course, one of the chief characteristics of melodrama. (For examples of writing that, less adeptly handled, could easily have slipped into sentimentality, see Twain, Catton, Staples, Curtin, Simpson, Gansberg, Greene.)

Simile (See *Figures of Speech*.)

Slang (See *Colloquial Expressions*.)

Specific and **General** terms, and the distinctions between the two, are similar to concrete and abstract terms (as discussed under their own heading), and for our purpose there is no real need to keep the two sets of categories separated. Whether *corporation* is thought of as "abstract" and *Ajax Motor Company* as "concrete," or whether they are assigned to "general" and "specific" categories, the principle is the same: in most writing, *Ajax Motor Company* is better.

But "specific" and "general" are relative terms. For instance, the word *apple* is more specific than *fruit* but less so than *Winesap*. And *fruit,* as general as it certainly is in one respect, is still more specific than *food*. Such relationships are shown more clearly in a series, progressing from general to specific: *food, fruit, apple, Winesap;* or *vehicle, automobile, Ford, Mustang*. Modifiers and verbs can also have degrees of specificity: *bright, red, scarlet;* or *moved, sped, careened.* It is not difficult to see the advantages to the reader—and, of course, to the writer who needs to communicate an idea clearly—in "the scarlet Mustang careened through the pass," instead of "the bright-colored vehicle moved through the pass."

Obviously, however, there are times when the general or the abstract term or statement is essential—e.g., "A balanced diet includes some fruit," or "There was no vehicle in sight." But the use of specific language whenever possible is one of the best ways to improve diction and thus clarity and forcefulness in writing.

(Another important way of strengthening general, abstract writing is, of course, to use examples or other illustrations. See Section 1.)

Style and **Tone** are so closely linked and so often even elements of each other that it is best to consider them together.

But there is a difference. Think of two young men, each with his girlfriend on separate moonlit dates, whispering in nearly identical tender and loving tones of voice. One young man says, "Your eyes, dearest, reflect a thousand sparkling candles of heaven," and the other says, "Them eyes of yours—in this light—they sure do turn me on." Their *tones* were the same; their *styles* considerably different.

The same distinction exists in writing. But, naturally, with more complex subjects than the effect of moonlight on a lover's eyes, there are more complications in separating the two qualities, even for the purpose of study.

The tone is determined by the *attitude* of writers toward their subject and toward their audience. Writers, too, may be tender and loving, but they may be indignant, solemn, playful, enthusiastic, belligerent, contemptuous—the list could be as long as a list of the many "tones of voice." (In fact, wide ranges of tone may be illustrated by essays in this book. Compare, for example, those of the two parts of Twain; Eiseley and Mitford; Viorst and Lynn; Staples and Ehrenreich; Reed and Goodall.)

Style, on the other hand, expresses the author's individuality through choices of words (see *Diction*), sentence patterns (see *Syntax*), and selection and arrangement of details and basic materials. (All these elements of style are illustrated in the contrasting statements of the moonstruck lads.) These matters of style are partially prescribed, of course, by the adopted tone, but they are still bound to reflect the writer's personality and mood, education and general background.

(Some of the more distinctive styles—partially affected by and affecting tone—represented by selections in this book are those of Viorst, Wolfe, Buckley, White, Noda, Soto, Anzaldúa, Eiseley, Quindlen, Staples, Walker, and Ackerman.)

Subjective Writing (See *Objective/Subjective.*)

Symbol refers to anything that although real itself also suggests something broader or more significant—not just in greater numbers, however, as a person would not symbolize a group or even humankind itself, although a person might be typical or representative in one or more abstract qualities. On the most elementary level, even words are symbols—e.g., *bear* brings to mind the furry beast itself. But more important is that things, persons, or even acts may also be symbolic, if they invoke abstract concepts, values, or qualities apart from themselves or their own kind. Such symbols, in everyday life as well as in literature and the other arts, are generally classifiable according to three types, which, although terminology differs, we may label *natural, personal,* and *conventional.*

In a natural symbol, the symbolic meaning is inherent in the thing itself. The sunrise naturally suggests new beginnings to most people, an island is almost synonymous with isolation, a cannon automatically suggests war; hence these are natural symbols. It does not matter that some things, by their nature, can suggest more than one concept. Although a valley may symbolize security to one person and captivity to another, both meanings, contradictory as they might seem, are inherent, and in both respects the valley is a natural symbol.

The personal symbol, depending as it does on private experience or perception, is meaningless to others unless they are told about it or allowed to see its significance in context (as in literature). Although the color green may symbolize the outdoor life to the farm boy trapped in the gray city (in this respect perhaps a natural symbol), it can also symbolize romance to the young woman proposed to while wearing her green blouse, or dismal poverty to the woman who grew up in a weathered green shanty; neither of these meanings is suggested by something *inherent* in the color green, so they are personal symbols. Anything at all

could take on private symbolic meaning, even the odor of mari-
golds or the sound of a lawnmower. The sunrise itself could mean
utter despair, instead of fresh opportunities, to the man who has
long despised his daily job and cannot find another.

Conventional symbols usually started as personal symbols,
but continued usage in life or art permits them to be generally
recognized for their broader meanings, which depend on custom
rather than any inherent quality—e.g., the olive branch for peace,
the flag for love of country, the cross for Christianity, the raised
fist for revolutionary power.

Symbols are used less in expository and argumentative writing than in fiction and poetry, but a few authors represented in
this book have either referred to the subtle symbolism of others
or made use of it in developing their own ideas. Eiseley says that
the old men clung to their seats as if they were symbols.

Syntax is a very broad term—too broad, perhaps, to be very useful—
referring to the arrangement of words in a sentence. Good syntax
implies the use not only of correct grammar but also of effective
patterns. These patterns depend on sentences with good unity,
coherence, and emphasis, on the use of subordination and parallel construction as appropriate, on economy, and on a consistent
and interesting point of view. A pleasing variety of sentence
patterns is also important in achieving effective syntax.

Theme (See *Unity.*)

Thesis In an argumentative essay, the central theme is often referred
to as the thesis, and to make sure that readers recognize it, the
thesis is often summed up briefly in a *thesis statement.* In a very
important sense, the thesis is the center of an argument because
the whole essay is designed to make the reader agree with it and,
hence, with the author's opinion. (See *Unity.*)

Tone (See *Style/Tone.*)

Transition is the relating of one topic to the next, and smooth transition is an important aid to the coherence of a sentence, a paragraph, or an entire piece of writing. (See *Coherence.*)

The most effective coherence, of course, comes about naturally with sound development of ideas, one growing logically
into the next—and that depends on sound organization. But
sometimes beneficial even in this situation, particularly in going
from one paragraph to the next, is the use of appropriate transitional devices.

Readers are apt to be sensitive creatures, easy to lose. (And, of course, the writers are the real losers since they are the ones who presumably have something they want to communicate.) If the readers get into a new paragraph and the territory seems familiar, chances are that they will continue. But if there are no identifying landmarks, they will often begin to feel uneasy and will either start worrying about their slow comprehension or take a dislike to the author and the subject matter. Either way, a communication block arises, and very likely the author will soon have fewer readers.

A good policy, then, unless the progression of ideas is exceptionally smooth and obvious, is to provide some kind of familiar identification early in the new paragraph, to keep the reader feeling at ease with the different ideas. The effect is subtle but important. These familiar landmarks or transitional devices are sometimes applied deliberately but more often come naturally, especially when the prospective reader is kept constantly in mind at the time of writing.

An equally important reason for using some kinds of transitional devices, however, is a logical one: while functioning as bridges between ideas, they also assist the basic organization by pointing out the *relationship* of the ideas—and thus contributing still further to readability.

Transitional devices useful for bridging paragraph changes (and, some of them, to improve transitional flow within paragraphs) may be roughly classified as follows:

1. *Providing an "echo"* from the preceding paragraph. This may be the repetition of a key phrase or word, or a pronoun referring back to such a word, or a casual reference to an idea. (See Wolfe, especially from pars. 1 to 2 and 4 to 5; Mitford.) Such an echo cannot be superimposed on new ideas, but must, by careful planning, be made an organic part of them.

2. *Devising a whole sentence or paragraph* to bridge other important paragraphs or major divisions. (See Lynn, pars. 11, 20, and 21.)

3. *Using parallel structure* in an important sentence of one paragraph and the first sentence of the next. This is a subtle means of making the reader feel at ease in the new surroundings, but it is seldom used because it is much more limited in its

potential than the other methods of transition. (See Lawrence, pars. 1 to 2.)

4. *Using standard transitional expressions,* most of which have the additional advantage of indicating relationship of ideas. Only a few of those available are classified below, but nearly all the selections in this book amply illustrate such transitional expressions:

Time—soon, immediately, afterward, later, meanwhile, after a while.

Place—nearby, here, beyond, opposite.

Result—as a result, therefore, thus, consequently, hence.

Comparison—likewise, similarly, in such a manner.

Contrast—however, nevertheless, still, but, yet, on the other hand, after all, otherwise.

Addition—also, too, and, and then, furthermore, moreover, finally, first, second, third.

Miscellaneous—for example, for instance, in fact, indeed, on the whole, in other words.

Trite (See *Clichés.*)

Unity in writing is the same as unity in anything else—in a picture, a musical arrangement, a campus organization—and that is a *oneness*, in which all parts contribute to an overall effect.

Many elements of good writing contribute in varying degrees to the effect of unity. Some of these are properly designed introductions and closings; consistency of point of view, tone, and style; sometimes the recurring use of analogy or thread of symbolism; occasionally the natural time boundaries of an experience or event, as in the selections of Hall, Mitford, Simpson, Gansberg, and Orwell.

But in most expository and argumentative writing the only dependable unifying force is the *central theme,* which every sentence, every word, must somehow help to support. (The central theme is also called the *central idea* or the *thesis* when pertaining to the entire writing and is almost always called the *thesis* in argument. In an expository or argumentative paragraph it is the same as the *topic sentence,* which may be implied or, if stated, may be located anywhere in the paragraph, but is usually placed first.) As soon as anything appears that is not related to the central idea, there are *two* units instead of one. Hence unity is basic to all other virtues of good writing, even to coherence and emphasis, the other two organic essentials. (See *Coherence, Emphasis*.)

An example of unity may be found in a single river system (for a practical use of analogy), with all its tributaries, big or little, meandering or straight, flowing into the main stream and making it bigger—or at least flowing into another tributary that finds its way to the main stream. This is *one* river system, an example of unity. Now picture another stream nearby that does not empty into the river but goes off in some other direction. There are now two systems, not one, and there is no longer unity.

It is the same way with writing. The central theme is the main river, flowing along from the first capital letter to the last period. Every drop of information or evidence must find its way into this theme-river, or it is not a part of the system. It matters not even slightly if the water is good, the idea-stream perhaps deeper and finer than any of the others: if it is not a tributary, it has no business pretending to be relevant to *this* theme of writing.

And that is why most students are required to state their central idea or thesis, usually in solid sentence form, before even starting to organize their ideas. If the writer can use only tributaries, it is very important to know from the start just what the river is.

To the Student

Part of our job as educational publishers is to try to improve the textbooks we publish. Thus, when revising, we take into account the experiences of both instructors and students with the previous edition. At some time your instructor may be asked to comment extensively on *Patterns of Exposition 13*, but right now we want to hear from you. After all, though your instructor assigned this book, you are the one who paid for it.

Please help us by completing this questionnaire and returning it to Readers Editor, College English, HarperCollins Publishers Inc., 10 E. 53rd Street, New York, NY 10022.

School _____ Course title _____

Instructor's name _____

Other books assigned _____

	Liked Best				Liked Least	Didn't Read
Rooney, In and of Ourselves We Trust	5	4	3	2	1	_____
Hill, Waste Not, Want Not	5	4	3	2	1	_____
Goodall, The Mind of the Chimpanzee	5	4	3	2	1	_____
Buckley, Why Don't We Complain?	5	4	3	2	1	_____
Ehrenreich, What I've Learned from Men	5	4	3	2	1	_____
Viorst, What, Me? Showing Off?	5	4	3	2	1	_____
Tajima, Lotus Blossoms Don't Bleed	5	4	3	2	1	_____
Morris, Territorial Behaviour	5	4	3	2	1	_____
Marsh, Tribes	5	4	3	2	1	_____
Berger, The Assault of Squaw Peak	5	4	3	2	1	_____
Twain, Two Ways of Seeing a River	5	4	3	2	1	_____
Catton, Grant and Lee: A Study in Contrasts	5	4	3	2	1	_____
Croce, Scrambled Eggs and Cross-Purposes	5	4	3	2	1	_____
Tannen, It Begins at the Beginning	5	4	3	2	1	_____
Walker, Am I Blue?	5	4	3	2	1	_____
Eiseley, The Brown Wasps	5	4	3	2	1	_____
Rawls, Weeds	5	4	3	2	1	_____
Wolfe, O Rotten Gotham	5	4	3	2	1	_____
Haines, Snow	5	4	3	2	1	_____
Buhler/Graham, Give Juggling a Hand!	5	4	3	2	1	_____
Murray, The Maker's Eye	5	4	3	2	1	_____
Faraday, Unmasking Your Dream Images	5	4	3	2	1	_____
Ackerman, The Beholder's Eye	5	4	3	2	1	_____
Mitford, To Dispel Fears of Live Burial	5	4	3	2	1	_____
Greene, Thirty Seconds	5	4	3	2	1	_____
Mairs, On Being a Scientific Booby	5	4	3	2	1	_____
Perry/Dawson, What's Your Best Time of Day?	5	4	3	2	1	_____
Goodman, Children Lost and Found	5	4	3	2	1	_____
Kowinski, Kids in the Mall	5	4	3	2	1	_____
Winn, Television Addiction	5	4	3	2	1	_____
Klass, Anatomy and Destiny	5	4	3	2	1	_____

	Liked Best		Liked Least		Didn't Read
Welsch, Gypsies	5	4	3	2	1	_____
Noda, Growing Up Asian in America	5	4	3	2	1	_____
Atwood, Pornography	5	4	3	2	1	_____
Curtin, Aging in the Land of the Young	5	4	3	2	1	_____
Maynard, The Yellow Door House	5	4	3	2	1	_____
Simpson, The War Room at Bellevue	5	4	3	2	1	_____
Bourke-White, Dust Changes America	5	4	3	2	1	_____
White, Once More to the Lake	5	4	3	2	1	_____
Gansberg, 38 Who Saw Murder Didn't Call the Police	5	4	3	2	1	_____
Dillard, Prologue	5	4	3	2	1	_____
Orwell, A Hanging	5	4	3	2	1	_____
Soto, The Locket	5	4	3	2	1	_____
Hall, The Embrace of Old Age	5	4	3	2	1	_____
Reed, America: The Multinational Society	5	4	3	2	1	_____
Ehrenreich, Star Dreck	5	4	3	2	1	_____
Hamill, The Neverglades	5	4	3	2	1	_____
Edmondson, Making Yourself at Home	5	4	3	2	1	_____
Quindlen, Execution	5	4	3	2	1	_____
Perrin, War on the Farm	5	4	3	2	1	_____
Nocera, How the Middle Class Has Helped Ruin the Public Schools	5	4	3	2	1	_____
Lynn, Why Johnny Can't Read, but Yoshio Can	5	4	3	2	1	_____
Lawrence, Four-Letter Words Can Hurt You	5	4	3	2	1	_____
King, Letter from Birmingham Jail	5	4	3	2	1	_____
Finch, Death of a Hornet	5	4	3	2	1	_____
Holleran, Bedside Manners	5	4	3	2	1	_____
Anzaldúa, Tlilli, Tlapalli	5	4	3	2	1	_____
Berry, The Pleasures of Eating	5	4	3	2	1	_____

1. Are there any authors not included whom you would like to see represented? _____

2. Were the biographical sketches and introductions useful? _____
   How might they be improved? _____

   _____

3. Will you keep this book for your library? _____

4. Please include any additional comments or suggestions. _____

   _____

5. May we quote you in our promotional efforts for this book?

   yes _____   no _____

Date _____   Signature _____

Mailing address _____